No Stress Tech
Guide To
Crystal Reports XI: For Beginners

By Dr. Indera E. Murphy

No Stress Tech Guide To Crystal Reports XI: For Beginners

Published By:
Tolana Publishing
PO Box 719
Teaneck, NJ 07666 USA

Find us online at www.tolana.com
Inquiries may be sent to the publisher: tolanapub@yahoo.com

Our books are available online at amazon.com, www.lulu.com/tolanapub and www.barnesandnoble.com

ISBN-10: 0-9773912-3-X
ISBN-13: 978-0-9773912-3-3

Library of Congress Control Number: 2006904826

Printed and bound in the United States Of America

Notice of Liability
Every effort has been made to ensure that this book contains accurate and current information. However, the publisher and author shall not be liable to any person or entity with respect to any loss or damage caused or alleged to be caused directly or indirectly, as a result of any information contained herein or by the computer software and hardware products described in it.

Trademarks
All companies and product names are trademarks or registered trademarks of their respective companies. They are used in this book in an editorial fashion only. No use of any trademark is intended to convey endorsement or other affiliation with this book.

Cover designed by Mary Kramer, Milkweed Graphics, www.milkweedgraphics.com

Quantity Discounts

Quantity discounts are available for corporations, non-profit organizations and educational institutions for educational purposes, fundraising or resale. Please contact the publisher by email.

Discount On Future Books

To be notified when new titles are released, send an email with the subject "New Book Release". This will entitle you to a pre-publish discount, for new titles that are released.

About The No Stress Tech Workbook Series

The No Stress Tech Guide To Crystal Reports XI: For Beginners, is part of a growing series of computer software training workbooks that are designed to be used in a classroom setting, an online class or a self-paced learning tool. The workbooks in this series contain an abundance of screen shots to help reduce the "stress" often associated with learning new software.

Tolana Publishing believes that the following principals are important, when it comes to computer software training workbooks:

⇒   The text should be large enough that the reader does not have to squint.

⇒   The step-by-step instructions should really work and not leave something out.

⇒   Features or options that don't work as intended should be pointed out, not to bash the software company, but so that you don't think that you are crazy <smile>.

⇒   That there should be a realistic mix of theory, real world examples and hands-on exercises. It's important to know the past, because it helps you transition into the future with ease and dignity.

Why I Wrote This Workbook

I know that many books claim to have step-by-step instructions. If you have tried to follow books that claim this and you got lost or couldn't complete a task as instructed, it may not have been your fault. When I decided to write computer books, I vowed to really have step-by-step instructions that actually included every step <smile>. This includes steps like which file to open, which menu option to select, when to save a document, where the mouse pointer should be and more. In my opinion, it's this level of detail that makes a computer book easy to follow.

About The Author

Dr. Indera E. Murphy is an author, educator and IT professional that has over 18 years of experience in the Information Technology field. She has held a variety of positions including, programmer, consultant, technical writer, web designer, course developer and project leader. Indera has designed and developed software applications and web sites, as well as, manage IT Projects. In addition to being an Executive Director and consultant, Indera is also an online adjunct professor. She teaches courses in a variety of areas including technical writing, information processing, Access, HTML, Windows, Project Management, Word Processing, Spreadsheets, Dreamweaver and Critical Thinking.

Other Books And Forthcoming Titles

See the last page of this book

TABLE OF CONTENTS

GETTING STARTED WITH CRYSTAL REPORTS XI

Thank you for purchasing this workbook!

The easiest and fastest way to overcome an obstacle is to have someone that has been there, to be by your side every step of the way. That is the goal of this workbook - to be by your side every step of the way through learning Crystal Reports XI.

A hands-on approach is usually the best way to learn most things in life. This workbook is a visual guide that shows you how to create or modify over 200 reports. There are over 800 illustrations that practically eliminate the guess work and let you know that you are doing the steps correctly.

The table of contents takes the **HOW TO** approach, which makes it easier to find exactly what you are looking for. There is more to Crystal Reports than knowing how to open and print a report. Crystal Reports is robust and has a lot of features.

One goal of this workbook is to discuss report design issues and potential solutions on how to resolve them. The good thing is that you have taken a great first step towards learning Crystal Reports by purchasing this workbook. Now all you have to do is use this workbook to learn how to overcome the hurdles. From time to time, I will point out functionality that may not work as expected. When I do this, I am not complaining, merely pointing out things that you should be aware of.

It is my sincere hope that whatever your skill level is with Crystal Reports, that you will learn more about features that you are already familiar with as you go through this workbook and that you learn about features that you did not know existed. Learning new tips and shortcuts will let you work faster and smarter. The more you know about Crystal Reports, the easier your day to day report design experiences will be. So sit back and lets get started.

LESSON 1

About Crystal Reports XI

Crystal Reports XI is a software package that allows you to create reports. It is the report writing software that many companies use. Almost all businesses today that maintain data, have a need for reports to help them get their job done and to make business decisions. Reports allow one to be able to read and make sense of large amounts of information that is most often stored in a database. Most databases have limited reporting capabilities and only allow reports to be created in that "type" of database. Database types include Sybase, Microsoft SQL Server and Oracle, to name a few. These are often called SQL databases and are usually stored on a database server. Some of them do provide a desktop version that is used for learning purposes. If you need to create a report that has data (information) in both Oracle and Sybase databases for example, you would have to use Crystal Reports because neither database allows you to create reports that have data in other types of databases.

Crystal Reports XI (the XI stands for Extreme Insight) allows you to use data from a variety of database types and combine the data in one report. Crystal Reports can use databases of any size. In addition to the SQL databases mentioned above, you can also use mainframe databases and what I call desktop or PC databases like Microsoft Access and Visual FoxPro. This type of database usually contains a lot less data then the SQL databases and do not have the capacity to support hundreds or thousands of end-users, like SQL databases do. Crystal Reports also comes bundled with a lot of software development tools including Visual Studio. It also comes bundled with over 150 leading software packages like PeopleSoft, SAP, JD Edwards and many others. In addition to creating paper reports, you can export reports to a variety of formats including e-mail, Word, Excel, PDF and the Web. You can create almost any type of report that you can dream up.

Normally, Crystal Reports is a read-only program, meaning that when you create or modify reports, the data in the database is not changed. You can however, include SQL commands in the report, which will allow the report to edit, delete and add records to a database.

The primary goal of Crystal Reports is to allow a wide range of users to work with the raw data in databases to be able to create reports that allow data to be interpreted and analyzed. Crystal Reports makes creating basic reports easy enough for less technical people to use through the use of report wizards, which are similar to wizards that you may have used in other software packages. You can also create complex reports that include subreports, formulas, charts and much more.

What's New In Crystal Reports XI?

What you will notice that's new, depends on the previous version of Crystal Reports that you used, if any. The older the version of Crystal Reports that you are upgrading from, the more new features you will notice. The feature in Crystal Reports XI that you will probably notice first is the new interface, which includes the Start Page. It looks more like a web page. The following list does not include all of the new features, but it should be enough to make you want to learn more.

New Patch Installation

This feature will allow you to download and install any updates that are available for Crystal Reports XI.

Workbench

The Workbench allows you to keep projects organized and lets you group reports in folders based on your preference. You can store reports from different hard drive and server locations in the same folder. You can keep the Workbench open in the workspace so that you can easily access the reports that you need.

Report Export Configuration

This feature allows the export configuration options to be saved with the report, which means that the people that run the reports that you create, do not have to set up the export options each time the report needs to be exported.

RTF Export Format

A second RTF export format has been added. The new RTF export format allows end users to edit a report, without assistance from the person that actually created the report. It has been optimized for forms processing and accuracy. This means that you can select between the two RTF export formats depending on the needs of the report: either the ability to edit, or for accuracy, which is what the original RTF export format handles.

Updated Repository Explorer

This feature makes is easier to navigate in the Business Objects Enterprise System. You can share reports and other items with end-users and other report designers through the repository.

HTML Preview

This feature will let you view how your reports will look when they are published to the Web. You can view the report on the Web while you are designing it. You no longer have to publish a report to the Web before you are able to view it.

Enhanced Report Viewer

The report viewer toolbar has been modified to be more consistent. The resizable Group Tree improves report viewing for long group names.

N Value For Top N Style Reports

You can add parameter input options for these types of reports. This will allow one report to meet the needs of several users, which could reduce the number of reports that have to be created and maintained.

Drop And Drag Charts And Cross-Tabs

Crystal Reports can now automatically create a chart or Cross-Tab based on the data in the report. The charts are automatically updated when new data or variables are added to the report.

Single Sign-On

This feature allows Crystal Reports to be integrated into an existing security system, which means that multiple sign-ons are no longer a requirement.

Dynamic Image Location

With this new feature, it is no longer necessary to store images (graphic files) that are needed for a report, in the database. Images and pictures can now be placed on a report through a link in the database. This allows all of the images to be stored in one location or they can be used from their current location. The reference to the image is stored in the database, which helps keep the database size smaller.

Dynamic And Cascading Prompts

With this feature, you no longer have to use static prompt value lists for parameter fields. Dynamic lists can be populated from the database or from data stored in the repository each time the report is run. You can also have cascading prompts. This means that the options in one drop down list, control what you will see in another drop down list.

Updated Data Drivers

The following data drivers have been updated - DB2, IBM, JDBC and XML. This means that you can connect to more types of databases.

Other New Features

Report Application Server (RAS)
Report Designer Component (RDC)
Integration with Business Objects Enterprise XI

Workbook Objectives

This workbook is written to accommodate classroom and online training, as well as, to be used as a self-paced training course for the Crystal Reports Certified Program (CRCP). This workbook covers the topics that are on the RDCR201 exam. This exam has 45 questions. While there are no required prerequisites to successfully complete the exam or exercises in this workbook, having a general knowledge of any of the following would be helpful.

- ☑ Prior versions of Crystal Reports
- ☑ Database structures
- ☑ Basic programming
- ☑ Report design

Step-by-step instructions are included throughout this workbook. This workbook takes a hands-on, performance based approach to teaching you how to use Crystal Reports and provides the skills required to create reports efficiently. After completing this workbook, you will be able to perform the following tasks and more:

- ☑ Create a connection to a database and link tables
- ☑ Use the Online Help file
- ☑ Utilize report design and planning techniques
- ☑ Understanding database concepts
- ☑ Use the report wizards and create reports from scratch
- ☑ Create and apply templates to reports
- ☑ Modify existing reports
- ☑ Use multiple tables to create a report
- ☑ Format and edit reports
- ☑ Utilize the Workbench to organize reports that you work on
- ☑ Create report selection criteria
- ☑ Sort and group data
- ☑ Create charts
- ☑ Create reports that have subtotals, counts, running totals and summary information
- ☑ Export reports to other file formats
- ☑ Add Special Fields to reports
- ☑ Update Crystal Reports
- ☑ Incorporate drill down techniques in reports
- ☑ Create mailing labels using a wizard
- ☑ Create Cross-Tab and OLAP reports
- ☑ Use the Formula Editor and Formula Workshop to create formulas and use functions
- ☑ Use the Highlighting and Section Experts to format data conditionally
- ☑ Change the default report options
- ☑ Create If...Then...Else Statements
- ☑ Create parameter prompts and report alerts
- ☑ Use the Repository

Lesson 1 Objectives

After completing the exercises in this lesson you will be able to:

- ☑ Install and upgrade Crystal Reports XI
- ☑ Create an icon on your desktop for Crystal Reports
- ☑ Understand the options on the toolbars and menus
- ☑ Check for updates for Crystal Reports
- ☑ Remove toolbars
- ☑ Use the Online Help file

To pass the RDCR201 exam, you need to be familiar with and be able to:

- ☑ Understand the components of the design environment, like the toolbars

Conventions Used In This Workbook

I designed the following conventions to make it easier for you to follow the instructions in this workbook.

- ☑ The `Courier font` is used to indicate what you should type.
- ☑ **Drag** means to hold down the left mouse button while moving the mouse.
- ☑ **Click** means to press the left mouse button and release it immediately.
- ☑ **Double-click** means to quickly press the left mouse button twice and then release it.
- ☑ **Right-click** means to press the right mouse button once to open a shortcut menu.
- ☑ Click **OK** means to click the OK button on the dialog box.
- ☑ Press **Enter** means to press the Enter key on your keyboard.
- ☑ Press **Tab** means to press the Tab key on your keyboard.
- ☑ SMALL CAPS are used to indicate an option to click on or to bring something to your attention.
- ☑ This **NEW** icon indicates a new or modified feature in this version of Crystal Reports.
- ☑ This icon indicates a tip or additional useful information about the topic that is being discussed.
- ☑ This icon indicates a shortcut or another way to complete the task being discussed.
- ☑ This Exam icon indicates a concept that you will probably see on the RDCR201 certification exam or contains information about the exam.
- ☑ This icon indicates a warning that you need to pay attention to.
- ☑ When you see "YOUR SCREEN SHOULD LOOK LIKE THE ONE SHOWN IN FIGURE X.X", or something similar during the exercises in this workbook, check to make sure that your screen does look like the figure. If it does, continue with the next set of instructions. If your screen does not look like the figure, redo the steps that you just completed so that your screen does match the figure. Not doing so may cause you problems when trying to complete exercises later in the workbook.
- ☑ When you see this instruction "Right-click on a field", it means to right-click on the field in the details section of the report, unless noted otherwise.
- ☑ When you see this instruction "Select the database", it means to select the Xtreme database that comes with Crystal Reports. You will learn about this database in Lesson 2.
- ☑ [See Lesson 2, Figure 2-8] refers to a screen shot that you can use as a reference for the topic that is being discussed.
- ☑ [See Lesson 2, Database Concepts] refers to a section in this workbook that you can use as a reference for the topic that is being discussed.
- ☑ "Clear the (name of option) option" means to remove the checkmark from the option specified in the instruction.

☑ "L2.1 Report Name" is the naming convention for reports that you will create. L2.1 stands for Lesson 2, Exercise 1. You may consider some of the report file names to be long. I did this on purpose, so that it is easier to know what topic the report covers. If you don't like to type or don't want to type the full report name, you can just type the first part as the file name (Example, L5.8, L7.2 etc). That way when you have to find a report to complete another exercise, you will be able to find the correct report. For example, if the report name is L5.5 Orders Shipped Between 4-1-2004 and 6-30-2004, you can save the report as L5.5.

☑ "Save the L4.5 report as" means to open the L4.5 report and save it with the new report name that is specified in the instructions. Doing this lets you keep the original report.

☑ At the end of each lesson is a section called **TEST YOUR SKILLS**. This section can contain questions (fill in the blank, multiple choice or True/False). There can also be hands-on exercises for you to complete on your own. These exercises help reinforce what is covered in the lesson. If you are not familiar with working from what is known as "Business Requirements" or "Report Specs", these exercises will help you become familiar with this process because these types of documents do not include step-by-step instructions, like the exercises in the lessons have. The reports created in these hands-on exercises are used in other lessons as a starting point, which means that you need to complete them before going to the next lesson.

☑ **FILE ⇒ NEW ⇒ CROSS-TAB REPORT** means to open the **FILE** menu, select the option **NEW**, then select the option **CROSS-TAB REPORT**, as illustrated in Figure 1-1.

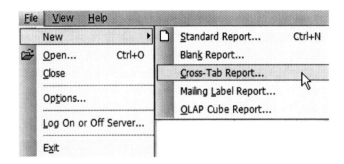

Figure 1-1 Menu navigation technique illustrated

 All of the web sites referenced in this workbook are listed on this page on our website: www.tolana.com/books/crxi/links.html. You can go to this page and click on the link that you want, instead of having to type the link in. See how nice I am. If you plan to use this page on our website, it is probably a good idea to bookmark the page, so that you can get to it quickly.

Assumptions

(Yes, I know one should never assume anything but . . . .)

☑ You have the standard, professional or developer version of Crystal Reports XI, which is also referred to as Crystal Reports Version 11.

☑ You are familiar with the Windows environment.

☑ You are comfortable using a mouse.

☑ You have access to a printer, if you want to print any of the reports that you will create. This is not a requirement for completing the exercises.

☑ You have installed or will install Crystal Reports on a desktop or laptop computer, instead of a server.

☑ You know that the operating system used to write this workbook is Windows XP Professional. If you are using Windows 2000 or Windows 2003 Server, it is possible that some of the screen shots may have a slightly different look.

☑ You have Crystal Reports open at the beginning of each lesson and create a folder in the Workbench for each lesson. You will learn how to create folders in the Workbench in Lesson 2.

☑ You have access to the Internet to download any files that you may need to complete the exercises and to download any updates to Crystal Reports that are available.

☑ You have the professional or developer edition of Crystal Reports XI, if you plan to take a CRCP exam. The standard edition does not have some of the features like the repository, that you need to learn for the exam. If you do not plan to use this workbook to take the exam, using the Standard edition will allow you to complete the majority of the exercises in this workbook.

☑ Optional: That you have Microsoft Word and Excel installed if you want to view the reports that will be exported to these formats. If you don't have either of these software packages, other options are covered in Lesson 8.

Interactive Messages

Like many other software packages, Crystal Reports will display interactive messages that require a response from you, to confirm an action. Table 1-1 shows the three types of interactive message symbols and what they mean.

Symbol	Name	This interactive message type . . . . .
(i)	Information	Provides information about an action that you just performed.
⚠	Warning	Usually requires you to make a decision.
⊗	Critical	Requires you to make a decision before moving on to the next step.

Table 1-1 Interactive message types explained

Crystal Reports Certification

The Crystal Reports Certified Professional (CRCP) certification requires you to take and pass two exams: RDCR201 and RDCR301. Unlike some certification programs, you are not required to take any specific courses. Prior to Crystal Reports XI, you had to pass three exams. The Certification Programs web page contains a list of objectives by exam and other information that you may find helpful. You can download the CRCP documents. The second document has a breakdown of what is covered on the exam.

Certification information http://www.businessobjects.com/services/training/certification.asp

If you purchased this workbook as part of your arsenal for preparing for the first certification exam, you may want to spend more time completing the exercises to make sure that you have an above average understanding of the concepts presented. Good Luck on the exam!

Differences Between The Standard And Professional Editions Of Crystal Reports XI

This workbook was written using the professional edition of Crystal Reports XI. Each edition of Crystal Reports XI has slightly different features. Table 1-2 shows the differences between the standard and professional editions. This table is a condensed version of the "Crystal Reports XI Feature Comparison By Version and Edition" document that is on the Business Objects web site. The table below only includes features that are different.

As you can see, there are not many features in the professional edition that are not in the standard edition. This means that if you have the standard edition, you will be able to complete almost all of the exercises in this workbook. If you have the developer edition, you have all of the features shown in the table and can complete all of the exercises in this workbook, just like you can with the professional edition.

Feature	Standard	Professional
OLAP Reports	N	Y
Repository for component reuse	(1)	Y
HTML Preview	N	Y
Enhanced support for Business Objects Universes	N	Y
Ad hoc SQL query tool	N	Y
Languages other than English	N	Y
Dynamic and Cascading Prompts	(2)	Y

Table 1-2 Differences between the editions of Crystal Reports XI

(1) This feature requires the Crystal Reports Server software, which does not come with the standard edition. The Crystal Reports Server software installation CD comes in the box with the professional and developer editions.

(2) This feature can be viewed in the standard edition, but not created.

Installing Crystal Reports

This exercise will show you how to install Crystal Reports on a computer opposed to a server, explain the upgrading options from a previous version of Crystal Reports, how to customize the installation and more. If you have already installed or upgraded to Crystal Reports XI, it would be a good idea to read through this section to ensure that you have installed all of the necessary components to complete the exercises in this workbook.

Installation Tips

① Running defrag before and after installing software is a good idea, especially if you are low on hard drive space, because this will allow your hard drive to open files faster.
② It is a good idea to create an image of your hard drive before installing software, or at a minimum, back up your important files, just in case the installation does not go smoothly.
③ Installing Crystal Reports requires Administrator rights because new registry entries are created and existing ones may be updated. Registry entries that come to mind that may be updated are the .NET and Java components, depending on the version of these components that are currently installed on your computer. Other system files may also be updated.
④ You should close as many programs and services that are currently open or running as possible, before installing Crystal Reports.

The installation process is not on the exam.

Minimum Installation Requirements

In addition to having a CD-ROM drive, Table 1-3 shows the minimum requirements needed to install Crystal Reports. More is better. In this exercise you will learn how to check the required components on your computer. If you are not sure whether your computer meets the minimum installation requirements, follow the steps below.

Component	Minimum Requirement
Processor	450 MHz Pentium II Processor (700 MHz Pentium III Processor or higher recommended)
RAM	128 MB (256 MB or higher recommended)
Hard Drive	350 MB free (600 MB free or higher recommended)
Operating System	Windows XP Professional, Windows 2000 with Service Pack 4 or higher or Windows 2003 Server

Table 1-3 Minimum installation requirements

1. On your desktop, right-click on the **MY COMPUTER** icon and select Properties. At the top of the General tab as illustrated in Figure 1-2, you will see the version of Windows and service pack if any, that is installed. At the bottom, you will see the processor and amount of RAM that you have. Close the System Properties dialog box.

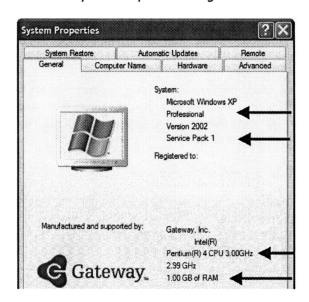

Figure 1-2 System Properties dialog box

2. Open Windows Explorer, then right-click on the C drive (or the letter of the drive that you plan to install Crystal Reports on) and select Properties. You should have at least 350 MB of free space as illustrated in Figure 1-3. Close the Disk Properties dialog box and Windows Explorer.

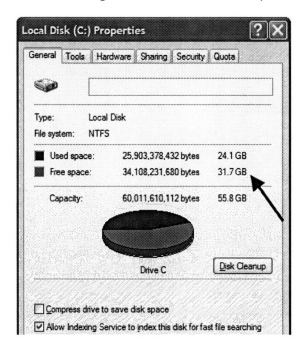

Figure 1-3 Disk Properties dialog box

Upgrading To Crystal Reports XI

If you already have version 8.5, 9 or 10 installed and you upgrade to Crystal Reports XI, this version can be installed in it's own directory. This means that you can have and run two versions of Crystal Reports on the same computer. The old version is not automatically uninstalled when Crystal Reports XI is installed.

Installation Overview

Crystal Reports provides a step-by-step process to install the software. If the **AUTO PLAY** feature is enabled (turned on) on your CD drive, when you put the installation CD in the drive you will see the screen shown below in Figure 1-4. If you do not see the screen, open Windows Explorer, click on the drive letter for your CD drive and double-click on the file, **SETUP.EXE**. If you purchased Crystal Reports online and downloaded the software, you will have to extract the files from the file that you downloaded and then double-click on the setup.exe file to start the installation process.

During the installation process, your hard drive will be searched to see if certain files are there and to determine if any system files need to be updated. If the installation detects that your operating system needs to be updated, you will be prompted to do so. You must complete this task so that Crystal Reports can be installed. There are two types of installations, as discussed below:

① **Typical** This installation installs the basic components of Crystal Reports, like the Report Designer.

② **Custom** This installation by default will install all of the basic components that the Typical option does, plus it will let you select additional options like data drivers and exporting options. You also have the ability to change some of the default options and not have them installed. This is not advised though, unless you have a very good understanding of all of the components that are installed by default.

How To Install Crystal Reports XI

The following instructions will show you how to install the professional edition of Crystal Reports XI on a computer that has Windows XP. If you are using a different edition of Crystal Reports XI or a different version of Windows, your steps may be slightly different. If you purchased Crystal Reports online and have downloaded the installation file, double-click on it now. This will create a directory structure like the one on the CD and will let you follow the steps below.

1.   If you have other applications open now, you should close (not minimize) them, then put the Crystal Reports XI CD into the CD-ROM drive, or double-click on the setup.exe file if you downloaded Crystal Reports. Select the option, **INSTALL CRYSTAL REPORTS** as shown in Figure 1-4.

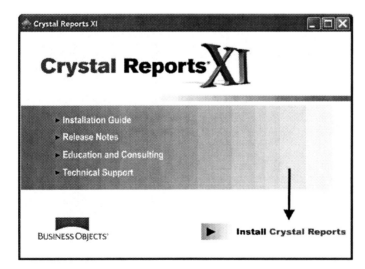

Figure 1-4 Crystal Reports installation option illustrated

 Depending on your computers configuration, you may see a dialog box that says that existing files need to be updated. If you see this dialog box, click Yes to let the installation wizard update the files. Your computer may be restarted after these files are updated.

2. Click Next on the Welcome Installation Wizard screen, then read and accept the license agreement illustrated in Figure 1-5 and click Next.

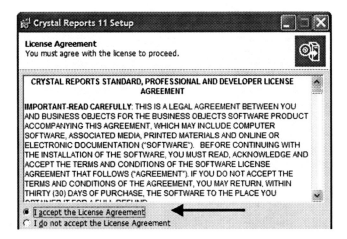

Figure 1-5 License Agreement screen

3. On the **USER INFORMATION** screen shown in Figure 1-6, type your name and Product Key Code. If you have a company name, type it in the Organization field and click Next.

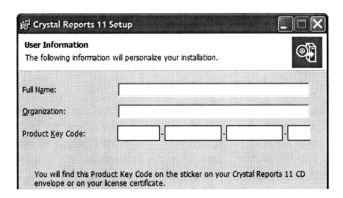

Figure 1-6 User Information screen

4. On the screen shown in Figure 1-7, select the type of installation that you want and click Next.

I always select **CUSTOM** just to see what the advanced options are, so that I will know which features will not be installed by default.

The **BROWSE** buttons shown in Figure 1-7 will let you select a different location to install the files to. Unless you have a really good reason, you should accept the default folder locations.

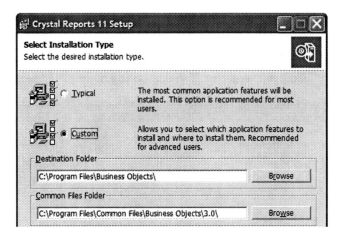

Figure 1-7 Select Installation Type screen

Installation Customization Options

The dialog box shown in Figure 1-8 lets you customize the installation. If you did not select the **CUSTOM** option shown above in Figure 1-7, you will not see this screen.

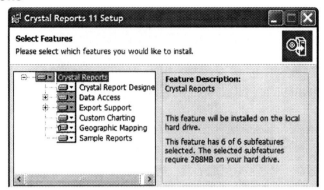

Figure 1-8 Custom installation options

You should be aware of the following when selecting the features that you want to install.

① The features with a + (plus sign) as shown above in Figure 1-8, indicate that there are additional options that can be installed.

② Features that have a white button like the Crystal Report Designer, means that all of the options under it will be installed if you selected the **TYPICAL** option shown earlier in Figure 1-7. The gray buttons mean that some or none of the options will be installed if the Typical option is selected.

③ A feature with a yellow number 1 (for example, the Geographic Mapping feature) means that it will be installed the first time that you use the feature, not during the initial installation process that you are completing now.

This is known as **INSTALL ON DEMAND**. When you are using Crystal Reports and select a feature that was not installed during the initial installation process, there will be a delay the first time that you attempt to use the feature and you will be prompted to install the option. If you want to have the feature installed during the initial installation, click on the button with the yellow number 1 and select either of the options illustrated in Figure 1-9.

④ Features that have a gray button like the **DATA ACCESS** option shown in Figure 1-10, means that there are additional features in the section that are not currently selected to be installed. The options under the Data Access node are all of the types of databases that Crystal Reports can be configured to work with. The "Access" option, is selected by default. This is the database type that you need to complete the exercises in this workbook. In Figure 1-10, the options JDBC Data Driver and ACT! will not be installed now, unless you change their options.

⑤ Features that have a red X as illustrated in Figure 1-11, mean that if you need the feature, you should select it and install it via the installation process that you are completing now. You cannot install it on first use, like you can the features that have a yellow number 1. You will need the CD if you decide to install it later.

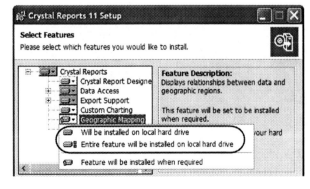

Figure 1-9 Options to install a feature illustrated

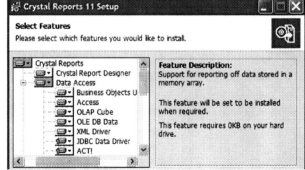

Figure 1-10 Features that will not be installed by default

When clicked, the **DISK COST** button will open the dialog box shown in Figure 1-12. This information is helpful if you added a lot of features to the installation and want to make sure that there is enough space on the hard drive to install them.

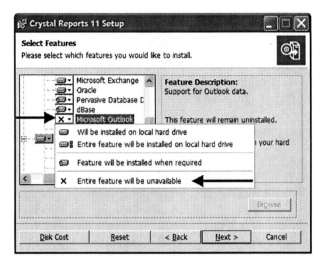

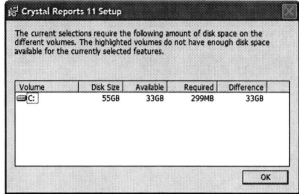

Figure 1-12 Disk drive options

Figure 1-11 Features that will not be available after the installation process

For now, you do not have to change any of the options. Any features that you need that will not be installed now, will be installed with the "On first use" utility. This will let you see how the Install On Demand utility works later in this workbook.

5. Click Next on the Select Features screen.

You will see the screen shown in Figure 1-13. This option, if installed will let you check to see if there are any product updates for Crystal Reports. This is similar to the software update feature that you may have seen or used in other software packages.

6. Click Next on the Web Update Service Option screen.

The screen shown in Figure 1-14 is asking if you are sure that you have selected the options that you need. If you are not sure, you can click the Back button to check.

7. When you are sure that you have the options that you need, click Next to install the software. If for some reason you need to stop the installation, click the **CANCEL** button shown in Figure 1-15. When the installation is complete, you will see the screen shown in Figure 1-16.

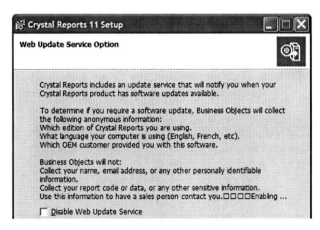

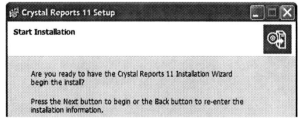

Figure 1-14 Start Installation screen

Figure 1-13 Web Update Service Option screen

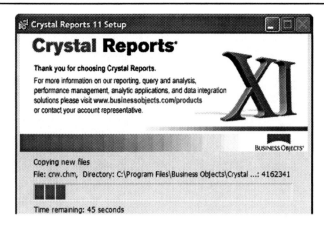

Figure 1-15 Crystal Reports Setup screen

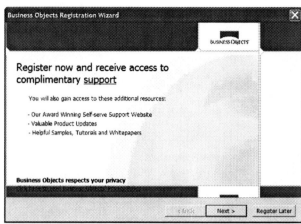

Figure 1-16 Register software screen

Product Registration Options

1. To register the software, click Next on the screen shown above in Figure 1-16. For now, click the **REGISTER LATER** button. You can register the software after you complete this lesson.

You will see the screen shown in Figure 1-17 if you selected the option to register later. Notice that the option to check for product updates is checked in the lower left hand corner.

Figure 1-17 Successful installation screen

2. Clear the option **CHECK FOR PRODUCT UPDATES**, then click Finish and remove the CD from the drive. You will learn how to check for updates when you open Crystal Reports later in this lesson.

Create An Icon For Crystal Reports

If you want to create an icon on your desktop for Crystal Reports, follow the steps below.

1. Start ⇒ Programs (or All Programs) ⇒ Business Objects 11 ⇒ Crystal Reports ⇒ Crystal Reports 11, as shown in Figure 1-18.

Figure 1-18 Path to Crystal Reports

2. Using the right mouse button, drag the Crystal Reports 11 menu option to the desktop and release the mouse button. You will see the shortcut menu shown in Figure 1-19. Select **COPY HERE**. You should see an icon for Crystal Reports 11 on your desktop.

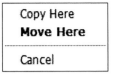

Figure 1-19 Shortcut menu

 If you want this icon on your Quick Launch bar on the Taskbar in Windows XP instead of on your desktop, drag it there with the **RIGHT** mouse button. You will see a shortcut menu similar to the one shown above in Figure 1-19. Select **MOVE HERE.** If you want the shortcut on your desktop and on the Quick Launch bar, select **COPY HERE.**

Changing The Installation Options

Depending on the projects that you work on, you may have the need to install additional components of Crystal Reports that were not installed during the initial installation or you may have the need to uninstall (remove) components. If either of these is the case, you have the two options discussed below:

① Put the installation CD in the drive and select the options that you need.
② Use the Windows Add Or Remove Programs utility.

Using The Add Or Remove Programs Utility To Install/Uninstall Components

1. Open the Control Panel in Windows and double-click on the Add or Remove Programs option.

2. Scroll down the list until you see the Crystal Reports 11 option as highlighted in Figure 1-20.

The **CHANGE** button will let you install additional components, remove components or reinstall Crystal Reports. The **REMOVE** button will let you uninstall Crystal Reports.

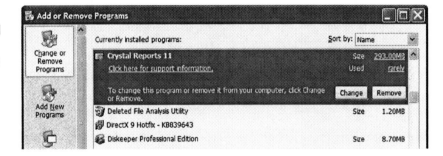

Figure 1-20 Add or Remove Programs dialog box

3. Click the Change button and you will see the dialog box shown in Figure 1-21. You will also see this dialog box if you use the installation CD. Select the option that you want and follow the instructions. Close all open dialog boxes and windows, when you are finished.

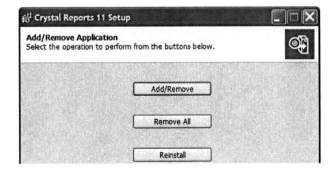

Figure 1-21 Crystal Reports Setup dialog box

ᴺᴱᵂ Start Page Overview

The Start Page provides a lot of options that you may find helpful. The options on this page should save you some time because you do not have to remember which menu they are on.

Open Crystal Reports

1. Double-click on the Crystal Reports 11 icon that you just created on the desktop. You will see the Register dialog box, if you have not registered the software yet. For now, click the **REGISTER LATER** button. You should see the window shown in Figure 1-22.

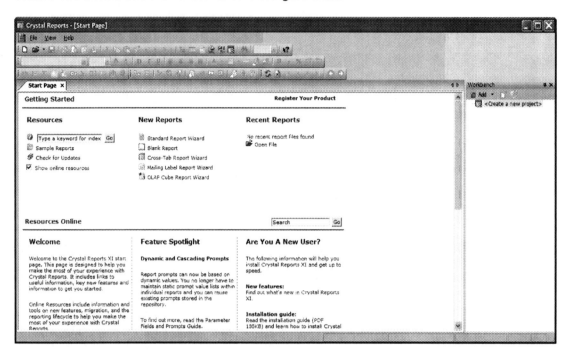

Figure 1-22 Crystal Reports window

When you open Crystal Reports, you will see the Start Page shown above in Figure 1-22. This replaces the Welcome dialog box in previous versions of Crystal Reports. As you can see, there are a lot of options on this page. On the right side of the Start Page, you should see the **WORKBENCH**. You will learn about this new feature in Lesson 2.

If the **SHOW ONLINE RESOURCES** option is checked, you will see the Resources Online section, as shown above in Figure 1-22. The purpose of this section is to keep you informed about updates for Crystal Reports and much more.

> Depending on the security that you have set in your firewall software, you may be prompted to grant Crystal Reports access to the Internet. It is probably a good idea to grant the access so that you can check for updates. Your firewall software will prompt you if either of the following options in Crystal Reports is selected.
>
> ① Show Online Resources option on the Start Page.
> ② Check for Updates on Start Up option on the Help menu.

Resources

The options in this section will let you search the help file, open the sample reports that come with Crystal Reports, check for updates and display or hide the Resources Online section, which is located at the bottom of the Start Page.

New Reports

The options in this section are the report wizards. Having them here makes them easy to get to. They are still on the File ⇒ New menu option, if you want to access them that way.

 The **BLANK REPORT** option is what you would select when you want to create a report from scratch (not use a wizard).

Recent Reports

This section displays the last five reports that you opened. The **OPEN FILE** link will open the last folder that you used in Crystal Reports. Clicking on this link lets you look for the report that you want to open. You can navigate to another folder, if the folder that opens is not the one that you need.

Start Page Menu Options

The Start Page menu contains some of the options available in Crystal Reports. The options on the File, View and Help menus are explained later in the workbook. This menu is a subset of the menus that are available when a report is open in Crystal Reports. For example, Figure 1-23 shows the options on the File menu on the Start Page. Figure 1-24 shows the options on the File menu when a report is open.

 If you close the Start Page either on purpose or by accident, you can still get to all of the options on the Start Page through the menu, toolbar or shortcuts.

 One difference in the location of items on the File menu that I noticed is the **LOG ON OR OFF SERVER** option. It is on the File menu on the Start Page as shown in Figure 1-23. When a report is open, this option is on the Database menu.

 Crystal Reports does not have a spell checker.

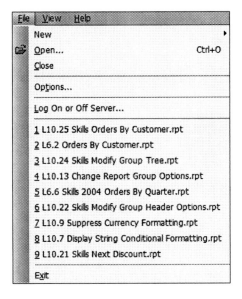

Figure 1-23 File menu options on the Start Page

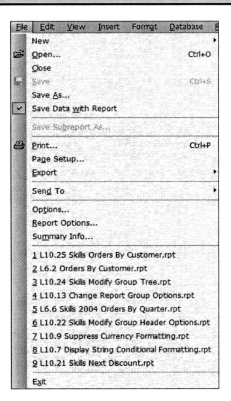

Figure 1-24 File menu options when a report is open

Checking For Software Updates

There are several ways that you can check for software updates as explained below.

① **Check for Updates on Start Up** If this option is selected, every time that you open Crystal Reports you will be prompted to check for updates. I don't know about you, but this would get on my nerves.

② **Check for Updates** This option lets you control when the check for updates will occur. This option is also on the Start Page.

③ Manually check the businessobjects.com web site for updates.

1. Open the Help menu. You will see the first two update options listed above, as illustrated in Figure 1-25.

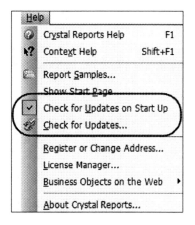

Figure 1-25 Update options illustrated

2. Clear the option CHECK FOR UPDATES ON START UP, if you do not want to check for updates every time that you open Crystal Reports.

How To Check For Updates

This exercise will show you how to check for and install updates.

1. Click on the link CHECK FOR UPDATES, on the Start Page. If updates are available, you will see a dialog box similar to the one shown in Figure 1-26.

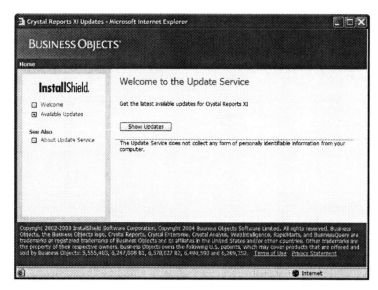

Figure 1-26 Crystal Reports Update window

. . . .

2. Click the **SHOW UPDATES** button or click the **AVAILABLE UPDATES** link on the left. You will see the window shown in Figure 1-27. You may have different updates that need to be installed, then the ones shown in the figure.

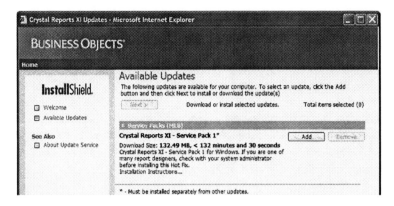

Figure 1-27 List of available updates

3. Click the **ADD** button next to each update that you want to install, then click the Next button. You will see the window shown in Figure 1-28.

The **INSTALL NOW** button will download and install the update(s) that you selected.

The **DOWNLOAD** button will download the update files, but will not install them. This option is helpful if you want to download the update files now and install them later.

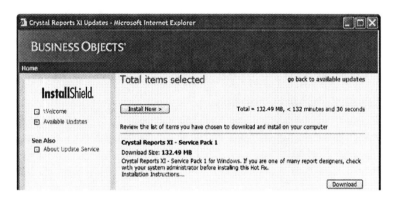

Figure 1-28 Items selected window

4. Click on the button for how you want to proceed and follow the directions given. If you do not want to do either now, close the browser window.

How To Manually Check For Updates

If the Show Online Resources option is checked on the Start Page and you scroll to the bottom of the page, you will see the Crystal Product Support, Product Updates and Training sections. You may have different options then the ones shown. These sections provide a lot of help and information about Crystal Reports. The Critical Updates, Monthly Hot Fixes and Service Packs links at the bottom of the window, as shown in Figure 1-29, are another way to manually check for updates.

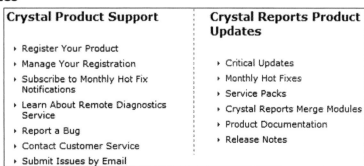

Figure 1-29 Crystal Product Support and Update options

As I am writing this workbook, there are two major updates that are available, as discussed below.

① **SERVICE PACK 1** Provides a lot of fixes. If you do not have this service pack installed, you may want to install it. The link below is for the Business Objects XI Service Packs. The **READ ME** link will open a pdf file that will let you view all of the updates in this service pack. http://support.businessobjects.com/downloads/updates/service_packs/boenterprise.asp

This service pack is for the entire Business Objects XI suite of products, not just Crystal Reports, but it will only update the components that you have installed.

② **CR XI RELEASE 2** You only need to install this release if you will be using Visual Studio 2005 with Crystal Reports, Crystal Reports Server or the Business Objects Enterprise and are upgrading from the bundled version of Crystal Reports that comes with Visual Studio 2005. This release includes an updated .NET engine for Visual Studio 2005.

Product Support Options

Below are some of the more popular support options for Crystal Reports.

Hot Fix Announcement

If you want to receive the free monthly hot fix e-mail announcement for Crystal Reports XI, click on the link **SUBSCRIBE TO MONTHLY HOT FIX NOTIFICATIONS,** shown above in Figure 1-29. You can also sign up on the link at the end of this paragraph. Signing up here will also allow you to post questions in the forums, which are explained in the next section. https://secure.businessobjects.com/login/login.asp

Crystal Reports Forums

If you have a question about Crystal Reports, you can post a message in the forum. The link below will take you to the home page of the Business Objects forum. If you do not already have an account, you will be prompted to create one. It's free. Business Objects does not provide staff to answer questions on the forum. The questions are answered by other Crystal Reports users.

http://support.businessobjects.com/forums/default.asp

Another web site, that in my opinion is much more active and helpful is Tek-Tips. They currently have four Crystal Reports forums. The Crystal Reports forums are under the Programmers ⇒ Reporting Solutions category. You have to register in order to post questions.

http://www.tek-tips.com

Newsgroups

There are newsgroups on the Internet that are specifically for Crystal Reports. Two of them are listed below. You will be able to post questions and receive answers. You will also learn how other people are living with and using Crystal Reports. Like the forums listed above, the questions on this newsgroup are also answered by other users. The reason Microsoft has a newsgroup for Crystal Reports, is because some Microsoft software packages like Visual Studio come bundled with Crystal Reports.

The newsgroup host is **MSNEWS.MICROSOFT.COM.**
The name of the newsgroup is **MICROSOFT.PUBLIC.VB.CRYSTAL.**

You will need to have a newsgroup reader installed like the one in Microsoft Outlook Express to use the newsgroups. You can also access the newsgroups online at Microsoft's web site. The web site address is http://www.microsoft.com/communities/newsgroups/default.mspx.

I was personally disappointed when I first started using Crystal Reports to find out that there really is not a newsgroup or forum that has staff to answer our questions. This is one reason why I decided to write a book on Crystal Reports XI, so that I would be able to provide as many tips and helpful information as possible. Hopefully by reading and completing the exercises in this workbook, you will not have to go through all of the trials and tribulations that I went through when I first learned Crystal Reports years ago.

Access The Newsgroups With Email Software

Many people prefer to use email software like Outlook Express (which you already have on your computer), that has a newsgroup reader to access the newsgroups instead of logging on to a website to access the newsgroups. If you want to do this, the link below provides instructions for setting up Outlook Express to use newsgroups. Don't worry, it is not difficult to set up.

http://www.microsoft.com/communities/guide/newsgroups.mspx

If you plan to participate in newsgroups either from the web site or using software like Outlook Express, you should not use your real email address. Most people that use their real email address suddenly wind up with more spam then they can handle. My advise is to set up a free email account with Yahoo or Hotmail or any free email service provider that you want and use that email account to post messages in newsgroups. If your ISP offers multiple email accounts, you can create another account under your primary account and use that one.

Download Center

The Download Center contains add-ons for Crystal Reports XI registered licensed users. The link below will take you to the add-ons.

http://www.businessobjects.com/products/downloadcenter/

Crystal Reports Toolbars

There are five main toolbars in Crystal Reports: Standard, Formatting, Insert Tools, Navigation Tools and Expert Tools, as discussed below. They are right below the menu that you learned about earlier in this lesson. Like toolbars in other applications, you can rearrange the toolbars by clicking on the dots at the beginning of the toolbar with the left mouse button and dragging the toolbar to a new location in the window. You cannot add or delete buttons on the toolbars, but you can turn off (remove) toolbars that you do not need or use. If you have used other Windows based applications, you are already familiar with many of the menu options. You will probably find that you will use the toolbar buttons more frequently then the options on the menus.

Keep in mind that the buttons on the toolbars are available based on what you are doing and the object that is selected. There are some differences between the toolbar buttons and their menu counterparts. These differences will be pointed out.

Standard Toolbar

The buttons on the Standard toolbar contain options from the File, Edit, Format, View, Report and Help menus. Table 1-4 explains the purpose of each button on the Standard toolbar.

Button	Purpose
	Creates a new report.
	Lets you open an existing report. If you click on the arrow at the end of the button, you will see the last nine reports that you opened.
	Saves the active report.
	Opens the Print dialog box.
	Displays the active report in the Preview window. This is the same as clicking on the Preview tab. You can click this button if the Preview tab is not visible.
	Displays the active report as a web page the HTML Preview window.
	Opens the Export dialog box which will let you export the report to one of several popular formats. [See Lesson 8, Export Format Options]
	Removes the selected object(s) and places it on the clipboard.
	Copies the selected object(s) to the clipboard.
	Pastes object(s) from the clipboard into the report.
	Lets you copy (absolute or conditional) formatting properties from one object to one or more other objects. This is a shortcut to the Format Painter command.
	Undoes an action. (3)
	Redoes the last action that was undone. (3)
	Toggles the Group Tree on and off on the Preview window.
	Opens the Field Explorer so that you can add fields and other objects to the report. (4)
	Opens the Report Explorer so that you can see the contents of the report in tree view. (4)
	Opens the Repository Explorer so that you can see the contents of the repository. (4)
	Opens the Dependency Checker so that you can check reports for errors.
	Displays or hides the Workbench so that you can see the contents of your workspace.
	Opens the Find dialog box, which lets you search for information in the report.
100%	Sets the zoom level for viewing a report. If you need a zoom percent that is not in the list, you can type over the 100% that is displayed and press Enter.
	If you click on this button and then click on something on the screen, the Online Help file will open.

Table 1-4 Standard toolbar buttons explained

(3) You can select how many changes that you want to undo and redo from the drop down list. This capability is not available from the Edit menu.

(4) Clicking this button a second time does not close the Explorer window.

Formatting Toolbar

The buttons on the Formatting toolbar contain options that let you format the object that is selected. Table 1-5 explains the purpose of each button on the Formatting toolbar.

Button	Purpose
Tahoma	Lets you select a font.
10	Lets you change the size for the font that is currently selected.
A	Increases the font size of the selected object, one point each time this button is clicked. (5)
A	Decreases the font size of the selected object, one point each time this button is clicked. (5)
B	Makes the selected object bold.
I	Makes the selected object italic.
U	Underlines the selected object.
	Aligns the selected object flush left.
	Centers the data in the selected object.
	Aligns the data in the selected object flush right.
	Justifies the data in the selected object between the length of the frame the object is in.
A	Applies the selected color to the object. This button allows you to select or define colors in the color dialog box. If you click on this button, the font color will change to the color that is on the line at the bottom of the button. Click on the arrow to change the color.
	Applies the selected border to the object. You can select from several border style options. Click on the arrow to change the border style.
	Suppresses the selected object. This means that the object will not print on the report.
	Locks or unlocks the formatting of an object so that it can't be changed accidentally.
	Locks the size and position of an object in relation to the object to its right.
$	Adds or removes the currency symbol in the selected numeric field.
,	Adds or removes the comma in the selected numeric field.
%	Adds or removes the percent sign in the selected numeric field.
.00	Moves the decimal point in the selected numeric field, one place to the right each time this button is clicked. (6)
00.	Moves the decimal point in the selected numeric field, one place to the left each time this button is clicked. (6)

Table 1-5 Formatting toolbar buttons explained

(5) There is no menu option that has this functionality.
(6) Rounding is set to the number of decimal places in the field.

Font Size Tip

If the font size that you want is not in the drop down list, highlight whatever size is showing in the font size drop down list and type in the size that you want. You can also type in half sizes like 9.5.

Insert Tools Toolbar

The buttons on the Insert Tools toolbar contain additional reporting options. Table 1-6 explains what each button lets you add to a report. These options are also available on the Insert menu.

Button	Lets You Insert A . . .
ab	text object
	group
Σ	summary field
	Cross-Tab object
	OLAP grid object
	subreport
	line
	box
	picture
	chart
	map

Table 1-6 Insert Tools toolbar buttons explained

NEW Navigation Tools Toolbar

The buttons on the Navigation Tools toolbar contain options to navigate in a report and refresh data. This toolbar is activated once you preview a report. Table 1-7 explains the purpose of each button on the Navigation Tools toolbar.

When you have a report open in the Preview window, you will see another navigation toolbar that has the first six buttons shown in Table 1-7. The second navigation toolbar is right above the report, which you will see in the next lesson.

Button	Purpose
	Refreshes the report data.
	Stops the processing of data and only displays the report with the data that has been processed, prior to clicking this button.
	Moves to the first page in the report.
	Moves to the previous page in the report.
	Moves to the next page in the report.
	Moves to the last page in the report.
	Returns to the previous page in the report on the Preview tab. (7)
	Moves to the next page in the report on the Preview tab. (7)

Table 1-7 Navigation Tools toolbar buttons explained

(7) These buttons do not work for me. I read a message in a forum that said to search the Help file for "What are report parts". Fortunately, these buttons are not needed to complete the exercises in this workbook.

Expert Tools Toolbar

The buttons on the Expert Tools toolbar provide access to the experts, including the database, group and template experts. The buttons on this toolbar open dialog boxes that provide options to complete a task. Table 1-8 explains the purpose of each button on the Expert Tools toolbar. These options are also available on the Report menu.

Button	Purpose
	Opens the Database Expert, which is used to select (or remove) data sources for the report.
	Opens the Group Expert which is used to create, modify and delete groups.
	Opens the Group Sort Expert, which will let you find the Top or Bottom N records or lets you sort the report on summary fields.
	Opens the Record Sort Expert which lets you set the order that the detail records will be sorted in.
	Opens the Select Expert which lets you create report selection criteria.
	Opens the Section Expert which lets you format any section of the report.
	Opens the Formula Workshop, which lets you create formulas and add functions to reports.
	Opens the OLAP Design Wizard, which lets you create a report that uses an OLAP Cube or CAR file.
	Opens the Template Expert, which lets you apply a template to a report.
	Opens the appropriate Format Editor, which will let you modify formatting properties of the selected object.
	Opens the Hyperlink tab on the Format Editor, which will let you insert a hyperlink in a report.
	Opens the Highlighting Expert, which lets you apply conditional formatting to an object.

Table 1-8 Expert Tools toolbar buttons explained

How To Remove Toolbars

Like many features in Crystal Reports, there is more than one way to remove toolbars. There are two ways to remove a toolbar, as discussed below.

① View ⇒ Toolbars. You will see the dialog box shown in Figure 1-30. Clear the checkmark for the toolbar option that you do not want and click OK.

② Right-click near the toolbars at the top of the Crystal Reports window. You will see the **TOOLBAR SHORTCUT MENU** shown in Figure 1-31. Click on the toolbar that you want to remove. Notice the **TOOLBARS** option at the bottom of the shortcut menu. Selecting this option will open the Toolbars dialog box shown above in Figure 1-30.

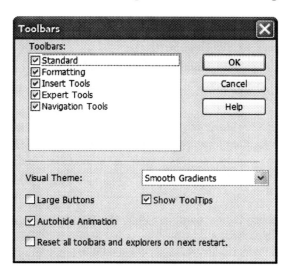

Figure 1-31 Toolbar shortcut menu

Figure 1-30 Toolbars dialog box

The Online Help File

The Help file in Crystal Reports is quite extensive. When you open the Help file, it opens in a new window instead of opening on the right side of the application window, like it does in other applications. To open the Help file, follow the instructions below.

1. Help ⇒ Crystal Reports Help. You will see the window shown in Figure 1-32. The **CONTENTS** tab is the online manual. This window is like a table of contents. Click on the plus sign in front of the topic that you want to know more about to see additional options.

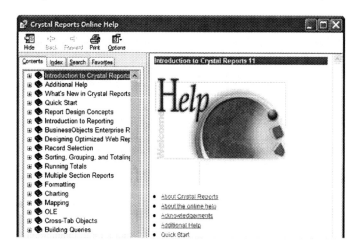

Figure 1-32 Contents tab options

You may have seen this style of help in other software applications. Each of the tabs (Contents, Index, Search and Favorites) provide help in a slightly different way.

Figure 1-33 shows the options on the Index tab. You can enter a keyword and click the **DISPLAY** button or scroll down the list of keywords and select the topic that you want.

Figure 1-33 Index tab options

2. Click on the **SEARCH** tab.

If you type in a keyword on the Search tab and click the **LIST TOPICS** button shown in Figure 1-34, you will see a list of topics that relate to the keyword that you entered.

Select the topic that is closest to what you are looking for and click the **DISPLAY** button or double-click on the topic.

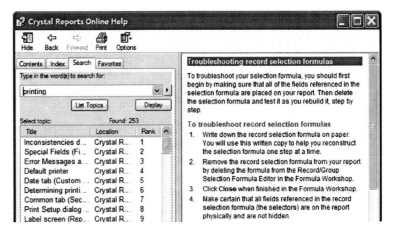

Figure 1-34 Search tab options

3. Click on the **FAVORITES** tab. This tab lets you view a list of the help topics that you have bookmarked, as shown in Figure 1-35.

 To add a topic to the Favorites tab, display the topic on the right side of any help window. Click on the Favorites tab. You should see the topic name in the **CURRENT TOPIC** field at the bottom on the left side of the window, as shown in Figure 1-35. Click the **ADD** button.

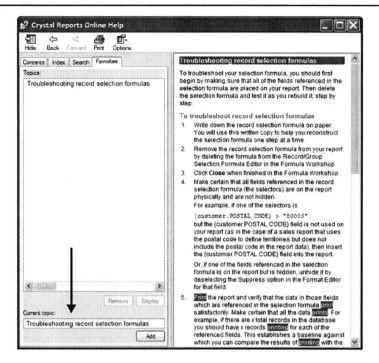

Figure 1-35 Favorites tab options

There are five buttons at the top of the help window as shown in Figure 1-36. The toolbar buttons are explained below.

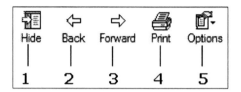

Figure 1-36 Help toolbar buttons

① The **HIDE** button will close the left side of the help window as shown in Figure 1-37. Compare this to the window shown earlier in Figure 1-35. To restore the left side of the window, click the **SHOW** button.

② The **BACK** button takes you back to the previous topic that you viewed. This option is only available after you have viewed at least one other help topic.

③ The **FORWARD** button works similar to the Back button. The Forward button will also take you to topics that you have already viewed.

④ The **PRINT** button will print the help topic that is displayed.

⑤ The **OPTIONS** button provides options to customize the help window. The options are shown in Figure 1-38.

Figure 1-37 Left side of the help window hidden

Figure 1-38 Help customization options illustrated

4. Close the Help window.

Create A Folder For Your Reports

You will create and modify several reports in this workbook. It would be a good idea to store all of them in the same folder on your hard drive so that you can find them easily. You will create the folder at the root of the C drive. If you want to create the folder in another location or under an existing folder, navigate to that location, prior to starting step 2 below.

1. Open Windows Explorer and click on the C drive.

2. File ⇒ New ⇒ Folder.

3. Type `Crystal Reports Workbook` as the folder name, press Enter, then close Windows Explorer.

All of the reports created in this workbook are located on this page of our web site in a zip file named crxi.zip (http://www.tolana.com/d/crxi/crfiles.html). They are provided as a reference in case you really get stuck. If you follow each step in the exercises, you probably will not need to look at these files.

Before you download this file, you should create a folder called `Exercises` in the Crystal Reports Workbook folder that you just created and extract the reports in the zip file to this folder. The zip file also contains reports that I created that are referenced in the workbook to illustrate a concept.

Backing Up Your Work

I cannot stress how important it is to back up your work frequently. Doing so will save you frustration in the event a power failure occurs or if you have a hardware failure. The majority of times that you lose work, it can't be recovered or if it can, it may cost you a few hundred dollars or more to recover it.

If you aren't already, you should also be saving your work to an external source like a CD, DVD, external hard drive or USB drive. Windows has a backup utility that you can use. I tell my students this in every class and it never fails that a student loses some, if not all of their work. Don't say that I didn't warn you <smile>.

Test Your Skills

1. Which toolbar has the option to let you open the Select Expert?

2. How many menu options are there that will let you check for updates for Crystal Reports?

3. How many menu options will let you refresh the data in a report?

4. Which section of the Start Page will let you open the Standard Report Wizard?

5. Which toolbar has the option to let you add a Summary field?

CREATE YOUR FIRST REPORT

In addition to creating your first report, after completing the exercises in this lesson, you will be able to:

- ☑ Have a foundation of database terminology
- ☑ Understand data types
- ☑ Have a foundation of Crystal Reports terminology
- ☑ Understand the report design process
- ☑ Understand the sections of a report
- ☑ Understand the report creation options
- ☑ Understand the save data report options
- ☑ Organize reports in the Workbench
- ☑ Use the Group Tree
- ☑ Use the Design and Preview windows

To pass the RDCR201 exam, you need to be familiar with and be able to:

- ☑ Understand database concepts
- ☑ Plan the layout and select content for a report
- ☑ Develop a report prototype
- ☑ Know the purpose of each section in a report
- ☑ Understand the design environment, including menus and the design and preview windows
- ☑ Connect to a data source
- ☑ Preview reports
- ☑ Save reports

LESSON 2

Database Terminology

Below are key terms that you need to understand about databases in order to work with them effectively.

① **Database** A database is a collection of information that is stored in one or more tables.

② **Relational Database** A relational database is a collection of **RELATED** information that is stored in one or more tables. It is important to note that there are different types of physical database structures.

③ **Table** A table is stored in a database and is a collection of records. Most databases have more than one table. Tables are linked on similar fields. Tables may remind you of a spreadsheet when viewed, because SQL databases have rows and columns, which Crystal Reports refers to as records and fields. Each table contains information about a specific topic. For example, a customer table would only contain information about customers. The customer table would not contain information about products.

④ **Record** A record has one or more fields. Each of the fields in a record are related. A record looks like a row of data in a spreadsheet.

⑤ **Field** A field contains one piece of information and is stored in a record. Examples of fields include customer name and customer address.

You need to understand all of the database terminology discussed above.

Database Concepts

There are several database concepts that you need to be aware of. Having an understanding of these concepts is necessary to create reports effectively.

Data Source A data source is where the data is stored. Examples of data sources are databases/tables, views and spreadsheets.

Data Dictionary A data dictionary contains detailed information about a data source and includes the following types of information: database and table names, field names, types, sizes, indexes and related files. A data dictionary can be a handwritten or typed document. It can also be generated by some database software packages.

Relationship A relationship is how two or more tables are joined (linked). Tables can be joined when they have at least one field that is the same in each table. For example, an invoice table can be joined to a products table because each invoice record will have at least one item from the products table. Crystal Reports has a **SMART LINKING** feature that will automatically join tables that have related information. Crystal Reports also has a built-in visual utility that will help you link tables.

Length Is used to set what the contents of the field cannot be longer than. If the length of a field is set to 20, the contents in the field cannot have more than 20 characters.

Null Any of the field data types discussed later in this lesson can be null (empty). Null means that the field does not have a value. Depending on the data source, an empty string may or may not be set to null. An empty numeric field is not equal to zero.

Index The purpose of indexes is to make the retrieval of records from tables faster. Knowing which fields in the table are indexed is important when you need to optimize a report. Crystal Reports can indicate which fields are indexed in some types of databases and in other types of databases it can't. If Crystal Reports does not recognize the indexes in the table(s) that you are using, you can get the information from the data dictionary for the database.

PRIMARY KEY FIELDS should always be indexed. **FOREIGN KEY FIELDS** are usually indexed. Other fields in a table that are used frequently to retrieve (select) records are also indexed. Fields that fall into this category are fields that are used to sort, group or link data.

 Databases that have too many indexes will retrieve records slower. Indexes are usually created by the DBA (Data Base Administrator). If you need to have an index created, contact the DBA, unless you have the rights to do so.

SQL (stands for Structured Query Language) This is the language that is most used to interact with databases. It is used to create and populate tables with data, modify data and retrieve data from a database. The **SQL SELECT** command is what is used to retrieve data. This is also known as a **QUERY**. Before you start to frown, the answer is no, you do not have to learn how to write SQL code to retrieve the data that you need for the reports that you will create. Crystal Reports provides tools, like the Select Expert and Group Expert, that allow you to retrieve the data from the tables. At some point you may have requests for functionality that these tools can't provide, which means that you will have to write code.

 Think of these tools as query generators. They let you "visually" select criteria that will retrieve the records based on the options that you select.

Business Views Many databases have the ability to present different views of the data. A view is a **RECORDSET** (the result) of a query. Views display a subset of the data. Views are stored in the database and are like tables, but they do not have the physical characteristics of a table. For example, records cannot be added or deleted from a view, fields cannot be added to a view or the length of a field cannot be changed in a view.

Views are one way to optimize reports that use tables that have a lot of data. For example, a customer table will hold all customers world wide. If there is a need to create several reports that are specific to a certain country for marketing or sales analysis purposes, create a view (a query) that retrieves all of the customer records for the country. When the reports are created for that country, select the "country view" if you will, as the data source, instead of the customer table. The report will run faster because it does not have to read the entire customer table to find the records for the specific country. Instead, the "view" is read.

Stored Procedures These are mini programs that are stored (saved) in the database. They are created when it is difficult to retrieve the data from a table or when a view cannot handle the processing that is needed. Stored procedures are saved on a database server. From a report designers perspective, they function and have the same characteristics as a view. Don't worry, most report designers do not create stored procedures. If you have to create a complex report and have trouble getting the data the way that you need it, talk to the DBA to get their recommendation for the best way to get the data that you need.

Data Types

Each field must have a data type. The data type determines what type of information can be stored in the field. Table 2-1 explains the data types that are available in most databases.

Data Type	Description
String	String fields primarily contain text. String fields can also have numbers, spaces and other special characters. String fields are also known as **TEXT FIELDS**. Numeric data that is stored in a string field is treated like text because there is no need to use the data in any type of calculation. An example of numeric data that is treated like text is zip codes. Numeric data stored in a string field cannot be formatted with any number type formatting options.
Number	This data type can only contain numbers and decimal points. This data type can be used in a calculation, like addition, multiplication and formulas.
Currency	This data type can only contain monetary data. You can use currency fields in calculations, just like number fields. Currency is a special number data type. By default, Crystal Reports will automatically display and print a dollar sign with this data type.
Date	Date fields are used to store dates, which can be stored in several formats. Date fields contain the month, day and year.
Time	This data type is used to store times, which can be stored in several formats. Time fields contain hours, minutes and seconds. Crystal Reports does not recognize fractional seconds even if the underlying data source has them.
Date and Time	Displays the date and time in one field, in this format - MM/DD/YYYY HH:MM:SS. You can hide the time portion of this data type on reports if you need to.
Boolean	Boolean fields are used to set a logical value of true/false, yes/no or 1/0.
Memo	The memo data type is a free form text field, meaning that it can store almost any type of information. This data type may not be available in all databases. Memo fields can contain large amounts of data and embedded formatting. Crystal Reports can recognize **RICH TEXT (RTF)** and **HTML FORMATTING** in memo fields. A common use for memo fields is to store comments about the data in the other fields in the record.
Picture	This data type stores an image file or as you learned earlier, a link to the location of the image file. [See Lesson 1, Dynamic Image Location] Crystal Reports recognizes the following image file types: bitmap, JPEG, TIFF, PNG and Windows Metafile. Some databases refer to this data type as a **BLOB** (Binary Large Object).

Table 2-1 Data types explained

 Crystal Reports recognizes all of the data types listed above. If you use a database that has data types other then the ones listed above in Table 2-1, they will be mapped to a data type that Crystal Reports recognizes.

Crystal Reports Terminology

Below are some key terms that you need to understand about Crystal Reports in order to work with databases effectively. The four field types discussed below are not stored in a database.

① **Formula Fields** Formula fields can include any of the 300 built-in functions that Crystal Reports has, or you can create a formula from scratch. The result of a calculated field is created on the fly, meaning that each time the report is run, the formula field will be recalculated. Formula fields are covered in detail in Lesson 9.

② **Special Fields** Special fields contain information that is system generated. Examples of system generated fields include the date the report was printed and page numbers. There are 25 special fields that you can use.

③ **Summary Fields** Summary fields are calculated fields and like formula fields, they are also calculated on the fly, each time the report is run. You create summary fields.

④ **Text Object Fields** This is a free form field that is used to place information on the report that can't be added to the report by the fields discussed above. Text objects are often used to create a report title or a heading for fields that you create.

The Repository

The repository allows you to store objects that you want to use in more than one report or share with other people. Examples of items that are commonly stored in the repository are SQL commands, logos, reports or functions.

Report Design Process

I know that you are anxious to create your first report, but there are several items that need to be addressed and worked out before you create a report, whether this is your first report or your 100th report. This section is an overview of the report design process and planning. Report design could be an entire chapter or two all by itself, but I am giving you the abridged version. The report design process is part of what is known as the "Business Requirements" phase of a project. As you gain experience, you will see that if you do not get the business requirements right, the project will be delayed, potentially be over budget and not produce the results that the business owner (requestor) or client is looking for. Many call this a "bad career move".

When you learn the concepts presented in this lesson, it will be easier for you to create reports in Crystal Reports. You should write down the answers to the questions that will be presented in the report design process. The more planning that you do before you create the report, the less you will have to modify the report after it is created. There are four primary steps to the report design process. Each step can have multiple tasks. You will see how these steps come together through the exercises in this workbook.

Step 1: Define The Purpose Of The Report

Yes, I know what you are saying - "How hard can it be to figure out the purpose of a report?". The answer is it depends on how well the person or group of people are able to explain what they want the report to provide and how well you understand what they tell you.

The majority of reports that you create will be used by someone other than yourself, which means that you should meet with the person or group of people that will use the report. These meetings are part of the requirement gathering process. Keep in mind that you may have to have more than one meeting to get a good idea of what the report needs to include, because the users may not tell you or be able to clearly articulate their needs in the one meeting. Reports are often used as a decision making tool, which means that poor decisions will be made or the decision making process will be ineffective due to missing or incorrect data that is presented on the report. The data must be presented in a logical manner in order to be an effective decision making tool.

 Keep in mind that one report can be used by people at different levels in the company. This means that at each level, people can have slightly different needs. If this is the case, you will have to plan and design the report accordingly, so that it meets the needs for all of the users.

Your role as the report designer is to gather the information needed, which will help the user(s) of the report to be able to read it easily, as well as, understand the data on the report. If the information is not presented in a way that works for the users, trust me, they will let you know and you will be spending a lot of time modifying the report.

In my opinion and experiences that I have had, the more that users have you modify a report, the quicker your credibility goes down hill. That is not something that you want to happen. What I have discovered, as well as, many other Information Technology professionals, is that if you create a prototype (which is discussed later in this lesson) of the report for the users, they can discuss what they like and do not like about the prototype report. Usually, you will gain valuable information that is often hard to get users to discuss in a regular meeting. The worst thing that you can do in many cases, is give the users the impression that you know more about their needs then they do. I am not saying that in some cases that you won't know more about their data, just don't give them that impression, if you know what I mean.

To define the expected outcome of the report, write a descriptive sentence or two about the purpose of the report or what the report needs to accomplish. Below are some sample purpose statements.

① The purpose of the report is to compare last years sales data to this years sales data by region.
② The purpose of the report is to show products that are low on inventory and need to be reordered.
③ The purpose of the report is to show the top 10 best selling products by sales team.

In addition to defining the expected outcome of the report, you have to take into consideration who will be using the report. It is very possible that managers and their staff will request similar reports. In many cases, it is better to create separate reports, even if there is only one field that is different, then to try and get multiple parties to try and come up with one report that works for both groups of users. As you gain report design experience, understand business requirements and know the requestors, you will be able to quickly determine which is the best option.

Step 2: Determine The Layout Of The Report

Now that you have determined the purpose of the report, you need to determine where each piece of data should be placed on the report. If you are creative, you will like this step. In addition to determining where the data should be placed, you need to determine some or all of the following:

① Create a list of fields that need to appear on the report. If you know what database or table each field is in, include that on the list. If the data does not currently exist, include it on the list also. You will use this list to complete tasks in future steps in the report design process.
② What should the report title be and where should it be placed on the report. Should it only be printed on the first page or on all pages of the report?
③ Does the report need page numbers or dates? If so, what format should they be in and where should they be placed on the report - in the page header or footer or someplace else?
④ Are any Special Fields other than the page number or date needed on the report?
⑤ Which fields or sections of the report need totals, summary, statistical information or some other type of calculated field? (**Hint**: Summary fields do not currently exist in a table).
⑥ An important question to answer during this step is what format the report needs to be in. This is known as the **DELIVERY METHOD** (for example, paper, PDF or web based). The way that a report needs to be distributed, can influence the layout of a report. You should also determine if the report needs to be distributed in more than one format.

Step 3: Find The Data For The Report

This step is very important because without the data, there is no report. As the person creating the report, life will be much easier for you if you are familiar with the data needed for the report and how it is organized. If you are not familiar with the data or are not technical, you may have to rely on Information Technology specialists like database administrators, to help you with the tasks in this step. There are three tasks that you have to work on, to complete this step successfully.

Task 1

The first task that you have to complete is to find out which databases and tables contain the data that you need for the report. Use the list of fields that you created in step 2, to find the databases and tables. You may also have to find out what servers the databases are on. There are several types of databases that the data can be stored in. The data may also be stored in a Crystal dictionary, an OLAP Cube or something other than a database. This task is known as finding the data source.

Task 2

This task involves selecting the actual fields in the tables that are needed for the report. Use the list that you created in step 2. Once the fields are selected, determine the formatting for each field and how the fields should be displayed on the report. You also have to determine if the field names in the table are the best choice for the field headings on the report. One example of when a field heading needs to be changed on a report is for fields that are known as ID fields, which you will learn about in Lesson 3.

Task 3

Now that you have found some of the data in the tables, there are probably fields left on the list that you created in step 2 that you have not found. Some may be special fields that you learned about earlier in this lesson. More than likely, many of the fields that are left on the list are calculated fields. This task involves writing out the formulas for the calculated fields. Some calculated fields may use a built-in function and others require a field that is in a data source, but will not be used on the report.

In order to be able to create calculated fields, you have to become familiar with the database field types and the Crystal Reports fields discussed earlier in this lesson. Several of the Crystal Reports functions are designed to only work with specific types of data. Examples of calculated fields include:

① Sales price x quantity
② Number of days between the order date and the ship date
③ How long the person has been employed at the company

Step 4: Organize The Data

This step involves organizing all of the data. Many of the options that you decide on in task 1 below, will automatically dictate which section of the report certain fields will be placed in.

Task 1

To complete this task, you have to organize all of the data, both from the tables and calculated fields, as well as, any other data source. Organizing the data means at a minimum, answering the following questions.

① Does the data need to be sorted? If so, which field(s) should the data be sorted on?
② Does the data need to be grouped? If so, which field(s) should the data be grouped on?
③ Does the report need summary data? Summary data is often a calculated field, like grand totals, averages and counts.
④ Does the report need to have any data flagged? If so, how should the data be flagged? The primary reason data would be flagged is so that it can be easily identified on a report. Make a list of data that needs to be flagged. Crystal Reports has several options including borders, symbols, changing the font size and other formatting techniques that you can use to indicate that the data is flagged.
⑤ Decide if the report needs any of the following: charts, cross-tabs, maps or alerts, which notify the person running the report that a specific condition has been met.

Task 2

To complete this task you have to determine which section of the report each field should be placed in. Task 1 had you make decisions on how to organize the data at a high level. There are several sections of a report that the data and objects can be placed in. The sections of a report are discussed later in this lesson.

Task 3

One way that you organize the data is selecting which records will actually appear on the report. This is important because most reports do not require that all records in a table appear on the report. For example, if the report needs to display sales (orders) for a specific sales rep, you would create selection criteria that would only allow orders for the particular sales rep to appear on the report. Another example would be to display all customers that purchased a specific product or group of products.

In addition to record selection, it may be necessary to create parameter fields, which will make the report more flexible in terms of record selection. Parameter fields allow the person running the report to select the criteria that will be used to retrieve the records that will appear on the report. Parameter fields allow one report to be run with a variety of selection criteria. An example of this would be an order report. If the report had parameter fields for the order date, order amount and sales rep fields, all of the following reports and more, could be run from the same report.

① A report to show all orders on a specific date.
② A report to show all orders for a specific sales rep.
③ A report to show all orders over or under a specific order amount.
④ A report to show all orders in a date range.
⑤ A report to show all orders in a certain date range for a specific sales rep.

Task 4

Depending on the company, it may be necessary to have the person or group of people sign a document that states that all of the tasks discussed above will produce the report that they need.

Report Prototype

Even though you will go through the entire report design process, it is very possible that the users are still somewhat unclear or cannot visualize what the finished report will look like. If that is the case, creating a report prototype will be a life saver. A prototype can be hand drawn on paper or you can create a sample report that displays the data based on the information that you gather during the report design process.

Some report designers create this prototype as each of the steps and tasks that were discussed above are completed. Other report designers will create the prototype right after the report design process is over. The reason prototypes are helpful is because the users will get a pretty good idea of what the finished report will look like, based on the information that they supplied.

The feedback that you receive from the users about the prototype is invaluable because users get to "see" what they asked for. I have found this process to be a very effective way for users to tell me what they like, don't like, need and don't need.

Sections Of A Report

There are seven sections of a report that you can place data and other objects in. If you place the same calculated field in different sections of the report, it will produce different results. It is important that you understand how each section of the report functions, because they function independently of each other. Keep the following items in mind when deciding where to place fields and objects on the report.

① Not all sections are needed for every report.
② If you create a report using a wizard, the majority of fields are automatically placed in the correct section of the report.
③ All of the report sections discussed below except the group header and footer, will appear in all reports. Grouping is optional.
④ The order of the default sections cannot be changed.
⑤ If a report does not need a section, it can be suppressed so that it does not display blank space on the report.
⑥ Sections can be resized as needed.

Formulas, charts and cross-tabs will display different results, depending on which section of the report they are placed in. These differences are explained in each report section.

 By default, the letters in parenthesis after each report section name discussed below, is what you will see to the left of the report when it is previewed. These are known as **SECTION SHORT NAMES**. In the design window, you will see the full section name. If you want to change either of these options, File ⇒ Options ⇒ Layout tab.

Section 1: Report Header (RH)

Data fields and other objects placed in this section will only print on the first page of the report. It is quite possible that many of the reports that you create will not have anything in this section. Something that you may want to include in this section of the report is the criteria and parameters of the report. If the report needs a cover page, the report header section can be used for the cover page. If this is what you need to do, add a page break after this section, so that the actual report starts on a new page.

FORMULAS are calculated for the entire report.
CHARTS and **CROSS-TABS** will contain data for the entire report.

 If the report header section requires more than one page, the information in the page header and footer sections of the report will not print until all of the information in the report header section has printed.

Section 2: Page Header (PH)

Data fields and other objects placed in this section will appear at the top of every page in the report. This is where most people put the report title. Other objects that are commonly placed in this section include the date, page number and headings for the fields in the details section of the report. Report wizards will automatically place field headings and the system generated "print date" field in this section.

FORMULAS are calculated at the beginning of every page of the report.
CHARTS and **CROSS-TABS** cannot be placed in this section.

Section 3: Group Header (GH)

This section is only used if data is grouped in the report. Data fields and other objects placed in this section will print at the beginning of each group section of the report. Each time the data in the field the group is based on changes, another group header and footer section is dynamically created. This section is always right above the details section. If a report is grouped on two or more fields, a new group header and footer section will be created for each field that the report is grouped on.

FORMULAS are calculated one time at the beginning of the group, based on the data in the group, not all of the data in the report.
CHARTS and **CROSS-TABS** will only display information based on the data in the group.

Section 4: Details (D)

Data fields and other objects placed in this section will print for each record that meets the selection criteria. The data fields and other objects in this section usually have field headings in the page header section. This section is automatically repeated once for each record that will be printed on the report.

FORMULAS are calculated for each record in this section, unless the record does not meet the condition of the formula.
CHARTS and **CROSS-TABS** cannot be placed in this section.

Section 5: Group Footer (GF)

This section is only used if data is grouped in the report. Data fields and other objects placed in this section will print at the end of each group. The group footer section often includes subtotals and other summary data for the group. This section is always right below the details section.

FORMULAS are calculated one time at the end of the group, based on the data in the group, not all of the data in the report.
CHARTS and **CROSS-TABS** will only display information based on the data in the group.

Section 6: Report Footer (RF)

Data fields and other objects placed in this section will print once at the end of the report. This is usually where grand totals and other types of report summary information is placed.

FORMULAS are calculated once at the end of the report.
CHARTS and **CROSS-TABS** will contain data for the entire report.

 If the report footer section requires more than one page, the page header and footer sections will print on the additional pages that the information in the report footer needs. This is the opposite of what happens if the report header requires more than one page. If you think about it though, that makes sense because by the time the report footer section is printed, the "switch" if you will, for the page header and footer sections is on.

Section 7: Page Footer (PF)

Data fields and other objects placed in this section will print at the bottom of each page of the report. The page footer section is similar to the page header section. Page numbers are often placed in this section. Report wizards will automatically place the page number in this section.

FORMULAS are calculated at the end of every page of the report. This would be useful if the report needs to have totals by page.
CHARTS and **CROSS-TABS** cannot be placed in this section.

 The five default sections of a report in order are: Report Header, Page Header, Details, Report Footer and Page Footer.

Report Creation Options

There are three ways (wizards, from an existing report and from scratch) that you can create a report. Each option has pros and cons. Once you understand all of the options, you can select the one that best meets the needs for the report that you have to create.

Wizards

This is the easiest way to create a new report. The wizards will walk you through all of the steps required to create a report. The wizards are helpful when learning the basics of Crystal Reports. Experienced report designers sometimes use the wizards to save time to create a basic report and then add advanced features manually. Keep in mind that the wizards do not provide all of the functionality that is needed to create many features that reports need. The wizards are limited because they use default options which often do not meet the needs of the report that you are creating. One of the things that comes to mind are the titles that summary fields and other total fields are given.

Based on your selections on the wizard screens, the fields are placed in the most appropriate section of the report. This does not mean that if you make a mistake when using the wizard, that the wizard will correct the mistake. It is possible to create a report that displays results that are different then you intended, when using a wizard. There are four report creation wizards that you can select from, that are discussed later in this lesson. What you will find, depending on the options that you select, is that additional fields are automatically added to the report, which you may not need. If this happens, you can delete the field(s) once you have the report open in the design window.

Create A Report Based Off Of An Existing Report

If a report exists that is similar to the report that you now need to create, select this report creation option. Save the existing report with a new name and make the necessary changes to the new report. An example of when to create a report based off of an existing report would be when two groups of people need to see the majority of the same fields and one group of people needs additional information that the other group does not need, or when one group needs the same fields in a different layout. You can also use one of the templates that come with Crystal Reports to format the report differently.

Create A Report From Scratch

This option gives you the most flexibility to create a report. You start with a blank canvas so to speak and add the fields, formulas and other objects without any assistance. For many, this can be intimidating, especially in the beginning, but being the fearless person that you are, I'm sure that when you get to the exercises that have you create a report from scratch, you will do just fine.

Wizard Types

As mentioned earlier, there are four report wizards that you can select from to create reports. They are discussed below.

① **Standard** This is probably the most used wizard because it provides the majority of options needed to create a wide variety of reports. The report wizards discussed below create specific types of reports.

② **Cross-Tab** This wizard will create a report that presents data in a grid. Cross-Tab reports resemble spreadsheets because they have rows and columns. The grid often contains totals at the end of each row and column. An example of when a cross-tab should be used would be if you needed to know how many of specific products were sold by each sales rep. You should only use this wizard if the cross-tab will be the only object on the report.

③ **Mailing Label** This wizard will walk you through the process of creating mailing labels. While you can format a report created with the Standard wizard to print labels, the advantage of using the mailing label wizard is that it has an option to select the label size that you need. This means that you will not have to manually format the report to match the dimensions of the label size that you need.

④ **OLAP Cube** This wizard lets you create a report that is similar to a cross-tab report. The difference is that this wizard lets you connect to OLAP data. You can filter the data and create a chart.

Using report wizards is not an objective on the exam.

Xtreme Database

The Xtreme database comes with Crystal Reports. This is the database that you will use as the basis for all of the reports that you will create in this workbook. It also contains sample reports, which you can use to get ideas for reports that you may need to create.

When Crystal Reports was installed, the Xtreme database also was installed. It is a Microsoft Access database. This database contains the data for a fictitious company called Xtreme Mountain Bikes. As the company name suggests, they sell mountain bikes and accessories. The database has tables that store the following types of information: Customers, Employees, Orders, Suppliers and Products.

Figure 2-1 shows the data model for the Xtreme database. The fields in bold are the Primary Key fields. Table 2-2 contains information for each table in the database that will be helpful when creating reports. You will learn more about primary keys in the next lesson.

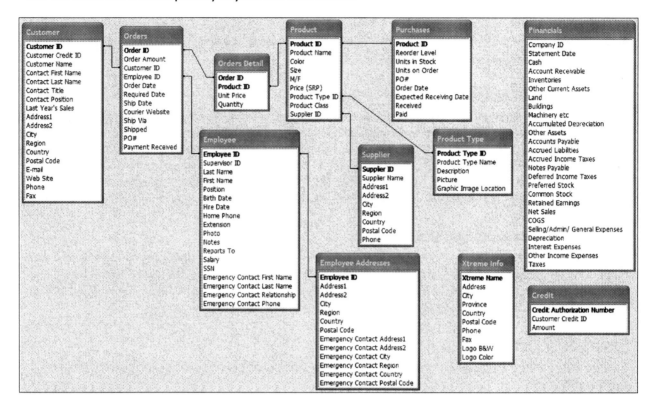

Figure 2-1 Xtreme database data model

Table	Primary Key	Indexed Fields	Records
Credit	Credit Authorization Number	Credit Authorization Number, Customer Credit ID	322
Customer	Customer ID	Customer ID, Postal Code	269
Employee	Employee ID	Employee ID, Supervisor ID, Reports To	15
Employee Address	Employee ID	Employee ID, Postal Code, Emergency Contact Postal Code	15
Financials	Company ID	Company ID	4
Orders	Order ID	Order ID, Customer ID, Employee ID	2,192
Orders Detail	Order ID, Product ID	Order ID, Product ID	3,684
Product	Product ID	Product ID, Product Type ID, Supplier ID	115
Product Type	Product Type ID	Product Type ID	8
Purchases	Product ID	Product ID	44
Supplier	Supplier ID	Supplier ID, Postal Code	7
Xtreme Info	Xtreme Name	Xtreme Name, Postal Code	1

Table 2-2 Xtreme database information

Xtreme Database Tables Explained

In order to help you become more familiar with the data contained in each table, this section provides a description of the data in each table. The table name is in bold.

Credit Contains credit limit information for customers.

Customer Contains contact and address information for all of the companies customers.

Employee Contains information for each employee. Some of the employees are sales reps for the company.

 The Supervisor ID field in the Employee table contains the Employee ID of a different person in the Employee table. The Supervisor ID field contains who the employee reports to. This is known as a **RECURSIVE JOIN**, which you will learn about in the next lesson.

Employee Addresses Contains the home address and emergency contact information for each person in the Employee table.

Financials Contains accounting information for the company.

Orders Contains information about each customer order. Fields that apply to the entire order, like the order date and order amount are in this table. This table is often referred to as the **ORDER HEADER** table. This table does not contain information about the items on the order.

Orders Detail Contains information about each item in each order. This is one of the smaller tables in the database in terms of the number of fields.

Product Contains information for each item that Xtreme sells. Each product only has one product type and supplier. This does not mean that there cannot be two suppliers that have the same product. For example, Supplier A has blue hats. Supplier B has blue hats and brown hats. There would be a record in the Product table for each of these three hats.

Product Type Contains the general categories for the products.

Purchases Contains information about purchases that Xtreme makes from their suppliers.

Supplier Contains information for the companies that Xtreme purchases the products from that they sell. Contact and address information for each supplier is stored in this table.

Xtreme Info Contains the Xtreme company contact information and the logo.

Viewing The Sample Reports

If you haven't already viewed any of the sample reports that come with the Xtreme database, this exercise will show you how to view them.

1. Click on the link, **SAMPLE REPORTS** in the "Getting Started" section of the Start Page.

2. On the **OPEN** dialog box you should see two folders, **FEATURE EXAMPLES** and **GENERAL BUSINESS**. Double-click on the Feature Examples folder. You will see the list of reports shown in Figure 2-2.

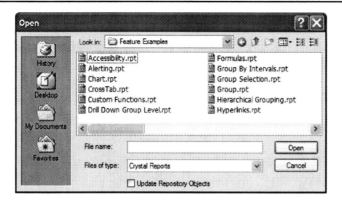

Figure 2-2 Reports in the Feature Examples folder

3. Double-click on the Accessibility report. The report should look similar to the one shown in Figure 2-3. The only difference should be the date and time under the report title.

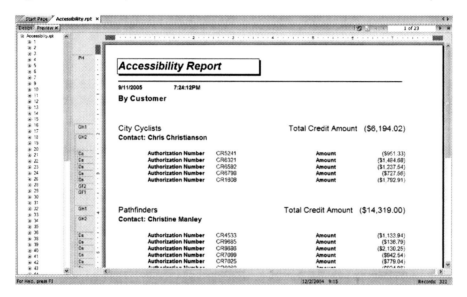

Figure 2-3 Accessibility Report

The Status Bar

The **STATUS BAR**, shown in Figure 2-4 is located below the report. The status bar is at the bottom of all Crystal Reports windows by default. It displays helpful information when you are designing and previewing reports. The information on the status bar will change, depending on what you are doing. It also displays tool tips when the mouse is hovered over an option on a menu or over a button on a toolbar. Like the toolbars, the status bar can also be turned off (View ⇒ Status Bar), but it can't be moved.

You should see the number of records in the report, towards the center of the status bar. The date and time shown, 12/2/2004 9:15 in Figure 2-4 is the last time that the data in the report that you are viewing was refreshed. If the data was refreshed or retrieved today, only the time will be displayed. If you clicked the **REFRESH** button, the date and time information will change. The percent shown in the far right corner is the percent of records that were retrieved. If an object is selected on the report, it's name will be displayed in the left hand corner of the status bar instead of the date and time, as shown in Figure 2-5. The object size and position are also displayed.

Figure 2-4 Status bar with report information

Field: Employee.Last Name	21:11	2.9 , 1.0 : 1.8 x 0.2

Figure 2-5 Status bar with field information

Preview And Design Tabs And Windows

When a report is opened, two tabs will appear below the Start Page tab: the preview and design tabs, which were shown earlier at the top of Figure 2-3. The majority of functionality available in the design window is also available in the preview window including the menus, toolbars and formatting options.

Preview Tab And Window

The preview window lets you view the report as it will look when it is printed. Reports can look different in this window depending on the printer that is selected. Also notice the following:

① That some of the toolbars at the top of the window that you learned about in Lesson 1 are now available.
② The report opened on it's own tab. The tab name is either the report file name or the report title.
③ The report has it's own Navigation toolbar, shown earlier in Figure 2-3 in the upper right hand corner. You can use the options on this toolbar to move from one page to another and to refresh the data in the report. The Navigation toolbar also lets you know what page of the report you are currently viewing and how many pages in total the report has. You can slide this toolbar to the left or to the right as needed.
④ The tan area to the left of the report contains the "sections" of the report. Having the sections visible, lets you know which section of the report each piece of data or object is in. You learned about the seven report sections earlier in this lesson.
⑤ The options down the far left side of the report are the groups that the report has. This section is called the **GROUP TREE**. It displays the groups and subgroups in the report. You can customize the group name, which you will learn how to do later in the workbook. The group tree will let you jump to a specific location in the report.
⑥ You can modify reports in the preview window. Unless stated otherwise, all reports that are modified in this workbook are written to be completed in the design window.

The preview tab will not automatically appear for a report that was created from the **BLANK REPORT** option or for a report that is open, but has not been refreshed. If you need the preview window and it is not visible, you can use one of the five options listed below.

① Click the **PRINT PREVIEW** button on the Standard toolbar.
② Click the **REFRESH** button on the Navigation Tools toolbar.
③ Press the **F5** key.
④ File ⇒ Print Preview.
⑤ File ⇒ Print ⇒ Preview Sample. You will learn more about this option in Lesson 8.

The Group Tree

This feature is helpful when you need to navigate through a report that has a lot of groups. You will not see the group tree if the report does not have groups. The group tree is located on the far left in the preview window. It displays all of the groups and subgroups in the report. Clicking on an option in the group tree will jump to the corresponding section in the report.

If a group has a subgroup, you will see a plus sign (+) in front of the group name, as shown earlier in Figure 2-3. Clicking on the plus sign will expand the group and show the subgroup as shown in Figure 2-6. The plus sign is also known as the **EXPAND BUTTON**. The minus sign is also known as the **COLLAPSE BUTTON**.

To turn the group tree on or off, click the **DISPLAY GROUP TREE** button on the Standard toolbar.

1. Click on the plus sign in front of the number 10, then click on the name under the group, as shown in Figure 2-6. You should now see the section for this person on page 3 of the report.

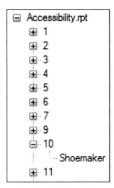

Figure 2-6 Group tree options illustrated

Group Tree Shortcut Menu

If you right-click in the group tree section of the preview window you will see the shortcut menu shown in Figure 2-7. The options are explained below.

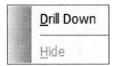

Figure 2-7 Group tree shortcut menu

① **Drill Down** This option will open another window as illustrated in Figure 2-8. This window contains the detail information for the branch in the group tree that you right-clicked on. The number on the tab represents the heading in the group tree that was right-clicked on.

② **Hide** This option will hide the branch that was selected before it was right-clicked on.

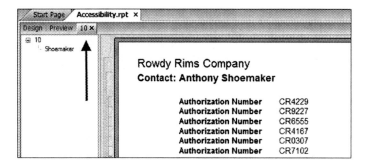

Figure 2-8 Drill Down result

 The Drill Down and Hide options are not available from the main menu.

Design Tab And Window

1. Click on the DESIGN tab. You will see the window shown in Figure 2-9.

The design window is where you will create and modify reports, as well as, easily see the structure of the report. Figure 2-10 illustrates the parts of the design window. Table 2-3 explains the parts of the design window.

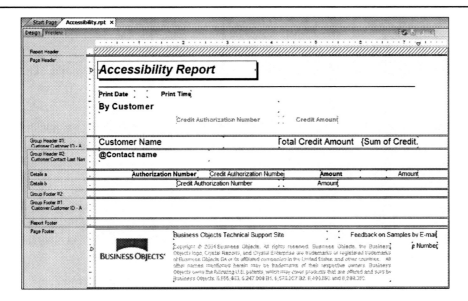

Figure 2-9 Design window

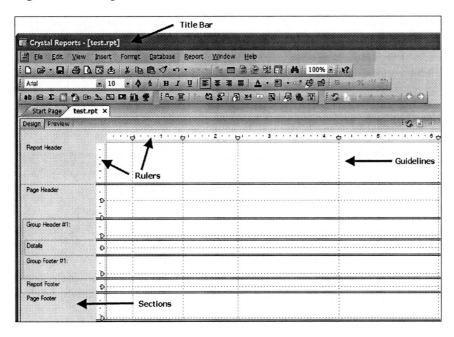

Figure 2-10 Parts of the design window illustrated

Option	Description
Title bar	Displays the name of the software followed by the file name of the report.
Sections	Like other parts of the design window, the section portion has a shortcut menu, which you access by right-clicking in the section that you want to work on. These are the report sections that you learned about earlier in this lesson.
Rulers	The rulers help you place fields in a specific location on the report.
Guidelines	The guidelines help you line up fields and other objects in the design area.
Design area	This is where you will add, change and format fields and other objects. The design area is all of the white space inside of the rulers. You can place objects as close to the edge of this area as necessary because this area is inside of the report page margins.

Table 2-3 Parts of the design window explained

Everything on a report is an object. Each object has its own set of properties. Almost all of these properties can be modified. The properties can also be modified based on a condition that you set. You will learn about conditional formatting in Lesson 9.

Report Sections

As shown above in Figure 2-10, the design window is divided into sections. The sections are divided by boundary lines, which are also called **SECTION BARS** and is how I will reference them. The sections can be resized by moving the section bar up or down. Figure 2-11 shows a smaller page header section and a larger details section, then shown above in Figure 2-10.

If you do not need to display data in a section of the report, you can **SUPPRESS** (hide) the section and it will not appear on the preview window or on the printed report. To resize a section of the report, place the mouse pointer over the section bar that you need to move, as illustrated in Figure 2-12. The mouse pointer will change to a double arrow as shown in Figure 2-12. Drag the section bar up or down.

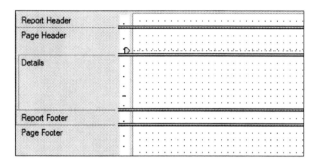

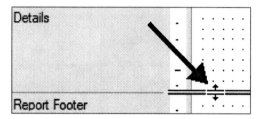

Figure 2-12 Mouse pointer in position to move the section bar

Figure 2-11 Sections of a report resized

 You cannot make a section of the report smaller than the objects that are in the section.

Design And Preview Window Differences

As much as these windows have in common, there are some differences between the windows that you should be aware of, as discussed below.

① The section names display differently. In the design window you can display the section names as long or short names. In the preview window, the section names can be hidden or displayed as short section names, but not long section names.
② Only the preview window has the group tree, page controls and refreshed data information.
③ If you select a field in the preview window, every occurrence of the field in the report is selected.
④ The design window has a vertical ruler for each section. The preview window has one vertical ruler for the entire report.
⑤ If you modify a field in the preview window, the report will take longer to be redisplayed then it will if you make the same change in the design window.
⑥ The design window does not display the page margins. In the preview window, the margins are displayed in light gray.

View Another Sample Report

1. Click on the Start Page tab, then click on the **SAMPLE REPORTS** link.

2. Double-click on the Feature Examples folder. Scroll until you see the Running Totals Group file and double-click on it. You will see the report shown in Figure 2-13.

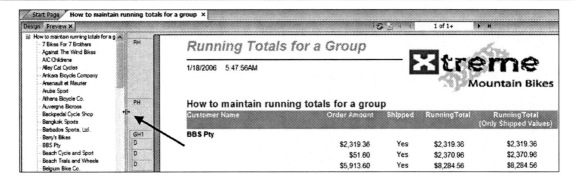

Figure 2-13 Preview of the Running Totals Group report

 If you can't see the groups on the left side of the window, place the cursor on the bar as illustrated above in Figure 2-13 and drag the bar over to the right as much as needed.

Notice that the report opened on it's own tab to the right of the Start Page tab. You can have several reports open at the same time. Also notice that you do not see the file name of the report on the tab. Instead, you see the report title on the tab. You will learn how to create report titles later in the workbook.

 The tab with the X indicates the active report window. To close a report click on the X. If changes were made to the report, you will be prompted to save them.

Report Navigation Toolbar

In Lesson 1 you learned about a navigation toolbar. [See Lesson 1, Navigation Tools Toolbar] Earlier I mentioned that the preview tab had it's own navigation toolbar. It is located in the upper right hand corner of the preview tab as shown above in Figure 2-13. This Report Navigation toolbar is shown in Figure 2-14. It has a **PAGE INDICATOR** that lets you know what page of the report you are currently viewing. As shown earlier in Figure 2-3, the page indicator lets you know that there are 23 pages in the report.

The plus sign in **1 OF 1+** shown in Figure 2-14 lets you know that Crystal Reports has not formatted all of the pages for the report. This means that the total number of pages is currently unknown.

Figure 2-14 Report Navigation toolbar

 If you see **1 OF 1+** and want to know how many pages the report has, click the **SHOW LAST PAGE** button on the navigation toolbar.

1. Click the **SHOW LAST PAGE** button on the Report Navigation toolbar. You should see the page shown in Figure 2-15. Scroll to the bottom of the report to see the grand totals.

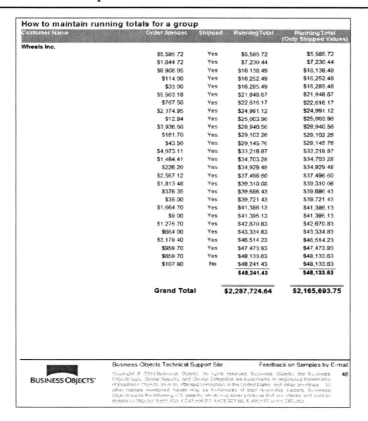

How to maintain running totals for a group			
Customer Name	Order Amount	Shipped	Running Total	Running Total (Only Shipped Values)
Wheels Inc.				
	$5,585.72	Yes	$5,585.72	$5,585.72
	$1,644.72	Yes	$7,230.44	$7,230.44
	$8,908.05	Yes	$16,138.49	$16,138.49
	$114.00	Yes	$16,252.49	$16,252.49
	$33.00	Yes	$16,285.49	$16,285.49
	$5,563.18	Yes	$21,848.67	$21,848.67
	$767.50	Yes	$22,616.17	$22,616.17
	$2,374.95	Yes	$24,991.12	$24,991.12
	$12.84	Yes	$25,003.96	$25,003.96
	$3,936.60	Yes	$28,940.56	$28,940.56
	$161.70	Yes	$29,102.26	$29,102.26
	$43.50	Yes	$29,145.76	$29,145.76
	$4,073.11	Yes	$33,218.87	$33,218.87
	$1,484.41	Yes	$34,703.28	$34,703.28
	$226.20	Yes	$34,929.48	$34,929.48
	$2,567.12	Yes	$37,496.60	$37,496.60
	$1,813.48	Yes	$39,310.08	$39,310.08
	$376.35	Yes	$39,686.43	$39,686.43
	$35.00	Yes	$39,721.43	$39,721.43
	$1,664.70	Yes	$41,386.13	$41,386.13
	$9.00	Yes	$41,395.13	$41,395.13
	$1,275.70	Yes	$42,670.83	$42,670.83
	$664.00	Yes	$43,334.83	$43,334.83
	$3,179.40	Yes	$46,514.23	$46,514.23
	$959.70	Yes	$47,473.93	$47,473.93
	$659.70	Yes	$48,133.63	$48,133.63
	$107.80	No	$48,241.43	$48,133.63
			$48,241.43	**$48,133.63**
	Grand Total		**$2,287,724.64**	**$2,165,693.75**

Figure 2-15 Last page of the Running Totals Group sample report

 Like the toolbars at the top of the Crystal Reports window can be moved, you can move the Report Navigation toolbar that is on the design and preview windows, if you do not like its current location. You can use the Report Navigation toolbar that is on the report window or the Navigation toolbar that is in the toolbar section of the Crystal Reports window. The biggest difference between the two navigation toolbars is that the toolbar on the design and preview windows provide the current page number and the total number of pages in the report. It would be nice if both navigation toolbars had all of the same options.

2. Close the Running Totals Group report by clicking on the X to the right of the report name. You may see the warning message shown in Figure 2-16.

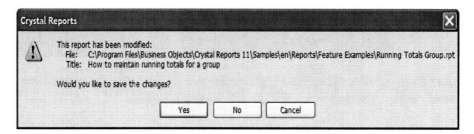

Figure 2-16 Report modified warning message

 File ⇒ Close, will also close the active report window.

Depending on what you have touched in the report, Crystal Reports will think that you have made changes. In this case, you didn't make any changes and if you did, you wouldn't want to save them in the sample report.

3. Click **NO** on the information window shown above in Figure 2-16. The report window will close. Close the Accessibility report. If prompted to save the changes, click No.

The **RECENT REPORTS** section of the Start Page will display the last five reports that you opened. You should see links for the two sample reports that you just opened, as shown in Figure 2-17. You will see additional reports listed if you opened reports prior to starting this exercise. The first report listed is the most recent one that you opened. I think that it would be great if there was an option to display the last nine reports, like the bottom of the File menu does.

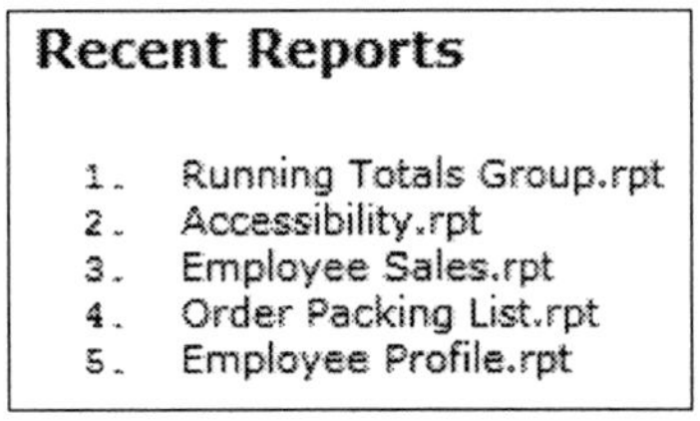

Recent Reports
1. Running Totals Group.rpt
2. Accessibility.rpt
3. Employee Sales.rpt
4. Order Packing List.rpt
5. Employee Profile.rpt

Figure 2-17 Recent Reports illustrated

NEW The Workbench

This feature will let you organize the reports that you create or are responsible for maintaining. The way that you organize the reports in the Workbench is by placing them in folders which Crystal Reports calls **PROJECTS**. You can also add **REPORT PACKAGES** to the Workbench if you are using the Crystal Reports Server or the Business Objects Enterprise.

Project folders can only contain reports. Unlike other file management tools, you cannot create a folder under an existing folder in the Workbench. A benefit of using the Workbench is that you will be able to access reports without having to know where they are located on your hard drive or which server they are on. The downside is that you have to add the reports one by one to the Workbench.

Once you have added reports to the Workbench, you can move them from one folder to another, by dragging the report. You can also rearrange the order of the project folders by dragging them to where you want them to be. You will create a folder in the Workbench for each lesson in this workbook. That way, should you need to go back to a report, it will be exactly like you left it at the end of that lesson.

> If you rename, delete or move the report (not the link in the Workbench), when you click on the link for it in the Workbench you will get an error message when you try to open the report. If this happens, you have to add the report to the Workbench again.

How To Create A Folder In The Workbench

The Workbench has been discussed as a way for you to organize the reports that you create.
In preparation for the first report that you will create, you will create a folder in the Workbench by following the steps below.

> View ⇒ Workbench, will display the Workbench if you do not see it on the Start Page. It is probably a good idea to leave the Workbench open all the time, because you will be using it throughout this workbook to open reports that you have already created.

1. Add ⇒ Add New Project, as shown in Figure 2-18.

2. Type `Lesson 2 Reports` as shown in Figure 2-19 and press Enter.

Workbench
Add
Add Existing Report...
Add New Project

Figure 2-18 Menu option to create a new project folder illustrated

Workbench
Add
Lesson 2 Reports

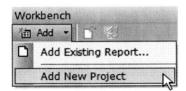

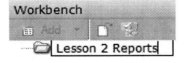

Figure 2-19 New project folder name illustrated

> Remember to create a folder in the Workbench at the beginning of each lesson.

Adding Reports To The Workbench

There are three ways to add reports to the Workbench as discussed below.

    ① Add ⇒ Add Existing Report.
    ② Right-click in the Workbench and select Add ⇒ Add Existing Report.
    ③ Drag a report from Windows Explorer to the Workbench.

The Workbench Toolbar

Table 2-4 explains the purpose of each button on the Workbench toolbar.

Button	Purpose
	The **Add Report** button lets you add three types of objects to the Workbench as discussed below. ① **Add Existing Report** Select this option if you want to add an existing report to the Workbench. ② **Add New Project** Select this option if you want to create a new project folder. ③ **Add Object Package** Selecting this option will prompt you to log into your Business Objects Enterprise System. After you log in, you can select an object to add to the Workbench. It is possible that you will not see this option when you click the Add Report button.
	The **Open** button lets you open a report that is in the Workbench. I find it easier to double-click on the report in the Workbench, then to click this button.
	The **Check Dependencies** button will start the Dependency Checker. This tool is used to check one report or all reports in a folder in the Workbench for the following types of errors: formula, hyperlink and repository.

Table 2-4 Workbench toolbar buttons explained

Report Packages

Earlier in this lesson I mentioned that Report Packages could be added to the Workbench. A report package is a group of related reports that are stored on a Crystal Reports Server or are in the Business Objects Enterprise. Report packages allow several reports to be viewed or scheduled as a single entity. Report packages are not stored in project folders.

In order to add a report package to the Workbench, you need to have a login account to the Crystal Reports Server or Business Objects Enterprise system. After you log in, there are two ways to add a report package as discussed below.

    ① Add ⇒ Add Object Package, from the Workbench toolbar.
    ② Right-click in the Workbench and select Add ⇒ Add Object Package.

Deleting Projects And Reports From The Workbench

Deleting projects and reports from the Workbench works similar to how you delete folders and files in other applications. Reports deleted from the Workbench are not deleted from the hard drive or server that they are stored on. You are only deleting the reference (link) to the report in the Workbench. There are two ways to delete items in the Workbench, as discussed below.

    ① Click on the project folder or report that you want to delete and press the DEL key on your keyboard.
    ② Right-click on the project folder or report that you want to delete and select REMOVE on the shortcut menu.

Maintaining The Workbench

The information for the Workbench is stored in the file **PROJECTEXPLORER.XML.** This file is saved in your personal folder under the Documents and Settings folder, which Windows XP creates. If you have to reinstall Crystal Reports, and want to retain your Workbench project folder and report links, you should copy this file to another location before reinstalling Crystal Reports and then copy the file back. If you get a new computer, you can copy this file to the new computer and you will have the same objects in the Workbench.

Learning To Create Reports

For some, learning to create reports can be intimidating. Learning to create reports requires time, patience and dedication. Crystal Reports is a very robust package and has a lot of features and options. As you go through the hands-on exercises in this workbook, take your time and try to understand how the concepts that you are learning can be applied to reports that you will create on your own, once you have completed this workbook. It is possible to go through this entire workbook in a few days if you already have above average report design experience with another software package or if you have used a previous version of Crystal Reports and have a solid foundation of relational databases.

The reality is that you will make some mistakes along the way. If you have a fear of making mistakes, this is the time to let go of the fear because the fear will prevent you from learning. It is also normal to initially get confused on what to do next. Even though you may not understand why you are being instructed to do something, the steps in each exercise will allow you to achieve the expected result. This is how you will begin to build a foundation for creating reports and learning Crystal Reports.

The first time that a concept or technique is presented, a lot of information is provided. Each subsequent time that you have to perform the same task, less and less information (aka hand holding) will occur. As you will see, there are a lot of repetitious tasks involved in creating reports. These are the tasks that less and less information will be provided for as you go through the workbook. The purpose behind this learning technique is to allow you to rely more on your knowledge, which in turn allows you to complete an exercise in less time.

Exercise 2.1: Create Your First Report

I suspect that this is the moment that you have been waiting for - to create your first report. The first report that you will create is a report that only uses data from one table. The report layout is basic, but you will use almost every screen on the wizard dialog box so that you can become familiar with all of the options. You will use the Standard Report Wizard to create the reports in this lesson.

Why Do I Have To Connect To A Data Source?

First, I should explain what a data source is. A data source contains the underlying data for the report that you will create or modify. The most common data source is a database. In addition to there being several types of data sources that you can connect to, there are multiple ways to connect to the same data source including the Xtreme database. You can connect to this database via the Access/Excel (DAO) connection type or the ODBC connection type. There are two reasons that you would need to connect to a data source as discussed below.

① Earlier in this lesson you viewed two of the reports that come with the Xtreme sample database. The reason that you were able to view data for these reports is because the reports were saved with the data. You will learn more about saving data with reports later in this lesson. If the data is not saved with the report, you would have to create a connection to the database(s) that the report gets its data from, to view data with the report.

② If you want to create a new report or modify an existing report that does not have the data saved with it.

Step 1: Create A Connection To The Data Source

There are several types of data sources that you can use in Crystal Reports. Figure 2-20 shows the categories of connection options that are available. Table 2-5 explains some of the more popular connection options.

Figure 2-20 Available connection options illustrated

 You may see different data source options depending on the data components that were selected when you installed Crystal Reports. You will also see data source options that you have added.

 If you do not see the **UNIVERSES** data source option shown above in Figure 2-20 and you need to use it, you can download the fix from this web page.
http://support.businessobjects.com/library/kbase/articles/c2017168.asp

Connection Option	Lets You Connect To . . .
Access/Excel (DAO)	Access databases and Excel files.
Database Files	Standard PC databases including FoxPro, Paradox, Clipper and dBASE.
ODBC (RDO)	Any ODBC complaint database including Oracle, Sybase, Access and Visual FoxPro.
OLAP	OLAP cubes and .CAR files. OLAP stands for Online Analytical Processing. CAR stands for Crystal Analysis file.
OLE DB (ADO)	Data link files that contain connection information that is saved in a file.
Universes	Business Objects query and analysis tools like Web Intelligence.
XML	XML files.
More Data Sources	Databases through ODBC drivers including ACT! 3.0, Btrieve, Informix, Oracle, Sybase and Web/IIS log files.

Table 2-5 Database and data sources explained

If you haven't created a connection (either for the Access/Excel (DAO) or the ODBC (RDO) connection type) for the Microsoft Access Xtreme sample database that comes with Crystal Reports, you will have to do that first. Follow the steps below to create an Access/Excel (DAO) connection. When Crystal Reports is installed, an ODBC connection for the Xtreme database should have been created. You can go to the section, Step 2: Select The Tables, if you already have a connection to the Xtreme database.

How To Create An Access/Excel (DAO) Connection
1. Click on the **STANDARD REPORT WIZARD** link on the Start Page.

2. Click on the plus sign in front of the **CREATE NEW CONNECTION** Data Source option. If this is the first Access/Excel (DAO) connection that you are creating, you will see the Access/Excel (DAO) connection dialog box.

3. Click on the button at the end of the **DATABASE NAME** field. Navigate to the following path: C:\Program Files\Business Objects\Crystal Reports 11\Samples\en\Databases, as shown in Figure 2-21. If you changed the default folders during the installation, navigate to the destination folder that you selected in Lesson 1 in Figure 1-7.

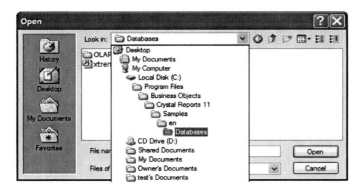

Figure 2-21 Path to the Xtreme sample database

4. Double-click on the **XTREME.MDB** database file. The database should have been added to the Database Name field on the dialog box as shown in Figure 2-22.

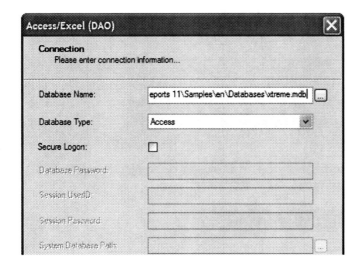

Figure 2-22 Xtreme sample database added to the Connection dialog box

 If you want to make sure that you added the correct database, click in the Database Name field and press the **END** key. You will be able to see the database name shown above in Figure 2-22.

 If the database required logon information, you would check the **SECURE LOGON** option shown above in Figure 2-22. The remaining fields on the dialog box would become available for you to enter the password information.

5. Click the **FINISH** button. You have completed creating your first connection to a database in Crystal Reports. That wasn't so bad, was it?

Step 2: Select The Tables

1. Click on the plus sign in front of the **CREATE NEW CONNECTION** folder, then click on the plus sign in front of the Access/Excel (DAO) folder or the ODBC folder depending on the connection type that you created for the Xtreme database.

2. Select the Xtreme database and click on the plus sign in front of the Tables folder. You should see the tables shown in Figure 2-23. These are all of the tables that are in the Xtreme database. They are the tables that are used in the sample reports that you viewed earlier in this lesson.

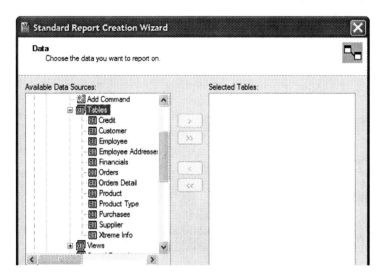

Figure 2-23 Tables in the Xtreme database

 The only reason that I can think of to click the **CANCEL** button shown above in Figure 2-23 on a screen in the wizard is if you decide that you no longer want to create the report. You will lose all of the options that you have selected if you click the Cancel button. It is better to use the **BACK** button to go back and make correct changes, because you cannot reopen the wizard to make changes or pick up where you left off.

3. Click on the **PRODUCT** table, then click the **>** button. The Product table should now be in the **SELECTED TABLES** section, as shown in Figure 2-24. Click Next.

Figure 2-24 Product table selected

All of the items in the **AVAILABLE FIELDS** section are the fields that are in the Product table that you selected on the previous screen.

View The Data In A Field

The **BROWSE DATA** button on the Fields screen will let you view data that is in the field that you select. Being able to view the data in a field is helpful if you are not familiar with the data in a table. This button is on several dialog boxes in Crystal Reports.

1. Click on the **PRODUCT NAME** field, then click the **BROWSE DATA** button. You will see the dialog box shown in Figure 2-25. The items in the scroll box is the data in the Product Name field.

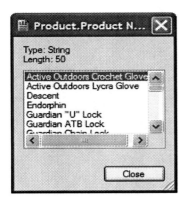

Figure 2-25 Data in the Product Name field

 Notice that the **FIELD TYPE** and **LENGTH** are displayed at the top of the dialog box shown above in Figure 2-25. This information is helpful because you can learn more about the field and the data stored in it.

2. Click the Close button when you are finished viewing the data.

 You can also view the data on the Design window. By default, the first 500 distinct values in the field are displayed. This default number of values cannot be changed, but the actual values that you see can be changed, by clearing the **SELECT DISTINCT DATA FOR BROWSING** option on the Database tab on the Options dialog box or on the Report Options dialog box if you only want the change to be for the report that you are currently working on. [See Lesson 8, Report Options] It probably is not a good idea to turn this option off because you will see duplicate data in the Browse Data dialog box shown above in Figure 2-25.

How To Find A Field

The **FIND FIELD** button will let you search for a field in the table. You will see this button on a few dialog boxes in Crystal Reports. I'm not sure that I understand the purpose of this button because all of the fields in a table are displayed on this dialog box. It could be helpful if you don't know which table a field is in.

Figure 2-26 Enter Search Name dialog box

The Find Field button will only find the first field that matches the text that you enter in the dialog box shown in Figure 2-26. You can also enter a partial field name. If the same field name is in more than one table, it does not continue searching. If you were creating a report on your own you would have already written down a list of fields and where they are located in the report design process, because you learned to do this earlier in this lesson <smile>.

Step 3: Select The Fields

1. Click on the Product Name field if it is not already selected and click the **>** button. You should see the field in the **FIELDS TO DISPLAY** section.

2. Add the following fields to the Fields To Display section: Size, Price (SRP) and Product Class. Figure 2-27 shows the fields that should have been added. Click Next.

To add all of the fields in the table at the same time, click the **>>** button. You do not have to select any fields before clicking this button.

To remove a field that you do not need on the report, click on the field in the Fields To Display section, then click the **<** button.

To remove all of the fields from the Fields to Display section, click the **<<** button.

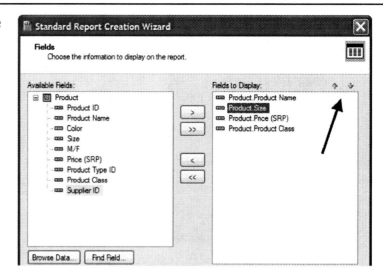

Figure 2-27 Fields selected

 You can add several fields at the same time by clicking on the first field that you want to add, then hold down the **CTRL** key and click on the other fields, one by one, that you want to add. When you have all of the fields selected that you want to add, click the **>** button.

The order that you add the fields to the Fields to Display section is the order that they will appear on the report in the details section from left to right. If you discover that the fields are not in the order that you want them to appear on the report, click on the field in the Fields To Display section and click the **UP** or **DOWN** arrow button illustrated above in Figure 2-27 to move the field to where it should be.

 The order that the fields are in will change automatically if at least one field is selected to group on. Fields that are grouped on are moved to the beginning of the details section. You can rearrange the fields after the wizard has created the report. This does not happen when you create a report from scratch that has groups.

Notice in Figure 2-27 above, that fields in the Fields To Display section have the table name in front of the field name. This is done to let you know which table the field is located in. This is helpful when you are using more than one table to create the report. Primary key fields in tables often have the same field name when the tables have related information. Without adding the table name, you would not know which table a field came from.

 Primary key fields are fields that are used to link one table to another table.

Step 4: Select The Grouping Options

As you learned earlier, grouping allows you to organize and sort the data. Grouping data forces all records that are related by the field that is being grouped on, to print together. Grouping data makes reports that have a lot of data easier to read. Grouping the data in a report is optional. You can group on more than one field. You can group on fields that have already been selected to print on the report, or you can select fields to group on that will not print on the report.

The Accessibility report that you viewed earlier in this lesson uses the grouping option. That report is grouped on customer name and contact name.

1. Add the Product Class field to the Group By section. The default grouping option **IN ASCENDING ORDER** is correct. Figure 2-28 shows the grouping options that you should have selected. Click Next.

There are two options that you can select from to group the records by, as discussed below. This is how you sort the values that are in the field that is being grouped on.

IN ASCENDING ORDER This is the default grouping option. The values in the field being grouped on will be sorted in A-Z order if the field is a string field. If the field being used to group on is numeric, the values will be sorted in 0-9 order.

IN DESCENDING ORDER The values in the field being grouped on will be sorted in Z-A order if the field is a string field. If the field being used to group on is numeric, the values will be sorted in 9-0 order.

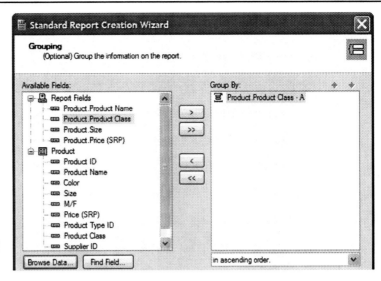

Figure 2-28 Field added to the Group By section

Step 5: Select The Summary Options

Creating summary fields is optional. Summary options usually involve calculated fields. By default, the wizard will create a summary field for all numeric fields that were selected to print on the report. There are 25 built-in summary functions that you can use. Many of them are shown at the bottom of Figure 2-29. The number of summary options that you see in the list, depends on the data type of the field that you are summarizing on. Not all data types can use all of the summary function options. Many of the summary functions are only for numeric fields.

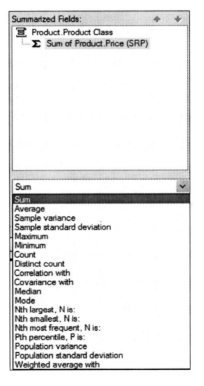

Figure 2-29 Summary options illustrated

1. Add the Product Class field to the **SUMMARIZED FIELDS** section.

2. Open the drop down list shown above in Figure 2-29 and select **COUNT**. Notice that the Product Class field has different options in the drop down list, then those shown above for the Product Price (SRP) field. Figure 2-30 shows the summary options that should be selected. Click Next.

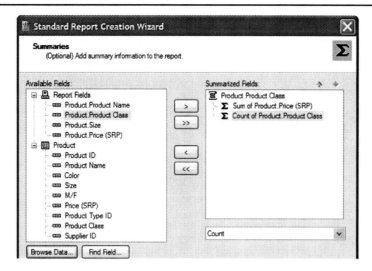

Figure 2-30 Summary options

3. Select the **TOP 5 GROUPS** option. Figure 2-31 shows the Group Sorting options that should be selected. Click Next.

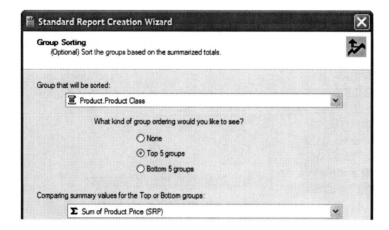

Figure 2-31 Group Sorting options

 The Top 5 Groups option will only display data for the five groups that have the highest value in the field selected in the **SUMMARY VALUES** field. Selecting **NONE**, which is the default, will display all groups. It is possible that you will not get the five groups that you think should appear on the report. This is because of the way that Crystal Reports processes data. In Lesson 7 you will create a Top 5 group report that illustrates unexpected results because a wizard was used to create the report.

Step 6: Select The Chart Type

Adding a chart to a report is optional. Once you select a chart type, the wizard will fill in information for the other fields on the dialog box. If you are not sure what options to select, accept the defaults, preview the report and then decide which chart options need to be modified.

1. Select the **PIE CHART** option. Figure 2-32 shows the chart options that should be selected. Click Next.

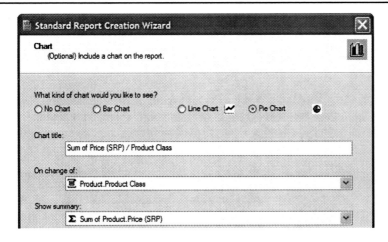

Figure 2-32 Chart options

Step 7: Select The Fields To Filter On

Creating filters is optional. Filters are another way that you can narrow down the number of records that will appear on the report. You can create as many filters as you need. In this step you will create a filter for the Product Size field to only display records that have a size, that is in a specific range.

1. Add the Product Size field to the **FILTER FIELDS** section, then open the drop down list and select **IS BETWEEN**.

2. Open the next drop down list and select 16, then open the last drop down list and select **XLRG**. Figure 2-33 shows the filter options that should be selected. Click Next.

 The data in the last two drop down lists is the actual data in the field that you are creating the filter for.

The filter that you just created will only display products that have a size that is between 16 and XLRG.

The filter options shown in Figure 2-33 are the same as what you would select on the **SELECT EXPERT** tool that you will learn how to use in Lesson 5.

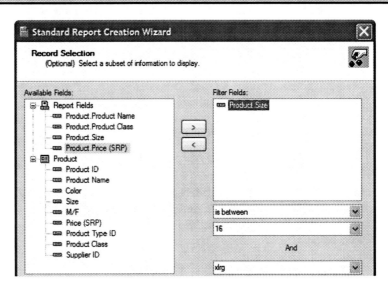

Figure 2-33 Filter options

Step 8: Select A Template

Selecting a template is optional. If you do not want to use a template, select the **NO TEMPLATE** option. You can preview what the other template options look like by clicking on them.

1. Select the **CORPORATE (BLUE)** template and click Finish. The first page of the report should look like the one shown in Figure 2-34. The top of the second page of the report should look like the one shown in Figure 2-35. As you scroll through the report, you may see things that you would like to rearrange on the report.

In Step 4, because grouping options were selected, the **GROUP TREE** shown down the left side of the report in Figure 2-34, is displayed. Clicking on the options in the group tree will take you to that section of the report. If for some reason the group tree is not visible or you do not want to see it, you can click the **TOGGLE GROUP TREE** button on the Standard toolbar, to turn it on or off.

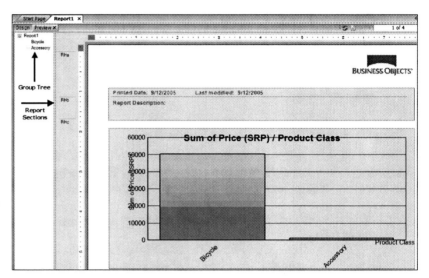

Figure 2-34 Page 1 of the report

Printed Date: 9/27/2005	Last modified: 9/12/2005		
Bicycle			
Product Class	**Product Name**	**Size**	**Price (SRP)**
Bicycle	Descent	22	$2,939.85
Bicycle	Descent	17	$2,939.85
Bicycle	Descent	17	$2,939.85
Bicycle	Descent	18.5	$2,939.85
Bicycle	Descent	18.5	$2,939.85
Bicycle	Descent	20	$2,939.85
Bicycle	Nicros	18	$329.85
Bicycle	Descent	20	$2,939.85

Figure 2-35 Page 2 of the report

Step 9: Save The Report

As shown earlier in Figure 2-34, the report was given a default name of **REPORT 1** which you can use. You should save the report with a name that is more meaningful. In addition to giving the report a meaningful name, you have to decide whether or not you want to save the data with the report, which is discussed below.

Options For Saving Data

Unless you changed the default options after Crystal Reports was installed, the data is saved with the report by default. Figure 2-36 illustrates the **SAVE DATA WITH REPORT** option selected on the File menu. There are pros and cons to saving data with a report as discussed below.

> If you do not want the **SAVE DATA WITH REPORT** option set as the default, File ⇒ Options. Click on the **REPORTING** tab. Clear the option, **SAVE DATA WITH REPORT** and click OK.

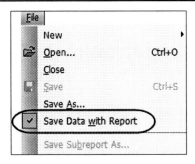

Figure 2-36 Save data option on the File menu

Save The Report With Data

As stated earlier, this is the default option. You can preview and print reports faster with this option because the data does not have to be retrieved. This option is also useful if you need to send the report to someone that does not have access to the data. One downside to saving the data with the report is that the report requires more hard drive or server space. A second downside is that anyone that runs the report with saved data will not be using the most current data. A third downside occurs if the database has security. Unless the report has been published to Crystal Reports Server, the security is bypassed and anyone that opens the report will have access to the data, whether they should or not.

Fields in tables are indexed to reduce the time it takes to retrieve the records needed to create the report. Fields that are used in the record selection criteria are often used as an index.

 Indexes are not usually helpful in reports that use saved data. The exception to this is reports that have parameter fields that the person running the report can use to change the record selection formula. The **REPORT BURSTING INDEXES** command will let you create indexes in reports that are saved with data.

Save The Report Without Data

Selecting this option requires less disk space. With this option you will be using live data each time the report is run. The downside is when you need to preview or print the report, it will take a little longer to process, because the data has to be retrieved. Most of the time, you will not notice the delay.

 From a report developers perspective if you have the space, it will save time, a considerable amount of time if there are thousands of records, if you save the data with the report while you are creating and modifying it. The danger that some developers have <not us of course> is that they forget to change the save data option before putting the report into production. Another danger is not testing the report with live data. Remember that most data is volatile, meaning that it changes frequently, is deleted and added to on a regular basis. Not testing with live data before putting the report into production could be a bad career move, if you know what I mean. Testing with live data before putting the report into production, also means that it won't go into production with the saved data.

Refreshing Report Data

As you just learned, you have to decide whether to save the data with the report or not. If you decide to normally save data with a report to save processing time while designing the report that's fine. Anytime that you want to work with the current data, click the **REFRESH** button on the navigation toolbar.

If the changes that you make to a report fall in the formatting category, like changing fonts, moving fields around on the report or adding titles to summary fields that were already saved with the report, you do not have to refresh the data.

Automatic Data Refreshing

If any of the items below occur after a report have been saved, the data will automatically be refreshed, regardless of the save data option that is associated with the report.

① A new field is added to the report.

② If a formula is added to the report that uses a field that was not already being used on the report.

③ If an existing formula is modified that uses a field that was not already being used on the report.

④ If any report criteria or parameter fields are added or changed that include a field that was not already being used on the report.

⑤ If the grouping is not done on a server, the detail record data will be refreshed.

> If you drill down on hidden data, the data is not a full refresh. If the grouping is taking place on a server, drilling down in the details section will only retrieve the new data required by the drill down for the details section.

Yes, I can sense that you are shaking your head about the save data with report options. Keep in mind that only the fields on the report and fields needed for formulas or functions that the report uses are saved with the report. Other fields in the table are not saved with the report. This is why you are prompted frequently to refresh data when the save data option is turned on. As you become more familiar with modifying reports, you will know which save data option is best suited for each report that you are modifying or creating.

Real World Data

Many companies have what is known as a "development server" that has a copy of "live data" and applications (live data is also known as production data). This is done so that anyone that is creating new applications, modifying existing applications or testing software, can do so without putting the companies data in danger. If this is the type of environment that you working in, keep in mind while going through this workbook, the differences between "live" and "refreshed" data, when these terms are referenced.

When creating reports on a development server and you click the **REFRESH** button in Crystal Reports, you are not getting a copy of the data from a production server. You are getting another copy of the data from the development server. The same is true if you have placed a copy of the production data on your hard drive. Usually, data on a development server is refreshed from a production server at pre-defined intervals (ex. daily, weekly monthly). If you want to know when the data on a development server is refreshed, ask the DBA or the person that manages the databases that you are using.

Save The Report

> The default file extension for reports is **.RPT** in Crystal Reports. Report file names can have up to 255 characters and can include spaces and special characters. Reports can be stored in almost any folder on your hard drive or server. You should not store reports in operating system folders.

1. File ⇒ Save As. Open the **SAVE AS** drop down list on the Save As dialog box and navigate to the Crystal Reports Workbook folder that you created in Lesson 1.

> You can also click the **SAVE** button on the Standard toolbar.

2. Type L2.1 My first report as the file name, as shown at the bottom of Figure 2-37 and press Enter or click the Save button.

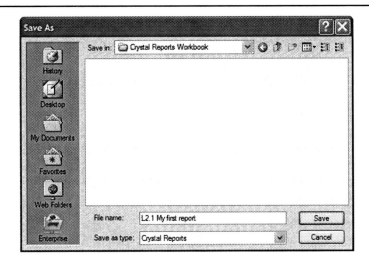

Figure 2-37 Save As options illustrated

 Report file names like the one shown above in Figure 2-37 are different then report titles. Report file names are what you save the report as. Report titles come from the DOCUMENT PROPERTIES dialog box.

The name on the design and preview tabs by default will display the report file name. If the report has a report title, that will be displayed on the tab instead. In the "View Another Sample Report" section, earlier in this lesson, you opened the "Running Totals Group" report. The tab for that report displays, "How To Maintain Running Totals For A Group". This is the report title.

Step 10: Add The Report To The Workbench

When you save a report, it is not automatically added to the Workbench. You have to manually add it. Follow the steps below to add the report to the Workbench.

1. Add ⇒ Add Existing Report, in the Workbench.

2. Navigate to the folder that has the report that you want to add to the Workbench. In this exercise, navigate to the Crystal Reports Workbook folder. Double-click on the report that you want to add. Double-click on the "L2.1 My first report" file. The report should now be under the Lesson 2 Reports folder in the Workbench, as shown in Figure 2-38. Close the report.

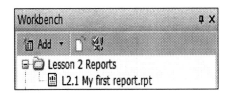

Figure 2-38 Report added to the Workbench

Additional Ways To Select A Data Source

In the previous exercise you selected the data source (in this case a database) under the CREATE NEW CONNECTION folder. There are other ways to select a data source that you have already created a connection for, as discussed below.

① If you opened the data source after you opened the current session of Crystal Reports, you can select the data source under the CURRENT CONNECTIONS folder shown in Figure 2-39. Once you close Crystal Reports, all data source connections in the Current Connections folder are closed.

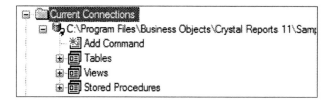

Figure 2-39 Current Connections folder option

② If you know that you will be using a data source on a regular basis, you should add it to the **Favorites** folder by right-clicking on the data source under another folder and selecting **ADD TO FAVORITES**, as illustrated in Figure 2-40.

Figure 2-40 Add to Favorites option illustrated

③ The **History** folder contains the last five data sources that were opened.

④ The **Repository** folder will let you select a Business Objects View or an SQL command. The repository lets you connect to data on the Crystal Reports Server or in the Business Objects Enterprise repository.

Report Bursting Indexes

The Report Bursting Indexes command (Report ⇒ Report Bursting Indexes) will let you create indexes in reports that have saved data. Figure 2-41 shows the **SAVED DATA INDEXES** dialog box, which is used to select the fields in the report to create indexes for the next time the report is refreshed. After the fields are selected, the report should be refreshed so that the indexes can be created.

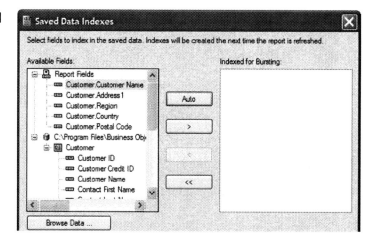

Figure 2-41 Saved Data Indexes dialog box

 Clicking the **AUTO** button will automatically add all of the fields that are used in the record selection criteria for the report to the Indexed for Bursting list.

Exercise 2.2: Create A Product List Report

In this exercise you will create a product list report that will print the Product ID, Product Name and Price fields.

1. Click on the Standard Report Wizard link on the Start Page.

2. Select the Xtreme database, then add the Product table to the Selected Tables section and click Next.

3. Add the Product ID, Product Name and Price (SRP) fields to the Fields to Display section and click Finish because the report does not require any of the options on the other wizard screens. Your report should look like the one shown in Figure 2-42.

```
11/19/20

Product ID  Product Name             Price (SRP)
    1,101  Active Outdoors Crochet Glo'    $14.50
    1,102  Active Outdoors Crochet Glo'    $14.50
    1,103  Active Outdoors Crochet Glo'    $14.50
    1,104  Active Outdoors Crochet Glo'    $14.50
    1,105  Active Outdoors Crochet Glo'    $14.50
    1,106  Active Outdoors Lycra Glove     $16.50
    1,107  Active Outdoors Lycra Glove     $16.50
    1,108  Active Outdoors Lycra Glove     $16.50
    1,109  Active Outdoors Lycra Glove     $16.50
    1,110  Active Outdoors Lycra Glove     $16.50
    1,111  Active Outdoors Lycra Glove     $16.50
    2,201  Triumph Pro Helmet              $41.90
    2,202  Triumph Pro Helmet              $41.90
```

Figure 2-42 L2.2 Product list report

4. Save the report as L2.2 Product list and close it.

Exercise 2.3: Create An Employee Contact List Report

The fields that are needed to create this report are stored in two tables. This report will be grouped by the Supervisor ID field so that each supervisor can have a list of their employees.

1. Open the Standard Report Wizard and select the Xtreme database.

2. Add the Employee and Employee Addresses tables, then click Next.

Linking Tables

You will see the screen shown in Figure 2-43. The options on this screen allow you to select the appropriate links for the tables that you have selected.

Most of the time, the link that is automatically selected is the one that you need. Fields are automatically linked if they have the same name and data type. In this exercise, the tables should be linked by the Employee ID field.

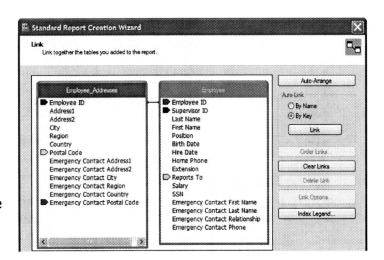

Figure 2-43 Link screen

 You may need to make the dialog box wider to see both tables. To make the dialog box wider, place the cursor on the right side of the dialog box and drag the border of the dialog box to the right. You can also make the tables longer if you want to see all of the fields.

If you right-click on a field shown above in Figure 2-43 and select **BROWSE FIELD,** as shown in Figure 2-44, you will be able to see the first 500 unique values for the field that you selected. If you see more than one occurrence of the same value, it means that you have turned off the Select Distinct Data For Browsing option on the Database tab on the Options dialog box or on the Report Options dialog box.

Figure 2-44 Link screen shortcut menu

Index Legend

As you can see in Figure 2-43 above, there are colored arrows next to some fields. If you click on the **INDEX LEGEND** button, you will see the index that each colored arrow represents, as shown in Figure 2-45.

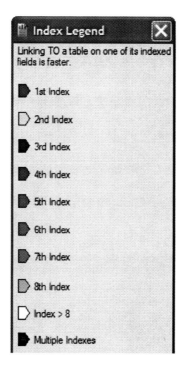

Figure 2-45 Index Legend dialog box

Add The Fields To The Report

1. Click Next on the dialog box shown earlier in Figure 2-43, then add the fields in Table 2-6 to the Fields to Display section. Figure 2-46 shows the order that the fields should be in. Click Next.

Employee	Employee Addresses
Supervisor ID	Region
First Name	
Last Name	
Home Phone	

Table 2-6 Fields to add to the report

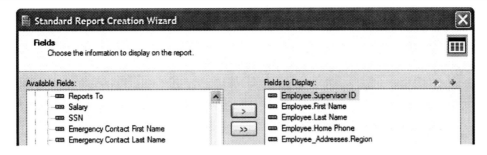

Figure 2-46 Fields selected for the report

Select The Grouping Options

This report would look better if it was grouped on the Supervisor ID field and within each Supervisor ID group, the employee names were sorted by last and first name. It would also be helpful if there was a count of employees per supervisor.

1. Add the Supervisor ID field to the **GROUP BY** section and click Next.

2. Add the Employee ID field to the **SUMMARIZED FIELDS** section. This field is in the Employee table.

3. Open the drop down list and select **COUNT**. Figure 2-47 shows the summary options that should be selected.

This option will count the number of employee ID's under each supervisor ID. When you want a count of records, you should select a field that has unique values. Each employee is assigned a unique ID.

Think of ID's as being the equivalent of social security numbers, where each persons social security number is unique.

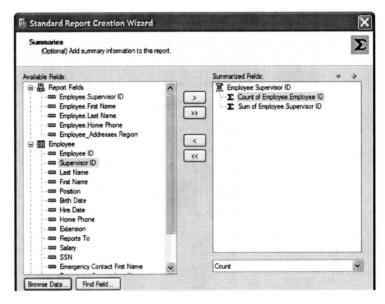

Figure 2-47 Summary options

4. Click Next. Click Next again on the Group Sorting dialog box because you do not need to change any of the options.

Select The Chart Options

1. Select the **BAR CHART** option.

2. Type `Count of employees per supervisor` in the **CHART TITLE** field. Figure 2-48 shows the chart options that should be selected. Click Next.

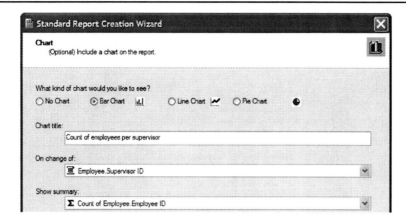

Figure 2-48 Chart options

Finish The Report

1. Click Next on the Record Selection screen because you do not need to select any fields to filter on.

2. Select **NO TEMPLATE** and click Finish. Your report should look like the one shown in Figure 2-49. It looks okay, but it needs to be modified. You will learn how to modify reports later in the workbook.

3. Close the report and save it as L2.3 Employee contact list.

 If there is an existing report that has some of the data that you need to create another report, open the existing report and use the File ⇒ Save As option. Save the report with a new name and modify it as needed.

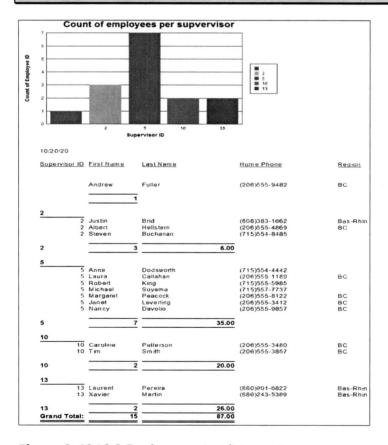

Figure 2-49 L2.3 Employee contact list report

Exercise 2.4: Saving Data

Earlier you learned that you have the option to save or not save data with the reports that you create. You also learned that saving data with the report will take more space. To give you a better idea of the difference in the file size between these options, follow the steps below.

1. Save the L2.1 report as L2.4 Data not saved.

2. File ⇒ Save Data With Report. This will clear (turn off) the option.

3. Click the REFRESH button, then click OK when prompted to refresh the data.

4. Save the report, then click the OPEN button.

5. Right-click on the L2.1 report and select Properties. You will see the dialog box shown in Figure 2-50. As you can see, the file size is 105 KB.

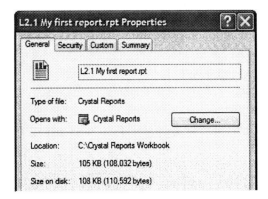

Figure 2-50 Properties of the L2.1 report

6. Right-click on the L2.4 report and select Properties. The file size is 100 KB. This report has a smaller file size, as shown in Figure 2-51.

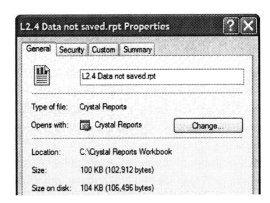

Figure 2-51 Properties of the L2.4 report

The difference is not significant in this report because the Xtreme database does not have a lot of records. The difference would be much more significant if the report had 100,000 records. Think monthly credit card or bank statements <smile>.

7. Close the L2.4 report.

Test Your Skills

1. Create a report using the Standard Wizard. The report should look like the one shown in Figure 2-52.

   - Add the Customers table to the report.
   - Add the Customer ID, Customer Name and Last Year's Sales fields to the report.
   - Group on the Last Years Sales field.
   - Select the Top 5 group sorting option.
   - Create a bar chart and type `Top 5 Customer Orders` as the chart title name.
   - Save the report as `L2.5 Skills Top 5 customer orders with chart`.

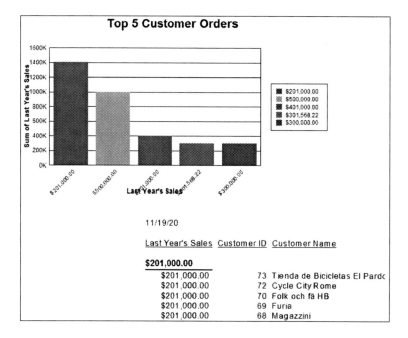

Figure 2-52 L2.5 Skills Top 5 customer orders with chart report

2. Add the following reports to the Lesson 2 Reports folder in the Workbench: L2.2 Product list, L2.3 Employee contact list, L2.4 Data not saved and L2.5 Skills Top 5 customer orders with chart.

3. Create a folder in the Workbench for Lesson 3. Type `Lesson 3 Reports` as the folder name.

CREATING REPORTS FROM SCRATCH

After completing the exercises in this lesson, you will be able to:

☑ Create basic reports from scratch
☑ Use the Database Expert
☑ Use the Field Explorer
☑ Understand the purpose of the Repository Explorer
☑ Add and remove tables in the Field Explorer window
☑ Dock and undock the explorers
☑ Understand relational databases
☑ Understand the different types of relationships
☑ Understand Linking, Join Types and Smart Linking techniques

To pass the RDCR201 exam, you need to be familiar with and be able to:

☑ Add tables to reports
☑ Add objects to a report

The Database Expert

The Database Expert (Database ⇒ Database Expert) shown in Figure 3-1 will display the options to select the data source that you need for the report.

As you can see, this dialog box is very similar to the Data screen in the Standard wizard that you used in the previous lesson. Like the Data screen, the Database Expert has a Links screen.

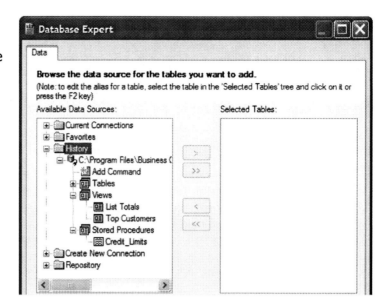

Figure 3-1 Database Expert dialog box

Data Source Options

Each of the four data source options (Commands, Tables, Views and Stored Procedures) provide a different way to access data for the reports that you create. As the report designer, for the most part, you will not be required to create or maintain the data sources. You do however, need a good understanding of them, so that you can select the best option, based on the requirements for the report.

Commands

Commands are queries (code that retrieves data from tables) that are created with a **STRUCTURED QUERY LANGUAGE (SQL)** and have been brought into Crystal Reports. These queries are often complex. They are created in another software package, usually by a DBA or programmer.

Using a command as a data source allows the report to process faster, because the selection of records for the report is already done before the report that you create is run. Commands are very useful when you (the report designer) need data from several databases to create one report. In this workbook, all of the reports are created from data in one database, so there probably wouldn't be a need to have a DBA or programmer create a command.

Tables

Tables are probably the most used of the four data sources because accessing the tables does not require any code or programming skills, like the other three data source options require.

Views

Views are less complex queries then the ones in the Command section. These queries are similar to what you can create in Crystal Reports when you use the sorting, grouping and data selection options to create a report. As you learned in a previous lesson, views are created when the same recordset, calculation or query needs to be used in several reports. If you know that you will create several reports that use the same sorting, grouping or data selection options, you could create and save a view, if you have the appropriate administrator rights to do so. Doing this means that you would not have to select the same options over and over again for each report. Instead of selecting all of the tables, fields and options, select the view that already has all of this information.

Business Views is the real name of this option. Business Views are a set of components, (Data Connections, Dynamic Data Connections, Data Foundations and Business Elements) that report designers and end-users can use to access the data that is needed to create the report. Business Views are created in the Business View Manager by a System Administrator, report designer or someone that has administrator rights to the databases. Business Views allow one to gather data from a variety of databases and combine the data into a "view". This makes it easier to access the data. The Xtreme database comes with two views that you can use. Figure 3-1 above shows the views. They are explained below.

① **List Totals** This view calculates the total order amount by multiplying the Quantity times the Unit Price. Both of these fields are in the Orders Detail table.

② **Top Customers** This view contains customers that have purchased $50,000 or more worth of products. The fields in this view are from the Customer table.

Stored Procedures

Stored procedures, like Commands and Views, do not contain data. They contain queries that are more complex then views, but less complex then commands. The majority of the time, stored procedures are created by a DBA or programmer. The Xtreme database comes with one stored procedure that you can use. Figure 3-1 above shows the stored procedure. It is explained below.

① **Credit_Limits** This view contains customer credit limits. It also has a parameter field that will let you specify the range limit that you need for the report that you are creating. The reason this view is in the stored procedure section is because views cannot have parameter fields in most databases. When Crystal Reports recognizes that a view has a parameter field, the view will be placed in the stored procedure section, because stored procedures can have a parameter field.

Explorers

Crystal Reports comes with three explorers that you can use to help create and manage reports. The one that you will probably use the most is the Field Explorer. The explorers are discussed below.

 The View menu shown in Figure 3-2, lets you select the explorers. Buttons for the explorers are also on the Standard toolbar.

Figure 3-2 Explorer options illustrated on the View menu

1. If the Field and Report Explorers are not visible below the Workbench or another location in the Crystal Reports window, add them now. The explorer windows should look similar to the ones shown in Figure 3-3.

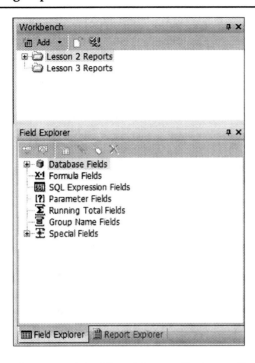

Figure 3-3 Field and Report Explorers illustrated

 By default, the Field Explorer is docked on the right side of the design window. Pay attention to the symbols (icons) that are next to each of the options in the Field Explorer. You will see them again when you learn how to create formulas.

Field Explorer

The Field Explorer lets you add the seven types of fields shown above in Figure 3-3, to a report. Table 3-1 explains each of the field types. Table 3-2 explains the buttons on the Field Explorer toolbar.

Field Type	Description
Database	The fields in this folder come from tables and are usually placed in the details section of the report. This is the only field type in the Field Explorer that is stored in a database.
Formula	These are calculated fields that you create using the Formula Workshop. [See Lesson 9, Formula Workshop Overview] They are recalculated every time the report is run or previewed. (1)
SQL Expression	This type of field is written in a language called SQL. This field type queries (searches) tables to select records that meet the criteria in the query. They are stored on and run from a server. (1)
Parameter	This field type is one that you create. Parameter fields prompt the person running the report to provide information. The information gathered from the parameter fields is used to query the tables to select records that meet the information gathered from the parameter fields.
	Parameter fields allow the person running the report to produce several versions of the report from one report file. An example of parameter fields are the questions that you answer when you use an ATM machine to withdraw or deposit money. (1)

Table 3-1 Field types explained

Field Type	Description
Running Total	This is a formula field that sums (adds) the values in a numeric field (or column of data). Later in this lesson, you will create a Customer Orders report. This report could have a running total for the quantity field to calculate how many items were sold. Running Total fields can be placed in the details section of the report and will provide a total up to the current record. Running Total fields can be reset to zero. They can be used to create totals by group or for the entire report. Summary fields can only be placed in the group header and footer, report header and footer sections of the report. (1)
Group Name	This field type is automatically created for each group the report has. When a group is created, by default the group name field is added to the group header section of the report and will display the value in the field. You can customize the group name to display something other than the value in the field. [See Lesson 6, How To Create A Custom Group Name] (1)
Special Fields	These are system generated fields. Some of the more popular special fields include, page number, print date and Page N of M. Special Fields can be formatted like the other field types discussed in this table. [See Lesson 4, Special Fields] (1)

Table 3-1 Field types explained (Continued)

(1) This field type is not stored in a database.

Button	Purpose
▭▾	The **INSERT TO REPORT** button lets you add a field to the report.
▨	The **BROWSE** button lets you view the data in the field that you select.
▤	The **NEW** button lets you create formula, parameter, SQL Expression or running total fields. (2)
✎	The **EDIT** button lets you modify formula, parameter, SQL Expression or running total fields. (2)
◇	The **RENAME** button lets you rename formula, parameter, SQL Expression or running total fields. (2)
✕	The **DELETE** button lets you delete formula, parameter, SQL Expression or running total fields. (2)

Table 3-2 Field Explorer toolbar buttons explained

(2) Before clicking on this button, click on the category of the field type that you want to use.

Field Type Symbols And Naming Conventions

In Table 3-1, you learned about several field types that you can add to a report. Four of these field types: Formula, SQL Expression, Parameter and Running Total, are fields that you create. Each of these field types must have a unique name. Crystal Reports will add a symbol to the beginning of the field name as discussed below. This is done to help you know what type of field it is, when you are viewing the field in the design window. Figure 3-4 shows what each field type looks like when displayed in the design window.

① **@ symbol** Is a formula field.
② **% sign** Is an SQL Expression field.
③ **? question mark** Is a parameter field.
④ **# sign** Is a Running Total (or summary) field.

Employee Name	Position	Birth Date	Hire Date
@Employee Name	%Position	?Birth Date	#Hire Date

Figure 3-4 Field types and symbols

Do not use the field type symbols discussed above as part of a field name that you create.

Formula, SQL Expression, Parameter and Running Total fields must have a unique name within each field type. Therefore, it is possible to use the same field name for a parameter, formula and running total field in the same report. This is why understanding what the field type symbols represent is important.

NEW Repository Explorer

The Repository Explorer is where you can save objects like images, queries and functions that you want to use in more than one report. When you use this explorer, you will be prompted to log on to the Business Objects Enterprise, as shown in Figure 3-5. The Repository Explorer can only be accessed through the Repository, which is stored in the Business Objects Enterprise. Prior versions of Crystal Reports came with all of the components required to use the Repository Explorer and did not require access to another system. Table 3-3 explains the buttons on the Repository Explorer toolbar.

You cannot store formulas in the Repository.

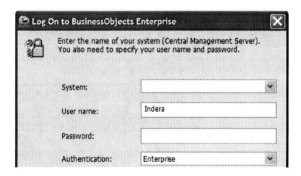

Figure 3-5 Business Objects Enterprise Log on dialog box

Button	Purpose
	The **CHANGE VIEW SETTINGS** button lets you select options that will change how the Repository Explorer window looks. It lets you limit the items that are displayed in the Repository Explorer.
	The **ADVANCED FILTERING** button allows you to only display items based on the author or by specific words.
	The **DELETE THE ITEM/FOLDER** button allows you to permanently delete a file or folder from the repository. If you delete a folder, all of the files in the folder are also deleted.
	The **INSERT A NEW FOLDER** button lets you add a new folder to the repository.
Logon...	The **LOGOFF SERVER** button lets you logon or logoff of the Business Objects Enterprise server.

Table 3-3 Repository Explorer toolbar buttons explained

Docking The Explorers

Docking explorers is not a requirement to complete the exercises in this workbook, but doing so will make the explorer windows easier to find and use. I find it easier to dock the explorers as shown in Figure 3-6. To accomplish this, follow the steps below.

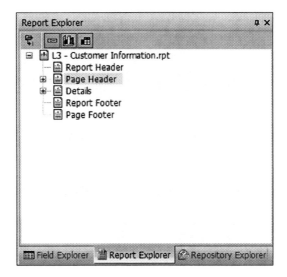

Figure 3-6 Docked explorer windows illustrated

1. Open two of the explorer windows as shown in Figure 3-7.

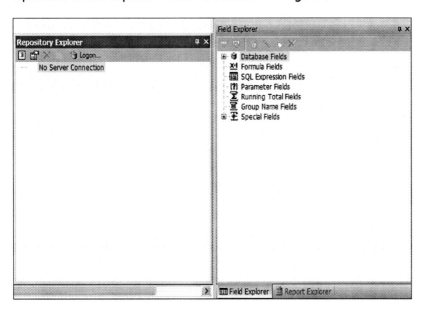

Figure 3-7 Two open explorer windows illustrated

 The Field Explorer and Report Explorer windows will usually be docked together on their own, because when Crystal Reports is installed, this is a default setting for these two explorers.

2. With the left mouse button, drag the explorer window that you want to dock, over to the explorer window that you want to dock it to and release the mouse button when the window has a tab for the explorer window that you moved. The docked window will now contain the explorer window that you added, as illustrated in Figure 3-8.

Figure 3-8 New window docked

Docking Tips

Below are several tips that you should find useful when using the explorers. It could be me, but when I mistakenly move an explorer window, I have difficulty getting it back to where it was. This truly drives me nuts. I hope a solution is available soon. The reason that I am telling you this is so that if you have trouble getting the explorers exactly where you want them, you know that aren't the only one that this bothers.

① To select the explorer that you want to use, click on the tab for it, as illustrated at the bottom of Figure 3-8 above.

② If you double-click on an explorer's title bar, it will toggle between being in docked and free floating modes.

③ If you double-click on the title bar of a free floating explorer window, it will go back to where it was the last time that you used Crystal Reports.

④ In free-floating mode, the explorer window can be moved to a new location in the Crystal Reports window.

⑤ The Workbench and Dependency Checker windows can also be docked with the explorers as shown in Figure 3-9. I prefer to keep the Workbench separate from the explorers because I use the Workbench frequently and like to always keep it open. If it was docked with the explorers, I would have to keep clicking on the tab to get to it. The Workbench and Dependency Checker windows can also be docked together as shown in Figure 3-10.

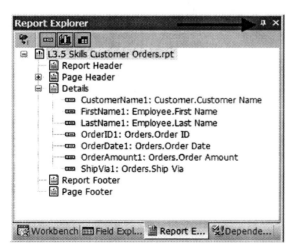

Figure 3-9 Workbench and Dependency Checker windows docked with the explorers

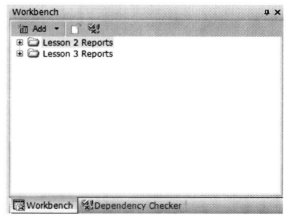

Figure 3-10 Workbench and Dependency Checker windows docked together

NEW The Push Pin

If you click on the push pin illustrated in the upper right hand corner of Figure 3-9 shown earlier, you will open the toolbar shown in Figure 3-11. This toolbar will give you more space to work on reports.

To access one of the explorers from this toolbar, hold the mouse over the icon and the corresponding explorer window will open. To close the toolbar and return to the docked explorer windows, open an explorer window from the toolbar and click on the push pin.

Figure 3-11 Explorer toolbar

Exercise 3.1: Create Your First Report From Scratch

1. Click on the **BLANK REPORT** link on the Start Page. You will see the Database Expert dialog box. It looks similar to the Data screen on the Standard Report wizard that you used in Lesson 2. All of the wizards have this screen except for the OLAP Cube Report wizard.

2. Select the Xtreme database.

3. Add the Customer table to the **SELECTED TABLES** section and click OK. You will see an empty Design window.

Additional Ways To Add The Fields To A Report

There are several ways to add fields in the Field Explorer to a report as discussed below. If you are not familiar with the techniques discussed, take some time to try them and see which one you like the best.

① Drag the field to the report.
② Select the field. Click the **INSERT FIELDS** button on the Field Explorer toolbar and then click in the report where you want to place the field.
③ Select the field. Press Enter, then click in the report where you want to place the field.
④ Right-click on the field that you want to add to the report and select **INSERT TO REPORT** on the shortcut menu, then click in the report where you want to place the field.
⑤ Double-click on the field, then click in the report where you want to place the field.

 If you add a field to the report from the preview window, the value in the field will be displayed instead of the field name.

Add The Fields To The Report

1. Click on the plus sign in front of the **DATABASE FIELDS** option on the Field Explorer window, then click on the plus sign in front of the Customer table. You will see all of the tables that you have added to the report. Clicking on the plus sign in front of a table name will display all of the fields in that table.

2. Click on the Customer Name field with the left mouse button and drag the field to the **DETAILS** section. Notice that a field heading is automatically added to the page header section.

 If you add a field to a section other then the details section, a field heading will not automatically be added to the page header section. Field headings are only added automatically when the field is added to the details section.

As you add fields to the report, you will see triangles called **GUIDELINES**, automatically being added to the beginning or end of the field. Text and date fields will have the guideline marker at the beginning of the field. Numeric fields will have the guideline marker at the end of the field. In Figure 3-12, the Customer Name and Order Date fields have the guideline markers at the beginning of the field. The Order ID and Unit Price fields have the guideline marker at the end of the field. These markers let you know visually where a field starts or ends on the report. Each field also has brackets around it to let you know how long the field is. You will learn more about guidelines in the next lesson.

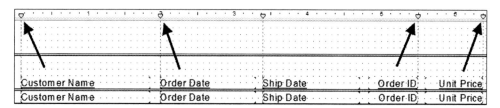

Figure 3-12 Guidelines illustrated

As a general rule, the brackets for one field should not be inside of the brackets for another field, unless you are combining objects and fields. Overlapping fields, as illustrated in Figure 3-13, will cause the fields to print on top of each other, as shown in Figure 3-14.

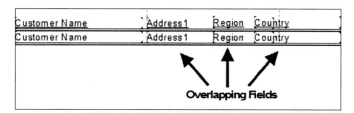

Figure 3-13 Fields overlapped in the report layout

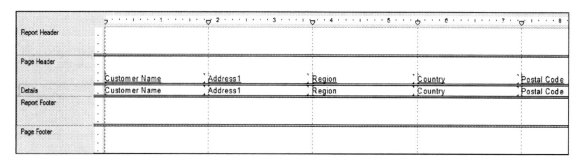

Figure 3-14 Overlapped fields illustrated in Preview mode

3. Add the following fields to the **DETAILS** section: Address1, Region, Country and Postal Code. When you are finished, the report layout should look like the one shown in Figure 3-15.

Report Header	
Page Header	
	Customer Name Address1 Region Country Postal Code
Details	Customer Name Address1 Region Country Postal Code
Report Footer	
Page Footer	

Figure 3-15 Report layout

The green checkmarks illustrated in the Field Explorer in Figure 3-16 indicate that the field has been added to the report or is being used in a formula field that is being used on the report.

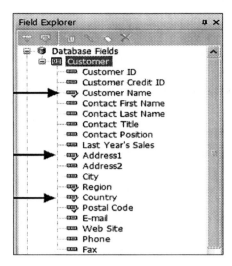

Figure 3-16 Checked fields illustrated

4. Save the report in the Crystal Reports Workbook folder.
Type L3.1 Customer information as the file name, then add the report to the Lesson 3 Reports Workbench folder.

Adding More Than One Field To The Report At The Same Time

There are two options that you can select from to add more than one field to the report at the same time.

① Click on a field, then hold down the **CTRL** key and click on the other fields that you want to add from the Field Explorer.
② Clicking on a field and holding down the **SHIFT** key will let you select fields that are next to each other. If you click on the Customer Name field and hold down the Shift key and then click on the Last Year's Sales field, all of the fields between these two fields will be selected.

Once you have selected all of the fields, drag them to the report.

Preview The Report

1. Click the **REFRESH** button or press the **F5** key. Your report should look like the one shown in Figure 3-17. Not bad for your first time creating a report from scratch.

Customer Name	Address1	Region	Country	Postal C
City Cyclists	7464 South Kingsway	MI	USA	48358
Pathfinders	410 Eighth Avenue	IL	USA	60148
Bike-A-Holics Anonymous	7429 Arbutus Boulevard	OH	USA	43005
Psycho-Cycle	8287 Scott Road	AL	USA	35818
Sporting Wheels Inc.	480 Grant Way	CA	USA	92150
Rockshocks for Jocks	1984 Sydney Street	TX	USA	78770
Poser Cycles	8194 Peter Avenue	MN	USA	55360
Spokes 'N Wheels Ltd.	3802 Georgia Court	IA	USA	50305
Trail Blazer's Place	6938 Beach Street	WI	USA	53795
Rowdy Rims Company	4861 Second Road	CA	USA	91341

Figure 3-17 L3.1 Customer information report

2. Close the report. If prompted to save the changes, click Yes.

Exercise 3.2: Create A Report Using Multiple Tables

In the previous exercise, the report that you created was based on one table. Many of the reports that you will need to create will use two or more tables. The report that you will create in this exercise will use more than one table.

Select The Tables

1. Open a blank report and add the Employee, Employee Addresses and Orders tables as shown in Figure 3-18.

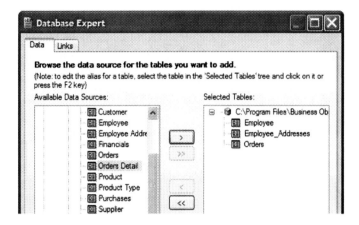

Figure 3-18 Tables selected for the report

 You can add more than one table at the same time by clicking on the first table that you want to add and then hold down the Shift key and select the other tables. You can also double-click on the table in the **AVAILABLE DATA SOURCES** section to add it to the Selected Tables section.

2. Click on the **LINKS** tab and make the screen larger. This will make it easier to see how the tables are linked. Notice that all of the tables have an Employee ID field.

 The Database Expert calls the screen that you link tables on, the **LINKS** screen. The wizards call the same screen the **LINK** screen. They both do the exact same thing, so I don't know why they have slight different names.

The **ORDER LINKS** button opens the dialog box shown in Figure 3-19. It allows you to verify the order of how the tables are connected. Most of the time, the order that is selected is what you need.

When you are using several tables, it is a good idea to check the link order to make sure that the links are correct, because an incorrect linking order will produce an outcome different then what you expect.

If you need to rearrange the order of the links, click on the link that you need to move and click the **UP** or **DOWN** arrow to move the link, as illustrated in Figure 3-19.

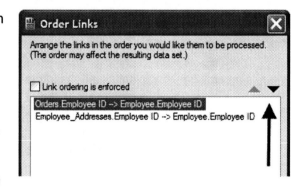

Figure 3-19 Order Links dialog box

If you are using a command or query as the basis of the report, you do not have to create or have links, because the links are created and stored in the command or query. Linking data in tables is an important concept to understand and will be covered in detail after you finish creating this report.

3. Close the Order Links dialog box, then click OK to close the Database Expert dialog box.

Add The Fields To The Report

1. Open the Field Explorer and add the following fields in the Employee table to the details section: Photo, First Name and Last Name. Figure 3-20 shows the report layout.

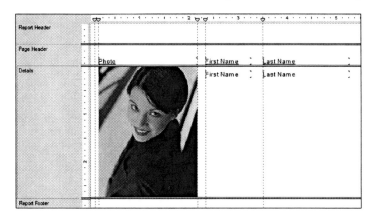

Figure 3-20 Fields from the Employee table added to the report

2. Add the following fields in the Employee Addresses table to the details section: Address1 and Region. Figure 3-21 shows the modified report layout. Notice that these fields are not on the same line as the name fields.

Figure 3-21 Fields from the Employee Addresses table added to the report

3. Save the report. Type L3.2 Employee list as the file name.

4. Add the report to the Workbench and leave the report open to complete the next exercise.

How To Add And Remove Databases And Tables

It is possible that during the report design process, you may need to add a database or table or delete one. You just realized that you do not need any fields from the Orders table and want to remove the table from the report. You can make changes like this in the design window by following the steps below.

1. Right-click on the **DATABASE FIELDS** option in the Field Explorer. You will see the shortcut menu shown in Figure 3-22.

The **REFRESH** option shown in Figure 3-22 works the same as the Refresh button on the Report Navigation toolbars that you learned about in the previous lesson.

If you click on the **SHOW FIELD TYPE** option shown, the field type and field length if applicable, will be displayed at the end of the field as illustrated in Figure 3-23.

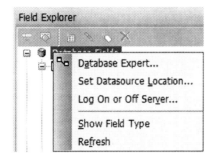

Figure 3-22 Field Explorer shortcut menu for databases, tables and fields

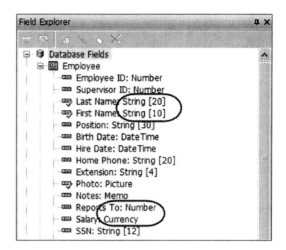

Figure 3-23 Field types and lengths illustrated

2.   Select the **DATABASE EXPERT** option on the shortcut menu.

Other Ways To Open The Database Expert

① Right-click on a table in the Field Explorer and select Database Expert.
② Right-click on a field in the Field Explorer and select Database Expert.
③ Click the Database Expert button on the Expert Tools toolbar.

3.   Click on the Orders table in the **SELECTED TABLES** section and click the < button, then click OK.

If you need to add a table, you would select it from the **AVAILABLE DATA SOURCES** section and add it to the Selected Tables section of the Database Expert dialog box.

4.   Click OK to close the Database Expert dialog box, then preview the report. Click OK if prompted to refresh the report data. Your report should look like the one shown in Figure 3-24. Save the changes and close the report.

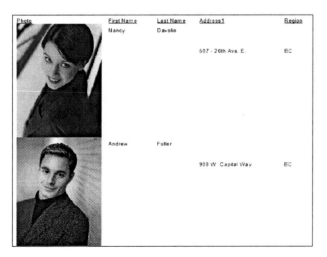

Figure 3-24 L3.2 Employee list report

Relational Databases

Earlier in this lesson you learned a little about linking tables. The reason tables can be linked is because there is a relationship between them, thus the term "Relational Databases". Yes, this is a complicated topic and there are a lot of books on the concepts associated with relational databases and how to create them, so I won't bore you with the details, but please hear me out and don't skip this section.

If the databases that you will use out in the real world are created properly, you will not have to learn a lot about linking or relational databases, because Crystal Reports will create the links that you need. This doesn't mean that you do not have to learn anything about these topics. A good introduction to databases would be to read Chapter 25, "Understanding Databases" in the Crystal Reports XI User Guide that is in the Docs folder on the Crystal Reports installation CD. The file name is UserGde.pdf. The more of that chapter that you understand, the easier it will be for you to create meaningful reports.

While databases are not the primary focus of this workbook, it is important that you understand a little more then the fundamentals that were covered in Lesson 2. The reason that you need to understand databases is because they are the foundation for the reports that you will create and modify. If you have never created a database, or have very little experience creating them, the next few sections in this lesson will be your crash course in databases, relationships and linking. In Lesson 2 you learned the basic database terminology. Now you will learn how all of the components fit together. Figures 3-25 and 3-26 illustrate the layout of two tables.

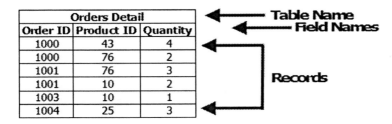

Figure 3-25 Orders table layout

Orders			
Order ID	Order Date	Order Amount	Cust ID
1000	1/2/2005	$263.99	48
1001	1/2/2005	$322.45	57
1002	1/3/2005	$196.00	3
1003	1/4/2005	$124.99	48

Figure 3-26 Orders Detail table layout

Orders Detail		
Order ID	Product ID	Quantity
1000	43	4
1000	76	2
1001	76	3
1001	10	2
1003	10	1
1004	25	3

Primary Key Fields

In Lesson 2 you saw a table that listed the primary keys for the tables in the Xtreme database. [See Lesson 2, Xtreme Database] The fields in the Primary Key column are the ID fields. You will see these two terms used interchangeably. I prefer to use the term ID field because primary key fields usually have "ID" as part of the field name.

 ID is short for identification. It is jargon that the programming community uses to reference a field that can be used to link the data in one table to the data in another table.

All of the tables that you will use in the Xtreme database have at least one ID field. Hopefully, you will find that this is also true out in the real world. The reason ID fields are used is because by design they provide a way for each record in the table to have a unique way to be identified.

I have taught several database classes and almost without fail, this topic causes a lot of confusion. For some reason, people want to create links on string (text fields). Please don't do that. It can cause you problems.

If you needed to create a report that showed all of the orders and what items were on each order, you would need a way to link the Orders and Orders Detail tables. Think of "linking" as having the ability to combine two or more tables "virtually" and being able to display the result of this "virtual linking" on a computer screen or on a printed report.

In Figures 3-25 and 3-26 above, the common ID field is the Order ID field. If you look at the data in the Orders Detail table, you will see that some records have the same Order ID number. That's okay. This means that some customers placed orders with more than one item. Each record in the Orders Detail table represents one item that a customer ordered. If you were to "virtually" join the data in the tables shown in Figures 3-25 and 3-26 above, it would look like the table shown in Figure 3-27.

| Orders | | | | Orders Detail | | |
Order ID	Order Date	Order Amount	Cust ID	Order ID	Product ID	Quantity
1000	1/2/2005	$263.99	48	1000	43	4
1000	1/2/2005	$263.99	48	1000	76	2
1001	1/2/2005	$322.45	57	1001	76	3
1001	1/2/2005	$322.45	57	1001	10	2
1002	1/3/2005	$196.00	3			
1003	1/4/2005	$124.99	48	1003	10	1
				1004	25	3

Figure 3-27 Virtually joined tables

This "virtual" join is what happens when tables are LINKED. If all of this data was stored in one table instead of two, at the very minimum, the Order Date and Order Amount fields would be repeated for every record that is in the Orders Detail table. Repetition of data is why this information is stored in two tables instead of one. It is considered poor table design to have the same information (other than fields that are used to join tables) stored in more than one table.

> More then likely if you see a record in the Orders Detail table, like Order ID 1004 shown above in Figure 3-27, or any child table that is in a parent-child relationship, there is a problem with the data in at least one of the tables because all of the records in the child table should have at least one matching record in the parent table. Parent tables are used to get data from a child table.

Types Of Relationships

The Employee report that you just created required two tables. These tables are linked by a common field, the Employee ID field. This field is what connects (joins) data from both tables and allows you to use data from both tables.

The Employee ID field in the Employee table is how you find the matching record (known as a ONE-TO-ONE RELATIONSHIP) or records (known as a ONE-TO-MANY RELATIONSHIP, which is the most popular type of relationship) in the Employee Addresses table. These are two of the most common types of relationships. The MANY-TO-MANY RELATIONSHIP is a third type of relationship. It is not used as much as the other two.

How Linking Works

More than likely, most reports that you create will require data from more than one table. Reports like the Product List report that you created in Lesson 2, only used one table, so there is no linking involved. For reports that require two or more tables, the tables need to be linked. The tables are usually linked in the database. The links that you see on the Link screen are the same as the links in the database. When you create a report and need to view or modify the links, you can do so by opening the Database Expert and clicking on the Link tab. Even though most of the time the links that you need are created for you, it is important to understand what is going on behind the scenes, as they say.

> You need to understand the linking concept.

The best way to understand the basic concept of linking tables is to look at the records or a portion of the records in the tables that need to be linked. When you create a report that you are not familiar with the data that is needed, you should take the time to look at the data in the tables. Figures 3-28 and 3-29 show the records in the Employee and Employee Addresses tables. As mentioned earlier, the field that these tables have in common is the Employee ID field, as shown below.

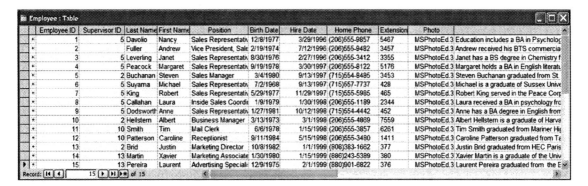

Figure 3-28 Data in the Employee table

Figure 3-29 Data in the Employee Addresses table

Fields that are used to link tables must be the same data type. [See Lesson 2, Table 2-1] You could not create a link between a date field and a string field.

Depending on the table structure, tables can have more than one field that they can be linked by. An example of this would be the Orders Detail table. This table has an ID field that would let you link it to the Orders table. There is a Product ID field in the Orders Detail table, that would let you retrieve the Product Name from another table (the Product table) to print on the report, instead of printing the Product ID number. Displaying the product name on the report is more meaningful to the people that read the report then the Product ID field, which contains a number. If you are asking why the Product Name is not stored in the Orders Detail table, there are two reasons.

① The ID field takes up less space, thereby keeping the size of the Orders Detail table smaller.
② If a Product Name has to be changed for any reason, it only has to be changed in the Product table. Every place that the Product Name field is used on any report, would automatically be updated with the revised product name. If the product name was stored in the Orders Detail table, every record in the Orders Detail table that had that product name would have to be changed, as well as, any other table that stored the product name. That would be a lot of work.

Join Types

Hopefully, you are still with me. Don't worry, the relational database "lecturette" is almost over.
There are several types of links that can be created. These different types of links are called JOIN TYPES.
Crystal Reports has several join types that you can select from. Each join type will return different results
from the same tables, which you will see in Figures 3-30 to 3-33. INNER joins are the most common.
If you use any of the three OUTER join types discussed below, the order that the tables are added to the
report is important. The four join types that are explained in Table 3-4 are the ones that are automatically
created and are the most common. The other join types have to be created manually.
They are covered later in this lesson.

Join Type	Description
Inner	Records that have matching records in both tables, as illustrated in Figure 3-30.
Left-Outer	Selects all records from one table (usually the left most table on the Links tab) and only matching records in the table on the right, as illustrated in Figure 3-31.
Right-Outer	Selects all records from the right table and only matching records from the table on the left, as illustrated in Figure 3-32. This join type works the opposite of the Left-Outer join type.
Full-Outer	Selects all records from both tables whether or not there are matching records in the other table, as illustrated in Figure 3-33. Full-Outer joins are also known as a **UNION** join type.

Table 3-4 Join types explained

 The "matching" discussed above in Table 3-4 is usually done on **ID** fields.

In the Orders and Orders Detail tables, the Orders table is known as the LEFT table and should be added
to the list of tables for the report first. The Orders Detail table is known as the RIGHT table and should be
added to the list of tables after the Orders table. The reason the tables need to be added in this order is
because for each record in the Orders table, there can be multiple records in the Orders Detail table that
have the same ID. Earlier in this lesson you learned about the Order Links dialog box. If the tables were
added incorrectly, you can use the options on the Order Links dialog box to change the order.

Join Type Examples

When walking through these examples, compare the data in the example to the data shown earlier in
Figure 3-27. The examples in this section illustrate how the same data would be retrieved differently
depending on the join type that is selected. This is why it is important to understand linking and join
types.

In Figure 3-30, the record for Order ID 1002 in the Orders table would not be retrieved in an Inner join
because there is no related record in the Orders Detail table. The arrows between the tables represent
the flow of the data.

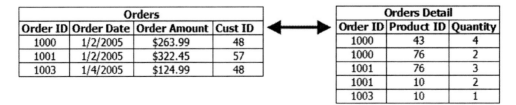

Figure 3-30 Inner join recordset

In Figure 3-31, the record for Order ID 1004 would not be retrieved from the Orders Detail table in a Left-
Outer join because there is no related record in the Orders table.

Orders			
Order ID	Order Date	Order Amount	Cust ID
1000	1/2/2005	$263.99	48
1001	1/2/2005	$322.45	57
1002	1/3/2005	$196.00	3
1003	1/4/2005	$124.99	48

Orders Detail		
Order ID	Product ID	Quantity
1000	43	4
1000	76	2
1001	76	3
1001	10	2
1003	10	1

Figure 3-31 Left-Outer join recordset

In Figure 3-32, the record for Order ID 1002 in the Orders table would not be retrieved in a Right-Outer join because there is no related record in the Orders Detail table.

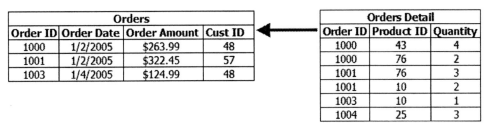

Orders			
Order ID	Order Date	Order Amount	Cust ID
1000	1/2/2005	$263.99	48
1001	1/2/2005	$322.45	57
1003	1/4/2005	$124.99	48

Orders Detail		
Order ID	Product ID	Quantity
1000	43	4
1000	76	2
1001	76	3
1001	10	2
1003	10	1
1004	25	3

Figure 3-32 Right-Outer join recordset

In Figure 3-33, all records would be retrieved in a Full-Outer join whether there is a related record in the other table or not.

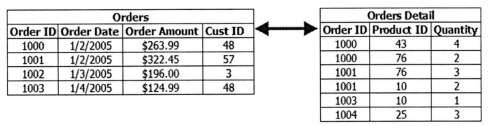

Orders			
Order ID	Order Date	Order Amount	Cust ID
1000	1/2/2005	$263.99	48
1001	1/2/2005	$322.45	57
1002	1/3/2005	$196.00	3
1003	1/4/2005	$124.99	48

Orders Detail		
Order ID	Product ID	Quantity
1000	43	4
1000	76	2
1001	76	3
1001	10	2
1003	10	1
1004	25	3

Figure 3-33 Full-Outer join recordset

Tables Without A Link

If you added the Orders and Orders Detail tables to a report but did not link them, Crystal Reports would not know which record in the Orders table went with which record in the Orders Detail table. The result would be that each order record would be displayed (matched) with each of the records in the Orders Detail table as shown in Figure 3-34. In total, 24 records would print on the report. When a report uses more than one table, this is usually not what you want.

Orders			
Order ID	Order Date	Order Amount	Cust ID
1000	1/2/2005	$263.99	48
1000	1/2/2005	$263.99	48
1000	1/2/2005	$263.99	48
1000	1/2/2005	$263.99	48
1000	1/2/2005	$263.99	48
1000	1/2/2005	$263.99	48
1001	1/2/2005	$322.45	57
1001	1/2/2005	$322.45	57
1001	1/2/2005	$322.45	57
1001	1/2/2005	$322.45	57
1001	1/2/2005	$322.45	57
1001	1/2/2005	$322.45	57

⁞

| 1003 | 1/4/2005 | $124.99 | 48 |

Orders Detail		
Order ID	Product ID	Quantity
1000	43	4
1000	76	2
1001	76	3
1001	10	2
1003	10	1
1004	25	3
1000	43	4
1000	76	2
1001	76	3
1001	10	2
1003	10	1
1004	25	3

⁞

| 1004 | 25 | 3 |

Figure 3-34 Tables not joined recordset

The reports shown in Figures 3-35 and 3-36 have the same three fields: Customer Name, Product ID and Order ID. The report shown in Figure 3-35 has the **LEFT-OUTER** join between the Customer and Orders tables. The report shown in Figure 3-36 has the **RIGHT-OUTER** join between the Orders and Orders Detail tables. As you can see, the output is completely different for these reports. Hopefully, these reports demonstrate why understanding table structures, types of relationships, linking and join types is important.

Customer Name	Product ID	Order ID
City Cyclists	2,201	1
Deals on Wheels	5,205	1,002
Deals on Wheels	102,181	1,002
Warsaw Sports, Inc.	2,213	1,003
Warsaw Sports, Inc.	5,402	1,003
Bikes and Trikes	402,002	1,004
SAB Mountain	1,101	1,005
Poser Cycles	1,107	1,006
Poser Cycles	5,208	1,006
Poser Cycles	5,402	1,006
Spokes	1,109	1,007

Figure 3-35 Left-Outer join report

Customer Name	Product ID	Order ID
City Cyclists	2,209	1,387
City Cyclists	3,305	1,387
City Cyclists	302,201	1,387
City Cyclists	1,108	2,277
City Cyclists	2,207	2,277
City Cyclists	1,101	1,033
City Cyclists	1,105	1,033
City Cyclists	102,181	1,033
City Cyclists	2,214	2,402
City Cyclists	7,402	2,402
City Cyclists	301,161	2,772
City Cyclists	301,201	1,366

Figure 3-36 Right-Outer join report

Recursive Join

In addition to the join types discussed above, there is another join type called **RECURSIVE JOIN**. This type of join is not always obvious when looking at the table structures. A recursive join occurs when the same data is stored in two different ID fields in the same table. This is not the same as a parent/child (also known as a master/detail) relationship because this type of relationship does not require two tables like the Orders and Orders Detail tables that you read about earlier in this lesson.

An example of a recursive join is in the Employee table. The Supervisor ID field in the Employee table contains the Employee ID of another record in the Employee table. This is because supervisors are also employees. Refer back to Figure 3-28. Seven employees have the number 5 in the Supervisor ID field (the second field from the left). This is because they all have the same supervisor, Steven Buchanan, whose Employee ID is number 5. Recursive joins are used to create hierarchical reports, which you will learn how to create in Lesson 13.

Smart Linking

Smart linking is turned on by default. Crystal Reports uses this feature to create links based on an index or common fields in tables. You can change the default smart linking option on the Database tab of the Options dialog box. [See Lesson 5, Figure 5-56] Some people turn this option off and always create the links manually to make sure that the correct join type is selected. The reason people turn this feature off is because tables are joined on fields that have the same name and data type, which may not be what you want.

View The Current Links

1. Open a blank report and add the Customer, Orders and Orders Detail tables.

2. Click on the Links tab and click the **CLEAR LINKS** button. Click Yes, when prompted if you are sure.

How To Manually Create Links

When you have the need to manually create links, follow the steps below.

1. Select a field in one table and drag it to the field in the other table. In this example, select the Quantity field and drag it to the Customer Name field.

Both fields must have the same data type. If there is something wrong with the link that you are trying to create, you will see a warning message similar to the one shown in Figure 3-37. This message lets you know that the link that you are trying to create is not valid.

Figure 3-37 Link error warning message

2. Click OK to close the Visual Linking Editor message window shown above in Figure 3-37.

Manual Join Types

As discussed earlier, there are other join and link types that can be used to link tables. Table 3-5 explains the enforce join type options. Table 3-6 explains the link types.

Enforce Join Type	Description
Not Enforced	Selecting this option doesn't mean that the link will be included in the SQL statement. At least one field must be used to join tables in order for the linking criteria to be included in the SQL statement.
Enforced From	Selecting this option forces the link to the right table. When a field from the right table is used, but not one from the left table, the SQL statement requires that both tables be referenced.
Enforced To	This option forces the link from the left table, whether or not a field is used from the right table. This means that the SQL statement will include both tables.
Enforced Both	This option forces the link between the tables, regardless of where the fields that are used in the report are stored.

Table 3-5 Enforce Join types explained

Link Type	Description
Equal Link =	Creates a recordset where the link field has related records in the left and right tables.
Greater Than Link >	Creates a recordset where the link field from the left table is greater than the linked field in the right table.
Greater Than or Equal To Link >=	Creates a recordset where the link field from the left table is greater than or equal to the linked field in the right table.
Less Than Link <	Creates a recordset where the link field from the left table is less than the linked field in the right table.
Less Than or Equal To Link <=	Creates a recordset where the link field from the left table is less than or equal to the linked field in the right table.
Not Equal Link !=	Creates a recordset where the link field from the left table does not match the linked field in the right table.

Table 3-6 Link Types explained

Exercise 3.3: Create A Customer Orders Report

In this exercise you will create a report that displays customers and their orders.

1. Open a blank report and add the Customer and Orders tables, then click Finish to close the Database Expert dialog box.

2. Delete the Print Date field in the page header section of the report.

Add The Fields

1. Add the Customer Name field in the Customer table to the details section.

2. Add the Order Date and Ship Date fields in the Orders table to the details section.

Add Another Table

You have decided that the report would look better if it also had fields from the Orders Detail table. To add a table to the report, follow the steps below.

1. Right-click on the **DATABASE FIELDS** option in the Field Explorer and select Database Expert.

2. Add the Orders Detail table and click OK. When you see the **LINKS** tab, Click OK.

3. Click OK to refresh the data. You will see the Orders Detail table in the Field Explorer window.

Add More Fields

1. Click on the design tab and add the Order ID, Unit Price and Quantity fields in the Orders Detail table to the details section. Your report layout should look like the one shown in Figure 3-38.

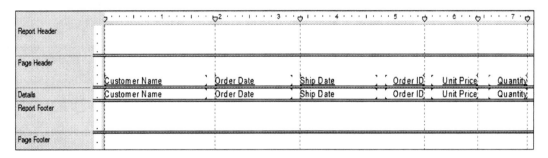

Figure 3-38 Customer orders report layout

Preview The Report

1. Save the report. Type `L3.3 Customer orders` as the file name.

2. Click the **PRINT PREVIEW** button on the Standard toolbar. Your report should look like the one shown in Figure 3-39. Close the report.

The reason that the information in the Customer Name, Order Date, Ship Date and Order ID fields is repeated, is because on some orders the customer ordered more than one item. (See Order ID 1002 and 1003). As you can see, all of the reports that you have created in Lessons 2 and 3 need to be edited and formatted, so that they are more presentable. You will learn how to edit reports in the next lesson.

Customer Name	Order Date	Ship Date	Order ID	Unit Price	Quantity
City Cyclists	12/2/2003 12:00:00A	12/10/2003 5:32:23F	1	$41.90	1
Deals on Wheels	12/2/2003 12:00:00A	12/2/2003 6:45:32AI	1,002	$33.90	3
Deals on Wheels	12/2/2003 12:00:00A	12/2/2003 6:45:32AI	1,002	$1,652.86	3
Warsaw Sports, Inc.	12/2/2003 12:00:00A	12/5/2003 12:10:12A	1,003	$48.51	3
Warsaw Sports, Inc.	12/2/2003 12:00:00A	12/5/2003 12:10:12A	1,003	$13.78	3
Bikes and Trikes	12/2/2003 12:00:00A	12/2/2003 3:24:54PI	1,004	$274.35	3
SAB Mountain	12/3/2003 12:00:00A	12/3/2003 1:54:34AI	1,005	$14.50	2
Poser Cycles	12/3/2003 12:00:00A	12/5/2003 7:58:01PI	1,006	$16.50	1
Poser Cycles	12/3/2003 12:00:00A	12/5/2003 7:58:01PI	1,006	$33.90	1
Poser Cycles	12/3/2003 12:00:00A	12/5/2003 7:58:01PI	1,006	$14.50	1
Spokes	12/3/2003 12:00:00A	12/3/2003 9:05:46AI	1,007	$16.50	3
Clean Air Transportation Co.	12/3/2003 12:00:00A	12/7/2003 10:10:12P	1,008	$726.61	2
Clean Air Transportation Co.	12/3/2003 12:00:00A	12/7/2003 10:10:12P	1,008	$431.87	1
Clean Air Transportation Co.	12/3/2003 12:00:00A	12/7/2003 10:10:12P	1,008	$329.85	1
Extreme Cycling	12/3/2003 12:00:00A	12/10/2003 6:47:47A	1,009	$14.50	2
Cyclopath	12/3/2003 12:00:00A	12/3/2003 11:11:11P	1,010	$2,939.85	3
Cyclopath	12/3/2003 12:00:00A	12/3/2003 11:11:11P	1,010	$2,645.87	2
Cyclopath	12/3/2003 12:00:00A	12/3/2003 11:11:11P	1,010	$253.67	3

Figure 3-39 L3.3 Customer orders report

Test Your Skills

1. Create a Product report from scratch that uses the Product, Supplier and Product Type tables. Add the fields in Table 3-7 in the order they are shown in the report. The report should look like the one shown in Figure 3-40. Type L3.4 Skills Product report as the file name.

Product	Supplier	Product Type
Product ID	Supplier Name	Product Type Name
Product Name		

Table 3-7 Fields to add to the report

Product ID	Product Name	Product Type Name	Supplier Name
1,101	Active Outdoors Crochet Glo\	Gloves	Active Outdoors
1,102	Active Outdoors Crochet Glo\	Gloves	Active Outdoors
1,103	Active Outdoors Crochet Glo\	Gloves	Active Outdoors
1,104	Active Outdoors Crochet Glo\	Gloves	Active Outdoors
1,105	Active Outdoors Crochet Glo\	Gloves	Active Outdoors
1,106	Active Outdoors Lycra Glove	Gloves	Active Outdoors
1,107	Active Outdoors Lycra Glove	Gloves	Active Outdoors
1,108	Active Outdoors Lycra Glove	Gloves	Active Outdoors
1,109	Active Outdoors Lycra Glove	Gloves	Active Outdoors
1,110	Active Outdoors Lycra Glove	Gloves	Active Outdoors
1,111	Active Outdoors Lycra Glove	Gloves	Active Outdoors
2,201	Triumph Pro Helmet	Helmets	Triumph
2,202	Triumph Pro Helmet	Helmets	Triumph
2,203	Triumph Pro Helmet	Helmets	Triumph
2,204	Triumph Pro Helmet	Helmets	Triumph

Figure 3-40 L3.4 Skills Product report

2. Create a Customer Orders report from scratch that uses the Customer, Employee and Orders tables. Add the fields in Table 3-8 in the order they are shown in the report. The Last Name field may not fit on the report. It's okay to let it hang off of the right edge of the report for now. Later you will learn how to resize fields so that they fit on the report. The report should look like the one shown in Figure 3-41. Type L3.5 Skills Customer orders as the file name.

Customer	Employee	Orders
Customer Name	First Name	Order ID
	Last Name	Order Date
		Order Amount
		Ship Via

Table 3-8 Fields to add to the Customer orders report

Customer Name	Order ID	Order Date	Order Amount	Ship Via	First Name	Last
City Cyclists	1	12/2/2003 12:00:00A	$41.90	UPS	Nancy	Dav
Deals on Wheels	1,002	12/2/2003 12:00:00A	$5,060.28	Pickup	Janet	Levi
Warsaw Sports, Inc.	1,003	12/2/2003 12:00:00A	$186.87	UPS	Margaret	Pea
Bikes and Trikes	1,004	12/2/2003 12:00:00A	$823.05	Pickup	Margaret	Pea
SAB Mountain	1,005	12/3/2003 12:00:00A	$29.00	Loomis	Janet	Levi
Poser Cycles	1,006	12/3/2003 12:00:00A	$64.90	Purolator	Margaret	Pea
Spokes	1,007	12/3/2003 12:00:00A	$49.50	Parcel Post	Anne	Dod
Clean Air Transportation Co.	1,008	12/3/2003 12:00:00A	$2,214.94	Purolator	Margaret	Pea
Extreme Cycling	1,009	12/3/2003 12:00:00A	$29.00	Loomis	Margaret	Pea
Cyclopath	1,010	12/3/2003 12:00:00A	$14,872.30	UPS	Nancy	Dav
BBS Pty	1,011	12/3/2003 12:00:00A	$29.00	Purolator	Margaret	Pea
Piccolo	1,012	12/3/2003 12:00:00A	$10,259.10	Loomis	Nancy	Dav
Pedals Inc.	1,013	12/3/2003 12:00:00A	$1,142.13	Parcel Post	Margaret	Pea
Spokes 'N Wheels Ltd.	1,014	12/4/2003 12:00:00A	$29.00	Purolator	Nancy	Dav
Cycle City Rome	1,015	12/4/2003 12:00:00A	$43.50	UPS	Anne	Dod
SAB Mountain	1,016	12/4/2003 12:00:00A	$563.70	FedEx	Janet	Levi
Tyred Out	1,017	12/5/2003 12:00:00A	$72.00	Purolator	Margaret	Pea
Has Been Bikes (consignmer	1,018	12/5/2003 12:00:00A	$115.50	Loomis	Janet	Levi

Figure 3-41 L3.5 Skills Customer orders report

3. Add the following reports to the Workbench: L3.3, L3.4 and L3.5.

FORMATTING AND EDITING 101

As the title of this lesson indicates, you will learn basic formatting and editing techniques that you can use to make the reports that you create look better. Lessons 9 and 10 will teach you other ways to format reports. After completing the exercises in this lesson you will be able to:

- ☑ Understand the formatting options on various shortcut menus
- ☑ Select objects
- ☑ Align objects
- ☑ Use Guidelines
- ☑ Understand the purpose of the Grid
- ☑ Resize objects
- ☑ Add graphics to a report
- ☑ Use the Format Editor
- ☑ Use the Format Painter
- ☑ Use the Section Expert
- ☑ Add Special Fields to a report
- ☑ Understand how the Report Explorer works

To pass the RDCR201 exam, you need to be familiar with and be able to:

- ☑ Position and size objects
- ☑ Add graphics to a report
- ☑ Use the Format Painter

LESSON 4

Shortcut Menus

Crystal Reports has several shortcut menus that you can use instead of selecting menu options or clicking on toolbar buttons. As you will see, you will spend a lot of time formatting and editing reports. A great time saver in completing these tasks is using the options on the shortcut menus.

The options will change on the shortcut menu depending on the object that is right-clicked on.

In addition to the object shortcut menu, there is a general shortcut menu available when you right-click on an empty space in the design or preview window as shown in Figure 4-1. Several of the options on this shortcut menu are explained in detail later in this lesson. The options that aren't, are explained below.

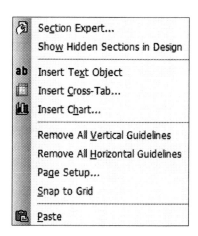

Figure 4-1 General shortcut menu

① **Show Hidden Sections In Design** By default, this option is turned on. It allows you to see hidden sections of the report in the design window. Hidden sections will have vertical lines, as shown in Figure 4-2. If this option is turned off (not checked), hidden sections have a small space between the sections, as shown in Figure 4-3.

② **Insert Cross-Tab** Lets you add a cross-tab object to the report.

③ **Insert Chart** Lets you add a chart to the report.

④ **Remove All Vertical Guidelines** Selecting this option will hide (not delete) vertical guidelines (1).

⑤ **Remove All Horizontal Guidelines** Selecting this option will hide (not delete) horizontal guidelines (1).

⑥ **Page Setup** [See Lesson 8, Page Setup Options]

 (1) These options are not the same as clearing the **GUIDELINES** option on the Layout tab of the Options dialog box.

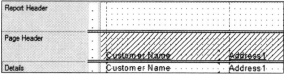

Figure 4-2 Page header section with vertical lines

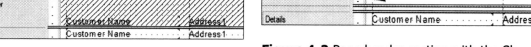

Figure 4-3 Page header section with the Show Hidden Sections In Design option turned off

Selecting Fields And Objects

A lot of the report editing that you will do requires fields and other objects to be selected. Often, you will have the need to apply the same changes to several fields or objects. To select a single field or object, click on it with the left mouse button. When an object is selected, you will see a blue frame around it, as illustrated in Figure 4-4. You will also see squares. These squares are called **SIZE HANDLERS**. They allow you to change the size of the object to make it wider, longer, shorter or smaller. You will learn how to resize objects later in this lesson.

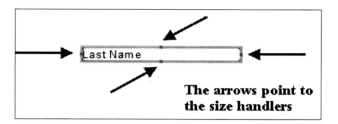

Figure 4-4 Field selected and size handlers illustrated

When I use the word "field", I am referring to a field in the details section of the report, or a field from a table or a calculated field that you create. "Objects" refer to items like the field heading, a text field or an image.

Selecting Multiple Fields And Objects

There are three ways to select the fields that you need, as discussed below.

① Click on one field or object. Press and hold down the **CTRL** or **SHIFT** key and click on the other fields or objects that you need to select.

② Draw what is called a **MARQUEE** or **LASSO** around the fields or objects with the mouse. To do this successfully, the objects need to be near each other, either side by side or up and down from each other. Click outside of the first field or object. Hold the left mouse button down and draw around the objects that you need to select. You will see a frame being drawn. When you are finished selecting the objects and release the mouse button, you will see that several objects have been selected.

③ If you need to select all of the objects in one section of the report, right-click in the corresponding report (tan) section (page header, details, etc.) on the far left side of the design window and select the option, **SELECT ALL SECTION OBJECTS** as shown in Figure 4-5. The first option at the top of the shortcut menu lets you know which section of the report you are about to select all of the objects in. As shown in Figure 4-5, the objects that will be selected are in the page header section.

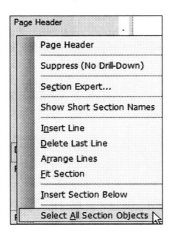

Figure 4-5 Report section shortcut menu

Exercise 4.1: Moving Objects

One of the tasks that you will do from time to time is rearrange fields and other objects on a report. This exercise will show you how to move fields and objects on a report.

1. Save the L3.4 report as `L4.1 Moving fields`. Make sure that you save the report in the Crystal Reports Workbook folder.

2. Click on the design tab. Using the guideline marker, move the **PRODUCT TYPE NAME** field in the details section to the right, as close to the Supplier Name field as possible. Notice that the field heading moved with the field.

 Interestingly enough, when you have multiple objects selected, the last one that you select is the **MAIN OBJECT**. The main object is the one that the other selected objects emulate (follow). If you have multiple objects selected and you move the main object to a place in the report where it does not fit, none of the objects that are selected will be moved. If you move multiple objects to a location where some objects will fit, including the main object, the objects that will fit in the new location will be moved and those that will not fit, will not be moved.

Aligning Objects

In addition to moving objects, you will have the need to have multiple objects line up. The **ALIGNMENT** option will help you line up several objects at the same time. Follow the steps below to learn how to align objects. Because everything on the report is currently aligned, you need to move an object to get it out of alignment to complete this exercise.

1. Click on the Product Type Name field heading and drag it to the right as shown in Figure 4-6.

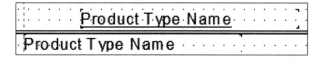

Figure 4-6 Field heading moved to the right

2. Select the Project Type Name field and heading, then right-click on the Project Type Name field.

 In the step 2, you have to right-click on the object that has the alignment that you want duplicate. In this exercise, you want to align the field heading with the field in the details section. If you right-clicked on the field heading in the step above and selected Align ⇒ Rights, the field in the details section would have been aligned on the right with the field heading.

You can right-click on any object and select the **ALIGN** option. Just remember which object that you right-click on before selecting an align option, because you may get results different then what you expected. The alignment of the object that you right-click on will be applied to the other objects that are selected.

3. Align ⇒ Lefts, as shown in Figure 4-7. The field and heading should be where it was before you started this exercise. Table 4-1 explains the alignment options.

 At the top of the shortcut menu if you see the words **MULTIPLE SELECTION**, it means that you have multiple objects selected. When selecting multiple fields or objects, whatever change you make will be applied to all of the selected fields or objects as long as the change can be applied to the data type. Not all data types can have the same changes.

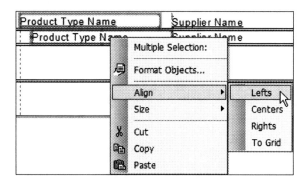

Figure 4-7 Alignment options illustrated

Align Option	How It Aligns
Lefts	Aligns on the left side of the object.
Centers	Aligns on the center of the object.
Rights	Aligns on the right side of the object.
To Grid	Aligns to the closest grid point of the object that you right-click on. You need to have the **GRID** option turned on to see how this feature works.

Table 4-1 Alignment options explained

4.   Save the changes and leave the report open to complete the next exercise.

Aligning Objects Horizontally

This type of alignment is very similar to the alignment options that you just learned about. The horizontal alignment option is useful when you manually add fields or objects to a report. If you rush and add fields to a report like I do, meaning that you just drop them on the report without paying attention to whether or not they are lined up properly. If this sounds like the way you work, you will really appreciate this exercise. In order to demonstrate how this feature works, you need to rearrange objects on the report first.

1.   Drag the Product ID and Product Type Name field headings up in the page header section, as shown in Figure 4-8.

Page Header		Product ID				Product Type Name	
			Product Name				
Details		Product ID	Product Name			Product Type Name	
Report Footer							

Figure 4-8 Field headings moved

2.   Select the Product ID, Product Name and Product Type Name field headings, then right-click on the Product Name heading.

3.   Align ⇒ Bottoms, as shown in Figure 4-9. The field headings should be back where they were before you started this exercise. Table 4-2 explains the options on the shortcut menu.

The alignment options shown in Figure 4-9 are only available when all of the selected objects are in the same section of the report.

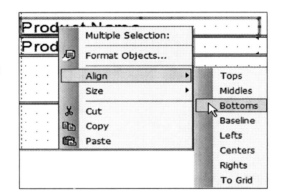

Figure 4-9 Horizontal alignment options

Align Option	How It Aligns
Tops	Aligns on the top of the object.
Middles	Aligns on the middle of the object.
Bottoms	Aligns on the bottom of the object.
Baseline	Aligns on the bottom of the text, not the bottom of the frame like all of the other alignment options discussed in this table. The baseline alignment option is useful when you are aligning objects that have a different font, font size or frame size.
Lefts	Aligns on the left side of the object.
Centers	Aligns on the center of the object.
Rights	Aligns on the right side of the object.
To Grid	Aligns to the closest grid point of the object that you right-click on. You need to have the **GRID** option turned on to see how this works.

Table 4-2 Horizontal alignment options explained

4.   Save the changes and leave the report open to complete the next exercise.

Guidelines

It may not always be easy to move or align objects. The guidelines feature helps you move and align objects easily. Guidelines let you move all objects that are anchored to the guideline at the same time. This means that you can move the field in the details section, the field heading in the page header section and all calculated or summary fields in other sections that are anchored to the guideline at the same time, without selecting them.

Guidelines are the **TRIANGLE BUTTONS** on the ruler at the top of the report, that are illustrated in Figure 4-10. The dotted lines that you see coming down from the guidelines in the page header and group header sections are **MARKERS** on the ruler. The reason you do not see the markers in the report header section in Figure 4-10 is because the section has a chart. The lines for the markers are behind the chart.

 By default, the **VERTICAL GUIDELINE** option is enabled. To verify, File ⇒ Options ⇒ Click on the Layout tab. The **INSERT DETAIL FIELD HEADINGS** option should be checked.

If you moved the guideline that is anchored to the Last Name field all of the following objects would move at the same time: the field heading, the Sum of Employee.Supervisor ID field in the first group footer section and the Count of Employee.Home Phone field in the report footer section.

Guidelines are automatically added to a report if any of the follow actions occur:

① A field is added to the details section.
② You right-click in the **REPORT SECTION** of the design window as shown earlier in Figure 4-5 and select **ARRANGE LINES**.
③ A summary field is added to the report.

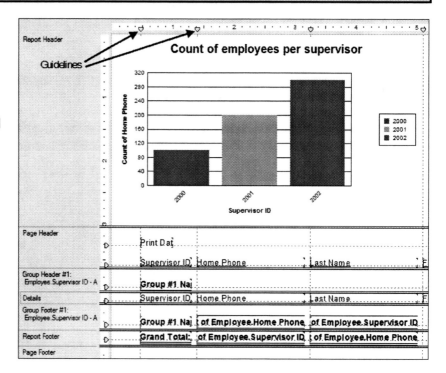

Figure 4-10 Guidelines illustrated

You will see red marks on the side of objects that the guideline is on, if the object is anchored to a guideline. If you do not see the red marks, drag the object towards the guideline or drag the guideline towards the object.

Turning The Guidelines On

If you do not see the guidelines, View ⇒ Guidelines ⇒ Design, will turn the guidelines on (on the design window), as shown in Figure 4-11. The **PREVIEW** option will turn the guidelines on, on the preview window.

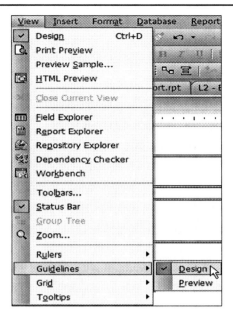

Figure 4-11 Option selected to turn the guidelines on

 By default, reports created with a wizard other than the **BLANK REPORT WIZARD** will have horizontal guidelines inserted automatically. You can manually add horizontal guidelines to reports created with the Blank Report wizard. The horizontal guidelines for all fields are at the top or bottom of the field or the baseline of the text in the field.

How To Manually Add Guidelines

If the need arises that you have to manually add guidelines, you can select one of the options below.

① Click on the horizontal ruler where you want to add a guideline.
② Click on the vertical ruler where you want to add a guideline.

 To remove a guideline, drag the triangle marker off of the ruler. Removing guidelines does not delete the objects attached to it.

Using Guidelines To Move Objects

You can move all of the objects that are associated to the same guideline at the same time, by following the steps below.

1. Click on the guideline marker for the Supplier Name field on the L4.1 report and drag the marker to the right, to the 5.5 inch mark on the ruler, as illustrated in Figure 4-12. The field and field heading should have moved. If there were other objects anchored to this marker, like a total or summary field, they would have moved also.

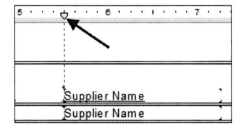

Figure 4-12 Supplier Name field marker moved

Guideline Issues

Depending on how much you use guidelines, you may notice that a few strange things happen with the guidelines. The ones that I have noticed are discussed in Table 4-3.

Issue	Solution
You delete objects from the report, but the guidelines stay.	Delete the guidelines that are no longer needed.
You moved an object, but the guideline did not move with it.	Move the object towards the guideline until the object snaps to the guideline.
You resized or moved an object and the object now appears to be attached to two guidelines.	Move the object away from the guideline that you do not want the object attached to and then resize the object and attach it to the guideline that you want.

Table 4-3 Guideline issues explained

Using The Grid

When you need to have greater precision over lining up objects on a report then the guidelines provide, you can turn on the **GRID** option. This option is not on by default. In addition to the grid option, turning on the **SNAP TO GRID** option provides additional precision. The **SNAP TO GRID** option affects the guidelines.

View ⇒ Grid ⇒ Design, will turn on the grid on the design window, as shown in Figure 4-13. The grid is the dot pattern in the background. When new fields or objects are added to the report manually, they are automatically placed on the closest grid position to where you release the mouse button. If you need to change any of the grid settings, they are located on the Layout tab on the Options dialog box.

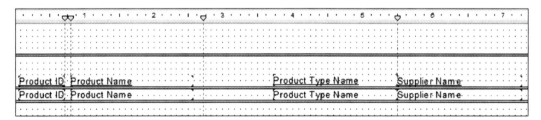

Figure 4-13 Report layout with the grid option turned on

Sizing Objects

When fields are added to a report, the size is the larger of the field or the field heading. It appears that Crystal Reports estimates the horizontal space needed for string fields. Sometimes this works and sometimes the data in a string field in the details section of the report gets cut off using this method. I suspect this happens because there is not enough space in the row to display all of the fields, so text fields are often truncated. This is what happened with the Product Name field on the report illustrated in Figure 4-14.

To fix this you need to resize the field. Depending on how close you placed the fields on the report, you may have to move the Product Type Name field to the right, before starting this exercise. To resize a field, follow the steps below.

1. Click on the field that you need to resize. In this exercise, click on the Product Name field.

2. Place the mouse pointer on the right side of the field as illustrated in Figure 4-15. The mouse pointer will change to a double arrow, as illustrated in Figure 4-15. Drag the **RESIZE HANDLE** that you saw earlier in Figure 4-4 to the right. You will see the color on the ruler change over the field, as illustrated in Figure 4-16. This may make it easier to see the size that you are adjusting the field to. Notice that the field heading was also resized.

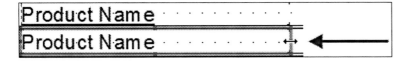

Product ID	Product Name		Product Type Name
1,101	Active Outdoors Crochet Glo		Gloves
1,102	Active Outdoors Crochet Glo		Gloves
1,103	Active Outdoors Crochet Glo	Truncated Data	Gloves
1,104	Active Outdoors Crochet Glo		Gloves
1,105	Active Outdoors Crochet Glo		Gloves
1,106	Active Outdoors Lycra Glove		Gloves
1,107	Active Outdoors Lycra Glove		Gloves

Figure 4-14 Truncated data illustrated

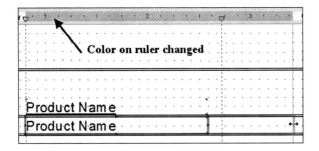

Figure 4-15 Mouse pointer in position to resize the field

Figure 4-16 Color on ruler illustrated

3. Preview the report to see if you can now see all of the data in the Product Name field as shown in Figure 4-17. Save the changes and leave the report open to complete the next exercise.

 If the Product Name field is selected on the preview window, click on a blank space in the report to deselect it. To keep this from happening, click on a blank space in the design window before previewing the report.

Product ID	Product Name	Product Type Name
1,101	Active Outdoors Crochet Glove	Gloves
1,102	Active Outdoors Crochet Glove	Gloves
1,103	Active Outdoors Crochet Glove	Gloves
1,104	Active Outdoors Crochet Glove	Gloves
1,105	Active Outdoors Crochet Glove	Gloves
1,106	Active Outdoors Lycra Glove	Gloves
1,107	Active Outdoors Lycra Glove	Gloves

Figure 4-17 Product Name field resized

 It is a good idea to scan through several pages of the report while previewing it, to make sure that you do not see any data cut off (truncated) in the field that you are resizing. It is possible that the resized field may still not be wide enough.

The Size And Position Dialog Box

In addition to resizing a field manually, you can also use the Size and Position option on the shortcut menu by following the steps below.

1. Right-click on the field that you want to resize and select **SIZE AND POSITION** as shown in Figure 4-18. In this exercise, right-click on the Product Type Name field.

Notice that the options on the shortcut menu are different then the ones shown earlier in Figure 4-7.

The options on the menu change, depending on how many objects are selected or the type of object that is selected.

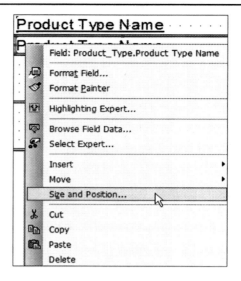

Figure 4-18 Object shortcut menu

2. Change the **WIDTH** to 1.0, as shown in Figure 4-19 and click OK. Save the changes and leave the report open to complete the next exercise.

This change will make the field shorter. If you enter a larger number, the field will be longer. If you do not have a need for such field size precision, you will probably not have a need to use the options on this dialog box. I have been using Crystal Reports for years and other then writing this exercise, I have never used this dialog box.

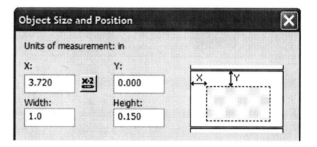

Figure 4-19 Object Size and Position dialog box

 The options that you change on the Object Size and Position dialog box will **NOT** automatically be applied to the field title.

Nudging Objects

So far in this lesson you have learned how to move and resize objects using the mouse. You can also move and resize objects using the keyboard. This is helpful if you use a laptop and do not use a mouse. Using the keyboard to move or resize objects is known as **NUDGING** an object.

 If the **SNAP TO GRID** option is turned on, the arrow key will move the object one grid point each time you press an arrow key.

How To Move An Object By Nudging It

1. Select the object that you want to move.

2. Use one of the four arrow keys on the keyboard to move the object in the direction that you need to move the object.

How To Resize An Object Using The Nudge Feature

1. Click on the object that you need to resize, then press and hold down the **SHIFT** key.

2. Use the arrow key that points in the direction that you want to resize the object. If you used the nudging feature on the L4.1 report, close the report but do not save the changes.

Formatting And Editing Overview

It can take an hour or more to create a report. You may struggle to write the formulas, make sure that the sorting and grouping options meet the report requirements and come up with an appropriate title for the report. You are pleased that you were able to accomplish all of these tasks and give a copy of the report to the person that requested it. You see them frown, but can't figure out why, especially because you checked the formulas by hand and know that the data is correct. You ask why they are frowning and they say, "Some of the fields are not lined up and there are too many fonts." As they say, "Perception is everything." Take from this what you will.

Crystal Reports provides a variety of options that you can use to make the reports that you design look better. You can draw boxes, apply templates, add color (probably best suited for reports that will be viewed as a web page or printed on a color printer) and more. You can also apply formatting conditionally to fields or sections of the report depending on whether the value in a field meets specific criteria. This type of formatting can be applied to any field that is on the report including summary, formula, group name, running total and SQL Expression fields.

Earlier in this workbook you learned that everything on a report is an object, including charts, data fields, headings and formulas. I realize that this may take some getting use to. The good news is that each type of object has it's own set of properties that you can modify. The options on the Standard, Formatting and Insert Tools toolbars, shown in Figures 4-20, 4-21 and 4-22 respectively, contain many of the options that are covered in the next few exercises in this lesson.

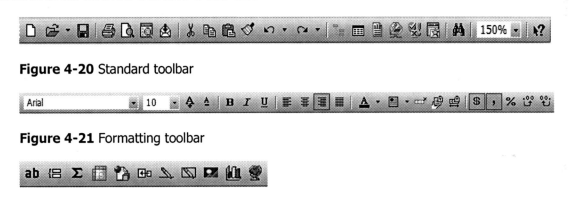

Figure 4-20 Standard toolbar

Figure 4-21 Formatting toolbar

Figure 4-22 Insert Tools toolbar

Adding And Editing Text Objects

Text objects are used to add additional information to a report. Text objects include field headings, report titles or any text that you want to add to a report that is not created based on a field in a table.

Exercise 4.2: How To Edit Text Objects

In this exercise you will learn how to edit text objects.

1. Save the L3.5 report as L4.2 Text objects.

The majority of the field headings on the report are clear and easy to understand. The one field heading that would be easier to understand is the Order ID field. Most end-users (people that will read the report) would not understand the term "ID", so it would be better to change this field heading.

2. Right-click on the Order ID field heading in the page header section and select **EDIT TEXT**.

You can also double-click on the Order ID field heading to change the text.

3. Select (highlight) the text shown in Figure 4-23, then type `Order  #` and click on a blank space on the report.

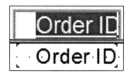

Figure 4-23 Text selected to change

 You can also select a portion of the text in a field and change that. For example, you could select "ID" in Figure 4-23 above and just change that.

 Pressing the **ENTER** key does not end the editing session like it does in other software packages. Pressing Enter in Crystal Reports starts a new line in the text object. When you finish adding or editing text, click outside of the text object to end the edit session.

Make The Page Header Section Longer

The report that you have open does not have a report title. As you can see, there is not a lot of space in the page header section above the field headings to add the report title. The page header section needs to be longer. Follow the steps below to learn how to make a section of the report longer.

1. Click on the section bar below the page header section. The mouse pointer is in the right position when you see the double arrow illustrated in Figure 4-24. Drag the section bar down below the details section.

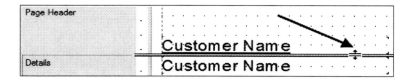

Figure 4-24 Mouse pointer in position to make the page header section longer

2. Move all of the field headings in the page header section down, then click on a blank space on the report.

 The easiest way to move all of the field headings at one time is to select all of them first and then move them at the same time.

 If you need to make a section in the report shorter, drag the section bar up.

How To Add A Text Object

1. Click the **INSERT TEXT OBJECT** button on the Insert Tools toolbar. The mouse pointer will change to a plus sign.

2. Click in the page header section and type `Customer  Orders  Report` in the text object, then click on a blank space on the report.

 You can right-click on a blank space in the report and select **INSERT TEXT OBJECT** as shown earlier in Figure 4-1.

When selecting fonts to use on a report, it is best to use the default fonts that come with Windows, otherwise the report will look different on computers that do not have the font that you selected. If you have to use a font that does not come with Windows, you should export the report to Adobe PDF format. Doing that will allow the report to be seen with the font that you selected.

How To Format A Text Object

As you can see, the text object is too small for the text that you entered. Follow the steps below to learn how to format a text object.

1. Click on the object that you want to apply formatting to. In this exercise, click on the report title that you just created.

2. Click the **BOLD** button and change the font size to 14, then make the object longer and wider so that you can see all of the text.

3. Move the report title so that it is centered (left to right) across the page header section. The top of the report should look like the one shown in Figure 4-25. Save the changes and close the report.

Customer Orders Report					
Customer Name	Order #	Order Date	Order Amount	Ship Via	First Name	Last
City Cyclists	1	12/2/2003 12:00:00A	$41.90	UPS	Nancy	Dav
Deals on Wheels	1,002	12/2/2003 12:00:00A	$5,060.28	Pickup	Janet	Leve
Warsaw Sports, Inc.	1,003	12/2/2003 12:00:00A	$186.87	UPS	Margaret	Pea
Bikes and Trikes	1,004	12/2/2003 12:00:00A	$823.05	Pickup	Margaret	Pea

Figure 4-25 Modified page header section

I use to find it difficult to center text like a report title across a page. I finally came up with the steps below to center a report title across the page.

① Make the report title object the width of the report as shown in Figure 4-26.

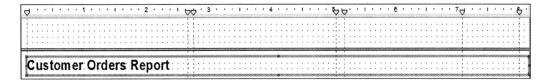

Figure 4-26 Text object resized to the width of the report

② Click the **ALIGN CENTER** button.

If you do not see the font size that you need in the font size drop down list, you can type it in. In the font drop down list, there is no option for font size 21. You can type it into the field on the toolbar and press Enter as shown in Figure 4-27.

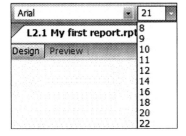

Figure 4-27 Font size changed to one not in the drop down list

How To Import A Text File Into A Text Object

If there is text in a file that you want to add to a text object in the report, you can, by following the steps below.

1. Add a text object to the report, then double-click in the text object to go into edit mode.

2. Right-click in the text object and select **INSERT FROM FILE** as shown in Figure 4-28.

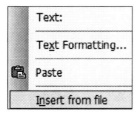

Figure 4-28 Text object shortcut menu

3. Find the file on your hard drive or in another location and double-click on it. The content of the text file will be added to the text object. Save the changes.

Combining Text Objects And Database Fields

Text objects are more powerful then they may appear. If you have spent any time trying to get a text object and a field to line up side by side with spacing that looks right, but have had trouble doing so, you are in luck. Text objects can have data fields embedded in them. Text objects will automatically resize to accommodate the embedded field so that there is no extra space. The steps below explain how to embed a database field in a text object.

1. Add a text object to the report, then add the text to the object.

2. Drag a database field either from the report or from the Field Explorer into the text object as shown in Figure 4-29, then release the mouse button. You will see a flashing cursor in the text object before you release the mouse button. This is where the database field will be added.

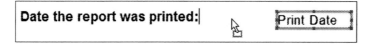

Figure 4-29 Database field being added to a text object

Combining Text Objects Tips

① You can edit the combined field or add more text or another database field to the text object.
② You can format part of a text object. If this is what you need to do, only select (highlight) the part that you want to format.
③ If you discover that you have added the wrong field to the text object, click on the database field in the text object, then press the **DEL** key.

Exercise 4.3: Adding Graphics To A Report

The sample reports that you viewed in Lesson 2 had a logo. This exercise will show you how to add a logo or any graphic file to a report that is not stored in a table. There are two options discussed below for navigating to the Open dialog box shown in Figure 4-30.

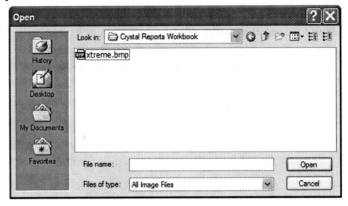

① Click the **INSERT PICTURE** button on the Insert Tools toolbar.
② Insert ⇒ Picture.

Figure 4-30 Insert Picture Open dialog box

Believe it or not, the logo that you saw in the sample reports does not come with this version of Crystal Reports. You can download it from the Business Objects web site, from the link below. The web page says that the logo is for version 10, but it is the same logo that is used in the sample reports in Crystal Reports XI. When you download the zip file, extract the xtreme.bmp file and put it in the Crystal Reports Workbook folder.

http://support.businessobjects.com/communityCS/FilesAndUpdates/cr_xtremelogo.zip.asp

 If you can't find the logo on the web site, you can open a sample report that has the logo, like the Charting report in the Feature Examples sample reports folder and copy it to the report that you create.

1. Save the L3.4 report as `L4.3 Insert picture`.

2. Make the page header section longer by dragging the section bar (below the section) down almost to the end of the page footer section. You will need that amount of space for the logo. Move the field headings down.

3. Open the Insert Picture dialog box shown above in Figure 4-30 and navigate to the folder or location where the graphic is, that you want to use. For this exercise, navigate to the Crystal Reports Workbook folder. You may have to change the Files of type field at the bottom of the Open dialog box to **ALL FILES** to be able to see the logo file.

4. Double-click on the file, xtreme.bmp. The mouse pointer should have changed to a shadow box (which is the actual size of the graphic), as shown in Figure 4-31.

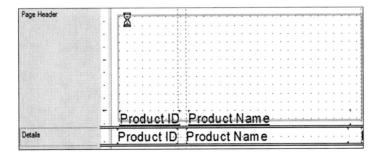

Figure 4-31 Mouse pointer in the Insert Picture mode

5. Click in the upper left corner of the page header section. You should see the logo. Save the changes and leave the report open to complete the next part of the exercise.

How To Resize A Graphic

The logo would look better if it were smaller. The default size of the logo is too large. Follow the steps below to resize the logo.

1. Select the logo if it is not already selected. If the Product ID and Product Name field headings are covered by the logo, click on the lower right corner of the logo and drag the mouse up and over to the left, until you can see the field headings.

2. The report should look like the one shown in Figure 4-32. If you look at other pages in the report, you will see the logo at the top of the page because it was placed in the page header section of the report, which prints on every page. Save the changes and close the report.

Figure 4-32 L4.3 Insert picture report with the logo added

Exercise 4.3A: Adding Graphics From Fonts

In addition to being able to add graphic images to a report, you can also add graphics that are stored in fonts like the Wingdings font. Fonts that have graphics can be accessed from the Character Map application in Windows. These graphics have to be placed in a text object. In this exercise you will add a graphic from a font to a report.

1. Save the L4.2 report as L4.3A Graphics from fonts.

2. Delete the first and last name fields from the report.

3. In Windows XP, click the Start button, then select All Programs (or Programs) ⇒ Accessories ⇒ System Tools ⇒ Character Map.

4. Open the Font drop down list on the Character Map dialog box and select WINGDINGS, if it is not already selected. You should see the dialog box shown in Figure 4-33.

5. Double-click on the document picture (the third picture from the right in the first row), then click the Copy button and close the dialog box.

6. Add a text object to the details section after the Ship Via field, then press the CTRL+ V keys to paste the picture in the text object. Click on a blank space on the report. Save the changes. The report should look like the one shown in Figure 4-34.

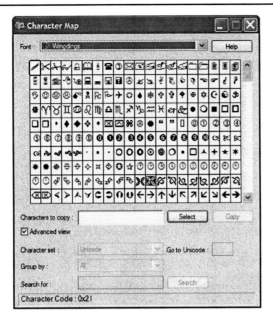

Figure 4-33 Character Map dialog box

One reason to add an image next to each detail record is to create a hyperlink to another section of the report or to open a document or another report that has information that relates to the detail record.

Customer Name	Order #	Order Date	Order Amount	Ship Via	
City Cyclists	1	12/2/03	$41.90	UPS	
Deals on Wheels	1002	12/2/03	$5,060.28	Pickup	
Warsaw Sports, Inc.	1003	12/2/03	$186.87	UPS	
Bikes and Trikes	1004	12/2/03	$823.05	Pickup	

Figure 4-34 L4.3A Graphics from fonts report

The Format Editor

So far in this lesson all of the formatting that you have learned about is considered basic formatting. For many reports that is all of the formatting that is required. When you need to create additional formatting, you can use the Format Editor. If the standard options on the Format Editor do not handle your needs, you can write conditional formulas. As you will see, many options on the Format Editor have a Formula button. Clicking on this button will let you apply conditional formatting to the option. You will learn how to do this in Lesson 10. The Format Editor provides a lot of options for changing how objects look on a report.

The options that are on the Format Editor dialog box will vary, depending on the type of object that is selected. When you open the Format Editor, you will only see tabs that can be used for the field type that is selected. Table 4-4 lists all of the tabs on the Format Editor and what data type each tab is for.

 If you need to make the same change to several objects, select all of the objects that need the same change, prior to opening the Format Editor.

In the next few exercises you will learn how to use the Format Editor. There are three ways to open the Format Editor AFTER selecting at least one object in the report, as discussed below.

    ① Click the **FORMAT** button on the Expert Tools toolbar.
    ② Right-click and select **FORMAT <OBJECT TYPE>** as shown in Figure 4-35. Depending on the object that is selected, you will see a different format option type. If the selected object is a graphic, you would see **FORMAT GRAPHIC**. The option for the Format Editor is always the first "Format" option on the shortcut menu. Notice that the icons to the left of the menu options shown in Figure 4-35 are the same icons that are on the buttons on the Expert Tools toolbar.
    ③ Format ⇒ Format <object type>.

Tab	Data Type	Purpose
Common	All	These options, shown in Figure 4-36 can be used by most objects on a report. Table 4-5 explains the options on the Common tab.
Border	All	Add lines and drop shadows to fields.
Font	All except OLE & graphic objects	Select font, font size, font color, underlining, strike out and character spacing. Most of the options on this tab are also on the Formatting toolbar.
Hyperlink	All	Lets you use the selected object as a link to a web site, file, email address or a field on a web page.
Paragraph	String & Memo fields	Formats paragraphs that are stored in string or memo fields.
Number	Number & currency	Lets you apply formatting options that are only for number fields. (2)
Date & Time	Date & Time fields	Lets you apply formatting options that are only for date and date/time fields. (2)
Picture	Graphic	Lets you crop, scale, reset and resize graphic images.
Boolean	Boolean	Lets you select how Boolean values will be displayed.

Table 4-4 Format Editor tab options explained

(2) Options on this tab support custom formatting.

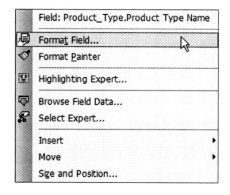

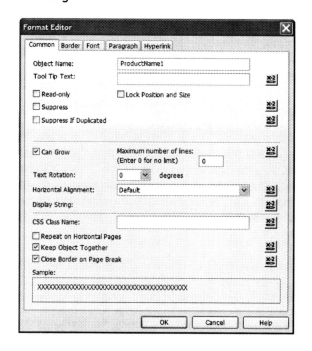

Figure 4-35 Format Editor menu option illustrated

Figure 4-36 Common tab options

You should know where options are on the Format Editor.

Option	Description
Option Name	This field is filled in by default. You can accept the default name unless you have a need to use it in a formula and want to use a shorter or more descriptive name. It is not necessary to change the option name.
Tool Tip Text	Enter text in this field that you want displayed when the mouse pointer hovers over the field in Preview mode.
Read-only	Prevents the object from having additional formatting applied.
Lock Position and Size	Prevents the object from being moved or resized.
Suppress	Hides the object.
Suppress If Duplicated	Hides the object if it has the same value as the one in the prior record.
Suppress Embedded Field Blank Lines	Suppresses the field if it does not have data. This prevents blanks lines from appearing on the report. This option is only for text fields which is why it is not visible in Figure 4-36 above.
Can Grow	Lets the field expand to accommodate more data.
Text Rotation	Lets you change the angle of the field.
CSS Class Name	If the field will be formatted with a style sheet, enter the CSS Class Name that should be applied to the object.
Repeat on Horizontal	This option is mostly used with a cross-tab or OLAP grid that will print horizontally across more than one page.
Keep Object Together	Keeps the object from printing on more than one page. The object will be printed on the next page if it does not fit at the bottom of the previous page.
Close Border on Page Break	This option is used for fields that will print on more than one page and have a border. This option will print the bottom of the border of the object on the first page and print another border around the remaining data in the field that prints on the next page.

Table 4-5 Common tab options explained

Format A Text Object

1. Open the L4.2 report and right-click on the report title, then select **FORMAT TEXT**.

2. Click on the **BORDER** tab. You will see the options shown in Figure 4-37. Table 4-6 explains the options on this tab. Change the **LINE STYLE** to single for the Left, Right and Top options. Notice at the bottom of the dialog box in the **SAMPLE** section that you can see the options that you have applied to the object.

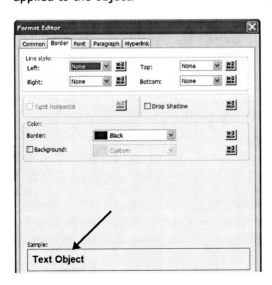

Figure 4-37 Border tab options on the Format Editor dialog box

Option	Description
Line Style	These four options let you select the line style for each side of the object.
Tight Horizontal	Moves the border of the object closer to the object.
Drop Shadow	Adds the shadow effect to the lower right corner of the object.
Border Color	Lets you select a color for the border and drop shadow.
Background Color	Lets you select the color for the background of the object.
	The Formula button opens the Formula Workshop, which lets you create a formula to use with the option. You can also attach an existing formula to the option. You would use a formula when you need to control when the option is turned on or off, based on a condition. For example, if you wanted to highlight the order amount field on records that were in a certain dollar amount range.

Table 4-6 Border tab options explained

3. Check the **DROP SHADOW** and **BACKGROUND** options, then open the drop down list across from the Background option and select **YELLOW** as shown in Figure 4-38.

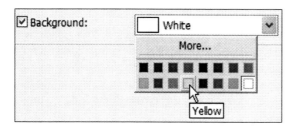

Figure 4-38 Background color options

> If selected, the **MORE** option shown above in Figure 4-38 will open the Color dialog box, which will let you select additional colors or create a custom color.

4. Click OK to close the Format Editor. The report should look like the one shown in Figure 4-39. Save the changes and leave the report open to complete the next part of the exercise.

Customer Orders Report							
Customer Name	Order #	Order Date	Order Amount	Ship Via		First Name	Last
City Cyclists	1	12/2/2003 12:00:00A	$41.90	UPS		Nancy	Dav
Deals on Wheels	1,002	12/2/2003 12:00:00A	$5,060.28	Pickup		Janet	Leve
Warsaw Sports, Inc.	1,003	12/2/2003 12:00:00A	$186.87	UPS		Margaret	Pea
Bikes and Trikes	1,004	12/2/2003 12:00:00A	$823.05	Pickup		Margaret	Pea

Figure 4-39 L4.2 Text Objects report with formatting applied to a text object

The Can Grow Option

Earlier in this exercise I mentioned that one reason data gets truncated is because there may not be enough room in the section of the report to accommodate all of the data. In the part of the exercise that you just completed, there was enough room to make the field longer. If you have tried everything possible to get all of the data to fit, the option **CAN GROW**, should fix the problem. This option will cause the data in the field to wrap to a new line, only when needed. Fields that have this option enabled, will only grow longer, not wider. Follow the steps below to learn how to turn this option on.

> The Can Grow option can only be used with string fields, text objects and memo fields.

1. Right-click on the object(s) that you want to apply the Can Grow option to and select **FORMAT FIELD**. You will see the Format Editor dialog box. For this exercise, right-click on the Product Name field.

 You can also click on the field and then click the **FORMAT** button on the Expert Tools toolbar to open the Format Editor.

2. Click on the **COMMON** tab, then check the **CAN GROW** option and click OK.

If you want to limit the maximum number of lines that a field can print on the report, enter it in the **MAXIMUM NUMBER OF LINES** field to the right of the Can Grow field. For example, if you are applying the Can Grow option to a memo field that could have 500 characters or more of text, you may not want to have all of the text in the field print on the report. If this is the case, you would enter a number in the Maximum number of lines field so that only the first two or three lines of information in the field will actually print on the report. The Can Grow option, even when enabled will only be activated when needed. It does not force every record to expand to the number entered in the field.

If you use the Can Grow option on a field and there is another field below it, it is possible that the field below will be overwritten. To prevent this, the following options are available.

① Put the field with the Can Grow option at the bottom of the section.
② Not as effective as the first option, but you can check the spacing to make sure that the field with the Can Grow option is not close to other fields.

3. Resize the Product Name field so that it ends at the 2 inch mark. The report should look similar to the one shown in Figure 4-40. Save the changes.

Product ID	Product Name	Product Type Name
1,101	Active Outdoors Crochet Glove	Gloves
1,102	Active Outdoors Crochet Glove	Gloves
1,103	Active Outdoors Crochet Glove	Gloves
1,104	Active Outdoors Crochet Glove	Gloves

Figure 4-40 Report with the Can Grow option applied to the Product Name field

Text Rotation

There may be times when some of the text on a report will look better if it is rotated. Figure 4-41 shows the degrees that you can rotate text. Select the text that you want to rotate, then select the degree rotation and click OK. Figure 4-42 shows the Product ID heading rotated 90 degrees.

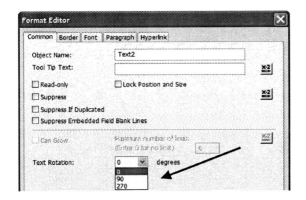

Product ID	Product Name	Product Type Name
1,101	Active Outdoors Crochet Glove	Gloves
1,102	Active Outdoors Crochet Glove	Gloves

Figure 4-42 Product ID heading rotated 90 degrees

Figure 4-41 Text rotation options illustrated

Format Editor Paragraph Tab

When you are applying formatting to a text object, string or memo field, you will see the Paragraph tab shown in Figure 4-43. The options on this tab let you select how text fields that have multiple lines of data or text will be formatted.

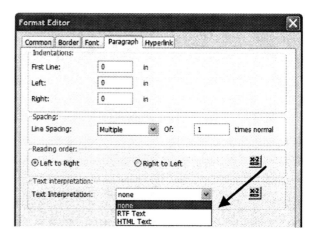

Figure 4-43 Paragraph tab on the Format Editor

 The **TEXT INTERPRETATION** option illustrated in Figure 4-43 is not available for text objects. These options are helpful if the field has HTML (Hypertext Markup Language) formatting, which is used for web pages or RTF (Rich Text Format) formatting for text that may have special formatting from word processing or publishing software.

Format A Numeric Object

Usually, order numbers do not have any formatting. As you saw earlier in Figure 4-39, the Order Number field has a comma. This field would look better if it did not have any formatting. Follow the steps below to change the formatting of the Order Number field.

1. Right-click on the Order ID field in the details section and select **FORMAT FIELD**. You will see the dialog box shown in Figure 4-44.

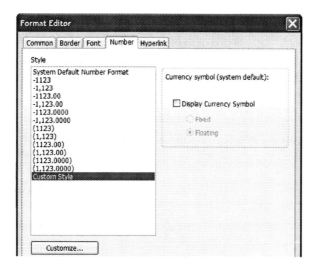

Figure 4-44 Number tab options

2. Click on the second option **-1123** from the top. The minus sign will only print if the number is negative. Click OK and preview the report. The Order ID field should not have a comma in it. Save the changes and leave the report open to complete the next part of the exercise.

If none of the options shown above in Figure 4-44 meet your needs to format currency or number fields, click the **CUSTOMIZE** button.

You will see the options shown in Figure 4-45 if the field that you are formatting is a currency field. You will see the options shown in Figure 4-46 if the field that you are formatting is a number field.

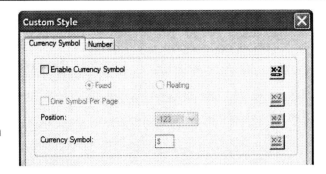

Figure 4-45 Currency symbol custom style options

 Usually, the **DECIMALS** and **ROUNDING** options shown in Figure 4-46 are set to the same number of decimal places.

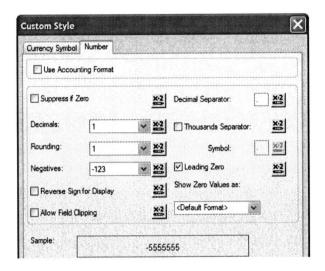

Figure 4-46 Number custom style options

 If you think determining if a field is a string field or a numeric field based on the name is difficult or confusing, you can clear the **SHOW FIELD NAMES** option on the Layout tab of the Options dialog box. [See Lesson 5, Figure 5-54] Clearing this option will display X's in string fields and 5's in numeric fields as shown in Figure 4-47.

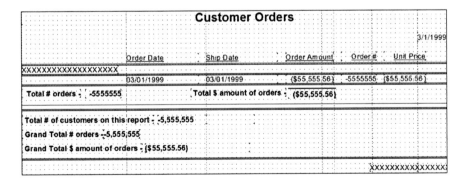

Figure 4-47 Fields without field names

Format A Date Field

Displaying the time as part of the Order Date field is not needed on the report that you are working on. To keep the time portion of the field from printing on the report, the data needs to be formatted. Follow the steps below to change the formatting of the Order Date field.

1. Right-click on the Order Date field and select Format Field. You will see the dialog box shown in Figure 4-48.

   If you click the **CUSTOMIZE** button you will see the dialog box shown in Figure 4-49, which will let you change the formatting for a date field or the date portion of a date/time field. The options shown on Figure 4-50 let you change the formatting for the time portion of a date/time field.

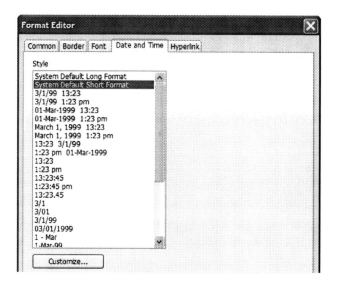

Figure 4-48 Date and Time tab options

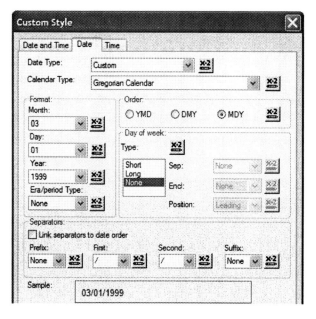

Figure 4-49 Date custom style options

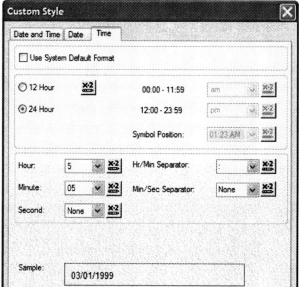

Figure 4-50 Time custom style options

2. Click on the option **3/1/99** on the Date and Time tab and click OK. The report should look like the one shown in Figure 4-51. You should not see the time on the Order Date field like you did earlier in Figure 4-39. Save the changes and close the report.

Customer Orders Report					
Customer Name	Order #	Order Date	Order Amount	Ship Via	First Name	Last
City Cyclists	1	12/2/03	$41.90	UPS	Nancy	Dav
Deals on Wheels	1002	12/2/03	$5,060.28	Pickup	Janet	Leve
Warsaw Sports, Inc.	1003	12/2/03	$186.87	UPS	Margaret	Pea
Bikes and Trikes	1004	12/2/03	$823.05	Pickup	Margaret	Pea

Figure 4-51 L4.2 Text objects report with the Order Number and Order Date fields modified

Format A Graphic

Earlier in this lesson you added a logo (graphic) to the L4.3 Insert Picture report. The logo would look better if it had a border and was scaled down.

Resize The Logo

1. Open the L4.3 report, then right-click on the logo and select Format Graphic. Click on the **PICTURE** tab. You will see the dialog box shown in Figure 4-52. Table 4-7 explains the options on the Picture tab.

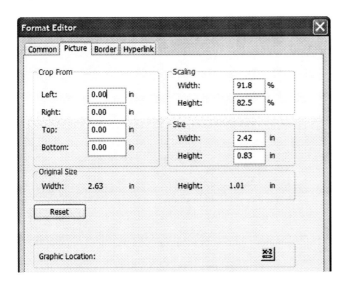

Figure 4-52 Picture tab options

Option	Description
Crop From	Allows you to remove part of the image. The part of the image that is removed, is the part on the outside of the crop lines that are created when you enter the dimensions in any or all of the four crop options (left, right, top or bottom).
Scaling	Allows you to enlarge or reduce the image by a percent.
Size	Allows you to change the width and height of the image.
Reset	Removes all of the formatting that was applied to the image on the Picture tab. When you crop, scale or size an image, the original image file is not changed. It is only displayed differently on the report, based on the options that are selected.

Table 4-7 Picture tab options explained

2. Change the scaling **WIDTH** option to 60, then change the scaling **HEIGHT** option to 60 and click OK. Preview the report. Figure 4-53 shows the logo before it was scaled. Figure 4-54 shows the logo after scaling. Save the changes and leave the report open to complete the next part of the exercise.

Figure 4-53 L4.3 Insert picture report with the image before scaling

Figure 4-54 L4.3 Insert picture report with the image after scaling

Add A Border To The Logo

1. Click on the logo, then open the Format Editor and click on the Border tab.

2. Change all four **LINE STYLE** options to Dotted and click OK. The logo should look like the one shown in Figure 4-55. Save the changes and leave the report open to complete an exercise later in this lesson.

Figure 4-55 L4.3 Insert picture report with the image border modified

Exercise 4.4: Format A Boolean Field

In this exercise you will change how the data in a Boolean field is displayed on a report.

1. Create a new report and add the following fields from the Orders table: Order ID, Order Date, Shipped and Payment Received.

2. Save the report as `L4.4 Boolean formatting`. The report should look like the one shown in Figure 4-56.

The Shipped and Payment Received fields are Boolean fields. As you can see, they both are displaying true or false. You will format these fields so that they display Yes and No instead. Doing this does not change the data in the table.

Order ID	Order Date	Shipped	Payment Received
1	12/2/2003 12:00:00A	True	True
1,002	12/2/2003 12:00:00A	True	True
1,003	12/2/2003 12:00:00A	True	True
1,004	12/2/2003 12:00:00A	True	True
1,005	12/3/2003 12:00:00A	True	True
1,006	12/3/2003 12:00:00A	True	True

Figure 4-56 L4.4 Boolean formatting report

3. Select both fields, right-click and select Format Objects, then click on the Boolean tab.

4. Open the **BOOLEAN TEXT** drop down list and select Yes or No as shown in Figure 4-57, then click OK.

5. Preview the report. The value in the Shipped and Payment Received fields is now displayed as Yes or No instead of True and False. If you go to page 29, you will see that not all of the data in these fields is Yes, as shown in Figure 4-58. Save the changes and close the report.

 Instead of clicking on the right arrow 28 times, you can type 29 in the Report Navigation toolbar as illustrated in Figure 4-58 and press Enter.

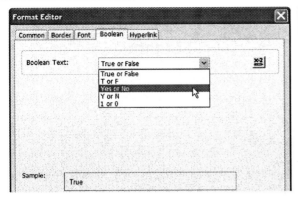

Figure 4-57 Boolean tab options

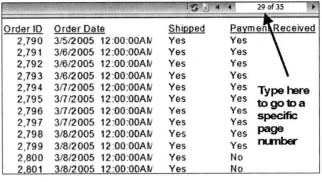

Figure 4-58 Boolean fields displayed differently on the L4.4 Boolean formatting report

The Format Painter

This is a pretty cool feature. It allows you to copy the formatting from one object to several other objects with a mouse click. Formatting properties like font, font size, font color and borders can be taken from a text object and applied to a numeric object. This is because this type of formatting is not specific to a data type. Usually, number specific formatting cannot be applied to other data types. There are three ways to start the Format Painter as discussed below, **AFTER** you have clicked on the object that has the formatting that you want to apply (copy) to other objects.

① Right-click on the object and select **FORMAT PAINTER.**
② Click the **FORMAT PAINTER** button on the Standard toolbar.
③ Format ⇒ Format Painter.

There are some things that the Format Painter cannot do as discussed below.

① The Format Painter cannot copy a format that is created with the Highlighting Expert. [See Lesson 10, Highlighting Expert Overview]
② Formatting cannot be copied from text objects or templates to fields in a table.
③ Formatted objects in the repository can be copied to reports. Formatting from reports cannot be copied to objects in the repository.
④ The Format Painter does not copy hyperlink properties.
⑤ The Format Painter will copy all formatting to other objects of the same data type. If formatting is copied from one data type to a different data type, only the formatting options that the objects have in common will be copied.

Change The Formatting Of An Object

In order to use this feature you need to change the formatting of an object.

1. Open the L4.3 report.

2. Change the font of the Product Name heading to Times New Roman, Size 10 and Bold.

Apply The Formatting To Other Objects

1. With the Product Name field selected, open the Format Painter.

2. When you hold the mouse pointer over the Product ID heading, it will change to a **PAINT BRUSH**, as illustrated in Figure 4-59.

Figure 4-59 Mouse pointer in position to apply formatting

3. Click on the Product ID heading. The formatting from the Product Name heading should have been applied to the Product ID heading.

 You should know the steps required to use the Format Painter.

Using The Format Painter On Multiple Objects

If you need to apply the same formatting to more than one object, follow the steps below.

1. Select the object that has the formatting that you want to apply to other objects. For this exercise, click on the Product ID heading.

2. Open the Format Painter, then press and hold down the **ALT** key.

3. Click on the first object that you want to change. In this exercise, click on the Product Type Name heading, then click on the Supplier Name heading. The headings should all have the same formatting. Save the changes and close the report.

If you tried to apply this formatting to the logo, the mouse pointer would change to the symbol illustrated in Figure 4-60.

This symbol lets you know that the formatting cannot be applied to the object that you are holding the mouse pointer over.

Figure 4-60 Symbol indicating that the formatting cannot be applied to the object

Exercise 4.5: Center Data Under A Heading

The report would look better if the following changes were made.

① Center the region field under the heading.
② Put a line under each detail record to make the report easier to read.

1. Save the L3.1 report as L4.5 Modified customer information.

2. Select the Region field and heading, then click the **ALIGN CENTER** button on the Standard toolbar.

3. Resize the Region field and heading to make them smaller. The data should now be centered under the heading.

How To Add Horizontal Lines To A Report

One way to make the data in the details section of a report easier to read is to place a line under the fields in this section. Like other objects, you can format lines that you add to a report. There are two ways to open the **LINE** tool as discussed below.

① Click the **INSERT LINE** button on the Insert toolbar.

② Insert ⇒ Line.

Follow the steps below to add a line to the details section.

1. Move the details section bar down a little. Move it to the first row of dots in the report footer section.

2. Open the **LINE** tool. The mouse pointer will change to a pencil. Draw a line under the fields in the details section.

It is easier to draw a long line like this if you can see the entire width of the report. To do this, I often change the **ZOOM CONTROL** option on the Standard toolbar to 75%.

Format The Line

Follow the steps below to learn how to format a line.

1. Right-click on the line in the details section and select **FORMAT LINE**. You will see the dialog box shown in Figure 4-61.

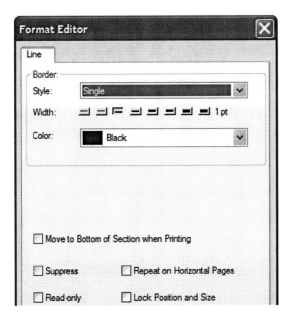

Figure 4-61 Format Editor line options

The **MOVE TO BOTTOM OF SECTION WHEN PRINTING** option is often used for lines in a section of the report that has a field with the Can Grow option turned on, like a Notes field. Checking this option will force the line to print at the bottom of the section, which is what you usually want. You can test how this option works by checking it. Then make the section of the report longer that has the line and preview the report.

2. Open the **STYLE** drop down list and select Single, if it is not already selected.

3. Click on the first button in the **WIDTH** section. You should see the word **HAIRLINE** at the end of the Width options. Click OK. The report should look like the one shown in Figure 4-62. Notice that the Region field data is centered under the heading. Save the changes and close the report.

Customer Name	Address1	Region	Country	Postal C
City Cyclists	7464 South Kingsway	MI	USA	48358
Pathfinders	410 Eighth Avenue	IL	USA	60148
Bike-A-Holics Anonymous	7429 Arbutus Boulevard	OH	USA	43005
Psycho-Cycle	8287 Scott Road	AL	USA	35818
Sporting Wheels Inc.	480 Grant Way	CA	USA	92150
Rockshocks for Jocks	1984 Sydney Street	TX	USA	78770

Figure 4-62 L4.5 Modified customer information report with the details section modified

Exercise 4.6: Add Vertical Lines To A Report

In the previous exercise you learned how to add horizontal lines to a report. In this exercise you will learn how to add vertical lines to a report.

1. Save the L3.1 report as `L4.6 Vertical lines`.

2. Make the Region, Country and Postal Code fields smaller, then move the Country and Postal Code fields over to the left.

3. Insert ⇒ Line. Draw a vertical line in the details section, after the Customer Name field.

4. Right-click on the vertical line that you just created and select Copy, then right-click anyplace in the report and select Paste. The mouse pointer will have a picture of the line next to it.

5. Click at the end of the next field (the Address field) on the report.

6. Repeat steps 4 and 5 to place a vertical line after every field in the details section, then save the changes. The report should look like the one shown in Figure 4-63. Close the report.

Customer Name	Address1	Region	Country	Postal Code
City Cyclists	7464 South Kingsway	MI	USA	48358
Pathfinders	410 Eighth Avenue	IL	USA	60148
Bike-A-Holics Anonymous	7429 Arbutus Boulevard	OH	USA	43005
Psycho-Cycle	8287 Scott Road	AL	USA	35818
Sporting Wheels Inc.	480 Grant Way	CA	USA	92150
Rockshocks for Jocks	1984 Sydney Street	TX	USA	78770
Poser Cycles	8194 Peter Avenue	MN	USA	55360
Spokes 'N Wheels Ltd.	3802 Georgia Court	IA	USA	50305
Trail Blazer's Place	6938 Beach Street	WI	USA	53795
Rowdy Rims Company	4861 Second Road	CA	USA	91341
Clean Air Transportation Co	1867 Thurlow Lane	PA	USA	19453
Hooked on Helmets	7655 Mayberry Crescent	MN	USA	55327

Figure 4-63 L4.6 Vertical lines report

You can also draw vertical lines through sections of the report. In the report that you just added vertical lines to, make the vertical lines longer by clicking on the line and dragging the top blue square on the line up, so that it is above the field heading in the page header section. The report should look like the one shown in Figure 4-64.

Customer Name	Address1	Region	Country	Postal Code
City Cyclists	7464 South Kingsway	MI	USA	48358
Pathfinders	410 Eighth Avenue	IL	USA	60148
Bike-A-Holics Anonymous	7429 Arbutus Boulevard	OH	USA	43005
Psycho-Cycle	8287 Scott Road	AL	USA	35818
Sporting Wheels Inc.	480 Grant Way	CA	USA	92150
Rockshocks for Jocks	1984 Sydney Street	TX	USA	78770
Poser Cycles	8194 Peter Avenue	MN	USA	55360
Spokes 'N Wheels Ltd.	3802 Georgia Court	IA	USA	50305
Trail Blazer's Place	6938 Beach Street	WI	USA	53795
Rowdy Rims Company	4861 Second Road	CA	USA	91341
Clean Air Transportation Co.	1867 Thurlow Lane	PA	USA	19453
Hooked on Helmets	7655 Mayberry Crescent	MN	USA	55327

Figure 4-64 L4.6 Vertical lines report with lines extended into the page header section

If an object has the Can Grow option turned on, the object will grow, but the vertical line will not grow by default, as shown in Figure 4-65. You will see breaks in the vertical line. To fix this, check the **EXTEND TO BOTTOM OF SECTION WHEN PRINTING** option shown in Figure 4-66.

Customer Name	Address1	Region	Country	Postal Code
City Cyclists	7464 South Kingsway	MI	USA	48358
Pathfinders	410 Eighth Avenue	IL	USA	60148
Bike-A-Holics Anonymous	7429 Arbutus Boulevard	OH	USA	43005
Psycho-Cycle	8287 Scott Road	AL	USA	35818
Sporting Wheels Inc.	480 Grant Way	CA	USA	92150
Rockshocks for Jocks	1984 Sydney Street	TX	USA	78770

Figure 4-65 Can Grow option and vertical lines

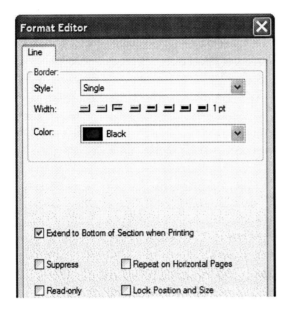

Figure 4-66 Format Editor options for a vertical line

Subsections

As you saw in the L3.5 Skills Customer orders report, all of the fields in the details section did not fit. Crystal Reports allows you to split any section of the report into **SUBSECTIONS**. One reason that you would create subsections is to be able to spread the fields out so that they are easier to read. This allows fields to be in multiple rows. Yes, you can make the section longer, but depending on the requirements of the report, creating subsections may be a better solution. One reason that comes to mind that this is a better solution is because you may need to apply conditional formatting to some fields in a section. When a section of the report is split, the subsections are labeled, A, B, C, etc, as shown in Figure 4-67.

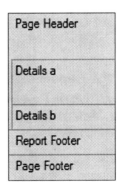

Figure 4-67 Details subsections

Exercise 4.7: How To Create Subsections

1. Save the L3.5 report as `L4.7 Subsections`.

2. Make the details section a little longer, then place the mouse pointer over the vertical ruler in the section that you want to split. In this exercise, place the mouse pointer over the vertical ruler in the details section. The mouse pointer will change to a vertical arrow as shown in Figure 4-68.

Figure 4-68 Mouse pointer in position to split a section

3. Press the left mouse button and hold it down until you see a gray line, as shown in Figure 4-69. This shows the start of the new section. Move the gray line to where you want to split the section, then release the mouse button. The details section should look like the one shown in Figure 4-70.

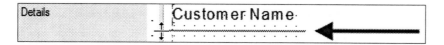

Figure 4-69 Gray line illustrated

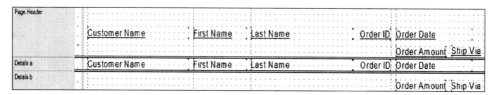

Figure 4-70 Details section split

4. Rearrange the fields in the details section as shown in Figure 4-71 and save the changes.

Page Header						
	Customer Name	First Name	Last Name		Order ID	Order Date
						Order Amount Ship Via
Details a	Customer Name	First Name	Last Name		Order ID	Order Date
Details b						Order Amount Ship Via

Figure 4-71 Fields rearranged in the details section

 There are three other ways to add subsections to a report as described below.

① Use the Section shortcut menu. Right-click on the section on the left that you want to split and select **INSERT SECTION BELOW**, as shown earlier in Figure 4-5.
② Click the Section Expert button on the Expert Tools toolbar.
③ Report ⇒ Section Expert.

Add Sections To The Report With The Section Expert

The benefit of using the Section Expert to add a new section to the report is that you can apply other options to the section. These options are on the right side of Figure 4-72. You will learn about the options on the Section Expert in Lesson 10.

1. Open the Section Expert and click on the report section that you want to add a section to as shown in Figure 4-72, then click the **INSERT** button. For this exercise, select the details section. You will see the section that you added, as shown in Figure 4-73.

2. Add a new section to the page header section, then click OK to close the Section Expert. The report layout should look like the one shown in Figure 4-74. Save the changes and leave the report open to complete the next exercise.

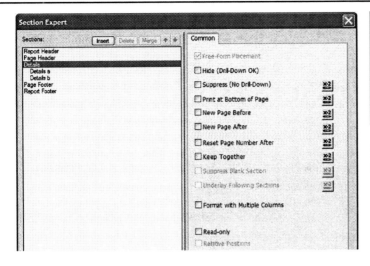

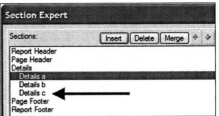

Figure 4-73 Section added to the details section

Figure 4-72 Section Expert

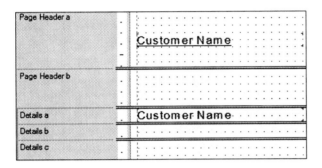

Figure 4-74 L4.7 Subsections report with new sections

Exercise 4.7A: Add A Background Color To A Report Section

In some of the sample reports that come with Crystal Reports, the field headings have a background color applied. Many reports have other objects in the page header section in addition to the field headings. If you applied a background color to the page header section, all of the objects in the section would have the background. Fortunately, there is a solution for this. If you only want the background color applied to the field headings and not the other objects in the page header section, you have to move the field headings to a new section.

1. Save the L4.3 report as L4.7A Section background color.

2. Insert a new page header section, then click on the Color tab for the new section.

3. Check the Background Color option, then open the drop down list, select the color Gray and click OK.

4. Select all of the field headings and change the color to white. Remove the underline and move the fields to the new page header section. Save the changes. The report should look like the one shown in Figure 4-75.

Product ID	Product Name	Supplier Name	Product Type Name
1,101	Active Outdoors Crochet Glo	Active Outdoors	Gloves
1,102	Active Outdoors Crochet Glo	Active Outdoors	Gloves
1,103	Active Outdoors Crochet Glo	Active Outdoors	Gloves
1,104	Active Outdoors Crochet Glo	Active Outdoors	Gloves
1,105	Active Outdoors Crochet Glo	Active Outdoors	Gloves
1,106	Active Outdoors Lycra Glove	Active Outdoors	Gloves

Figure 4-75 L4.7A Section background color report

Exercise 4.8: Add A Border To A Field

So far in this lesson you have learned several formatting techniques that you can use to make reports look better. Another technique that you can use is to put borders around a field. Borders are often used to make a field stand out on the report. In this exercise, you will add a border to the Notes field. Earlier in this lesson you learned about the Can Grow option. A notes field is a good field to use this option on.

1. Save the L4.7 report as `L4.8 Border around field`.

2. Add the Notes field in the Employee table to the details b section of the report under the Customer Name field. Make the Notes field longer and wider.

3. Right-click on the Notes field and select Format Editor. Check the **CAN GROW** option on the Common tab.

4. Click on the Border tab and check the **DROP SHADOW** option.

5. Change the Line Style to **DOTTED** for the Left and Right options, then change the Top and Bottom Line Style options to **SINGLE**. You should have the options selected that are shown in Figure 4-76. Click OK and save the changes. The report should look like the one shown in Figure 4-77. Close the report.

 It may be a good idea to check the **CLOSE BORDER ON PAGE BREAK** option on the Common tab on the Format Editor for fields that have a border, because it is possible that the field could print on more than one page, especially a field that has the Can Grow option.

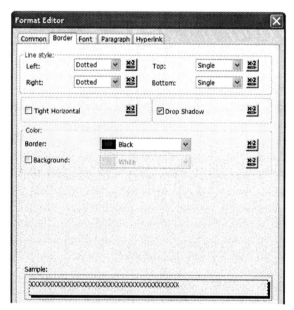

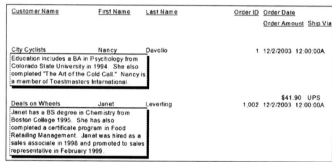

Figure 4-77 L4.8 Border around field report

Figure 4-76 Border options

Exercise 4.9: Adding Boxes To A Report

Earlier in this lesson you learned how to add lines to a report. If you need to make something on a report stand out or you want to put a more decorative border around a field or heading, then the border options that you learned about in Exercise 4.8, you can use the options on the Box tab on the Format Editor. In this exercise you will add a box to a field and a box to a report title. There are two ways to open the Box tool as discussed below.

① Click the **INSERT BOX** button on the Insert toolbar.
② Insert ⇒ Box.

Add The Box

1. Save the L4.7 report as L4.9 Box around objects.

2. Add the Notes field in the Employee table to the details b section of the report under the Customer Name field. Make the Notes field longer and wider.

3. Apply the **CAN GROW** option to the Notes field and click OK.

4. Open the Box tool and draw a box around the Notes field.

5. Right-click on the box and select Format Box. As you can see, the Box tab has many of the same options that the Line tab has. Table 4-8 explains the options that are different on the Box tab.

If you have trouble selecting the Box, open the Report Explorer and select it from there.

Box Option	Description
Fill Color	If checked, this option will let you apply a background color to the box.
Always Close Border	This option will close a box by adding additional lines if a box goes to the next page of the report. The box at the bottom of the page will have a bottom line added to the border. The box at the top of the page will have a line at the top of the box added automatically.
Extend to Bottom of Section when Printing	Checking this option will allow the box to extend to the bottom of the section as the field that it is being used for extends (grows).

Table 4-8 Box tab options explained

6. Select the **DOTTED** Border Style, then check the **FILL COLOR** option and select Silver as the color.

7. Check the **EXTEND TO BOTTOM OF SECTION WHEN PRINTING** option. You should have the options selected that are shown in Figure 4-78. Leave the Format Editor open to complete the next part of the exercise.

Figure 4-78 Box tab options

Use The Rounding Options

The options on the Rounding tab will let you change the corners of the box to make them round.

1. Click on the Rounding tab and change the **ROUNDING PERCENT** to 50. Your dialog box should look like the one shown in Figure 4-79.

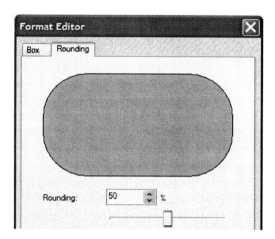

Figure 4-79 Rounding tab options

2. Click OK and save the changes. Leave the report open to complete the next part of the exercise.

 | If you move the slider all the way to the right, the box will change to a circle. |

Add A Box Around A Text Object

Just like you can place a box around a data field, you can place a box around a text object.

1. Place a text object at the top of the report header section. Type `Customer Orders` in the text object.

2. Make the border of the text object smaller, so that it is close to the content.

3. Draw a box around the text object, then open the Format Editor for the box.

4. Accept the default options on the Box tab. Change the rounding percent to 100 on the Rounding tab. Click OK and save the changes. The report should look like the one shown in Figure 4-80. Close the report.

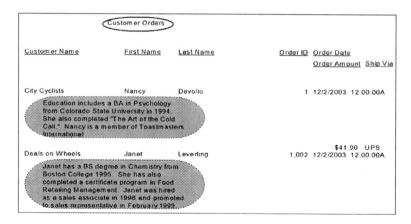

Figure 4-80 L4.9 Box around objects report

Deleting Objects From The Report Layout

There are three ways to delete one object or several objects from a report as discussed below.
When deleting fields in the details section, the field heading in the page header section is also deleted.

    ① Right-click on the object(s) and select Delete.
    ② Select the object(s) and press the Delete key.
    ③ Select the object(s), then Edit ⇒ Delete.

Special Fields

Crystal Reports has 25 built-in fields that you can add to reports. You can drop and drag these fields from
the Field Explorer to the report, just like you drop and drag fields from tables in the Field Explorer to the
report. Figure 4-81 shows the Special Fields that you can add. Because these are system fields, the data
can change each time the report is run. Table 4-9 explains what each of the Special Fields contains.

You should know what the Special Fields are and what they will print.

Special fields, like the fields from a table that are added to the details section, have headings
automatically created in the page header section.

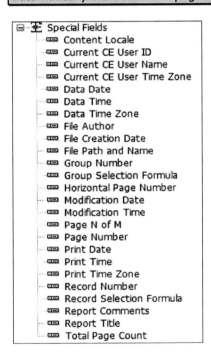

Figure 4-81 Special Fields

Special Field	The Field Will Print The . . .
Content Locale	Information in the **LOCATION** field. This data comes from the Regional & Language Options dialog box (which is part of Windows) shown in Figure 4-82. (3)
Current CE User ID	ID number of the Business Objects user. (3)
Current CE User Name	Name of the Business Objects user. (3)
Current CE User Time Zone	Time zone that the Business Objects user is in. (3)
Data Date	Date the data was last refreshed in the report.
Data Time	Time the data was last refreshed in the report.
Data Time Zone	Time Zone that the data was last refreshed in the report.
File Author	Information in the **AUTHOR** field. (4)
File Creation Date	Date the report was first created.
File Path And Name	File path and name of the report. (The location on the hard drive or server). For example: C:\Crystal Reports Workbook\L3.2 Employee list.rpt.
Grouping Number	Number of each group in the group header or footer. If the report does not have any groups, this field will print a "1". This number is created each time the report is run.
Group Selection Formula	Group selection formula if applicable.
Horizontal Page Number	Page number by objects like cross-tabs and OLAP Grids that print on more than one page horizontally.
Modification Date	Date the report was last modified. This would be helpful during the report creation and modification process.
Modification Time	Time the report was last saved.
Page N of M	Page number and total number of pages in this format - Page 3 of 24. (5)
Page Number	Current page number.
Print Date	Date the report was printed. (3)
Print Time	Time the report was printed. (3)
Print Time Zone	Time zone the report was printed in. This data comes from the Date & Time Properties dialog box (which is part of Windows) shown in Figure 4-84. (3)
Record Number	System generated number that is a counter for each detail record. It is based on the sort order in the report.
Record Selection Formula	Record Selection formula that was created in the Record Selection Formula Editor.
Report Comments	Information in the **COMMENTS** field. (4)
Report Title	Information in the **TITLE** field. (4)
Total Page Count	Total number of pages in the report. (5)

Table 4-9 Special Fields explained

(3) This data comes from the computer that the report is run from.
(4) This data comes from the Summary tab on the Document Properties dialog box shown in Figure 4-83.

(5) The Page N of M and Total Page Count fields add to the processing time when the report is generated. If the report has hundreds of pages, you may notice a delay while the data is being processed, but it is bearable.

To view the dialog box shown in Figure 4-82, open the Control Panel in Windows, then double-click on the **REGIONAL AND LANGUAGE OPTIONS** icon.

File ⇒ Summary Information, will let you view the dialog box shown in Figure 4-83.

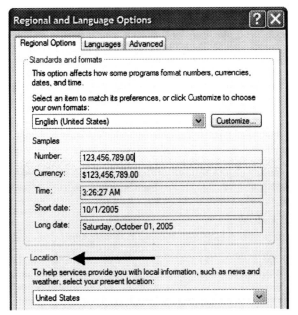

Figure **4-82** Location option illustrated

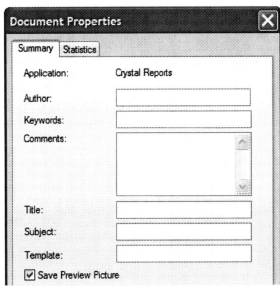

Figure **4-83** Summary tab options

 To view the dialog box shown in Figure 4-84, open the Control Panel in Windows. Double-click on the **DATE AND TIME** option, then click on the Time Zone tab.

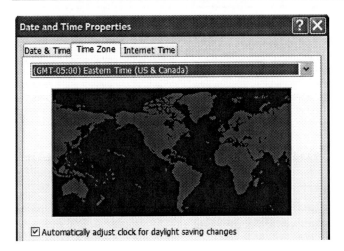

Figure **4-84** Time Zone options

Exercise 4.10: Add Special Fields To A Report

As you learned in Table 4-9 above, there are several "Date" and "Time" fields. To better understand what each of these fields will print, you will add all of them to one report in this exercise.

1. Save the L3.4 report as `L4.10 Date special fields`.

2. Make the report header section longer by dragging the section bar down to the fourth row of grid dots in the page header section.

3. Open the Special Fields section of the Field Explorer and drag the **DATA DATE** field to the upper right corner of the report header section.

4. Drag the **DATA TIME** field to the upper right corner of the report header section and place it below the Data Date field.

Adding Text Objects

As you noticed, the headings were not created for the special fields that you added to the page header section. You have two options for using a text object with Special Fields, as discussed below. I tend to use the second option because I find it easier to move the objects when they are combined, but you can use either option.

① Create a text object. Enter a title for the field and place the text object next to the special field.
② Complete ① above, then press the **SPACE BAR** and drag the special field into the text object.

1. Create two text objects in the report header section.
   Type `Date the data was last refreshed:` in one of the text objects.
   Type `Time the data was last refreshed:` in the other text object.
   Make both text objects bold.

2. Rearrange the fields and text objects so that they look like the ones shown in Figure 4-85.
   Save the changes and leave the report open to complete the next part of the exercise.

 You may need to use the **ALIGN** options that you learned about earlier in this lesson to line up the objects that you just added to the report. This would be a good use of the Align ⇒ Baseline option so that you can line up the text object and the corresponding field because the text object is bold and the field is not.

	Date the data was last refreshed: 9/24/2005
	Time the data was last refreshed: 9:05:15AM

Product ID	Product Name	Product Type Name	Supplier Name
1,101	Active Outdoors Crochet Glo	Gloves	Active Outdoors
1,102	Active Outdoors Crochet Glo	Gloves	Active Outdoors

Figure 4-85 Fields and text objects arranged on the report

Add More Date And Time Special Fields

1. In the report header section, add the Special Fields and Text Objects in Table 4-10. Arrange the objects so that they look like the ones shown in Figure 4-86.

Special Field	Text For The Text Object
File Creation Date	Date the report was designed:
Modification Date	Date the report was last saved:
Modification Time	Time the report was last saved:
Print Date	Date the report was printed:

Table 4-10 Fields and text objects to add to the report

 You can select all of the special fields and then drag them to the report header at the same time.

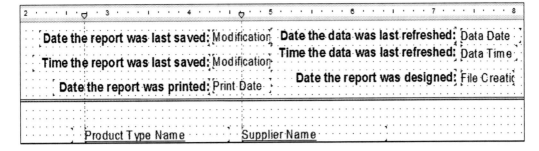

Figure 4-86 Special Fields and text objects arranged on the report

2. Save the changes and preview the report. If prompted to refresh the data, click **NO**. Make any changes that are needed. The report should look similar to the one shown in Figure 4-87. Write down the dates and times that are displayed in the report. You can write them next to the headings in Figure 4-87.

Date the report was last saved: 10/1/2005   Date the data was last refreshed: 9/24/2005
Time the report was last saved: 4:18:14AM   Time the data was last refreshed: 9:05:15AM
Date the report was printed: 10/1/2005   Date the report was designed: 9/24/2005

Product ID	Product Name	Product Type Name	Supplier Name
1,101	Active Outdoors Crochet Glo	Gloves	Active Outdoors
1,102	Active Outdoors Crochet Glo	Gloves	Active Outdoors

Figure 4-87 L4.10 Date special fields report run on day one

3. Tomorrow, run this report twice as follows:

    ① Run the report without refreshing the data. Compare the dates and times to those that you wrote down in step 2 above. My report looks like the one shown in Figure 4-88. The only fields that should have changed are the **TIME THE REPORT WAS LAST SAVED** and the **DATE THE REPORT WAS PRINTED**.

    ② Move the Print Date field and title to the upper left hand corner of the report and save the changes. Refresh the data and run the report. Compare the data to what you wrote down in step 2 above. My report looks like the one shown in Figure 4-89. The only field that should still have the same data is the **DATE THE REPORT WAS DESIGNED**, as shown in Figure 4-87 above.

Date the report was last saved: 10/1/2005   Date the data was last refreshed: 9/24/2005
Time the report was last saved: 4:26:58AM   Time the data was last refreshed: 9:05:15AM
Date the report was printed: 10/2/2005   Date the report was designed: 9/24/2005

Product ID	Product Name	Product Type Name	Supplier Name
1,101	Active Outdoors Crochet Glo	Gloves	Active Outdoors
1,102	Active Outdoors Crochet Glo	Gloves	Active Outdoors

Figure 4-88 L4.10 Date special fields report run on day two without modifications

Date the report was printed: Date the report was last saved: 10/2/2005   Date the data was last refreshed: 10/2/2005
10/2/2005   Time the report was last saved: 12:48:25AM   Time the data was last refreshed: 12:47:46AM
                                                                              Date the report was designed: 9/24/2005

Product ID	Product Name	Product Type Name	Supplier Name
1,101	Active Outdoors Crochet Glo	Gloves	Active Outdoors
1,102	Active Outdoors Crochet Glo	Gloves	Active Outdoors

Figure 4-89 L4.10A Date special fields report run on day two with modifications

4. Save the changes and close the report.

Report Explorer

By default, the Report Explorer displays the following report sections, whether or not they are actually being used in the report: report header, page header, details, report footer and page footer.

Figure 4-90 shows the Report Explorer window. At the top of the tree structure is the report name. Each of the branches in the tree represents one section of the report. If you click on an object in the Report Explorer, it is automatically selected in the design area. You may find it easier to locate the object that you need to edit or format in this window, then in the Field Explorer once it has been added to the report. Like the Field Explorer, the Report Explorer lets you see all of the fields on the report. The Report Explorer also displays all of the other objects that are on the report, like charts and images.

A magnifying glass icon next to a report section indicates that the section is hidden on the report. I find it hard to tell one icon from the next for the report sections. The field shortcut menus are the same as the ones in the Field Explorer. Table 4-11 explains the buttons on the Report Explorer toolbar. The last three buttons on the toolbar let you filter the object types, which means that you do not have to display all of the objects in the Report Explorer.

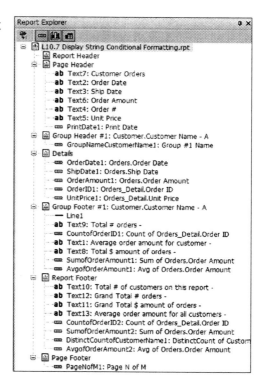

Figure 4-90 Report Explorer window

 The group header and footer sections are only displayed in the Report Explorer if they are being used.

Button	Purpose
	The **EXPAND** button opens all of the sections in the Report Explorer that have a plus sign.
	The **SHOW/HIDE DATA FIELDS** button will display or hide the data objects.
	The **SHOW/HIDE GRAPHICAL OBJECTS** button will display or hide the lines, boxes, charts, maps and images (like photos or logos).
	The **SHOW/HIDE GRIDS AND SUBREPORTS** button will display or hide the cross-tabs, OLAP Grids and subreports.

Table 4-11 Report Explorer toolbar buttons explained

 You can delete objects in the Report Explorer, but you cannot add new objects.

If you right-click on an object in the Report Explorer, you will see the shortcut menu editing options shown in Figure 4-91. The shortcut menu options vary depending on the object that is selected. Figure 4-92 shows the shortcut menu if you right-click in the Report Explorer and an object is not selected.

If you need to make the same change to more then one field or object, select all of the fields and objects that require the change and then open the shortcut menu shown in Figure 4-91. The fields that you select should be the same data type, to make the best use of editing multiple fields. If you select multiple fields that have different data types, the shortcut menu options that you can use will be limited to those that work for all of the data types of the fields that you have selected.

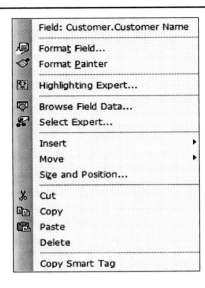

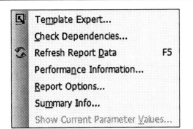

Figure 4-92 Report Explorer shortcut menu options when an object is not selected

Figure 4-91 Report Explorer shortcut menu editing options for a data field

Report Explorer Section Shortcut Menu

This shortcut menu has options that you can use to manage the sections of the report. Many of the options on the Report Explorer section shortcut menu, shown in Figure 4-93 are the same as the options on the Report Section shortcut menu that you saw earlier in Figure 4-5. Depending on the section that you right-click on in the Report Explorer, you will see different options.

Table 4-12 explains all of the options on the Report Explorer Section Shortcut menu, regardless of which section you right-click on.

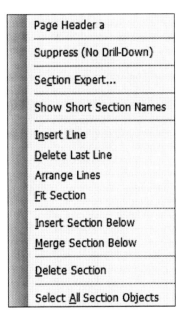

Figure 4-93 Report Explorer Section shortcut menu

Option	Description
Hide/Show (Drill-Down OK)	Hides the section when the report is printed. The section can be viewed on the preview window.
Suppress (No Drill-Down)	The section that this option is applied to will not be printed and cannot be viewed on the preview window.
Section Expert	Opens the Section Expert.
Show Short/Long Section Names	Toggles between long and short section names.
Insert Line	Adds a guideline to the section that is selected.
Delete Last Line	Deletes the last guideline that was added to the section.
Arrange Lines	Spaces the guidelines in a section evenly.
Fit Section	Moves the bottom section bar up to the lowest object in the section.
Insert Section Below	Creates a new section below the selected section. The new section is the same type of section as the selected section.
Merge Section Below	Combines the fields in the selected subsection with the subsection below it.
Delete Section	Deletes a subsection of the report. (6)
Hide Area	Hides a subsection of the report. (6)
Suppress Area	Suppress a subsection of the report. (6)
Don't Suppress Area	When selected, the subsection cannot be suppressed. (6)
Select All Section Objects	Selects all of the objects in the section. This is useful when you need to apply the same formatting or change to all of the objects in a section.

Table 4-12 Report Explorer section shortcut menu options explained

(6) This option is only available for a report section that has at least one subsection.

Test Your Skills

1. Save the L4.5 report as `L4.11 Skills Customer information`. Make the changes below. Your report should look like the one shown in Figure 4-94.

   - Add space below the field headings.
   - Center the Region field under it's heading.
   - Change the Line Style to Dotted in the details section.
   - Make the Customer Name field smaller.
   - Move the Country field over to the left and make it smaller.
   - Move the Postal Code field over to the left.
   - Apply the Can Grow option to the Customer Name and Address1 fields. Do not limit the number of lines.

Customer Name	Address1	Region	Country	Postal Code
City Cyclists	7464 South Kingsway	MI	USA	48358
Pathfinders	410 Eighth Avenue	IL	USA	60148
Bike-A-Holics Anonymous	7429 Arbutus Boulevard	OH	USA	43005
Psycho-Cycle	8287 Scott Road	AL	USA	35818
Sporting Wheels Inc.	480 Grant Way	CA	USA	92150
Rockshocks for Jocks	1984 Sydney Street	TX	USA	78770
Poser Cycles	8194 Peter Avenue	MN	USA	55360

Figure 4-94 L4.11 Skills Customer information report

2. Save the L4.2 report as `L4.12 Skills Editing`. Make the changes below. Your report should look like the one shown in Figure 4-95.

   - Center the Order ID field under it's heading.
   - Make the Order Date and Ship Via fields shorter.
   - Add the logo to the upper right hand corner of the page header section, above the report title.
   - Add the Page N of M special field below the logo.
   - Apply the Can Grow option to the Customer Name field.
   - Change the Top border line style of the report title to Dotted.
   - Change the report title border color to red.
   - Move the Order Amount, Ship Via, First Name and Last Name fields over to the left so that they all fit on the page.

Xtreme Mountain Bikes

Page 1 of 48

Customer Orders Report

Customer Name	Order #	Order Date	Order Amount	Ship Via	First Name	Last Name
City Cyclists	1	12/2/03	$41.90	UPS	Nancy	Davolio
Deals on Wheels	1002	12/2/03	$5,060.28	Pickup	Janet	Levering
Warsaw Sports, Inc.	1003	12/2/03	$186.87	UPS	Margaret	Peacock
Bikes and Trikes	1004	12/2/03	$823.05	Pickup	Margaret	Peacock
SAB Mountain	1005	12/3/03	$29.00	Loomis	Janet	Levering
Poser Cycles	1006	12/3/03	$64.90	Purolator	Margaret	Peacock
Spokes	1007	12/3/03	$49.50	Parcel Post	Anne	Dodsworth
Clean Air Transportation Co.	1008	12/3/03	$2,214.94	Purolator	Margaret	Peacock
Extreme Cycling	1009	12/3/03	$29.00	Loomis	Margaret	Peacock
Cyclopath	1010	12/3/03	$14,872.30	UPS	Nancy	Davolio

Figure 4-95 L4.12 Skills Editing report

3. Save the L4.3 report as `L4.13 Skills Product report`. Make the changes below. Your report should look like the one shown in Figure 4-96.

   - Change the Product ID heading to `Product #`.
   - Format the Product ID field to not have a comma.
   - Use the Format Painter to make the field headings italic and bold.
   - Remove the underline from the headings.
   - Add the Print Date field above the logo.
   - Add the Record Number special field in front of the Product ID field. Change the font on the Record Number field and heading to the one that the other fields and headings use.
   - Add a double border line above and below the field headings.
   - Add a Page Number to the page footer section in the lower left corner.

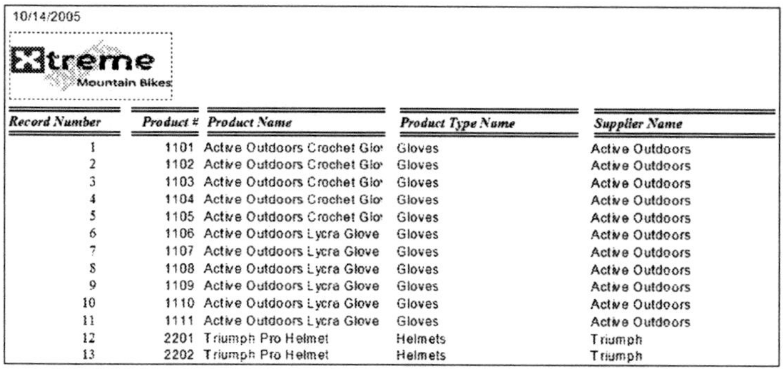
10/14/2005

Xtreme Mountain Bikes

Record Number	Product #	Product Name	Product Type Name	Supplier Name
1	1101	Active Outdoors Crochet Glo	Gloves	Active Outdoors
2	1102	Active Outdoors Crochet Glo	Gloves	Active Outdoors
3	1103	Active Outdoors Crochet Glo	Gloves	Active Outdoors
4	1104	Active Outdoors Crochet Glo	Gloves	Active Outdoors
5	1105	Active Outdoors Crochet Glo	Gloves	Active Outdoors
6	1106	Active Outdoors Lycra Glove	Gloves	Active Outdoors
7	1107	Active Outdoors Lycra Glove	Gloves	Active Outdoors
8	1108	Active Outdoors Lycra Glove	Gloves	Active Outdoors
9	1109	Active Outdoors Lycra Glove	Gloves	Active Outdoors
10	1110	Active Outdoors Lycra Glove	Gloves	Active Outdoors
11	1111	Active Outdoors Lycra Glove	Gloves	Active Outdoors
12	2201	Triumph Pro Helmet	Helmets	Triumph
13	2202	Triumph Pro Helmet	Helmets	Triumph

Figure 4-96 L4.13 Skills Product report

4. Create a new report. This report will print orders by sales rep. Save the report as `L4.14 Skills Orders by sales rep`. Your report should look like the one shown in Figure 4-97.

   - Add the tables and fields in Table 4-13 to the report.

Employee	Orders	Order Details
Employee ID	Order ID	Product ID
First Name	Order Date	Unit Price
Last Name		Quantity

Table 4-13 Tables and fields for the Orders by sales rep report

   - Add the logo to the center of the page header section.
   - Print the date in the left corner, across from the logo.
   - Add the Page number to the center of the page footer section.
   - Format the Order Date, Order ID and Product ID fields as shown in the report.

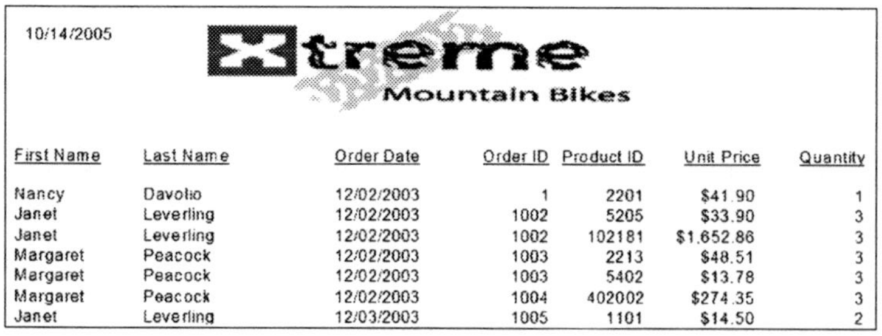
10/14/2005

Xtreme Mountain Bikes

First Name	Last Name	Order Date	Order ID	Product ID	Unit Price	Quantity
Nancy	Davolio	12/02/2003	1	2201	$41.90	1
Janet	Leverling	12/02/2003	1002	5205	$33.90	3
Janet	Leverling	12/02/2003	1002	102181	$1,652.86	3
Margaret	Peacock	12/02/2003	1003	2213	$48.51	3
Margaret	Peacock	12/02/2003	1003	5402	$13.78	3
Margaret	Peacock	12/02/2003	1004	402002	$274.35	3
Janet	Leverling	12/03/2003	1005	1101	$14.50	2

Figure 4-97 L4.14 Skills Orders by sales rep report

5. Add all of the reports that were created in this lesson to the Workbench.

SELECTING RECORDS

After completing the exercises in this lesson you will be able to use the following techniques to control which records will appear on a report:

- ☑ Select, filter and query records
- ☑ Create report summary information
- ☑ Add summary information to a report

It is possible that you could create reports for a long time and not have to open any of the menus in Crystal Reports. It is also possible that you will not have the need to change the default Crystal Reports environment options. If you plan to take any of the Crystal Reports certification exams, learning more about the menus and environment options is a requirement. These topics will be covered in this lesson.

To pass the RDCR201 exam, you need to be familiar with and be able to:

- ☑ Understand the report design environment (including menu options)
- ☑ Determine what the record selection criteria should be
- ☑ Understand the features on the Select Expert
- ☑ Create and modify record selection criteria
- ☑ Create date/time record selection criteria
- ☑ Know the difference between saved and refreshed data
- ☑ Add multiple record selection criteria to the same report

LESSON 5

Selecting Records Overview

So far you have learned to create a variety of basic reports. All of the reports that you created without a wizard retrieved all of the records in the tables. As you saw, many of the reports contained 500 or more detail records. Most of the time reports provide specific information, which means that all of the records in the tables selected should not be on every report that is created. For reports that use tables similar to the size of the ones in the Xtreme database, this may not be a problem, but if the report is using tables or other data sources with thousands or millions of records (think credit card statements), the report will take a long time to run. Not only will you notice this on your computer, which may run out of memory, the network will also take a performance hit.

One way that Crystal Reports lets you narrow down the records that will appear on the report is through a selection process. This selection process uses the **SELECT EXPERT**. This tool allows you to specify which records will appear on the report by entering **CRITERIA** that a record must meet. Records that do not meet the criteria will not appear on the report. This process is also known as **FILTERING RECORDS** or **QUERYING THE DATABASE**. Other ways to select records include writing formulas and using functions.

In Lesson 2 when you used a wizard to create the L2.1 report, you created a filter on the Record Selection screen. [See Lesson 2, Figure 2-33] The Record Selection screen has similar functionality to the Select Expert that you will learn how to use in this lesson.

Examples of the types of information that can be retrieved when selecting, filtering records or querying the database, include the following:

① Orders that were placed during a specific date range, like the month of June.
② Customers that purchased a specific product.
③ Orders that are over a certain dollar amount.
④ Products that need to be reordered.

Selecting, filtering or querying the database lets you ask a question about the data and then retrieve the records that meet the criteria that you specify. The records that are retrieved are known as a **RECORDSET**. The examples above are only asking one question. You can ask more than one question in the same query. You can ask the following types of multi-part questions.

① Orders that were placed during a specific date range and were more than $500.
② Customers that purchased a specific product and live in a specific state.
③ Orders that are over a certain dollar amount that were taken by a certain salesperson.
④ Customers that have a credit limit of $1,000 or more and have placed at least one order over $2,500, that shipped during a specific date range.
⑤ Orders that were placed or shipped during a specific date range.

In Lesson 3 you learned a little about SQL. Like SQL, the selection process produces the same results. Think of the Select Expert as an SQL code generator, without actually having to write code. The Select Expert creates the SQL code for you, which makes the Select Expert easy to use. The SQL code is what Crystal Reports uses to select records for the report.

In addition to selecting individual records, the Select Expert can also select groups. A group selection example would be to only display records in states that have an order total amount between $100,000 and $400,000.

The Select Expert provides two ways to select records as discussed below:

① Use the built-in **OPERATORS**. Table 5-1 explains the operators that are available. Not all of the operators listed in the table are available for all field types.
② **FORMULAS** let you write the SQL code. This is not a contradiction to what I said earlier about not having to write code to use the Select Expert, because writing code in the Select Expert is not mandatory.

Operator	This Operator Selects Records That . . .
Is Equal To	Are equal to (the same as) the value that you specify.
Is Not Equal To	Are not equal to the value that you specify. This operator works the opposite of the "Is Equal To" operator.
Is One Of	Match at least one of the values that you specify. If the criteria is NY, NJ or PA for the state field, any record that has one of these values in the state field would appear on the report.
Is Not One Of	Are not one of the values that you specify. This operator works the opposite of the "Is One Of" operator.
Is Less Than	Are less than the value that you specify. If you want to see products that have a reorder level of less then 10 items in stock, enter 10 in the criteria field and the report will display products with a reorder level of nine or less. (1)
Is Less Than Or Equal To	(Works similar to "Is Less Than"). The difference is that this operator will also select records that have the value that you specify. In the less than example above, the report would not display records with a reorder level of 10 items. The less than or equal to operator will. (1)
Is Greater Than	Are greater than the value that you specify. If you want to see all orders with an order amount over $500, enter $500 in the criteria field and the report will display records with an order amount of $500.01 or more.
Is Greater Than Or Equal To	(Works similar to "Is Greater Than"). The difference is that this operator will also select records that have the value that you specify. In the greater than example above, the report would not display records with an order amount of exactly $500. The greater than or equal to operator will.
Is Between	Fall between two values. If you want to see order amounts between $1,000 and $5,000 or orders between 6/1/05 and 6/15/05, this is the operator that you would use. This operator also selects records equal to the two values that you enter for the range.
Is Not Between	Are not in the range of values that you enter. This operator works the opposite of the "Is Between" operator.
Starts With	Begins with a specific character or set of characters. If you want to retrieve records of employees whose last name starts with the letter "M", use this operator. (2)
Does Not Start With	Do not start with the character or set of characters that you specify. This operator works the opposite of the "Starts With" operator. (2)
Is Like	Meet the wildcard criteria that you specify. The wildcard characters that you can use are a ? (question mark) and an * (asterisk). (2)
Is Not Like	Do not meet the criteria that you specify with the wildcards. This operator works the opposite of the "Is Like" operator. (2)
Is In The Period	Meet the criteria of one of the functions explained in Table 5-2. These functions will save you a lot of time because you do not have to figure out what the formula should be. (3)
Is Not In The Period	Are not in the period that you select. This operator works the opposite of the "Is In The Period" operator. (3)
Is True	Have a value of true in the Boolean field. (4)
Is False	Have a value of false in the Boolean field. (4)
Formula	Lets you write the code for the records that need to be selected for the report.

Table 5-1 Select Expert operator options explained

(1) This operator can also be used with a string field.
(2) This operator can only be used with a string field.
(3) This operator can only be used with date and date/time fields.
(4) This operator can only be used with a Boolean field.

In addition to the operators listed above in Table 5-1, there is another operator, **IS ANY VALUE**, which is the default operator that you see when the Select Expert is first opened. This operator does not apply any condition to the field that it is associated to. In reports that you create and do not select any criteria for the report, this is the operator that is used by default when the report is run.

The functions in Table 5-2 provide a date range. You can create the same criteria using the "Is Between" operator, but using these built-in functions is easier and does not require dates to be hard coded.

Function	When It Starts And Ends
Week To Date From Sun	From last Sunday to today
Month To Date	From the beginning of the current month to today
Year To Date	From the first day of the current year to today
Last 7 Days	From 7 days ago to today
Last 4 Weeks To Sun	From 4 weeks prior to last Sunday to last Sunday
Last Full Week	From Sunday of last week to Saturday of last week
Last Full Month	From the first day of last month to the last day of last month
All Dates To Today	From the earliest date in the table up to and including today
All Dates To Yesterday	From the earliest date in the table up to and including yesterday
All Dates From Today	From today forward
All Dates From Tomorrow	From yesterday forward
Aged 0 To 30 Days	From 30 days ago to today
Aged 31 To 60 Days	From 31 days ago from today to 60 days ago
Aged 61 To 90 Days	From 61 days ago from today to 90 days ago
Over 90 Days	More than 90 days ago
Next 30 days	From today to 30 days in the future
Next 31 To 60 Days	From 31 days from today to 60 days in the future
Next 61 To 90 Days	From 61 days from today to 90 days in the future
Next 91 To 365 Days	From 91 days from today to 365 days in the future
Calendar 1st Qtr	From January 1 of the current year to March 31 of the current year
Calendar 2nd Qtr	From April 1 of the current year to June 30 of the current year
Calendar 3rd Qtr	From July 1 of the current year to September 30 of the current year
Calendar 4th Qtr	From October 1 of the current year to December 31 of the current year
Calendar 1st Half	From January 1 of the current year to June 30 of the current year
Calendar 2nd Half	From July 1 of the current year to December 31 of the current year
Last Year MTD	From the first day of the current month last year to the same month and day last year
Last Year YTD	From January 1 of last year to today's month and day last year

Table 5-2 Is in the period criteria functions explained

Using The Select Expert

For the most part using the Select Expert is point and click. The only time that you have to type, is if the value that you want to use is not in the drop down list. This usually happens because the drop down list only displays the first 500 unique values in a field. Any field that has multiple values that are identical will only display the value once in the drop down list. An example of this would be a date field, because it is possible that multiple records have the same date in the same field.

If you want to create a customer order report and only want to display records for the Wheels Company, this company name may not appear in the drop down list because there could be more than 500 companies in the table and this company name is near the end of the alphabet. This is an example of when you would have to type something in the Select Expert.

The other time that you would need to type something in the Select Expert is if you are using a value that you know is not one of the values for the field. For example, if you want to select records that have an order amount greater than $600. You may have to type 600 in the field if the order amount field does not have that value in any of the first 500 values that are in the drop down list.

There are three ways to open the Select Expert as discussed below:

① Right-click on the field that you want to create criteria for and select, **SELECT EXPERT**.
② Click the **SELECT EXPERT** button on the Expert Tools toolbar.
③ Report ⇒ Select Expert.

If you click on the field that you want to create the criteria for before you select option two or three above, the Select Expert will open with the field selected and you can start to create the selection criteria.

 You can also use the Select Expert in the preview window.

The first nine exercises in this lesson will teach you how to create a variety of queries using the operators that you learned about earlier in Table 5-1. Hopefully, this will make you feel comfortable using the Select Expert.

Exercise 5.1: Using The Is Equal To Operator

In this exercise you will use the Select Expert to find customers that are in the CA region. The region field contains the same data as a state field.

1. Save the L4.5 report as `L5.1 Region = CA`.

2. Preview the report. Notice that there are 269 records in the report. The number of records is in the lower right hand corner of the Crystal Reports window.

3. Use one the last two options discussed earlier to open the Select Expert. You will see the dialog box shown in Figure 5-1. You will learn how to use the first option in the next exercise.

The reason that you see the Choose Field dialog box is because a field was not selected in the report, prior to opening the Select Expert.

The **REPORT FIELDS** section at the top of the dialog box lists the fields that are currently on the report. Below that section, you will see all of the data sources that are associated with in the report.

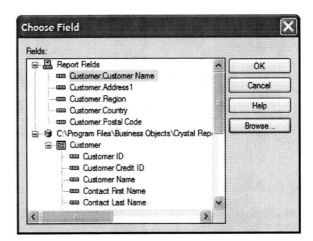

Figure 5-1 Choose Field dialog box

 You can use any field in the Choose Field dialog box shown above in Figure 5-1, whether or not it is being displayed on the report, as a field for the selection criteria.

4. Click on the **CUSTOMER.REGION** field in the Report Fields section and click OK. You will see the dialog box shown in Figure 5-2.

Notice that the field that you selected is the name on the first tab. Multiple tabs means that there is more than one set of selection criteria for the report.

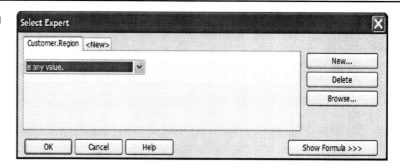

Figure 5-2 Select Expert dialog box

The **NEW** button opens the Choose Field dialog box.
The **DELETE** button deletes the tab that is selected.
The **BROWSE** button will let you view data in the field that is selected.
The **SHOW FORMULA** button will display the formula that was created by the selection criteria that you created.

5. Open the next drop down list and select **IS EQUAL TO**.

You will now see another drop down list. This drop down list is connected to the field that is selected. The values in the second drop down list are from the region field in the table, as shown in Figure 5-3. As you learned earlier, drop down lists that are connected to a field, only display the first 500 unique values in the field.

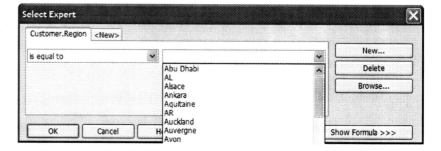

Figure 5-3 Data from the region field illustrated

6. Select **CA** from the drop down list shown above in Figure 5-3. Figure 5-4 shows the criteria that should be selected. When the report is run, it will use this criteria to find records that have CA (the state) in the Region field. Click OK and preview the report. You may see the message shown in Figure 5-5.

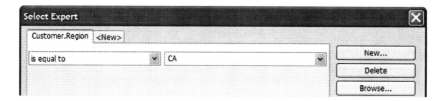

Figure 5-4 Criteria for the report

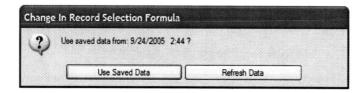

Figure 5-5 Change In Record Selection Formula message

This message is asking if you want to use the data that is currently saved with the report or if you want to refresh the data. It also tells you the date and time the data was last refreshed. If you know that the data in the report is current or you want to use the data that is saved with the report, click the **USE SAVED DATA** button. If you are not sure, click the **REFRESH DATA** button. When in doubt, refresh the data.

If you were creating this report and using live data, you would probably select the Refresh Data option the first time that you run the report after creating the selection criteria. Keep in mind that refreshing data can take a little longer than using saved data if there are thousands of records in the table. Under certain conditions you may have to refresh the data, regardless of how long it takes. Don't worry, even with thousands of records, it only takes a few seconds. If the record selection criteria changes, Crystal Reports does not know if the database has to be re-queried. When this is the case, you will see the message shown above in Figure 5-5.

If you changed the selection criteria to include more records then the original selection criteria, you should refresh the data, so that the additional records that meet the criteria can be retrieved from the database. If you do not refresh the data when the modified selection criteria includes more records, the report will not display all of the records that should be on the report. It is also possible that no records will be displayed on the report depending on the revised selection criteria, if the data is not refreshed.

7. Click the **REFRESH DATA** button. The report should look like the one shown in Figure 5-6. Notice that there are six records displayed on the report. This means that there are only six records in the Customers table in the CA region. Save the changes and close the report.

Customer Name	Address1	Region	Country	Postal Code
Sporting Wheels Inc.	480 Grant Way	CA	USA	92150
Rowdy Rims Company	4861 Second Road	CA	USA	91341
Changing Gears	1600 Hyde Crescent	CA	USA	92750
Off the Mountain Biking	192 St. Luke Boulevard	CA	USA	92725
Tyred Out	3687 Kernsdale Street	CA	USA	92721
Bike Shop from Mars	7071 Dundas Crescent	CA	USA	91338

Figure 5-6 L5.1 Region = CA report

Exercise 5.2: Using The Is One Of Operator

In the previous exercise you used the "Is Equal To" operator to find customers in one region. In this exercise you will use the Is One Of operator to find customers that are in the OH or FL region.

1. Save the L4.5 report as L5.2 Region = OH or FL.

2. Right-click on the **REGION** field and select, **SELECT EXPERT**.

3. Open the drop down list and select **IS ONE OF**, then open the next drop down list and select **OH**.

 If you type in the first letter of the value that you are looking for in the drop down list, the list will jump to the first value that starts with that letter that you type in. You can also type in the exact value that you want.

4. Open the same drop down list that you just used and select **FL**. Figure 5-7 shows the criteria that should be selected. Click OK.

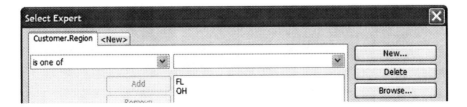

Figure 5-7 Criteria for the report

5. Move the Postal Code field over to the left so that it fits on the page. You may need to make the Country field smaller, so that the Postal Code field will fit on the page.

6. Preview the report. Click the **USE SAVED DATA** button. Your report should look like the one shown in Figure 5-8. Save the changes and close the report.

Customer Name	Address1	Region	Country	Postal Code
Bike-A-Holics Anonymous	7429 Arbutus Boulevard	OH	USA	43005
Wheels and Stuff	2530 Bute Avenue	FL	USA	34666
Uni-Cycle	1008 Kerr Street	OH	USA	43042
Extreme Cycling	1925 Glenaire Avenue	FL	USA	34638
Karma Bikes	1516 Ohio Avenue	OH	USA	43092

Figure 5-8 L5.2 Region = OH or FL report

Exercise 5.3: Using The Is Greater Than Or Equal To Operator

In this exercise you will use the "Is Greater Than Or Equal To" operator to find all orders that were placed on or after 6/24/2003.

1. Save the L3.3 report as `L5.3 Order Date GTE 6-24-2003`.
    (GTE is an abbreviation for greater than or equal to that I made up).

2. Preview the report. The report should have 3,683 records.

3. Open the Select Expert to use with the Order Date field.

4. Select the "Is greater than or equal to operator", then open the next drop down list and select 6/24/2003. You can type the value in if you want to. Figure 5-9 shows the criteria that should be selected.

Figure 5-9 Criteria for the report

5. Click OK. The report should look like the one shown in Figure 5-10. The report should have 3,602 records. Notice that there are fewer records then before the selection criteria was applied. Save the changes and leave the report open to complete the next exercise.

Customer Name	Order Date	Ship Date	Order ID	Unit Price	Quantity
City Cyclists	12/2/2003 12:00:00A	12/10/2003 5:32:23F	1	$41.90	1
Deals on Wheels	12/2/2003 12:00:00A	12/2/2003 6:45:32AP	1,002	$33.90	3
Deals on Wheels	12/2/2003 12:00:00A	12/2/2003 6:45:32AP	1,002	$1,652.86	3
Warsaw Sports, Inc.	12/2/2003 12:00:00A	12/5/2003 12:10:12A	1,003	$48.51	3
Warsaw Sports, Inc.	12/2/2003 12:00:00A	12/5/2003 12:10:12A	1,003	$13.78	3
Bikes and Trikes	12/2/2003 12:00:00A	12/2/2003 3:24:54PP	1,004	$274.35	3
SAB Mountain	12/3/2003 12:00:00A	12/3/2003 1:54:34AP	1,005	$14.50	2
Poser Cycles	12/3/2003 12:00:00A	12/5/2003 7:58:01PP	1,006	$16.50	1
Poser Cycles	12/3/2003 12:00:00A	12/5/2003 7:58:01PP	1,006	$33.90	1

Figure 5-10 L5.3 Order Date GTE 6-24-2003 report

Exercise 5.4: Modify Selection Criteria

In the previous exercise you created criteria to find orders that have an order date greater than or equal to a specific date. In this exercise you will add to this criteria to filter out orders that have an order amount less than $2,500.00.

Adding additional criteria via the Select Expert will reduce or increase the number of records that will appear on the report. As you have probably noticed, the report that you just added selection criteria to does not have the order amount field. If you need to have additional fields on the report you can add them at anytime. If you need to create a filter on a field, but do not need to see the field on the report, you can create a filter without adding the field to the report.

> Creating the criteria IS GREATER THAN 2499.99 will produce the same results as creating the criteria, IS GREATER THAN OR EQUAL TO 2500.00.

1. Save the L5.3 report as
   L5.4 Order Date GTE 6-24-03 and Order Amt GT 2499.99.

2. Delete the Quantity field, then add the Order Amount field from the Orders table and place it after the Ship Date field as shown in Figure 5-11.

Page Header						
	Customer Name	Order Date	Ship Date	Order Amount	Order ID	Unit Price
Details	Customer Name	Order Date	Ship Date	Order Amount	Order ID	Unit Price

Figure 5-11 Order Amount field added to the report

3. Open the Select Expert to use with the Order Amount field. Notice that you see existing criteria on the Select Expert dialog box. This is the criteria that you created in the previous exercise. Open the drop down list and select IS GREATER THAN, then type 2499.99 in the next drop down list. Figure 5-12 shows the criteria that should be selected.

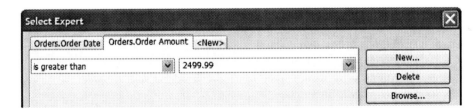

Figure 5-12 Criteria for the report

4. Click OK and preview the report. Because you changed the selection criteria, you should refresh the data. The report should look like the one shown in Figure 5-13. The report should have 1,142 records. Save the changes and close the report.

Customer Name	Order Date	Ship Date	Order Amount	Order ID	Unit Price
Deals on Wheels	12/2/2003 12:00:00A	12/2/2003 6:45:32AP	$5,060.28	1,002	$33.90
Deals on Wheels	12/2/2003 12:00:00A	12/2/2003 6:45:32AP	$5,060.28	1,002	$1,652.86
Cyclopath	12/3/2003 12:00:00A	12/3/2003 11:11:11P	$14,872.30	1,010	$2,939.85
Cyclopath	12/3/2003 12:00:00A	12/3/2003 11:11:11P	$14,872.30	1,010	$2,645.87
Cyclopath	12/3/2003 12:00:00A	12/3/2003 11:11:11P	$14,872.30	1,010	$253.67
Piccolo	12/3/2003 12:00:00A	12/5/2003 4:59:00PP	$10,259.10	1,012	$2,939.85
Piccolo	12/3/2003 12:00:00A	12/5/2003 4:59:00PP	$10,259.10	1,012	$2,939.85
Piccolo	12/3/2003 12:00:00A	12/5/2003 4:59:00PP	$10,259.10	1,012	$479.85

Figure 5-13 L5.4 Order Date GTE 6-24-2003 and Order Amt GT 2499.99 report

Exercise 5.5: Using The Is Between Operator

In this exercise you will use the "Is Between" operator to find all of the orders that were shipped between 4/1/2004 and 6/30/2004.

1. Save the L3.3 report as
    L5.5 Orders shipped between 4-1-2004 and 6-30-2004.

2. Preview the report. There should be 3,683 records in the report. Open the Select Expert to use with the Ship Date field.

3. Select the "Is between" operator, then open the top drop down list on the right and select 4/1/2004. If the date is not in the drop down list, you can type it in.

4. Open the bottom drop down list and select 6/30/2004. If the date is not in the drop down list, you can type it in. Click OK and preview the report. The report should have 780 records. Save the changes and close the report.

Exercise 5.6: Using Multiple Selection Criteria

In this exercise you will create a new report that selects records that meet the following criteria: Country = USA, the Order Date is between 4/1/2005 and 4/30/2005 and the order was not shipped.

☑ Table 5-3 contains the tables and fields for the report. The table names are in bold.
☑ Figure 5-14 shows the report layout.
☑ Figure 5-15 shows the selection criteria formula. Click the **SHOW FORMULA** button on the Select Expert dialog box to view the formula. Depending on the tab that is selected prior to clicking on the Show Formula button, the formula will be in a different order then what is shown in Figure 5-15. The Country tab was selected for this exercise.
☑ Figure 5-16 shows the report, which should have 44 records. Save the report as
L5.6 US orders not shipped in April 2005.

Customer	Orders
Customer Name	Order Date (5)
Country	Order Amount
	Shipped

Table 5-3 Tables and fields to add to the report

(5) Change the format of this field to xx/xx/xxxx on the report.

Steps
① Open a new report, then add the tables and fields.
② Add the selection criteria.
③ Save the report.

Page Header					
	Customer Name	Country	Order Date	Order Amount	Shipped
Details	Customer Name	Country	Order Date	Order Amount	Shipped

Figure 5-14 L5.6 report layout

 Once you open the Select Expert and create the first set of criteria, you do not have to close it to add additional criteria. Click on the **NEW** tab to add more criteria.

If the syntax in your formula looks different then what is shown in Figure 5-15 and your report looks exactly like the one shown in Figure 5-16, you are probably using the **BASIC SYNTAX** formula language instead of **CRYSTAL SYNTAX**. [See Lesson 9, Syntax]

```
{Customer.Country} = "USA" and
not {Orders.Shipped} and
{Orders.Order Date} in DateTime (2005, 04, 01, 00, 00, 00) to DateTime (2005, 04, 30, 00, 00, 00)
```

Figure 5-15 Selection criteria formula

 The zeros at the end of the date/time fields in the formula, represent the time in HH MM SS format (hours, minutes, seconds).

Customer Name	Country	Order Date	Order Amount	Shipped
City Cyclists	USA	04/29/2005	$63.90	False
Pathfinders	USA	04/26/2005	$3,185.42	False
Rockshocks for Jocks	USA	04/25/2005	$8,933.25	False
Rockshocks for Jocks	USA	04/30/2005	$31.00	False
Poser Cycles	USA	04/14/2005	$83.80	False
Trail Blazer's Place	USA	04/18/2005	$107.80	False
Trail Blazer's Place	USA	04/25/2005	$39.80	False
Hooked on Helmets	USA	04/20/2005	$2,797.25	False
Hooked on Helmets	USA	04/25/2005	$1,971.53	False

Figure 5-16 L5.6 US orders not shipped in April 2005 report

Using Wildcard Characters As Selection Criteria

Earlier in the lesson you learned that you could use the ? and the * as selection criteria using the "Is Like" and "Is Not Like" operators. Wildcard characters provide another way to retrieve records. Wildcards are characters that you can use to substitute all or part of the data in a field. You can also use wildcards to search for data that has a pattern. You can use these wildcard characters at the beginning or end of the search criteria that you enter.

① The question mark is used to replace one character in the data. If you entered t?n in the criteria field, the selection criteria would return records that have ten, tan, tune and ton, but not toon in the field.

② The asterisk is used to replace more than one character in the data. If you entered s*r in the criteria field, the selection criteria would return records that have star, start and sour, or any records that had the letter "s" come before the letter "r" in the field that the selection criteria is based on. This wildcard character selection criteria is more flexible, but often returns a lot of results that are not needed.

Viewing Formulas

Earlier in this lesson you created criteria that selected an order date greater than or equal to 6/24/2003. In another exercise you modified that criteria to only retrieve records that had an order amount greater than $2,499.99. To view the formula, click the **SHOW FORMULA** button on the Select Expert. The formulas for the selection criteria are similar.

Figure 5-17 shows the formula that was created for the selection criteria shown earlier in Figure 5-9. Figure 5-18 shows the formula that was created for the report shown earlier in Figure 5-13. Figure 5-18 shows all of the criteria that must be met. At the end of the first line of the formula, you see the word **AND**. If you changed the "and" to **OR**, the report would look like the one shown in Figure 5-19. If you made this change and ran the report, you would see that there are 3,622 records in this report, compared to the 1,142 records in the report shown earlier in Figure 5-13.

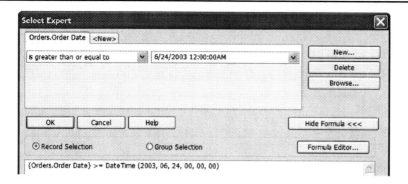

Figure 5-17 Formula for the selection criteria shown earlier in Figure 5-9

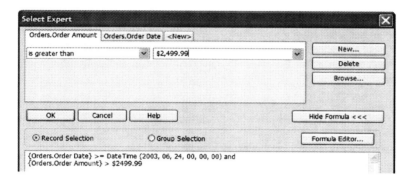

Figure 5-18 Formula for the selection criteria for the report shown earlier in Figure 5-13

Customer Name	Order Date	Ship Date	Order Amount	Order ID	Unit Price
City Cyclists	12/2/2003 12:00:00A	12/10/2003 5:32:23F	$41.90	1	$41.90
Deals on Wheels	12/2/2003 12:00:00A	12/2/2003 6:45:32AI	$5,060.28	1,002	$33.90
Deals on Wheels	12/2/2003 12:00:00A	12/2/2003 6:45:32AI	$5,060.28	1,002	$1,652.86
Warsaw Sports, Inc.	12/2/2003 12:00:00A	12/5/2003 12:10:12A	$186.87	1,003	$48.51
Warsaw Sports, Inc.	12/2/2003 12:00:00A	12/5/2003 12:10:12A	$186.87	1,003	$13.78
Bikes and Trikes	12/2/2003 12:00:00A	12/2/2003 3:24:54PI	$823.05	1,004	$274.35
SAB Mountain	12/3/2003 12:00:00A	12/3/2003 1:54:34AI	$29.00	1,005	$14.50
Poser Cycles	12/3/2003 12:00:00A	12/5/2003 7:58:01PI	$64.90	1,006	$16.50
Poser Cycles	12/3/2003 12:00:00A	12/5/2003 7:58:01PI	$64.90	1,006	$33.90
Poser Cycles	12/3/2003 12:00:00A	12/5/2003 7:58:01PI	$64.90	1,006	$14.50
Spokes	12/3/2003 12:00:00A	12/3/2003 9:05:46AI	$49.50	1,007	$16.50
Clean Air Transportation Co.	12/3/2003 12:00:00A	12/7/2003 10:10:12P	$2,214.94	1,008	$726.61

Figure 5-19 L5.4A Order Date GTE 6-24-2003 OR Order Amt GT 2499.99 report

As you have learned, a report can have more than one selection criteria. When this is the case, in order for records to appear on the report, they have to meet all of the selection criteria. That is because by default, Crystal Reports uses the logical **AND** operator on the Select Expert. If you need to create selection criteria where only one of the selection criteria options must be true in order for a record to appear on the report, you have to use the logical **OR** operator. To change the operator, you have to manually edit the selection formula that is created by the Select Expert.

How To Delete Selection Criteria

After you have created selection criteria you may decide that one or more of the criteria that you set up is not needed. You do not have to delete everything and start over. The steps below will show you how to delete specific criteria on the Select Expert dialog box.

1.   Open the report that has the selection criteria that you want to delete.

2.   Open the Select Expert and click on the tab that has the selection criteria that you want to delete and click the **DELETE** button shown earlier in Figure 5-18.

3.   Click OK to close the Select Expert and save the changes.

Understanding How Date/Time Fields Work In Selection Criteria

In Exercise 5.4, a date/time field was used as part of the selection criteria. You entered a date and the records that have an order date greater than or equal to 6/24/2003 were retrieved, even though you did not enter a time for the date that you selected. That is because Crystal Reports will use midnight as the time when a date is entered without a time. This is fine for selection criteria that only uses a date/time field once. If the selection criteria uses the **IS BETWEEN** operator for example (or any operator that requires two dates be entered for the selection criteria), the records that are retrieved may not be exactly what you are expecting.

The first date in the selection criteria will be compared to midnight as the time, meaning that all records that have a time of midnight or later will be included. So far, so good. The problem is with the second date in the selection criteria. If a time is not entered for the second date, only records that have midnight as the time will be retrieved. This means that a record that has the same date as the second date field in the criteria, but the time is something other then midnight, it will not appear on the report. To include all records on the date in the second date field, you should enter 23:59:59 (or 11:59:59 PM) as the time after the date. If you enter 17:00:00 (or 05:00:00 PM) as the time, for the second date, records that have a time that is greater than 5 PM will not be included on the report.

If you were going to modify the L5.6 report to show all of the orders that were shipped between 1/1/2004 and 1/15/2004, Figure 5-20 shows what many people would enter as the selection criteria. When the report is run with this selection criteria, 49 records will be retrieved. This is incorrect because it does not account for records that have a time other than midnight on the Ship Date field.

Figure 5-20 Incorrect selection criteria

If the selection criteria shown in Figure 5-21 was entered, the report would retrieve 58 records. As you can see in Figure 5-22, the times on the Ship Date field are different. Notice that there are nine records that have a ship date of 1/15/2004.

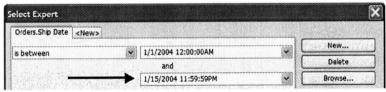

Figure 5-21 Correct selection criteria

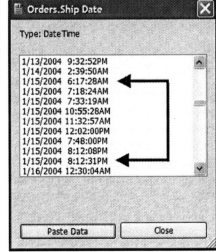

Figure 5-22 Ship Date field data

If the second Ship Date field has the time entered as 03:00:00 PM as shown in Figure 5-23, the last three records shown above in Figure 5-22 would not be displayed on the report because the time for these three records is after 3 PM.

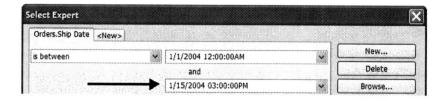

Figure 5-23 Criteria to show orders that were shipped between 1/1/2004 and 1/15/2004 by 3 PM

If you want to try this yourself, save the L5.6 report as L5.6A Time Problem (Incorrect Criteria) and delete all of the current selection criteria, then create the criteria shown above in Figure 5-20. Add the Ship Date field to the report and sort this field in ascending order. Refresh the data and run the report. If you scroll to the end of the report, you will see that the last record on the report has a ship date of 1/14/2004. There are no records for 1/15/2004 on the report.

Save the L5.6A report as L5.6B Time Problem (Correct Criteria). Use the criteria shown above in Figure 5-21. If you scroll to the end of the report, you will see that there are nine records on 1/15/2004. These are the records that you were expecting to appear on the report when you entered the criteria shown above in Figure 5-21.

Save the L5.6A report as L5.6C Time criteria with a specific time. Use the criteria shown above in Figure 5-23. If you scroll to the end of the report, you will see that there are 55 records on 1/15/2004. This is what you were expecting because the time on the criteria was 3 PM.

I don't know about you, but when I first figured this out it was somewhat scary. You have two options. You can always type in the time that you need on the second date field or you can type in the day after the last day that you want to include records for on the report. Instead of typing 1/15/2004 for the second date, you could type 1/16/2004 and let the time default to 00:00:00 AM and you will get the same result. Keep this in mind when you are creating reports on your own. In an effort to save time, when you create reports in this workbook that have similar selection criteria, you do not have to enter a time on the Select Expert dialog box.

Being able to enter a time is helpful for reports that are time sensitive. If you needed to create a report that displayed a list of medications that were dispensed to patients between 8 AM and 2 PM, you could enter the times as part of the selection criteria.

More Practice Creating Report Criteria

By now I think that you have figured out how important it is to understand how to create selection criteria to meet the requirements of the report. If the wrong criteria is created for the report, the output will not be what the user is expecting. This means that they could make decisions off of incorrect data and not know that the data is incorrect. If you aren't familiar with the data, it is a good idea to open the tables and look at the raw data. The next three exercises will allow you to gain more practice creating report selection criteria.

Each of the three practice exercises below is worded slightly different on purpose to help you learn how to take report specs and create selection criteria from them. Remember that each person that requests a report or asks for changes to an existing report will convey their needs differently.

Exercise 5.7: Practice Exercise 1

In this exercise you will create a new report that will find all products that the suppliers Craze and Triumph offer.

☑ Table 5-4 contains the tables and fields for the report.
☑ Figure 5-24 shows the report layout.
☑ Figure 5-25 shows the selection criteria formula.
☑ Figure 5-26 shows the report. The report should have 86 records.
☑ Save the report as L5.7 Products that suppliers Craze and Triumph offer.
   You may see a dialog box that says, "The saved data is incomplete". If so, click Yes.

Product	Supplier
Product Name	Supplier Name
M/F	
Price (SRP)	

Table 5-4 Tables and fields to add to the report

Product Name	M/F	Supplier Name	Price (SRP)
Product Name	M/F	Supplier Name	Price (SRP)

Figure 5-24 L5.7 report layout

{Supplier.Supplier Name} in ["Craze", "Triumph"]

Figure 5-25 Selection criteria formula

Product Name	M/F	Supplier Name	Price (SRP)
Mozzie		Craze	$1,739.85
Descent		Craze	$2,939.85
Descent		Craze	$2,939.85
Descent		Craze	$2,939.85
Descent		Craze	$2,939.85
Descent		Craze	$2,939.85
Descent		Craze	$2,939.85
Endorphin		Craze	$899.85
Descent		Craze	$2,939.85
Xtreme Gellite Ladies Saddle	ladies	Craze	$23.50

Figure 5-26 L5.7 Products that suppliers Craze and Triumph offer report

Exercise 5.8: Practice Exercise 2

In this exercise you will add selection criteria to the L3.5 report. You will modify the report so that it will only retrieve customers whose order amount is between $2,000 and $5,000 and was not shipped via the carrier Purolator.

Save the L3.5 report as L5.8 Orders between 2-5000 and not shipped by Purolator.

Figure 5-27 shows the report. The report should have 281 records.

The report needs the following criteria and changes.

① Change the format of the Order Date field to look like the one shown in the report.
② The Order Amount is between $2,000 and $5,000.
③ The order was not shipped by Purolator.

Customer Name	Order ID	Order Date	Order Amount	Ship Via	First Name	Last
Belgium Bike Co.	1,022	12/07/2003	$2,792.86	Parcel Post	Janet	Leve
The Great Bike Shop	1,027	12/07/2003	$2,972.85	UPS	Michael	Suyi
City Cyclists	1,033	12/08/2003	$3,520.30	Loomis	Janet	Leve
The Bike Cellar	1,036	12/10/2003	$2,014.20	Loomis	Michael	Suyi
Cyclopath	1,043	12/11/2003	$2,179.83	UPS	Margaret	Pea
The Bike Cellar	1,045	12/11/2003	$3,764.04	FedEx	Michael	Suyi
Cycle City Rome	1,055	12/12/2003	$2,459.40	Parcel Post	Nancy	Dav
Cycle City Rome	1,057	12/12/2003	$3,638.01	Loomis	Janet	Leve
To The Limit Biking Co.	1,063	12/12/2003	$2,497.05	Loomis	Anne	Dod

Figure 5-27 L5.8 Orders between 2-5000 and not shipped by Purolator report

Exercise 5.9: Practice Exercise 3

In this exercise you will add selection criteria to the L3.5 report. This report will only retrieve orders from 2004 that were shipped by the carrier Purolator or were picked up.

Save L3.5 the report as `L5.9 2004 Orders shipped by Purolator or Pickup`.

Figure 5-28 shows the report. The report should have 483 records.

The report needs the following criteria and changes.

① Change the format of the Order Date field to look like the one shown in the report.
② The Ship Via field must have Pickup or Purolator.
③ The Order Date is in 2004.

Customer Name	Order ID	Order Date	Order Amount	Ship Via	First Name	Last
Clean Air Transportation Co.	1,123	01/02/2004	$5,219.55	Pickup	Janet	Leve
Off the Mountain Biking	1,124	01/02/2004	$59.70	Purolator	Margaret	Pea
BBS Pty	1,127	01/02/2004	$520.35	Pickup	Robert	King
Paris Mountain Sports	1,134	01/05/2004	$43.80	Pickup	Anne	Dod
C-Gate Cycle Shoppe	1,136	01/05/2004	$3,209.53	Pickup	Michael	Suyi
Furia	1,137	01/05/2004	$6,040.95	Purolator	Margaret	Pea
Cyclopath	1,147	01/06/2004	$1,830.35	Purolator	Michael	Suyi
Magazzini	1,148	01/07/2004	$157.11	Pickup	Janet	Leve
Biking's It Industries	1,150	01/08/2004	$83.80	Pickup	Robert	King

Figure 5-28 L5.9 2004 Orders shipped by Purolator or Pickup report

Edit An Existing Formula

In Exercise 5.9, the criteria for the Ship Via field is that it has to contain one of two values. If you needed to add another value, you could use the Select Expert to add the value from the drop down list or you could edit the formula that is at the bottom of the Select Expert dialog box.

If you type in the **FORMULA** field, Crystal Reports will disable the top portion of the Select Expert dialog box as shown in Figure 5-29. Compare this to the Select Expert dialog box shown earlier in Figure 5-18.

In Figure 5-29, you do not see anything in the top portion of the dialog box. That is because I typed "UPS" in the formula field at the bottom of the dialog box.

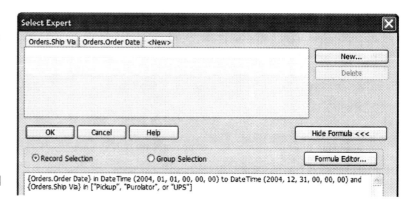

Figure 5-29 Top half of the Select Expert dialog box disabled

The reason Crystal Reports disables the top half of the Select Expert when you create or edit a formula at the bottom of the dialog box is because the formula can't be duplicated by the options that the Select Expert has.

Opening The Formula Editor From The Select Expert

If you can create or edit the formula at the bottom of the Select Expert shown above in Figure 5-29, you do not have to use the Formula Editor. If you cannot remember the function or need help creating the formula, there are two ways that you can open the Formula Editor from the Select Expert as discussed below. You will learn more about the Formula Editor in Lesson 9.

① Click the **FORMULA EDITOR** button shown above in Figure 5-29.
② Open the operator drop down list, scroll to the bottom of the list and select the **FORMULA** option, as shown in Figure 5-30. The Select Expert will change as shown in Figure 5-31 to let you create a formula.

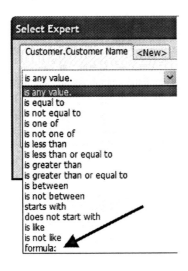

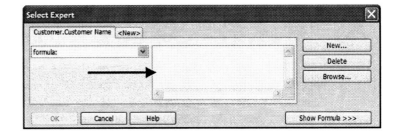

Figure 5-31 Select Expert with formula field

Figure 5-30 Formula option illustrated

Record Selection Performance Considerations

The type of database that the report is using determines the record selection process that Crystal Reports uses. Databases that are stored on a database server or desktop databases that use an ODBC connection have more performance issues then desktop databases that are local or are on a network drive, as discussed below.

① If the database is on a server, Crystal Reports creates a WHERE clause and adds the clause to the query and sends the query to the database server. The query is run on the server and returns the records to Crystal Reports to use, to generate the report. If the database is on a server, performance improves if this record selection process is used.
② If the database is local or is a desktop database that is stored on a network drive (which is different then a database server), Crystal Reports runs the query that is created from the record selection criteria itself. Depending on the number of records, the report selection process can take some time.

 Making changes to a formula created with the Select Expert via the **SHOW FORMULA** button can really slow down the record selection process if the database is on a database server, especially if the underlying tables have a lot of records.

The **USE INDEXES OR SERVER FOR SPEED** option if selected, will improve performance. If you want to use this option for the current report, it is on the Report Options dialog box. [See Lesson 8, Report Options] If you want this option to be the default for all reports that you will create going forward, select the option on the Database tab of the Options dialog box, which you will learn about later in this lesson.

In Lesson 2 you learned about indexes. Using indexed fields will improve performance during the record selection process, especially when using tables that have a lot of records. When possible, you should use indexed fields for the record selection process because the fields index, stores all of the values that are in the field, in sorted order, which makes it faster to retrieve records.

Case Sensitive Considerations

When Crystal Reports is installed, case insensitivity is set as the default. This means that entering "new orleans" or "New Orleans" will retrieve the same records. When creating selection criteria on text fields, keep the following in mind.

① PC and SQL databases that are connected to, via an ODBC connection usually ignores case sensitivity in Crystal Reports.

② Some databases and ODBC drivers may not support case insensitivity when used with Crystal Reports, even though the **DATABASE SERVER IS CASE-INSENSITIVE** option is turned on.

③ If the server that the database is stored on is set to be case sensitive, you cannot override it by turning on the **DATABASE SERVER IS CASE-INSENSITIVE** option on the Options dialog box. If you select the same option on the Report Options dialog box, you can turn the option on, only for the report that you are currently working with. If this is the case, you would have to convert the text field that you need to create the selection criteria for to all upper case and enter the criteria to support all upper case.

④ If the database is not stored on a server that is set to case sensitive and the database is set for case insensitivity, you can use the **DATABASE SERVER IS CASE-INSENSITIVE** option to control what the selection criteria returns.

 If you want the **DATABASE SERVER IS CASE-INSENSITIVE** option applied to reports that have already been created, you have to open each of the reports and select the option on the Report Options dialog box.

Document Properties

In Lesson 4 you learned about **SPECIAL FIELDS** and that they can be added to a report. You also learned that some of the special fields come from the Summary tab on the Document Properties dialog box. The next two exercises will show you how to create summary information and save it, as well as, add the summary information to a report.

Exercise 5.10: How To Create Report Summary Information

1. Save the L5.1 report as `L5.10 Region = CA with summary info.` Notice the name of the report on the tab.

2. File ⇒ Summary Info. Type your name in the **AUTHOR** field.

3. Type `This report has summary information` in the **COMMENTS** field, then type `L5.10 Region = CA` in the **TITLE** field. Figure 5-32 shows the options that should be filled in.

4. Click OK and save the changes. Look at the tab for the report. It should have changed to what you entered in the Title field on the Summary tab. Leave the report open to complete the next part of the exercise.

The information that is entered on this tab is used for identification purposes. These are properties of Windows files and are not specific to Crystal Reports. Other software packages have similar dialog boxes. For example, Microsoft Word has the "Properties" dialog box.

The **TEMPLATE** field shown in Figure 5-32 currently does not provide any use. It does not let you apply a template to the report or save the active report as a template. If the report is based off of a template, you could enter the template name in this field so that you will know which template the report is using.

The **SAVE PREVIEW PICTURE** option if checked, will let you view a thumbnail size picture of the first page of the report in the Open dialog box of Crystal Reports, as shown in Figure 5-33 or in Windows Explorer, as shown in Figure 5-35.

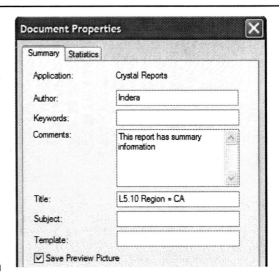

Figure 5-32 Summary tab options

You should know how to add summary property information to a report and how to save a preview picture of a report.

To view a thumbnail of the first page of the report on the Open dialog box, click the **PREVIEW** button illustrated in Figure 5-33.

To view the Summary tab options on the Open dialog box in Crystal Reports, click the **PROPERTIES** button illustrated in Figure 5-34.

To view a thumbnail of the first page of the report in Windows Explorer, open the **VIEWS** drop down list in Windows Explorer and select Thumbnails. You will see similar options to those shown in Figure 5-35.

To view the Summary tab options in Windows Explorer, hold the mouse pointer over the report file in Windows Explorer. You will see similar options to those shown in Figure 5-36.

Figure 5-33 Thumbnail of a report in Crystal Reports

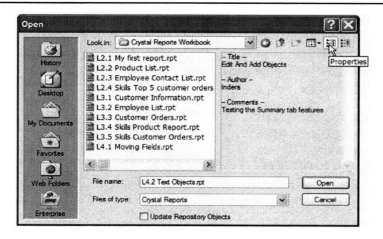

Figure 5-34 Summary options of a report in Crystal Reports

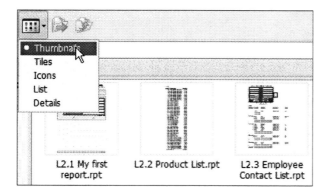

Figure 5-35 Thumbnail view of reports in Windows Explorer

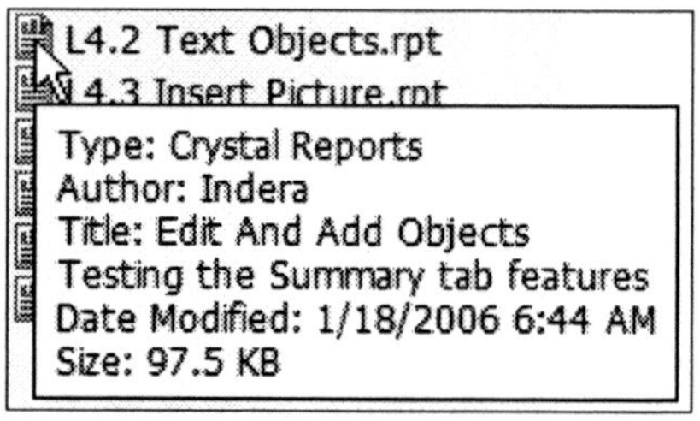

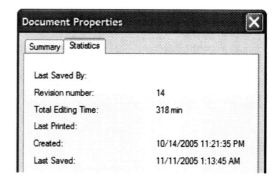

Figure 5-36 Summary options of a report in Windows Explorer

Statistics Tab

1. Open the Document Properties dialog box and click on the Statistics tab.

The options shown in Figure 5-37 are **READ-ONLY**, which means that you cannot modify them manually.

The **REVISION NUMBER** is incremented each time the report is saved. If you are modifying a report that you did not create, the information on this tab may be helpful. The **TOTAL EDITING TIME** field lets you know how long the report has been open and whether it has been edited.

Figure 5-37 Statistics tab options

2. Close the Document Properties dialog box.

Add Summary Information To A Report

1. Add the **FILE AUTHOR** and **REPORT TITLE** Special Fields to the report header section. The report should look similar to the one shown in Figure 5-38. Save the changes and close the report.

Indera		L5.10 Region = CA		
Customer Name	**Address1**	**Region**	**Country**	**Postal Code**
Sporting Wheels Inc.	480 Grant Way	CA	USA	92150
Rowdy Rims Company	4861 Second Road	CA	USA	91341

Figure 5-38 L5.10 Region = CA report with summary information added

Crystal Reports Menus

Tables 5-5 to 5-15 explain the Crystal Reports menu options. Many of the menu options will be familiar from the toolbars that you learned about in Lesson 1.

File Menu Options

The options on the File menu allow you to open, close, print and save files.

Menu Option	Description
New	Lets you create a new report as shown in Figure 5-39.
Open	Lets you open an existing report. The default setting is to only display Crystal Reports files in the dialog box. You can change this setting and open other types of files. If checked, the **UPDATE REPOSITORY OBJECTS** option shown earlier in Figure 5-34 will cause objects in a report that is connected to the repository to be updated when the report is opened.
Close	Closes the active report. (6)
Save	Saves the active report. If the report is new, you will be prompted to give the report a file name. (6)
Save As	Lets you save the active report with a new name.
Save Data With Report	[See Lesson 2, Options For Saving Data]
Save Subreport As	This option lets you save an existing report as a subreport with it's own file name, even if it has already been inserted into another report.
Print	[See Lesson 8, Printer Options]
Page Setup	[See Lesson 8, Page Setup Options]
Export	[See Lesson 8, Export Report Overview]
Send To	This option lets you send the active report via email using the dialog box shown in Figure 5-40 or to an Exchange mail folder. The first time that you use the Mail Recipient option, you may be prompted to insert the Crystal Reports CD to install the required components.
Options	Opens the Options dialog box, which is covered in detail later in this lesson.
Report Options	[See Lesson 8, Report Options]
Summary Info	[See Lesson 5, Document Properties]
Exit	Closes Crystal Reports. (6)

Table 5-5 File menu options explained

(6) If changes were made to the report you will be prompted to save them.

As you learned earlier, the Recent Reports section of the Start Page will display the last five reports that you opened. The section above the Exit option on the File menu will display the last nine reports that were opened, as shown in Figure 5-39.

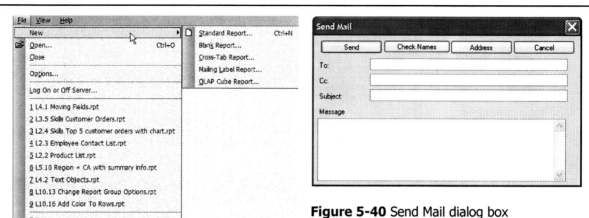

Figure 5-40 Send Mail dialog box

Figure 5-39 Report options

 The **ADDRESS** button on the **SEND MAIL** window will open the default address book that is associated with the email software that you use. To send a report via email, you must use a MAPI compliant email software package. [See Lesson 8, Table 8-3]

Edit Menu Options

Many of the options on the Edit menu may be familiar, especially if you have used a word processing software package. Some of the options on the Edit menu require an object to be selected before the menu option is available.

Menu Option	Description
Undo	It will let you undo the last action that you did. If the menu option is grayed out, the last action cannot be undone. (7)
Redo	It will let you redo the last action that you did. If the menu option is grayed out, the last action cannot be repeated. (7)
Cut	Deletes the selected object(s) from the report and places it on the clipboard.
Copy	Copies the selected object(s) and places them on the clipboard.
Paste	Pastes object(s) from the clipboard into the report.
Paste Special	This option is primarily used for OLE (Object Linking and Embedded) objects because it gives more control then the Paste option on how an object is pasted into the report.
Delete	Deletes the selected object(s) from the report. Unlike the Cut option, the Delete option does not send the object to the clipboard.
Select All	Lets you select all of the objects in the report at one time. This will let you perform the same task to all of the objects at the same time.
Find	This option opens the dialog box shown in Figure 5-42. The options let you search for text in the report. The **ADVANCED FIND** button opens the dialog box shown in Figure 5-43. These options let you search for data (values in a field in the report). It is similar to the Select Expert that you learned about earlier in this lesson, because you can search in more than one field at the same time. These options work best from the preview window.
Go To Page	The dialog box shown in Figure 5-44 will let you jump to any page in the report. Type in the page number that you want to go to in the field across from the Page field and click OK.

Table 5-6 Edit menu options explained

Menu Option	Description
Edit Report Object	The name of this menu item will change depending on the type of object that is selected. Other than a text object, a dialog box will open. Figure 5-45 shows the Edit Parameter dialog box and Figure 5-46 shows the Formula Editor.
Subreports Links	This option is only available in reports that have a subreport. The subreport links dialog box will let you check and modify the link between the subreport and main report.
Object	This option is only available in reports that have an OLE object that is selected. This option will let you edit the OLE object.
Links	Lets you modify the Link properties of the OLE object that is selected.

Table 5-6 Edit menu options explained (Continued)

(7) The Undo and Redo menu options will change depending on the action (what you did) right before you opened the Edit menu. Figure 5-41 shows the Undo and Redo menu options after an action was taken.

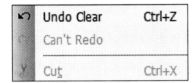

Figure 5-41 Edit menu after an action was taken

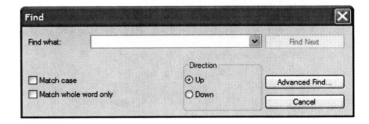

Figure 5-42 Find dialog box

The difference between the Search Expert and the Select Expert is that the Search Expert searches through the data in the report. It does not search the records in the database like the Select Expert does.

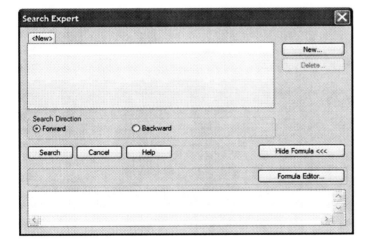

Figure 5-44 Go To dialog box

Figure 5-43 Search Expert

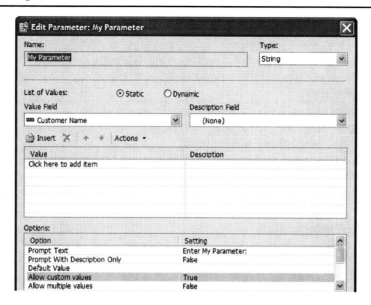

Figure 5-45 Edit Parameter dialog box

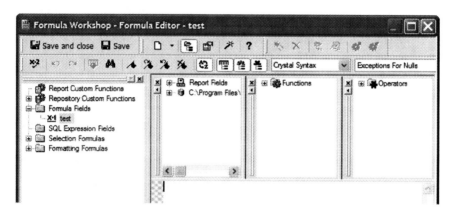

Figure 5-46 Formula Editor

View Menu Options

The options on the View menu let you select how you want to use many of the tools in Crystal Reports.

Menu Option	Description
Design	Opens the design window.
Preview	Opens the preview window.
Print Preview	This option is only available on the design window. It lets you view the report. This is the same as clicking on the preview tab.
Preview Sample	Lets you preview the report with limited data. [See Exercise 8.6]
HTML Preview	Lets you preview the report in HTML format. You may have to set some of the options on the Smart Tag & HTML Preview tab on the Options dialog box before you can use this option.
Close Current View	Closes the active tab.
Field Explorer	Opens the Field Explorer so that you can add fields and other objects to the report.
Repository Explorer	Lets you add an item from the repository to the report. It opens the Repository Explorer.

Table 5-7 View menu options explained

Menu Option	Description
Repository Explorer	Lets you add an item from the repository to the report. It opens the Repository Explorer.
Dependency Checker	Opens the Dependency Checker so that you can see the results of running the Check Dependencies application.
Workbench	Displays or hides the Workbench.
Toolbars	Lets you customize the toolbars.
Status Bar	Displays or hides the status bar at the bottom of the Crystal Reports window. The status bar provides additional information about the object that you are holding the mouse over, as well as, other information about the active report.
Group Tree	Toggles the group tree on and off on the preview window.
Zoom	Lets you set the zoom level for viewing a report. You can change the zoom percent on the dialog box shown in Figure 5-47, or you can type the zoom percent in the Zoom field on the Standard toolbar.
Rulers	Lets you turn the rulers on or off. (8)
Guidelines	Lets you turn the guidelines on or off. (8)
Grid	Lets you turn the grid on or off. (8)
Tool tips	Lets you turn the tool tips on or off. (8)

Table 5-7 View menu options explained (Continued)

(8) This option works on the design and preview windows.

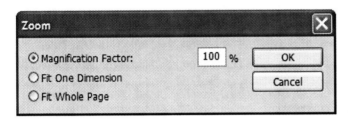

Figure 5-47 Zoom dialog box

Insert Menu Options

The options on the Insert menu let you add objects to a report. Many of these objects are available on the shortcut menu for the object.

Menu Option	Description
Text Object	Lets you add a text object to the report.
Summary	Lets you add a summary field to the report.
Field Heading	Lets you create a field heading for the selected field. If the **INSERT DETAIL FIELD HEADINGS** option is checked on the Layout tab of the Options dialog box, you will probably not have the need to use the field heading option because field headings will be created automatically for fields that are added to the details section.
Group	Lets you add a group to the report.
OLAP Grid	Opens the OLAP Expert, which allows you to create an OLAP grid. (9)
Cross-Tab	Opens the Cross-Tab Expert, which allows you to create a cross-tab object. (9)
Subreport	Opens the Insert Subreport dialog box, which lets you create a subreport or select an existing report to use as a subreport.

Table 5-8 Insert menu options explained

Menu Option	Description
Line	Lets you draw lines on the report. You can draw horizontal or vertical lines. Lines can also be drawn across sections of the report.
Box	Lets you draw a box on the report. Boxes can also be drawn across sections of the report.
Picture	Lets you add graphic files to a report. The supported file types are .bmp, jpeg, png, tiff and Windows metafile.
Chart	Lets you create a chart using the Chart Expert.
Map	Lets you create a map using the Map Expert.
OLE Object	Lets you add an OLE object to the report.
Template Field Object	This object is used as a placeholder for a field in a template. Template field objects are not connected to fields in a database. [See Lesson 13, Template Field Objects]

Table 5-8 Insert menu options explained (Continued)

(9) There can be more than one OLAP grid or cross-tab object in the same report.

Format Menu Options

The options on the Format menu let you change the appearance of the objects on the report.

Menu Option	Description
Format Field	Opens the appropriate Format Editor to modify the properties of the selected object.
Format Painter	This option is used to copy the formatting options from one object to another.
Hyperlink	Lets you insert a hyperlink.
Use Expert	This option opens an expert, based on the object that is selected, so that you can edit the object.
Highlighting Expert	Opens the Highlighting Expert which lets you apply conditional formatting to a field.
Line Height	This option is used to adjust the height of a section of the report if the **FREE FORM PLACEMENT** option on the Section Expert is turned off.
Text Formatting	Lets you apply formatting to a text field.
Move	Lets you move a field from one location to another on the report.
Align	Lets you line up objects. [See Lesson 4, Aligning Objects]
Make Same Size	Let you make two or more objects the same size by width, height or both.
Size and Position	Opens the Object Size And Position dialog box which gives you greater control over the size and position of an object, then you get if you size the object manually.
Pivot OLAP Grid	This option is used to change the row and column dimensions of an OLAP grid.
Pivot Cross-Tab	This option is used to change the row and column dimensions of a cross-tab grid.

Table 5-9 Format menu options explained

You may find it easier to right-click on an object and select the expert that you want to use, instead of selecting the object and then opening the Format menu.

Database Menu Options

The options on the Database menu provide options that you may need to set for the databases that you will use.

Menu Option	Description
Database Expert	Opens the Database Expert, which is used to add or delete data sources to or from the report.
Set Data Source Location	Lets you select a different database for the report or a different location for the database that the report is currently using. This option is useful when you are using a copy of the database to create and test the report(s) and are now ready to move the report(s) into production (go live). For example, this feature will let you change the database to the one on a production server.
Log On or Off Server	Lets you log on or off of an SQL or ODBC server, set database options and maintain the Favorites folder. Most of the tasks that you can complete on the Data Explorer window can be done another way.
Browse Data	Lets you view data in a field. This is the same as the Browse button that you have seen on different dialog boxes.
Set OLAP Cube Location	Lets you change the location of the OLAP Cube in the report.
Verify Database	Lets you compare the structure of the data source that is used in the report to the structure of the actual database.
Show SQL Query	This option will let you view SQL queries if the report is using any. Parameter fields are included if they are used in the selection formula. Figure 5-48 shows the dialog box.
Perform Grouping on Server	If checked and the report has a group and the details section of the report is hidden, the grouping process will be done on a server.
Select Distinct Records	If checked, duplicate records will not appear on the report. A duplicate record has the same data in every field in both records.

Table 5-10 Database menu options explained

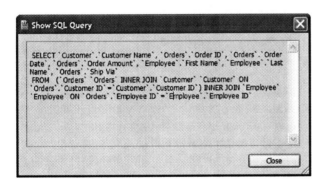

Figure 5-48 Show SQL Query dialog box

Each of the exercises that you have completed so far in this lesson created an SQL query, similar to the one shown above in Figure 5-48.

Report Menu Options

Many of the options on the Report menu will open an Expert. Some of the wizard screens that you have used look similar to some of the Experts.

Menu Option	Description
Select Expert	Opens the Select Expert which lets you create selection criteria to filter records.
Selection Formulas	The **RECORD** selection option opens the Record Selection Formula Editor, which lets you edit the record selection formula. The **GROUP** selection option opens the Group Selection Formula Editor, which lets you edit the group selection formula.
Formula Workshop	Opens the Formula Workshop, which allows you to create, edit and view formulas and functions.
Alerts	Lets you create and edit alerts.
Report Bursting Indexes	This option is only available on reports that have saved data. It lets you create indexes on the saved data. This improves the record selection process time. [See Lesson 2, Report Bursting Indexes]
Section Expert	Opens the Section Expert which lets you format any section of the report. [See Lesson 10, The Section Expert]
Group Expert	Opens the Group Expert which is used to create, modify and delete groups.
Group Sort Expert	Lets you sort the groups in the report by group summary fields.
Record Sort Expert	Opens the Record Sort Expert which lets you select the order that the detail records will be sorted in. [See Lesson 6, Sorting Records]
XML Expert	Lets you modify the format of exported XML files.
Template Expert	Opens the Template Expert. You can create custom templates using this expert.
OLAP Design Wizard	Opens the OLAP Expert. This menu option is only available after an OLAP grid is selected in the report.
Hierarchical Grouping Options	Lets you create a hierarchical report. [See Lesson 13, Hierarchical Group Reports]
Show Current Parameter Values	Opens the Current Parameter Values Dialog box, which will let you view the parameter values that were selected the last time that the report was run, as shown in Figure 5-49.
Check Dependencies	Opens the Dependency Checker so that you can see the results of running the Check Dependencies tool.
Refresh Report Data	Lets you refresh the data in the report. If the report has parameter fields, you can select the parameter options that you want to use.
Set Print Date and Time	Lets you override the values that would print if the Print Date or Print Time special fields are on the report. [See Lesson 8, Using The Set Print Date And Time Options]
Performance Information	Displays information similar to what is shown in Figure 5-50, which may help you troubleshoot report performance problems.

Table 5-11 Report menu options explained

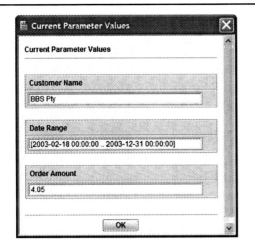

Figure 5-49 Current Parameter Values dialog box

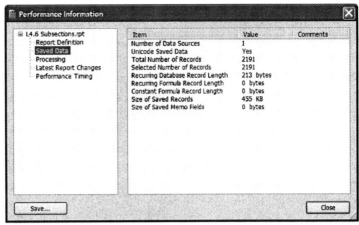

Figure 5-50 Performance Information dialog box

Chart Menu Options

The options on the Chart menu let you customize a chart. This menu is only available when a chart is selected on a report.

Menu Option	Description
Format Background	Lets you change the color or font of the selected item.
Chart Options	Opens the Chart Options dialog box.
Axis Options	Lets you change the grid options.
Series Options	Lets you change the options for the chart series that is selected.
3D Viewing Angle	Lets you change the viewing angle of a 3D chart.
Edit Axis Label	Lets you change the axis label that is selected.
Trendlines	Lets you modify the trendlines.
Auto-Arrange Chart	Lets you arrange all of the objects on the chart.
Apply Changes To All Charts	Lets you apply the same formatting to all similar group level chart objects.
Discard Custom Changes	Lets you delete all customizations that you made to the chart.
Load Template	Lets you select a template to apply to the chart.
Save As Template	Lets you save the chart as a user defined template.
Select Mode	Prevents accidental zooming or panning on the chart.
Zoom In	Lets you zoom in closer on the chart.
Zoom Out	Lets you zoom out on the chart.
Pan	This option is only available when a chart has been zoomed in on. It lets you move through the data in the chart.

Table 5-12 Chart menu options explained

Map Menu Options

The options on the Map menu let you customize a Geographic map. In order to use the options on this menu or view a report that has a map, you have to install the Map DLL's. This menu is only available when a map is selected on a report.

Menu Option	Description
Select Mode	This option is enabled as soon as you click on a map on the preview tab. Once enabled, the Map menu is visible.
Zoom In	Lets you zoom in closer on the map.
Zoom Out	Lets you zoom out on the map.
Pan	This option is only available when a map has been zoomed in on. It lets you move through the data in the map.
Center Map	Lets you center a map in its frame. You may need to use this option after you have used the pan option.
Title	Lets you add or change a title on the map.
Type	Lets you change the type of map.
Layers	Opens the Layer Control dialog box, which will let you change the order of the layers, so that the map can have more or less detail.
Resolve Mismatch	Opens the Resolve Map Mismatch dialog box which lets you select the map that you want to have the data values associated with.
Map Navigator	Turns the Map Navigator on and off. You can use the Map Navigator to center, zoom and pan.

Table 5-13 Map menu options explained

Window Menu Options

The options on the Window menu let you change the default layout of the open windows in Crystal Reports. These options work the same way that they do in Windows XP.

Menu Option	Description
Tile Vertically	Arranges all open windows side by side.
Tile Horizontally	Arranges all open windows in rows so that they do not overlap.
Cascade	Arranges all open windows so that the title bar of each window is visible.
Arrange Icons	Arranges the icons at the bottom of the window.
Close All	Closes all open windows. You will be prompted to save any reports that have been modified or have never been saved.

Table 5-14 Window menu options explained

Open Reports

At the bottom of the Window menu, you will see a list of all of the reports that are currently open, as shown in Figure 5-51. The report that is active has a check mark in front of it. If you want to switch to a different report that is open, you can select it from the bottom of the Window menu.

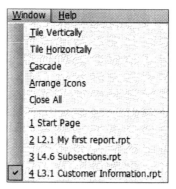

Figure 5-51 Open reports on the Window menu illustrated

Help Menu Options

The options on the Help menu provide several ways to get assistance. The other options let you register and manage the software.

Menu Option	Description
Crystal Reports Help	Opens the Online Help file.
Context Help	Displays help for windows, buttons and menus that you click on. After selecting this option, click on an item in the Crystal Reports workspace and a tool tip will appear that explains the item that you clicked on. For example, select this option and then click on a button on any toolbar. The Help file will open. On the right side of the window, you will see a page for the button that you clicked on.
Report Samples	Will let you open the sample reports that come with Crystal Reports.
Show Start Page	Displays the Start Page if it is closed.
Check for Updates on Start Up	If checked, this option will automatically check for software updates each time that you open Crystal Reports.
Check for Updates	If checked, this option will let you check for software updates when you want to.
Register or Change Address	Opens the registration wizard which lets you register your copy of Crystal Reports or change your address.
License Manager	Lets you add and remove Crystal Reports license numbers and Integration kit licenses.
Business Objects On the Web	Will take you to several web pages on the Business Objects web site.
About Crystal Reports	Opens the About dialog box which displays information about the version of Crystal Reports that is installed. Clicking on the MORE INFO button shown in Figure 5-52, will let you see the Loaded Modules, as shown in Figure 5-53. This information could be helpful if you have to troubleshoot some types of report problems. In Lesson 8 you will install DLL files that will be added to the list shown in Figure 5-53.

Table 5-15 Help menu options explained

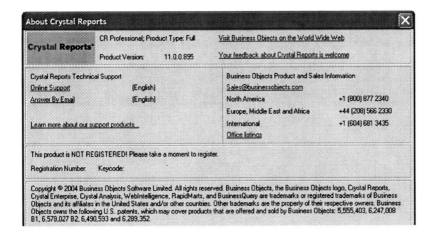

Figure 5-52 About Crystal Reports dialog box

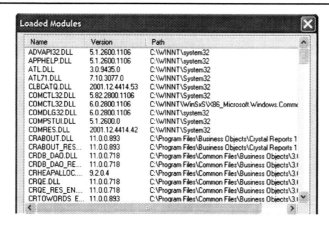

Figure 5-53 Loaded Modules

Customizing Crystal Reports Design Environment

If you need to customize the design environment, you can, by following the steps below. These options let you set the default settings for the majority of features that you will use to create and modify reports. Once you have used the software for a while and find yourself always having to change an option, you should come back to this section and review all of the options on the Options dialog box and change the ones that you use, to better meet your needs.

 While looking at the options, pay particular attention to the options on the layout, database and reporting tabs, as they contain the options that you are likely to need to change first, because they contain the options that most effect the functionality in the design window.

 The changes that you make on the Options dialog box, affect all of the reports that you create or modify once the changes on this dialog box are saved. Any changes that are made will not be picked up by reports that were saved prior to the changes made on the Options dialog box. If you want to apply changes that you make on the Options dialog box to existing reports, delete the object from the report that the change will effect and then add the object back to the report.

1. File ⇒ Options. You will see the dialog box shown in Figure 5-54.

2. To find out more about a specific option, click the **HELP** button shown above in Figure 5-54. You will see the Help window shown in Figure 5-55, which explains all of the settings on the tab.

 Notice that the Online Help file automatically opens to the page for the options on the tab that you have open. In this example, the help button was clicked on the Layout tab shown in Figure 5-54.

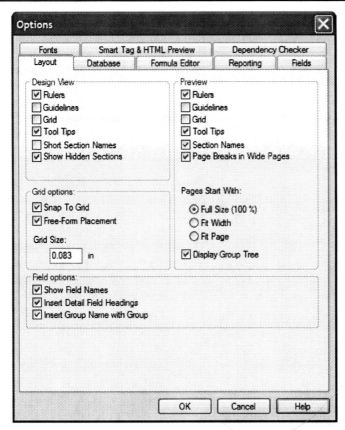

The Layout options determine how reports are displayed.

The options in the Design View section determine the look and functionality of the Design window.

The options in the Preview section determine the look and functionality of the Preview window.

The options in the Grid Options section determine how the grid will or will not be displayed in the Design window.

The options in the Field Options section determine how fields are displayed in the Design window. If the **SHOW FIELD NAMES** option is not checked, characters will be displayed in fields in the design window instead of the field name.

Figure 5-54 Layout options

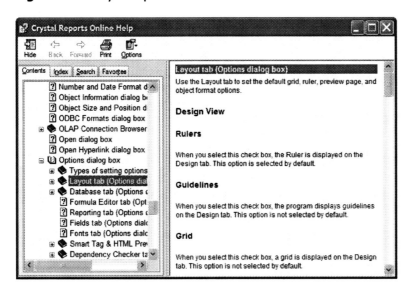

Figure 5-55 Help window

3. Figures 5-56 to 5-62 show all of the other options that you can change. When you are finished viewing the options, close the dialog box.

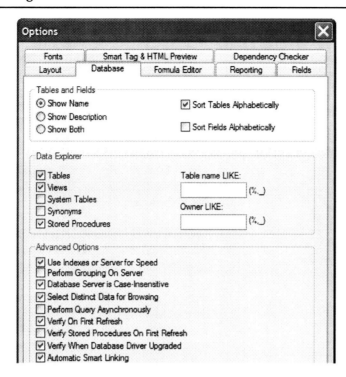

Figure 5-56 Database options

The Database options determine how data appears and how queries are processed.

The options in the Tables and Fields section let you configure how tables and fields are displayed.

The options in the Data Explorer section determine how database objects are displayed in the Database Expert.

The options in the Advanced Options section determine how queries will be run and when changes in the database structure will be checked.

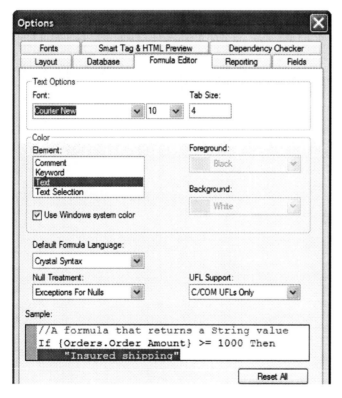

Figure 5-57 Formula Editor options

The Formula Editor options let you customize the Formula Editor. [See Lesson 9, Formula Editor]

The **DEFAULT FORMULA LANGUAGE** option will let you select the default syntax language for the formulas that you create. [See Lesson 9, Syntax]

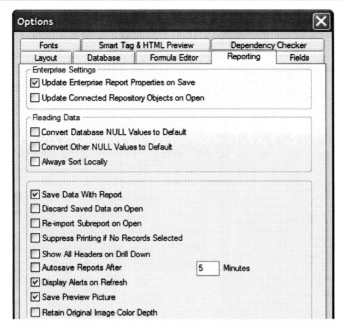

Figure 5-58 Reporting options

The Reporting options determine how the data is stored and retrieved in the report. These settings can be changed on a report by report basis on the Report Options dialog box. [See Lesson 8, Report Options]

The options in the Enterprise Settings section determine report functionality in the Business Objects Enterprise environment.

The options in the Reading Data section determine how null values and sorting features will be handled.

The remaining options apply to a variety of report features.

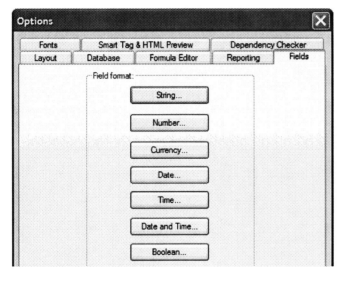

Figure 5-59 Field options

The Field format options let you select the default options for the field types that Crystal Reports supports.

You may want to click on these buttons now to become familiar with the default options. One option that you may want to change after completing the exercises in this workbook is the default date format, if you think that you will use the same date format for the majority of reports that you will create. You do not have to change anything to complete the exercises in this workbook.

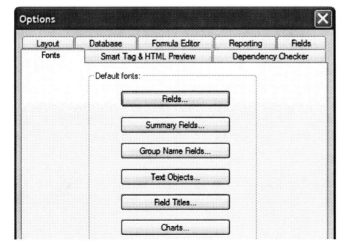

Figure 5-60 Font options

The Font options let you select the default font options for a variety of fields and objects that Crystal Reports supports.

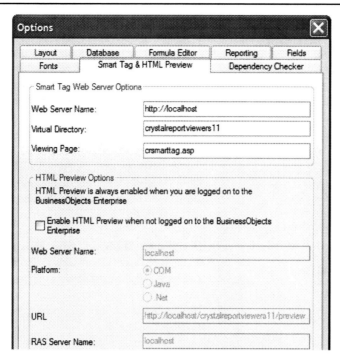

The Smart Tag & HTML Preview options let you select how Crystal Reports Smart Tags will be used in Microsoft Office Applications.

The HTML Preview Options let you select and configure how reports will be displayed as web pages.

If your reports are not stored in the Business Objects Enterprise you may want to check the **ENABLE HTML PREVIEW** option so that you can preview reports as web pages.

Figure 5-61 Smart Tag & HTML Preview options

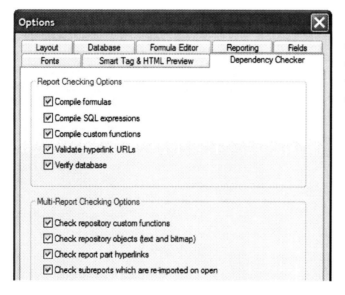

The Dependency Checker options let you select what conditions you want to verify when you check for formula errors, broken links and database issues in reports.

Figure 5-62 Dependency Checker options

Customizing The Interface Of Crystal Reports

In addition to being able to change the default values and options in Crystal Reports that you just learned about, you can also change the interface of Crystal Reports. The default interface reminds me of Microsoft Office 2003 because of the blue gradient layout and shading. There are other themes and layout options that you can select. They are on the lower half of the Toolbars dialog box, that you learned about in Lesson 1.

1. View ⇒ Toolbars. You will see the dialog box shown in Figure 5-63. The options shown in the **VISUAL THEME** drop down list are the other layouts that you can select. Figure 5-64 shows the toolbars with the **CLASSIC FLAT STYLE** layout option selected.

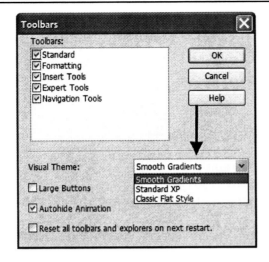

Figure 5-63 Toolbars dialog box

Figure 5-64 Classic Flat Style layout option

2. Make any changes that you want and click OK.

Test Your Skills

You should refresh the data before previewing the reports that have selection criteria.

1. Save the L4.1 report as `L5.11 Skills Product type filter`.

    - Create a filter that only displays the gloves, saddles and kids product types.

    Your report should look like the one shown in Figure 5-65. The report should have 33 records.

Product ID	Product Name	Product Type Na	Supplier Name
1,101	Active Outdoors Crochet Glove	Gloves	Active Outdoors
1,102	Active Outdoors Crochet Glove	Gloves	Active Outdoors
1,103	Active Outdoors Crochet Glove	Gloves	Active Outdoors
1,104	Active Outdoors Crochet Glove	Gloves	Active Outdoors
1,105	Active Outdoors Crochet Glove	Gloves	Active Outdoors
1,106	Active Outdoors Lycra Glove	Gloves	Active Outdoors
1,107	Active Outdoors Lycra Glove	Gloves	Active Outdoors
1,108	Active Outdoors Lycra Glove	Gloves	Active Outdoors
1,109	Active Outdoors Lycra Glove	Gloves	Active Outdoors
1,110	Active Outdoors Lycra Glove	Gloves	Active Outdoors
1,111	Active Outdoors Lycra Glove	Gloves	Active Outdoors

Figure 5-65 L5.11 Skills Product type filter report

2. Save the L3.5 report as `L5.12 Skills Ship Via filter`.

    - Create a filter that displays all orders where the Ship Via field does not have **PICKUP** or **LOOMIS**.

    Your report should look like the one shown in Figure 5-66. The report should have 1,445 records.

Customer Name	Order ID	Order Date	Order Amount	Ship Via	First Name	Last
City Cyclists	1	12/2/2003 12:00:00A	$41.90	UPS	Nancy	Dav
Warsaw Sports, Inc.	1,003	12/2/2003 12:00:00A	$186.87	UPS	Margaret	Pea
Poser Cycles	1,006	12/3/2003 12:00:00A	$64.90	Purolator	Margaret	Pea
Spokes	1,007	12/3/2003 12:00:00A	$49.50	Parcel Post	Anne	Dod
Clean Air Transportation Co.	1,008	12/3/2003 12:00:00A	$2,214.94	Purolator	Margaret	Pea
Cyclopath	1,010	12/3/2003 12:00:00A	$14,872.30	UPS	Nancy	Dav
BBS Pty	1,011	12/3/2003 12:00:00A	$29.00	Purolator	Margaret	Pea
Pedals Inc.	1,013	12/3/2003 12:00:00A	$1,142.13	Parcel Post	Margaret	Pea
Spokes 'N Wheels Ltd.	1,014	12/4/2003 12:00:00A	$29.00	Purolator	Nancy	Dav
Cycle City Rome	1,015	12/4/2003 12:00:00A	$43.50	UPS	Anne	Dod
SAB Mountain	1,016	12/4/2003 12:00:00A	$563.70	FedEx	Janet	Leve

Figure 5-66 L5.12 Skills Ship Via filter report

3. Save the L4.2 report as `L5.13 Skills Order filter`.

    - Create a filter that displays order amounts that are >= $1,000 and were **SHIPPED** between 1/01/04 and 1/31/04 in the USA.
    - Delete the First and Last Name fields. Add the Region field after the Ship Via field.

    Your report should look like the one shown in Figure 5-67. The report should have 40 records.

Customers Order Report					
Customer Name	Order #	Order Date	Order Amount	Ship Via	Region
City Cyclists	1246	1/30/04	$3,884.25	Pickup	MI
Bike-A-Holics Anonymous	1097	12/27/03	$1,439.55	Loomis	OH
Sporting Wheels Inc.	1181	1/15/04	$5,912.96	UPS	CA
Sporting Wheels Inc.	1220	1/22/04	$5,879.70	UPS	CA
Rockshocks for Jocks	1161	1/11/04	$1,799.70	Parcel Post	TX
Rowdy Rims Company	1090	12/22/03	$1,529.70	Loomis	CA
Rowdy Rims Company	1186	1/15/04	$1,110.70	Purolator	CA
Clean Air Transportation Co.	1123	1/2/04	$5,219.55	Pickup	PA
Clean Air Transportation Co.	1228	1/25/04	$2,181.86	Loomis	PA
Hooked on Helmets	1122	1/1/04	$1,025.40	Loomis	MN
C-Gate Cycle Shoppe	1136	1/5/04	$3,209.53	Pickup	VA

Figure 5-67 L5.13 Skills Order filter report

4. Save the L3.5 report as L5.14 Skills Employee report.

   - Create a filter that displays orders that do not have an Order Date in 2004.
   - Do not display the time on the Order Date field.
   - Modify the report so that all of the fields fit in the details section.

   Page 12 of your report should look like the one shown in Figure 5-68. The report should have 629 records.

Customer Name	Order ID	Order Date	Order Amount	Ship Via	First Name	Last Name
Souzel Bike Rentals	3,189	12/12/2003	$31.00	Loomis	Robert	King
Tom's Place for Bikes	3,190	12/12/2003	$53.90	Pickup	Robert	King
Coastal Line Bikes	3,191	12/12/2003	$101.70	Parcel Post	Anne	Dodsworth
Hikers and Bikers	3,192	12/12/2003	$959.70	UPS	Nancy	Davolio
Mountain View Sport	3,193	12/12/2003	$23.80	Parcel Post	Nancy	Davolio

Figure 5-68 L5.14 Skills Employee report

5. Add all of the reports that were created in this lesson to the Workbench.

GROUPING, SORTING AND SUMMARIZING RECORDS

After completing the exercises in this lesson, you will be able to use the following techniques to control which records appear on a report and how they are organized:

- ☑ Grouping records
- ☑ Sorting records
- ☑ Create summary subtotals and group totals
- ☑ Organize the records that will appear on the reports
- ☑ Create percent calculations
- ☑ Create a custom group name
- ☑ User defined sort order
- ☑ User defined groups
- ☑ Use the Group Expert

To pass the RDCR201 exam, you need to be familiar with and be able to:

- ☑ Group records
- ☑ Sort records

LESSON 6

Grouping And Sorting Overview

Sorting rearranges the order that records will appear on the report. Grouping takes sorting one step further by displaying records that have the same value in a field or a value that is in a range of values together. After all of the records in a group print, there are often totals or some type of summary information about the records in the group. You can sort records whether or not there are groups on the report. In Exercise 2.1 you created a report that grouped the data using a wizard.

Grouping Records

Grouping displays records together that meet specific criteria. Consider the following two examples:

① In the L5.2 Region = OH or FL report, at a glance, it is hard to tell how many records are in the OH region versus how many are in the FL region. If the report was modified to print all of the records in the same region together, it would be easier to see how many records are in each region. This is known as grouping records.

② In the L5.6 US orders not shipped in April 2005 report, you cannot tell how many orders were not shipped on any particular day. If the records were grouped by ship date, you would be able to create a count summary field to show how many orders were not shipped by day. You could also have a total by day of the total dollar amount, based on the order amount field, of orders that were not shipped.

There are three main tasks that need to be completed when records in a report need to be grouped. The three tasks are listed below and are discussed in detail in this lesson.

① Select the fields to group on. [See Lesson 2, Report Design Process Step 4]

② Decide if the detail records in each group need to be sorted.
[See Lesson 2, Report Design Process Step 4]

③ Decide if any fields in the details section of the report need summary information.
[See Lesson 2, Report Design Process Step 2]

You learned about the group header and footer sections in Lesson 2. The name of the group is usually placed in the group header section and the summary information, which is not a requirement, is usually placed in the group footer section.

Being able to add this type of functionality to reports will make them much more useful in many cases, then the reports that were created in Lesson 5. Reports that have groups can also use the drill down feature. In addition to creating the groups, Crystal Reports also provides summary functions including statistical, averaging and totals that you can add to a report.

Records are placed together because they have the same value in a field (or fields). This is how the group header and footer sections are automatically re-created each time the value in a field the report is grouped on changes. You will not see this in the design window. The process of creating another group each time the value changes is dynamic processing that happens behind the scenes, as they say. This is how you can create totals for a group. If you are shaking your head, after you complete the first exercise in this lesson, this should make more sense.

Grouping Tips

Below are some tips that I follow to help determine if a report needs a group and if so, which fields to group on.

① Reports that retrieve hundreds or thousands of records, probably would be easier to read, if nothing else, if there were one or two groups.

② If you need to provide a count or subtotal for a field.

③ If the report needs statistical information.

Insert Group Dialog Box

The options on the **COMMON** tab are used to create the groups. At a minimum, the field to group on (the first drop down list shown in Figure 6-1) and the sorting order of the group (the second drop down list shown in Figure 6-1) have to be selected. Date and Boolean fields have an additional option that can be set. The **OPTIONS** tab will be discussed later. There are two ways to open the **INSERT GROUP** dialog box, as discussed below.

     ① Click the **INSERT GROUP** button on the Insert Tools toolbar.

     ② Insert ⇒ Group.

The **GROUP BY** field is the first drop down list on the Common tab. It contains all of the fields that the report can be grouped by. This list contains the fields that are on the report and the fields in tables that are associated with the report. You can also use formula fields as the field to group on.

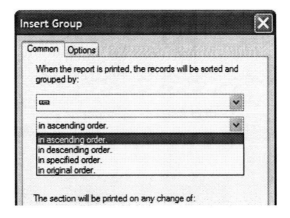

Figure 6-1 Insert Group dialog box

 Memo fields will not appear in the group by drop down list because they cannot be used as a field to group on.

The **GROUP SORT ORDER** field is the second drop down list on the Common tab. The sort order determines the order that the groups will appear on the report. Table 6-1 explains the group sorting options. The first four options in the table are in the second drop down list on the Insert Group dialog box.

Sorting Option	Description
In Ascending Order	Text fields will be sorted in A-Z order. Numeric fields will be sorted in low to high order. Date group fields will be sorted in oldest to most recent date order.
In Descending Order	Text fields will be sorted in Z-A order. Numeric fields will be sorted in high to low order. Date group fields will be sorted in most recent to oldest date order.
In Specified Order	This option allows you to select the order of the groups. This is known as **CUSTOM GROUPING** and is discussed below. An example of a custom group would be to rank customers by the amount of sales they placed last year.
In Original Order	This option will leave the data in the order that it is retrieved from in the database. It may be me, but I don't find this option very useful.
Use A Formula As Group Sort Order	Check this option if you want to allow the person running the report to be able to sort the groups in ascending or descending order.

Table 6-1 Group sorting options explained

 Once a field is selected to be grouped on, it will appear under the text, **THE SECTION WILL BE PRINTED ON ANY CHANGE OF** at the bottom of the Insert Group dialog box.

The **DATE/TIME** option is only available when a date or date/time field is selected in the Group By drop down list. Figure 6-2 shows the options for date/time fields.

The **BOOLEAN** option is only available when a Boolean field (ex. true/false or yes/no field) is selected in the group by drop down list. The Boolean sort process does not work like the other sort options. Boolean fields sort false before true, when the ascending sort order is selected. The groups are created when there are changes from yes to no, or from true to false in the report data. The exception to this is the **ON ANY CHANGE** option. Figure 6-3 shows the options for Boolean fields. Table 6-2 explains the Boolean options.

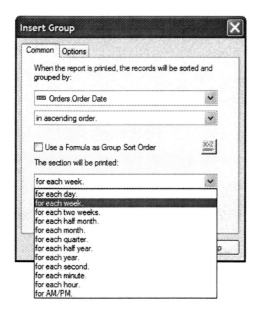

Figure 6-2 Date/Time field options

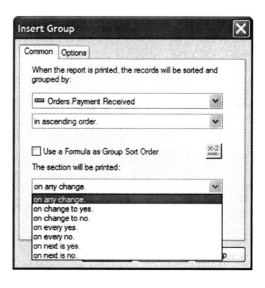

Figure 6-3 Boolean field options

 In addition to using the Insert Group dialog box to create and edit groups, you can also use the Group Expert to create and edit groups.

Option	Description
On any change	This is the default option and will sort the values and place them next to each other.
On change to yes	Creates a new group each time a **True** value comes after a False value. (1)
On change to no	Creates a new group each time a **False** value comes after a True value. (1)
On every yes	This option creates a group that always ends with a True value and includes any records in the middle that have a False value, back to the previous True value. (1)
On every no	This option creates a group that always ends with a False value and includes any records in the middle that have a True value, back to the previous False value. (1)
On next is yes	This option creates groups that always start with a True value and includes all records in the middle that have a False value until the next record with a True value is found. (1)
On next is no	This option creates groups that always start with a False value and includes all records in the middle that have a True value until the next record with a False value is found. (1)

Table 6-2 Boolean field options explained

(1) The records are not sorted if this option is selected.

Custom Grouping

If the ascending and descending sort options are not sufficient, you can create custom groups by selecting the **IN SPECIFIED ORDER** option in the second drop down list shown earlier in Figure 6-1. There are two custom group options available on the Insert Group dialog box: User defined sort order and User defined groups, which will be covered later in this lesson.

User Defined Sort Order

When you select this option, a tab called **SPECIFIED ORDER** will appear on the Insert Group dialog box as shown in Figure 6-4.

The **NAMED GROUP** drop down list contains all of the values for the group field. Select the values in the order that you want the groups to appear in on the report, as shown in Figure 6-5.

Once you add one value to the Named Group list, the **OTHERS** tab shown in Figure 6-6 will open. The options on this tab allow you to determine what you want to happen to the group values that are not added to the Named Group list on the Specified Order tab. Table 6-3 explains the options on the Others tab.

Figure 6-4 Specified Order tab

 You do not have to order all of the group values. You can select just the ones that you need.

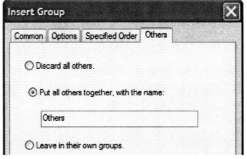

Figure 6-6 Others tab options

Figure 6-5 Values placed in order

Option	Description
Discard all others	Selecting this option causes the group values (and their detail records) that are not selected on the Specified Order tab to not be displayed on the report.
Put all others together, with the name	Selecting this option allows you to put all of the group values that are not selected on the Specified Order tab together under one group name that you type in the text box.
Leave in their own groups	Selecting this option will print all of the group values that you selected on the Specified Order tab first on the report. The remaining group values will be printed after, in ascending order.

Table 6-3 Others tab options explained

Sorting Records

Sorting records is the second task that has to be completed. Like grouping, sorting allows you to rearrange the order that records appear on the report. Data can be sorted by any database field, formula or SQL Expression. Data cannot be sorted by a memo field. There are two types of sorting, as discussed below.

① You can sort the report as it is. The L5.1 report could be sorted by customer name. Another way to sort this report would be by postal code.

② You can sort the records within a group. After the groups for a report have been determined, you may decide that the report would be more meaningful if the detail records in the group were sorted. If you do not specify a sort order, the records in each group will print in the order that they are retrieved from the table.

The **RECORD SORT EXPERT** dialog box shown in Figure 6-7 lets you select the options to sort the records in the details section of the report.

The Record Sort Expert will show group fields in the Sort Field list box. This is done to show that the detail records will be sorted within the group. Group field sorting is done before detail record sorting. This expert does not sort groups. You can sort in ascending or descending order on each field. There are two ways to open the dialog box as discussed below.

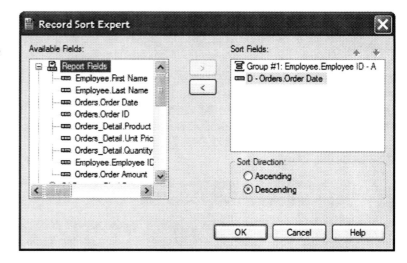

Figure 6-7 Record Sort Expert dialog box

① Click the **RECORD SORT EXPERT** button on the Expert Tools toolbar.

② Report ⇒ Record Sort Expert.

 In addition to clicking on a field in the Available Fields section and clicking the arrow button to add it to the Sort Fields list box, you can also drag fields to the Sort Fields dialog box.

What I found interesting is that if you click on a group field in the Sort Fields list, all of the buttons become disabled on the dialog box. I suspect that this is because Crystal Reports is trying to protect you from changing the group order. Don't worry. If you need to change the order of the groups, you can change them on the design window by dragging them or you can use the Group Expert.

 The order that fields are added to the **SORT FIELDS** section of the Record Sort Expert is the order that the records will be sorted in. If you discover that the fields are in the wrong order in the Sort Fields section, click on the field that is not in the correct place, then click the Up or Down arrow buttons that are across from the words "Sort Fields", to move the field to the correct location.

Summary Information

This is the third major task that has to be completed when groups are created. One reason that groups are created is to make the report easier to read. Another reason groups are created is to provide summary information for fields in the details section of the report.

These summary calculated fields are usually placed in the group footer section of the report. As you learned in Lesson 2, formulas, in this case, summary fields can also be placed in the group header section. Students have asked me how it is possible that summary fields that are in the group header section contain accurate totals. The answer is somewhat beyond the scope of this workbook, but I will answer the question because it may help some people understand and allow them to use summary fields in the group header section with confidence, when needed.

Crystal Reports actually builds (processes) the entire report before it is printed. This means that values for summary fields, regardless of where they are placed on the report, are calculated before the report prints.

The two types of calculations that you can perform on text (string) data is counting records in a group and determining the frequency of records in the group. These summary calculations are often also placed in the report footer section to create what is known as a grand total, report total or RUNNING TOTAL. Summary fields that are in the report header or footer section are not dependant on groups. You can create summary calculation fields in the report header and footer if the report does not have any groups. Summary fields in the report header and footer contain totals for all records on the report.

Instead of having to manually count the number of orders that are printed on a report that each customer placed, a calculated field can be added to the report that would count the number of orders and display the number on the report. Each summary field has to be created separately.

> To create a group summary field, the report must have at least one group. If you select the option to create a summary field and the report does not have a group, you will be prompted to create a group. If you place the same summary field in different sections of the report, it will produce different total amounts, which is what should happen.

There are three ways to open the Insert Summary dialog box shown in Figure 6-8 AFTER you have selected the field that you need to create a summary calculation field for, as discussed below. If the field that you need to create a summary calculation for is not on the report, you have to select option two or three below.

① Right-click and select Insert Summary.
② Click the INSERT SUMMARY button on the Insert Tools toolbar.
③ Insert ⇒ Summary.

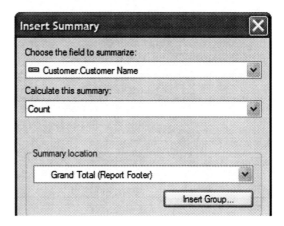

Figure 6-8 Insert Summary dialog box

There are two categories of summary calculations that you can create, as discussed below.

① The **Text** field summary calculation options are explained in Table 6-4. Text fields can only create the calculations in Table 6-4.
② The **Numeric** field summary calculation options are explained in Table 6-5. They can also be used with currency fields. Numeric fields can also create the calculations in Table 6-4.

Text Summary Calculation Options	
Calculation	**Description**
Count	Counts all of the records in the group.
Distinct Count	Counts all of the unique values in the selected field in the group.
Maximum	Finds the highest value in the field that is being grouped on.
Minimum	Finds the lowest value in the field that is being grouped on.
Mode	Finds the most frequently used value in the field that is being grouped on.
N^{th} Largest, N is:	Lets you select a number (the N is a value) and calculate the Nth largest value in the selected field in the group. An example would be if you wanted to find out what the third (N^{th} largest) largest order amount (N) is in the group.
N^{th} Most Frequent, N is:	Lets you select a number (the N is a value) and calculate the Nth most frequently occurring value in the selected field in the group. An example would be if you wanted to find out which product was ordered the most in the group, you would enter a 1 in this field. This is similar to the Mode function, but it is not limited to the frequent occurrences.
N^{th} Smallest, N is:	Lets you select a number (the N is a value) and calculate the Nth smallest occurring value in the selected field in the group. An example would be if you wanted to find out what the fifth (N^{th} smallest) smallest order amount (N) is in the group. You would enter a 5 in this field.

Table 6-4 Text summary calculation options explained

Numeric Summary Calculation Options	
Calculation	**Description**
Average	Finds the average value of all of the values in the field that is being grouped on.
Correlation With	Finds the relationship between the selected field and another field in the database or on the report.
Covariance With	Finds the difference (often called the variance) between the selected field and another field in the database or on the report.
Median	Finds the middle value of all the values in the field that is being grouped on.
Mode	Finds the most frequently used value in the field that is being grouped on.
P^{th} percentile, P is:	Lets you select a percent (the P is value) between 0 and 100 and calculates that percentile of the values in the field that is being grouped on.
Population Standard Deviation	Calculates how far from the mean (the average) each value in the selected field deviates.
Population Variance	Divides the sum of the number of items in the population. The result is the population variance.
Sample Standard Deviation	Calculates the mean (the average) value for the items in the sample.
Sample Variance	Calculates the square of the standard deviation of the sample.
Sum	Adds the values in the selected field to get a total.
Weighted Average With	Calculates the average, by the number of times the value in the selected field is in the group.

Table 6-5 Numeric summary calculation options explained

Date and Boolean fields can only be used in the following types of calculations: count, distinct count, maximum, minimum, mode, N^{th} largest, N^{th} most frequent and N^{th} smallest.

In addition to the summary options that you learned about in Tables 6-4 and 6-5 above, the summary options in Table 6-6 are also available. They are located at the bottom of the Insert Summary dialog box.

Option	Description
Summary Location	This option allows you to select the section of the report where you want to place the summary field. If you open the drop down list, you will see the options that are available. The good thing is that you are not limited to the options in the drop down list. You can manually copy or move the summary field to another section of the report in the design window.
Show as a percentage of	This option will calculate a comparison of the percent of one group that is part of a larger group. If selected, this option lets you select the group or total that you want the comparison to be based on. For example, this option can calculate the percent of sales for June compared to the sales for the entire year. The result that would display will tell you (out of 100%), what percent the sales in June accounted for, compared to the sales for the entire year. This option is not available for all types of calculations. (2)
Insert across hierarchy	On reports that have hierarchical groups (groups that have parent/child relationships), an identical summary field will be added to all subgroups under the primary hierarchical group. An example of a report that could have hierarchical groups would be one that displays a list of department managers (the parent group) and the employees (the child group) that are in each department.

Table 6-6 Summary options explained

 (2) Percentage summaries cannot be placed in the report footer section.

 Headings are not automatically created for group summary fields like they are for fields in the details section.

 Many of the exercises in this lesson will have you create a title for the report or a title for a field. When you see the phrase "Create a title", that means to add a text object to the report and type in the specified text. Report titles should be placed in the page header section unless stated otherwise. They should also be centered across the report.

If all of the summary calculation options seem a little confusing right now don't worry, you will only see options in the drop down list that are available for the field type that you select to create the calculation for.

Creating Groups

The first five reports that you modify in this lesson will show you how to apply a variety of group and sorting options effectively. The name of each exercise describes how the data will be grouped. You will also learn more formatting techniques. As you will see, the more data that you add to a report, the more the report needs to be formatted.

Exercise 6.1: Group Customer Information By Region

In this exercise you will modify a report to include the following group and sorting options. These options also allow you to create totals for the group.

① Group the data by the region field and sort the group in ascending order.
② Sort the detail records in each group in ascending order by the Postal Code field.

③ Create a count of detail records in each group.

1. Save the L4.11 report as `L6.1 Customer info by region`.

2. Open the Insert Group dialog box.

3. Open the first drop down list and select the **REGION** field from the Customer table, then click OK.

Notice that a **GROUP HEADER** and **FOOTER** section have been added to the report, as illustrated in Figure 6-9. If you also wanted to group this report on a second field, you would see a second set of group header and footer sections, as shown in Figure 6-10.

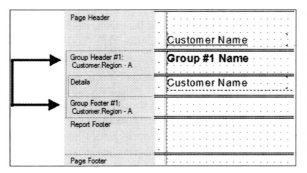

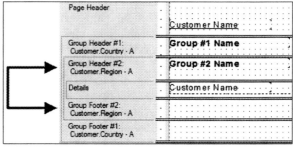

Figure 6-9 Group header and footer sections added to the report

Figure 6-10 Two sets of group header and footer sections

 If you cannot see the entire group name on the left side of the design window as shown above in Figure 6-10, you can drag the section bar below the group section down until you can see the full name. Keep in mind that doing this will cause additional space to be added to that section of the report when you preview or print it. A better solution would be to turn on the **SHORT SECTION NAMES** option, by following the steps below.

How To Turn The Short Section Names On

1. Right-click in the **REPORT SECTION** of the design window. You will see the shortcut menu shown in Figure 6-11. Select the option **SHOW SHORT SECTION NAMES**. The report section should look like the one shown in Figure 6-12.

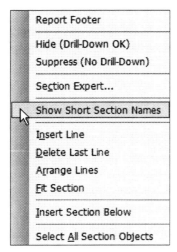

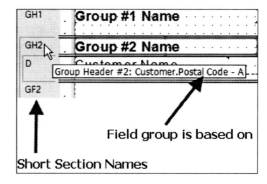

Figure 6-12 Report section with the short section names option turned on

Figure 6-11 Report section shortcut menu

If you hold the mouse over the **GROUP SECTION NAME** as illustrated above in Figure 6-12, you will be able to see which field the group is based on and the order that the group is sorted in.

2.   Preview the report. It should look like the one shown in Figure 6-13.

	Customer Name	Address1	Region	Country	Postal Code
	Abu Dhabi				
	UAE Cycle	Post Box: 278	Abu Dhabi	United Arab Emirate	3453
	AL				
	Psycho-Cycle	8287 Scott Road	AL	USA	35818
	The Great Bike Shop	1922 Beach Crescent	AL	USA	35857
	Benny - The Spokes Person	1020 Oak Way	AL	USA	35861
	Alsace				
	Sports Alsace	11, rue Clemenceau	Alsace	France	67100
	Mulhouse Vélos	4 avenue de la Liberation	Alsace	France	68100
	Ankara				
	Ankara Bicycle Company	PO Box 2121	Ankara	Turkey	443665

Figure 6-13 Customer information grouped by region

Notice that the group name is bold on the report. This makes it easier to know where each group starts. If you look in the group tree section on the left of Figure 6-13 above, you will see all of the groups that the report has. If you scroll down the list of groups and click on the **PA** group, the report will jump to that page and will display the customer information in the PA region, as shown in Figure 6-14.

				9 of 9+
OR				
Whistler Rentals	4501 Third Street	OR	USA	97051
Rad Bikes	8217 Prince Edward Place	OR	USA	97068
PA				
Clean Air Transportation Co.	1867 Thurlow Lane	PA	USA	19453
Insane Cycle	5198 Argus Place	PA	USA	19442
Backpedal Cycle Shop	743 Three Rivers Way	PA	USA	19178
Rocky Roadsters	1430 Hastings Boulevard	PA	USA	19440
Tek Bikes	8018 Meacon Crescent	PA	USA	19144

Figure 6-14 Customers in the PA region

 By default, group name fields are added to the group header section of the report. If at some point you decide that you do not want the group name to automatically be added to the group header section, you can turn the **INSERT GROUP NAME WITH GROUP** option off on the Layout tab on the Options dialog box. If you turn this option off and then need to add a group name to a specific report, you can, without turning this option back on.

Sort The Detail Records

As you can see in Figure 6-13 shown earlier, the detail records in each group are not sorted on any field. Unless you specify a sort order, the detail records will appear in the report based on the order they are stored in the database. In this part of the exercise you will sort the detail records by the Postal Code field (the Zip Code).

1.   Open the Record Sort Expert dialog box and click on the Postal Code field in the **AVAILABLE FIELDS** section, then click the **>** button. Select the **ASCENDING** sort order, if it is not already selected. Figure 6-15 shows the sort options that you should have selected. Click OK.

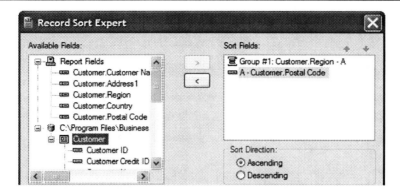

Figure 6-15 Report sort options

Notice that the group information for the report is the first entry in the **SORT FIELDS** section of the Record Sort Expert dialog box shown above in Figure 6-15. This is done to outline the sort order for the entire report. The first way that the report will be sorted is by group. Remember that the group is sorted in ascending order, which is denoted by the **A** at the end of the group field. If the field was sorted in descending order, you would see a **D** at the end of the field.

 If you need to sort a report by a persons name and the name is in two fields, you should sort on the last name field first and then sort on the first name field.

The detail records in each group will be sorted in ascending order by the Postal Code field. If you wanted to sort on other fields in the group, you can do that also, as shown in Figure 6-16. In this example, adding the Country field means that within each group, the detail records would be sorted by Postal Code first and then within each Postal Code in the group, the records would be sorted by Country. In reality, these sort options would produce strange results. It is shown here for illustration purposes only.

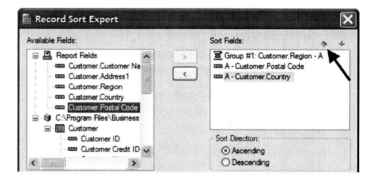

Figure 6-16 Second field in group to be sorted on

A better way to sort on these two fields would be to sort on the Country field first in each group, because there are several Postal Codes within each Country. If you wanted to sort on the Country field first, instead of the Postal Code field, you would click on the Country field and then click the **UP** arrow, as illustrated above in Figure 6-16. This would move the Country field up, as shown in Figure 6-17.

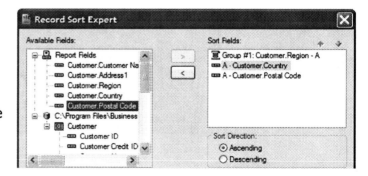

Figure 6-17 Sort order of the detail records changed

2. Save the changes. You will see the message shown in Figure 6-18. Click **YES** to generate (refresh) the data for the report.

This message is letting you know that the changes that you have made to the report may require the data to be refreshed because you may not have all of the data based on the modified sorting and grouping options that have been selected. You will get this message when you sort records and have the **SAVE DATA WITH REPORT** option turned on.

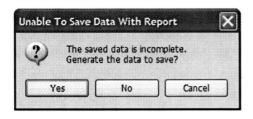

Figure 6-18 Generate data message

3. Preview the report. Go to the PA group. You should see the records shown in Figure 6-19. Notice the different order of the detail records in this version of the report, compared to the order of the detail records in the report shown earlier in Figure 6-14. Leave the report open to complete the next part of the exercise.

PA				
Tek Bikes	8018 Meacon Crescent	PA	USA	19144
Backpedal Cycle Shop	743 Three Rivers Way	PA	USA	19178
Rocky Roadsters	1430 Hastings Boulevard	PA	USA	19440
Insane Cycle	5198 Argus Place	PA	USA	19442
Clean Air Transportation Co.	1867 Thurlow Lane	PA	USA	19453

Figure 6-19 Report with detail record sort order added

Count Summary Field Overview

As you learned earlier in this lesson, creating summary fields is the third step in the grouping and sorting process. In this part of the exercise you will create a summary field that will count the number of detail records in each group.

Create The Count Summary Field

1. On the Insert Summary dialog box, open the first drop down list and select the Customer ID field.

2. Open the second drop down list and select **COUNT**. You should see all of the options that were discussed earlier in Tables 6-4 and 6-5 for Customer ID field because it is a numeric field.

 Notice that you can create a group from this dialog box. If you click the **INSERT GROUP** button, you will see the Insert Group dialog box that you saw earlier in Figure 6-1.

3. Open the **SUMMARY LOCATION** drop down list and select the Group 1 option. Figure 6-20 shows the summary options that you should have selected.

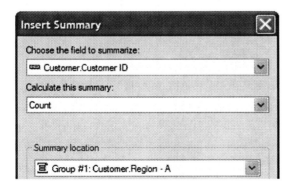

Figure 6-20 Summary options

4. Click OK. The summary field should be in the group footer section. Save the changes. If prompted to generate the data, click Yes, then preview the report. It should look like the one shown in Figure 6-21. The number in bold below the dotted lines is the count field that you just created.

Customer Name	Address1	Region	Country	Postal Code
Abu Dhabi				
UAE Cycle	Post Box: 278	Abu Dhabi	United Arab Emirate	3453
		1		
AL				
Psycho-Cycle	8287 Scott Road	AL	USA	35818
The Great Bike Shop	1922 Beach Crescent	AL	USA	35857
Benny - The Spokes Person	1020 Oak Way	AL	USA	35861
		3		
Alsace				
Sports Alsace	11, rue Clemenceau	Alsace	France	67100
Mulhouse Vélos	4 avenue de la Liberation	Alsace	France	68100
		2		

Figure 6-21 Report with the summary field added

When used with detail level fields, summary functions like Average and Count will not include records when the detail level field is null because null fields do not contain anything, which is different then an empty string or a zero.

For example, if you were creating a summary field that counts on the city field and some records did not have any data in the city field and the database was set to use **NULL VALUES**, records that fall into this category would print on the report, but would not be included in the count summary calculation.

Often, this may not be what you want to happen. If this is the case, checking the **CONVERT DATABASE NULL VALUES TO DEFAULT** option on the Report Options dialog box will automatically convert the null values in the database to an empty string for string fields or zero for numeric fields. Selecting this option will include records in the count or average summary calculation. If you want this to be the default option for all reports, check the same option on the Reporting tab on the Options dialog box.

Modify The Report
The report would look better if the following changes were made.

① Add a report title, print date and page number.
② Change the Postal Code heading to Zip Code.
③ Change the Address1 heading to Address.
④ Delete the Region field from the details section of the report. The field is not needed in this section because it is the field that the report is grouped on.
⑤ Create a title for the summary field that you created.
⑥ Create a grand total for the number of customers that are displayed on the report. Place this field in the report footer section.
⑦ Rearrange the fields in the details section so that the report is easier to read.

Add A Report Title, Date And Page Number
1. Make the page header section of the report longer, so that you will have room to add the report titles. Move all of the headings in the page header section down.

2. Create a report title and type `Customer Information Grouped By Region` in the object. Make the font size 16 and make the title bold.

3. Create a second report title and type `Sorted By Zip Code` in the object. Make the font size 14 and make the title bold.

4. Center both of these titles across the page.

5. Add the Print Date special field to the page header section below the second report title, on the left, then add the Page N of M special field across from the Print Date field on the right and right align the Page Number field.

Change The Field Headings And Delete Fields

1. Change the Address1 field heading to `Address`, then change the Postal Code field heading to `Zip Code`.

2. Delete the Region field from the details section.

3. Move the Address field and heading over to the right and make the Customer Name field wider.

Create A Title For The Summary Field

1. Create a title for the summary field and type `Total # of customers in region -` in the object. Right align the title.

2. Move the summary field over and place the field title that you just created before it, then remove the bold from the summary field and left align the field.

3. Make the group footer section a little longer so that there will be more blank space on the report before the next group prints.

Create A Grand Total Summary Field

Grand totals are also known as **RUNNING TOTALS** because they keep a total for all of the detail records that are included on the report. Earlier in this lesson you learned how to create group summary totals, which are also known as "subtotals". The difference between a group summary total and a running total is that a running total field cannot be summarized.

Another difference between group summary total fields and running total fields is that group summary total fields are automatically reset to zero each time a new group is started, as shown earlier in Figure 6-21. Running Total fields have the option of being reset to zero.

Grand or running total fields that are placed in the report footer section include all of the records in the report, regardless of which group the detail records are in. Earlier in this lesson, I stated that depending on the section of the report that the summary field is placed in, you will get different results. The summary field that you will copy to the report footer section in this exercise will demonstrate this.

1. Right-click on the summary field in the group footer section and select **COPY**.

2. Right-click in the report and select **PASTE**, then click in the report footer section where you want to place the field.

3. Create a title for the summary field in the report footer section and type `Grand Total # of customers on this report -` in the object. Place this title at the 2 inch mark.

4. Move the grand total field to the right of the title.

You could create another summary field by using the Insert Summary dialog box, just like the one you created for the group footer section and place it in the report footer section. I find it easier to copy the field and place the second field in the section that I need it in. You can also create a summary field by right-clicking on the field in the details section and selecting Insert ⇒ Summary or Insert ⇒ Running Total.

Rearrange The Fields

1. Rearrange the fields in the details section so that the Customer Name field starts at the half inch mark.

2. Delete the dotted line in the details section. The report layout should look like the one shown in Figure 6-22. Save the changes.

   Page 1 should look like the one shown in Figure 6-23.
   The last page of the report should look like the one shown in Figure 6-24. The total number of pages in the report depends on the spacing that you have in each section of the report. Adjust the spacing if necessary, so that it is readable.

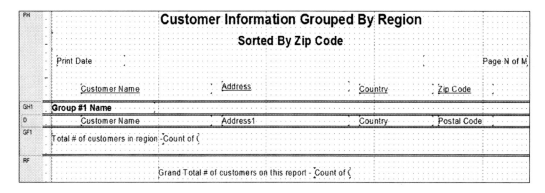

Figure 6-22 L6.1 report layout

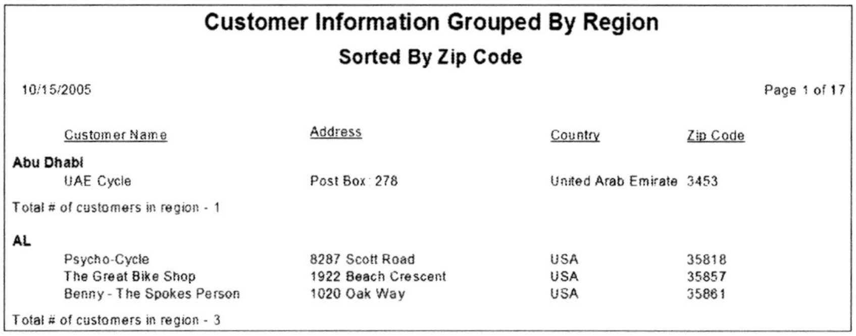

Figure 6-23 Page 1 of the L6.1 Customer Info By Region report

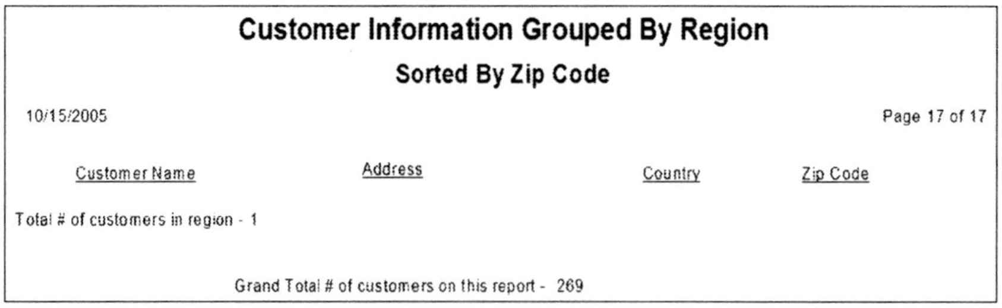

Figure 6-24 Last page of the L6.1 Customer Info By Region report

3. If you open the Field Explorer and click on the plus sign in front of the **GROUP NAME FIELDS** option, you will see the Region group that you created, as illustrated in Figure 6-25. Close the report.

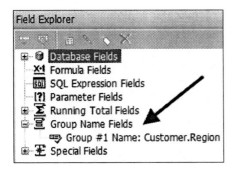

Figure 6-25 Group Name Fields section of the Field Explorer illustrated

You can drag the group name object from the **GROUP NAME FIELDS** section of the Field Explorer on to the report. If you prefer to keep the data in the group header or footer section visible, but not display it on the report, you can suppress the section.

Exercise 6.2: Group Orders By Customer

In this exercise you will modify a report to include the following group and sorting options.

① Group on the Customer Name field and sort the group in ascending order.
② Sort the detail records in each group in ascending order by Order Date.
③ Provide a count of detail records for each customer in each group.
④ Create a total amount per customer based on the order amount field. This will let the reader of the report know the total amount of the orders placed by each customer.

These options will create counts and totals for the group. The changes that you will make to the report will place all of the orders for each customer together. This will make the report more effective, because you will be able to see all of a customers orders in one place.

In Exercise 6.1 you created a group based on a field that was not being printed on the report. Groups are often created on fields that are printed on the report, but it is not a requirement.

1. Save the L5.4 report as `L6.2 Orders by customer`.

2. On the Insert Group dialog box, open the first drop down list and select the **CUSTOMER NAME** field, if it is not already selected. Click OK. The report should look like the one shown in Figure 6-26.

Customer Name	Order Date	Ship Date	Order Amount	Order ID	Unit Price
Alley Cat Cycles					
Alley Cat Cycles	1/8/2004 12:00:00AM	1/8/2004 1:30:00AM	$5,879.70	1,151	$2,939.85
Alley Cat Cycles	9/28/2004 12:00:00A	9/30/2004 12:00:00A	$2,559.63	2,157	$539.85
Alley Cat Cycles	9/28/2004 12:00:00A	9/30/2004 12:00:00A	$2,559.63	2,157	$313.36
Alley Cat Cycles	10/27/2004 12:00:00.	11/6/2004 12:00:00A	$2,699.55	2,272	$899.85
Alley Cat Cycles	1/31/2005 12:00:00A	2/3/2005 12:00:00AM	$9,290.30	2,664	$2,792.86
Alley Cat Cycles	1/31/2005 12:00:00A	2/3/2005 12:00:00AM	$9,290.30	2,664	$455.86
Alley Cat Cycles	2/19/2005 12:00:00A	2/22/2005 12:00:00A	$8,819.55	2,735	$2,939.85
Alley Cat Cycles	2/19/2005 12:00:00A	2/22/2005 12:00:00A	$8,819.55	2,735	$2,939.85
Aruba Sport					
Aruba Sport	6/5/2004 12:00:00AM	6/8/2004 12:00:00AM	$5,879.70	3,079	$2,939.85
Athens Bicycle Co.					
Athens Bicycle Co.	6/8/2004 12:00:00AM	6/18/2004 12:00:00A	$8,819.55	3,097	$2,939.85

Figure 6-26 Orders grouped by customer

Sort The Detail Records

As you can see in Figure 6-26 above, the report is now grouped by customer. The detail records in each group are not sorted. Because orders are entered into the database in the order that they are received, they are often already in date order. There are exceptions to this, including orders that may get changed some how during the ordering process.

Other exceptions that have to be accounted for include how the tables are linked and how the database sends the records to Crystal Reports. To be on the safe side, it is best to control the sort order. In this exercise that means that you should sort the records by the Order Date field to ensure that they are in date order, if that is what the requirement of the report calls for.

1. On the Record Sort Expert dialog box, click on the Order Date field, then click the **>** button.

2. Select the ascending sort order, if it is not already selected. Figure 6-27 shows the sort options that should be selected. Click OK. Save the changes and refresh the data.

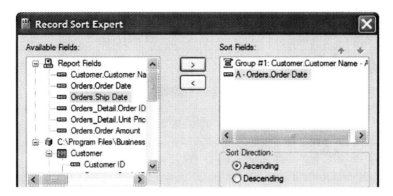

Figure 6-27 Sort options

Total Summary Fields Overview

In this part of the exercise you will create a summary field that will create a total dollar amount of orders for each customer. You will also create a count to show the number of orders for each customer.

 The default summary type is **SUM** for numeric fields.
The default summary type is **MAXIMUM** for Boolean, date and string fields.

Create The Total Summary Field

This summary field will create a total dollar amount of orders for each customer.

1. On the Insert Summary dialog box, open the first drop down list and select the Order Amount field, then open the second drop down list and select **SUM**.

2. Open the Summary Location drop down list and select the Group 1 option. Figure 6-28 shows the summary options that should be selected. Click OK. The order amount summary field should be in the group footer section.

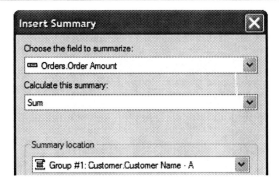

Figure 6-28 Summary options

Create The Count Summary Field

This summary field will create a count of the number of orders for each customer.

1. On the Insert Summary dialog box, open the first drop down list and select the Order ID field, then open the second drop down list and select **COUNT**.

2. Open the Summary Location drop down list and select the Group 1 option. Click OK. The count summary field should be in the group footer section.

Create The Distinct Count Summary Field

The distinct count summary will only count the information in a field once. If there are 20 orders for one customer, the distinct count will only count that customer once. This will let you create a count for the total number of customers that are on the report.

1. On the Insert Summary dialog box, open the first drop down list and select the Customer Name field, if it is not already selected, then open the second drop down list and select **DISTINCT COUNT**. Notice that the only options that are available for this text field are the ones discussed earlier in Table 6-4.

2. Open the Summary Location drop down list and select the **GRAND TOTAL (REPORT FOOTER)** option, if it is not already selected. The distinct count only needs to appear once, at the end of the report. Figure 6-29 shows the summary options that should be selected. Click OK. The distinct count summary field should be in the report footer section.

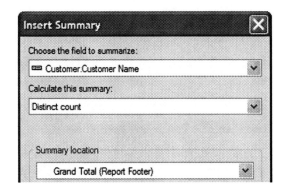

Figure 6-29 Distinct count summary options

3. Save the changes and refresh the data. The report should look like the one shown in Figure 6-30. As you can see, the report needs a little work.

Customer Name	Order Date	Ship Date	Order Amount	Order ID	Unit Price
Alley Cat Cycles					
Alley Cat Cycles	1/8/2004 12:00:00AM	1/8/2004 1:30:00AM	$5,879.70	1,151	$2,939.85
Alley Cat Cycles	9/28/2004 12:00:00A	9/30/2004 12:00:00A	$2,559.63	2,157	$539.85
Alley Cat Cycles	9/28/2004 12:00:00A	9/30/2004 12:00:00A	$2,559.63	2,157	$313.36
Alley Cat Cycles	10/27/2004 12:00:00.	11/6/2004 12:00:00A	$2,699.55	2,272	$899.85
Alley Cat Cycles	1/31/2005 12:00:00A	2/3/2005 12:00:00AM	$9,290.30	2,664	$2,792.86
Alley Cat Cycles	1/31/2005 12:00:00A	2/3/2005 12:00:00AM	$9,290.30	2,664	$455.86
Alley Cat Cycles	2/19/2005 12:00:00A	2/22/2005 12:00:00A	$8,819.55	2,735	$2,939.85
Alley Cat Cycles	2/19/2005 12:00:00A	2/22/2005 12:00:00A	$8,819.55	2,735	$2,939.85
			$49,918.21	**8**	
Aruba Sport					
Aruba Sport	6/5/2004 12:00:00AM	6/8/2004 12:00:00AM	$5,879.70	3,079	$2,939.85
			$5,879.70	**1**	
Athens Bicycle Co.					
Athens Bicycle Co.	6/8/2004 12:00:00AM	6/18/2004 12:00:00A	$8,819.55	3,097	$2,939.85
			$8,819.55	**1**	

Figure 6-30 Orders by customer report

If you view the last page of the report, you will see the number 102. This is the distinct count summary field that you just created, which shows how many customers are on the report. In the next part of this exercise you will create a title for this field.

Modify The Report

The report would look better if the following changes were made.

    ① Add a report title, print date and page number.
    ② Create titles for the summary fields.
    ③ Create a grand total field and title for the order amount field and for the grand total count of order summary field. Place these fields in the report footer section.
    ④ Remove the time from the order date and ship date fields.
    ⑤ Add a line above all of the summary fields.
    ⑥ Rearrange the fields in the details section so that the report is easier to read.

1. Create a report title and type `Customer Orders` in the object. Make the font size 16 and the title bold. Center the title across the page.

> If a report has selection criteria, it is a good idea to incorporate the selection criteria in the report. Doing this lets the reader know what criteria the report is using. This report will print records for orders that were placed after a specific date and have a specific minimum order amount. How, or if you incorporate this information is up to you and the requestors of the report. Keep in mind that business decisions are based off of the data in reports, so providing as much helpful and useful information as possible, is a good thing.

2. Add the Print Date special field to the page header section below the report title on the right, then add the Page N of M special field to the page footer section in the right hand corner and right align this field.

3. Copy both of the summary fields in the group footer section and place them in the report footer section.

> If you select both fields before you select the **COPY** command, you can copy both fields at the same time.

4. Create the field titles in Table 6-7 for the summary fields. The section column refers to the section in the report where the title should be placed.

Summary Field	Section	Title
Order Amount	Group Footer	Total $ amount of orders - (Make the title bold.)
Order ID	Group Footer	Total # orders -
Customer Name	Report Footer	Total # of customers on this report -
Order Amount	Report Footer	Grand Total $ amount of all orders -
Order ID	Report Footer	Grand Total # of orders -

Table 6-7 Field titles for Exercise 6.2

If I know that the report needs several field titles with the same formatting, I create one and then copy it and just change the text. For me, this is quicker than using the Format Painter. Over time, you will find a process that works best for you.

I usually right align titles for calculated fields, when the title is placed right before the calculated field. Doing this reduces the amount of white space between the title and the calculated field. When I do this, I also left align the calculated field to further reduce the space between the field and the title. The other option is to drag the calculated field into the text object.

5. Remove the time from the Order Date and Ship Date fields. Delete the Customer Name field in the details section and remove the bold from the Group Name field.

Group Name objects can be formatted like any other object in the report.

6. Change the Order ID heading to `Order  #`, then format the Order ID and Order ID count summary fields to display as a whole number without a comma.

7. Add a line at the bottom of the group footer section. Change the size of the line to 0.5 pt. Save the changes and leave the report open to complete the next part of the exercise.

Add A Line Above The Summary Fields

1. Move the summary fields in the group footer section down, so that you have room to add the line.

2. Right-click on the Order Amount summary field and select **FORMAT FIELD**, then click on the Border tab. Open the **TOP** drop down list, select **SINGLE** and click OK.

You can also use the **LINE** tool to draw a line. The advantage of using the line option on the Border tab for a field is that if you move or resize the field, the line is automatically re-adjusted. If you use the Line tool and you move or resize the field, you will also have to move or resize the line.

3. Rearrange the fields so that they look like the layout shown in Figure 6-31.

Figure 6-31 L6.2 report layout

4. Save the changes and refresh the data. Page 1 should look like the one shown in Figure 6-32. The report footer section on the last page should look like the one shown in Figure 6-33.

 If you see **###'s** in a field, make the field wider.

Customer Orders

10/14/2005

	Order Date	Ship Date	Order Amount	Order #	Unit Price
Alley Cat Cycles					
	01/08/2004	01/08/2004	$5,879.70	1151	$2,939.85
	09/28/2004	09/30/2004	$2,559.63	2157	$539.85
	09/28/2004	09/30/2004	$2,559.63	2157	$313.36
	10/27/2004	11/06/2004	$2,699.55	2272	$899.85
	01/31/2005	02/03/2005	$9,290.30	2664	$2,792.86
	01/31/2005	02/03/2005	$9,290.30	2664	$455.86
	02/19/2005	02/22/2005	$8,819.55	2735	$2,939.85
	02/19/2005	02/22/2005	$8,819.55	2735	$2,939.85
Total # orders - 8		Total $ amount of orders -	$49,918.21		
Aruba Sport					
	06/05/2004	06/08/2004	$5,879.70	3079	$2,939.85
Total # orders - 1		Total $ amount of orders -	$5,879.70		
Athens Bicycle Co.					
	06/08/2004	06/18/2004	$8,819.55	3097	$2,939.85
Total # orders - 1		Total $ amount of orders -	$8,819.55		

Figure 6-32 Page 1 of the L6.2 Orders by customer report

Total # of customers on this report - 102

Grand Total # of orders - 1,142

Grand Total $ amount of all orders - $ 6,424,118.58

Figure 6-33 Last page of the L6.2 Orders by customer report

5. Make any changes that are needed. Leave the report open to complete the next exercise.

Exercise 6.3: Group Orders By Customer With Averages

It may be useful to the reader of the report to know the average order amount for each customer. The steps below will show you how to create an average summary field.

1. Save the L6.2 report as L6.3 Orders by customer with averages.

2. On the Insert Summary dialog box, open the first drop down list and select the Order Amount field, then open the second drop down list and select **AVERAGE**. Open the Summary Location drop down list and select the Group 1 option, then click OK. The order amount percent summary field should be in the group footer section.

3. Move the percent summary field over to the right, then copy the percent summary field in the group footer section and place the copy in the report footer section. Place it below the last summary field.

4. Create a title for the Order Amount summary field in the group footer section and type Average order amount for customer - in the object. Make the title bold.

5. Create a title for the Order Amount summary field in the report footer section and type Average order amount for all customers - in the object. Make the title bold. Save the changes. The last page of the report should look like the one shown in Figure 6-34. If you need to make any changes, make them now, then close the report.

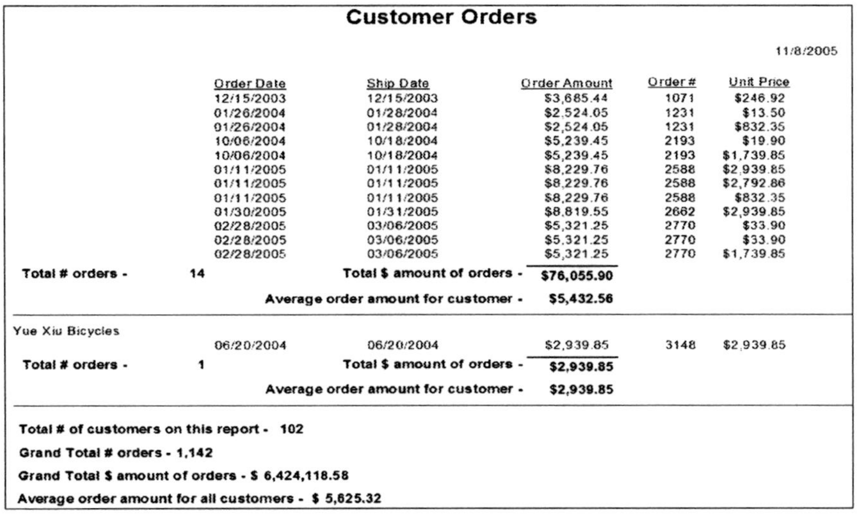

Figure 6-34 L6.3 Orders by customer with averages report

Exercise 6.4: Group 2004 Orders By Shipping Method

In this exercise you will modify a report to include the following group and sorting options. These options also allow you to create totals for the group.

① Group on the ship via field and sort the groups in ascending order.
② Sort the detail records in ascending order on the Order Date field.
③ Create a count of orders in each ship via group.
④ Create a total per customer in each ship via group.

This report currently only displays orders between $2,000 and $5,000. All of the shipping methods are printed, except for Purolator. In order to get a count of detail records for each group and a total per customer, two groups need to be created. To get an accurate count of orders for each shipping method in 2004, the existing selection criteria needs to be deleted and new criteria has to be created.

Create The Ship Via And Customer Name Groups

1. Save the L5.8 report as L6.4 2004 Orders by shipping method.

2. On the Insert Group dialog box, open the first drop down list, select the **SHIP VIA** field and click OK.

3. On the Insert Group dialog box, open the first drop down list and select the **CUSTOMER NAME** field, if it is not already selected and click OK. You should have two groups in the report layout as shown in Figure 6-35.

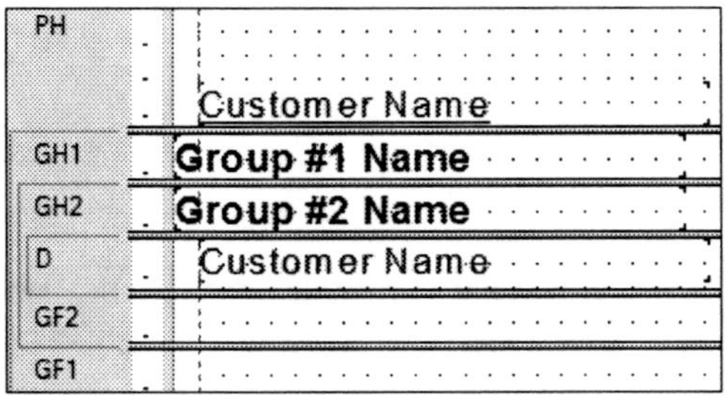

Figure 6-35 Two groups added to the report

Sort The Detail Records

1. On the Record Sort Expert dialog box, click on the Order Date field and click the **>** button.

2. Select the Ascending sort order, if it is not already selected. Figure 6-36 shows the sort options that should be selected. Click OK and save the changes. You do not have to generate the data because you are not finished making changes.

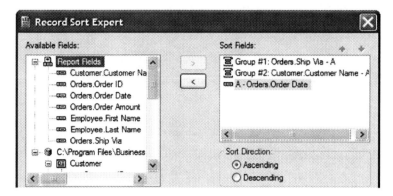

Figure 6-36 Sort options

Change The Selection Criteria

The report that this one is based off of, has selection criteria that is not needed in the report that you are modifying now. This report needs criteria to only display records from 2004.

1. Open the Select Expert and delete all of the current criteria.

2. Create criteria to only include orders placed in 2004.

Create The Summary Fields

This report requires two summary fields: a count of orders and a total dollar amount of orders per customer.

Create The Order ID Count Summary Field

This count summary field will create a total number of orders per customer. It will also be copied to the report footer section to create a grand total number of orders on the report.

1. On the Insert Summary dialog box, open the first drop down list and select the Order ID field. Open the second drop down list and select **COUNT**. Open the Summary Location drop down list and select the Group 2 option. This will place the summary field in the customer name group footer section. Click OK.

Create The Order Amount Summary Field

This summary field will create a total dollar amount per customer. It will also be copied to the report footer section to create a grand total order amount on the report.

1. On the Insert Summary dialog box, open the first drop down list and select the Order Amount field, then open the second drop down list and select **SUM**. Open the Summary Location drop down list and select the Group 2 option, then click OK.

 Summary fields are available in the **REPORT EXPLORER** and **FORMULA WORKSHOP**. They are not available in the Field Explorer.

2. Save the changes and refresh the data. The report should look like the one shown in Figure 6-37.

Customer Name	Order ID	Order Date	Order Amount	Ship Via	First Name	Last
FedEx						
Alley Cat Cycles						
Alley Cat Cycles	2,207	10/11/2004	$72.00	FedEx	Janet	Leve
Alley Cat Cycles	2,301	10/31/2004	$1,664.70	FedEx	Michael	Suy
Alley Cat Cycles	2,361	11/17/2004	$389.65	FedEx	Robert	King
	3		**$2,126.35**			
Backpedal Cycle Shop						
Backpedal Cycle Shop	1,311	02/19/2004	$6,233.05	FedEx	Robert	King
Backpedal Cycle Shop	1,802	07/02/2004	$3,479.70	FedEx	Anne	Dod
Backpedal Cycle Shop	2,198	10/08/2004	$93.50	FedEx	Janet	Leve
	3		**$9,806.25**			
BBS Pty						
BBS Pty	1,776	06/25/2004	$5,913.60	FedEx	Margaret	Pea
BBS Pty	2,067	09/03/2004	$51.60	FedEx	Michael	Suy
	2		**$5,965.20**			

Figure 6-37 L6.4 Orders by shipping method report

Modify The Report

The report would look better if the following changes were made.

① Add a report title, print date and page number.
② Create titles for the summary fields.
③ Create a grand total field and title for the order amount and count of orders summary fields. Place the fields in the report footer section.
④ Rearrange the fields in the details section so that the report is easier to read.

1. Create a report title and type 2004 Orders By Shipping Method in the object. Make the font size 16.

2. Add the Print Date field to the page header section below the report titles on the right, then add the Page N of M field to the page footer section in the right hand corner. Right align the field.

3. Add the logo to the upper left hand corner of the page header section. Change the Order ID field heading to Order #. Format the Order ID field to display as a whole number without a comma.

4. Delete the Customer Name and Ship Via fields from the details section. Remove the bold from the Group 2 Header field and make the field wider. Remove the bold from the summary fields in the Group 2 Footer section.

5. Move the First Name and Last Name fields over to the left. Delete the existing name field headers and create one that says Salesperson. Center this header over the two name fields in the details section.

6. Copy both of the summary fields in the Group 2 Footer section and place them in the Group 1 Footer and report footer sections.

7. Add a line under the totals in the Group 1 and 2 Footer sections. Change the size of the line to 0.5, then make the line in the Group 1 Footer section dotted.

8. Create the field titles in Table 6-8 for the summary fields.

Summary Field	Section	Title
Order Amount	Group 1 Footer	Total order amount for customers -
Order ID Count	Group 1 Footer	Total # orders for customers
Order Amount	Group 2 Footer	Total order amount for customer -
Order ID Count	Group 2 Footer	Total # orders for customer -
Order Amount	Report Footer	Total order amount for all customers -
Order ID	Report Footer	Total # orders for all customers -

Table 6-8 Field titles for Exercise 6.4

9. Copy the Group 1 Header field and place the copy in the Group 1 Footer section, then remove the bold from the field in the Group 1 Footer section.

10. Create a title for the Group 1 Footer section and type `Totals For:` in the object. Create a title for the report footer section and type `Report Grand Totals:` in the object. Make both objects bold.

11. Arrange the fields so that they look like the layout shown in Figure 6-38.

12. Save the changes and refresh the data.
Page 1 should look like the one shown in Figure 6-39.
Page 13 should look like the one shown in Figure 6-40. Notice the totals for the shipping method for FedEx.
The last page should look like the one shown in Figure 6-41.

Leave the report open to complete the next exercise.

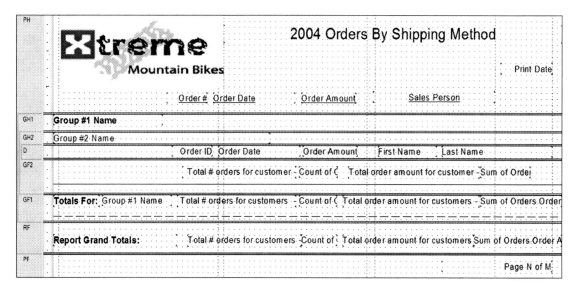

Figure 6-38 L6.4 report layout

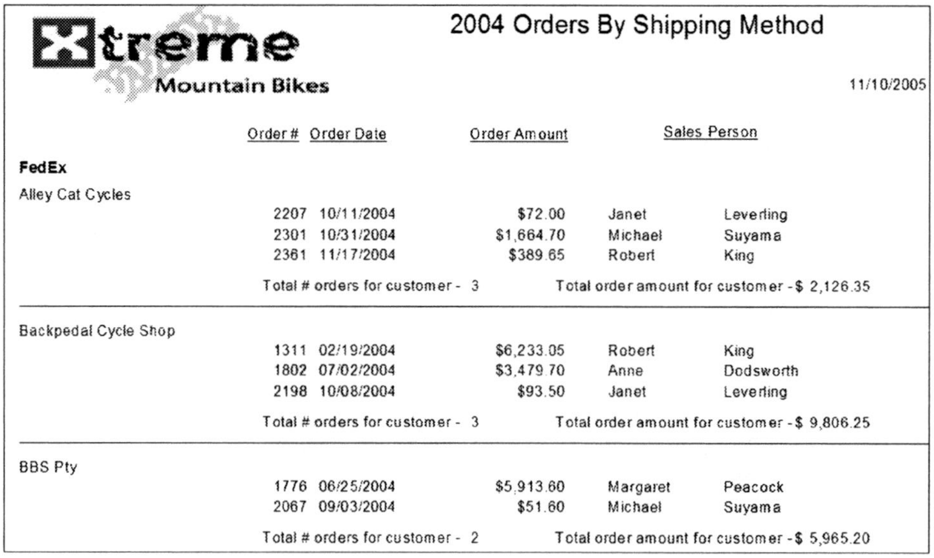

Figure 6-39 Page 1 of the L6.4 2004 Orders by shipping method report

Yue Xiu Bicycles				
	3148 06/20/2004	$2,939.85	Nancy	Davolio
	Total # orders for customer - 1		Total order amount for customer - $ 2,939.85	
Totals For: FedEx	Total # orders for customers - 271		Total order amount for customers - $ 495,054.99	
Loomis				
Alley Cat Cycles				
	1939 08/05/2004	$1,409.55	Margaret	Peacock
	2157 09/28/2004	$2,559.63	Janet	Leverling
	2300 10/30/2004	$1,784.32	Michael	Suyama
	2477 12/11/2004	$1,718.60	Nancy	Davolio
	Total # orders for customer - 4		Total order amount for customer - $ 7,472.10	

Figure 6-40 Page 13 of the L6.4 2004 Orders by shipping method report

Yokohama Biking Fans				
	3174 06/25/2004	$33.90	Nancy	Davolio
	Total # orders for customer - 1		Total order amount for customer - $ 33.90	
Totals For: UPS	Total # orders for customers - 255		Total order amount for customers - $ 540,760.37	
Report Grand Totals:	Total # orders for customers - 1,562		Total order amount for customers $ 2,861,205.48	

Figure 6-41 Last page of the L6.4 2004 Orders by shipping method report

Exercise 6.5: Change The Group Order

The L6.4 report that you just completed is grouped on two fields: Ship Via and Customer Name. If after viewing the report you decide that the groups should be in the opposite order, meaning that the first group should be the Customer Name, you could open the Record Sort Expert and change the group order or you could drag the Customer Name group header (or footer) section of the design window up. You can do this by following the steps below.

1. Save the L6.4 report as L6.5 Change group order.

2. In the design window, click in the Group Header 2 section on the left side of the window, as shown in Figure 6-42 and drag the section up above the Group Header 1 section.

Figure 6-42 Group Header 2 report section selected

Notice that Group Header 1 is now grouped on the Customer Name field. This is now the first field that the report will be grouped on, as shown in Figure 6-43. Refer back to Figure 6-39. The report is no longer grouped by the shipping method first. If you look at the last page of the report, you will see that the report grand totals are the same, but in the L6.5 report, the totals for the shipping method are per customer.

3. Save the changes and close the report.

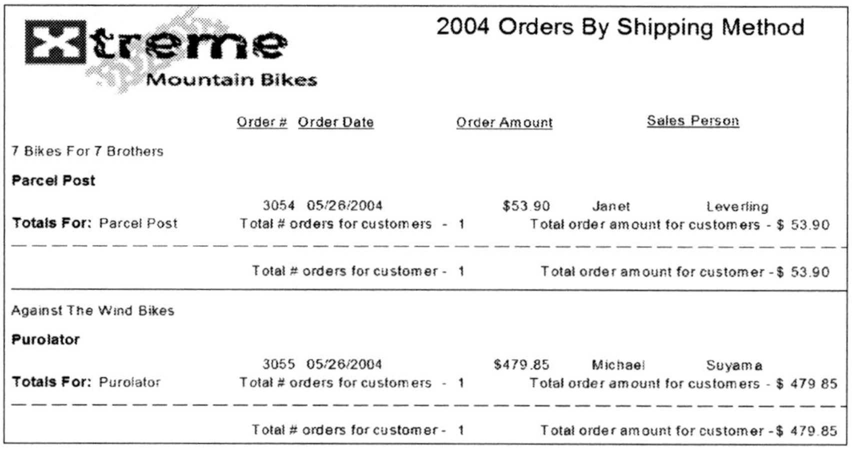

Xtreme Mountain Bikes

2004 Orders By Shipping Method

	Order #	Order Date	Order Amount	Sales Person	
7 Bikes For 7 Brothers					
Parcel Post					
	3054	05/26/2004	$53.90	Janet	Leverling
Totals For: Parcel Post	Total # orders for customers - 1		Total order amount for customers - $ 53.90		
	Total # orders for customer - 1		Total order amount for customer - $ 53.90		
Against The Wind Bikes					
Purolator					
	3055	05/26/2004	$479.85	Michael	Suyama
Totals For: Purolator	Total # orders for customers - 1		Total order amount for customers - $ 479.85		
	Total # orders for customer - 1		Total order amount for customer - $ 479.85		

Figure 6-43 Page 1 of the L6.5 Change group order report

Exercise 6.6: Another Change The Group Order Report

You have already learned that if the same summary field is placed in different sections of the report, it can display a different total. This exercise will demonstrate the differences when the same summary field is placed in different group footer sections of the report.

1. Create a new report. Add the Customer Name, Region and Country fields from the Customer table to the report.

2. Delete the date field in the page header section, then insert a group for the region. Insert another group for the country.

3. Create a summary count field for the region field and place it in the Group Footer 1 section, then create a summary count field for the country field and place it in the Group Footer 1 section.

4. Format the country summary field so that it only displays whole numbers (meaning no decimal points), then duplicate the country summary count field and place it in the Group Footer 2 section.

5. Left align the three summary count fields, then save the report as `L6.6 Change group order`. The report should look like the one shown in Figure 6-44.

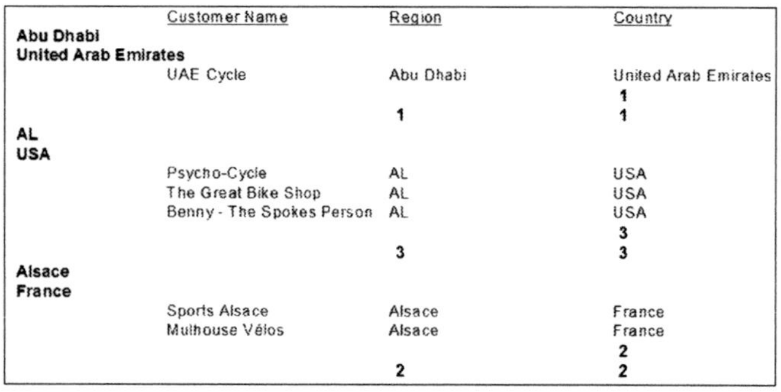

	Customer Name	Region	Country
Abu Dhabi			
United Arab Emirates			
	UAE Cycle	Abu Dhabi	United Arab Emirates
			1
		1	**1**
AL			
USA			
	Psycho-Cycle	AL	USA
	The Great Bike Shop	AL	USA
	Benny - The Spokes Person	AL	USA
			3
		3	**3**
Alsace			
France			
	Sports Alsace	Alsace	France
	Mulhouse Vélos	Alsace	France
			2
		2	**2**

Figure 6-44 L6.6 Change group order report with summary count fields

6. In the design window, click in the Group Footer 2 section on the left side of the window and drag the section below the Group Footer 1 section. The report should look like the one shown in Figure 6-45. Save the changes and close the report.

	Customer Name	Region	Country
Argentina			
Mendoza			
	Bicicletas Buenos Aires	Mendoza	Argentina
		1	**1**
			1
Aruba			
St. George			
	Aruba Sport	St. George	Aruba
		1	**1**
			1
Australia			
New South Wales			
	Down Under Bikes	New South Wales	Australia
	Canberra Bikes	New South Wales	Australia
		2	**2**
Queensland			
	Koala Road Bikes	Queensland	Australia
		1	**1**

Figure 6-45 L6.6 Change group order report with the group sections rearranged

If you moved the region count summary field to the Group Footer 1 section, the report would look like the one shown in Figure 6-46. Notice the difference in totals at the bottom of the reports shown in Figures 6-45 and 6-46. This is why it is important to understand what the report specifications require. Just by looking at the two reports, you can't tell which is the one that is being requested.

	Customer Name	Region	Country
Argentina			
Mendoza			
	Bicicletas Buenos Aires	Mendoza	Argentina
			1
		1	**1**
Aruba			
St. George			
	Aruba Sport	St. George	Aruba
			1
		1	**1**
Australia			
New South Wales			
	Down Under Bikes	New South Wales	Australia
	Canberra Bikes	New South Wales	Australia
			2
Queensland			
	Koala Road Bikes	Queensland	Australia
			1

Figure 6-46 L6.6 Change group order report with the region count field moved to the Group Footer 1 section

7. Save the changes and close the report.

Exercise 6.7: Group 2004 Orders By Month

In this exercise you will modify a report to include the following group and sorting options. These options also allow you to create totals and counts so that the records will be grouped by the month the orders were placed.

① Group on the Order Date field.
② Sort the detail records in ascending order on the Order Date field.
③ Provide a count of orders per month.

The goal of this exercise is to create a report that displays all of the orders from 2004 and to have a subtotal for each month. In order to create a subtotal of orders for each month, the report needs to be grouped on the Order Date field.

As you will see, when you group on a date or date/time field, the Insert Group dialog box will display the option, **THE SECTION WILL BE PRINTED**. This option will allow you to create the group by month, day, quarter, year and more.

Create The Order Date Group

1. Save the L4.14 report as L6.7 2004 Orders by month.

2. On the Insert Group dialog box, open the first drop down list and select the **ORDER DATE** field. Open the last drop down list and select **FOR EACH MONTH**. Figure 6-47 shows the group options that should be selected. Click OK.

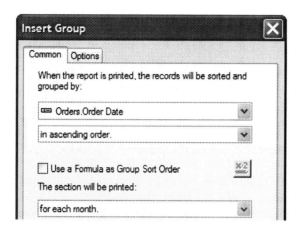

Figure 6-47 Group options

Sort The Detail Records

1. On the Record Sort Expert, click on the Order Date field, then click the **>** button.

2. Select the Ascending sort order, if it is not already selected. Click OK and save the changes.

Select The Records

In this part of the exercise you will create criteria to select all of the orders in 2004.

1. Click on the Order Date field in the details section.

2. Open the Select Expert and select the **IS BETWEEN** operator, then type 01/01/2004 in the first field. Type 12/31/2004 in the last field and click OK.

Create The Order ID Count Summary Field

This count summary field will create a total for the number of orders per month. It will also be copied to the report footer section to create a grand total of orders for the entire report.

1. On the Insert Summary dialog box, open the first drop down list and select the Order ID field, then open the second drop down list and select **DISTINCT COUNT**. Open the Summary Location drop down list and select the Group 1 option, then click OK.

Create The Order Amount Summary Field

This summary field will create a total dollar amount per month. It will also be copied to the report footer section to create a grand total order amount.

1. Delete the Product ID, Unit Price and Quantity fields from the report.

2. Add the Order Amount field in the Orders table to the report. Place it after the Order ID field in the details section.

3. On the Insert Summary dialog box, open the first drop down list and select the Order Amount field, then open the second drop down list and select **SUM**. Open the Summary Location drop down list and select the Group 1 option and click OK.

How To Create Percent Calculations

Percent calculations are very useful when you have the need to show what percent each group on the report represents in comparison to the grand total value of the report. For example, on a report that shows the sales for an entire year, there could be a percent calculation by month on the Order Amount field. This would tell the person that reads the report the percent of sales each month represents for the year. Another example on a yearly sales report would be the percent of sales each salesperson had per month, per year or both.

You can only create percent calculations on summary fields that have a numeric value. This means that if you are creating a count summary of customers based on the Customer Name field, which is a text field, you can create a percent calculation, because the count calculation field is a numeric value.

Each percent calculation on a report requires its own percent summary calculation field. The process of creating a percent summary calculation starts off the same as the calculations that you have already created in this lesson. The options to create percent calculations are at the bottom of the Insert Summary dialog box. To create a percent calculation check the **SHOW AS A PERCENTAGE OF** option, then select the group or total that you want the percent comparison based on.

If you need a total field and a percent calculation field that are based off of the same field, you have to create two summary calculation fields: one for the total amount and one for the percent.

In the previous part of the exercise you created the Order Amount summary field. Now you will create the Order Amount percent calculation field.

1. On the Insert Summary dialog box, open the first drop down list and select the Order Amount field, then open the second drop down list and select **SUM**. Open the Summary Location drop down list and select the Group 1 option, then check the **SHOW AS A PERCENTAGE OF** option. Figure 6-48 shows the summary options that should be selected. Click OK.

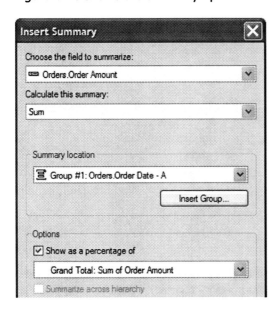

Figure 6-48 Insert Summary dialog box options

2. Move the percent summary field over to the right. On my report, it is currently on top of the Order Amount summary field that you just created. Save the changes and refresh the data. Page 3 of the report should look like the one shown in Figure 6-49. Notice that the percent summary field is already formatted with a percent sign.

First Name	Last Name	Order Date	Order ID	Order Amount
Robert	King	01/24/2004	1226	$10.71
Margaret	Peacock	01/24/2004	1227	$101.70
Nancy	Davolio	01/25/2004	1228	$2,181.86
Robert	King	01/25/2004	1229	$17.50
Nancy	Davolio	01/25/2004	1230	$1,668.36
Janet	Leverling	01/26/2004	1231	$2,524.05
Anne	Dodsworth	01/27/2004	1232	$8,174.25
Robert	King	01/27/2004	1233	$139.48
Michael	Suyama	01/27/2004	1234	$1,723.22
Anne	Dodsworth	01/27/2004	1235	$1,642.05
Janet	Leverling	01/27/2004	1236	$989.55
Robert	King	01/27/2004	1237	$998.35
Robert	King	01/28/2004	1238	$1,024.01
Robert	King	01/28/2004	1239	$101.70
Robert	King	01/28/2004	1240	$3,635.34
Robert	King	01/28/2004	1241	$4,849.86
Michael	Suyama	01/29/2004	1242	$2,993.75
Michael	Suyama	01/29/2004	1243	$128.20
Janet	Leverling	01/30/2004	1244	$24.00
Michael	Suyama	01/30/2004	1245	$3,419.25
Margaret	Peacock	01/30/2004	1246	$3,884.25
Margaret	Peacock	01/31/2004	1247	$36.00
			127	$211,265.10	7.37%

Figure 6-49 L6.7 2004 Orders by month report

How To Check Or Edit Summary Fields

Sometimes reports will have more than two or three summary fields and you may not remember what each summary field is calculating. If a summary field is not producing the output that you think it should, it is possible that you selected an option that you should not have. If either of these is the case, all is not lost. You do not have to delete the field and start over. You can follow the steps below.

1. Right-click on the percentage summary field and select **EDIT SUMMARY** as shown in Figure 6-50. You will then see the dialog box shown in Figure 6-51. You can make any changes that are necessary.

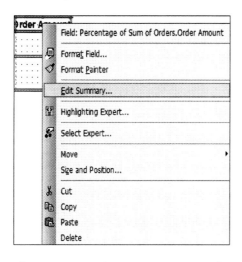

Figure 6-50 Edit Summary option illustrated on the shortcut menu

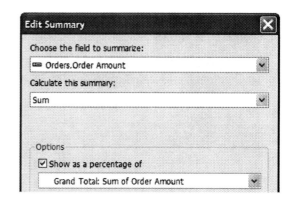

Figure 6-51 Edit Summary dialog box

The Edit Summary dialog box is almost identical to the Insert Summary dialog box. The difference is that you cannot change the location of the summary field. If you need to move a summary field from one section of the report to another, you will have to do it manually.

Modify The Report

The report would look better if the following changes were made.

① Add a report title.
② Create titles for the summary fields.

③ Create a grand total field and title for the order amount and count of orders summary fields. Place the fields in the report footer section.

④ Rearrange the fields in the details section so that the report is easier to read.

1. Create a report title and type `2004 Orders By Month` in the object. Make the font size 16 and place the title above the field headings.

2. Change the Order ID field heading to `Order #` and center the Order ID field.

3. Delete the existing First Name and Last Name field titles and create one that says `Salesperson`. Center this title over the two name fields in the details section.

4. Format the Order ID field in the Group 1 Footer section to display as a whole number without a comma.

5. Copy the Order ID and Order Amount summary fields in the Group 1 Footer section and place the copies in the report footer section.

6. Add a line under the totals in the Group 1 Footer section. Change the size of the line to 0.5.

7. Create the field titles in Table 6-9 for the summary fields.

Summary Field	Section	Title
Order Amount	Group 1 Footer	Total order amount for the month -
Order ID Count	Group 1 Footer	Total # orders for the month
Order Amount Percent	Group 1 Footer	Percent of yearly sales -
Order Amount	Report Footer	Total order amount for the year -
Order ID	Report Footer	Total # orders for the year -

Table 6-9 Field titles for Exercise 6.7

8. Copy the Group 1 Header field and place the copy in the Group 1 Footer section. Remove the bold from the field in the Group 1 Footer section.

9. Create a title for the Group 1 Footer section and type `Totals For:` in the object. Create a title for the report footer section and type `Report Grand Totals:` in the object.

10. Arrange the fields so that they look like the layout shown in Figure 6-52. Save the changes and refresh the data. Leave the report open to complete the next part of the exercise.

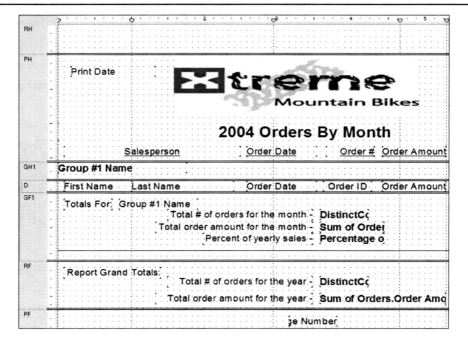

Figure 6-52 L6.7 report layout

You will see the months in the group tree section of the report. If you click on the 1/2004 group as illustrated in Figure 6-53, you will see the orders that were placed in January. Later in this lesson you will change the group name to display the name of the month instead of the month number. The Percent of yearly sales field lets you know that the orders in January represent 7.37% of the total sales in 2004.

First Name	Last Name	Order Date	Order ID	Order Amount
Robert	King	01/24/2004	1226	$10.71
Margaret	Peacock	01/24/2004	1227	$101.70
Nancy	Davolio	01/25/2004	1228	$2,181.86
Robert	King	01/25/2004	1229	$17.50
Nancy	Davolio	01/25/2004	1230	$1,668.36
Janet	Leverling	01/26/2004	1231	$2,524.05
Anne	Dodsworth	01/27/2004	1232	$8,174.25
Robert	King	01/27/2004	1233	$139.48
Michael	Suyama	01/27/2004	1234	$1,723.22
Anne	Dodsworth	01/27/2004	1235	$1,642.05
Janet	Leverling	01/27/2004	1236	$989.55
Robert	King	01/27/2004	1237	$998.35
Robert	King	01/28/2004	1238	$1,024.01
Robert	King	01/28/2004	1239	$101.70
Robert	King	01/28/2004	1240	$3,635.34
Robert	King	01/28/2004	1241	$4,849.86
Michael	Suyama	01/29/2004	1242	$2,993.75
Michael	Suyama	01/29/2004	1243	$128.20
Janet	Leverling	01/30/2004	1244	$24.00
Michael	Suyama	01/30/2004	1245	$3,419.25
Margaret	Peacock	01/30/2004	1246	$3,884.25
Margaret	Peacock	01/31/2004	1247	$36.00

Totals For: 1/2004

Total # of orders for the month - **127**
Total order amount for the month - **$ 211,265.10**
Percent of yearly sales - **7.37%**

Figure 6-53 Page 3 of the L6.7 2004 Orders by month report

How To Create A Custom Group Name

As you can see in Figure 6-54, the Order Date group name displays the month and year. The report would look better if the group name displayed the actual month name instead (January, February, March, etc.)

First Name	Last Name	Order Date	Order ID	Order Amount
1/2004 ←				
Anne	Dodsworth	01/01/2004	1121	$851.77
Michael	Suyama	01/01/2004	1122	$1,025.40
Janet	Leverling	01/02/2004	1123	$5,219.55

Figure 6-54 Order Date group name illustrated

The Format Editor has an option that you can use to display the month name. You could create a formula to accomplish this task, but using the Format Editor is easier. The steps below will show you how to create a custom group name.

1. Right-click on the **GROUP 1 NAME** field and open the Format Editor, then click the **CUSTOMIZE** button on the Date and Time tab.

2. Open the **ORDER** drop down list and select Date. Figure 6-55 shows the option that you should have selected.

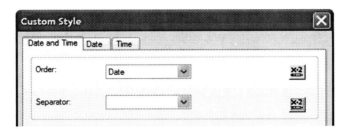

Figure 6-55 Date and Time tab options

3. Click on the Date tab and open the Month drop down list and select **MARCH**, then select **NONE** for the Day and Year options. Figure 6-56 illustrates the options that you should have selected. Click OK twice, to close both dialog boxes.

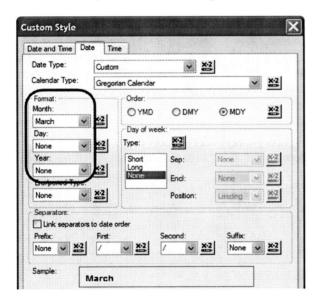

Figure 6-56 Date tab options illustrated

4. Format the Group Name field in the group footer section to have the same formatting as the one in the group header section and save the changes. Go to the last page of the report. The totals for December and the report grand totals should look like the ones shown in Figure 6-57. Leave the report open to complete the next exercise.

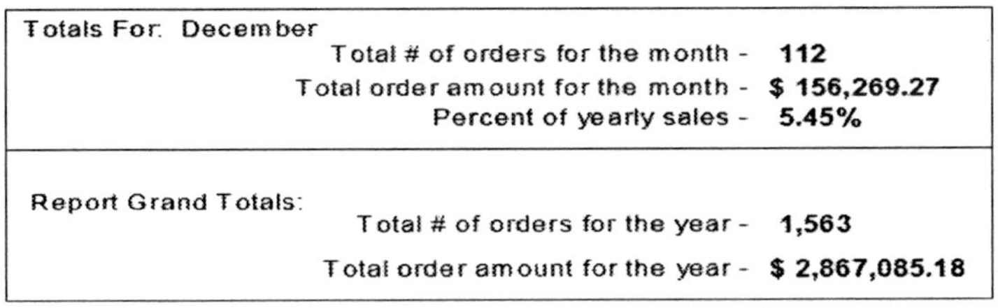

Totals For: December
Total # of orders for the month - **112**
Total order amount for the month - **$ 156,269.27**
Percent of yearly sales - **5.45%**

Report Grand Totals:
Total # of orders for the year - **1,563**
Total order amount for the year - **$ 2,867,085.18**

Figure 6-57 Last page of the L6.7 2004 Orders by month report

Exercise 6.8: Create Selection Criteria On Summary Fields

In Lesson 5 you learned about record selection. **GROUP SELECTION** is similar. The difference is that group selection is done on summary fields, instead of fields in the details section. If a report is grouping the orders by state, each state would include an order total amount.

In Exercise 6.7 you created a report that grouped the orders by month. At the end of each month are summary calculations for the total number of orders and total order amount for the month. In this exercise you will learn how to create selection criteria on group summary fields. The report that you created in Exercise 6.7 displays data for every month in 2004. In this exercise, you will use the Select Expert to modify that report to only display months where the total monthly sales is greater than $250,000.

1. Save the L6.7 report as L6.8 2004 Monthly total orders over 250K.

2. Right-click on the Sum of Orders field in the group footer section and select, Select Expert.

3. Open the drop down list and select **IS GREATER THAN OR EQUAL TO**, then type 250000 in the second field and click OK. Notice that the field name on the tab does not display a table name. Instead it displays information that lets you know that this is a summary field.

4. Change the report title to 2004 Monthly Total orders over $250,000, then save the changes.

As shown in Figure 6-58, the first page of the report is for June. Notice that all of the groups are still visible in the group tree. If you click on the 02/2004 option in the group tree, you will not see the data for February. That is because the monthly total for February is less than $250,000. I don't know about you, but I would prefer that the only options that appear in the group tree are the ones that meet the criteria. This happens because of the way Crystal Reports processes data. Remember that the group header information is processed before the totals for the summary calculations in the group footer are processed. This is why all of the months appear in the group tree.

L6.6 2004 Monthly Total Orders					
1/2004	**2004 Monthly Total Orders Over $250,000**				
2/2004					
3/2004		Salesperson	Order Date	Order #	Order Amount
4/2004					
5/2004					
6/2004	**June**				
7/2004					
8/2004	Anne	Dodsworth	06/01/2004	1665	$161.20
9/2004	Margaret	Peacock	06/01/2004	1666	$10,662.75
10/2004	Robert	King	06/01/2004	1667	$959.70
11/2004	Janet	Leverling	06/01/2004	1668	$1,138.09
12/2004	Anne	Dodsworth	06/01/2004	1669	$8,945.25

Figure 6-58 L6.8 2004 Monthly total orders over 250K

Know the difference between the detail level **RECORD SELECTION**, which was covered in Lesson 5 and **GROUP SELECTION**.

User Defined Groups

Earlier in this lesson you learned about the User defined sort order. In Exercise 6.7 you learned how to create a custom group name. Custom group names allowed you to rename existing group names. Custom groups must be based on a single field in the report. User defined groups are similar to custom group names. The major difference is that the user defined group name is free form. In addition to being able to create a free form group name, you can create custom groups. Below are examples of user defined groups.

① Orders placed between the first and the 15th of the month.
② Group a customer based on their year to date sales (example Gold, Bronze and Silver levels).

③ Create sales territories and associate states to a territory (example Northeast, Southeast and Midwest).

There are four steps to creating a user defined group as discussed below:

① Select the field that you want to create the user defined group for and then select the option, **IN SPECIFIED ORDER** in the second drop down list on the Common tab of the Insert Group dialog box. Once this option is selected, other tabs (the Specified Order and Others tabs) will appear on the dialog box.

② Type in the name for the first group name that you need in the **NAMED GROUP** drop down list shown in Figure 6-59, then click the **NEW** button.

③ The **DEFINE NAMED GROUP** dialog box is similar to the Select Expert. The difference is that each tab on the Define Named Group dialog box is for the same field. User defined groups cannot use parameter fields and the formula cannot be modified. You would type in the criteria for the user defined group, as shown in Figure 6-60.

④ Click OK and repeat steps 2 and 3 until you have created all of the user defined groups that the report needs.

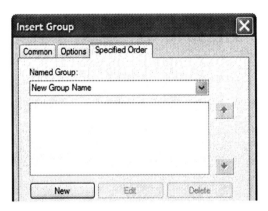

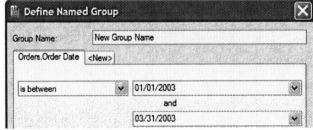

Figure 6-60 Criteria for user defined group

Figure 6-59 Specified order options

If you wanted to group orders by specific order date ranges like 1/1/04 to 1/15/04, 2/1/04 to 2/15/04 and 3/1/04 to 3/15/04, you would create three named groups, for example, Jan 04, Feb 04 and Mar 04. For each named group you would select the Order Date field, the operator "Is between" and the date range for the named group. The report would show the three groups and the detail records that have an order date that falls into one of the three date ranges.

If one group or all groups need additional criteria, click on the New tab and add the next piece of criteria for the group. You can only add criteria for the same field. For example, if you also wanted to see orders for 1/15/04 to 1/25/04, you would add this criteria on the New tab as shown in Figure 6-61. The criteria for each group name is joined using the OR operand. This means that as long as the record meets one of the sets of criteria for the group name, it will appear on the report.

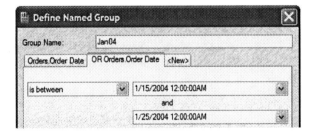

Figure 6-61 Additional criteria added to the named group

The options on the Others tab, which you will learn about in the next exercise will let you select what you want to do with the records that do not meet the criteria for any of the named groups.

Exercise 6.9: Create A User Defined Group Report

In this exercise you will modify the L6.1 report to include the following region user defined groups: CA, IL and PA.

1. Save the L6.1 report as L6.9 User defined groups.

2. Right-click on the group header section and select **CHANGE GROUP**.

3. Select the option **IN SPECIFIED ORDER** in the second drop down list. You should now see the **SPECIFIED ORDER** tab.

4. Select CA, IL and PA in the **NAMED GROUP** drop down list. Make sure that the states are in the order shown in Figure 6-62. If they are not in the order shown, use the up and down arrow buttons to put the states in the order shown.

5. Click on the **OTHERS** tab and select the option **DISCARD ALL OTHERS**, as shown in Figure 6-63, then click OK to close the dialog box.

Selecting the Discard all others option means that records that are not in any of the groups that you selected on the Specified Order tab will not appear on the report.

The **PUT ALL OTHERS TOGETHER, WITH THE NAME** option, will put all of the other records that do not meet the criteria on the Specified Order tab in the report under a new group name that you enter on the field below the option. This group will appear at the end of the report.

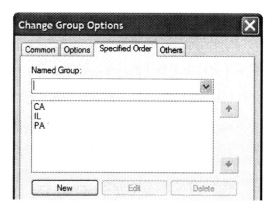

Figure 6-62 Change Group Options dialog box

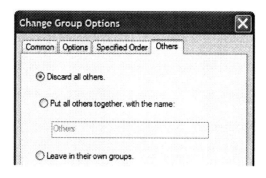

Figure 6-63 Others tab options

6. Preview the report. You should only see the CA, IL and PA groups in the group tree as shown in Figure 6-64. Save the changes and leave the report open to complete the next exercise.

Exercise 6.10: Create A Custom Group Name Report

In the previous exercise, the User Defined Group report displayed the two character state name. In this exercise you will modify that report so that the state names are spelled out.

1. Save the L6.7 report as L6.10 Custom group name.

2. Right-click on the group header report section and select **CHANGE GROUP**, then click on the Specified Order tab and delete all of the Named Groups.

3. Click the **NEW** button and type California in the Group Name field.

4. Open the first drop down list and select **IS EQUAL TO**, then select CA from the second drop down list. You should have the options selected that are shown in Figure 6-65. Click OK.

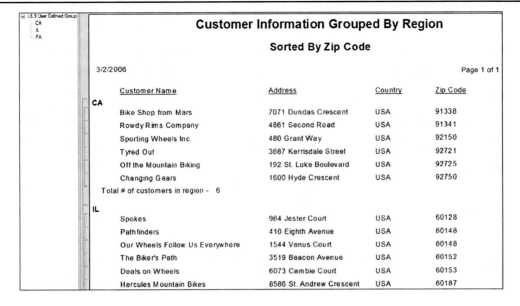

Figure 6-64 L6.9 User defined groups report

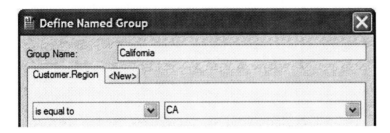

Figure 6-65 Defined Name Group options for CA

5. Repeat steps 3 and 4 for IL and PA. Leave the Change Group Options dialog box open when you are finished.

6. Click on the **OTHERS** tab and select the option **PUT ALL OTHERS TOGETHER, WITH THE NAME**, then type `Other States`, as shown in Figure 6-66.

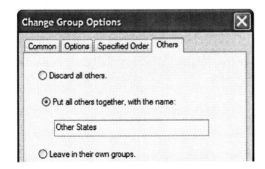

Figure 6-66 Others tab options

7. Click OK and save the changes. The report should look like the one shown in Figure 6-67. Notice that the state names are spelled out and that there is a new group called Other States in the group tree. This group contains all of the records that meet the selection options for the report, but are not in CA, IL or PA.

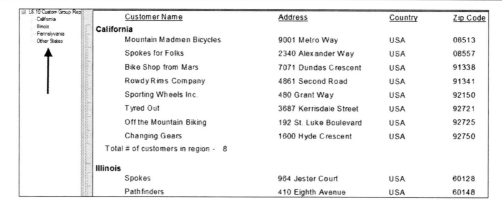

Figure 6-67 L6.10 Custom group name report

Using The Group Expert

All of the groups that you have created in this lesson were created using the Insert Group dialog box. You can also create groups using the Group Expert shown in Figure 6-68.

There are two ways to open the Group Expert as discussed below.

① Click the Group Expert button on the Expert Tools toolbar.
② Report ⇒ Group Expert.

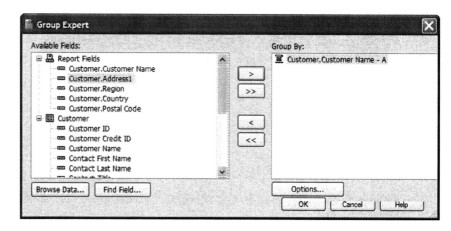

Figure 6-68 Group Expert

One benefit of using the Group Expert is that you can create all of the groups for the report without having to re-open a dialog box to create each group. Another benefit is if you need to see the data in a field, you can click the Browse Data button.

The **OPTIONS** button will open the Change Group Options dialog box shown in Figure 6-69. It is the same as the Insert Group dialog box shown earlier in Figure 6-47.

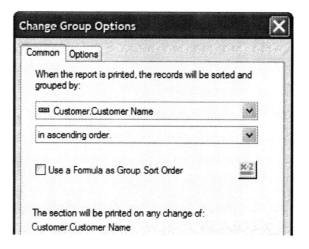

Figure 6-69 Change Group Options dialog box

Test Your Skills

1. You will modify a monthly report so that it is grouped by quarter, instead of by month. Save the L6.7 report as `L6.11 Skills 2004 orders by quarter`.

   - Change the report title to `2004 Orders By Quarter`.
   - Modify the report to group by quarter instead of by month.
   - Change the titles in the group footer section to `Quarter` instead of month.
   - Delete the Group 1 field in the group footer section.
   - Add `The Quarter` to the end of the "Totals For" text object in the group footer section.

   Figure 6-70 shows the last page of the report. Notice the Quarter totals and that the report grand totals are the same as the ones shown earlier in Figure 6-57. Also notice that there are only four groups instead of 12.

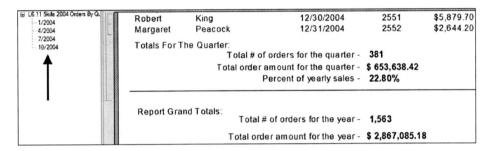

Figure 6-70 Last page of the L6.11 Skills 2004 orders by quarter report

2. You will modify a report to include the salary field. Save the L3.2 report as `L6.12 Skills Employee list`.

   - Delete the Photo field and make the details section shorter.
   - Move all of the fields over to the left in the details section and line them up.
   - Add the Salary field after the Region field.
   - Group the report by region.
   - Sort the report on the salary field in descending order in each region.

   Your report should look like the one shown in Figure 6-71. The report should have 15 records.

First Name	Last Name	Address1	Region	Salary
Steven	Buchanan	14 Garrett Hill		$ 50,000.00
Robert	King	Edgeham Hollow		$ 37,000.00
Anne	Dodsworth	7 Houndstooth Rd.		$ 35,000.00
Michael	Suyama	Coventry House		$ 30,000.00
Bas-Rhin				
Justin	Brid	2 impasse du Soleil	Bas-Rhin	$ 75,000.00
Xavier	Martin	9 place de la Liberté	Bas-Rhin	$ 50,000.00
Laurent	Pereira	7 rue Nationale	Bas-Rhin	$ 45,000.00

Figure 6-71 L6.12 Skills Employee list report

3. You will modify the Orders By Employee report so that it only displays orders in 2004, grouped by sales rep. Save the L4.14 report as
    `L6.13 Skills 2004 monthly orders by sales rep`.

    - Create selection criteria that displays orders that have an order date in 2004.
    - Group the report by the Employee ID.
    - Sort the records by Order Date in descending order.

    Create the following three summaries in the group footer section.

    ① A count of Customer Orders (use the Order ID field).
    ② A total per customer.
    ③ A sum order amount field to calculate a total of the number of pieces shipped per customer.

    - Format the fields appropriately.
    - Move the Employee Name fields to the group header section.
    - Change the First Name field title to `Salesperson`, then delete the Last Name field title.

    The last page of the report should look like the one shown in Figure 6-72. The report should have 2,617 records.

Totals for:	Anne Dodsworth	
	Total # of orders -	**434**
	Total # of pieces shipped -	**888**
	Total amount of orders -	**$ 1,076,651.52**
Report Totals:	Total # of orders -	**2,617**
	Total # of pieces shipped -	**5,395**
	Total amount of orders -	**$ 5,835,909.95**

Figure 6-72 L6.13 Skills 2004 Monthly orders by sales rep report

4. You will modify the sort order of a report. Save the L6.1 report as
    `L6.14 Skills Customers sorted by country and zip code`.

    - Change the existing sort criteria to sort by Country first and then by Postal Code.
    - Change the Postal Code field title to `Zip Code`.

    Preview the **DISTRITO FEDERAL** region section of the report. It should look like the one shown in Figure 6-73.

Distrito Federal			
Brasília Bikes Inc.	Rua Fernando, 991	Brazil	23293-300
Bicycles Alex	Rufino Tamayo 395	Mexico	03853
Deportes Mexico City	Vía Morelos 3343	Mexico	24421
Tienda de Repuestos Caracas	Av San Jorge 2011	Venezuela	32111
Harare Cycle	4290 Shell Aveneue	Zimbabwe	403943
Total # of customers in region - 5			

Figure 6-73 L6.14 Skills Customers sorted by country and zip code report

5. You will modify a report to only display months that have less than 125 orders. Save the L6.7 report as `L6.15 Skills Monthly number of orders under 125`.

    - Change the report title to `2004 Months With Less Than 125 Orders`.
    - Create selection criteria to only display months where the total number of orders is less than 125. The report should look like the one shown in Figure 6-74. The only months that should appear on the report are February, March, April, July, September and December.

2004 Months With Less Than 125 Orders

Salesperson		Order Date	Order #	Order Amount
February				
Margaret	Peacock	02/01/2004	1248	$5,938.40
Michael	Suyama	02/02/2004	1249	$18.00
Margaret	Peacock	02/02/2004	1250	$2,497.05
Janet	Leverling	02/03/2004	1251	$45.00
Anne	Dodsworth	02/03/2004	1252	$70.50
Janet	Leverling	02/03/2004	1253	$2,683.82
Michael	Suyama	02/03/2004	1254	$2,497.05
Nancy	Davolio	02/03/2004	1255	$33.00
Janet	Leverling	02/04/2004	1256	$70.50

Figure 6-74 L6.15 Skills Monthly number of orders under 125 report

6. You will modify a report to create groups and summary fields. Save the L4.14 report as `L6.16 Skills 2003 orders by sales rep.`

- Add the Order Amount field after the Order ID field.
- Add the Customer ID field after the Order Amount field.
- Group on the Employee ID field, then group on the Order Date field and then group on the Customer ID field. Sort the groups in ascending order.
- Sort the detail records on the Customer ID, Order Amount and Order Date fields in ascending order.
- Create a count of orders per day, per sales rep. Place the count in both group footer sections and in the report footer section. (Use the Order ID field).
- Create a total amount of orders per day, per sales rep (Employee). Place the total in both group footer sections and in the report footer section. (Use the Order Amount field).
- Create selection criteria to only include orders in 2003.
- Create a report title and type `2003 Orders By Sales Rep` in the object. Make the font size 16. Make the title bold and center the title across the page.
- Add a line under the totals in all of the group footer sections. Change the size of the line to 0.5.
- Center the Quantity field.
- Move the First Name and Last Name fields to the Group Header 1 section. Change the field title to `Salesperson.`
- Change the Order ID field heading to `Order #` and center the field.
- Change the Customer ID field heading to `Customer #` and center the field.
- Change the Product ID field heading to `Product #.`
- Create titles for all of the summary fields.

Page 1 should look like the one shown in Figure 6-75.
The last page of the report should look like the one shown in Figure 6-76. Notice the totals for the sales rep. As you can see, the total order amount for each customer is not correct. You will modify this report in Lesson 9.

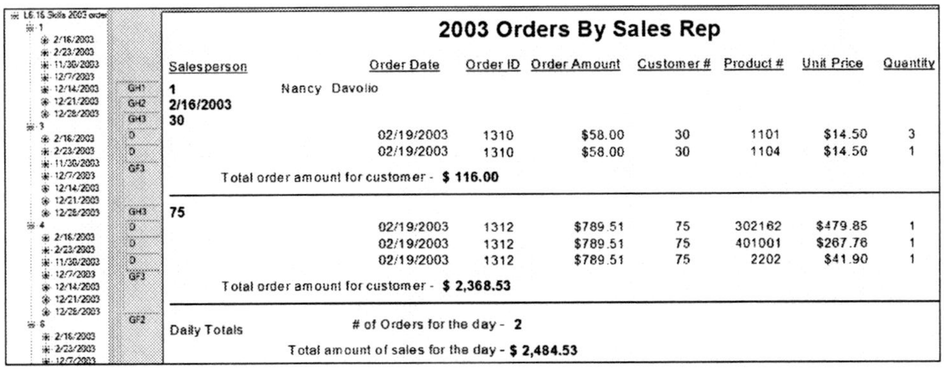

2003 Orders By Sales Rep

Salesperson		Order Date	Order ID	Order Amount	Customer #	Product #	Unit Price	Quantity
1	Nancy Davolio							
2/16/2003								
30								
		02/19/2003	1310	$58.00	30	1101	$14.50	3
		02/19/2003	1310	$58.00	30	1104	$14.50	1
	Total order amount for customer - **$ 116.00**							
75								
		02/19/2003	1312	$789.51	75	302162	$479.85	1
		02/19/2003	1312	$789.51	75	401001	$267.76	1
		02/19/2003	1312	$789.51	75	2202	$41.90	1
	Total order amount for customer - **$ 2,368.53**							
Daily Totals	# of Orders for the day - **2**							
	Total amount of sales for the day - **$ 2,484.53**							

Figure 6-75 Page 1 of the L6.16 Skills 2003 orders by sales rep report

33							
	12/27/2003	1101	$982.65	33	2204	$41.90	3
	12/27/2003	1101	$982.65	33	402002	$274.35	3
	12/27/2003	1101	$982.65	33	5204	$33.90	1

Total order amount for customer - **$ 2,947.95**

Daily Totals	# of Orders for the day - **2**
	Total amount of sales for the day - **$ 3,031.95**

12/28/2003							
5							
	12/29/2003	1112	$161.70	5	2215	$53.90	3
	12/30/2003	1115	$9.00	5	3301	$4.50	2

Total order amount for customer - **$ 170.70**

Daily Totals	# of Orders for the day - **2**
	Total amount of sales for the day - **$ 170.70**

Salesperson Totals	# of Orders for salesperson - **37**
	Total amount of sales for salesperson - **$ 54,138.44**

Report Totals	# of Orders - **181**
	Total amount of sales - **$ 515,252.18**

Figure 6-76 Last page of the L6.16 Skills 2003 orders by sales rep report

7. You will modify a report to include a custom group.
   Save the L5.11 report as `L6.17 Skills Supplier custom group.`

   - Group the report on the Supplier Name field.
   - Create a custom group called `Top Suppliers.`
   - Add the following suppliers to the Defined Named Group dialog box using the **IS ONE OF** operator: Craze, Roadster, Triumph and Vesper. Group all of the other suppliers under the group Other Suppliers.
   - The first page of the **Top Suppliers** group should look like the one shown in Figure 6-77. The first page of the **Other Suppliers** group should look like the one shown in Figure 6-78.

Product ID	Product Name	Product Type Name	Supplier Name
Top Suppliers			
2,201	Triumph Pro Helmet	Helmets	Triumph
2,202	Triumph Pro Helmet	Helmets	Triumph
2,203	Triumph Pro Helmet	Helmets	Triumph
2,204	Triumph Pro Helmet	Helmets	Triumph
2,205	Triumph Pro Helmet	Helmets	Triumph
2,206	Triumph Pro Helmet	Helmets	Triumph
2,207	Triumph Vertigo Helmet	Helmets	Triumph
2,208	Triumph Vertigo Helmet	Helmets	Triumph
2,209	Triumph Vertigo Helmet	Helmets	Triumph
2,210	Triumph Vertigo Helmet	Helmets	Triumph
2,211	Triumph Vertigo Helmet	Helmets	Triumph
2,212	Triumph Vertigo Helmet	Helmets	Triumph
2,213	Triumph Vertigo Helmet	Helmets	Triumph
2,214	Triumph Vertigo Helmet	Helmets	Triumph
2,215	Triumph Vertigo Helmet	Helmets	Triumph
5,201	Xtreme Adult Helmet	Helmets	Craze
5,202	Xtreme Adult Helmet	Helmets	Craze

Figure 6-77 Page 1 of the Top Supplier group on the L6.17 Skills Supplier custom group report

Product ID	Product Name	Product Type Name	Supplier Name
Other Suppliers			
1,101	Active Outdoors Crochet Glove	Gloves	Active Outdoors
1,102	Active Outdoors Crochet Glove	Gloves	Active Outdoors
1,103	Active Outdoors Crochet Glove	Gloves	Active Outdoors
1,104	Active Outdoors Crochet Glove	Gloves	Active Outdoors
1,105	Active Outdoors Crochet Glove	Gloves	Active Outdoors
1,106	Active Outdoors Lycra Glove	Gloves	Active Outdoors
1,107	Active Outdoors Lycra Glove	Gloves	Active Outdoors
1,108	Active Outdoors Lycra Glove	Gloves	Active Outdoors
1,109	Active Outdoors Lycra Glove	Gloves	Active Outdoors
1,110	Active Outdoors Lycra Glove	Gloves	Active Outdoors
1,111	Active Outdoors Lycra Glove	Gloves	Active Outdoors
3,301	Guardian Chain Lock	Locks	Guardian
3,302	Guardian "U" Lock	Locks	Guardian

Figure 6-78 Page 1 of the Other Suppliers group on the L6.17 Skills Supplier custom group report

8. Add all of the reports that were created in this lesson to the Workbench.

REPORT WIZARDS AND TEMPLATES

Lesson 2 provided an overview of how to create reports and charts using a wizard. In this lesson you will learn more about the wizards. In the last few lessons, all of the reports that you created were created from scratch. I figured that I would give you a break in this lesson from creating reports from scratch. In addition to learning more about the wizards, you will learn how to use the templates. After completing the exercises in this lesson you will be able to:

☑ Understand the options on the common wizard screens
☑ Know the types of reports that each wizard can create
☑ Use the Mailing Label wizard
☑ Use the Cross-Tab wizard
☑ Use the OLAP Cube wizard
☑ Understand how templates work
☑ Use the predefined templates
☑ Add a template to the available list of templates

To pass the RDCR201 exam, you need to be familiar with and be able to:

☑ Apply a template to a report
☑ Remove a template from a report

LESSON 7

Report Wizard Overview

Now that you have used several report creation and modification features and were able to see the completed reports, many of the options on the wizard screens will hopefully make more sense. Selecting the wrong option in the wizard or not selecting an option that you need, will cause you to have to fix the report manually. That's okay though, as wizards can be used as a starting point for a report that you can modify as needed. I think that it is important to understand sorting, grouping and summary options before using a wizard to create a report. One reason that I think this is important is because many of the wizard screens are scaled down versions of an expert screen. This is why this lesson comes after lessons that had you create reports that demonstrate how to sort, group and summarize records.

Table 7-1 explains the type of report that each wizard creates. As you learn to use each of the report wizards, you will see that they have a core set of common screens. Table 7-2 illustrates the common screens and the screens that are unique to a specific report wizard.

Wizard	Type Of Report It Creates
Standard	Allows you to create a variety of reports because it is a generic report wizard. It is similar to creating a report from scratch.
Cross-Tab	Allows you to create reports that look like spreadsheets. The Cross-Tab and Grid Style screens let you create and format the Cross-Tab.
Mailing Label	Allows you to create reports in a column layout, which can be used to create any size mailing label that you need.
OLAP Cube	This wizard is similar to the Cross-Tab wizard because it displays the data in a grid, which is similar to a spreadsheet. While the output from a report created with the OLAP Cube wizard is similar to a Cross-Tab report, the process is different because of the requirements of working with OLAP data sources.

Table 7-1 Report Wizards explained

Screen	Standard	Cross-Tab	Mailing Label	OLAP
Data	X	X	X	
Link	X	X	X	
Fields	X		X	
Grouping	X			
Summaries	X			
Group Sorting	X			
Record Selection	X	X	X	
Chart	X	X		X
Template	X			
Cross-Tab		X		
Grid Style		X		
Label			X	
OLAP Data				X
Rows/Columns				X
Slice/Page				X
Style				X

Table 7-2 Report wizard screens

You should be familiar with many of the wizard screens because in Exercise 2.1 you created a report using a wizard that selected options on every screen of the wizard. This was done to demonstrate all of the options in the wizard. The reports that you create with wizards in this lesson will be more focused. Many of the reports that you will create in this lesson are reports that you have already created from scratch. The reason for this is two-fold:

    ① So that you will be able to determine which method (by wizard or by scratch) is better suited for a specific type of report.
    ② So that you can decide which way you like best.

The wizards are designed to make what may seem like a complicated task, a little easier to complete. What you may not realize is that there is often more going on behind the scenes of a wizard then you realize. By that I mean, wizards can have default options that you may not be aware of. In Exercise 7.7 you will see an example of this.

Unless you are very familiar with the data that is being used to create the report, you or the person using the report may not know that the data on the report is not 100% accurate. I personally try not to use wizards because of this. I may reconsider using wizards if there was documentation that thoroughly explains the inner workings and defaults that are set.

Common Wizard Screens

As you saw above in Table 7-2, several of the report wizards use the same screens. The majority of reports that you will create with a wizard will be created using the standard wizard. This section will explain the purpose and features of the screens that provide the foundation for many of the wizards.

Some of the wizard screens including the Record Selection, Chart and Cross-Tab have less functionality then the "Expert" that it was taken from. If you find that there is a task that you can't complete using the wizard, check the options on the Expert toolbar to see if there is an option that will help you complete the task.

Data Screen

Figure 7-1 shows the Data screen. This is the first screen that many wizards use. This screen is used to select the data sources that are needed to create the report. The Data screen provides the same functionality as the Database Expert that you learned about. [See Lesson 3, The Database Expert]

Figure 7-1 Data screen

Fields Screen

Figure 7-2 shows the Fields screen. This is where you select the fields that are needed for the report.

The fields that you select on this screen will be placed in the details section of the report.

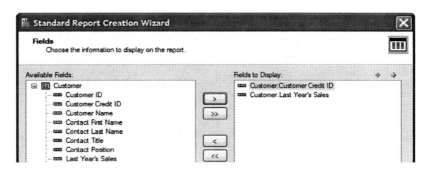

Figure 7-2 Fields screen

Grouping Screen

Figure 7-3 shows the Grouping screen. The options on this screen let you select the fields to group on. Creating groups is optional. Grouping options if selected, will create the group header and footer sections of the report. This screen is the equivalent of the Insert Group dialog box that you learned about in Lesson 6.

You cannot sort the detail records on this wizard screen. If you need to sort records in a report that does not have a group, you will have to do that through the Record Sort Expert, after the report has been created with the wizard.

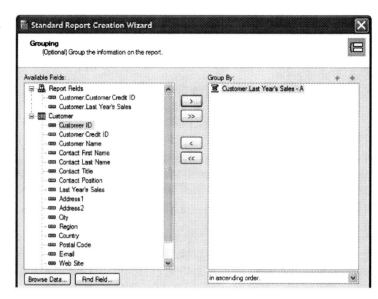

Figure 7-3 Grouping screen

 Keep in mind that when you create a group using the wizard, the field(s) that are being grouped on, are automatically moved to the beginning of the report. The fields do not stay in the order that you add them to the report on the Fields screen.

Summaries Screen

The Summaries screen is only available if at least one field is being grouped on. By default, the numeric fields that you select on the Grouping screen are automatically added to the **SUMMARIZED FIELDS** section, as shown in Figure 7-4. The fields in the Summarized Fields section will automatically have grand total fields created and placed in the report footer section of the report.

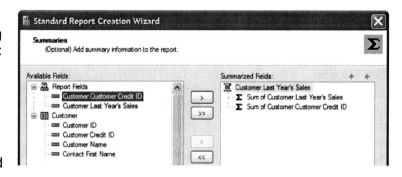

Figure 7-4 Summaries screen

The Summaries screen is the equivalent of the Insert Summary dialog box that you learned about. If you do not need a summary field for a field that is in the Summarized Fields section, click on the summary field that is not needed and then click the < button. If you need to add a field to summarize on, select it here.

Group Sorting Screen

The Group Sorting screen is only available if at least one field was selected on the Grouping and Summaries screens. Figure 7-5 shows the options that you can select as needed, to change the order of the groups based on the value from the selection on the Summaries screen. The Group Sorting screen is a scaled down version of the Group Sort Expert.

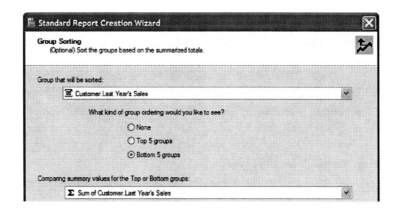

Figure 7-5 Group Sorting screen

There are three group ordering options that you can select from, as discussed below.

① **None** This is the default group ordering option. This option will leave the group order the way it is. Most of the time, this is the option that you want.

② **Top 5 Groups** This option will only print the five groups that have the highest value in the field that is being grouped on. The other groups will not print on the report.

③ **Bottom 5 Groups** This option will only print the five groups that have the lowest value in the field that is being grouped on. The other groups will not print on the report.

If the Top 5 groups or Bottom 5 groups option is selected, the **COMPARING SUMMARY VALUES FOR THE TOP OR BOTTOM GROUPS** option is turned on. This option lets you select the summarized field to base the sort on. The options available in the drop down list come from the summary fields that you created on the Summaries screen.

Top and Bottom N reports, commonly known as Top N reports, allow you to show the first N or bottom N records in a group. Instead of displaying all orders in a certain date range, you could only show the largest 10 orders in the date range. The wizard does not allow you to select the value of N. It always uses five. If you use the Group Sort Expert to create a Top or Bottom N report, you can select the value of N, by typing it in or using a parameter field to get the value of N each time the report is run. [See Lesson 12, Parameter Fields Overview] You can use the Group Sort Expert to edit a Top N report that you created with a wizard. [See Lesson 13, Group Sort Expert]

Chart Screen

The options shown in Figure 7-6 will let you add a chart to the report. Adding a chart is optional. In order to add a chart, the report has to have at least one group.

Compared to the Chart Expert, the options and chart types on the Chart screen are limited, which means that most of the time you will have to modify the chart after the wizard creates it.

Figure 7-6 Chart screen

The other major drawback to creating a chart using a report wizard is that you have to create the chart from fields that will print on the report. The Chart Expert allows you to create a chart with fields that do not print on the report. Once you select a chart type in the wizard, the three options discussed below are available to help you customize the chart.

① **Chart Title** The information that you enter here will be printed at the top of the chart.
② **On Change Of** This option defaults to a field that the report is being grouped on.
③ **Show Summary** This option defaults to the summary field for the field that is in the On Change Of field.

Record Selection Screen

The options shown in Figure 7-7 allow you to create selection criteria like you did in Lesson 5 when you learned how to use the Select Expert. Selecting options on this screen is optional. As you saw in Lesson 5, a formula is created when you use the Select Expert. A formula is created on the Record Selection screen if criteria is added. The difference is that you cannot see the formula that is created from the wizard screen. You can view it after the report is created with the wizard by opening the Select Expert. This will let you edit the formula if necessary. Like the Select Expert, you can create as many filters as you need.

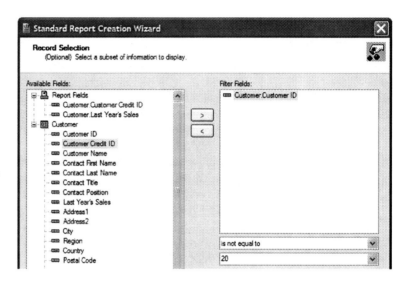

Figure 7-7 Record Selection screen

Template Screen

The options shown in Figure 7-8 allow you to apply a template (a pre-formatted style) to the report. Applying a template to a report is optional. You can also create your own templates. If there is a template that you want to use that is not shown in the Available Templates list, click the BROWSE button. This will let you navigate to the location where the template is that you want to use.

I would like to have the ability to preview the report before the wizard creates it. This would let you know how "close" you are to getting the output that you want.

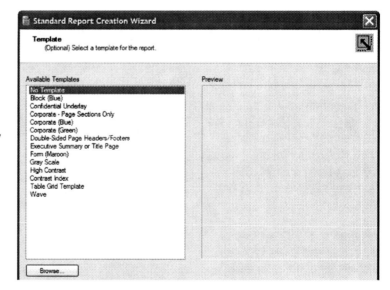

Figure 7-8 Template screen

If you make a mistake or leave something out, you would not have to start all over again because you could click the Back button and fix the mistake or add what you need, because you could see what the report would look like before clicking the Finish button.

Exercise 7.1: Create The Region = OH Or FL List Report

As you learned in Lesson 2, list reports are one of the easiest types of reports to create. In Lesson 6 you learned how to select records. The report that you will create in this exercise is a list report that selects certain records. The L2.2 list report that you created displayed all of the product records. In this exercise you will select options on the wizard that will filter the data in the customers table to retrieve customers that are in OH or FL.

1. Open the Standard Report Wizard and add the Customer table, then click Next.

2. Add the following fields: Customer Name, Address1, Region, Country and Postal Code, then click Next.

3. Click Next on the Grouping screen because this report does not have any grouping requirements. Add the Region field to the **FILTER FIELDS** section of the Record Selection screen.

4. Open the drop down list and select **IS ONE OF**, then open the next drop down list and select **OH** or you can also type it in. Click the **ADD** button.

5. Open the same drop down list that you just used and select **FL** or you can type it in. Click the **ADD** button. Figure 7-9 shows the filter options that should be selected.

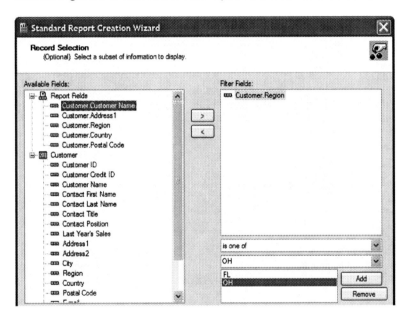

Figure 7-9 Record Selection screen options

6. The report does not require a template. Click **FINISH**. Your report should look like the one shown in Figure 7-10. Notice that a date field was automatically added to the report, but it gets cut off. Save the report as L7.1 Region = OH or FL list, then close the report.

11/11/20				
Customer Name	Address1	Region	Country	Postal Code
Bike-A-Holics Anonymous	7429 Arbutus Boulevard	OH	USA	43005
Wheels and Stuff	2530 Bute Avenue	FL	USA	34666
Uni-Cycle	1008 Kerr Street	OH	USA	43042
Extreme Cycling	1925 Glenaire Avenue	FL	USA	34638
Karma Bikes	1516 Ohio Avenue	OH	USA	43092

Figure 7-10 L7.1 Region = OH or FL list report

Exercise 7.2: Create The Order Date And Order Amount Report

In this exercise you will create a report that selects criteria on fields from three tables. You will create a filter that will select records that have an order date greater than or equal to 6-24-03 and has an order amount greater than 2499.99. [See Exercise 5.4]

1. Open the Standard Report Wizard and add the Customer, Orders and Orders Detail tables, then click Next. The reason that you see the **LINK** screen is because more than one table being used to create the report. The default links between the tables are correct. Click Next.

2. Add the following fields: Customer Name, Order Date, Ship Date, Order Amount, Order ID and Unit Price.

3. Click Next, then click Next on the Grouping screen because this report does not have any grouping requirements. Add the Order Date field to the **FILTER FIELDS** section.

4. Open the drop down list and select **IS GREATER THAN OR EQUAL TO**, then open the next drop down list and select **6/24/2003** or you can type in the date. Click the **ADD** button.

5. Add the Order Amount field to the **FILTER FIELDS** section, then open the drop down list and select **IS GREATER THAN**.

6. Type 2499.99 in the next drop down list and click **FINISH**. Your report should look like the one shown in Figure 7-11.

11/11/20					
Customer Name	Order Date	Ship Date	Order Amount	Order ID	Unit Price
Deals on Wheels	12/2/2003 12:00:00A	12/2/2003 6:45:32AI	$5,060.28	1,002	$33.90
Deals on Wheels	12/2/2003 12:00:00A	12/2/2003 6:45:32AI	$5,060.28	1,002	$1,652.86
Cyclopath	12/3/2003 12:00:00A	12/3/2003 11:11:11P	$14,872.30	1,010	$2,939.85
Cyclopath	12/3/2003 12:00:00A	12/3/2003 11:11:11P	$14,872.30	1,010	$2,645.87
Cyclopath	12/3/2003 12:00:00A	12/3/2003 11:11:11P	$14,872.30	1,010	$253.67
Piccolo	12/3/2003 12:00:00A	12/5/2003 4:59:00PI	$10,259.10	1,012	$2,939.85
Piccolo	12/3/2003 12:00:00A	12/5/2003 4:59:00PI	$10,259.10	1,012	$2,939.85
Piccolo	12/3/2003 12:00:00A	12/5/2003 4:59:00PI	$10,259.10	1,012	$479.85
Canal City Cycle	12/6/2003 12:00:00A	12/12/2003 7:30:23/	$5,237.55	1,021	$9.00
Canal City Cycle	12/6/2003 12:00:00A	12/12/2003 7:30:23/	$5,237.55	1,021	$1,739.85
Belgium Bike Co.	12/7/2003 12:00:00A	12/7/2003 5:40:35AI	$2,792.86	1,022	$2,792.86
SAB Mountain	12/7/2003 12:00:00A	12/8/2003 11:23:43A	$8,819.55	1,025	$2,939.85
The Great Bike Shop	12/7/2003 12:00:00A	12/7/2003 6:42:00PI	$2,972.85	1,027	$16.50
The Great Bike Shop	12/7/2003 12:00:00A	12/7/2003 6:42:00PI	$2,972.85	1,027	$2,939.85
Trail Blazer's Place	12/8/2003 12:00:00A	12/14/2003 4:14:07F	$12,323.10	1,032	$2,939.85
Trail Blazer's Place	12/8/2003 12:00:00A	12/14/2003 4:14:07F	$12,323.10	1,032	$2,939.85
Trail Blazer's Place	12/8/2003 12:00:00A	12/14/2003 4:14:07F	$12,323.10	1,032	$281.85

Figure 7-11 L7.2 Order Date GTE 6-24-2003 and Order Amt GT 2499.99 report

7. Save the report as L7.2 Order Date GTE 6-24-2003 and Order Amt GT 2499.99, then close the report.

Exercise 7.3: Create A Group Report

In Lesson 6 you learned how to create reports that had groups. In this exercise you will create a report that has a group. The records will be grouped by the product that was ordered.

1. Open the Standard Report Wizard and add the Orders Detail and Product tables, then click Next. The reason that you are adding the Product table is so that you can print the name of the product instead of the Product ID number that is in the Orders Detail table. Click Next on the Link screen because the link options do not need to be changed.

2. Add the following fields: Product Name, Quantity and Order ID, then click Next.

3. Add the Product Name field to the Group By section. The default sort order for the group will cause the Product Names to be sorted in ascending order. No other options need to be selected. Click Finish. Your report should look like the one shown in Figure 7-12.

11/21/20		
Product Name	Quantity	Order ID
Active Outdoors Crochet G		
Active Outdoors Crochet Glo'	2	1,326
Active Outdoors Crochet Glo'	1	1,891
Active Outdoors Crochet Glo'	1	1,850
Active Outdoors Crochet Glo'	1	1,655
Active Outdoors Crochet Glo'	3	1,610
Active Outdoors Crochet Glo'	3	1,537
Active Outdoors Crochet Glo'	3	1,512
Active Outdoors Crochet Glo'	3	1,501
Active Outdoors Crochet Glo'	3	3,000

Figure 7-12 L7.3 Orders grouped by product name report

4. Save the report as `L7.3 Orders grouped by product name`, then close the report.

Exercise 7.4: Create A Summary Report

The report that you just created lets you see how many orders for each product there are. If you wanted to know how many customers ordered a specific product you would have to manually count the detail records in each group. You can add a count summary field to the report that will display the total number of orders for each product. In this exercise, you will create a report that has a count summary field.

1. Repeat the first three steps in Exercise 7.3 and click Next on the Grouping screen in step 3, instead of clicking the Finish button.

As you can see in Figure 7-13, two summary fields were automatically added to the Summarized Fields section. By default, numeric fields are automatically selected to be summarized on in the wizard. You need to remove the fields in the Summarized Fields section that you do not need. To count the number of orders for each product, you can use the Order ID field or the Product Name field because each will print in the details section of the report. The Quantity summary field is not needed.

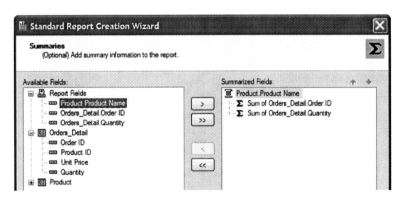

Figure 7-13 Group and summary options

2. Remove the Quantity summary field, then click on the Sum Order ID field.

3. Open the drop down list below the Summarized Fields section and select Count. You should have the options selected that are shown in Figure 7-14. Click Finish. Your report should look like the one shown in Figure 7-15.

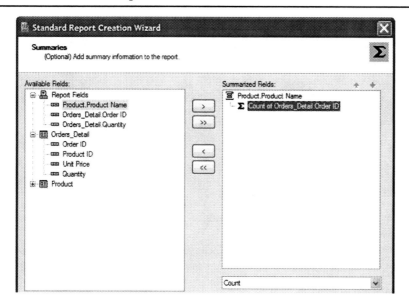

Figure 7-14 Modified summary options

If you look in the group tree section you will see a list of all of the products that were purchased by product name, instead of by Product ID number. This makes it easy to find out how many orders were placed for a certain product. Figure 7-16 shows the total number of orders for the first product on the report.

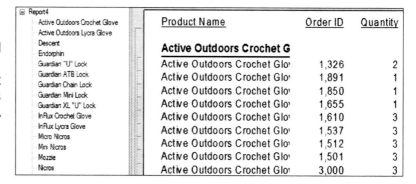

Figure 7-15 L7.4 Product summary report

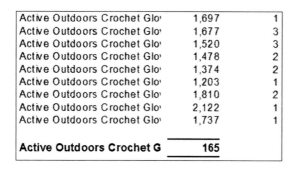

Figure 7-16 Total number of orders for the first product on the report

4. Save the report as L7.4 Product summary, then close the report.

Exercise 7.5: Create The Customer Information By Region Report

In this exercise you will create a report that groups the data by region. The report will also have summary information and a bar chart.

1. Open the Standard Report Wizard, then add the Customer table and click Next.

2. Add the following fields: Customer Name, Address1, Region, Country and Postal Code, then click Next.

3. Add the Region field to the **GROUP BY** section. Within each region, the report needs to be sorted by Postal Code. Add the Postal Code field to the Grouping screen. Figure 7-17 shows the options that should be selected.

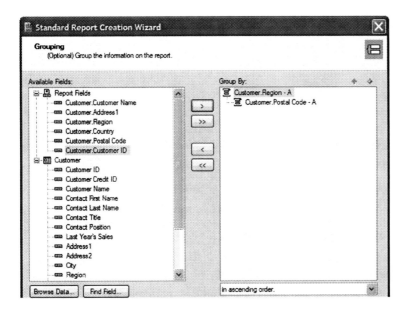

Figure 7-17 Grouping and sorting options selected

4. Click Next and add the Customer ID field, then open the drop down list and select **COUNT**. Click Next. You will see the Group Sorting screen. No options need to be selected on this screen.

5. Click Next, then select the **BAR CHART** option on the Chart screen and type Customers Per Region in the Chart Title field. Figure 7-18 shows the options that should be selected.

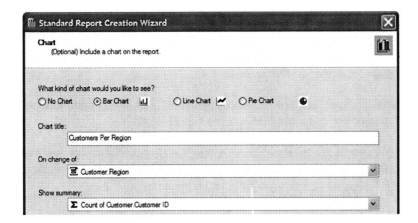

Figure 7-18 Chart screen options

6. This report does not require any filters or criteria. Click Finish. Your report should look like the one shown in Figure 7-19.

Notice that the fields are not in the same order on the report as the order that you added them to the Fields to Display section on the Fields screen. The wizard rearranges the fields and puts the fields that are being grouped on, at the beginning of the details section. As you can see, the chart would need to be modified to be meaningful.

7. Save the report as L7.5 Customer information by region with chart, then close the report.

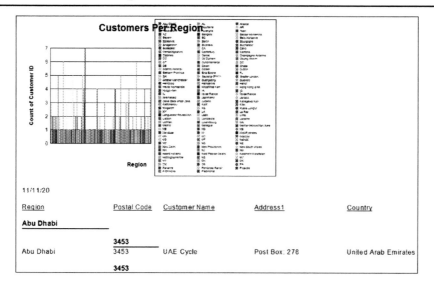

Figure 7-19 L7.5 Customer information by region with chart report

Exercise 7.6: Create The Orders By Customer Report

The report that you will create in this exercise is similar to the report that you created in Exercise 6.2.

1. Open the Standard Report Wizard and add the Customer, Orders and Orders Detail tables. Click Next, then click Next on the Link screen.

2. Add the following fields: Customer Name, Order Date, Ship Date, Order Amount, Order ID and Unit Price, then click Next.

3. Add the Customer Name field to the **GROUP BY** section and click Next.

4. Click on the Order ID field in the Summarized Fields section and select **COUNT** from the drop down list, then remove the Unit Price field from the Summarized Fields section.

5. Click on the Order ID field in the **AVAILABLE FIELDS** section, then click the > button. This will let you create another summary for the Order ID field.

6. With the second Order ID field still selected, open the drop down list and select **DISTINCT COUNT**. Figure 7-20 shows the Summarized Field options that should be selected.

7. Click Next. Click Next again because none of the options on the Group Sorting screen are needed for this report. Click Next again because none of the options on the Chart screen are needed for this report.

8. Add the Order Date field to the Filter Fields section. Open the drop down list and select **IS GREATER THAN OR EQUAL TO,** then open the next drop down list and select **6/24/2003** or you can type it in.

9. Add the Order Amount field to the Filter Fields section. Open the drop down list and select **IS GREATER THAN,** then type 2499.99 in the next drop down list and click Finish. Your report should look like the one shown in Figure 7-21. Have you noticed that you can't create a title for the report in the wizard?

10. Save the report as L7.6 Orders by customer, then close the report.

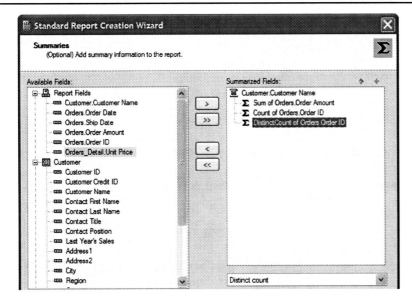

Figure 7-20 Summaries screen options

11/12/20					
Customer Name	Order Date	Ship Date	Order Amount	Order ID	Unit Price
Alley Cat Cycles					
Alley Cat Cycles	9/28/2004 12:00:00A	9/30/2004 12:00:00A	$2,559.63	2,157	$539.85
Alley Cat Cycles	10/27/2004 12:00:00.	11/6/2004 12:00:00A	$2,699.55	2,272	$899.85
Alley Cat Cycles	2/19/2005 12:00:00A	2/22/2005 12:00:00A	$8,819.55	2,735	$2,939.85
Alley Cat Cycles	2/19/2005 12:00:00A	2/22/2005 12:00:00A	$8,819.55	2,735	$2,939.85
Alley Cat Cycles	1/31/2005 12:00:00A	2/3/2005 12:00:00AN	$9,290.30	2,664	$455.86
Alley Cat Cycles	1/31/2005 12:00:00A	2/3/2005 12:00:00AN	$9,290.30	2,664	$2,792.86
Alley Cat Cycles	1/8/2004 12:00:00AN	1/8/2004 1:30:00AM	$5,879.70	1,151	$2,939.85
Alley Cat Cycles	9/28/2004 12:00:00A	9/30/2004 12:00:00A	$2,559.63	2,157	$313.36
Alley Cat Cycles	**$49,918.21**			8	5

Figure 7-21 L7.6 Orders by customer report

Exercise 7.7: Create A Top N Report

In previous exercises in this lesson, you created reports that grouped the data. By default, the groups are sorted on the value in the group field. For example, in Exercise 7.6 the orders were grouped by the values, (the actual customer names) in the summary customer name field.

There is another way to sort groups on a report. In Lesson 5, you learned how to filter (select) which records would appear on the report. Just like you filtered the detail records in Lesson 5, you can filter the groups. One way to explain Top N reports is that this sort method is sorting the groups on the value of a group summary field instead of the values in the group by field.

> The Group Sorting screen allows you to limit the number of groups on the report to five by selecting the Top 5 or Bottom 5 group option. No more or no less. The Group Sorting Expert does not have a group number limitation.

> The grand totals that appear on a report when the top or bottom five group sorting option is used, are not the real totals for the detail records on the report. They are the totals for all records that meet the other report criteria before the top or bottom five group sort option is applied.

In this exercise you will create a report that will display the top five days in June 2004 with the largest daily order totals. You will also create a pie chart that displays the top five order days.

1. Open the Standard Report Wizard, then add the Customer and Orders tables and click Next. Click Next on the Link screen.

2. Add the following fields: Customer Name, Order ID, Order Amount and Order Date, then click Next.

3. Add the Order Date field to the **GROUP BY** section and click Next.

4. Remove the Order ID field from the Summarized Fields section and click Next.

5. Select the **TOP 5 GROUPS** option on the Group Sorting screen and click Next.

6. Select the Pie chart option on the Chart screen and type `Top 5 Order Days In June 2004` in the Chart Title field and click Next.

7. Add the Order Date field to the Filter Fields section on the Record Selection screen. Open the drop down list and select **IS BETWEEN**, then type `6/01/2004` in the next drop down list. In the last drop down list, type `6/30/2004`. Figure 7-22 shows the options that should be selected.

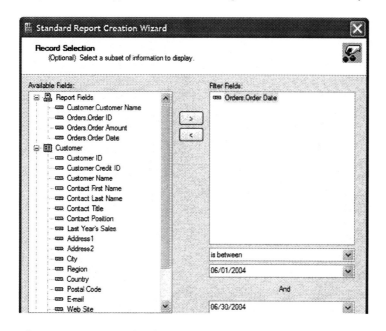

Figure 7-22 Record Selection options

8. Click Finish. Your report should look like the one shown in Figure 7-23. You will only see detail information for the top five order days.

As you can see, one of the dates in the group tree is in May. If you click on that link, you will see orders for June. No, I did not lead you astray. This is one of the features of the wizards that do not work as intended and is why many report designers tend to stay away from the report wizards. There are options that are preset that you don't know about, that can produce unexpected results. If you plan to use this wizard on a regular basis for something other then a basic report, hopefully you see how important it is to understand the data that the report should produce. That should lead you in the direction of how to fix any problem that the wizard creates.

9. Save the report as `L7.7 Top 5 order days in June 2004` and leave it open to complete the next exercise.

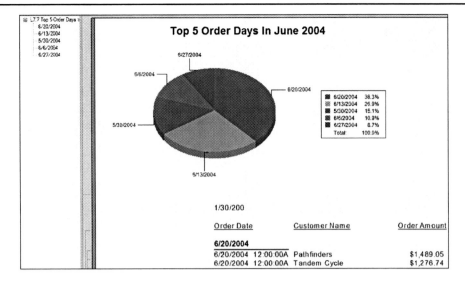

Figure 7-23 L7.7 Top 5 order days in June 2004 report

Exercise 7.7A: How To Fix The L7.7 Top 5 Order Days Report

When I looked at the data in the report, I noticed that each of the five groups actually had more than one days worth of data. Each group actually had a weeks worth of data, even though I was expecting to only see data for one day in each group. Because the data is grouped on the Order Date field, I realized that the wizard must have a group default set to weekly. I opened the Group Expert (which is a different expert then the Group Sort Expert) and sure enough, the option was set to weekly.

This is an example of how a wizard will produce unexpected results. What scares me is that I get the feeling that because the majority of people that use wizards use them without questioning the results, this is something that could easily be missed. What would be helpful on the Standard Wizard would be if the Group Sorting wizard screen had an option to let you select how you want the data to be grouped, by day, week, month, year etc. After looking at the options on the Group Sort Expert, I noticed that it did not have this option either, so because the Group Sorting wizard screen is a subset of the Group Sort Expert, it made a little sense.

Even though the wizard produces results that you may not want, I do not know about you, but I can do without this type of help from a wizard. The best advise that I can give you if you insist on using a wizard is after the wizard creates the report, open each corresponding expert for a screen that you selected options on in the wizard and look at the options. While this is good advise, if you think for a minute, you will realize that even that advise would not have helped you detect this error because options from the Group Expert are not used in this wizard. The good news is that this report can be fixed by following the steps below.

1. Save the L7.7 report as L7.7A Fixed Top 5 order days in June 2004.

2. Report ⇒ Group Expert, then click the **OPTIONS** button. You will see the Change Group Options dialog box. In the last drop down list, you will see that the option **FOR EACH WEEK IS** selected.

3. Open **THE SECTION WILL BE PRINTED** drop down list and select **FOR EACH DAY** as shown in Figure 7-24. As you can see, knowing about this option would allow you to create a variety of reports, just by changing this option. Click OK twice to close both dialog boxes.

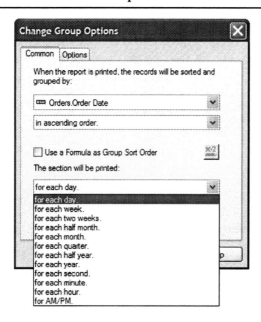

Figure 7-24 Change Group Options dialog box

4. Refresh the data and preview the report. It should look like the one shown in Figure 7-25. You should now see five days in June (opposed to four as shown earlier in Figure 7-23) in the group tree section of the report. All of the detail records in each group should have the same order date. Save the changes and close the report.

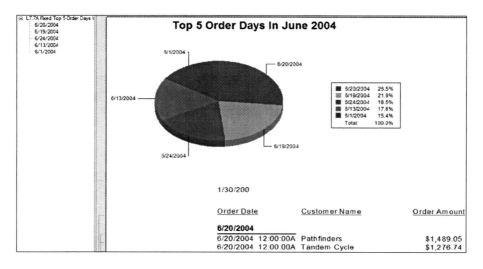

Figure 7-25 L7.7A Fixed Top 5 order days in June 2004 report

Exercise 7.8: Use The Mailing Label Report Wizard

This wizard allows you to create a column layout report, which many people use to print labels. You can use this wizard to create other types of columnar reports besides mailing labels. In this exercise you will learn how to create a report that can be used to print labels. The report will print shipping labels for customers that placed an order in June 2004, that are in the US. Many of the screens in this wizard are the same as the ones that you have used in the Standard Report wizard.

1. Open the Mailing Label Report wizard and add the Customer and Orders tables, then click Next. Click Next again, because the links are correct.

2. Add the following fields: Customer Name, Address1, Address2, City, Region and Postal Code, then click Next.

3. Open the **MAILING LABEL TYPE** drop down list and select Avery 5153. Figure 7-26 shows the options that should be selected.

The **MAILING LABEL TYPE** drop down list has an option, **USER DEFINED LABEL**, that will let you create a custom size label.

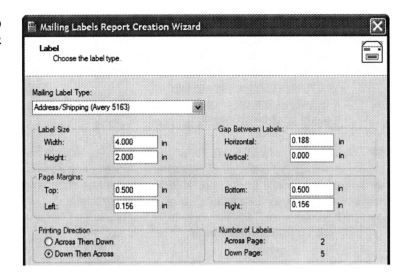

Figure 7-26 Label screen options

4. Click Next and add the Country field to the Filter Fields section. Open the drop down list and select **IS EQUAL TO**, then open the next drop down list and select **USA** or you can type it in.

5. Add the Order Date field to the Filter Fields section. Open the drop down list and select **IS BETWEEN** and type 6/01/2004 in the first drop down list, then type 6/30/2004 in the last drop down list. Click Finish. Your report should look like the one shown in Figure 7-27. The report should have 108 records.

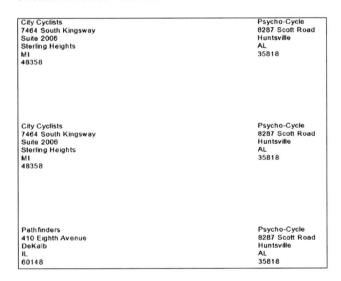

Figure 7-27 L7.8 Customer labels for June 2004 report

 This label report uses two address lines. What many people do is modify the label layout and put both address fields on the same line. That is not a requirement for this exercise.

Because the date criteria was for a month, you see duplicate customer names. More than likely, the labels would be printed daily, which means that you would not see duplicate customer names in the labels, unless a customer placed more than one order on the same day.

6. Save the report as L7.8 Customer labels for June 2004, then close the report.

Cross-Tab Reports

As you saw earlier in Table 7-2, the Cross-Tab wizard has many of the same screens as the Standard Report wizard. The major differences between the Standard and Cross-Tab wizards are listed below.

① There are no detail records in a cross-tab report.
② The functionality of the Standard wizards grouping and summary screens are combined on one Cross-Tab wizard screen.
③ Cross-Tabs are most often placed in the report header or footer section, but they can be placed in other sections.

Cross-Tabs, like the Select Expert allow you to retrieve records that meet specific criteria. The cross-tab report takes the Select Expert that you learned about in Lesson 5, one step further because it allows you to summarize the data that is in the detail section of standard reports. Cross-Tab reports are often used for comparison analysis. Examples of cross-tab reports are:

① Sales by sales rep by year.
② Sales by region.
③ Summarizing how many orders by year and by zip code, each sales rep has.
④ Sales of a specific product by sales rep, by month.
⑤ Summarizing how many customers by region purchased certain products by month or by year.

Cross-Tab reports often give new report designers difficulty. I suspect that this is because this type of report requires one to think in dimensions. Like spreadsheets, cross-tab reports have rows and columns. Each cell in a spreadsheet contains one piece of data. In a cross-tab object, the cell contains one piece of summary data (count, sum, average etc).

Behind the scenes, cross-tab objects take the detail records that you are use to seeing, as well as, the groups and summarizes the detail data and places the result in a cell. Hopefully the following scenario will make the concept of cross-tab objects easier to understand.

Going From Standard Reports To Cross-Tab Reports

This scenario will use the first cross-tab example mentioned above - Sales by sales rep by year. The goal of this cross-tab report from a standard report perspective is to show sales for a year by sales rep.

The report shown in Figure 7-28 is a basic list report that sorts the sales, by sales rep and by year. This report is in the zip file that you downloaded in Lesson 1. The file name is L7 Cross-tab basic sort report combined.

Sales By Rep By Year

Last Name	First Name	Order Date	Order Amount	Customer Name
Davolio	Nancy	02/19/2003	$789.51	Belgium Bike Co.
Davolio	Nancy	02/19/2003	$58.00	Spokes for Folks
Davolio	Nancy	02/26/2003	$68.90	Mountain Madmen Bicycles
Davolio	Nancy	02/27/2003	$2,698.53	Pedals Inc.
Davolio	Nancy	02/27/2003	$1,079.70	Mountain Madmen Bicycles
Davolio	Nancy	02/27/2003	$1,529.70	Cycle City Rome

Last Name	First Name	Order Date	Order Amount	Customer Name
Suyama	Michael	02/14/2005	$5,893.20	Crazy Wheels
Suyama	Michael	02/19/2005	$6,005.40	Off the Mountain Biking
Suyama	Michael	02/19/2005	$7,685.25	To The Limit Biking Co.
Suyama	Michael	02/22/2005	$1,664.70	Bike-A-Holics Anonymous
Suyama	Michael	02/24/2005	$138.70	Tienda de Bicicletas El Pardo
Suyama	Michael	02/25/2005	$893.55	Whistler Rentals
Suyama	Michael	02/28/2005	$1,529.70	Belgium Bike Co.

Figure 7-28 Basic sorted report of sales by sales rep by year

The report shown above in Figure 7-28 contains all of the data one would need to determine sales by sales rep, by year, but because there aren't any totals for the groups, it would take a while to manually do the math, especially if there were hundreds of sales reps. Yes, I know what you are thinking, create a report that groups the data by sales rep, then by year. Figure 7-29 shows that report.

Can you tell me how many saddles Robert King sold in total? Or can you tell me who had the lowest number of sales in 2004? Okay, I'll wait while you open the report shown in Figure 7-29 and get a calculator to add up the totals for the two sales reps. (It's in the zip file. The file name is L7 Cross-tab grouped report.) I can wait. I have patience <smile>.

Like the report shown above in Figure 7-28, the report in Figure 7-29 has all of the information that you need to answer these questions.

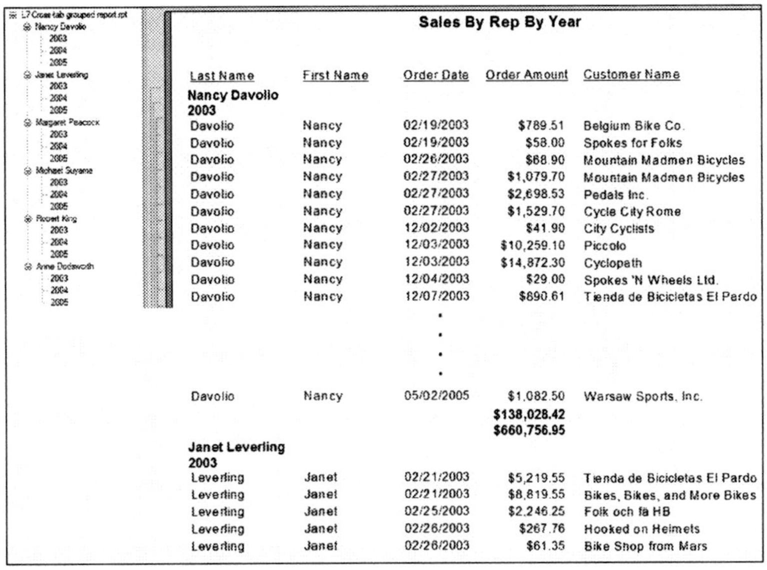

Figure 7-29 Data grouped by sales rep by year

The problem is that it is spread out over several pages in the report, which makes it difficult for comparison analysis. As you will see after completing Exercise 7.9, this same data in a cross-tab report will be in an easy to read format. With a cross-tab report you can quickly answer questions like how many sales Robert King had for three products and who had the lowest number of sales in 2004.

How To Create This Cross-Tab

Yes, I hear you grumbling and saying, "Great, I now see the advantages of creating a cross-tab report, but how do I get the data shown earlier in Figures 7-28 and 7-29 into cross-tab format?" Okay, here goes:

① Usually, the field down the left side of a cross-tab (that creates the rows) is the data element that there are more occurrences of. In this example, there are more sales reps then years. You can put the sales reps across the top and still get the same results.

② The field that goes across the top (that creates the columns) represents the data element that there are less occurrences of.

③ The cells in the middle of the cross-tab are the sum (in this example, a count) of orders that the sales rep had for the year. This is the equivalent to grouping and sorting data.

④ The totals at the bottom of the cross-tab report will tell you how many sales are for each year and a grand total number of sales for the entire report in the lower right hand corner of the cross-tab. These totals are automatically calculated in a cross-tab report.

⑤ I have saved the best for last - the placement of the fields on the Cross-Tab screen. The fields for the row and column were answered above. That leaves the field for the cells in the middle of the cross-tab report. Recall the original statement - Sales by sales rep, by year. You have already determined that the sales rep field (Employee Name field in the table), is what will be used for the rows. You have also determined that the Order Date will be used for the columns. The only field left is the sales (the orders). This is what goes in the Summary field section of the Cross-Tab screen. In this example, the cells represent a count of orders. The default calculation is Sum. You would change that to **DISTINCT COUNT** for the Order ID field.

Cross-Tab Screen

Now that you have a foundation of cross-tab reports, the options on the Cross-Tab and Grid Style screens will hopefully make sense. Figure 7-30 shows the Cross-Tab screen. Figure 7-31 shows the Grid Style screen.

The **AVAILABLE FIELDS** section lets you select the fields that are needed to create the report.

The **ROWS** section contains the field(s) that will be displayed down the left side of the report.

The **COLUMNS** section contains the field(s) that will be displayed across the top of the report.

The **SUMMARY FIELDS** section contains the field(s) that will have the calculation (sum, count, average etc).

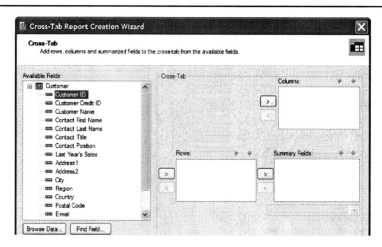

Figure 7-30 Cross-Tab screen

The Grid Style screen contains options that let you add formatting to the report, similar to templates.

Like other reports, you can format a cross-tab report manually.

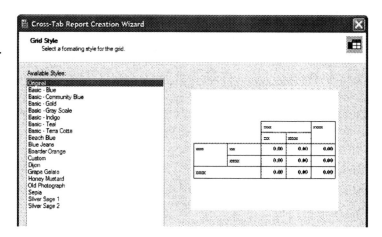

Figure 7-31 Grid Style screen

Exercise 7.9: Create A Cross-Tab Product Report

In this exercise you will create a cross-tab report that shows the number of sales for three classes of products: gloves, kids and saddles by sales rep.

1. Click on the Cross-Tab Report Wizard link on the Start Page.

2. Add the Employee, Orders, Orders Detail and Product Type tables, then click Next. Click Next on the Link screen.

3. Click on the Last Name field in the Employee table, then click the right arrow button next to the **ROWS** section.

4. Move the Product Type Name field in the Product Type table to the **COLUMNS** section.

> 💡 You can click on the field in the Available Fields section and drag it to the section of the Cross-Tab screen that you need.

5. Move the Quantity field in the Orders Detail table to the **SUMMARY FIELDS** section.

6. Select **COUNT** from the drop down list under the Summary Fields section. The Cross-Tab screen should have the options selected that are shown in Figure 7-32.

7. Click Next, then select the **NO CHART** option, if it is not already selected and click Next.

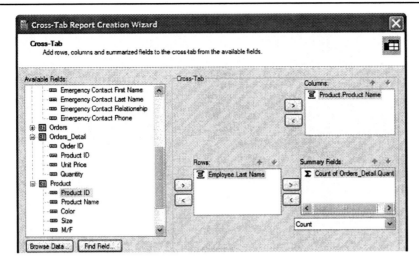

Figure 7-32 Cross-Tab screen options

 The reason that you added the Orders table and did not use any fields from the table is because it is the "link" between the Orders Detail table and the Employee table to get the Employee Name for each order.

8. This report needs to be filtered because you only want totals for three classes of products: gloves, kids and saddles. Add the Product Type Name field from the Product Type table to the Filter Fields section, then open the drop down list and select **IS ONE OF**.

9. Open the next drop down list and select gloves, kids and saddles. You should have the options selected that are shown in Figure 7-33.

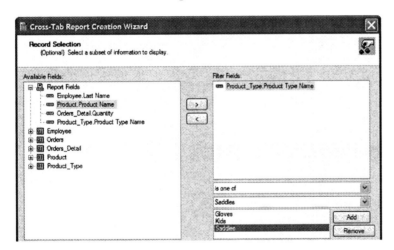

Figure 7-33 Record Selection options

10. Click Next, then click on the **ORIGINAL** grid style, if it is not already selected, as shown earlier in Figure 7-31. Click Finish. Your report should look like the one shown in Figure 7-34. Now can you tell me how many saddles Robert King sold in total?

	Gloves	Kids	Saddles	Total
Davolio	85	18	49	152
Dodsworth	101	19	58	178
King	97	23	58	178
Leverling	84	25	56	165
Peacock	105	20	59	184
Suyama	84	25	56	165
Total	556	130	336	1,022

Figure 7-34 L7.9 Cross-Tab report

11. Save the report as L7.9 Cross-Tab, then close the report.

Exercise 7.10: Create A Sales Per Year Per Sales Rep Cross-Tab Report

Earlier I asked if you could tell how many sales in total Robert King had and who had the lowest total sales in terms of the order amount. I was wondering if you came up with the answer yet? If not, this exercise will show you how to find out how many sales per year each sales rep had.

1. Click on the Cross-Tab Report Wizard link on the Start Page.

2. Add the Employee and Orders tables and click Next, then click Next on the Link screen.

3. Click on the Last Name field in the Employee table, then click the right arrow button next to the **ROWS** section and add the Order Date field to the **COLUMNS** section.

4. Open the drop down list under the Columns section and select **FOR EACH YEAR**. This will create a column for each year that there are orders in the Orders table.

5. Add the Order Amount field to the Summary Fields section. You should have the options selected that are shown in Figure 7-35. This cross-tab report does not need to select (filter) any records. Click Finish. Your report should look like the one shown in Figure 7-36. Leave the report open to complete the next part of the exercise.

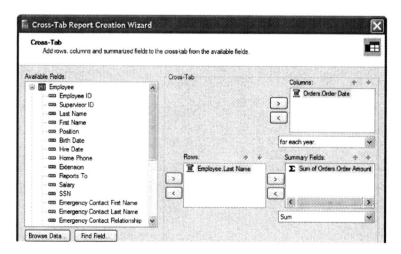

Figure 7-35 Cross-Tab screen options

 If the Orders table had 10 years worth of data and you only wanted to show some of the years on the report, you would select the Order Date field on the Record Selection screen and enter the date range for the years that you wanted to display on the report.

	2003	2004	2005	Total
Davolio	$71,862.70	#########	#########	#########
Dodsworth	$29,049.94	#########	#########	#########
King	$21,093.75	#########	#########	#########
Leverling	$44,121.64	#########	#########	#########
Peacock	$38,458.39	#########	#########	#########
Suyama	$54,804.22	#########	#########	#########
Total	#########	#########	#########	#########

Figure 7-36 Sales by year cross-tab report

Modify The Cross-Tab Report

As you can see, the grid is too small to handle the sales total amounts. This part of the exercise will show you how to modify the cross-tab report.

1. In the design window, select all four of the Order Amount fields as shown in Figure 7-37, then make the fields wider by dragging them to the right.

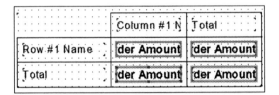

Figure 7-37 Order Amount fields selected

2. Center the Column #1 Name field and Total object.

3. The report should look like the one shown in Figure 7-38. Save the report as L7.10 Sales Per Year Per Sales Rep Cross-Tab. Now you should be able to figure out who had the lowest sales amount each year. Close the report.

	2003	2004	2005	Total
Davolio	$71,862.70	$450,865.83	$138,028.42	$660,756.95
Dodsworth	$29,049.94	$513,545.52	$140,253.75	$682,849.21
King	$21,093.75	$512,406.60	$215,255.59	$748,755.94
Leverling	$44,121.64	$447,235.19	$157,745.16	$649,101.99
Peacock	$38,458.39	$446,150.56	$147,190.82	$631,799.77
Suyama	$54,804.22	$496,881.48	$158,715.78	$710,401.48
Total	$259,390.64	$2,867,085.18	$957,189.52	$4,083,665.34

Figure 7-38 L7.10 Sales Per Year Per Sales Rep Cross-Tab report

OLAP Reports

OLAP reports look similar to cross-tab reports because they present the data in a summarized format in rows and columns. OLAP reports use an OLAP cube as the data source. The difference between OLAP data and the data that a cross-tab report uses is that OLAP data has already been summarized before it is placed in the cube structure that you use as the data source for a report. OLAP data must be on a server. The OLAP Cube does not have to be on a server, but it usually is. You should only use the OLAP wizard if the OLAP data is the only object on the report.

| The **OLAP CUBE** contains the data. The **OLAP** grid is where the data is placed. |

Exercise 7.11: Create An OLAP Report

In this exercise you will create an OLAP report that will display customer order totals by country, by state and by month. This information has already been summarized. If you selected the default options, it would present a lot of data. A benefit of OLAP data is that you can select which customers, states and months you want to display on the report.

There are three basic steps to creating an OLAP report. The steps are: create an OLAP connection, select options on the Rows/Columns screen and modify the report.

The requirements for this report are:

① Display totals for January, February and March.
② All customers in CA, IL and PA.
③ Include the following products: Active Outdoors Lycra Glove, Descent and Mozzie.

Step 1: Create An OLAP Connection

1. Click on the OLAP Cube Report Wizard link on the Start Page. You will see the screen shown in Figure 7-39.

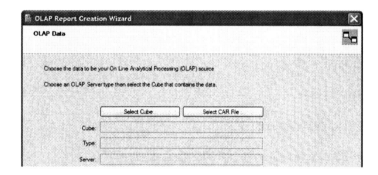

Figure 7-39 OLAP Data screen

The **OLAP Data** screen lets you select the data source for the report. There are two types of data sources that you can select, as discussed below.

① **Select Cube** This option lets you select an OLAP Cube to use as the data source.
② **Select CAR File** This option will let you select a CAR file, which will use a Crystal Analysis application file as the data source.

2. Click the **SELECT CUBE** button. You will see the dialog box shown in Figure 7-40.

If you see the OLAP Connection that you need on this dialog box, you would click on it here and then click **OPEN**. If not, you have to create a connection for the OLAP cube that you need, which is what you will do now.

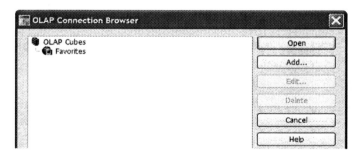

Figure 7-40 OLAP Connection Browser dialog box

3. Click the **ADD** button. You will see the dialog box shown in Figure 7-41.

The **CONNECTION PROPERTIES** dialog box lets you create OLAP connections.

The **SERVER OPTIONS** will vary depending on the connection type.

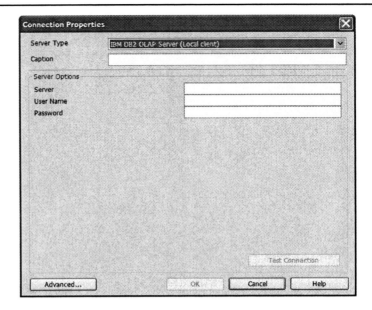

Figure 7-41 Connection Properties dialog box

You have to select a server type and create a caption for every connection type.

4. Open the Server Type drop down list and select **HOLOS HDC CUBE (LOCAL CLIENT)**, then type `Exercise 7.11 OLAP` in the **CAPTION** field.

5. Click the button at the end of the **SERVER OPTIONS** field and navigate to the following path: C:\Program Files\Business Objects\Crystal Reports 11\Samples\en\Databases\OLAP Data\, then double-click on the Xtreme.hdc file, as shown in Figure 7-42.

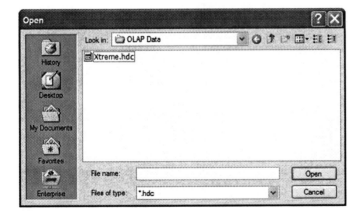

Figure 7-42 OLAP Data file

If you do not see this file, you probably changed the default installation path when you installed Crystal Reports. If that is the case, navigate to the path that you selected during the installation. If you still can't find the file, you can use the Search tool in Windows and search for the Xtreme.hdc file.

6. Click the **TEST CONNECTION** button on the Connection Properties dialog box to confirm that your connection is working. Click OK when you see the "Connected Successfully" message. Your Connection Properties dialog box should have the options shown in Figure 7-43.

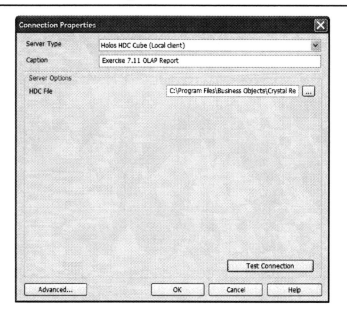

Figure 7-43 Connection Properties options

7. Click OK to close the Connection Properties dialog box. You should see the connection to the Xtreme cube as illustrated in Figure 7-44. Click on the Xtreme cube connection, then click the OPEN button. Your OLAP Data screen should have the options shown in Figure 7-45. Click Next.

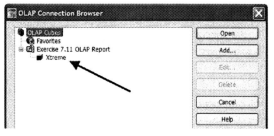

Figure 7-44 Xtreme cube connection

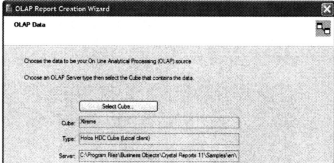

Figure 7-45 OLAP Data screen options

Step 2: Select Options On The Rows/Columns Screen

In this part of the exercise you will select the dimensions, rows and columns for the report. Figure 7-46 shows the Rows/Columns screen.

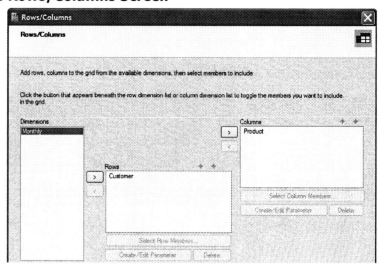

Figure 7-46 Rows/Columns screen

The **DIMENSIONS** section determines how the data will be grouped on the report. The dimensions listed are all of the ones that have not already been added to the rows or columns sections. In this exercise the only available dimension that you can select is Monthly. If you added the monthly dimension to the Columns section, the report would be grouped by Product. If you wanted the product data grouped by month, the monthly dimension would have to be the first item in the Columns section.

The **ROWS** and **COLUMNS** sections basically work the same as they do on the Cross-Tab wizard. Like cross-tabs, you should put the item that has the most data down the left side of the OLAP grid and the item with the least data, across the top of the OLAP grid.

With OLAP data, I find it easier to figure out the layout order by working from the inside of the grid (the cells) out. The goal of this report is to show what products customers purchased by country, by state and by month. The data in this OLAP cube has the totals at the state level.

The way that you select the months, customers and products that will appear on the report is by clicking on the **SELECT ROW MEMBERS** or **SELECT COLUMN MEMBERS** buttons. These buttons let you select the specific months, customers and products that will appear on the report. For example, if you want two customers in PA, two customers in NC and one customer in CA, that is what you would select for the Customer row options. If you want to only show the activity for the customers just mentioned for the first quarter of the year, you would select the months January, February and March. Each of these options is known as a **MEMBER**.

Select The Row Dimension Options

1. Add the Monthly dimension to the **ROWS** section, then move the Customer field below the Monthly dimension by clicking on the down arrow button.

2. Click on the Monthly dimension, then click the **SELECT ROW MEMBERS** button. The Member Selector dialog box is how you select which months (in this exercise) that you want totals for.

3. Click on the plus sign in front of the **YEAR TOTAL** option, then check the months Jan, Feb and Mar as shown in Figure 7-47. Click OK.

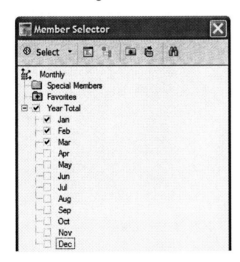

Figure 7-47 Months selected for the report

4. Click on the Customer row option, then click the Select Row Members button.

5. Click on the plus sign in front of USA. This report needs to include all customers in three regions: CA, IL and PA. Click on each of these regions, then check each company under each of these three regions as shown in Figure 7-48. Click OK to close the Member Selector dialog box.

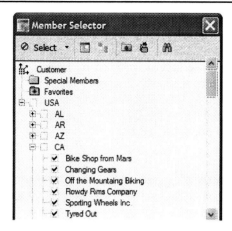

Figure 7-48 Three regions selected

Select The Column Dimension Options

In this part of the exercise you will select the products that you want to appear on the report.

1. Click on the Product field, then click the Select Column Members button.

2. Open the Product list and select the following products: Active Outdoors Lycra Glove, Descent and Mozzie, as shown in Figure 7-49, then click OK to close the Member Selector dialog box. Click Finish. Your report should look like the one shown in Figure 7-50. The report needs to be modified.

3. Save the report as `L7.11 OLAP`, then click on the Design tab.

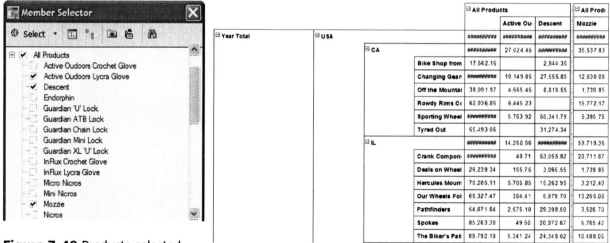

Figure 7-49 Products selected

Figure 7-50 L7.11 OLAP report (before formatting)

Step 3: Modify The OLAP Report

The following changes need to be made to the report:

> ① The Year Total, Country and Region columns need to be made smaller.
> ② The Customer section needs to be made larger.
> ③ All of the columns with numeric values need to be wider.

1. Select the two monthly level fields and make them smaller.

2. Select the first two customer level fields and make them smaller. Make the third customer level field wider. This is the Company Name field.

3. Select all six **VALUE** fields and the bottom Product Level field and make them wider.

4. Make the bottom Product Level field longer because the name of the first product is not totally visible. Save the changes. Page 1 should look like the one shown in Figure 7-51.

			All Products	Active Oudoors	Descent	Mozzie
Year Total	US		4,066,527.25	137,838.58	1,080,017.63	413,665.31
	CA		401,785.03	27,024.45	125,935.88	35,537.83
		Bike Shop from Mars	17,562.16		2,944.35	
		Changing Gears	106,990.36	10,149.85	27,555.85	12,630.06
		Off the Mountaing Biking	38,091.97	4,665.45	8,819.55	1,739.85
		Rowdy Rims Company	62,036.86	6,445.23		15,772.17
		Sporting Wheels Inc.	121,610.59	5,763.92	55,341.79	5,395.75
		Tyred Out	55,493.06		31,274.34	
	IL		531,187.19	14,260.56	151,984.20	59,719.36
		Crank Components	139,687.84	48.71	53,055.82	20,711.87
		Deals on Wheels	26,239.34	155.75	3,065.55	1,739.85
		Hercules Mountain Bikes	70,205.11	5,705.85	15,262.95	3,212.40
		Our Wheels Follow Us Everyw	65,327.47	384.41	5,879.70	13,255.06
		Pathfinders	54,671.84	2,575.10	29,398.50	3,526.70
		Spokes	85,263.38	49.50	20,972.67	6,785.42
		The Biker's Path	89,792.19	5,341.24	24,349.02	10,488.06

Figure 7-51 L7.11 OLAP report page 1

OLAP Grand Total Section Explained

Figure 7-52 illustrates the grand total section of the report.

① Grand totals for the entire report.
② Grand totals for the region CA (state) for the entire report.
③ Grand totals for one company for the entire report.
④ This lets you know what time frame the totals are for. In this case, the totals are for the entire year.

			All Products	Active Oudoors	Descent	Mozzie
Year Total	USA	① →	4,066,527.25	137,838.58	1,080,017.63	413,665.31
	CA	② →	401,785.03	27,024.45	125,935.88	35,537.83
		Bike Shop from Mars	17,562.16		2,944.35	
		Changing Gears	106,990.36	10,149.85	27,555.85	12,630.06
④		Off the Mountaing Biking	38,091.97	4,665.45	8,819.55	1,739.85
		Rowdy Rims Company	62,036.86	6,445.23		15,772.17
		Sporting Wheels Inc.	121,610.59	5,763.92	55,341.79	5,395.75
		Tyred Out ③ →	55,493.06		31,274.34	

Figure 7-52 Grand totals illustrated

Sections Of An OLAP Report Explained

Figure 7-53 illustrates the sections for each month.

   ① This column lets you know what month the totals are for.
   ② This column lets you know what country the monthly totals are for.
   ③ This column lets you know what region the monthly totals are for.
   ④ These are the monthly totals for one company. The number in the All Products column is the grand total for that company for the month of January. The other amounts in the row are the totals for the company for each product. Empty cells means that the company did not purchase any of that product during the month.
   ⑤ These are the totals for all of the companies in PA for the month of January.

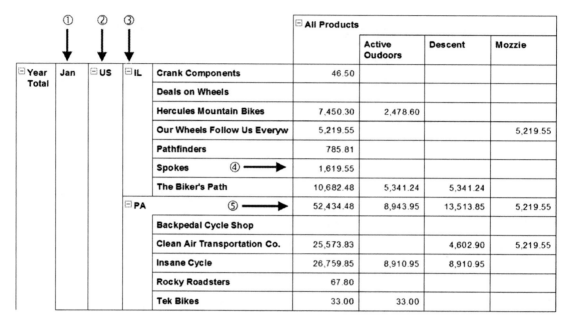

Figure 7-53 Sections of the OLAP report illustrated

When you reopen an OLAP report, the **SHOW/HIDE** (plus and minus) buttons will not be visible. To display these buttons, you have to refresh the report. When you close the report you will be prompted to save the changes. If you didn't make any changes, you do not have to save the report.

Figure 7-52 shown earlier does not display the Show/Hide buttons. They are displayed in Figure 7-53 above. Any section of the report that can be hidden will have the minus sign symbol next to it. Figure 7-54 shows the report after the Show/Hide button was clicked on each of the region sections on the first page of the report. The customer rows are now hidden. The amounts that you see now are the totals for each region (state) by month. This view is an OLAP summary report.

All Products					Active Oudoors	Descent	Mozzie
Year Total	⊟US			4,066,527.25	137,838.58	1,080,017.63	413,665.31
		⊞CA		401,785.03	27,024.45	125,935.88	35,537.83
		⊞IL		531,187.19	14,260.56	151,984.20	59,719.36
		⊞PA		401,492.63	18,967.36	124,507.28	46,115.50
Jan	⊟US			310,900.38	21,491.72	70,962.05	17,573.15
		⊞CA		26,926.60		11,792.66	
		⊞IL		25,804.19	7,819.84	5,341.24	5,219.55
		⊞PA		52,434.48	8,943.95	13,513.85	5,219.55
Feb	⊟US			365,829.00	15,717.29	133,585.59	30,329.80
		⊞CA		90,700.06	3,705.60	34,586.38	6,743.27
		⊞IL		25,554.06		17,639.10	
		⊞PA		34,888.20		6,233.05	8,763.75

Figure 7-54 Customer (product) rows hidden in the report

Report Template Overview

In prior versions of Crystal Reports, STYLES allowed you to format reports like templates do now.
The downside to styles was that you could not create your own. Templates have replaced styles and as you will learn, they have some functionality that styles do not have. Templates also allow you to provide a consistent look for the reports that you create. Templates allow you to change the "look" of the report quickly, without having to format objects on the report manually.

Templates can apply a variety of formatting options including: shading, adding color, lines and borders.
If you have formatted a report, you can use it as a template to apply to other reports. Crystal Reports comes with 12 templates that you can use.

How Templates Work

The layout, format of the fields, text objects, group and summary fields in the template are applied (copied) to the corresponding objects in the report. Conditional formatting formulas, graphics, lines, special fields, group charts and boxes in the template are also applied to the report.

Template Types

There are three types of templates that can be applied to a report. They are explained below.

① **Predefined templates** These are the templates that come with Crystal Reports. You can apply these templates from the Standard Report Wizard or from the Template Expert.
② **Use an existing report as a template** If you have created a report that has the formatting that you would like to apply to other reports, you can use the report as a template.
③ **Create a template** If neither of the two options listed above have a template that you like or need, you can create your own template. Templates that you create are not connected to a data source. Instead of formatting fields from a table, you add TEMPLATE FIELD OBJECTS to the template and format the objects.

The biggest tip that I can give you about templates that you create, is to include formatting for as many object types as possible. The reason is because if the report has an object that doesn't have a matching object in the template, the object will not be formatted, which may or may not be what you want. An object in the report can be deleted because the template does not have a corresponding matching object. For example, if there is a field in the details section that does not have a matching field in the template, another details section is created and the field will be moved to the new details section. The remaining objects in the details section will have the template formatting applied.

Exercise 7.12: Using Predefined Templates

You have already applied a predefined template to a report using the Standard Report Wizard. This exercise will focus on applying predefined templates using the Template Expert. There are two ways to open the Template Expert, as discussed below.

① Click the **TEMPLATE EXPERT** button on the Expert Tools toolbar.

② Report ⇒ Template Expert.

 The only difference between the Template screen in the Standard Report Wizard and the Template Expert is that the Template Expert allows you to undo a template or re-apply a template.

1. Save the L2.2 report as L7.12 Product List Template 1.

2. Open the Template Expert and select the **TABLE GRID TEMPLATE** option, then click OK. The report should look like the one shown in Figure 7-55. Close the report and save the changes.

Product ID	Product Name	Price (SRP)
1,101	Active Outdoors C	$14.50
1,102	Active Outdoors C	$14.50
1,103	Active Outdoors C	$14.50
1,104	Active Outdoors C	$14.50
1,105	Active Outdoors C	$14.50
1,106	Active Outdoors L	$16.50
1,107	Active Outdoors L	$16.50
1,108	Active Outdoors L	$16.50
1,109	Active Outdoors L	$16.50

Figure 7-55 L7.12 Product List Template 1 report

Exercise 7.13: Apply A Predefined Template To A Report

One thing that I found interesting about templates is that if there is an object in the template that is not in the report that the template is being applied to, the template adds the object to the report. In this exercise you will apply a template that has a chart to a report that does not have a chart.

1. Save the L6.4 report as
   L7.13 2004 orders by shipping method report with template.
   As you can see, the report does not have a chart.

2. Apply the Corporate (Green) template to the report. The first page of the report should look like the one shown in Figure 7-56. Notice that a chart has been added to the report. The chart takes the characteristics of the chart in the template. If you do not need the chart from the template, you can delete the chart and keep the other template formatting. When you are finished looking at the report, close it and save the changes.

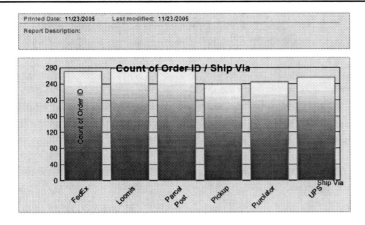

Figure 7-56 Page 1 of the L7.13 2004 orders by shipping method report with template

Where Are The Predefined Templates Stored?

The templates listed on the Template Expert or Template wizard screen in the **AVAILABLE TEMPLATES** list are stored in this location, if Crystal Reports was installed on your hard drive:
C:\Program Files\Business Objects\Crystal Reports 11\Templates\en.

 If you create templates and want them to appear in the Available Templates list on the Template Expert or the Template wizard screen, you have to place the templates that you create in this location or the location that is designated for templates in the registry of your computer.
The path in the registry is
HKEY_LOCAL_MACHINE\Business Objects\Suite 11.0\Crystal Reports\Templates

Exercise 7.14: Using The Undo Current Template Option

As mentioned earlier, if you apply a template but do not like it, you can remove it. In this exercise you will learn how to remove a template from a report.

1. Save the L2.2 report as L7.14 Product List Template 2.

2. Open the Template Expert, select any template in the list and click OK.

3. Open the Template Expert, then select the **UNDO THE CURRENT TEMPLATE** option, illustrated in Figure 7-57 and click OK. The dialog box will close and the template will be removed. Close the report. When prompted to save the changes, click No.

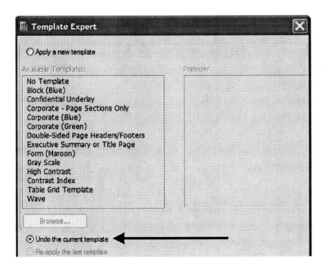

Figure 7-57 Undo the current template option illustrated

The **UNDO THE CURRENT TEMPLATE** option only undoes one template. If you applied more than one template to the report and do not want any of them, close the report and do not save the changes.

Test The Undo Current Template Option

In the previous exercise you learned how to use the Undo the current template option if no changes were made to the report. In this exercise you will learn how this option works if you make a change to the report or save it, after the template has been applied.

1. Open the L7.14 report and apply a template to it, then delete a field on the report and save the changes.

2. Open the Template Expert, select the Undo the current template option and click OK. You will see the message shown in Figure 7-58.

If you click Yes, the template will be removed and the field that you deleted will be added back to the report. If you click No, the report will retain the template and changes that were made.

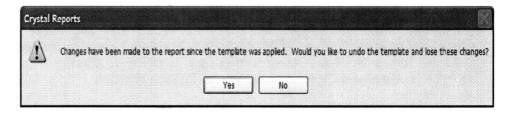

Figure 7-58 Template changes message

3. Click No on the message box shown above in Figure 7-58. Close the report and reopen it, then open the Template Expert. Notice that the option to remove the template is not available. If you save the report and leave it open, you can still go back and remove the template. Once you close the report, you can no longer remove the template. Close the report.

Before applying a template, you should save the report. If you apply a template but do not like how it looks, or it produces unexpected results, you can remove the template as long as the report has not been saved, by closing the report and not saving the changes. You may find this easier then using the Undo Current Template option.

Using Existing Reports As A Template

As you learned earlier, you can use the formatting of an existing report as a template. There are two ways that you can use an existing report as a template, as discussed below.

① Select the report that you want to use as a template by clicking the Browse button on the Template Expert dialog box or on the Template screen in the Standard Report Wizard and navigate to the location of the report that you want to use as a template.
② Save an existing report and give it a new name, then modify the options on the Document Properties dialog box and add the report to the Available Templates list.

By now you know that you will learn both ways <smile>. By the time you complete the next two exercises, you will be a pro at using an existing report as a template.

Exercise 7.15: Use The Browse Button To Apply A Template

Using the Browse button to apply a template means that the template that you want to use is not stored in the same folder as the templates that come with Crystal Reports. Only templates that are stored in the default template folder in Crystal Reports or another folder that has been designated as the template folder will recognize a file as a template.

1. Save the L7.1 report as `L7.15 Region List Template`.

2. Open the Template Expert and click the **BROWSE** button, then navigate to the Crystal Reports Workbook folder and double-click on the L5.13 file. You can see a preview of the formatting that will be applied to the report on the right side of Figure 7-59. Click OK to apply the template.
Figure 7-60 shows the report after the template is applied to the report. Figure 7-61 shows the report before the template was applied.

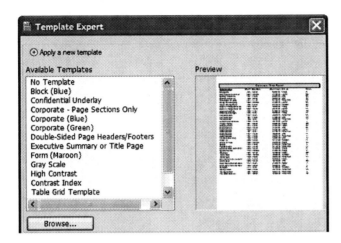

Figure 7-59 Preview of the formatting that will be applied to the report

Customers Order Report				
Customer Name	Address1	Region	Country	Postal Code
Bike-A-Holics Anonymous	7429 Arbut	OH	USA	43005
Wheels and Stuff	2530 Bute	FL	USA	34666
Uni-Cycle	1008 Kerr :	OH	USA	43042
Extreme Cycling	1925 Glen:	FL	USA	34638
Karma Bikes	1516 Ohio	OH	USA	43092

Figure 7-60 L7.15 Region List Template report with a template applied

11/24/20

Customer Name	Address1	Region	Country	Postal Code
Bike-A-Holics Anonymous	7429 Arbutus Boulevard	OH	USA	43005
Wheels and Stuff	2530 Bute Avenue	FL	USA	34666
Uni-Cycle	1008 Kerr Street	OH	USA	43042
Extreme Cycling	1925 Glenaire Avenue	FL	USA	34638
Karma Bikes	1516 Ohio Avenue	OH	USA	43092

Figure 7-61 L7.15 Region List Template report before the template was applied

Notice that the text in the report title in Figure 7-60 above is not accurate for the report. The report title shown comes from the L5.13 report. Also notice that the date field has been deleted from the report. That is because the template report does not have a date field.

3. Change the report title to `Region = OH or FL List`, then save the changes and close the report.

Modify Existing Reports To Use As A Template

Before you go any further, it would be a good idea to save existing reports with a new file name, modify the Document Properties and add the reports to the Templates folder, so that they can be used as templates in exercises that you will complete in this lesson.

Exercise 7.16: Modify The L2.1 Report

1. Save the L2.1 report as L7.16 My First Template.

2. Open the Document Properties dialog box (File ⇒ Summary Info) and enter the information shown in Figure 7-62 and click OK.

Figure 7-62 L7.16 My First Template document properties

3. Save the changes and close the report.

Exercise 7.17: Modify The L7.7 Report

1. Save the L7.7 report as L7.17 Top 5 Order Days Template.

2. Open the Document Properties dialog box. Enter the information shown in Figure 7-63 and click OK. Save the changes and close the report.

 The information in the Title field is what will appear in the Available Templates list on the wizard screen and the Template Expert. If this field is left blank, it will appear as **UNNAMED TEMPLATE 1** as illustrated in Figure 7-64.

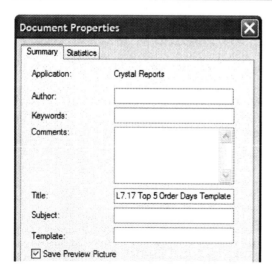

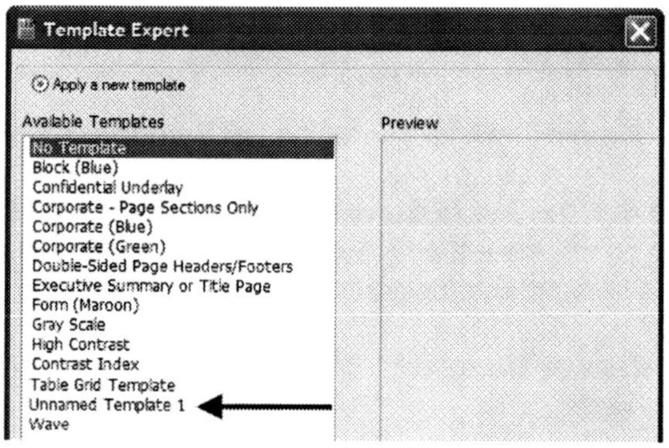

Figure 7-64 Template with the title field left blank

Figure 7-63 L7.17 template document properties

3. Open Windows Explorer and navigate to the Crystal Reports Workbook folder, then select both of the template reports that you just saved.

4. Edit ⇒ Copy. Navigate to C:\Program Files\Business Objects\Crystal Reports 11\Templates\, then click on the **EN** folder illustrated in Figure 7-65. Edit ⇒ Paste. You should see the two reports as illustrated in Figure 7-66. Close Windows Explorer.

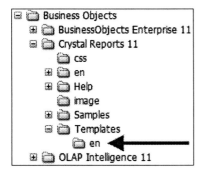

Figure 7-65 Path to template folder

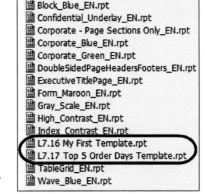

Figure 7-66 Report templates copied to the templates folder

 In the steps above, you could have just saved the reports to the folder shown earlier in Figure 7-65. It would save a few steps, but I didn't want to loose anyone, plus I wanted you to have all of the reports that you created, saved in the Crystal Reports Workbook folder so that you would know where they were.

Exercise 7.18: Use An Existing Report As A Template

In the previous exercise you modified two reports that can be used as templates. In this exercise you will apply those templates to reports that have already been created.

1. Save the L7.6 report as `L7.18 Orders by customer with template`.

2. Apply the L7.17 template to the report. Notice that the two templates that you added to the Templates folder are in the Available Templates list as illustrated in Figure 7-67. Save the changes and preview the report. It should look like the one shown in Figure 7-68. As you can see, the report would need to be modified because the chart is too hard to read. Close the report.

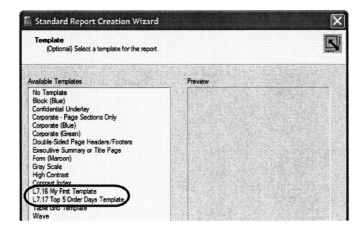

Figure 7-67 Templates added to the list

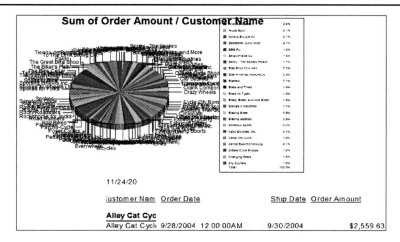

Figure 7-68 L7.18 Orders by customer with template report

Exercise 7.19 And 7.20: Use An Existing Report As A Template

In these exercises you will apply the same template to two reports to see how one template can cause reports to look different even though the same template is applied to both reports.

1. Save the L7.1 report as L7.19 Region List Template 2.

2. Save the L7.6 report as L7.20 Orders By Customer With Template.

3. Apply the L7.16 template to both of these reports and save the changes.

Figure 7-69 shows the L7.19 report. The reason that you see all of the blank space in the middle of the page is because the template has a placeholder for a chart. You could delete the placeholder or suppress the section of the report that the chart is in. Figure 7-70 shows the L7.20 report.

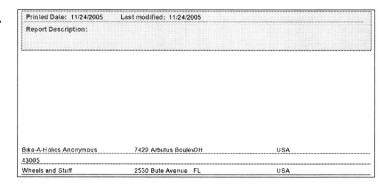

Figure 7-69 L7.19 Region List Template 2 report

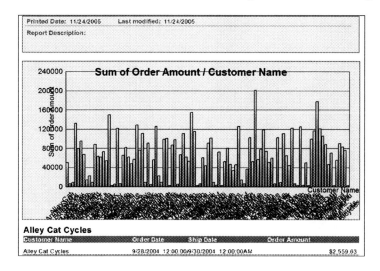

Figure 7-70 L7.20 Orders By Customer With Template report

Test Your Skills

1. Create the L5.11 Skills Product type filter report using the Standard Wizard. Your report should look similar to the one shown in Figure 7-71. The report should have 33 records.

   - Save the report as `L7.21 Skills Product type filter`.
   - The Product, Product Type and Supplier tables are needed to create this report.
   - Create a filter that only displays the gloves, saddles and kids product types.
   - Apply the Block (Blue) template to the report.

			BUSINESS OBJECTS'
Report Description:			
1101	Active Outdoors Crochet Glove	Gloves	Active Outdoors
1102	Active Outdoors Crochet Glove	Gloves	Active Outdoors
1103	Active Outdoors Crochet Glove	Gloves	Active Outdoors
1104	Active Outdoors Crochet Glove	Gloves	Active Outdoors
1105	Active Outdoors Crochet Glove	Gloves	Active Outdoors
1106	Active Outdoors Lycra Glove	Gloves	Active Outdoors
1107	Active Outdoors Lycra Glove	Gloves	Active Outdoors
1108	Active Outdoors Lycra Glove	Gloves	Active Outdoors
1109	Active Outdoors Lycra Glove	Gloves	Active Outdoors
1110	Active Outdoors Lycra Glove	Gloves	Active Outdoors
1111	Active Outdoors Lycra Glove	Gloves	Active Outdoors
4101	InFlux Crochet Glove	Gloves	InFlux
4102	InFlux Crochet Glove	Gloves	InFlux

Figure 7-71 L7.21 Skills Product type filter report

2. Create the L5.12 Skills Ship Via filter report using the Standard Wizard. Your report should look similar to the one shown in Figure 7-72. The report should have 40 records.

   - Save the report as `L7.22 Skills Orders filter`.
   - The Customer and Orders tables are needed to create this report.
   - Create a filter that displays order amounts that are >= $1,000 and were shipped between 1/1/2004 and 1/31/2004 in the USA.

Customer Name	Order ID	Order Date	Order Amoun	Ship Via	Region
City Cyclists	1,246	1/30/2004 12:00:00	$3,884.25	Pickup	MI
Bike-A-Holics Anonymous	1,097	12/27/2003 12:00:0	$1,439.55	Loomis	OH
Sporting Wheels Inc.	1,181	1/15/2004 12:00:00	$5,912.96	UPS	CA
Sporting Wheels Inc.	1,220	1/22/2004 12:00:00	$5,879.70	UPS	CA
Rockshocks for Jocks	1,161	1/11/2004 12:00:00	$1,799.70	Parcel Post	TX
Rowdy Rims Company	1,090	12/22/2003 12:00:0	$1,529.70	Loomis	CA
Rowdy Rims Company	1,186	1/15/2004 12:00:00	$1,110.70	Purolator	CA
Clean Air Transportation C	1,123	1/2/2004 12:00:00A	$5,219.55	Pickup	PA
Clean Air Transportation C	1,228	1/25/2004 12:00:00	$2,181.86	Loomis	PA
Hooked on Helmets	1,122	1/1/2004 12:00:00A	$1,025.40	Loomis	MN
C-Gate Cycle Shoppe	1,136	1/5/2004 12:00:00A	$3,209.53	Pickup	VA
Alley Cat Cycles	1,151	1/8/2004 12:00:00A	$5,879.70	Parcel Post	MA
Alley Cat Cycles	1,204	1/19/2004 12:00:00	$1,583.05	UPS	MA
The Bike Cellar	1,129	1/2/2004 12:00:00A	$2,997.25	Parcel Post	VA

Figure 7-72 L7.22 Skills Orders filter report

3. Create a report using the Standard Wizard that groups and counts employees by position. Your report should look like the one shown in Figure 7-73. The report should have 15 records.

   - Add the following fields from the Employee table: Position, First Name, Last Name, Hire Date and Reports To.
   - Save the report as `L7.23 Skills Employees by position`.

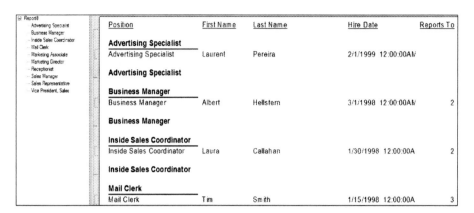

Figure 7-73 L7.23 Skills Employees by position report

4. Create a report using the Standard Wizard to create a Bottom N report that only selects records in the Customer table in the USA. Your report should look like the one shown in Figure 7-74. Notice that there are 251 records, but only five are displayed.

   - Add the following fields from the Customer table: Customer ID and Customer Name.
   - Add the following fields from the Orders table: Order Amount, Order Date and Ship Via.
   - Group on the Order Amount field.
   - Remove the Customer ID summary field.
   - The orders must have Pickup in the Ship Via field.
   - Use the Bottom 5 groups option and sort the groups on the order amount field.
   - Save the report as `L7.24 Skills Bottom 5 orders`.

Order Amount	Customer ID	Customer Name	Order Date	Ship Via
$10.71				
$10.71	40	Cyclist's Trail Co.	1/24/2004 12:00:00A	Pickup
$10.71	**$10.71**			
$13.50				
$13.50	36	Road Runners Paradise	10/20/2004 12:00:00.	Pickup
$13.50	**$13.50**			
$13.95				
$13.95	31	To The Limit Biking Co.	11/27/2004 12:00:00.	Pickup
$13.95	**$13.95**			
$14.50				
$14.50	55	Tandem Cycle	8/8/2004 12:00:00A	Pickup
$14.50	**$14.50**			
$14.73				
$14.73	9	Trail Blazer's Place	4/4/2004 12:00:00A	Pickup
$14.73	**$14.73**			
Grand Total:	#########			

Figure 7-74 L7.24 Skills Bottom 5 orders report

5. Add all of the reports that were created in this lesson to the Workbench.

You have created and modified a lot of reports in the previous lessons. So far, the reports that you have created have not been printed or shared with anyone. As the report designer, after you create the reports, they are put into production so that other people can use them. There are several ways that other people can use the reports, including: printing them if they have Crystal Reports installed, use a Crystal Reports viewer or export the reports to a file type that other people can use. Most users will not have Crystal Reports installed on their computer, so they will not be able to open the report file and print it like you can. After completing the exercises in this lesson, you will be able to use the following printing, exporting options and techniques:

☑ Page Setup dialog box options
☑ Printer options
☑ Use the Set print date and time options
☑ Use the Preview Sample option
☑ Diagnose printing problems
☑ Report Options dialog box
☑ Export reports to a variety of file formats
☑ CrystalReports.com

To pass the RDCR201 exam, you need to be familiar with and be able to:

☑ Export reports

Printing Options

Crystal Reports has the majority of printing options for reports that you have already used in word processing and other types of software packages. As you learned, most people that run the reports that you create will not have Crystal Reports installed. Even if they do have Crystal Reports installed, do you think that every user will be able to set the printing and page setup options correctly without calling you? And if they can, you should still select the appropriate printing options so that the report will print as you intended it to.

Page Setup Options

As shown in Figure 8-1, there are several options that you can select from to change the printed page layout to what is best suited for the report. The options shown are the defaults that are set when Crystal Reports is installed. The graphic at the top of the dialog box will change as the options are changed.

Table 8-1 explains the Page Setup options (File ⇒ Page Setup) that you may not be familiar with.

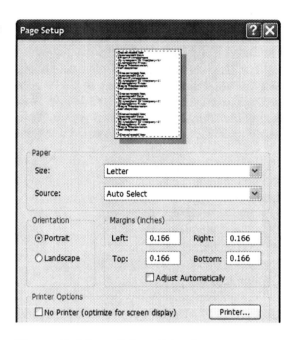

Figure 8-1 Page Setup dialog box

Setup Option	Description
No Printer	Select this option if the report will not be printed. This option will optimize the report to be viewed on a screen. It can also be used to resolve printing problems, as you will learn later in this lesson.
Adjust Automatically	If checked, this option will cause the margins to change automatically, when the paper size or orientation is changed.

Table 8-1 Page Setup dialog box options explained

Exercise 8.1: Change The Page Orientation

As shown above in Figure 8-1, the default orientation is **PORTRAIT**. You can fit more fields across the page if the orientation is **LANDSCAPE**. Some of the reports that you have created had a field that was hanging off of the right side of the report. When you previewed the report, all of the data in the last field could not be displayed.

1. Save the L3.5 report as L8.1 Landscape orientation. If you preview the report, you will see that the Ship Via field is cut off.

2. File ⇒ Page Setup. Select the **LANDSCAPE** orientation option. Notice that the graphic at the top of the Page Setup dialog box has changed, as shown in Figure 8-2 from what it was in Figure 8-1. The dotted line represents the margins. Click OK. The report should look like the one shown in Figure 8-3. Save the changes and leave the report open to complete the next exercise.

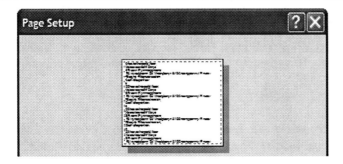

Figure 8-2 Page Setup graphic changed

Customer Name	First Name	Last Name	Order ID	Order Date	Order Amount	Ship Via
City Cyclists	Nancy	Davolio	1	12/2/2003 12:00:00A	$41.90	UPS
Deals on Wheels	Janet	Leverling	1,002	12/2/2003 12:00:00A	$5,060.28	Pickup
Warsaw Sports, Inc.	Margaret	Peacock	1,003	12/2/2003 12:00:00A	$186.87	UPS
Bikes and Trikes	Margaret	Peacock	1,004	12/2/2003 12:00:00A	$823.05	Pickup
SAB Mountain	Janet	Leverling	1,005	12/3/2003 12:00:00A	$29.00	Loomis
Poser Cycles	Margaret	Peacock	1,006	12/3/2003 12:00:00A	$64.90	Purolator
Spokes	Anne	Dodsworth	1,007	12/3/2003 12:00:00A	$49.50	Parcel Post
Clean Air Transportation Co.	Margaret	Peacock	1,008	12/3/2003 12:00:00A	$2,214.94	Purolator
Extreme Cycling	Margaret	Peacock	1,009	12/3/2003 12:00:00A	$29.00	Loomis
Cyclopath	Nancy	Davolio	1,010	12/3/2003 12:00:00A	$14,872.30	UPS
BBS Pty	Margaret	Peacock	1,011	12/3/2003 12:00:00A	$29.00	Purolator
Piccolo	Nancy	Davolio	1,012	12/3/2003 12:00:00A	$10,259.10	Loomis
Pedals Inc.	Margaret	Peacock	1,013	12/3/2003 12:00:00A	$1,142.13	Parcel Post
Spokes 'N Wheels Ltd.	Nancy	Davolio	1,014	12/4/2003 12:00:00A	$29.00	Purolator
Cycle City Rome	Anne	Dodsworth	1,015	12/4/2003 12:00:00A	$43.50	UPS
SAB Mountain	Janet	Leverling	1,016	12/4/2003 12:00:00A	$563.70	FedEx
Tyred Out	Margaret	Peacock	1,017	12/5/2003 12:00:00A	$72.00	Purolator
Has Been Bikes (consignmer	Janet	Leverling	1,018	12/5/2003 12:00:00A	$115.50	Loomis
Spokes for Folks	Anne	Dodsworth	1,019	12/5/2003 12:00:00A	$43.50	Parcel Post

Figure 8-3 L8.1 Landscape orientation report

Exercise 8.2: Change The Margins

The report that you just modified would look better if the data did not begin so close to the left margin. Reports often look better if there is a half inch or 1 inch margin on all four sides.

1. Save the L8.1 report as `L8.2 Change margins`.

2. File ⇒ Page Setup. Change the **LEFT** and **RIGHT** margins to 1 inch. Change the **TOP** and **BOTTOM** margins to `0.50` (which is ½ inch).

3. Click OK. The report should look like the one shown in Figure 8-4. Save the changes and close the report.

Customer Name	First Name	Last Name	Order ID	Order Date	Order Amount	Ship Via
City Cyclists	Nancy	Davolio	1	12/2/2003 12:00:00A	$41.90	UPS
Deals on Wheels	Janet	Leverling	1,002	12/2/2003 12:00:00A	$5,060.28	Pickup
Warsaw Sports, Inc.	Margaret	Peacock	1,003	12/2/2003 12:00:00A	$186.87	UPS
Bikes and Trikes	Margaret	Peacock	1,004	12/2/2003 12:00:00A	$823.05	Pickup
SAB Mountain	Janet	Leverling	1,005	12/3/2003 12:00:00A	$29.00	Loomis
Poser Cycles	Margaret	Peacock	1,006	12/3/2003 12:00:00A	$64.90	Purolator
Spokes	Anne	Dodsworth	1,007	12/3/2003 12:00:00A	$49.50	Parcel Post
Clean Air Transportation Co.	Margaret	Peacock	1,008	12/3/2003 12:00:00A	$2,214.94	Purolator
Extreme Cycling	Margaret	Peacock	1,009	12/3/2003 12:00:00A	$29.00	Loomis
Cyclopath	Nancy	Davolio	1,010	12/3/2003 12:00:00A	$14,872.30	UPS
BBS Pty	Margaret	Peacock	1,011	12/3/2003 12:00:00A	$29.00	Purolator
Piccolo	Nancy	Davolio	1,012	12/3/2003 12:00:00A	$10,259.10	Loomis
Pedals Inc.	Margaret	Peacock	1,013	12/3/2003 12:00:00A	$1,142.13	Parcel Post
Spokes 'N Wheels Ltd.	Nancy	Davolio	1,014	12/4/2003 12:00:00A	$29.00	Purolator
Cycle City Rome	Anne	Dodsworth	1,015	12/4/2003 12:00:00A	$43.50	UPS
SAB Mountain	Janet	Leverling	1,016	12/4/2003 12:00:00A	$563.70	FedEx
Tyred Out	Margaret	Peacock	1,017	12/5/2003 12:00:00A	$72.00	Purolator
Has Been Bikes (consignmer	Janet	Leverling	1,018	12/5/2003 12:00:00A	$115.50	Loomis
Spokes for Folks	Anne	Dodsworth	1,019	12/5/2003 12:00:00A	$43.50	Parcel Post

Figure 8-4 L8.2 Change margins report

Exercise 8.3: Change The Paper Size

As shown earlier in Figure 8-1, the default paper size is **LETTER**. Some reports, in particular, financial reports may need to be printed on legal paper. This exercise will show you how to change the paper size.

1. Save the L6.16 report as `L8.3 Legal paper`.

2. Open the Page Setup dialog box and change the Paper Size to **LEGAL**, then change the Orientation to **LANDSCAPE**. Figure 8-5 shows the options that should be selected. Click OK. The report should look like the one shown in Figure 8-6. When you are finished viewing the report, save the changes and leave the report open to complete the next exercise.

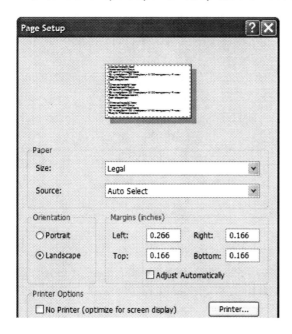

Figure 8-5 Paper size and orientation options changed

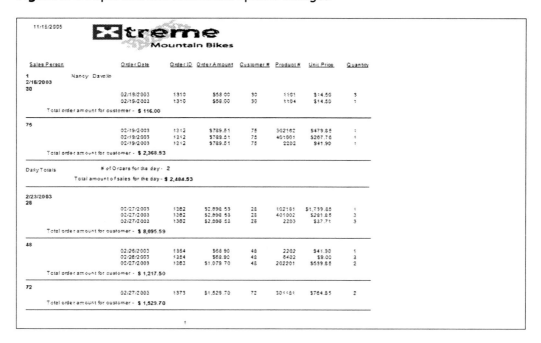

Figure 8-6 L8.3 Legal paper report

Exercise 8.4: Use The Adjust Automatically Option

In the previous exercise you changed the paper size and orientation. In a prior exercise you changed the margins manually. As you learned earlier in this lesson, when you change the paper size or orientation, the margins do not change. In this exercise you will learn how to make the margins change automatically when the paper size is changed.

1. Save the L8.3 report as `L8.4 Adjust margins automatically`.

2. Open the Page Setup dialog box and check the option **ADJUST AUTOMATICALLY**, then click OK and save the changes. Close the report and reopen it.

3. Change the Paper Size to Letter. Notice that the margins automatically changed. Save the changes and close the report.

Printer Options

The Page Setup dialog box has a **PRINTER** button. This button opens the dialog box shown in Figure 8-7. I'm not sure why it is called the Page Setup dialog box, when it has options for printers. These options allow you to select a printer and its options, which are the same options that you have probably used in other software packages.

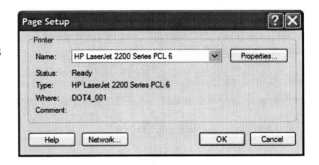

Figure 8-7 Printer options dialog box

 If you used Crystal Reports 10, you will notice that the Printer dialog boxes have changed slightly.

If you have more than one printer installed, the default printer that you have selected in Windows will appear in the **NAME** drop down list shown above in Figure 8-7. If the printer shown is not the one that you want to use, open the drop down list and select the printer that you want. The **PROPERTIES** button will let you select options for the printer that is selected.

Figure 8-8 shows another printer dialog box. It allows you to select options for the active report. File ⇒ Print, will open this dialog box.

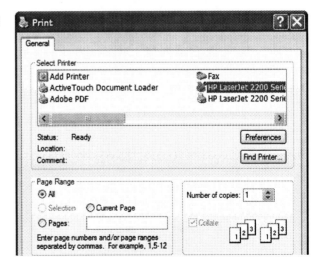

Figure 8-8 Print dialog box

Exercise 8.5: Use The Set Print Date And Time Options

The Set Print Date and Time options are useful when you use the Print Date or Print Time special fields on a report and have the need to override these dates when the report is printed. The options on the dialog box will let you set these fields to a date or time, other than the current date or time.

1. Save the L4.8 report as `L8.5 Set print date`.

2. Run the report. Notice the date in the **DATE THE REPORT WAS PRINTED** field. It should be today's date.

3. Report ⇒ Set Print Date and Time, then select the **OTHER** option and type 1/1/2003 in the Date field as shown in Figure 8-9.

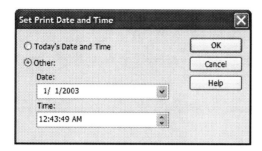

Figure 8-9 Set Print Date and Time dialog box

4. Click OK and save the changes. You should see 1/1/2003 in the Date the report was printed field, as shown in Figure 8-10.

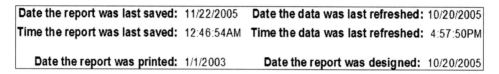

Date the report was last saved:	11/22/2005	Date the data was last refreshed:	10/20/2005
Time the report was last saved:	12:46:54AM	Time the data was last refreshed:	4:57:50PM
Date the report was printed:	1/1/2003	Date the report was designed:	10/20/2005

Figure 8-10 L8.5 Set print date report with the print date changed

5. Close the report. The 2003 date will print every time the report is run until you remove it from the Set Print Date and Time dialog box.

Exercise 8.6: Use The Preview Sample Option

If the report has hundreds or thousands of records and you do not want to see all of them when you are creating the report, you can specify the number of records that you want to see. The default for this is all records, which is why you have seen all of the records that met the criteria in every report that you have previewed so far in this workbook.

1. Save the L6.4 report as L8.6 Preview sample option. Notice that there are 1,562 records.

2. View ⇒ Preview Sample. Select the **FIRST** option and type 525 in the **RECORDS** field. Figure 8-11 shows the options that should be selected. Click OK. The report will automatically re-open in the Preview window. Notice that there are 525 records being displayed in the report.

Figure 8-11 Preview Sample options selected

If you look in the group tree section, you will see that only two shipping methods are included in the report, as shown in Figure 8-12. If you look at the original report shown in Figure 8-13, you will see that six shipping methods are on the report. The Preview Sample option will stay in effect until it is removed.

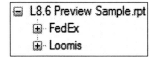

Figure 8-12 L8.6 Preview sample option report

Figure 8-13 L6.4 2004 Orders by shipping method report

 Keep in mind that when you select to preview a sample number of records, that they may not be the same first **N** number of records that will appear when you view all of the records. (N is the number that you enter on the Preview Sample dialog box shown earlier in Figure 8-11). In the exercise above, 525 records were selected to be previewed. If you preview the original report, some or all of the records that you see at the beginning of the report could be different.

3. Save the changes and close all of the open reports.

Printing Problems

If you have an inkjet printer and have opened a document that was created by someone that has a laser jet printer, you may have noticed that sometimes the spacing is off. If so, the topics discussed in this section will be helpful. If you have experienced formatting issues (when it comes to printing a document) using other software, many of those problems are also found in Crystal Reports, as discussed below.

While the reports that you create may look good on your computer monitor and look good when you print them, that may not be the case when the reports go into production. This is because information like printer drivers and monitor resolution come from the options that are on your computer. Technical people tend to install printer and video driver updates, while end-users do not. This can cause reports to print differently, even if you have the same model printer as the person printing the report.

This information is saved with the report. This is why someone that does not have the exact same settings on their computer as you do, will sometimes get different printed or visual screen results when they run the report. The list below discusses several printing concepts that you should be aware of that can effect how the reports that you create, look on a computer monitor and how they look when printed.

① Crystal Reports uses information from the printer driver that was the default, when the report was created (meaning the one on your computer). The printer driver determines the character width and height of the information printed on a report.
② The video driver resolution and operating system used when the report was created can also effect the report when it is viewed on a different monitor.
③ It is important to note that some of the layout options of reports that you create come from the options on the Page Setup and Print Setup dialog boxes. The default margins from the Page Setup dialog box are used for the reports that you create.
④ The length of the report page comes from the type of printer that is selected, which is usually your default printer. This is important to know because each printer model has limits on how close to the edge of the paper it can print.

Okay, I can imagine that the information that you just read is cause for concern. The suggestions below will help resolve many of the printing problems discussed above.

    ① Set the margins for the report instead of using the default printer driver margins.
    ② Use the **CAN GROW** option for fields that contain a lot of data, like memo fields. Putting memo fields in their own subsection of the report would also be helpful.
    ③ Use common True Type fonts, like Arial, Garamond and Times New Roman, that come standard on Windows based computers. If you need to use a non standard font, you should export the report to Adobe Acrobat PDF format, which you will learn about later in this lesson. Creating a PDF file is the best option to use, because this file type can be read on any computer that has the free Adobe Acrobat Reader.
    ④ Select the **NO PRINTER (OPTIMIZE FOR SCREEN DISPLAY)** option shown earlier in Figure 8-5. Selecting this option is best if the report will be printed on several different printer models. Doing this helps keep the formatting generic enough so that the report can be printed on a variety of printers. If you know that a report will be printed on a printer that is different from the printer that you have, select the No Printer option.
    ⑤ Select the computer monitor video resolution that most of the people that will view the report have. If this is not possible, consider converting the report to HTML format, so that more people can view the report as intended.

Report Viewers

If you do not have Microsoft Word or Excel, you can download the free viewers and use them to view some of the reports that you will create later in this lesson. If the web pages listed below have changed and you can't find the files, search for the file in parenthesis on Microsoft's web site.

Word 2003 Viewer - (wdviewer.exe)
office.microsoft.com/search/redir.aspx?AssetID=DC011320141033&Origin=HH100152641033&CTT=5

Excel 2003 Viewer - (xlviewer.exe) office.microsoft.com/downloads/2000/xlviewer.aspx

Report Options

The settings on the Options dialog box are global report options that are set. They are automatically applied to every report that you create. There are also options that you can set on a report by report basis, as shown in Figure 8-14. (File ⇒ Report Options) The options that are checked, are the default report options.

Many of the default options on this dialog box come from options that are checked on the Options dialog box. Some default (checked) options, like the **DATABASE SERVER IS CASE-INSENSITIVE** is checked here because it is set as a global default on the Options dialog box.

Changes that you make on the Reporting tab on the Options dialog box will change the default options on the Report Options dialog box. The options selected on the Report Options dialog box override the corresponding option on the Options dialog box (when applicable), for the active report. This means that the options on the Report Options dialog box will always be applied to the report, while the options on the Options dialog box will only be applied if there is no corresponding option on the Report Options dialog box.

You should understand the difference between the Report Options dialog box shown in Figure 8-14 and the Options dialog box (File ⇒ Options) that was covered in Lesson 5.

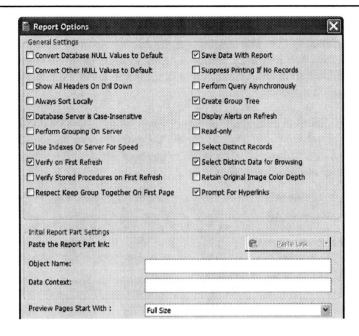

Figure 8-14 Report Options dialog box

Export Report Overview

A report designer is not only responsible for creating and modifying reports, they can also be responsible for distributing the reports. There are five main ways that an end-user can access and run reports that you create, as discussed below.

① Purchase and install Crystal Reports for every end-user that needs to run a report. This is probably not the best solution, especially if there are hundreds or thousands of people in the company that need to run or print reports. This option could cost tens of thousands of dollars in hardware upgrades, software purchases, training and tech support.

② Hire someone to run reports all day, print them and send them via inter-office mail or email to end-users. This may sound good until you realize that end-users may not get the reports in a timely manner if they are sent via inter-office mail.

③ If the reports are part of an application that is being developed in a software package like Visual Basic or C++, the reports can be added to menu options or be attached to screens in the application. If this is the case, that's great, because your job is done.

④ Save the reports to Crystal Reports Server, the Business Objects Enterprise or crystalreports.com.

⑤ If none of the options discussed above are appropriate, all is not lost. There is one more option. Exporting reports is cost effective and is something that a report designer can set up. The DBA would have to create a script that runs the exported report and place the exported report on a server. The only downside to this solution is that the reports will not necessarily have the most current data. If this is a problem, you will have to select one of the options above.

Export Format Options

Crystal Reports supports over 15 formats that reports can be exported to. Many of them are installed by default when Crystal Reports is installed. Exporting reports is a two step process, as discussed below.

① Select the **EXPORT** format. This determines the format that the exported report will be saved in.

② Select the **DESTINATION**. This determines where the report will be saved.

Reports can be exported to more than one format if needed. Some export formats are better suited for certain types of reports then others. For example, some Word and Excel export format options are better suited for reports that may need to be edited by the end-user. Table 8-2 explains the export format options. The software in brackets in the description column in the table is the most commonly used software to open the corresponding exported file format.

Some of the formats in the table do a better job of duplicating the report then others. I've noticed that sometimes reports that are exported to Excel get shifted a little. If the data does not need to be edited by the person using the exported report, the best format to use is PDF because it retains all of the formatting that you see when the report is viewed in Crystal Reports.

Format	Description
Adobe Acrobat (PDF)	This format will create a PDF file, which is one of the most popular export formats because it can be read by both PC and MAC computers. If you want the report to retain its look after it is exported, select this format. [Adobe Acrobat or the free reader] (1)
Crystal Reports (RPT)	This format can only be read by Crystal Reports or a report viewer from Crystal Reports Server, the Report Application Server (RAS) or a program that was created in Visual Basic, C++ or another application development tool that supports a runtime viewer. [Crystal Reports]
HTML 3.2	Select this option if you want to display the report on the Web. This format can be read by web browsers that use HTML v3.2 or higher. By today's standards, browsers that cannot use anything higher than HTML v3.2 are considered obsolete. [Web browser or HTML Editor] (2)
HTML 4.0	Select this option if you want to display the report on the Web. This format can be read by web browsers that use HTML v4.0 or higher. This format has better formatting capabilities then the HTML v3.2 format. [Web browser or HTML Editor] (2)
Excel 97-2000 (XLS)	Select this format if you want to export the report to a spreadsheet and keep as much of the formatting as possible. This format will not include any formulas from the report, just the result of the formula. [Microsoft Excel]
Excel 97-2000 (XLS) Data Only	Select this format if you want to export the report to a spreadsheet. Don't select this format if the report has charts or maps that you also need to export. Any data that is suppressed will not be exported. [Microsoft Excel]
Word (RTF)	This format will create an RTF document, which requires Microsoft Word or the viewer. RTF stands for Rich Text Format. [Microsoft Word]
Word (RTF) Editable	This format will create an RTF document. It allows the user to edit the report in Microsoft Word. [Microsoft Word]
ODBC	This format allows the report to be exported to any ODBC database.
Record Style (columns no spaces)	Select this format when you want to export the data to an ASCII fixed length format, without spaces. (3)
Record Style (columns with spaces)	Select this format when you want to export the data to an ASCII fixed length format, with spaces. (3)
Report Definition	This format produces a report that contains a description of the report's design. This includes the sections, selection criteria, object formats, groups and more. [Notepad] (4)
Rich Text Format (RTF)	This RTF export option retains the formatting of the report including graphics. Select this option if the report will be opened in a word processor other than Word. [Microsoft Word]

Table 8-2 Export format options explained

Format	Description
Separated Values (CSV)	This format is similar to the two ASCII Record Style formats discussed above. The difference is that in this format the fields are separated by commas. This is often called a "Comma Delimited" file. CSV stands for Comma Separated Values. [Microsoft Excel]
Tab Separated Text (TTX)	This format is similar to the Separated Values format because it separates the fields. The difference is that the fields are separated by tab spaces. [Notepad]
Text (TXT)	This format creates a plain text file. [Notepad] (5)
XML	This format will create an XML data file from the data in the report. Style sheets can be applied to the XML file, so that the data can be used in another application or on the web. XML stands for Extensible Markup Language. [Web browser]

Table 8-2 Export format options explained (Continued)

(1) The drill down feature and hyperlinks will not work with this report format.
(2) Left justified is the only justification that will work.

(3) This format is often used to move data into older applications.
(4) This report format is usually for technical people. It does not export the data in the report. It exports information about the report.
(5) Text (TXT) reports do not retain any formatting like bold, italic or underline.

Understand Excel Export formats.

There are two ways to open the Export dialog box shown in Figure 8-15, as discussed below.

① Click the **EXPORT** button on the Standard toolbar.
② File ⇒ Export ⇒ Export Report.

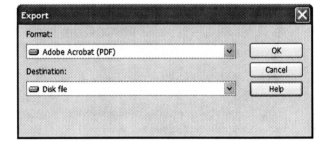

Figure 8-15 Export dialog box

The list shown in Figure 8-16 are the export format options. You may see the same or different options, then those shown. Some of the export format options shown in Figure 8-16 have an icon with the number 1 next to them. This means that the export format was not installed when Crystal Reports was installed. You will need the Crystal Reports CD to install any of these formats. Later in this lesson, you will learn how to install an export format DLL file that is needed for an export file type.

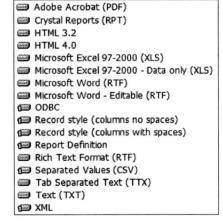

Figure 8-16 Available export options

Export Destination Options

In addition to selecting an export format, a destination for the report also has to be selected. The destination options that are available by default are discussed in Table 8-3. Some of the options may not be installed. You may have other options in addition to the ones in the table.

Option	Description
Application	Select this option when the export format is the Adobe Acrobat Reader or a Windows based application like Word or Excel. Selecting this option causes the application that is associated with the export format to open after the report is exported. Exported files that use this destination option are automatically saved in the TEMP directory. You can move the file to another location. If you want to change the default location, you have to modify the path in the ExportDirectory key in the registry. The path to this value is HKEY_CURRENT_USER\Software\Business Objects\Crystal Reports\Export as shown in Figure 8-17.
Disk File	This option lets you select a folder, either on a hard drive or on a server (which is also known as a Network drive), where the exported report will be placed. This destination option does not automatically open the application associated with the export file type.
Exchange Folder	This option allows the exported report to be placed on a public or private Exchange mail server.
Lotus Domino	This option will export the report to a Lotus Domino database, which requires that the correct form that the exported data will go to is already created in the Lotus database. (6)
Lotus Domino Mail	This option is used to send the exported report as an attachment to a Lotus email message. (6)
MAPI	This option is used to send the exported report as an attachment to a MAPI compliant email. To use this option, email software like Outlook Express or Outlook has to be installed and configured on your computer.

Table 8-3 Destination options explained

(6) To use this option, the appropriate Lotus mail client software must be installed and configured on your computer.

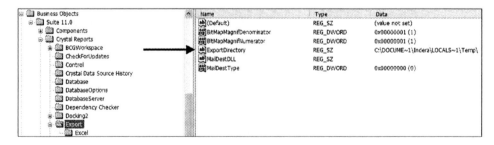

Figure 8-17 Path in the registry to change the default application export folder

Export Formatting Tips

I have found that by making sure that the export format tips listed below are followed, the exported file, regardless of the format, will look more like the report does in Crystal Reports.

① Make sure that all of the data fields in the same column have the same alignment (left or right). This is especially important for number and currency fields. If the fields in the same column have a different alignment option, some fields may appear in a different column in the exported report.

② Clear the **FREE FORM PLACEMENT** option on the Section Expert dialog box for all sections of the report. Turning this option off allows you to attach all objects to a guideline.

③ All objects in the same column should be attached (snapped) to the same guideline.

④ Remove any space that is not needed in each section of the report by moving all of the objects in each section up, as much as possible.

Report Export Formats

The exercises in this lesson will show you how to create some of the more popular report export formats. To demonstrate the differences between the export format output options, you will export the same report to create all of the export formats covered in this lesson.

The L6.7 2004 Orders by month report is the report that you will use to create all of the export reports. You should open this report and then open the Export dialog box shown earlier in Figure 8-15, prior to starting each exercise, unless instructed otherwise. Unless stated otherwise, save each exported report in the Crystal Reports Workbook folder.

Exercise 8.7: Create An Adobe Acrobat PDF Export File

This export file type will create a PDF (Portable Document Format) file of the report. End-users that need to open reports in this file type will need to have the Adobe Acrobat Reader installed. This software is free and can be downloaded from http://www.adobe.com/products/acrobat/readstep2.html. (You do not have to download and install the toolbar or Photoshop Album software for the Acrobat Reader software to work.) This export file type can also be opened and viewed with Adobe Acrobat, which is the full version of the software that lets you create PDF files.

1. Select the Adobe Acrobat (PDF) format, if it is not already selected, then open the Destination drop down list and select **DISK FILE**. Figure 8-15 shown earlier, has the export options that should be selected. Click OK.

> If you select the **APPLICATION** destination option, you will get the same PDF export file. The difference is that the Application option will not let you select where the export file will be saved initially. Once the report is exported you can save it to a different location. In Windows XP, the exported file will automatically be stored in this location: C:\Documents and Settings\{username}\Local Settings\Temp\
>
> Usually the files are not automatically deleted from this folder so you may want to check this folder from time to time and delete the files.
>
> The Disk File option will let you select where you want to save the export file.

The dialog box shown in Figure 8-18 will let you select whether you want to include all or some of the pages from the report in the PDF export file that you are about to create. If you were going to send each sales rep their stats for the month from the report, you would enter the corresponding page numbers in the From and To fields in the dialog box. If the report has **PARAMETER FIELDS**, you would not have to do this to get a specific sales reps stats.

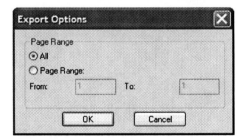

Figure 8-18 Export page range options

2. Click OK to include all of the pages. You will see the dialog box shown in Figure 8-19. This dialog box lets you select where you want to store the export file.

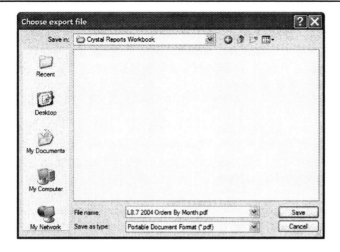

Figure 8-19 Choose Export File dialog box

3. Navigate to the Crystal Reports Workbook folder, as shown above in Figure 8-19 and type L8.7 2004 Orders By Month exported PDF file as the file name and press Enter or click the Save button.

You will see the dialog box shown in Figure 8-20. This dialog box lets you know that the export file is being created and how many records will be exported. When the export is complete, you can open the PDF file in either the Adobe Acrobat Reader or Adobe Acrobat. The exported PDF file should look similar to the one shown in Figure 8-21.

4. Close the PDF report.

Figure 8-20 Exporting Records dialog box

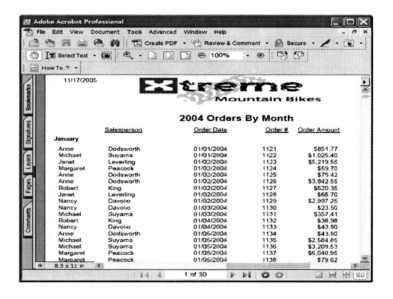

Figure 8-21 L8.7 2004 Orders By Month exported PDF file

Exercise 8.8: Create An Excel 97-2000 Export File

This export file type will create an Excel file of the report. To open this exported file type, Microsoft Excel or the free Excel viewer needs to be installed. As you read in Table 8-2, there are two Excel export formats. The Excel export format options provide a different output of the data. You will use both export options, so that you can see the differences.

1. Select the first Excel 97-2000 format, then open the Destination drop down list and select **APPLICATION**. Figure 8-22 shows the options that should be selected. Click OK.

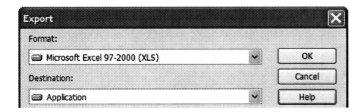

Figure 8-22 Export format options

You will see the dialog box shown in Figure 8-23. As you can see, there are several options that you can select, which will determine how the data will be formatted in Excel. Table 8-4 explains the options.

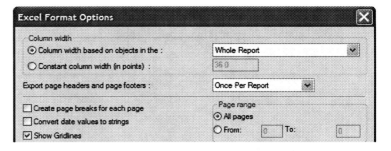

Figure 8-23 Excel 97-2000 Format Options dialog box

Option	Description
Column Width	These options let you select the column widths in Excel. ① The **COLUMN WIDTH BASED ON OBJECTS IN THE** option lets you select the column width in Excel based on a section in the report. ② The **CONSTANT COLUMN WIDTH (IN POINTS)** option lets you select a free form column width.
Export page headers and page footers	This option lets you select whether or not the information in the page header and footer sections on the report will be exported to Excel. If the page header and footer information is exported, the options in the drop down list determine where the information will be placed in the Excel file. ① **ONCE PER REPORT** causes the header information to only print at the top of the first page and the footer information to only print at the bottom of the last page. ② **ONCE PER PAGE** causes the header and footer information to print on each page of the report.
Create page breaks for each page	If selected, page breaks will be added to the exported Excel file in the same place they would appear in Crystal Reports. This may cause the report to break someplace other then at the end of the printed page. If you want the page breaks to happen automatically in Excel, do not check this option.
Convert date values to strings	If selected, this option will keep the date formatting in Crystal Reports when the report is exported to Excel. If this option is not checked, the formatting for the date fields when the report is exported will come from the date formatting options in the copy of Excel that the exported file is opened with. This means that if different people have different date settings in their copy of Excel, the dates in the exported file will appear differently.
Show Gridlines	If selected, this option forces gridlines in the exported copy of the report.
Page range	These options let you select how many pages of the report will be exported.

Table 8-4 Excel 97-2000 export format options explained

2. Select the **SHOW GRIDLINES** option that is shown above in Figure 8-23 and click OK. You will see the records being processed/exported. When the export is complete, Excel will open and you will see the report shown in Figure 8-24.

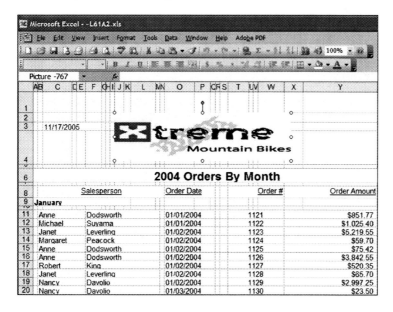

Figure 8-24 L8.8 2004 orders by month exported Excel file

3. Scroll down to row 142 and click in cell S131, the Total # of orders for the month cell.

If you look in the Formula Bar at the top of the spreadsheet window shown in Figure 8-25, you will not see the summary calculation (formula). One reason to use this export format is if you do not want the end-user to be able to change or see the formulas. For other end-users, it would be helpful if the formulas that are used in the report were also exported. You will learn how to export formulas in the next exercise.

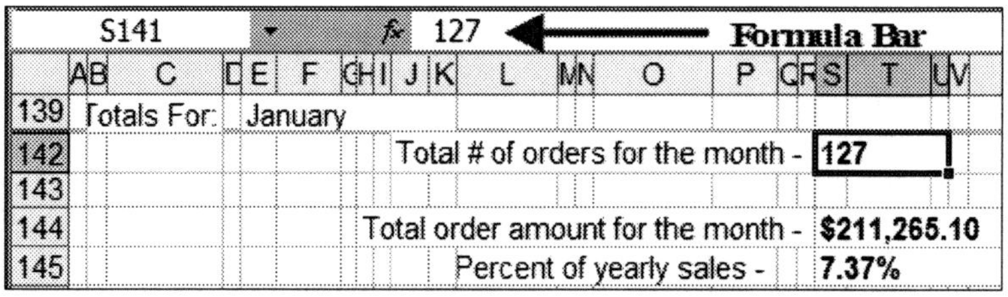

Figure 8-25 Formula Bar illustrated

4. Save the exported file as `L8.8 2004 orders by month exported file`, then close the spreadsheet.

Exercise 8.9: Create An Excel 97-2000 Data Only Export File

As you noticed in the previous exercise, the calculations were not included in the spreadsheet.
In order to have the calculations in the export file, you have to select the Excel Data Only export format.

If the **DETAILS** option was selected in the Column Width drop down list on the Excel Format Options dialog box instead of the **WHOLE REPORT** option shown earlier in Figure 8-23, the spreadsheet would look the way that many Excel users are use to seeing it. They would just have to turn the **GRIDLINES** option on.

1. Select the **EXCEL 97-2000 DATA ONLY** format, then open the Destination drop down list and select **DISK FILE** and click OK. You will see the dialog box shown in Figure 8-26. The typical and minimal options pre-select some options on the bottom portion of the dialog box for you. Table 8-5 explains the Excel format options.

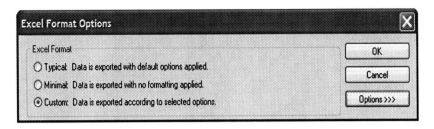

Figure 8-26 Excel 97-2000 Data Only Format Options dialog box

Format	Description
Typical	This option pre-selects the most common options in the bottom section of the dialog box, which are shown in Figure 8-27.
Minimal	This option pre-selects the basic options shown in Figure 8-28, to export the report without any formatting options.
Custom	This option lets you select the export options.

Table 8-5 Excel Data Only export format options explained

The pre-selected options shown in Figures 8-27 and 8-28 can be used as a starting point. You can select one of these options and then add or remove options as needed. This may be helpful if one of these export formats has a few of the options that you need. Selecting one of these options and then making changes to it may save you some time.

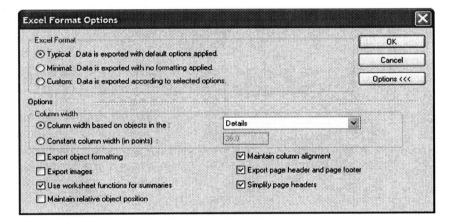

Figure 8-27 Typical pre-selected default options

Changing an option after selecting the typical or minimal option changes the format to custom.

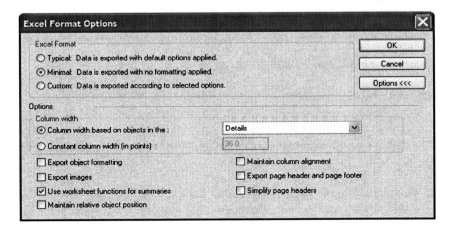

Figure 8-28 Minimal pre-selected default options

2. Click the **OPTIONS** button. You will see the options shown in Figure 8-29. Table 8-6 explains the options.

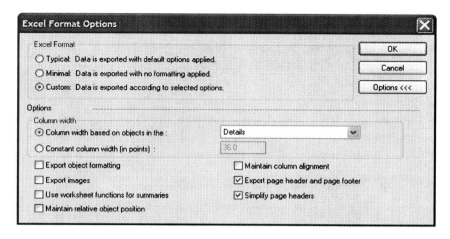

Figure 8-29 Extended Excel 97-2000 Data Only dialog box options

Option	Description
Column Width	These options let you select the column widths in Excel. ① The **COLUMN WIDTH BASED ON OBJECTS IN THE** option lets you select the column width in Excel based on a section in the report. ② The **CONSTANT COLUMN WIDTH (IN POINTS)** option lets you select a free form column width.
Export object formatting	Check this option to export as much formatting as possible.
Export images	Check this option to export any images that are in the report.
Use worksheet functions for summaries	Check this option if you want Crystal Reports to try and convert summary fields to Excel functions. If a matching function is not found, the summary field will be exported as a number without the formula.
Maintain relative object position	Check this option if you want Crystal Reports to add rows and columns as needed to keep objects in the exported Excel file in the same location/position that they are in the report.
Maintain column alignment	Check this option to force summary fields to appear in the correct column in Excel. By default, the export process ignores blank spaces to the left of fields, which causes fields to be shifted.
Export page header and page footer	Check this option if you want the information in the page header and footer sections to be exported.
Simplify page headers	Check this option if you only want the last row of the page header section to be exported. Usually the last row of the page header section contains the field headings.

Table 8-6 Excel Data Only export options explained

3. Check the option **USE WORKSHEET FUNCTIONS FOR SUMMARIES** and click OK, then save the exported file as `L8.9 2004 orders by month data only exported file`.

4. Open the L8.9 2004 orders by month data only spreadsheet in Excel and make columns A through H wider.

5. Scroll down to row 130 and click in cell F130, then look in the Formula Bar. You will see the equivalent of the summary calculation that was created in the report, as shown in Figure 8-30. Save the changes and close the spreadsheet.

	F130	▼	*fx*	=SUM(E3:E129)

	E		F
127	$3,419.25		
128	$3,884.25		
129	$36.00		
130	Total order amount for the month -		$211,265.10

Figure 8-30 Summary calculation in the Formula Bar

🆕 Exercise 8.10: Creating Default Export Options

If you know that you always want a certain report to use the same export format by default, you can save the export options by following the steps below. The default export options that you select are what will appear in the Format drop down list on the Export dialog box. Each report can have its own default export options.

1. Open the report that you want to set the default options for. In this exercise, open the L6.7 2004 Orders by month report, if it is not already open.

2. File ⇒ Export ⇒ Report Export Options, then open the Format drop down list and select the option, **MICROSOFT EXCEL 97-2000 - DATA ONLY (XLS)**. Click OK.

3. Check the **EXPORT IMAGES** and **USE WORKSHEET FUNCTIONS FOR SUMMARIES** options on the Excel Format Options dialog box shown in Figure 8-31 and click OK. In this exercise, these are the default options that you want to save for the export.

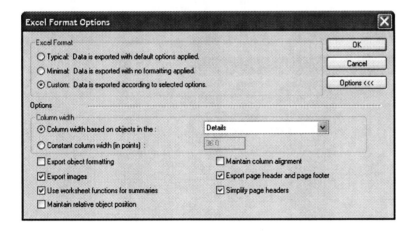

Figure 8-31 Default options that you want for the report

4. Save the exported file as L8.10 Saved export options. Close the report. Now when you need to export the report with the data only options, you can open this report, then open the Export dialog box, click OK twice (You will see the default options that you selected above in Figure 8-31.) and save the spreadsheet. Close Excel.

Exercise 8.11: Create A Word (RTF) Export File

This file type will export the report to a Word document. To open this exported file type, Microsoft Word or the free Word viewer needs to be installed.

1. Select the first Word (RTF) format, then open the Destination drop down list and select **APPLICATION**. Click OK.

2. Click OK to export all of the pages in the report. The report will now be exported to a Word document. Because you selected the Application destination, the report will open in Word (or the viewer) as shown in Figure 8-32. If you scroll down to page 3, you will be able to see the totals for January.

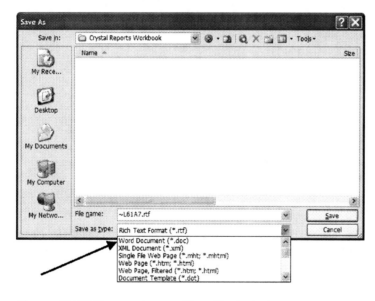

	Salesperson	Order Date	Order #	Order Amount
11/17/2005				
2004 Orders By Month				
January				
Anne	Dodsworth	01/01/2004	1121	$851.77
Michael	Suyama	01/01/2004	1122	$1,025.40
Janet	Leverling	01/02/2004	1123	$5,219.55
Margaret	Peacock	01/02/2004	1124	$59.70
Anne	Dodsworth	01/02/2004	1125	$75.42
Anne	Dodsworth	01/02/2004	1126	$3,842.55
Robert	King	01/02/2004	1127	$520.35
Janet	Leverling	01/02/2004	1128	$65.70
Nancy	Davolio	01/02/2004	1129	$2,997.25
Nancy	Davolio	01/03/2004	1130	$23.50
Michael	Suyama	01/03/2004	1131	$357.41

Figure 8-32 L8.11 2004 orders by month exported file in Word (RTF) format

3. Save the exported file as L8.11 2004 orders by month report in Word (RTF) exported file, then close the Word document.

 If you wanted to save the report in the standard Word file format of .doc, open the **SAVE AS TYPE** drop down list at the bottom of the Save As dialog box and select Word Document (*.doc) as illustrated in Figure 8-33.

Figure 8-33 Save as type options illustrated

NEW Exercise 8.12: Create A Word Editable (RTF) Export File

This file type will export the report to a Word document. If you think that the end-users will need to edit the report in Word, this is the export option that you should select. In this exercise you will only select the first 10 pages of the report to be exported to Word.

1. Select the Word Editable (RTF) format, then open the Destination drop down list and select **APPLICATION**. Click OK.

2. Select the page options shown in Figure 8-34. Click OK and the report will be created. Your report should look like the one shown in Figure 8-35.

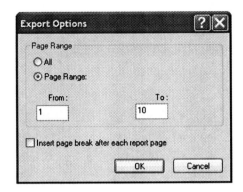

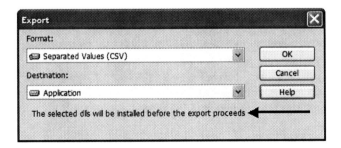

January					
Anne	Dodsworth	01/01/2004	1121	$851.77
Michael	Suyama	01/01/2004	1122	$1,025.40
Janet	Leverling	01/02/2004	1123	$5,219.55
Margaret	Peacock	01/02/2004	1124	$59.70
Anne	Dodsworth	01/02/2004	1125	$75.42
Anne	Dodsworth	01/02/2004	1126	$3,842.55
Robert	King	01/02/2004	1127	$520.35
Janet	Leverling	01/02/2004	1128	$65.70
Nancy	Davolio	01/02/2004	1129	$2,997.25
Nancy	Davolio	01/03/2004	1130	$23.50
Michael	Suyama	01/03/2004	1131	$357.41
Robert	King	01/04/2004	1132	$38.98
Nancy	Davolio	01/04/2004	1133	$43.50
Anne	Dodsworth	01/05/2004	1134	$43.80
Michael	Suyama	01/05/2004	1135	$2,584.85

Figure 8-35 L8.12 2004 orders by month exported file in Word Editable (RTF) format

Figure 8-34 Page range export options

Notice that even though you selected the first 10 pages, there are 12 pages in the Word document. That is because the page length is different in Crystal Reports then it is in Word. If you scroll down the pages, you will see a blank line between some of the records.

That blank line is where the data would print on a new page in Crystal Reports. Earlier I mentioned that if the **CREATE PAGE BREAKS FOR EACH PAGE** option was checked, you may see page breaks in places other then at the bottom of the page. This report is an example of what I was referring to.

3. Save the exported file as
L8.12 2004 orders by month report in Word Editable (RTF) exported file, then close the Word document.

Exercise 8.13: Create A Separated Values (CSV) Export File

In this exercise you will create a CSV export file. You will also learn how to install an export file type. You will need the Crystal Reports CD to complete this exercise.

1. Select the **SEPARATED VALUES (CSV)** format, then open the Destination drop down list and select **APPLICATION**. As you can see at the bottom of Figure 8-36, this export file type has not been installed. Also notice that the dialog box tells you that the required DLL files will be installed. Click OK.

Figure 8-36 Export file type not installed message illustrated

How To Install DLL's For An Export File Type

Once you click OK on the Export dialog box shown above in Figure 8-36, you will be prompted to put the Crystal Reports CD in the drive.

1. Insert the CD into the drive and click OK on the dialog box shown in Figure 8-37.

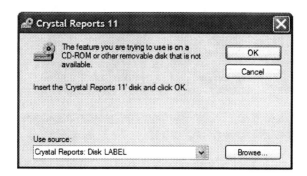

Figure 8-37 Insert CD dialog box

2. When the installation is complete, you will see the dialog box shown in Figure 8-38. Take the CD out of the drive.

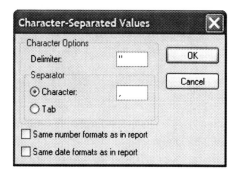

Figure 8-38 Character Separated Values dialog box

Continue Creating The CSV Export File

The options on the dialog box shown above in Figure 8-38 let you select the format for how you want the data from the report to be exported. The options that you select depend on how the data will be used.

If you do not want to have to reformat the number and date fields after the CSV export file is created, check both options, **SAME NUMBER FORMATS AS IN REPORT** and **SAME DATE FORMATS AS IN REPORT**.

1. For this exercise, check both options and click OK. This will let you see what the output will look like. Because the Application destination option was selected, the CSV file will be opened in Excel, unless you have another software package associated with .CSV files.

2. Any columns with the pound signs, as shown in Figure 8-39, means that the column is not wide enough for the data that it contains. To make the column wider, double-click on the line after the column that you want to widen, as illustrated in Figure 8-39.

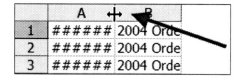

Figure 8-39 Mouse pointer in position to widen the column

After the column is made wider, it should look like the one shown in Figure 8-40. Notice that some of the columns (B, C and D for example) don't have data. They have field titles. That's because everything is exported. You can delete the columns that aren't needed.

	A	B	C	D
1	11/19/2005	2004 Orders By Month	Salesperson	Order Date
2	11/19/2005	2004 Orders By Month	Salesperson	Order Date
3	11/19/2005	2004 Orders By Month	Salesperson	Order Date
4	11/19/2005	2004 Orders By Month	Salesperson	Order Date
5	11/19/2005	2004 Orders By Month	Salesperson	Order Date
6	11/19/2005	2004 Orders By Month	Salesperson	Order Date

Figure 8-40 L8.13 CSV exported file with column A made wider

3. Save the file as L8.13 Exported CSV file. You will see the message shown in Figure 8-41. This message is asking if you want to keep the formatting. For this exercise, click Yes.

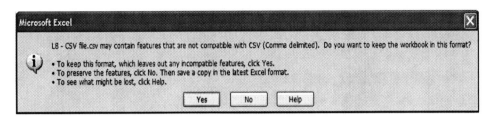

Microsoft Excel

L8 - CSV file.csv may contain features that are not compatible with CSV (Comma delimited). Do you want to keep the workbook in this format?

• To keep this format, which leaves out any incompatible features, click Yes.
• To preserve the features, click No. Then save a copy in the latest Excel format.
• To see what might be lost, click Help.

[Yes] [No] [Help]

Figure 8-41 Excel formatting message

4. Close Excel. You will be prompted to save the file again. Save it with the same name.

Exercise 8.14: Create A Report Definition Export File

In this exercise you will create a Report Definition export file. This export file type will be useful if you want to know how the report was created. Sometimes I use it to help troubleshoot a problem that I am having with a report. It can also be used as documentation for the report.

1. Select the Report Definition format, then select Application destination, if it is not already selected.

2. Like the Separated Values (CSV) export file option, the Report Definition option is not installed by default either. Follow the instructions that you used earlier to install the DLL's for the Report Definition export file type. When the installation is complete, you will see the document shown in Figure 8-42. If you scroll down to the bottom of the report, you will see all of the fields that are in the details section of the report, as shown in Figure 8-43.

```
        Crystal Report Professional v11.0 (32-bit) - Report Definition
1.0 File Information
        Report File:
        Version: 11.0
2.0 Record Sort Fields
        A - {Orders.Order Date}
3.0 Group Sort Fields
4.0 Formulas
4.1 Record Selection Formula
        {Orders.Order Date} in DateTime (2004, 01, 01, 0, 0, 0) to DateTime (2004, 12, 31, 0, 0, 0)
4.2 Group Selection Formula
4.3 Other Formulas
5.0 Sectional Information
5.1 Page Header Section
        Visible, Keep Together

        PrintDate
            Date, Visible, Default Alignment, Top Alignment,
            Keep Together, Using System Default Formatting, windows Default Type: Use windows Short Date, Date Order: Month Day
Year, Year Type: Long, Month Type: Numeric Month, Day Type: Numeric Day, Leading Day Type: None, First Separator: '/', Second Separator:
'/', Leading Day Separator: '

        2004 Orders By Month
            String, Visible, Horizontal Centre Alignment, Top Alignment,
            Keep Together
```

Figure 8-42 L8.14 Report definition report

```
5.7 Details Section
        Visible

        Subsection.1
                Visible, Keep Together

        {Employee.First Name}
                String, Visible, Default Alignment, Top Alignment,
                Keep Together, Using System Default Formatting, Word Wrap

        {Employee.Last Name}
                String, Visible, Default Alignment, Top Alignment,
                Keep Together, Using System Default Formatting, Word Wrap

        {Orders.Order Date}
                Date Time, Visible, Default Alignment, Top Alignment,
                Keep Together, Date Time Order: Date Only, Separator: ' '
```

Figure 8-43 Details section of the L8.14 Report definition report

3. Save the exported file as L8.14 Report definition, then close the document.

Exercise 8.15: Create An HTML Export File

This exercise will show you how to create a web page from the report.

1. Select the **HTML 4.0** format, then select Application destination and click OK. You will see the dialog box shown in Figure 8-44.

 Selecting the Application destination with the export file type will force your default web browser to open and display the web pages.

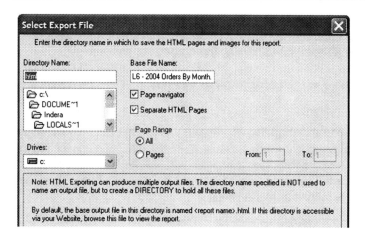

Figure 8-44 HTML Export options

The options on this dialog box let you configure the following:

① Where the web pages will be saved.
② How many pages of the report should be exported.
③ Whether or not the web pages should have navigation links.
④ Should the report be exported as one really long web page (if the report has a lot of pages) or a separate web page for each page of the printed report.

2. In the scroll box under the **DIRECTORY NAME** field, navigate to the Crystal Reports Workbook folder and double-click on it.

3. Type `L8.15_2004_Orders_Report` in the Directory Name field and click OK. You will see the web page shown in Figure 8-45. If you scroll to the bottom of the page, you will see the navigation links shown in Figure 8-46. Click on the links to go from page to page. Close the web browser when you are finished viewing the report.

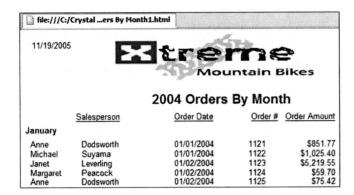

Figure 8-45 L8.15 Web page

If you look in the Crystal Reports Workbook folder you will see all of the files (60 files) in a folder named **L8.15_2004_ORDERS_REPORT** for the report.

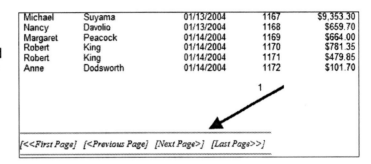

Figure 8-46 Navigation links on the web page illustrated

ODBC Export Format

If you select the ODBC export format, the destination option is grayed out on the Export dialog box. This is because this format exports the data from the report to a table. When you click OK on the Export dialog box, you will see the dialog box shown in Figure 8-47. You may be prompted to install the DLL files like you did for the CSV export file type. Select the ODBC database that you want to export the report to and click OK. You will then see the dialog box shown in Figure 8-48. Enter the name for the table that you will export the data to and click OK. The table will be created in the database that you selected and the data will be exported to the table.

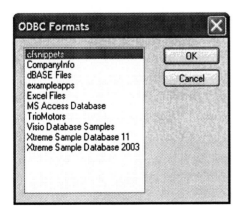

Figure 8-47 ODBC database format options

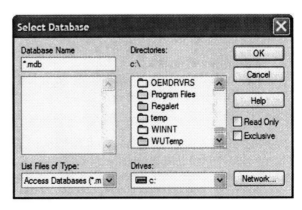

Figure 8-48 ODBC table name options

Text Export Format

Selecting this export format will prompt you to select the **CHARACTERS PER INCH** and the **NUMBER OF LINES PER PAGE** that you want for the exported file, as shown in Figure 8-49. To me, the characters per inch option is similar to selecting the font size.

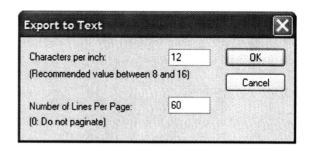

Figure 8-49 Export To Text dialog box

XML Export Format

This export format is similar to the HTML export format that you learned about earlier in this lesson, because it is also web based. Like the HTML format, the XML (which stands for Extensible Markup Language) export format requires you to create a folder to store the XML files in. XML uses **TAGS** that will format the data or content for the report. Figure 8-50 shows the XML options. If you need to customize the tags, you can use the XML Expert (Report ⇒ XML Expert) that is shown in Figure 8-51.
The people that will view a report in XML format will need software that recognizes XML files.

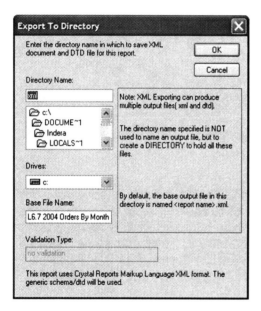

Figure 8-50 XML export options

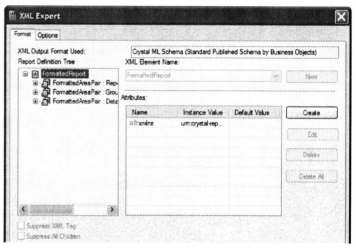

Figure 8-51 XML Expert

NEW Crystalreports.com

This is a new way to share reports on the Internet. It was introduced after Crystal Reports XI was released. You may have seen information about it on the Start page of Crystal Reports. It is easy to use and it is secure.

You can share up to 60 reports with 10 users including yourself, for free, as long as you have a Crystal Reports XI key code, which you have, if you purchased Crystal Reports XI. If you need to share more then 60 reports or give more then 10 people access, there is a premium service plan that you or your company can purchase. The premium service plan allows you to place reports in other formats like Word and Adobe PDF on the web site. Users can also put reports on the website with the premium service.

There is no software to install. You have complete control over who has access to the reports that you place on crystalreports.com. After you create your account, the steps below outline what you have to do.

① Create or refresh the report you want to upload.

② Upload it to crystalreports.com.

③ Add the names and email addresses of the people that you want to have access to the report. The people will automatically be notified that there is a new or revised report available for them to view.

Test Your Skills

1. Create a report definition for the L7.7 report. Save the report definition as `L8.16 Skills Top 5 orders report definition export file`. The report should look like the one shown in Figure 8-52.

```
        Crystal Report Professional v11.0 (32-bit) - Report Definition
1.0 File Information

        Report File:
        Version: 11.0

2.0 Record Sort Fields

3.0 Group Sort Fields
        D - Sum ({Orders.Order Amount}, {Orders.Order Date}, "weekly")

4.0 Formulas

4.1 Record Selection Formula
        {Orders.Order Date} in DateTime (2004, 06, 01, 00, 00, 00) to DateTime (2004, 06, 30, 00, 00, 00)

4.2 Group Selection Formula


4.3 Other Formulas

5.0 Sectional Information

5.1 Page Header Section
        Visible, Keep Together

        Order Date
                String, Visible, Left Alignment, Top Alignment,
                Keep Together
```

Figure 8-52 L8.16 Skills Top 5 orders report definition export file

2. Create a PDF file for the L7.7A report. Save the PDF file as
   `L8.17 Skills Top 5 orders PDF export file`. The PDF should look like the one
   shown in Figure 8-53.

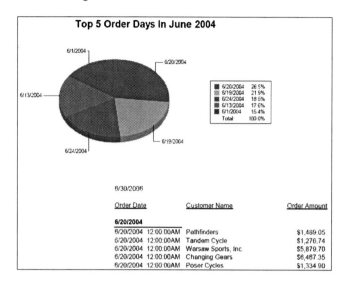

Figure 8-53 L8.17 Skills Top 5 orders PDF export file

3. Create a Data Only "Typical" Excel export file for the L7.7 report.
   Save the Excel file as `L8.18 Skills Top 5 orders export file`. The report should
   look like the one shown in Figure 8-54.

	A	B	C
1			
2	Order Date	Customer Name	Order Amount
3	6/20/2004		
4	6/20/2004 12:00:00 AM	Pathfinders	$1,489.05
5	6/20/2004 12:00:00 AM	Tandem Cycle	$1,276.74
6	6/20/2004 12:00:00 AM	Warsaw Sports, Inc.	$5,879.70
7	6/20/2004 12:00:00 AM	Changing Gears	$6,467.35
8	6/20/2004 12:00:00 AM	Poser Cycles	$1,334.90
9	6/20/2004 12:00:00 AM	Tandem Cycle	$1,784.75
10	6/20/2004 12:00:00 AM	Crank Components	$8,819.55

Figure 8-54 L8.18 Skills Top 5 orders export file

FORMULAS AND FUNCTIONS

After completing the exercises in this lesson, you will be able to:

☑ Understand the difference between formulas and functions
☑ Know what the formula rules are
☑ Select a Syntax Editor
☑ Use the Formula Workshop and know the purpose of its toolbar buttons
☑ Customize the Formula Editor window
☑ Use the Workshop Tree
☑ Understand the formula evaluation order
☑ Create numeric formulas
☑ Create string formulas
☑ Use functions in string formulas
☑ Create date formulas
☑ Use the Truncate function

To pass the RDCR201 exam, you need to be familiar with and be able to:

☑ Know what a formula is
☑ Understand Control Structures
☑ Use operators and functions
☑ Create numeric formulas
☑ Create string formulas
☑ Manipulate string fields
☑ Create date formulas

Formulas And Functions Overview

Formulas and functions are some of the most powerful features in Crystal Reports. Ironically, many people that are first learning Crystal Reports think that they are one of the most dreaded features because there is math and logic involved. If you fall into this category, hopefully this lesson will help you overcome some of the fear.

In Lesson 2 as part of the report design process, you learned that not all fields that are needed for a report exist in tables. In Lesson 6 you learned how to create summary fields, which are not stored in tables. While summary fields provide a quick way to create totals, that's about as far as they go.

For example, summary fields will not let you add two fields together, nor can you multiply a field in a table by a constant value, like calculating the sales tax for an order. When you have exhausted all other math related options, it's time to turn to formulas and functions. Formulas are created in the Formula Workshop, which you will learn about later in this lesson.

Actually, you have two options for creating formulas: The Formula Workshop and writing SQL Expressions. This type of field is what would be placed in the SQL Expression Fields section of the Field Explorer. If you are already freaking out about creating formulas, for now you should focus on using the Formula Workshop, because you would need to learn the version of SQL that works with the database that you are using for the reports that you are creating or modifying. If you recall, in Lesson 1, I listed several types of databases. Also keep in mind that some companies use a variety of database types from the list. [See Lesson 1, About Crystal Reports XI]

While creating SQL Expressions is more efficient then creating formulas in the Formula Workshop, SQL Expressions are evaluated (processed) on the server and sent back to Crystal Reports. The SQL for some types of databases is limited and can have fewer options then Crystal Reports has. For example, if you have to create a formula that needs to process or refer to (as in lookup) a record, other than the current record, you would have a problem if the database does not have any analytical functionality. I'm not saying this to scare you away from learning SQL, merely pointing out something that you may not be aware of.

What Is The Difference Between Formulas And Functions?

One of the questions that I am asked a lot is, "What is the difference between formulas and functions?" Formulas are calculations or some type of data manipulation that you create. Functions are built-in formulas or procedures that have already been created. If there is a built-in function that meets your needs, use it because there is no point reinventing the wheel, as they say. If you have created or used formulas or functions in spreadsheet software, you are already familiar with the basics of using them in Crystal Reports.

Formula Overview

Formulas let you create new fields. If you need to include data on a report that is not stored in the tables, many times you will need to create a formula to get the data. An example of this would be the line item total on an order report. Line item information is not stored in an Order Detail table, but the price and quantity ordered are stored in the table. These are the fields that you would use to create the formula to calculate the line item total. A line item total is sometimes referred to as the "Extended Price". If there is a built-in function that has the calculation that you need, you can use that. Formulas allow you to create the following types of calculations, comparisons, manipulations and much more.

① Solve math problems
② Convert data from one format to another
③ Compare or evaluate data
④ Join two or more text fields into one field
⑤ Join text and data fields

You may be thinking or asking why all of this information is not stored in tables. There are many reasons including the following, why data that falls into these categories is not stored in tables.

①	It would take a lot of hard drive or server space to store all of the data for these fields.
②	Applications that share data have slightly different data needs, which means that some tables would have empty fields.
③	Some data is only needed once or the data changes constantly, so it is more efficient to calculate it when it is needed.
④	The more data that has to be written (added or changed) to a table or tables, the slower the application will run. This "slowness" is often referred to as a performance issue.

Syntax Rules

Formulas have rules (also known as syntax rules) that have to be followed. Basically, the rules require that items be placed in a certain order, so that the formula will work. Table 9-1 provides the rules for Crystal Syntax, that if followed, will make learning how to write formulas easier. The items listed below are the parts of the formula.

Item	Syntax
//	The double slash lets you add comments to a formula. This is helpful when you need to document the formula. (1)
Case Sensitive	Formulas are not case sensitive.
Hard Returns	Pressing the Enter key to continue the formula on another line to make the formula more readable is acceptable. This is usually done on long formulas to make them easier to read. The one time that this will cause an error is if there is a hard return between quotation marks in a formula.
Operators	Placing a space before or after an operator is acceptable, but is not required. Many people include spaces to make the formulas easier to read. The spaces are ignored when the formula is executed. The operators are similar to the ones that you learned about earlier. The difference is that symbols are used in formulas, instead of words. = < > + - are some of the operators that you can use when creating formulas.
Fields	They must be surrounded by braces. For example, {Table.Field Name}.
Functions	Each function requires at least one argument. Each argument must be followed by a comma, except the last one. Arguments must be entered in this format: FunctionName (Argument 1, Argument 2).
Numbers	Numbers must be entered without any formatting. 5600 or 56000 is correct. 5,600 or 56,000.00 is incorrect.
Text	Text must be entered inside of quotation marks. Examples: "Help" would be printed as Help. ' "Help" ' would be printed as "Help". Notice the difference in the output, when different types of quotes are used.

Table 9-1 Syntax rules explained

(1) Comments should be added to formulas to explain the purpose of the formulas and to provide documentation. If the comment needs more than one line, each line must start with two slashes, otherwise Crystal Reports will treat the line as part of the formula, which will generate a syntax error. You may think that you will remember what the formula does six months from now, but it may take you a minute or so to remember. I have learned that it is easier to add comments to formulas and give them a descriptive name when they are first created.

Functions Overview

Functions are prewritten, built-in formulas or procedures. Software that supports functions have built-in functions, plus allow you to create your own. Functions have been thoroughly tested and from what I can tell, they are error free in Crystal Reports. However, this does not mean that if there is bad data in a table that you won't have a problem with the function. If you do not follow the syntax rules or fill in the arguments correctly when using the function, you will get an error.

Crystal Reports has over 300 functions that you can use. Sum, Average, Count and Distinct Count are functions that you have already learned to use. Many of the Special Fields that you have learned about are also functions, as are the Document Properties that you learned about. You also read about the Date Range functions. [See Lesson 5, Table 5-2] This lesson covers some of the more popular functions that you may have a need to use. For more information on functions, you can type `functions` on the Index tab of the Help window in Crystal Reports. You will see a list of function categories. Select the category that has the function that you want to learn more about.

Syntax

You can select the syntax language that you want to use. If you are already familiar with one, by all means continue to use it. If you have used a previous version of Crystal Reports, you may already be familiar with Crystal Syntax. You can create formulas and incorporate functions in both languages and both can be used in the same report. The good thing is that you do not have to be a programmer to create formulas or use functions in the Formula Workshop. Each language has its own rules for the Control Structures, functions and other syntax. In order to create a formula, you need to select one of the following languages:

① **Crystal Syntax** This language has been included in every version of Crystal Reports and is the default language that is selected when Crystal Reports is installed. The formulas that you viewed at the bottom of the Select Expert dialog box were written in Crystal Syntax, unless you have changed the default language to Basic Syntax prior to working on the exercises in this workbook. Some say that Crystal syntax is more user-friendly than Basic syntax. The exercises in this workbook use Crystal Syntax.

② **Basic Syntax** If you have developed applications in Visual Basic, you will find this syntax language familiar. The main difference that you will notice between Visual Basic and Basic Syntax is that the Basic Syntax language has extensions for creating reports. Figures 9-1 and 9-2 show the same formula using different syntax editors.

```
// This formula combines the Supplier ID and Supplier Name fields
ToText ({Supplier.Supplier ID},0 )+ " - " +{Supplier.Supplier Name}
```

Figure 9-1 Formula using Crystal Syntax

```
'This formula combines the Supplier ID and Supplier Name fields
formula = ToText ({Supplier.Supplier ID},0)+ " - " + {Supplier.Supplier Name}
```

Figure 9-2 Formula using Basic Syntax

You should know that Crystal Reports supports two syntax languages (Crystal Syntax and Basic Syntax) that can be used to create formulas.

Statements Depending on the environment that you work in, you may hear the term "Statement" and have a different interpretation of what a statement is then the context that I will present it in. That's fine, I just don't want you to think that either interpretation is incorrect. You may have also heard the term EXPRESSION. I believe that the terms statement and expression mean the same thing, but some will argue that there is a difference. Formulas in Crystal Reports and other software tools as well, consider a statement a combination of fields, operators, functions and other variables that provide an answer or value. I think of statements in Crystal Reports as sentences. Formulas have at least one statement.

Control Structures are how Crystal Reports processes a formula. The process starts at the beginning of the formula and moves from one statement to the next. Control structures evaluate expressions or conditions. The result of this evaluation is known as the RETURN VALUE. Formulas must return a value. The result of the last statement executed in the formula contains the result value. It is important to note that the last statement executed may not be the last physical line of code in the formula.

Types of control structures include WHILE DO/DO WHILE, SELECT CASE STATEMENTS and IF STATEMENTS, which are also known as If Then Else or Nested If statements. You will learn to create If statements in Lesson 10.

Formula Workshop Overview

The Formula Workshop shown in Figure 9-3 is the tool that you will use to create and manage formulas. You can also work with record and group selection formulas in the Formula Workshop. Notice that it does not have any menus. Depending on how you open the Formula Workshop, you will either see the Formula Editor as shown in Figure 9-3 or the Formula Expert. If you do not like the toolbars at the top of the window, you can move them. Each section of the Formula Workshop is explained below. Table 9-2 explains the buttons on the General Formula Workshop toolbar. Table 9-3 explains the buttons on the Workshop Tree toolbar. Table 9-4 explains the buttons on the Expression Editor toolbar.

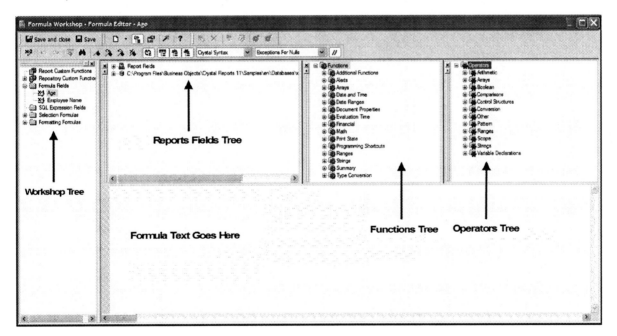

Figure 9-3 Formula Workshop

Button	Purpose
Save and close	Closes the Formula Workshop after prompting you to save changes if necessary. (2)
Save	Saves the formula and leaves the Formula Workshop open. (2)
	The New button lets you create a new formula based on the category selected from the drop down list shown in Figure 9-4.
	The Show/Hide Workshop Tree button shows or hides the Formula Workshop Tree.
	The Toggle Properties Display button toggles between displaying the Custom Function Editor and Custom Function Properties dialog box. Custom functions and formulas (where possible) are displayed in the selected mode until this button is clicked again.
	The Use Expert/Editor button toggles between the Formula Editor and the Formula Expert. Use the Formula Expert to create a formula based on a custom function. This button is not available when creating a custom function.
?	Opens the online help for the Formula Workshop, Formula Editor or Formula Expert, depending on which is currently displayed or where the cursor is.

Table 9-2 General Formula Workshop toolbar buttons explained

(2)   When you save the changes, the formula, custom function or SQL Expression is checked for errors.

Figure 9-4 New formula options

Button	Purpose
	Lets you rename the selected formula, custom function, or SQL Expression.
X	Deletes the selected formula, custom function, or SQL Expression.
	Expands the selected node(s) in the Workshop Tree.
	The Show Formatting Formulas button shows or hides all of the report objects in the Formatting Formulas folder or only the objects that have a formatting formula.
	The Add To Repository button opens the Add Custom Function To Repository dialog box so that you can select the repository to add the custom function to.
	The Add To Report button adds the selected repository custom function to the report.

Table 9-3 Workshop Tree toolbar buttons explained

Button	Purpose
x-2	The Check button tests the syntax of the formula or custom function and identifies syntax errors.
⤺	The Undo button undoes the last action made to the formula.
⤻	The Redo button redoes the last action that was made to the formula.
🗐	The Browse Data button lets you view the data in a field in the Report Fields window. (3)
🔍	The Find or Replace dialog box shown in Figure 9-5 searches the formula, fields, functions or operators for words or expressions. You can also replace text in formulas using this dialog box. The EDIT TEXT option is where you type in the formula.
⚓	The Bookmark button inserts a bookmark in the current line of the selected formula. Click the button again to remove the bookmark. Bookmarks let you mark a line of code as important. The bookmark feature is helpful in long formulas when you have to go from one part of the formula to another.
⚓	The Next Bookmark button will place the cursor at the next bookmark in the formula.
⚓	The Previous Bookmark button place the cursor at the previous bookmark in the formula.
⚓	The Clear All Bookmarks button deletes all bookmarks in the current formula.
🔤	This toggle button sorts the options in the Report Fields, Functions and Operators trees in alphabetical order or returns them to their original order.
▦	Displays or hides the Report Fields tree. (3)
▦	Displays or hides the Functions tree.
▦	Displays or hides the Operators tree.
Crystal Syntax ▼	Lets you to select CRYSTAL SYNTAX or BASIC SYNTAX as the formula syntax editor.
Exceptions For Nulls ▼	This option allows you to select EXCEPTIONS FOR NULLS or DEFAULT VALUES FOR NULLS as the method for dealing with null values in the data. Fields in a formula that have a null value will return invalid data or generate an error. Selecting the Default values for nulls option will replace data that has a null value, with default value for the field type. String fields are changed to an empty string. Number fields are changed to zero. If you don't know how or do not want to write code to test for nulls or check for errors, select this option.
//	Lets you add comments to a formula. Commented lines are not evaluated as part of the formula. I type the // into the Formula Text section when writing the formula because I find it faster then clicking this button.

Table 9-4 Expression Editor toolbar buttons explained

(3) This button is not available for custom functions.

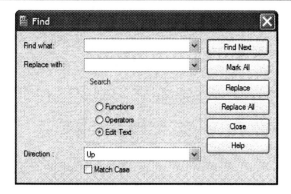

Figure 9-5 Find dialog box

Workshop Tree

This section of the Formula Workshop contains all of the formulas that are in the report and includes formulas that are in the repository that can be used in the report. Items under the Selection Formulas folder are ones that you have created with the Select Expert.

NEW Formula Editor

The Formula Editor itself is not new. What's new is that it has been incorporated into the Formula Workshop interface. The contents of each of the trees in the Formula Editor change to show the options that are available for the type of database that the report is based on. The Formula Editor allows you to create formulas by double-clicking on the functions, operators and fields that you need to include in the formula. The Formula Editor will allow you to create at least 90% of the formulas that you need. The Formula Editor contains the three trees discussed below. You may want to open some of the categories (nodes) in each tree to become familiar with the options.

① **Report Fields Tree** This tree displays all of the fields that are on the report, including groups, summary fields, running totals, parameters, formulas and the tables that the report uses. This tree is similar to the Field Explorer. You can use any of these fields in a formula.

② **Functions Tree** This tree contains the built-in functions. The functions are divided into categories, which makes it easier to find the function that you need.

③ **Operators Tree** This tree contains all of the operators (logical and mathematical) that you can use to create formulas. The operators are grouped by type to make them easier to find. Operators use symbols instead of words.

 When you first open the Formula Workshop, you will not see the Formula Editor. You can do either of the following to open the Formula Editor.

① Select an option in a folder under the Formula Fields, SQL Expression Fields or Selection Formulas in the Workshop Tree.

② Select one of the formula or function options on the New button menu shown earlier in Figure 9-4.

Formula Text Window

In addition to the three trees, the blank portion below the trees is where you type in the formula. This section is called the Formula Text window. Depending on the field selected in the Workshop Tree, the Formula Editor can change to a different editor, because each formula type has its own editor.

You can use the **AUTO COMPLETE** feature in the formula text window by typing in the first few letters of the function that you need and then press the **CTRL** and **SPACE BAR** keys. You will see a list that has functions that start with the letters that you typed in, as shown in Figure 9-6. If you type in enough letters to only display the function that you want, the drop down list will not be displayed. Instead, the function will be filled in for you. If you press the CTRL and Space bar keys before typing any letters, you will see all of the functions in the list.

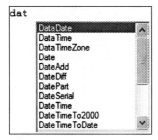

Figure 9-6 Auto complete list

Formula Expert

The Formula Expert shown in Figure 9-7 allows you to create custom functions. The functions that you create in the Formula Expert can be used in other reports if they are saved in the repository. By design, the Formula Expert will help you create a formula without having to use the Crystal Reports syntax programming language. While this may sound appealing to those that are new to Crystal Reports or do not want to write code, the Formula Expert only creates formulas that use one custom function. You cannot use the math operators or the Crystal Reports syntax programming language in the Formula Expert.

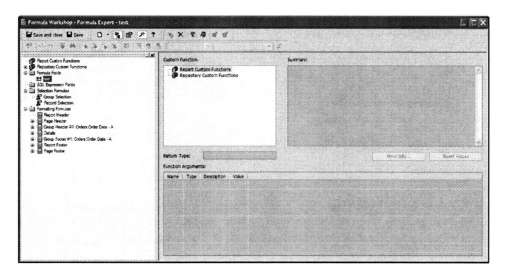

Figure 9-7 Formula Expert

Formula Editor Versus Formula Expert

The main difference between the two is that formulas created in the Formula Editor are saved with the report that they are created in and can only be used in that report. Formulas created in the Formula Expert can be saved as a **CUSTOM FUNCTION** in the repository and can be used in any report.

If you find yourself creating the same formula in several reports, copy it to the Formula Expert and save it as a custom function. I often also save the custom functions that I create in a Microsoft Word document because I find it easier to get to them that way, instead of logging into the repository. If you work from home, you will understand what I mean. Many will say that this is not a good technique.

There are valid reasons not to save custom functions in a document. I will leave it up to you to decide what works best for you in the environment that you will create reports in.

How To Open The Formula Workshop

Like many other tools in Crystal Reports, there is more than one way to open the this tool. The Formula Workshop is no exception. This tool has more ways that it can be opened then most tools.

    ① Click the **FORMULA WORKSHOP** button on the Expert Tools toolbar.
    ② Report ⇒ Formula Workshop.
    ③ Right-click on a formula or SQL Expression field in the design (or preview) window and select Edit.
    ④ Right-click on a formula or SQL Expression field in the Field Explorer and select New or Edit.
    ⑤ Click on a formula or SQL Expression field and click the **NEW** button on the Field Explorer toolbar.
    ⑥ Click the **FORMAT** button on any tab of the Format Editor dialog box.
    ⑦ Open the Select Expert, click the Show Formula button, then click the **FORMULA EDITOR** button.

Customizing The Formula Editor

You can customize the Formula Editor by doing any or all of the following:

    ① You can resize any of the tree sections by dragging the bar illustrated in Figure 9-8.
    ② Close a tree by clicking on the ⚏ button to the left of the section that you want to close.
    ③ Expand a tree by clicking on the ◂ button to the left of the section that you want to expand.
    ④ Make the Formula Text section longer or shorter by dragging the section bar above it, up or down.

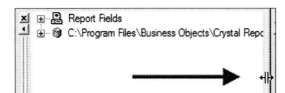

Figure 9-8 Mouse pointer in position to resize a tree

The Workshop Tree

As you saw earlier in Figure 9-3, the Workshop Tree contains several sections called **NODES** or **CATEGORY** folders that formulas can be saved in. In addition to being able to create formulas, you can also rename and delete formulas, just like you can in the Field Explorer. Each of the categories in the Workshop Tree is explained below.

    ① **Report Custom Functions** If you create a function or copy a function from the repository into the report, this is where it would be stored. The functions in this category can be used by any formula in your report. Custom functions are used in reports just like the built-in functions that come with Crystal Reports.
    ② **Repository Custom Functions** The functions stored in this category are stored in the repository. To use a repository custom function, it has to be added to the report so that it will become a report custom function.
    ③ **Formula Fields** The formulas in this category are server based and are the same ones that are in the Field Explorer in the Formula Fields, Parameter Fields, Running Total Fields and Group Name Fields sections.

④ **SQL Expression Fields** The formulas in this category are the same expression fields that are in the SQL Expression Fields section of the Field Explorer. If you create a new expression or modify an existing expression, the SQL Expression Editor will open with the Formula Workshop instead of the Formula Editor. The options in the Report Fields Tree, Functions Tree and Operators Tree will change and display the options that are available for the type of database that the report is using. It has been reported that the SQL Expression Editor may not reflect all of the operators and functions that are really available for certain database types.

⑤ **Selection Formulas** The formulas in this category are created when you use the Select Expert or the selection formula options on the Report menu. You can also create selection formulas in the Formula Workshop. If you click on the Group Selection option, the GROUP SELECTION FORMULA EDITOR will open. If you click on the Record Selection option, the RECORD SELECTION FORMULA EDITOR will open. The only difference that you will notice is that the title bar of the Formula Workshop will change as shown in Figure 9-9. Compare this title bar to the one shown earlier in Figure 9-3.

Figure 9-9 Record Selection Formula Editor title bar

⑥ **Formatting Formulas** This category has a folder for each section of the report. All of the objects from each section of the report are listed here. Formatting formulas like changing the color, font or font size for objects in the report are stored in this category.

Formula Evaluation Order

Many of the formulas that you will create will use more than one operator. The order that the formula is written in from left to right may not be the order that the formula is calculated or evaluated in.
Some operations are processed first, regardless of where they are in the formula. This is known as the ORDER OF PRECEDENCE. The formula evaluation order is:

① The portion of the formula that is in parenthesis.
② Exponential.
③ Multiplication and division. (4) (5)
④ Integer division.
⑤ MOD.
⑥ Addition and subtraction. (4)

(4) If the operators (3 and 6 above) are on the same level, they are evaluated from left to right. See the examples below.

Example #1: $3 + 4 / (2 + 19) = 3.19$
Example #2: $3+ (4 / 2) + 19 = 24$

The first example calculates the (2+19) first, then divides that by 4 and then adds 3.

The second example calculates the (4/2) first, then adds 3 and then adds 19.

(5) In Crystal syntax, percents are evaluated at the same level as multiplication and division.

You may find it helpful to write the formula on paper and use data in the tables to test the formulas to see if you get the results that you are expecting from the formula. As you saw in the examples above, the same data and operators can produce different results.

I have noticed in the workplace and in classes that I teach that this is one area where many people have a lot of trouble. I think this is because they are not willing to write out the formula and test it prior to opening the Formula Workshop. Yes, I am fully aware that doing this takes more time up front, but experience shows that the more time you spend "preparing", the less time you will spend debugging reports in the future. Trust me, a year from now, you will not remember why you wrote a formula the way that you did <smile>.

Keep the following in mind when creating formulas:

① Formulas must have an equal number of left and right parenthesis.
② Arguments must be the same data type.

Formula Naming Conventions

The naming conventions for formulas is free form. You should use as descriptive a name as possible, one that will make sense to you a year from now. The name you select is what you will see when the formula field is added to the report. Formula names can be up to 256 characters. You can use upper and lower case letters, spaces and the underscore. You should not use characters like the slash, dollar or percent sign in the formula name.

The company that you work for may have naming conventions. You should check to find out. One convention that many companies have is that they do not want spaces in object names. When this is the case, most companies use the underscore in place of spaces in object names.

Create Numeric Formulas

The exercises in this section will teach you how to create numeric formulas.

Exercise 9.1: Create A Formula Field

In Exercise L6.16, you created a report that displayed an order total per customer. As you saw, the order total was not correct. In this exercise you will modify the report and create a formula that will calculate the amount for each item. This is known as the line item amount. The formula is Unit Price * Quantity. This will allow the report to have the correct total amount.

1. Save the L6.16 report as `L9.1 Formula field for line item totals`.

2. Click on the **FORMULA FIELDS** option in the Field Explorer, then click the **NEW** button.

3. Type `Line Item Total` in the dialog box as shown in Figure 9-10 and click OK.

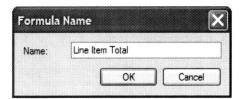

Figure 9-10 Formula Name dialog box

4. In the Report Fields tree, double-click on the Unit Price field in the Orders Detail table. You should see the field in the Formula Text section of the Formula Editor, as shown at the bottom of Figure 9-11.

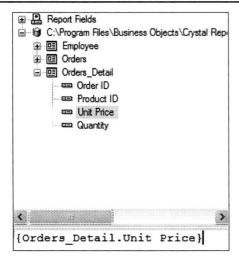

Figure 9-11 Field added to the Formula Text section

 You can also drag the field to the Formula Text section.

5. Type a * after the Unit Price field, then double-click on the Quantity field.

 You can use the **MULTIPLY** Arithmetic operator illustrated in Figure 9-12 instead of typing the operator.

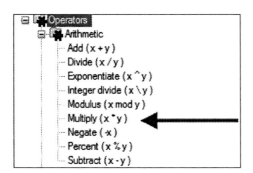

Figure 9-12 Multiply arithmetic operator illustrated

6. Add a blank line above the formula and type the following comment.
   // This formula calculates the Line Item Total.
   Your formula should look like the one shown in Figure 9-13.

```
// This formula calculates the Line Item Total
{Orders_Detail.Unit Price} *{Orders_Detail.Quantity}
```

Figure 9-13 Line Item Total formula

 Notice that the comment line is a different color then the formula line. This is one way to know that you have entered the comment correctly. Comments do not have to go at the beginning of a formula.

7. Click the **CHECK (X-2)** button on the Expression Editor toolbar. You should see the message shown in Figure 9-14.

Figure 9-14 No errors found message

 The message shown above in Figure 9-14 means that Crystal Reports did not find a syntax error. This does not mean that the formula will produce the results that you are expecting.

If you do not see this message, there is an error in your formula. Check to make sure that your formula looks like the one shown earlier in Figure 9-13. Figure 9-15 shows one error message that you could see. If there is an error, the flashing insertion bar will be at the location in the formula where Crystal Reports thinks the error is. The part of the formula where the syntax checker stopped understanding the formula will also be highlighted, as illustrated in Figure 9-15.

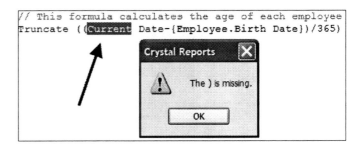

Figure 9-15 Formula error message

8. Click OK, then click the **SAVE AND CLOSE** button.

 If you need to work on another formula, click the **SAVE** button instead of the Save and close button. Doing this will leave the Formula Workshop open. When you save a formula it becomes a field, which you can then add to the report or use in another formula.

Using Formula Fields In Reports

You can use formula fields in reports, just like you use fields from a table. Formula fields can be placed in any section of the report. You can create counts and summary fields that are based on formula fields. You can also use formula fields as selection criteria.

Add The Line Item Formula Field To The Report

In this part of the exercise you will add the formula field that you just created to the report.

1. Delete the Order Amount field and heading, then move the four fields after the Order Amount field over to the left.

2. Add the Line Item Total field to the report. (**Hint:** The field is in the Field Explorer in the Formula Fields section.) The report should look like the one shown in Figure 9-16. Save the changes and leave the report open to complete the next exercise.

Sales Person		Order Date	Order ID	Customer #	Product #	Unit Price	Quantity	Line Item Total
1	Nancy Davolio							
2/16/2003								
30								
		02/19/2003	1310	30	1101	$14.50	3	$43.50
		02/19/2003	1310	30	1104	$14.50	1	$14.50
	Total order amount for customer - **$ 116.00**							
75								
		02/19/2003	1312	75	302162	$479.85	1	$479.85
		02/19/2003	1312	75	401001	$267.76	1	$267.76
		02/19/2003	1312	75	2202	$41.90	1	$41.90
	Total order amount for customer - **$ 2,368.53**							
Daily Totals		# of Orders for the day - **2**						
	Total amount of sales for the day - **$ 2,484.53**							

Figure 9-16 L9.1 Formula field for line item totals

As you can see, the Total Order Amount for each customer is still not correct. That is because the Total Order Amount field is adding the values in the Order Amount field, even though that field is no longer on the report. The Total Order Amount field should be adding the values in the Line Item Total formula field. One of the skills exercises in this lesson will have you modify this.

Exercise 9.2: Create A Sales Tax Formula

Many orders (or purchases) require sales tax to be collected. This exercise will show you how to create a sales tax formula. You will create a formula that calculates 6% of the line item total. As you know, not all items are taxable. If all items were taxable, you could create a sales tax formula that used the order total times the sales tax rate. In this exercise, you will modify a customer order report and create a sales tax formula that will use the Line Item Total field instead of the Order Total field.

> In the real world, the product table would have a field that is used to signify if each product is taxable or not. In that case, you would have to create a conditional formula that checked the field to see if the product is taxable. If it is taxable, then calculate the sales tax.

1. Save the L9.1 report as L9.2 Sales tax formula.

2. Open the Formula Workshop. Create a formula field and name it Line Item Sales Tax.

3. Double-click on the Line Item Total field in the Report Fields tree and type *.06 at the end of the field. Check the formula to make sure that the syntax is correct by clicking the Check (X-2) button. Your formula should look like the one shown in Figure 9-17. Save the formula and close the Formula Workshop.

```
{@Line Item Total}* .06
```

Figure 9-17 Line Item Sales Tax formula

4. Move all of the fields except for the Salesperson field to the left, then add the Line Item Sales Tax field at the end of the details section.

5. Change the field title for the Line Item Sales Tax field to Sales Tax. Your report should look similar to the one shown in Figure 9-18. Save the changes and leave the report open to complete the next exercise.

Sales Person	Order Date	Order ID	Customer #	Product #	Unit Price	Quantity	Line Item Total	Sales Tax
1 **2/16/2003** **30**	Nancy Davolio							
	02/19/2003	1310	30	1101	$14.50	3	$43.50	$2.61
	02/19/2003	1310	30	1104	$14.50	1	$14.50	$0.87
	Total order amount for customer - **$ 116.00**							
75								
	02/19/2003	1312	75	302162	$479.85	1	$479.85	$28.79
	02/19/2003	1312	75	401001	$267.76	1	$267.76	$16.07
	02/19/2003	1312	75	2202	$41.90	1	$41.90	$2.51
	Total order amount for customer - **$ 2,368.53**							
Daily Totals	# of Orders for the day - **2**							
	Total amount of sales for the day - **$ 2,484.53**							

Figure 9-18 L9.2 Sales tax formula report

Exercise 9.2A: Create A Summary Formula

In Lesson 6 you learned how to create summary fields. All of the summary fields that you created were based off of fields in a table. In this exercise you will create a summary field that is based off of a formula field.

1. Save the L9.2 report as L9.2A Summary formula.

2. Right-click on the Line Item Total formula field and select Insert ⇒ Summary.

3. Select the Average summary type, then select the Group 2 Orders Date section as the section to place the field in and click OK.

4. Click on the preview tab. You will see the average sales tax amount for the daily totals as illustrated in Figure 9-19. If you want, you can add a title for the field so that the person reading the report knows what the number is. Save the changes and close the report.

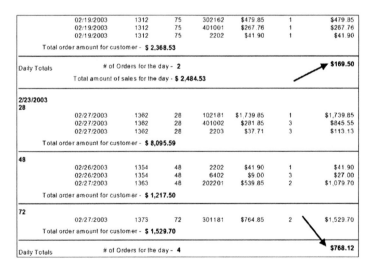

Figure 9-19 L9.2A Summary formula report

Exercise 9.3: Create A Weekly Salary Formula

In this exercise you will create a formula that will calculate each employees weekly salary. The annual salary field is stored in the Employee table. You will use this field to calculate the weekly salary.

1. Save the L6.12 report as L9.3 Employee list with weekly salary formula.

2. Open the Formula Workshop. Create a formula field and name it Weekly Salary.

3. Double-click on the Salary field in the Employee table and then drag the DIVIDE (X/Y) Arithmetic Operator to the Format Text section.

4. Type 52 after the slash. Check the formula to make sure that the syntax is correct. Your formula should look like the one shown in Figure 9-20. Save the formula and close the Formula Workshop.

```
{Employee.Salary} / 52
```

Figure 9-20 Weekly Salary formula

5. Delete the Region field, then add the Weekly Salary field before the Salary field. The report should look like the one shown in Figure 9-21. Save the changes and leave the report open to complete the next exercise.

First Name	Last Name	Address1	Weekly Salary	Salary
Steven	Buchanan	14 Garrett Hill	$961.54	$ 50,000.00
Robert	King	Edgeham Hollow	$711.54	$ 37,000.00
Anne	Dodsworth	7 Houndstooth Rd.	$673.08	$ 35,000.00
Michael	Suyama	Coventry House	$576.92	$ 30,000.00

Figure 9-21 L9.3 Employee list with weekly salary formula report

Exercise 9.4: Use A Formula Field As Selection Criteria

Earlier you learned that you can use a formula field as selection criteria. In this exercise, you will use the Weekly Salary formula field to only display employees that have a weekly salary between $500 and $750.

1. Save the L9.3 report as L9.4 Formula field used as selection criteria.

2. Create the selection criteria for the Weekly Salary formula field. The report should look like the one shown in Figure 9-22. There should be five records on the report. Save the changes and close the report.

First Name	Last Name	Address1	Weekly Salary	Salary
Robert	King	Edgeham Hollow	$711.54	$ 37,000.00
Anne	Dodsworth	7 Houndstooth Rd.	$673.08	$ 35,000.00
Michael	Suyama	Coventry House	$576.92	$ 30,000.00
BC				
Margaret	Peacock	4110 Old Redmond Rd.	$673.08	$ 35,000.00
Janet	Leverling	722 Moss Bay Blvd.	$634.62	$ 33,000.00

Figure 9-22 L9.4 Formula field used as selection criteria report

Create String Formulas

The exercises in this section will teach you how to create formulas that use String fields or literals. The most used string formulas allow you to convert date and numeric fields to text, select specific portions of a field and trim fields. A common string formula that is used is one that will concatenate (combine) the first and last name fields. Names are usually stored in two or more fields in a table. There are several string formula operators and functions that you can use, as explained in Tables 9-5 and 9-6.

Operator	What It Does
+ or &	These are known as concatenation operators. They are used to combine text fields. The plus sign requires that all arguments be string fields. Crystal Reports will automatically convert every argument to a string when the ampersand (&) operator is used.
[ ]	Subscript operators let you select specific characters from a text field.
" " or ' '	Quotes will treat the text inside of them as a literal. If a string or text field contains numeric data and you need to use it in a formula, you have to put the numeric data in quotes.
If Then Else	This operator allows different actions to be taken based on a condition. (6)

Table 9-5 String operators explained

Date/Time literals must be in one of these formats: #6/24/2005# or #June 24, 2005#.

Keep in mind that while the + (plus sign) operator allows you to join text and data fields, it does not add a space between the fields that are being joined. You have to type + " " + to add a space between the fields that you are joining. There is a space between the quotes in the syntax above.

Function	What It Does
Is Null	This function checks to see if a field has a value. It is often used with the If...Then...Else operator. If the function is used alone, it returns a value of True or False (Boolean). (6)
Length (str)	This function counts the number of characters in a string. It can be used to determine if a value in a field is a certain length. (6)
Lower Case (str)	This function converts the text to all lower case letters. Use **LOWERCASE** for Crystal Syntax. Use **LCASE** for Basic Syntax.
Picture (str, picture)	This function lets you format a string field. This is similar to the "mask" feature found in some database software packages.
To Text	This function is used to convert non text fields like Date, Number and Currency to a text string. This function can have multiple arguments, as shown in Figure 9-23. The only argument that requires a value is X.
Trim (str)	This function removes spaces before and after the data in a string argument. Use **TRIMLEFT** if you only want to remove spaces to the left of the string argument. Use **TRIMRIGHT** if you only want to remove spaces to the right of the string argument.
Upper Case (str)	This function converts the text to all upper case letters. Use **UPPERCASE** for Crystal Syntax. Use **UCASE** for Basic Syntax.

Table 9-6 String functions explained

(6) You will learn how to use this operator in Lesson 10.

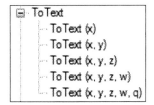

Figure 9-23 To Text functions

Exercise 9.5: Combine Two String Fields

Earlier in this lesson you modified an employee report. That report would look better if the employee first and last names were closer together. This produces the same result as dragging one field into another as you learned in Lesson 4. One reason that you would write code to combine the name fields is if you only needed to combine fields if a certain condition was met. Another reason to write code to combine fields is if there is a possibility that at least one of the fields is null.

1. Save the L9.1 report as `L9.5 Combine string fields`.

2. Create a formula field and name it `Employee Full Name`, then add the Employee First Name field from the Employee table to the Formula Text section.

3. Click after the First Name field and type + " " +
   This will add a space after the First Name. Make sure that there is a space between the quotes.

4. Add the Last Name field to the formula.

5. Add a blank line above the formula and type // This formula combines 2 fields, then check the formula for errors. The formula should look like the one shown in Figure 9-24. Save the formula and close the Formula Workshop.

```
// This formula combines 2 fields
{Employee.First Name} + " " +{Employee.Last Name}
```

Figure 9-24 String formula

Add The Employee Full Name Formula Field To The Report

1. Delete the First and Last name fields in the Group 1 Header section, then add the Employee Full Name field in place of the two fields that you just deleted.

2. Create a field title and call it `Employee`. Place it above the Employee Full Name field.
   The report should look like the one shown in Figure 9-25. Save the changes and leave the report open to complete the next exercise.

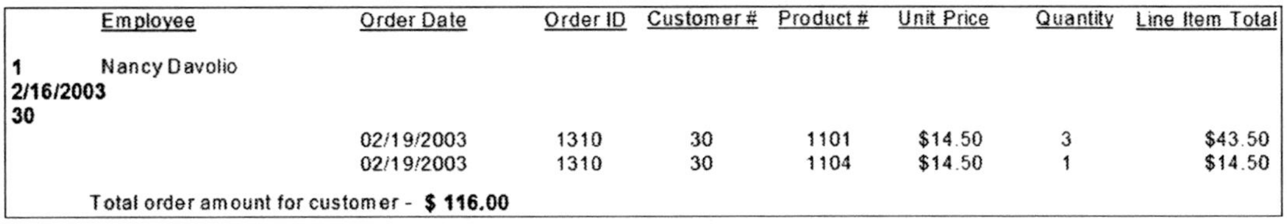

Employee	Order Date	Order ID	Customer #	Product #	Unit Price	Quantity	Line Item Total
1 Nancy Davolio **2/16/2003** **30**							
	02/19/2003	1310	30	1101	$14.50	3	$43.50
	02/19/2003	1310	30	1104	$14.50	1	$14.50
Total order amount for customer - **$ 116.00**							

Figure 9-25 L9.5 Combine string fields report

Exercise 9.6: Use The Subscript Operator

The subscript operator allows you to extract specific characters in a field based on their position in the field. In Exercise 9.5 you learned how to combine the first and last name fields. If you needed to modify that formula to only display the first letter of the first name, you would use the subscript operator. The subscript [1] means to select the first character in the field from the left. Subscript [3] means to select the third character in the field from the left. In this exercise, you will add the subscript operator to an existing formula.

1. Save the L9.5 report as `L9.6 Subscript`.

2. Modify the Employee Full Name formula so that it looks like the one shown in Figure 9-26.

```
// This formula combines 2 fields and only uses the first letter
// of the First Name field
{Employee.First Name}[1] + " " +{Employee.Last Name}
```

Figure 9-26 Subscript formula

3. Save the changes. The report should look like the one shown in Figure 9-27. Notice that only the first letter of the first name is displayed. Close the report.

Employee	Order Date	Order ID	Customer #	Product #	Unit Price	Quantity	Line Item Total
1 N Davolio							
2/16/2003							
30							
	02/19/2003	1310	30	1101	$14.50	3	$43.50
	02/19/2003	1310	30	1104	$14.50	1	$14.50
Total order amount for customer - **$ 116.00**							

Figure 9-27 L9.6 Subscript report

Exercise 9.7: Combine A Text And Numeric Field

In the reports that you have created with totals, you created a text object for the title of the summary field. If you had trouble either getting the text object and total field to line up or getting the two fields to be close together, this exercise will show you how to combine these fields using a formula, which means that you will not have to align the field and text object.

 If the numeric field that you will use needs to be formatted, you should not combine it with a text field because text fields cannot be formatted with numeric formatting options.

1. Save the L6.1 report as `L9.7 Combine text and numeric fields`.

2. Create a formula field and name it `Total Field`.

3. Add the comment `This formula combines text with a numeric field`.

4. Type `"Total # of customers in region - "` in the Formula Text section.

5. Open the **STRINGS** operator node and drag the **CONCATENATE (x&y)** operator illustrated on the right in Figure 9-28, to the formula.

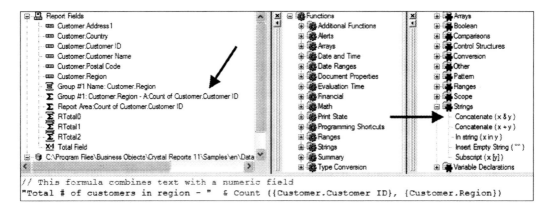

Figure 9-28 Group 1 Customer ID field added to the formula

6. Add the Group 1 Customer ID field illustrated above in Figure 9-28 to the formula, then check the formula for errors. Save the formula and close the Formula Workshop.

Add The Total Formula Field To The Report

1. Delete both objects in the group footer section.

2. Add the Total Field formula field to the group footer section. The report should look like the one shown in Figure 9-29. Notice that there is a decimal point in the number. You cannot format the number. Save the changes and close the report.

Customer Information Grouped By Region

Customer Information Grouped By Region

Sorted By Zip Code

12/29/2005   Page 1 of 17

Customer Name	Address	Country	Zip Code
Abu Dhabi			
UAE Cycle	Post Box: 278	United Arab Emirate	3453
Total # of customers in region - 1.00			
AL			
Psycho-Cycle	8287 Scott Road	USA	35818
The Great Bike Shop	1922 Beach Crescent	USA	35857
Benny - The Spokes Person	1020 Oak Way	USA	35861
Total # of customers in region - 3.00			

Figure 9-29 L9.7 Combine text and numeric fields report

Use Functions In String Formulas

You may have the need to combine data that is stored in different data types or format data differently then it is stored in the table. The next two exercises will show you how to incorporate functions in string formulas.

Exercise 9.8: Use The Picture Function

The phone numbers in the Supplier table are stored in the format shown in Figure 9-30. Notice that there are also international phone numbers in the table. When you want to print US phone numbers, they will look better if they are printed like this **(704) 555-5555**. In this exercise you will use the Picture function to format phone numbers in the Supplier table.

Figure 9-30 Phone numbers stored in the table

1. Create a new report. Add the Supplier table, but do not add any fields to the report. Save the report as `L9.8 Picture function`.

2. Create a formula field and name it `Supplier Phone`, then add the comment `This formula formats the Phone Number field` to the formula.

3. Open the Reports Field tree, then open the Supplier table.

4. Open the **ADDITIONAL FUNCTIONS** category in the Functions tree, then open the **SAMP1** category and double-click on the **PICTURE** function, as shown in Figure 9-31.

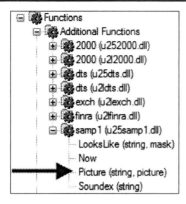

Figure 9-31 Picture function illustrated

5. Double-click on the Phone field in the Reports Field tree, then click after the comma in the formula and type " (XXX) XXXXXXX". Your formula should look like the one shown in Figure 9-32. Save the formula and leave the Formula Workshop open to complete the next part of the exercise.

```
//This formula formats the phone number field
Picture ({Supplier.Phone},"(XXX)XXXXXXX")
```

Figure 9-32 Phone number formula

 The brackets { } in a formula are used for data fields. The parenthesis ( ) are used to control the order that the formula is evaluated in.

In Figure 9-30 shown earlier, you saw the phone numbers that are stored in the Supplier table. All of the phone numbers will not work with the mask that you just created in the formula. In order to be able to accommodate international phone numbers, the formula would have to be modified to also use the **LENGTH** function and have another mask to accommodate phone numbers of a different length. This is known as conditional formatting, which you will learn how to do in the next lesson.

Use The ToText Function

The ToText function is one of the more popular functions. It lets you convert dates, numbers and more to a string/text field. In this part of the exercise you will combine the Supplier ID and Supplier Name fields. In order to combine a numeric and string field, you have to convert the numeric field to text. The **TOTEXT** function will let you do this.

1. Create a formula field and name it `Supplier ID & Name`, then add the comment `This formula combines the Supplier ID and Supplier Name fields` to the formula.

2. Open the Strings category in the Functions tree and double-click on the ToText (x,y) function.

3. Click inside of the parenthesis and add the Supplier ID field.

4. Move the insertion bar to the right of the comma in the formula and type a zero. The zero means that the number should not display any decimal places, if there are any in the field.

5. Click outside of the formula on the right and type + " - " +, then add the Supplier Name field. Your formula should look like the one shown in Figure 9-33. Save the formula and close the Formula Workshop.

```
// This formula combines the Supplier ID and Supplier Name fields
ToText ({Supplier.Supplier ID},0 )+ " - " +{Supplier.Supplier Name}
```

Figure 9-33 Supplier ID and Name formula

6. Add both of the formula fields to the report. The report should look like the one shown in Figure 9-34. Save the changes and close the report.

Supplier ID & Name	Supplier Phone
1 - Active Outdoors	(503) 555-9931
2 - Triumph	(313) 555-5735
3 - Guardian	(81)3 3555-5011
4 - InFlux	(81)6 431-7877
5 - Craze	(604) 681 3435
6 - Roadster	(44)171 555-2222
7 - Vesper	(514) 555-9022

Figure 9-34 L9.8 Picture function report

Using The Ampersand To Concatenate Strings

In the exercise that you just completed, you used the ToText function and the plus sign operator to concatenate string fields. The benefit of using the ToText function with the plus sign is that you can control the formatting. If you do not need to control the formatting, use the ampersand operator instead of the plus sign.

Formatting Strings With A Mask

In Exercise 9.8 you formatted a phone number field with the Picture function, which used a mask to format the field. Masks use characters including x, d, m and y as placeholders for the data, which determines how the data will be formatted when it is converted to a string. Table 9-7 lists some of the mask placeholders that are used the most for date fields. Table 9-8 provides placeholder examples for the date 6/1/05.

Placeholder	Description
d	Day of the month in numeric format without a leading zero.
dd	Day of the month in numeric format with a leading zero.
dddd	Full (character) name of the day.
M	Month in numeric format without a leading zero.
MM	Month in numeric format with a leading zero.
MMMM	Full (character) name of the month.
y	Last two digits of the year.
yyyy	Four digits of the year.

Table 9-7 Placeholder options

Mask	Displays
dd, MM, yy	01, 06, 05
MMMM dd yyyy	June 01, 2005
dddd MMMM, d, yyyy	Wednesday June 1, 2005
M, d, yy	6 1, 05

Table 9-8 Mask options

Create Date Formulas

Table 9-9 provides an overview of some of the date functions. The exercises in this section will show you how to create some of the more popular date formulas using functions.

Function	Description
ChrW(x)	This function returns the character that represents the Unicode value of (x).
CurrentDate	This function uses the system date on your computer.
DateAdd	This function allows you to increment a date field by intervals, including days, weeks, months and years.
DateDiff	Calculates the difference between the start and end dates in the function. (7)
Day	Extracts the day from a Date or Date/Time field and returns a whole number.
Month	Extracts the month from a Date or Date/Time field and returns a whole number.
ToText	This function allows you to format any or all parts of a date field. This function also allows you to convert a date field to a text value.
Year	Extracts the year from a Date or Date/Time field and returns a whole number.

Table 9-9 Date functions explained

(7) The DateDiff function has arguments that you can use to determine how you want to calculate the difference between two date fields. For a full list of arguments, type `DateDiff` on the Index tab of the Help application. The most common arguments are:

D will calculate the difference in days
M will calculate the difference in months
YYYY calculate the difference in years

Exercise 9.9: Create A Date Formula To Calculate The Order Processing Time

In this exercise you will create a formula to find out how long it is between the day an order is placed and when the order was shipped. This is known as the order processing time.

1. Save the L5.3 report as `L9.9 Calculate order processing time.`

2. Create a formula field and name it `Delay In Days To Ship`.

3. Expand the Date and Time function folder, then expand the **DATEDIFF** function folder and double-click on the first DateDiff function.

4. Type a "`d`" before the first comma in the formula.

5. Add the Order Date field to the formula after the first comma, then add the Ship Date field to the formula after the second comma. Your formula should look like the one shown in Figure 9-35. Check the formula for errors, then save the formula and close the Formula Workshop.

```
DateDiff ("d",{Orders.Order Date},{Orders.Ship Date})
```

Figure 9-35 Delay in days to ship formula

Add The Delay In Days To Ship Formula Field To The Report

1. Remove the time from the Order Date and Ship Date fields. Make these fields smaller, then move them to the left.

2. Add the Delay In Days To Ship formula field to the report and format it so that it does not have any decimal places. The report should look like the one shown in Figure 9-36. Save the changes and close the report.

Customer Name	Order Date	Ship Date	Order ID	Unit Price	Quantity	Delay In Days To Ship
City Cyclists	12/02/2003	12/10/2003	1	$41.90	1	8
Deals on Wheels	12/02/2003	12/02/2003	1,002	$33.90	3	0
Deals on Wheels	12/02/2003	12/02/2003	1,002	$1,652.86	3	0
Warsaw Sports, Inc.	12/02/2003	12/05/2003	1,003	$48.51	3	3
Warsaw Sports, Inc.	12/02/2003	12/05/2003	1,003	$13.78	3	3
Bikes and Trikes	12/02/2003	12/02/2003	1,004	$274.35	3	0
SAB Mountain	12/03/2003	12/03/2003	1,005	$14.50	2	0

Figure 9-36 L9.9 Calculate order processing time report

 A zero in the Delay In Days To Ship Field means that the order was shipped within 24 hours of when it was placed. Depending on the time an order was placed and shipped, the Ship Date could be the next day and still have a zero in the Delay In Days To Ship field because the order was shipped in less than 24 hours. Remember that the fields used in this formula are Date/Time fields.

Exercise 9.10: Calculate The Employee Age

One of the more popular date functions will allow you to calculate a persons age, if you have their date of birth. In this exercise you will create an employee birthday list report. You will create a formula to calculate the age of the employees. In the Formula Overview section earlier in this lesson, I listed four reasons why certain types of data are not saved in a table. A persons age is a good example of the type of data that should not be saved in a table. The reason is because the age changes every year. This would mean that the field would have to be updated once a year on each persons birthday. This is why it is best to calculate the age, each time the report is run.

1. Create a new report and add the following fields from the Employee table: Position, Birth Date and Hire Date.

2. Remove the time from the Birth Date and Hire Date fields, then save the report as L9.10 Calculate age formula.

3. Create a formula field to combine the first and last name fields. Name the formula Employee Name.

4. Create another formula field and save it as Age.

5. Add the Current Date function from the Date and Time Category to the Age formula, then type a – (minus sign).

6. Add the Birth Date field to the formula and check the formula for errors. Save the formula and close the Formula Workshop.

Modify The Report

1. Add the Employee Name formula field to the beginning of the details section, then add the Age formula field to the report after the Birth Date field.

2. Sort the report by the Last Name field. The report should look like the one shown in Figure 9-37.

Employee Name	Position	Birth Date	Age	Hire Date
Justin Brid	Marketing Director	10/08/1982	8,483.00	01/01/1999
Steven Buchanan	Sales Manager	03/04/1980	9,431.00	09/13/1997
Laura Callahan	Inside Sales Coordinator	01/09/1979	9,851.00	01/30/1998
Nancy Davolio	Sales Representative	12/08/1977	10,248.00	03/29/1996
Anne Dodsworth	Sales Representative	01/27/1981	9,102.00	10/12/1998
Andrew Fuller	Vice President, Sales	02/19/1974	11,636.00	07/12/1996
Albert Hellstern	Business Manager	03/13/1973	11,979.00	03/01/1998
Robert King	Sales Representative	05/29/1977	10,441.00	11/29/1997
Janet Leverling	Sales Representative	08/30/1976	10,713.00	02/27/1996
Xavier Martin	Marketing Associate	11/30/1980	9,160.00	01/15/1999
Caroline Patterson	Receptionist	09/11/1984	7,779.00	05/15/1998
Margaret Peacock	Sales Representative	09/19/1978	9,963.00	03/30/1997
Laurent Pereira	Advertising Specialist	12/09/1975	10,978.00	02/01/1999
Tim Smith	Mail Clerk	06/06/1978	10,068.00	01/15/1998
Michael Suyama	Sales Representative	07/02/1968	13,694.00	09/13/1997

Figure 9-37 Age field added to the report

Modify The Age Formula

As you can see, the function did not return the age in the format that you expected. The age shown on the report is in days, not years. This is because the Current Date function calculates in days. The formula will have to be modified so that the age is displayed in years.

1. Right-click on the Age formula field and select Edit Formula.

You may be thinking that the only thing that you have to do is click after the Birth Date field and type /365 and the age would be converted to years. Just adding this to the formula will not calculate the age. Instead, you will see the message shown in Figure 9-38.

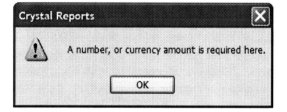

Figure 9-38 Calculation warning message

 The reason that you will see this message is because you are trying to divide the Birth Date field which is a Date/Time field by 365, which is a numeric field. As you learned earlier, arguments must be the same data type to use them in a formula. This is not the case in this formula.

Another reason that this formula will not work is because of the formula evaluation order. The evaluation order must be forced in this exercise. The way to force it is by adding parenthesis around the portion of the formula that has to be evaluated first. The order needed in this exercise is to force the Birth Date to be subtracted from the Current Date **BEFORE** the division takes place.

2. Type parenthesis around the formula, then type /365 after the last parenthesis and check the formula.

Use The Truncate Function

When you previewed the report, you saw that the age field has a decimal place, as shown earlier in Figure 9-37. The decimal place represents part of the year. This is not what you want. The Truncate function will remove that portion of the field.

1. Add the comment `This formula calculates the employees age.`

2. Expand the Math function node, then expand the Truncate function node.

3. Click in front of the formula in the Formula Text section, then double-click on the Truncate (x) function.

TRUNCATE(X) truncates a field. TRUNCATE (X, #PLACES) determines how many decimal places to keep before truncation occurs.

4. After the truncate function, you will see parenthesis. Delete the right parenthesis and add it to the end of the formula. Your formula should look like the one shown in Figure 9-39. Check the formula for errors, then save and close the formula. The report should look like the one shown in Figure 9-40.

```
// This formula calculates the age of each employee
Truncate ((CurrentDate-{Employee.Birth Date})/365)
```

Figure 9-39 Age formula

Employee Name	Position	Birth Date	Age	Hire Date
Justin Brid	Marketing Director	10/08/1982	23	01/01/1999
Steven Buchanan	Sales Manager	03/04/1980	25	09/13/1997
Laura Callahan	Inside Sales Coordinator	01/09/1979	26	01/30/1998
Nancy Davolio	Sales Representative	12/08/1977	28	03/29/1996
Anne Dodsworth	Sales Representative	01/27/1981	24	10/12/1998
Andrew Fuller	Vice President, Sales	02/19/1974	31	07/12/1996
Albert Hellstern	Business Manager	03/13/1973	32	03/01/1998
Robert King	Sales Representative	05/29/1977	28	11/29/1997

Figure 9-40 L9.10 Calculate age formula report

You may see a different age for some or all of the employees. This will happen if you run the report after an employees birthday has past. For example, I ran the report shown above in Figure 9-40 in late December 2005. I ran the report shown in Figure 9-41 in early March 2006, almost three months later. Notice that the age for some of the employees has changed. That is because some people had a birthday since I ran the report shown above in Figure 9-40.

Employee Name	Position	Birth Date	Age	Hire Date
Justin Brid	Marketing Director	10/08/1982	23	01/01/1999
Steven Buchanan	Sales Manager	03/04/1980	26	09/13/1997
Laura Callahan	Inside Sales Coordinator	01/09/1979	27	01/30/1998
Nancy Davolio	Sales Representative	12/08/1977	28	03/29/1996
Anne Dodsworth	Sales Representative	01/27/1981	25	10/12/1998
Andrew Fuller	Vice President, Sales	02/19/1974	32	07/12/1996
Albert Hellstern	Business Manager	03/13/1973	32	03/01/1998
Robert King	Sales Representative	05/29/1977	28	11/29/1997
Janet Leverling	Sales Representative	08/30/1976	29	02/27/1996
Xavier Martin	Marketing Associate	11/30/1980	25	01/15/1999
Caroline Patterson	Receptionist	09/11/1984	21	05/15/1998
Margaret Peacock	Sales Representative	09/19/1978	27	03/30/1997
Laurent Pereira	Advertising Specialist	12/09/1975	30	02/01/1999
Tim Smith	Mail Clerk	06/06/1978	27	01/15/1998
Michael Suyama	Sales Representative	07/02/1968	37	09/13/1997

Figure 9-41 L9.10 Calculate age formula report run almost three months later

If you need to use the same formula in more than one report, you can copy it from one report and paste it in another report.

Run-Time Errors

No one likes to talk about errors, but they do happen. Earlier in this lesson you learned about syntax errors and that if a formula passes the syntax checker, errors can still occur. These errors occur when the report is run (previewed). Run-time errors usually occur when a data type being used is not what the formula expected.

Examples of run-time errors include null values in a field or formula that returns zero (Divide By Zero). You can debug these errors using the **CALL STACK**. If you get a run-time error, you will see the error message in the Formula Workshop, which will display the formula that triggered the error. The call stack shown on the left of Figure 9-42 shows the formula with the error. You will also see all of the fields in the formula and the values in the field of the record that was being processed when the run-time error occurred. The value in the field is displayed after the field name as illustrated. Being able to see the data may help you figure out what caused the error.

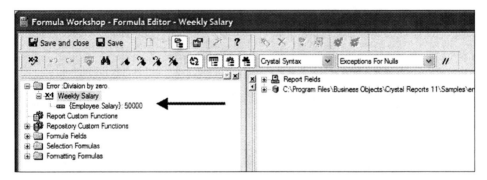

Figure 9-42 Run-time error call stack illustrated

Test Your Skills

1. Save the L9.3 report as `L9.11 Skills Calculate monthly salary`.

   - Create a formula to calculate the employees monthly salary and name it `Monthly Salary`. Place the formula on the report after the Weekly Salary formula field.
   - Create a formula called `Combined Name` that combines the Employee ID, first and last name fields. (**Hint**: Use the ToText (x,y) function)
   - Add a dash after the Employee ID field in the formula.
   - Create a title on the report for the field called `Employee`.
   - Delete the Address1 field.
   - Change the sort order to sort on the Employee ID field.
   - The report should look like the one shown in Figure 9-43.

Employee	Weekly Salary	Monthly Salary	Salary
5 - Steven Buchanan	$961.54	$4,166.67	$ 50,000.00
6 - Michael Suyama	$576.92	$2,500.00	$ 30,000.00
7 - Robert King	$711.54	$3,083.33	$ 37,000.00
9 - Anne Dodsworth	$673.08	$2,916.67	$ 35,000.00
Bas-Rhin			
13 - Justin Brid	$1,442.31	$6,250.00	$ 75,000.00
14 - Xavier Martin	$961.54	$4,166.67	$ 50,000.00
15 - Laurent Pereira	$865.38	$3,750.00	$ 45,000.00

Figure 9-43 L9.11 Skills Calculate monthly salary report

2. Save the L9.5 report as `L9.12 Skills Calculate sales tax`.

   - Modify the Total order amount for customer, Total amount of sales for the day, Total amount of sales for salesperson and Total amount of sales fields to use the Line Item Total field for the summary, instead of the Order Amount field. (**Hint**: Use the Edit Summary option)
   - Create a `Sales Tax` formula field that calculates 8.25% sales tax. Use the Group 3 Sum of Line Item Total field.
   - Create a formula field called `Order Total`. Add the Group 3 Sum of Line Item Total field and the Sales Tax field.
   - Add the Sales Tax and Order Total fields to the report. Place them in the Group 3 Footer section after the summary field.
   - Move the Total order amount for customer title in front of the Order Total field.
   - Create a field title called `Sub Total` and place it in front of the first summary field in the Group 3 Footer section. Take the bold off of the summary field in this section.
   - Create a field title called `Sales Tax` and place it in front of the Sales Tax field.

   Page 1 of the report should look like the one shown in Figure 9-44.
   The last page of the report should look like the one shown in Figure 9-45.

	Employee	Order Date	Order ID	Customer #	Product #	Unit Price	Quantity	Line Item Total
1	Nancy Davolio							
2/16/2003								
30								
		02/19/2003	1310	30	1101	$14.50	3	$ 43.50
		02/19/2003	1310	30	1104	$14.50	1	$ 14.50
		Sub Total $ 58.00		Sales Tax $ 4.79		Total order amount for customer - $ 62.79		
75								
		02/19/2003	1312	75	302162	$479.85	1	$ 479.85
		02/19/2003	1312	75	401001	$267.76	1	$ 267.76
		02/19/2003	1312	75	2202	$41.90	1	$ 41.90
		Sub Total $ 789.51		Sales Tax $ 65.13		Total order amount for customer - $ 854.64		
Daily Totals		# of Orders for the day - **2**						
		Total amount of sales for the day - **$ 847.51**						

Figure 9-44 Page 1 of the L9.12 Skills Calculate sales tax report

	Employee	Order Date	Order ID	Customer #	Product #	Unit Price	Quantity	Line Item Total
		12/27/2003	1101	33	402002	$274.35	3	$ 823.05
		12/27/2003	1101	33	5204	$33.90	1	$ 33.90
		Sub Total $ 982.65		Sales Tax $ 81.07		Total order amount for customer - $ 1,063.72		
Daily Totals		# of Orders for the day - **2**						
		Total amount of sales for the day - **$ 1,024.65**						
12/28/2003								
5								
		12/29/2003	1112	5	2215	$53.90	3	$ 161.70
		12/30/2003	1115	5	3301	$4.50	2	$ 9.00
		Sub Total $ 170.70		Sales Tax $ 14.08		Total order amount for customer - $ 184.78		
Daily Totals		# of Orders for the day - **2**						
		Total amount of sales for the day - **$ 170.70**						
Salesperson Totals		# of Orders for salesperson - **37**						
		Total amount of sales for salesperson - **$ 29,049.94**						
Report Totals		# of Orders - **181**						
		Total amount of sales - **$ 259,390.64**						

Figure 9-45 Last page of the L9.12 Skills Calculate sales tax report

If you refer back to Lesson 6, Figures 6-75 and 6-76, you will see the difference in the total amounts. Hopefully after completing this exercise you realize how easy it was in Lesson 6 to produce a report that looks good, but does not display the correct data. Many of the calculations in the report in Lesson 6 were incorrect, which in this case, inflated the totals.

People reading the report in Lesson 6 would think that the orders were a lot higher then they really are. Whatever decisions that would be made from the data on that report, may not be correct. Remember that the people reading the report normally do not see the formulas that are used in the report. This is why I know that it is important for the report designer (you) to understand the data for the report and to take the time to test the calculations to ensure that the calculations are correct. Okay, I will get off of my soap box now, as hopefully I have proven my point.

3. Save the L9.9 report as L9.13 Skills Ship delay GT 2 days.

   - Create selection criteria to only show orders that have a shipping delay of two or more days.

   Your report should look like the one shown in Figure 9-46. The report should have 1,977 records.

Customer Name	Order Date	Ship Date	Order ID	Unit Price	Quantity	Delay In Days To Ship
City Cyclists	12/02/2003	12/10/2003	1	$41.90	1	8
Warsaw Sports, Inc.	12/02/2003	12/05/2003	1,003	$48.51	3	3
Warsaw Sports, Inc.	12/02/2003	12/05/2003	1,003	$13.78	3	3
Poser Cycles	12/03/2003	12/05/2003	1,006	$16.50	1	2
Poser Cycles	12/03/2003	12/05/2003	1,006	$33.90	1	2
Poser Cycles	12/03/2003	12/05/2003	1,006	$14.50	1	2
Clean Air Transportation Co.	12/03/2003	12/07/2003	1,008	$726.61	2	4
Clean Air Transportation Co.	12/03/2003	12/07/2003	1,008	$431.87	1	4

Figure 9-46 L9.13 Skills Ship delay GT 2 days report

4. In this exercise you will combine two address fields and add the combined field to the report. You will also create totals for the reports.

    - Save the L9.3 report as `L9.14 Skills Combined address fields`.
    - Create a formula field called `Full Address` that combines the two address fields.
    - Create a count of employees per region.
    - Create a total dollar amount of weekly and monthly salaries per region.
    - Create a field title called `Totals for the region -` and place it in the Group 1 Footer section.
    - Create a field title called `# of employees` and place it in the Group 1 Footer section.
    - Add a line at the top of the Group 1 Footer section.

    Your report should look like the one shown in Figure 9-47. Notice that most of the addresses did not print on the report. That is because at least one of the address fields is null. In order to properly combine and print both address fields, conditional formatting needs to be applied that will force the address fields to print. You will learn how to create conditional formatting in the next lesson.

First Name	Last Name	Address	Weekly Salary	Salary
Steven	Buchanan		$961.54	$ 50,000.00
Robert	King	Edgeham Hollow	$711.54	$ 37,000.00
Anne	Dodsworth		$673.08	$ 35,000.00
Michael	Suyama		$576.92	$ 30,000.00
Totals for region -	# of employees **4**		**$ 2,923.08**	**$ 152,000.00**
Bas-Rhin				
Justin	Brid		$1,442.31	$ 75,000.00
Xavier	Martin		$961.54	$ 50,000.00
Laurent	Pereira		$865.38	$ 45,000.00
Totals for region -	# of employees **3**		**$ 3,269.23**	**$ 170,000.00**

Figure 9-47 L9.14 Skills Combined address fields report

When you have a formula that is combining fields and one or more fields is null, the formula will fail, which is what happened in this exercise.

5. Save the L4.13 report as `L9.15 Skills Convert case`.

    - Create a formula called `ProductTypeLowerCase` that changes the case of the Product Type Name field to all lower case letters.
    - Create a formula called `SupplierNameUpperCase` that changes the case of the Supplier Name field to all upper case letters.

    Your report should look like the one shown in Figure 9-48.

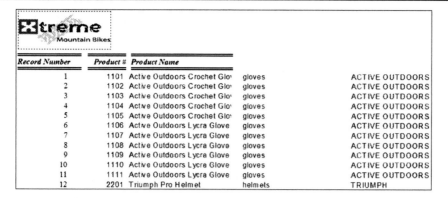

Figure 9-48 L9.15 Skills Convert case report

6. Add all of the reports that were created in this lesson to the Workbench.

CONDITIONAL FORMATTING

After completing the exercises in this lesson, you will be able to use the following tools and techniques to format fields and sections in a report.

- ☑ Highlighting Expert
- ☑ Apply conditional formats to fields
- ☑ Create If Then Else statements
- ☑ Suppressing fields and sections
- ☑ Section Expert

To pass the RDCR201 exam, you need to be familiar with and be able to:

- ☑ Create If Then Else statements

LESSON 10

Conditional Formatting Overview

In Lesson 4 you learned basic formatting techniques. In Lesson 9 you learned that data could be formatted or manipulated using formulas and functions. The techniques covered in those two lessons will handle a large percent of your report formatting needs. What you may have noticed is that the formatting that you have learned to create so far, is applied to every detail record. There will be times when the report does not need or require the same formatting to be applied to every detail record.

There are formatting techniques that you can use that will give you the option of applying the formatting only if a condition is met. This is known as **CONDITIONAL FORMATTING**. Examples of conditional formatting include the following:

① Highlighting records where the data in one field is greater than a constant value.
② Highlighting records with a specific color that have data missing in a field.
③ Check the value or length of a field and apply different formatting, depending on the value or length of the field.
④ Print a background color on every other detail record on the report.
⑤ Formatting one field with a border based on the value in another field.

The formatting techniques that you learned in Lesson 4 are known as **ABSOLUTE FORMATTING** because they are applied to every occurrence of the object. Conditional formatting starts off as absolute formatting, but goes a step further by setting up criteria to determine when the formatting should be applied.

> Conditional formatting is created using the Format Editor. Conditional formatting overrides absolute formatting that is created with the Format Editor. You can set the "on" and "off" properties conditionally.

There are two types of properties that conditional formatting can be applied to. The property type determines the type of conditional formula that has to be created for the option.

① **On-Off** properties like the Can Grow option or any option that has a check box on the Format Editor. On-off properties require **BOOLEAN** formulas.
② **Multiple choice** properties like the border line style option which is a drop down list on the Line tab of the Format Editor. Multiple choice properties require If Then Else or Select Case statements.

Highlighting Expert Overview

This tool allows you to easily create and apply font, background and border conditional formatting to fields on a report without having to write any code. The downside is that it does not provide a lot of options. The Highlighting Expert allows you to bring attention to certain values on the report. The way that the Highlighting Expert allows you to conditionally bring attention to values on the report is by changing one or some of the following:

☑ Font style
☑ Font color
☑ Background color
☑ Border style

> Conditional formatting that is created by the Highlighting Expert cannot be modified in the Formula Workshop which you learned about in Lesson 9.

An example of when to use the Highlighting Expert would be if you wanted to highlight the order amount if it is more than $1,000. Like many of the other experts, there are three ways to open the Highlighting Expert, shown in Figure 10-1.

① Right-click on the field that needs to meet a condition and select Highlighting Expert.
② Click the Highlighting button on the Experts toolbar.
③ Format ⇒ Highlighting Expert.

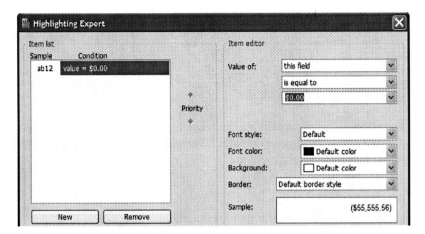

Figure 10-1 Highlighting Expert

As shown above in Figure 10-1, the Highlighting Expert has the following two sections:

① **Item List** Displays the conditional formatting formulas created by the Highlighting Expert for the field that is selected.
② **Item Editor** Allows you to create and view the conditional formatting formulas. This section also has the SAMPLE field that will let you see the highlighting that will be applied.

Item Editor Options

① The VALUE OF drop down list contains the fields, formulas and functions that are on the report or that are connected to the report, as shown in Figure 10-2. These are the fields that you can use to create the conditions for.

The THIS FIELD option lets you use the field that was selected before the Highlighting Expert was opened. Selecting a different field then the one that was selected prior to opening the Highlighting Expert means that you want to apply the formatting to the field selected prior to opening the Highlighting Expert, but you want the condition to be set based on the value in a different field.

The last option in the drop down list, OTHER FIELDS opens the Choose Field dialog box, which you can use to select another field from any data source connected to the report to use to create highlighting criteria for.

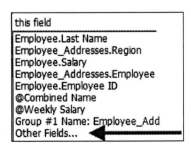

Figure 10-2 Field selection drop down list

② The COMPARISON drop down list contains the selection criteria options shown in Figure 10-3. You can use these operators to select which records will be highlighted.

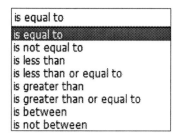

Figure 10-3 Comparison drop down list operators

③ The **COMPARE TO** drop down list is the third one from the top. It will display the values in the field that you select in the Value Of drop down list. This is like the Browse Data window. You can also type in the value that you want.

Item List Options

① The **PRIORITY** buttons let you change the order that the highlighting will be applied. Priority is important when there are multiple conditions set for the same field. For example, if you want to set the background of a date field to green if it is greater than 1/1/04 and another condition to place a border around the same date field if the date is greater than 6/24/05. If the date is 1/24/06, which of the two formatting conditions should be applied to the date field? If the greater than 1/1/04 is the first condition, all of the records that are greater than 1/1/04 would have a green background applied, even if the date is greater than 6/24/05. In some instances, multiple conditions can conflict. This is why setting a priority is important. It is how Crystal Reports resolves the conflicts.

② The **REMOVE** button will delete the highlighting criteria that is selected in the Item List.

> The Highlighting Expert does not work with **PARAMETER FIELDS,** which you will learn about in Lesson 12. The Highlighting Expert can only compare values in a table to set the conditional formatting.

The Highlighting Expert is similar to the Select Expert. One difference that I noticed is that the Highlighting Expert does not have as many operators as the Select Expert.

Create Reports That Highlight Data

The first two exercises in this lesson will show you how to highlight data using the Highlighting Expert.

Exercise 10.1: Use The Background Highlighting Option

In this exercise you will modify a report to highlight the background of the Delay In Days To Ship field for orders that were not shipped in two days or less.

1. Save the L9.9 report as
    L10.1 Highlight order delay shipping time conditionally.

2. Right-click on the Delay In Days To Ship field and select **HIGHLIGHTING EXPERT,** then click the **NEW** button on the Highlighting Expert dialog box.

3. Open the Comparison drop down list and select **IS GREATER THAN OR EQUAL TO,** then type a 3 in the last field.

4. Select **GRAY** as the background color. You should have the options selected that are shown in Figure 10-4.

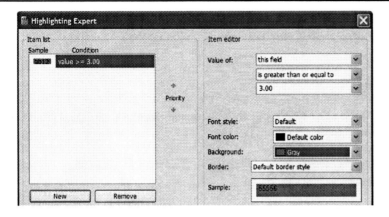

Figure 10-4 Highlighting options

5. Click OK and save the changes. The report should look like the one shown in Figure 10-5. Close the report.

Customer Name	Order Date	Ship Date	Order ID	Unit Price	Quantity	Delay In Days To Ship
City Cyclists	12/02/2003	12/10/2003	1	$41.90	1	
Deals on Wheels	12/02/2003	12/02/2003	1,002	$33.90	3	0
Deals on Wheels	12/02/2003	12/02/2003	1,002	$1,652.86	3	0
Warsaw Sports, Inc.	12/02/2003	12/05/2003	1,003	$48.51	3	
Warsaw Sports, Inc.	12/02/2003	12/05/2003	1,003	$13.78	3	
Bikes and Trikes	12/02/2003	12/02/2003	1,004	$274.35	3	0
SAB Mountain	12/03/2003	12/03/2003	1,005	$14.50	2	0
Poser Cycles	12/03/2003	12/05/2003	1,006	$16.50	1	2
Poser Cycles	12/03/2003	12/05/2003	1,006	$33.90	1	2
Poser Cycles	12/03/2003	12/05/2003	1,006	$14.50	1	2
Spokes	12/03/2003	12/03/2003	1,007	$16.50	3	0
Clean Air Transportation Co.	12/03/2003	12/07/2003	1,008	$726.61	2	
Clean Air Transportation Co.	12/03/2003	12/07/2003	1,008	$431.87	1	
Clean Air Transportation Co.	12/03/2003	12/07/2003	1,008	$329.85	1	
Extreme Cycling	12/03/2003	12/10/2003	1,009	$14.50	2	

Figure 10-5 L10.1 report with field background highlighting

Exercise 10.2: Use One Field To Highlight Another Field And Set A Priority

The Highlighting Expert allows you to create more than one highlighting condition per field. You can also use one field to highlight another field. If a field has multiple conditions, there may be a need to set a priority for the conditions. In this exercise you will create two conditions for the same field and set a priority for the conditions. You will create the following conditions:

① Bold the line items that have a quantity greater than or equal to three.
② Italicize the quantity if the unit price is greater than $500.

Create The Quantity Is Greater Than Condition

1. Save the L9.9 report as
   L10.2 Use multiple conditions to highlight a field.

2. Right-click on the Quantity field and open the Highlighting Expert, then click New.

3. Open the Comparison drop down list and select **IS GREATER THAN OR EQUAL TO**, then type 3 in the last field.

4. Select the bold font style. Leave the Highlighting Expert dialog box open to complete the next part of the exercise.

Create The Unit Price Is Greater Than Condition

1. Click New, then open the Value Of drop down list and select the Unit Price field.

2. Open the Comparison drop down list and select **IS GREATER THAN**, then type 500 in the last field.

3. Select the bold italic font style, then select red as the font color. Leave the Highlighting Expert dialog box open to complete the next part of the exercise.

Set The Priority

There could be a lot of records that meet both of the conditions that you just created. Unless it doesn't matter which order the conditions are applied to the field, you should set a priority. In this exercise, the most important criteria is on the Unit Price field.

1. Click on the Unit Price condition in the **ITEM LIST** and click the ⬆ (Priority Up) button. You should have the options selected that are shown in Figure 10-6.

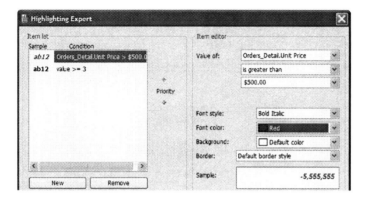

Figure 10-6 Highlighting conditions

2. Click OK and save the changes. The report should look like the one shown in Figure 10-7. Close the report.

Customer Name	Order Date	Ship Date	Order ID	Unit Price	Quantity	Delay In Days To Ship
City Cyclists	12/02/2003	12/10/2003	1	$41.90	1	8
Deals on Wheels	12/02/2003	12/02/2003	1,002	$33.90	3	0
Deals on Wheels	12/02/2003	12/02/2003	1,002	$1,652.86	3	0
Warsaw Sports, Inc.	12/02/2003	12/05/2003	1,003	$48.51	3	3
Warsaw Sports, Inc.	12/02/2003	12/05/2003	1,003	$13.78	3	3
Bikes and Trikes	12/02/2003	12/02/2003	1,004	$274.35	3	0
SAB Mountain	12/03/2003	12/03/2003	1,005	$14.50	2	0
Poser Cycles	12/03/2003	12/05/2003	1,006	$16.50	1	2
Poser Cycles	12/03/2003	12/05/2003	1,006	$33.90	1	2
Poser Cycles	12/03/2003	12/05/2003	1,006	$14.50	1	2
Spokes	12/03/2003	12/03/2003	1,007	$16.50	3	0
Clean Air Transportation Co.	12/03/2003	12/07/2003	1,008	$726.61	2	4
Clean Air Transportation Co.	12/03/2003	12/07/2003	1,008	$431.87	1	4
Clean Air Transportation Co.	12/03/2003	12/07/2003	1,008	$329.85	1	4
Extreme Cycling	12/03/2003	12/10/2003	1,009	$14.50	2	7

Figure 10-7 L10.2 Use multiple conditions to highlight a field report

Highlighting Expert Limitations

Despite being relatively easy to use, there are some features in Crystal Reports in my opinion, that could be improved. [See www.tolana.com/crxi/xi_wishlist.html] The Highlighting Expert is one feature that could be improved, similar to the inherent issues with some of the wizards. You should be aware of the following two facts about the Highlighting Expert.

① Formulas created by the Formula Expert override formulas in the Formula Workshop.
② Formulas created by the Highlighting Expert are not stored in the Formula Workshop. This means that you cannot see the formulas created by the Highlighting Expert and can easily forget that they exist.

 Any formula that you can create with the Highlighting Expert can be created in the Formula Workshop.

If...Then...Else Statements

This is one of the most used lines of programming code. This statement lets you set different options based on what you need to happen when the data is evaluated. The syntax below is for an If Then Else statement:

If **EXPRESSION/CONDITION** Then **TRUE STATEMENTS**
Else
FALSE STATEMENTS

Parts Of The If Then Else Statement Explained

① The **Expression/Condition** must evaluate to true or false.
② The **True Statements** will execute if the Expression/Condition is true.
③ The **Else** part of the statement is optional. If the Else clause is not included and the Expression/Condition is false, nothing will happen, which may be what you need. By "nothing happens", I mean that the If statement will default to the value for the data type. For example, if Field A is greater then 95, then textfield5 = "Great Job". If the variable "textfield5" was not declared to have a specific default value, the default value for a text field data type is " " (null), which is what would be displayed if Field A is not greater than 95.
④ The **False Statements** will execute if the Expression/Condition is false.

The plain English translation is: **IF** Choice A meets this condition, **THEN** do X, **ELSE** do Y.
Walk through the examples in Table 10-1 to gain a better understanding of If Then Else statements. Fill in the column on the right, based on the numbers in the Choice A column.

If Choice A is greater than 25, then Field B = 100, else Field B = 0.

Choice A	What Does Field B=
26	
1	
25	

Table 10-1 If Then Else examples

It may help to understand If...Then...Else statements if you think of them as a true or false test question. In the example above, the test question can be worded as "Is Choice A greater than 25?" There are two possible answers:

① Yes, it is (True). If it is, Field B would be set to 100.
② No, it isn't (False). If it isn't, Field B would be set to 0.

How Did You Do?

Table 10-2 contains the answers for the second column in Table 10-1. The third column explains the answer.

Choice A	Field B=	Reason
26	100	The answer is 100 because 26 is greater than 25.
1	0	The answer is 0 because 1 is less than 25.
25	0	The answer is 0 because 25 is not greater than 25.

Table 10-2 If Then Else answers for Table 10-1

You should know what value an If statement will return if the **EXPRESSION/CONDITION** is true and there is an Else part of the statement.

You should know what value an If statement will return if the **EXPRESSION/CONDITION** is false and there is no Else part of the statement.

To complicate If statements even more, there can be multiple true and false statements in the same If Then Else statement. When this is the case, they have to be enclosed in parenthesis, otherwise Crystal Reports will stop processing the statement after the first semi-colon, which often will produce a syntax error. Statements with multiple true and false statements are know as **NESTED IF STATEMENTS**.

Each statement except the last one in an If Then Else statement must end in a semi-colon.

Conditional Formatting Tips

As you will learn, you may not always need to apply the formatting that you create. This type of formatting is known as **CONDITIONAL FORMATTING**. The options on the Format Editor and Section Expert if checked, turn on what is known as **ABSOLUTE FORMATTING**, which means that the format will be applied to all values in the field. Absolute Formatting is not on if the option is not checked. This also applies to drop down lists and text fields on these dialog boxes.

When you create a formula for an option, this is known as conditional formatting because the formula will turn the option on and off. Boolean formulas are used for on-off options in conditional formatting. When creating conditional If...Then...Else statements, keep the following in mind:

① **CHECK BOX** formatting options are either on or off. This means that you do not have to type the entire If...Then...Else statement. Crystal Reports will turn the format option on if the test returns a true value. If the formula returns a false value the formatting is not turned on. This is when you would create a Boolean formula.
② **DROP DOWN LISTS AND TEXT BOXES** formatting options can have more than one choice. For this type of conditional formatting you have to type the entire If...Then...Else statement to specify what you want to happen if the test is true and if the test is false.

Conditional Formatting Warnings

You should be aware of the following when creating conditional formatting:

① If a field has formatting that is created with the Highlighting Expert and with conditional formatting, the Highlighting Expert formatting takes precedence. If the conditional formatting does not change the formatting created by the Highlighting Expert, the conditional formatting will be applied.
② Conditional formatting overrides absolute formatting even if the result of the conditional formatting is false.
③ Keep in mind that Crystal Reports does not require the "Else" part of an If Then Else statement.
④ If absolute and conditional formatting are applied to a field and the If Then Else statement for the conditional formatting does not have an Else clause and the conditional formatting does not return a "True" value, neither the conditional formatting or the absolute formatting is applied.
⑤ In addition to If Then Else statements you can also use **SELECT CASE** statements as long as the formatting property is in the Function Tree.

As you can see, it can be difficult to apply both absolute and conditional formatting to the same field. Even with the best intentions and code, you can get unexpected results. There are two things that you can do to help ensure that you get the output that you need, when you have to combine absolute and conditional formatting. I have found the second option below to be more effective, but if the first option fits your needs, you should use it.

① Use the "Else" clause on If statements or the **DEFAULT** clause on Select Case statements.
② Use the "Else" clause with the **DEFAULTATTRIBUTE** function. To do this, select the default (absolute) option on the Format Editor dialog box and use the DefaultAttribute as the Else part of the If statement. For example, if you need to set the default value for a field to green on the Format Editor, use the following If Then Else statement.

```
If {Employee.Salary}/52 <= 750
    Then crRed
        Else
            DefaultAttribute
```

This formula will display salaries that are less than or equal to $750 in red and the other salaries in green if the salary field is set to green on the Format Editor.

Exercise 10.3: Use The If Then Else Statement And IsNull Function

In Lesson 9 Skills Exercise 4, you created a formula to combine the two address fields. The formula that you created in that exercise is fine as long as there is data in both address fields. Unless the fields are required to be filled in on a data entry form, you cannot be 100% sure that they will contain data. In Lesson 2, you learned about Null values in fields. The second address field is an example of a field that can have null values because all addresses do not require two fields.

While the Employee Addresses table only has a few records, you could manually check to see if both address fields contained data before creating the formula. If the table had 200,000 records, checking them manually probably is not a good idea and could be quite time consuming. There are two options as discussed below, that you can use to prevent a formula from failing, if a field is null (empty).

① The **ISNULL** function will let you test a field to see if it is null. If it is, you can make a decision on what to do. To make this decision, you need to use the If Then Else statement with the IsNull function.
② Turn on the **CONVERT DATABASE NULL VALUES TO DEFAULT** option on the Options dialog box. Turning this option on will convert null values to zero for numeric fields or blank for string fields. "Blank" is different than Null.

While Crystal Reports supports the **CONVERT DATABASE NULL VALUES TO DEFAULT** option, not all databases support it. If you want to use this option, you need to make sure that the database that you are working with supports it. If you can't or don't want to confirm whether or not a database supports this feature, you can use the **ISNULL** function. I personally find it easier to use the IsNull function all the time, so that I can "see" what is going on.

In this exercise you will create a formula that will combine the two employee address fields and check the Address2 field to see if it is null. The majority of the time, the second address field will be the one that will not have data. On the rare occurrence that the first address field is null, you would want the formula to fail so that the field would be blank on the report. Hopefully, the reader of the report will notice this and fix the data. You can also write code that will print a message in the combined address field if either of the address fields is empty.

The **ISNULL** function has to be placed inside the If Then Else statement because the check that it will perform on the Address2 field is the first part (the test question) that the If Then Else statement is evaluates. In "plain" English the formula that you will create is:

If the Address2 field does not have any data
then set the Full Address field (the name of the formula) to only display/print the Address1 field
else set the Full Address field to display/print the Address1 field and the Address2 field.

1. Save the L9.14 report as `L10.3 If Then Else Statement`.

2. Open the Full Address formula and delete the formula that is there. (**Hint**: You can right-click on the field in the report and select **EDIT FORMULA**.)

3. Open the **CONTROL STRUCTURES** category in the Operators tree and double-click on the **IF X THEN Y ELSE Z** statement, as illustrated in Figure 10-8.

Figure 10-8 If Then Else statement illustrated

4. Open the **PRINT STATE** category in the Functions tree and double-click on the **ISNULL** function, as illustrated in Figure 10-9. With the flashing insertion point between the parenthesis in the formula, double-click on the Address2 field in the Reports Field tree. This is the question part of the **IF** statement.

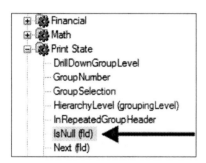

Figure 10-9 IsNull function illustrated

5. Click after the word **THEN** in the formula and double-click on the Address1 field, then press Enter. The word **ELSE** should be on the next line. This is the "true" part of the question, meaning that this is what you want to have print if the Address2 field is null.

6. Click after the word **ELSE** and add the Address1 field, then type + " " +.

7. Add the Address2 field. If you want to add a comment to the formula, you can. Check the formula for errors. It should look like the one shown in Figure 10-10.

```
// formula to check to see if the address2 field is null
if IsNull ({Employee_Addresses.Address2}) then {Employee_Addresses.Address1}
else {Employee_Addresses.Address1}+ " " +{Employee_Addresses.Address2}
```

Figure 10-10 If Then Else and IsNull formula

8. Save the formula and close the Formula Workshop. The report should look like the one shown in Figure 10-11. You will now see data in the Address field. Compare this report to the L9.14 report. Save the changes and close the report.

First Name	Last Name	Address	Weekly Salary	Salary
Steven	Buchanan	14 Garrett Hill	$961.54	$ 50,000.00
Robert	King	Edgeham Hollow	$711.54	$ 37,000.00
Anne	Dodsworth	7 Houndstooth Rd.	$673.08	$ 35,000.00
Michael	Suyama	Coventry House	$576.92	$ 30,000.00
Totals for region -	# of employees 4		$ 2,923.08	$ 152,000.00
Bas-Rhin				
Justin	Brid	2 impasse du Soleil	$1,442.31	$ 75,000.00
Xavier	Martin	9 place de la Liberté	$961.54	$ 50,000.00
Laurent	Pereira	7 rue Nationale	$865.38	$ 45,000.00
Totals for region -	# of employees 3		$ 3,269.23	$ 170,000.00

Figure 10-11 L10.3 If Then Else Statement report

Exercise 10.4: Use The Length Function

The Length function will check the number of characters in a field. Based on the length, you can assign different actions. For example, if a field has 10 characters you can display one message and if the same field in another record has 12 characters, you can display a different message.

In Exercise 9.8 you created a formula to format a phone number field. What you saw was that all of the phone numbers were not the same length. This caused some of the phone numbers to not be formatted properly. Using the Length function on the phone number field will allow you to use different formatting options based on the number of characters in the field. If you look at the data in the Phone field you will see that phone numbers are 12, 14 or 15 characters long.

In this exercise you will modify the Supplier Information report to check the number of characters in the Phone number field for each record and format the field based on the number of characters in the field.

Create A Formula For 12 Character Phone Numbers

In this part of the exercise you will create the formula that checks for 12 characters and creates the formatting for 12 character phone numbers.

1. Save the L9.8 report and as `L10.4 Length function.`

2. Open the Supplier Phone formula field and delete the formula, then open the **CONTROL STRUCTURES** catalog in the Operators tree and double-click on the If x then y else z statement.

3. Open the **STRINGS** category in the Functions tree and double-click on the **LENGTH(STR)** function, as shown in Figure 10-12. With the flashing insertion point between the parenthesis in the formula, add the Phone field, then click outside of the parenthesis on the right and type =12.

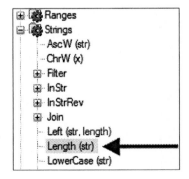

Figure 10-12 Length function illustrated

4. Click after the word **THEN** and press Enter. Open the **ADDITIONAL FUNCTIONS** category in the Functions tree and open the **SAMP1** category, then double-click on the **PICTURE** function.

5. Double-click on the Phone field in the Reports Field tree, then click after the comma in the formula and type " (XXX) XXXXXXX".

6. Place the insertion point before the word **ELSE** and press Enter. Leave the Formula Workshop open to complete the next part of the exercise.

Create A Formula For 15 Character Phone Numbers

In this part of the exercise, you will create the formula that checks for 15 characters and creates the formatting for phone numbers that have 15 characters. Most of the formula is the same as the one that you created for 12 characters. It is easier to copy the formula and change what's needed, then it is to create it again from scratch.

1. Copy the 12 character formula and paste it below the word **ELSE**.

2. Change the second =12 to =15, then change the Picture to XX-XXX-XXXXXXX.

In this exercise, if the phone number is not 12 or 15 characters, you just want the phone number printed without any formatting. You have complete control over which lengths you want to provide formatting for and which ones you don't.

3. Add the Phone field after the last **ELSE** in the formula. Your formula should look like the one shown in Figure 10-13.

```
//This formula formats the phone number field
if Length ({Supplier.Phone})=12 then
Picture ({Supplier.Phone},"(XXX)XXXXXXX" )
else
if Length ({Supplier.Phone})=15 then
Picture ({Supplier.Phone}," XX-XXX-XXXXXXX" )
else
{Supplier.Phone}
```

Figure 10-13 Phone number formula

4. Save the changes and close the Formula Workshop. The report should look like the one shown in Figure 10-14. Compare this report to the L9.8 report. Usually, phone numbers are entered with formatting so that they are lined up better than the data in the Supplier table. An example of this is the Customer Phone Number field in the Customers table. Save the changes and close the report.

Supplier ID & Name	Supplier Phone
1 - Active Outdoors	(503) 555-9931
2 - Triumph	(313) 555-5735
3 - Guardian	81 3 3555-5011
4 - InFlux	81 6 431-7877
5 - Craze	(604) 681 3435
6 - Roadster	44- 17-1 555-2222
7 - Vesper	(514) 555-9022

Figure 10-14 L10.4 Length function report

Exercise 10.5: Using Nested If Statements In Formulas

In the previous exercise, the formula that you created contained more than one If statement. This type of If statement is known as a **NESTED IF** statement. You can have as many If statements in a formula as you need. In this exercise you will create a Nested If statement to give customers a different discount on their next order based on the total amount of their last order.

1. Save the L4.2 report as L10.5 Nested If Statement.

2. Delete the first and last name fields from the report.

3. Create a formula field and name it `Order Discount`, then add the If Then Else statement to the formula.

4. Add the Order Amount field, then click outside of the brackets and type `>=10000`.

5. Click after the word **THEN** and type `"10% discount"`.

6. Copy the formula and paste it twice.

7. Change the middle Order Amount value to `>=5000`, then change the discount to `15%`. Change the last Order Amount value to `>=2500`, then change the discount to `20%`.

8. Click after the last **ELSE**, press Enter and type `"25% discount"`. Your formula should look like the one shown in Figure 10-15.

```
if {Orders.Order Amount} >=10000 then "10% discount" else
if {Orders.Order Amount} >=5000 then "15% discount" else
if {Orders.Order Amount} >=2500 then "20% discount" else
"25% discount"
```

Figure 10-15 Order Discount formula

9. Save the formula and close the Formula Workshop, then add the Order Discount formula field to the report after the Ship Via field. The report should look like the one shown in Figure 10-16. Save the changes and close the report.

Customer Orders Report					
Customer Name	Order #	Order Date	Order Amount	Ship Via	Order Discount
Spokes for Folks	1108	12/27/03	$5,219.55	Pickup	15% discount
Piccolo	1109	12/28/03	$25.98	Parcel Post	25% discount
Poser Cycles	1110	12/28/03	$161.70	Loomis	25% discount
Off the Mountain Biking	1111	12/28/03	$161.70	Loomis	25% discount
Sporting Wheels Inc.	1112	12/29/03	$161.70	Loomis	25% discount
Cyclist's Trail Co.	1113	12/29/03	$1,664.70	Pickup	25% discount
Bike Shop from Mars	1114	12/29/03	$161.70	Loomis	25% discount
Sporting Wheels Inc.	1115	12/30/03	$9.00	Loomis	25% discount
BBS Pty	1116	12/30/03	$1,095.75	UPS	25% discount
Spokes	1117	12/30/03	$6,539.40	Pickup	15% discount
Wheels and Stuff	1118	12/31/03	$49.50	Parcel Post	25% discount
C-Gate Cycle Shoppe	1119	12/31/03	$35.00	Loomis	25% discount

Figure 10-16 L10.5 Nested If Statement report

Because the Order Amount field is evaluated for each record, it will only match one of the If statements when the statement is set up correctly. If the Order Amount is $3,000, the formula will stop processing after the third statement. If the Order Amount is $6,500, the formula will stop processing after the second statement.

The order that you place the criteria values in is very important. If the statements were in a different order, the formula would not return the correct result because it is possible that the order amount would meet the criteria of another statement. For example, if the >=2,500 portion of the statement was above the >=10,000 portion of the statement and the order amount is $6,500, the formula would stop processing after the first If statement because $6,500 is >=2,500. That is not the outcome that you want though. You really want the $6,500 order to receive a 15% discount.

The rule of thumb is to put the criteria in high to low order. The option after the last else statement is the "catch all" statement. Sometimes, this will be an error message. In the example above, the customer would receive a 25% discount off of their next order if their last order was less then $2,500. In this example, the company is going to offer larger discounts to customers that placed smaller orders in hopes of having them place a larger order the next time that they order.

Suppressing Fields And Sections

There are times when there is no need to print the same data over and over again on a report. Sometimes not repeating the same data makes the report easier to read. There are also times when you will need to suppress a section of the report. Like the Highlighting Expert, the suppression of fields and sections in a report can be suppressed based on a condition. These conditions are created using Boolean formulas.

Exercise 10.6: Suppressing Fields

In this exercise you will learn how to suppress fields by creating a conditional formula for a field that has a salary greater than $50,000.

1. Save the L6.12 report as L10.6 Suppress salary GT 50000.

2. Right-click on the Salary field and select Format Field. Click on the Common tab, then check the **SUPPRESS** option as illustrated in Figure 10-17.

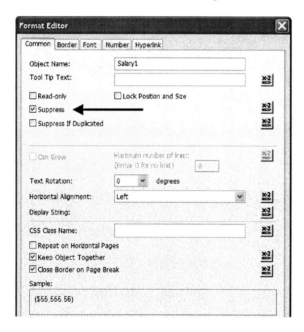

Figure 10-17 Common tab on the Format Editor

As you see in Figure 10-17 above, most of the options have a Formula button. When clicked, this button will open the Formula Format Editor in the Formula Workshop.

> The default color for the Formula button is blue, which means that the option does not have a formula. If the button is red, it means that the option does have a formula.
>
> You will also notice that the pencil is in a different position when the option has a formula.

> Formatting formulas that you create with the Section Expert, Format Editor or Formula Workshop will be applied whether or not the property option that it is attached to is checked. As long as the Formula button is red, which means that the property has a formula, the formula will be applied.

3. Click the **FORMULA** button across from the Suppress option on the Format Editor. You will see the Formula Workshop. Create a formula to suppress the salary if it is greater than $50,000. Add a comment that explains what the formula does. Save the changes and close the Formula Workshop.

4. Notice that the button across from the **SUPPRESS** option has red text. Click OK to close the Format Editor. Notice that the Salary field is dimmed out in the design window. This lets you know that this field will not always print on the report because of the suppression criteria. The report should look like the one shown in Figure 10-18. If your report does not look like the one shown, make sure that your formula looks like the one shown in Figure 10-19. You can refer back to Lesson 6, Figure 6-71 to see what the report looks like without the conditional formatting. Save the changes and close the report.

First Name	Last Name	Address1	Region	Salary
Steven	Buchanan	14 Garrett Hill		$ 50,000.00
Robert	King	Edgeham Hollow		$ 37,000.00
Anne	Dodsworth	7 Houndstooth Rd.		$ 35,000.00
Michael	Suyama	Coventry House		$ 30,000.00
Bas-Rhin				
Justin	Brid	2 impasse du Soleil	Bas-Rhin	Suppressed
Xavier	Martin	9 place de la Liberté	Bas-Rhin	$ 50,000.00
Laurent	Pereira	7 rue Nationale	Bas-Rhin	$ 45,000.00
BC				
Andrew	Fuller	908 W. Capital Way	BC	Suppressed
Albert	Hellstern	13920 S.E. 40th Street	BC	Suppressed

Figure 10-18 L10.6 Suppress salary GT $50000 report

```
// This formula will suppress the salary if it is > 50000
{Employee.Salary} >50000
```

Figure 10-19 Suppression formula

Comparison Conditional Formatting

You can use one field for the comparison criteria and a different field to apply the conditional formatting to. You will learn how to do this in the next three exercises.

Exercise 10.7: Compare Customer Averages

In Exercise 6.3 you created a report that printed the average order amount for each customer and the average order amount for all of the customers on the report. In this exercise you will modify that report to display a message if a customers average order amount is greater than the average order amount for all customers on the report. If the average order amount is less, no message will print. In order to print a message based on a condition, the formula has to be on the **DISPLAY STRING** option on the Format Editor.

 If you open the Formula Workshop from the Format Editor dialog box, you cannot create a different type of formula. You also cannot modify or delete existing formulas.

1. Save the L6.3 report as L10.7 Display string conditional formatting.

2. Right-click on the Average Order Amount field in the group footer section and select Format Field, then click on the Common tab.

3. Click the Formula button across from the **DISPLAY STRING** option, then add the If Then Else statement to the Formula Text section.

4. After the word **IF**, add the Group 1 Average Order Amount field, then type >= after the field.

5. Add the Report Area.Average Of Orders Order Amount field and press Enter.

6. Click after the word **THEN** and add the ToText(x) function.

7. Add the Group 1 Average Order Amount field inside of the ToText(x) function, then click outside of the parenthesis and type + " ** Above report average" and press Enter.

8. Copy the ToText portion of the formula and paste it after the **ELSE** clause, then type + " " at the end of the formula. Your formula should look like the one shown in Figure 10-20.

```
if Average ({Orders.Order Amount}, {Customer.Customer Name})>= Average ({Orders.Order Amount})
then ToText (Average ({Orders.Order Amount}, {Customer.Customer Name}))+" ** Above report average"
else ToText (Average ({Orders.Order Amount}, {Customer.Customer Name}))+ " "
```

Figure 10-20 Customer average comparison formula

9. Save the changes and close the Formula Workshop, then click OK to close the Format Editor.

10. Make the Average Order Amount field in the group footer section longer and preview the report.

Page 1 should look like the one shown in Figure 10-21.
The last page of the report should look like the one shown in Figure 10-22. Notice that there is no message next to these averages. This is because the customer average amount is less than $5,625.32, which is the average order amount for the report.

Save the changes and leave the report open to complete the next exercise.

 If the average amount field is not lined up, this is one of the rare times that I will modify a report in the preview window. To line up the Average Order Amount field, left align it and then drag it in the direction needed to line it up with the field above.

	Order Date	Ship Date	Order Amount	Order #	Unit Price
Alley Cat Cycles					
	01/08/2004	01/08/2004	$5,879.70	1151	$2,939.85
	09/28/2004	09/30/2004	$2,559.63	2157	$539.85
	09/28/2004	09/30/2004	$2,559.63	2157	$313.36
	10/27/2004	11/06/2004	$2,699.55	2272	$899.85
	01/31/2005	02/03/2005	$9,290.30	2664	$2,792.86
	01/31/2005	02/03/2005	$9,290.30	2664	$455.86
	02/19/2005	02/22/2005	$8,819.55	2735	$2,939.85
	02/19/2005	02/22/2005	$8,819.55	2735	$2,939.85
Total # orders -	8	Total $ amount of orders -	$49,918.21		
		Average order amount for customer -	$6,239.78 ** Above report average		
Aruba Sport					
	06/05/2004	06/08/2004	$5,879.70	3079	$2,939.85
Total # orders -	1	Total $ amount of orders -	$5,879.70		
		Average order amount for customer -	$5,879.70 ** Above report average		
Athens Bicycle Co.					
	06/08/2004	06/18/2004	$8,819.55	3097	$2,939.85
Total # orders -	1	Total $ amount of orders -	$8,819.55		
		Average order amount for customer -	$8,819.55 ** Above report average		

Figure 10-21 Page 1 of the L10.7 Display string conditional formatting report

	02/28/2005	03/06/2005	$5,321.25	2770	$33.90
	02/28/2005	03/06/2005	$5,321.25	2770	$1,739.85
Total # orders -	14	Total $ amount of orders -	$76,055.90		
		Average order amount for customer -	$5,432.56		

Yue Xiu Bicycles

	06/20/2004	06/20/2004	$2,939.85	3148	$2,939.85
Total # orders -	1	Total $ amount of orders -	$2,939.85		
		Average order amount for customer -	$2,939.85		

Total # of customers on this report - 102

Grand Total # orders - 1,142

Grand Total $ amount of orders - $ 6,424,118.58

Average order amount for all customers - $ 5,625.32

Figure 10-22 Last page of the L10.7 Display string conditional formatting report

Exercise 10.8: Font Color Conditional Formatting

In the previous exercise you compared the customer average amount to the average amount for the report. Detail records that are below the report average were not formatted. It may be helpful to change the color of customers that have an average less than the report average.

1. Save the L0.7 report as `L10.8 Font color conditional formatting`.

2. Right-click on the Average Customer Order Amount field in the group footer section and select Format Field, then click on the Font tab. Click the Formula button across from the **COLOR** option.

 The comments that you see in the Formula Text section are colors that you can use.

The formula that you need to create to change the font color is the opposite of the formula that you created in the previous exercise. Rather than type it in again, you can copy the formula that you created in the previous exercise and change it as needed.

3. Open the **FORMATTING FORMULAS** folder in the Workshop Tree. Under the Avg Of Order Amount1 section, you should see the **DISPLAY STRING** formula, as illustrated in Figure 10-23. Click on the Display String formula and select (highlight) the formula up to the first ToText function, then press the **CTRL** and **c** keys.

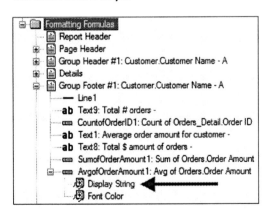

Figure 10-23 Formatting Formulas folder

4. Click on the Font color formula in the Workshop Tree and scroll to the end of the comments and paste the formula in, by pressing the **CTRL** and **v** keys.

5. Change the >= to <=, then type `crRed` after the word **THEN**. Save the changes and close the Formula Workshop, then click OK to close the Format Editor.

6. Go to the last page of the report. You should see the customer average dollar amounts in red. If you do not see the color red on the last page of the report, compare your font color formula to the one shown in Figure 10-24. Save the changes and close the report.

```
//
if Average ({Orders.Order Amount}, {Customer.Customer Name})<= Average ({Orders.Order Amount})
then crRed
```

Figure 10-24 Font color formula

Exercise 10.9: Suppress Currency Formatting

Every detail record on the L10.7 report prints the dollar sign for the Order Amount field. The report may look better if the dollar sign only printed for the first detail record for the customer. In this exercise, you will create conditional formatting to suppress the dollar sign on any record other than the first one for each customer.

1. Save the L10.7 report as `L10.9 Suppress currency formatting`.

2. Right-click on the Order Amount field in the details section and select Format Field, then click on the Customize button on the Number tab, then click on the **CURRENCY SYMBOL** tab.

3. Click the Formula button across from the **ENABLE CURRENCY SYMBOL** option and add the If Then Else statement to the Formula Text section.

4. Click after the word **IF** and add the **ONFIRSTRECORD** function, which is under the Print State category, then type the word `or` and press the space bar.

5. Add the Customer Name field and type `<> Previous`, then add the Customer Name field again and press Enter.

6. Delete the word **ELSE** and add the **CRFLOATINGCURRENCYSYMBOL** function. (**Hint:** You can copy this function from the comments above in the formula.)

7. Type two left parenthesis in front of the first Customer Name field and one parenthesis after the field, then type two left parenthesis in front of the second Customer Name field and three after the field. You may want to add a comment so that when you look at the formula later, you will know what it does.

8. Save and close the formula. Click OK twice to close both dialog boxes. The report should look like the one shown in Figure 10-25. As you can see, the dollar sign for the Order Amount field only prints on the first detail record for each customer. If your report does not look like the one shown, compare your formula to the one shown in Figure 10-26. Save the changes and close the report.

Formula Wrap Up

So how did you do creating and understanding the logic behind If Then Else statements? Hopefully you did okay. The reason that I am asking is because if you can understand and create If Then Else statements, you are on your way to becoming a Crystal Reports power report writer or a computer programmer. If you are curious about other statements that you can use, check out the following in the Help file: For Loop and my favorite, the Select Case statement.

	Order Date	Ship Date	Order Amount	Order #	Unit Price
Alley Cat Cycles					
	01/08/2004	01/08/2004	$5,879.70	1151	$2,939.85
	09/28/2004	09/30/2004	2,559.63	2157	$539.85
	09/28/2004	09/30/2004	2,559.63	2157	$313.36
	10/27/2004	11/06/2004	2,699.55	2272	$899.85
	01/31/2005	02/03/2005	9,290.30	2664	$2,792.86
	01/31/2005	02/03/2005	9,290.30	2664	$455.86
	02/19/2005	02/22/2005	8,819.55	2735	$2,939.85
	02/19/2005	02/22/2005	8,819.55	2735	$2,939.85
Total # orders - 8		Total $ amount of orders -	$49,918.21		
		Average order amount for customer -	$6,239.78 ** Above report average		
Aruba Sport					
	06/05/2004	06/08/2004	$5,879.70	3079	$2,939.85
Total # orders - 1		Total $ amount of orders -	$5,879.70		
		Average order amount for customer -	$5,879.70 ** Above report average		
Athens Bicycle Co.					
	06/08/2004	06/18/2004	$8,819.55	3097	$2,939.85
Total # orders - 1		Total $ amount of orders -	$8,819.55		
		Average order amount for customer -	$8,819.55 ** Above report average		
Backpedal Cycle Shop					
	02/08/2004	02/09/2004	$3,544.20	1279	$13.50
	02/08/2004	02/09/2004	3,544.20	1279	$12.00
	02/08/2004	02/09/2004	3,544.20	1279	$1,739.85

Figure 10-25 L10.9 Suppress currency formatting report

```
// This formula will suppress the dollar sign on all details records
// in each group, except for the first record
if OnFirstRecord or ({{Customer.Customer Name}} <> Previous ({{Customer.Customer Name}}))
then  crFloatingCurrencySymbol
```

Figure 10-26 Dollar sign suppression formula

Select Case Statement

Select Case is similar to If Then Else. I personally find Select Case statement easier to read and understand, especially easier then Nested If statements. For example, in Exercise 10.5 you created the nested If statement shown in Figure 10-27.

```
if {Orders.Order Amount} >=10000 then "10% discount" else
if {Orders.Order Amount} >=5000 then "15% discount" else
if {Orders.Order Amount} >=2500 then "20% discount" else
"25% discount"
```

Figure 10-27 Nested If statement

The following Select Case statement provides the same logic as the Nested If statement shown above in Figure 10-27. For whatever reason, I find this easier to read and understand.

Select {Orders.Order Amount}
   Case >= 10000:
      "10% discount"
   Case >= 5000:
      "15% discount"
   Case >= 2500:
      "20% discount"
   Default:
      "25% discount"

Boolean Formulas

In Lesson 2 you learned that Boolean fields have values of true/false or yes/no. **BOOLEAN EXPRESSIONS** return a value of true or false. In Lesson 4 you learned how to format a Boolean field. Earlier in this lesson I said that one way to understand If Then Else statements is to think of them as a true or false question. A Boolean formula is the test question portion of an If Then Else statement. Boolean formulas do not have to be created on Boolean fields. The value that a Boolean formula returns is either true or false. You can then format the result of the Boolean formula like you did in Exercise 4.4.

In Exercise 10.6 you created a formula that would suppress the salary if it was greater than $50,000. If the salary is greater than $50,000, the word "Suppressed" printed in the salary field. A Boolean formula could have been used to accomplish the same result. Figure 10-28 shows the formula. The difference would be the values printed in the salary field in the L10-6 report. Instead of printing the salary for some records and the word "Suppressed" for other records as shown earlier in Figure 10-18, the values true or false would have printed as shown in Figure 10-29.

```
{Employee.Salary} > 50000
```

Figure 10-28 Boolean formula

First Name	Last Name	Address1	Region	Salary > 50K
Steven	Buchanan	14 Garrett Hill		False
Robert	King	Edgeham Hollow		False
Anne	Dodsworth	7 Houndstooth Rd.		False
Michael	Suyama	Coventry House		False
Bas-Rhin				
Justin	Brid	2 impasse du Soleil	Bas-Rhin	True
Xavier	Martin	9 place de la Liberté	Bas-Rhin	False
Laurent	Pereira	7 rue Nationale	Bas-Rhin	False
BC				
Andrew	Fuller	908 W. Capital Way	BC	True

Figure 10-29 L10.6 report using a Boolean formula

The Section Expert

So far, all of the formatting techniques that you have learned were to change individual objects on the report. You can use the Section Expert to format an entire section of the report similar to how the Format Editor lets you format fields. You can also create formulas for many of the options on the Section Expert which is shown in Figure 10-30. With section formatting you can make the following types of changes to a report.

① Force each group to start at the top of a new page.
② Change the line spacing in the details section to something other than single spacing.
③ Create page breaks.
④ Conditionally suppress a section of the report.

Formatting options that are not available for the section of the report that is selected are dimmed out.

For example, in Figure 10-30, the **NEW PAGE BEFORE** option is not available for the Report Header section. There are three ways to open the Section Expert as discussed below.

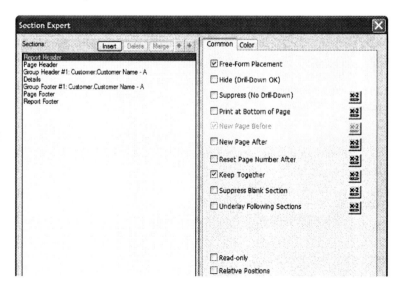

Figure 10-30 Section Expert

① Right-click on the section name on the left side of the design window and select Section Expert as shown in Figure 10-31.

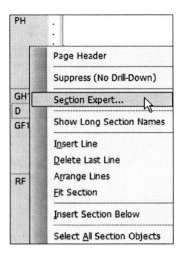

Figure 10-31 Section shortcut menu

② Click the Section Expert button on the Experts toolbar.
③ Report ⇒ Section Expert.

The advantage to using the first option above is that the section will be highlighted on the left side of the Section Expert dialog box when it is opened. Table 10-3 explains the formatting options on the Common tab. Table 10-4 explains the options that are only available for a specific section of the report.

Option	Description
Free form placement	This option lets you place fields on the report wherever you want. This option is checked by default. When checked, text objects will print where they are placed on the report. If the option is not checked, Crystal Reports will determine where text objects will be printed, which may be different then where you place them.
Hide (Drill-Down OK)	Hides the objects in the section when the report is printed. The section can be viewed on the preview window. If the section of the report that this option is applied to is part of a higher level group and the group is drilled into, the objects in the section will be visible on the drill-down tab. This option is not available for subsections.
Suppress (No Drill-Down)	The section that this option is applied to will not be printed and does not allow drill down and cannot be viewed on the preview window, even if a higher level section is drilled-down. This option is available for subsections.
Print at Bottom of Page	This option forces the section to be printed as close to the bottom of the page as possible, even if the detail records stop printing half way down the page.
New Page Before	This option forces a page break before the section prints. (1)
New Page After	This option forces a page break after the section prints. (1)
Reset Page Number After	Resets the page number back to one after the section has printed. This option also resets the Total Page Count special field.

Table 10-3 Common tab section formatting options explained

(1) This option is often used to force each group to start on a new page.

Option	Description
Keep Together	Keeps the section together on the same page when printed. This option is sometimes confused with the Keep Group Together option on the Group Expert dialog box. These options produce different results. [See Lesson 6, Using The Group Expert]
Suppress Blank Section	Prevents the section from printing when all of the objects in the section are blank.
Underlay Following Sections	This option causes the section to print in the same location that the section below it will print. This option will allow charts or images to print next to the section that follows.
Read-Only	Suppresses formatting in the section and prevents any formatting to the section. This option is similar to the **LOCK FORMAT** and **LOCK SIZE AND POSITION** options on the Format Editor and Formatting toolbar.
Relative Positions	This option will lock an object next to an object like a cross-tab or OLAP grid. If the cross-tab grows, the object will be repositioned so that it remains aligned with the grid object.
Background Color	This option is on the Color tab. It lets you select a color for the background of the section. This is different then the formatting that objects in the section have. You learned how to use this option in Exercise 4.7A.

Table 10-3 Common tab section formatting options explained (Continued)

Section	Option	Description
Page Footer	Reserve Minimum Page Footer	Select this option when you need to remove space in the page footer section to gain more space on the printed page.
Details	Format With Multiple Columns	This option allows you to display data in columns similar to a newspaper layout, instead of down the page. When checked, a new tab called **LAYOUT** will open, as shown in Figure 10-32. The options on the Layout tab let you set the size of the columns.

Table 10-4 Section specific formatting options explained

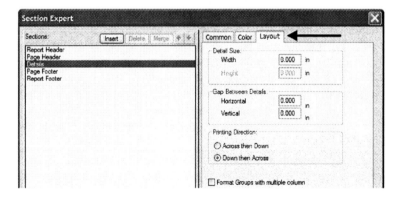

Figure 10-32 Layout tab illustrated

 If all of the detail sections have the Hide or Suppress option checked, the result is a Summary report.

Exercise 10.10: Create Page Breaks

Page breaks are one of the most used section formatting techniques. While the concept appears straight forward, it can be tricky and can produce unexpected results. Many page breaks are created when a new group starts on a report. In this exercise you will add a page break to a report that prints orders by month. The objective is to force a page break when the month of the order date changes in the group header section of the report.

1. Save the L6.7 report as `L10.10 2004 orders by month with page break`.

2. Open the Section Expert and click on the group header section, then check the **NEW PAGE BEFORE** option and click OK.

3. Preview the report. You should notice that the first page of the report is blank. More than likely, having the first page break occur before the detail records for the first group are printed on the report, is not what you had in mind. Save the changes and leave the report open to complete the next exercise.

Exercise 10.11: Conditionally Format The Page Break

As you saw in the previous exercise, selecting the **NEW PAGE BEFORE** option did not accomplish what you thought it would. In this exercise you will fix this problem. The problem with only selecting this option is that it causes a page break before any data prints.

Hopefully you are asking yourself, what is different about the first group of data. You may have looked through the functions to see if there is a function that you can use. If you have looked for a function, you won't find any that are specifically for sections on a report or for page breaks. You could create your own formula, but what would you write? You may have to think outside of the box on this one.

In case you are thinking that you could use the **NEW PAGE AFTER** option for the group header section, this option would cause the detail records to start on a different page, but the group header information would remain on the page before, as shown in Figure 10-33.

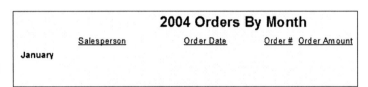

Figure 10-33 New Page After option turned on for the group header section

I know what you are thinking: Use the **NEW PAGE AFTER** option on the group footer section. That will give you the desired output of having each group start on a new page. The downside is that if the report has data in the report footer section, it will not print on the same page as the last group footer section of information. The information in the report footer section will be forced to a new page. If the report that you are creating does not have data in the report footer section or you want the information in the report footer section to print on a page by itself, using the New Page After option on the group footer section will work.

Earlier in this lesson you used a function called **ONFIRSTRECORD**. You could write code to see if the group contains the first record in the report. If it does, do not force a page break. This will work because only one group per report will contain the first record on the report. It just so happens that the first record is in the first group, which is the group that currently has a page break before it. Creating a formula to not force a break on the first record will cause the formatting (in this case a page break) to be turned off, on the first group. This is what you want to have happen.

1. Save the L10.10 report as `L10.11 Conditional page break`.

2. Open the Section Expert and click on the Formula button across from the New Page Before option for the group header section.

3. Type Not and press the space bar, then add the OnFirstRecord function, or you can type the function in. Save and close the formula, then click OK to close the Section Expert and preview the report. The first group (January), should be on page 1 of the report instead of on page 2, like it was in the previous exercise. If you look at the last page of the report, you will see that the report footer information is not on a page by itself. Save the changes and close the report.

Using The New Page After Option To Format A Page Break

Earlier, the idea of using the New Page After option was discussed as a way to force a page break. Adding the **NOTONLASTRECORD** funtion to the New Page After option on the group footer section will force each group to start on a new page, just like the exercise that you just completed.

Exercise 10.12: Resetting Page Numbers

Depending on the type of report that you create, you may have the need to have the page number reset after a certain condition has been met. A report that you may need this for is one that will be distributed to more than one person. An example of this would be a report like the monthly order report by sales rep that you created in Lesson 6. Resetting the page number to one when orders for a different sales rep prints, would allow the report to be distributed to each rep and have the page numbers make sense to the rep. Can you imagine receiving a report that started on page 75? You may think that you were missing pages. Using the **RESET PAGE NUMBER** section formatting option would prevent that from happening. In this exercise you will learn how to use this option.

1. Save the L6.13 report as L10.12 Reset page number.

2. Create a page break formula that does not cause a page break on the first record of the report, for the group header section.

3. Check the **RESET PAGE NUMBER AFTER** option for the group footer section, then click OK. The first page of the report should start on page 1. The page number is at the bottom of the report.

4. In the group tree, click on Group 3. In the navigation bar, you should see **9 OF 17+**. If you scroll down to the bottom of the page, you will see that the page number is 1. If you go to the next page, it will be page 2. This is what should happen. Save the changes and leave the report open to complete the next exercise.

Exercise 10.13: Using The Change Group Dialog Box Options

If you look at the second page for any group in the report that you just modified, you will notice that the group header information (the Salespersons name) only prints on the first page of each group. Figure 10-34 shows the second page of the first group. The report would look better if the group name printed on every page. Options on the **CHANGE GROUP** dialog box will let you force the group header information to print on every page.

Salesperson	Order Date	Order ID	Product ID	Unit Price	Quantity
	11/18/2004	2376	201161	$832.35	2
	11/18/2004	2367	401002	$281.85	2
	11/17/2004	2362	201201	$832.35	3
	11/17/2004	2362	303221	$329.85	2
	11/17/2004	2362	103171	$899.85	3
	11/15/2004	2356	6401	$12.00	2

Figure 10-34 Second page of the first group on the L10.12 Reset page number report

1. Save the L10.12 report as L10.13 Use Repeat Group Header option.

2. Right-click on the group header section on the left side of the design window and select **CHANGE GROUP**. Notice the Field Name at the top of the shortcut menu.

3. Click on the Options tab and check the **REPEAT GROUP HEADER ON EACH PAGE** option, as shown in Figure 10-35. This option will cause the group header information to print on every page of the report.

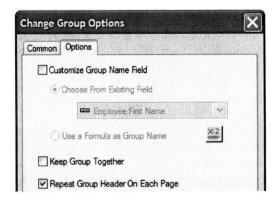

Figure 10-35 Change Group Options dialog box

 The purpose of the **KEEP GROUP TOGETHER** option shown above in Figure 10-35 is to force all records that are in the same group to print on the same page. If this option is checked and the first group on the report does not fit on the first page, the group will start printing on the second page and the first page of the report will be blank. If this happens, clear the **RESPECT KEEP GROUP TOGETHER ON FIRST PAGE** option on the Report Options dialog box.

The Keep Group Together option if checked, will cause all of the group sections (the group header, group footer and detail section for the group) to be printed on the same page. If all three sections will not fit on the current page, they will start printing on the next page. This is different then the **KEEP TOGETHER** option on the Section Expert, which only causes the section that the option is applied to, to print on the same page. [See Table 10.3] These options are best suited for reports that do not have a lot of detail records in each group. Groups that have a lot of records may require more than one page, which may result in the report having breaks in unexpected places.

4. Click OK. If you go to any page after the first page of a group, you will see the group header information, just like it is on the first page of each group. Save the changes and leave the report open to complete the next exercise.

How The Change Group Options Work

If checked, the **CUSTOMIZE GROUP NAME FIELD** option will let you create the name for the group, as you want it to appear in the group header section, or a different section if you copy or move the group header field to it.

 Do not check this option if you only want to display the data that is in the field that is being grouped on.

The **USE FORMULA AS GROUP NAME** option will let you write a formula which will control what appears in the Group Name field. This option is very helpful if you need to change what prints in the group name field based on data that appears in the report or data in a table that is connected to the report.

If checked, the **REPEAT GROUP HEADER ON EACH PAGE** option will cause the group header section to be printed at the top of each page that the group is printed on. This will let you know which group the details records and totals are for.

Exercise 10.13A: Using The InRepeatedGroupHeader Function

Prior to changing the group options in the previous exercise, it was easy to tell which was the first page for each group in the report. For this report, that is not exactly true because each group starts on page 1, but pretend that the page numbers are not reset. To help make reading the report easier, adding text on the pages in the group, other than the first page would resolve this issue. The **INREPEATEDGROUPHEADER** function will let you add conditional formatting to a group header or footer when the group prints on more than one page.

1. Save the L10.13 report as L10.13A Use the InRepeatedGroupHeader function.

2. Add a text object to the left of the Last Name field in the group header section and type (Continued) in the object. Change the font size of the text object to 8.

3. Right-click on the text object and select Format text, then click the Formula button across from the Suppress option and type Not InRepeatedGroupHeader in the Formula Text section.

4. Save the formula and close the Formula Workshop. Click OK to close the Format Editor and save the changes. Go to page 2 of the report. You should see (Continued), next to the salespersons name, as shown in Figure 10-36. Close the report.

	Salesperson	Order Date	Order ID	Product ID	Unit Price	Quantity
1	Nancy Davolio	(Continued)				
		11/18/2004	2376	201161	$832.35	2
		11/18/2004	2367	401002	$281.85	2
		11/17/2004	2362	201201	$832.35	3

Figure 10-36 Page 2 of the L10.13A Use the InRepeatedGroupHeader function report

 You should know how to use the **INREPEATEDGROUPHEADER** function.

Exercise 10.14: Suppress A Section Of The Report

There will be times when you need to permanently hide a section of a report. Often, this is done (on a second copy of an existing report) when you do not want some users to see certain information on a report. An example that comes to mind is the L6.13 Skills monthly orders by sales rep report that you modified in Exercise 10.12. Because the goal of the report in Exercise 10.12 was to distribute the sections of the report to the appropriate sales rep, there is no reason to display the Report Total information in the report footer section. This is what you will learn how to do in this exercise.

1. Save the L10.12 report as L10.14 Report footer suppressed.

2. Open the Section Expert and check the **HIDE (DRILL-DOWN OK)** option for the report footer section and click OK. The report footer section should look like the one shown in Figure 10-37. The lines indicate that the section is suppressed.

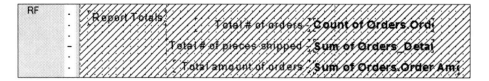

Figure 10-37 Report footer section suppressed

 You can also turn the suppression options on or off by selecting them on the Section shortcut menu.

3. On the last page of the report you should not see the report totals at the end of the report. Save the changes and close the report.

In Lesson 4 you learned how to add sections to a report. In the exercise that you just completed, you learned how to suppress a section of the report. If you have the need to create a report that uses more than one address field, often they are placed on separate rows in the details section. The second address field is often blank, which means that a blank row will print for the records when the second address field is blank, as illustrated in Figure 10-38.

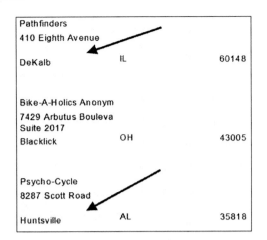

Figure 10-38 Blank row illustrated

When combined, the Suppress section option and adding a section with conditional formatting will allow you to suppress a section of the report based on a condition. You can combine these options and place the second address field in a section by itself, they conditionally hide the section if the second address field is blank. Remember that if you suppress a field in a section that has other objects, the entire section will be suppressed if the condition is true. Often, this is not what you want. If you move the second address field to its own section of the report, as shown in Figure 10-39, you can suppress the section if the address field is blank. This will cause the report to print like the one shown in Figure 10-40 instead of the one shown above in Figure 10-38.

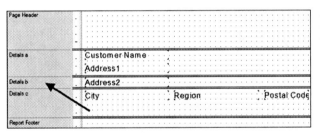

Figure 10-39 Address 2 field in a section by itself

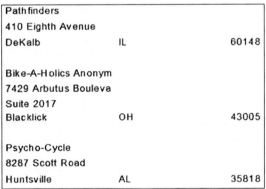

Figure 10-40 Report with the Address 2 field suppressed

Exercise 10.15: Suppress A Group

Depending on the amount of data that is displayed on a report, not all users may need to view all of the records. In this exercise you will modify a report to only print groups of data that meet specific criteria. You will modify a customer average report to only print groups that have a group total average amount that is less than $6,500.

1. Save the L6.3 report as
    L10.15 Suppress group if avg customer amount LT 6500K.

2. Open the Section Expert and add the formula shown in Figure 10-41 to the Suppress (No Drill-Down) option for the group header, details and group footer sections.

```
// This formula will suppress groups on the report where the
// average order amount of the customer is less than $6,500
//
// This formula is used on the Group Header, Details
// and Group Footer report sections
Average ({Orders.Order Amount}, {Customer.Customer Name})< 6500
```

Figure 10-41 Suppress group formula

Notice that the Formula Workshop displays the format option Suppress (No Drill-Down) in the title bar as shown in Figure 10-42.

Figure 10-42 Format Workshop title bar

3. Save the formulas and close the Formula Workshop. Click OK to close the Section Expert. The report should look like the one shown in Figure 10-43. Some of the groups (customers) that you should not see are the Alley Cat Cycles, Aruba Sport, BBS Party and Belgium. Compare it to the L6.3 report. Save the changes and close the report.

	Order Date	Ship Date	Order Amount	Order #	Unit Price
Athens Bicycle Co.					
	06/08/2004	06/18/2004	$8,819.55	3097	$2,939.85
Total # orders - 1		Total $ amount of orders -	$8,819.55		
		Average order amount for customer -	$8,819.55		
Backpedal Cycle Shop					
	02/06/2004	02/09/2004	$3,544.20	1279	$1,739.85
	02/08/2004	02/09/2004	$3,544.20	1279	$12.00
	02/08/2004	02/09/2004	$3,544.20	1279	$13.50
	02/19/2004	02/19/2004	$6,233.05	1311	$329.85
	02/19/2004	02/19/2004	$6,233.05	1311	$23.50
	02/19/2004	02/19/2004	$6,233.05	1311	$2,939.85
	07/02/2004	07/04/2004	$3,479.70	1802	$1,739.85
	08/15/2004	08/19/2004	$3,415.95	1972	$53.90
	08/15/2004	08/19/2004	$3,415.95	1972	$764.85
	08/15/2004	08/19/2004	$3,415.95	1972	$479.85
	11/16/2004	11/18/2004	$10,798.95	2358	$2,939.85
	11/16/2004	11/18/2004	$10,798.95	2358	$1,739.85
	11/16/2004	11/18/2004	$10,798.95	2358	$479.85
	12/18/2004	12/19/2004	$6,226.05	2507	$329.85
	12/18/2004	12/19/2004	$6,226.05	2507	$2,939.85
	12/18/2004	12/19/2004	$6,226.05	2507	$16.50
	01/04/2005	01/05/2005	$9,612.47	2560	$764.85
	01/04/2005	01/05/2005	$9,612.47	2560	$832.35
	01/04/2005	01/05/2005	$9,612.47	2560	$2,792.86
	02/02/2005	02/02/2005	$8,819.55	2685	$2,939.85
Total # orders - 20		Total $ amount of orders -	$131,791.26		
		Average order amount for customer -	$6,589.56		
Bikefest					
	05/21/2004	05/23/2004	$8,819.55	3033	$2,939.85
Total # orders - 1		Total $ amount of orders -	$8,819.55		

Figure 10-43 L10.15 Suppress group if avg customer amount LT 6500K report

Exercise 10.16: Using The Color Tab Section Expert Options

One of the more popular uses of the Color tab on the Section Expert is to add a color background to every other detail record on the report. If you have ever seen what is known as "green bar" computer paper, you understand the color effect that you will create in this exercise.

1. Save the L4.12 report as L10.16 Add color to rows.

2. Click the Section Expert button, then click on the details section and click on the Color tab.

3. Click the Formula button and type the formula shown at the bottom of Figure 10-44.

```
// This formula will print a silver background for all
// even number rows in the Details section of the report.
//
// RecordNumber mod 2 will return 0 for even row numbers
// and 1 for odd number row numbers
//
// DefaultAttribute is the default row color
//

If RecordNumber mod 2 = 0
then crSilver
Else DefaultAttribute
```

Figure 10-44 Row color formula

4. Save the formula and close the Formula Workshop. Click OK to close the Section Expert. The report should look like the one shown in Figure 10-45. Save the changes and close the report.

Customer Orders Report						
Customer Name	Order #	Order Date	Order Amount	Ship Via	First Name	Last Name
City Cyclists	1	12/2/03	$41.90	UPS	Nancy	Davolio
Deals on Wheels	1002	12/2/03	$5,060.28	Pickup	Janet	Leverling
Warsaw Sports, Inc.	1003	12/2/03	$186.87	UPS	Margaret	Peacock
Bikes and Trikes	1004	12/2/03	$823.05	Pickup	Margaret	Peacock
SAB Mountain	1005	12/3/03	$29.00	Loomis	Janet	Leverling
Poser Cycles	1006	12/3/03	$64.90	Purolator	Margaret	Peacock
Spokes	1007	12/3/03	$49.50	Parcel Post	Anne	Dodsworth
Clean Air Transportation Co.	1008	12/3/03	$2,214.94	Purolator	Margaret	Peacock
Extreme Cycling	1009	12/3/03	$29.00	Loomis	Margaret	Peacock

Figure 10-45 L10.16 Add color to rows report

 Some of the options on the Format Editor and Section Expert will be displayed with comments when they are opened in the Formula Workshop as shown in Figure 10-46. The comments that you see are for the four line style options for the Border tab on the Format Editor. The options in the comments let you know what values you can use in your formula. The row color formula that you just created had a list of colors at the top of the formula that you could select from to use as the background color.

```
// This conditional formatting formula must return one of the following Line Style Constants:
//
// crSingleLine
// crDoubleLine
// crDashedLine
// crDottedLine
// crNoLine
//
```

Figure 10-46 Default comments for the line style option

How The Row Color Formula Works

Now that you have created the row color formula, knowing how it works will be helpful, because you can modify the formula to meet other needs.

RECORDNUMBER is a special field that counts records in the details section.

MOD divides one number by another number and returns the remainder, instead of the result of the division.

IF RECORDNUMBER MOD 2=0 means to divide the record number by 2. If the remainder is zero, meaning that if the record number is evenly divisible by two, apply the color to the background of the detail row.

> If the report that you are applying the background row color formatting to has background formatting for objects in the section of the report that will have a background color, you should use **NOCOLOR** for the Else clause instead of using the color white, because NoColor produces a result that is similar to being transparent, which is what you want. Using the color white will cause the background color applied to individual fields to produce results that are not always visually appealing.
>
> If the report does not have any fields with background color formatting, using the **DEFAULT ATTRIBUTE** is fine.

You can change this formula to create a background pattern different then every other row.

Example #1 If RecordNumber mod 5 = 0 will shade every fifth row as shown in Figure 10-47.

Example #2 If RecordNumber mod 3 in [1,2] will shade the first two rows out of every three rows, as shown in Figure 10-48.

Example #3 If RecordNumber mod 10 in [3,5] will shade the third and fifth rows out of every ten rows, as shown in Figure 10-49.

Customer Name	Order #	Order Date	Order Amount	Ship Via	First Name	Last Name
City Cyclists	1	12/2/03	$41.90	UPS	Nancy	Davolio
Deals on Wheels	1002	12/2/03	$5,060.28	Pickup	Janet	Leverling
Warsaw Sports, Inc.	1003	12/2/03	$186.87	UPS	Margaret	Peacock
Bikes and Trikes	1004	12/2/03	$823.05	Pickup	Margaret	Peacock
SAB Mountain	1005	12/3/03	$29.00	Loomis	Janet	Leverling
Poser Cycles	1006	12/3/03	$64.90	Purolator	Margaret	Peacock
Spokes	1007	12/3/03	$49.50	Parcel Post	Anne	Dodsworth
Clean Air Transportation Co.	1008	12/3/03	$2,214.94	Purolator	Margaret	Peacock
Extreme Cycling	1009	12/3/03	$29.00	Loomis	Margaret	Peacock
Cyclopath	1010	12/3/03	$14,872.30	UPS	Nancy	Davolio
BBS Pty	1011	12/3/03	$29.00	Purolator	Margaret	Peacock
Piccolo	1012	12/3/03	$10,259.10	Loomis	Nancy	Davolio
Pedals Inc.	1013	12/3/03	$1,142.13	Parcel Post	Margaret	Peacock
Spokes 'N Wheels Ltd.	1014	12/4/03	$29.00	Purolator	Nancy	Davolio
Cycle City Rome	1015	12/4/03	$43.50	UPS	Anne	Dodsworth
SAB Mountain	1016	12/4/03	$563.70	FedEx	Janet	Leverling

Figure 10-47 Mod 5 = 0 output

Customer Name	Order #	Order Date	Order Amount	Ship Via	First Name	Last Name
City Cyclists	1	12/2/03	$41.90	UPS	Nancy	Davolio
Deals on Wheels	1002	12/2/03	$5,060.28	Pickup	Janet	Leverling
Warsaw Sports, Inc.	1003	12/2/03	$186.87	UPS	Margaret	Peacock
Bikes and Trikes	1004	12/2/03	$823.05	Pickup	Margaret	Peacock
SAB Mountain	1005	12/3/03	$29.00	Loomis	Janet	Leverling
Poser Cycles	1006	12/3/03	$64.90	Purolator	Margaret	Peacock
Spokes	1007	12/3/03	$49.50	Parcel Post	Anne	Dodsworth
Clean Air Transportation Co.	1008	12/3/03	$2,214.94	Purolator	Margaret	Peacock
Extreme Cycling	1009	12/3/03	$29.00	Loomis	Margaret	Peacock

Figure 10-48 Mod 3 in [1,2] output

Customer Name	Order #	Order Date	Order Amount	Ship Via	First Name	Last Name
City Cyclists	1	12/2/03	$41.90	UPS	Nancy	Davolio
Deals on Wheels	1002	12/2/03	$5,060.28	Pickup	Janet	Leverling
Warsaw Sports, Inc.	1003	12/2/03	$186.87	UPS	Margaret	Peacock
Bikes and Trikes	1004	12/2/03	$823.05	Pickup	Margaret	Peacock
SAB Mountain	1005	12/3/03	$29.00	Loomis	Janet	Leverling
Poser Cycles	1006	12/3/03	$64.90	Purolator	Margaret	Peacock
Spokes	1007	12/3/03	$49.50	Parcel Post	Anne	Dodsworth
Clean Air Transportation Co.	1008	12/3/03	$2,214.94	Purolator	Margaret	Peacock
Extreme Cycling	1009	12/3/03	$29.00	Loomis	Margaret	Peacock
Cyclopath	1010	12/3/03	$14,872.30	UPS	Nancy	Davolio

Figure 10-49 Mod 10 in [3,5] output

Exercise 10.17: Create Odd And Even Page Headers

As more and more word processing mail merge documents are being converted to reports, the need for odd and even page headers and footers is rising in reports. Some of these documents have header and footer information similar to the pages in this workbook. Documents that fall into this category are also often printed on printers that can print two pages on one side of a sheet of paper automatically on duplex printers.

In the previous exercise you learned that the MOD function can be used with a special field to determine an action based on the current record number. Creating odd and even page headers is similar. The difference is that for the page header, you need two page header sections and each one requires its own conditional MOD formula. These formulas are for the page number and determine if the current page number is odd or even. Each page of the report only needs the odd page header information or the even page header information. Therefore, each page header section has to be suppressed when the other page header section prints. The steps below outline the process.

Even page numbers have a remainder of zero. Odd page numbers have a remainder of one.

1. Open a new report and add the Customer Name and Address fields from the Customer table.

2. Create two page header sections, then delete the print date field.

3. In the first page header section add a text object and type "This is the left page header and should have an even page number". Move the Page Number field up to the upper right hand corner of the page header section, then place the text object to the left of the page number field.

4. Copy the field headings and page number field from the first page header section to the second page header section.

5. In the second page header section add a text object and type "This is the right page header and should have an odd page number". Move the Page Number field to the upper left hand corner, then place the text object to the right of the page number field.

6. Resize the page header sections so that they are the same size. The report layout should look like the one shown in Figure 10-50.

Report Header					
Page Header a			This is the left page header and should have an even page number	Page	
	D				
	Customer Na	Address	Address	City	Postal Code
Page Header b	mber This is the left page header and should have an odd page number				
	Customer Name	Address1	Address2	City	Postal Code
Details	Customer Name	Address1	Address2	City	Postal Code

Figure 10-50 L10.17 report layout

7. Add the following formula PageNumber mod 2 = 1 to the Page Header A Suppress (No Drill-Down) option on the Section Expert. You are adding this to the right page header section so that the left page header section will be suppressed when the right page header information is printed. Because the report does not have any groups, you do not have to check the Suppress (No Drill-Down) option.

8. Add the following formula to the left page header section so that the right page header section will be suppressed when the left page header section is printed. PageNumber mod 2 = 0.

9. Save the report. Type L10.17 Odd even page headers as the file name. The report should look like the one shown in Figures 10-51 and 10-52. Close the report.

1 This is the left page header and should have an odd page number				
Customer Name	Address1	Address2	City	Postal Code
City Cyclists	7464 South Kingsway	Suite 2006	Sterling Heights	48358
Pathfinders	410 Eighth Avenue		DeKalb	60148
Bike-A-Holics Anonymous	7429 Arbutus Boulevard	Suite 2017	Blacklick	43005
Psycho-Cycle	8287 Scott Road		Huntsville	35818

Figure 10-51 L10.17 report - odd page header

				This is the right page header and should have an even page number 2
Customer Name	Address1	Address2	City	Postal Code
Bike Shop from Mars	7071 Dundas Crescent	Suite 1730	Newbury Park	91338
Feel Great Bikes Inc.	3015 Delta Place	Suite 2601	Eden Prairie	55367
SAB Mountain	Hauptstr. 29		Bern	CH-3006
Platou Sport	Erling Skakkes gate 78		Stavanger	N-3290

Figure 10-52 L10.17 report - even page header

Test Your Skills

Use the Highlighting Expert to complete the first three skills exercises.

1. Save the L5.6 report as `L10.18 Skills US orders not shipped`.

    -   Highlight the order amount field in bold and red if the order amount is >=1500. Your report should look like the one shown in Figure 10-53. The second and third order amounts (plus others) should have the conditional formatting.

Customer Name	Country	Order Date	Order Amount	Shipped
City Cyclists	USA	04/29/2005	$63.90	False
Pathfinders	USA	04/26/2005	$3,185.42	False
Rockshocks for Jocks	USA	04/25/2005	$8,933.25	False
Rockshocks for Jocks	USA	04/30/2005	$31.00	False
Poser Cycles	USA	04/14/2005	$83.80	False
Trail Blazer's Place	USA	04/18/2005	$107.80	False
Trail Blazer's Place	USA	04/25/2005	$39.80	False
Hooked on Helmets	USA	04/20/2005	$2,797.25	False
Hooked on Helmets	USA	04/25/2005	$1,971.53	False

Figure 10-53 L10.18 Skills US orders not shipped report

2. Save the L9.9 report as `L10.19 Skills Order delay highlight`.

    -   Draw a box around the Order ID field if the Delay In Days To Ship field is >=5. Your report should look like the one shown in Figure 10-54.

Customer Name	Order Date	Ship Date	Order ID	Unit Price	Quantity	Delay In Days To Ship
City Cyclists	12/02/2003	12/10/2003	1	$41.90	1	8
Deals on Wheels	12/02/2003	12/02/2003	1,002	$33.90	3	0
Deals on Wheels	12/02/2003	12/02/2003	1,002	$1,652.86	3	0
Warsaw Sports, Inc.	12/02/2003	12/05/2003	1,003	$48.51	3	3
Warsaw Sports, Inc.	12/02/2003	12/05/2003	1,003	$13.78	3	3
Bikes and Trikes	12/02/2003	12/02/2003	1,004	$274.35	3	0
SAB Mountain	12/03/2003	12/03/2003	1,005	$14.50	2	0
Poser Cycles	12/03/2003	12/05/2003	1,006	$16.50	1	2
Poser Cycles	12/03/2003	12/05/2003	1,006	$33.90	1	2
Poser Cycles	12/03/2003	12/05/2003	1,006	$14.50	1	2
Spokes	12/03/2003	12/03/2003	1,007	$16.50	3	0
Clean Air Transportation Co.	12/03/2003	12/07/2003	1,008	$726.61	2	4
Clean Air Transportation Co.	12/03/2003	12/07/2003	1,008	$431.87	1	4
Clean Air Transportation Co.	12/03/2003	12/07/2003	1,008	$329.85	1	4
Extreme Cycling	12/03/2003	12/10/2003	1,009	$14.50	2	7
Cyclopath	12/03/2003	12/03/2003	1,010	$2,939.85	3	0

Figure 10-54 L10.19 Skills Order delay highlight report

3. Save the L10.5 report as `L10.20 Skills Customer discount`.

    -   Place a double underline border on the Order Amount field if the order discount is 15%.
    -   Place a yellow background on the Order Amount field if the discount is 10%. This should be the first priority. Your report should look like the one shown in Figure 10-55.

Customer Name	Order #	Order Date	Order Amount	Ship Via	Order Discount
City Cyclists	1	12/2/03	$41.90	UPS	25% discount
Deals on Wheels	1002	12/2/03	$5,060.28	Pickup	15% discount
Warsaw Sports, Inc.	1003	12/2/03	$186.87	UPS	25% discount
Bikes and Trikes	1004	12/2/03	$823.05	Pickup	25% discount
SAB Mountain	1005	12/3/03	$29.00	Loomis	25% discount
Poser Cycles	1006	12/3/03	$64.90	Purolator	25% discount
Spokes	1007	12/3/03	$49.50	Parcel Post	25% discount
Clean Air Transportation Co.	1008	12/3/03	$2,214.94	Purolator	25% discount
Extreme Cycling	1009	12/3/03	$29.00	Loomis	25% discount
Cyclopath	1010	12/3/03	$14,872.30	UPS	10% discount
BBS Pty	1011	12/3/03	$29.00	Purolator	25% discount
Piccolo	1012	12/3/03	$10,259.10	Loomis	10% discount

Figure 10-55 L10.20 Skills Customer discount report

4. Save the L5.14 report as L10.21 Skills Modify row color.

- Print the odd number detail rows with a Yellow background. Your report should look like the one shown in Figure 10-56.

2003 Orders By Sales Rep

	Order Date	Order ID	Product ID	Unit Price	Quantity
Nancy Davolio					
	02/19/2003	1312	302162	$479.85	1
	02/19/2003	1310	1101	$14.50	3
	02/19/2003	1310	1104	$14.50	1
	02/19/2003	1312	2202	$41.90	1
	02/19/2003	1312	401001	$267.76	1
	02/26/2003	1354	2202	$41.90	1
	02/26/2003	1354	6402	$9.00	3
	02/27/2003	1373	301181	$764.85	2

Figure 10-56 L10.21 Skills Modify row color report

5. Save the L9.13 report as L10.22 Skills Next discount.

- Delete the selection criteria.
- Create a formula called Next Discount. The purpose of this formula is to show the discount the customer will receive on their next order. The discount is based on their previous order.
- The Next Discount formula needs the following criteria:

  - Print "10% off your next order", if the quantity = 3.
  - Print "15% off your next order", if the quantity = 2.
  - Print "20% off your next order", if the quantity = 1.

- Delete the Unit Price field from the report.
- Add the Next Discount formula field after the Customer Name field. Your report should look like the one shown in Figure 10-57.

Customer Name	Next Discount	Order Date	Ship Date	Order ID	Quantity	Delay In Days To Ship
Hercules Mountain Bikes		01/19/2004	01/28/2004	1,207	1	9
Belgium Bike Co.	15% off your next order	01/19/2004	01/25/2004	1,208	3	6
Tyred Out	15% off your next order	01/19/2004	01/27/2004	1,209	3	8
Cyclist's Trail Co.		01/19/2004	01/21/2004	1,210	1	2
Cyclist's Trail Co.	20% off your next order	01/19/2004	01/21/2004	1,210	2	2
Cyclist's Trail Co.	15% off your next order	01/19/2004	01/23/2004	1,211	3	4
The Bike Cellar	15% off your next order	01/19/2004	01/23/2004	1,212	3	4
Bike Shop from Mars	15% off your next order	01/20/2004	01/28/2004	1,215	3	8
Clean Air Transportation Co.	15% off your next order	01/22/2004	02/02/2004	1,217	3	11
Clean Air Transportation Co.		01/22/2004	02/02/2004	1,217	1	11

Figure 10-57 L10.22 Skills Next discount report

6. Modify the L10.7 report to print the group header information at the top of the page if the group prints on more than one page. Save the report as
L10.23 Skills Modify group header options.

- Suppress the dollar sign on the Order Amount field on all but the first record in each group. Make the dollar sign fixed.

The bottom of page 1 should look like the one shown in Figure 10-58. Notice where the dollar sign is. The top of page 2 should look like the one shown in Figure 10-59.

BBS Pty					
	01/05/2004	01/07/2004	$ 2,654.56	1139	$854.86
	01/05/2004	01/07/2004	2,654.56	1139	$899.85
	03/30/2004	03/31/2004	3,734.10	1470	$764.85
	03/30/2004	03/31/2004	3,734.10	1470	$479.85
	06/19/2004	06/19/2004	8,819.55	1740	$2,939.85

Page 1 of 29

Figure 10-58 L10.23 Skills Modify group header options report bottom of page 1

	Order Date	Ship Date	Order Amount	Order #	Unit Price
BBS Pty					
	06/25/2004	06/28/2004	5,913.60	1776	$33.90
	06/25/2004	06/28/2004	5,913.60	1776	$2,939.85
	10/15/2004	10/16/2004	2,939.85	2221	$2,939.85
	10/21/2004	10/25/2004	3,479.70	2253	$1,739.85
	10/27/2004	11/03/2004	3,355.22	2280	$16.50
	10/27/2004	11/03/2004	3,355.22	2280	$1,652.86
	11/25/2004	11/30/2004	6,970.95	2426	$33.90
	11/25/2004	11/30/2004	6,970.95	2426	$2,939.85
	11/25/2004	11/30/2004	6,970.95	2426	$329.85
	04/19/2005	04/20/2005	6,209.55	2946	$2,939.85
	04/19/2005	04/20/2005	6,209.55	2946	$329.85
Total # orders -	16	Total $ amount of orders -	$79,886.01		
		Average order amount for customer -	$4,992.88		

Figure 10-59 L10.23 Skills Modify group header options report top of page 2

7. Modify the L6.11 report so that each quarter starts on a new page. Save the report as
L10.24 Skills 2004 orders by quarter with page break.

- Reset the page number when a new quarter begins.

Your report should look like the one shown in Figure 10-60.

		2004 Orders By Quarter			
	Salesperson	Order Date	Order #	Order Amount	
July					
Robert	King	07/01/2004	1799	$389.65	
Margaret	Peacock	07/01/2004	1800	$1,793.42	
Michael	Suyama	07/01/2004	1801	$3,327.67	
Anne	Dodsworth	07/02/2004	1802	$3,479.70	
Anne	Dodsworth	07/02/2004	1803	$823.05	
Janet	Leverling	07/10/2004	1849	$107.80	
Margaret	Peacock	07/10/2004	1850	$61.50	
Anne	Dodsworth	07/10/2004	1851	$35.00	
Janet	Leverling	07/10/2004	1852	$5,891.60	
Robert	King	07/11/2004	1853	$1,664.70	

1

Figure 10-60 L10.24 Skills 2004 orders by quarter with page break report

8. Modify the L10.13 report to display the Employee First and Last name in the group tree instead of the Employee ID. Save the report as `L10.25 Skills Modify group tree view.`

   - Do not display the Employee ID field in the group header section.
   - **Hint**: Create a formula to combine the employee first and last name fields on the Change Group options dialog box.

Page 2 of your report should look like the one shown in Figure 10-61. Notice the options in the group tree on the left.

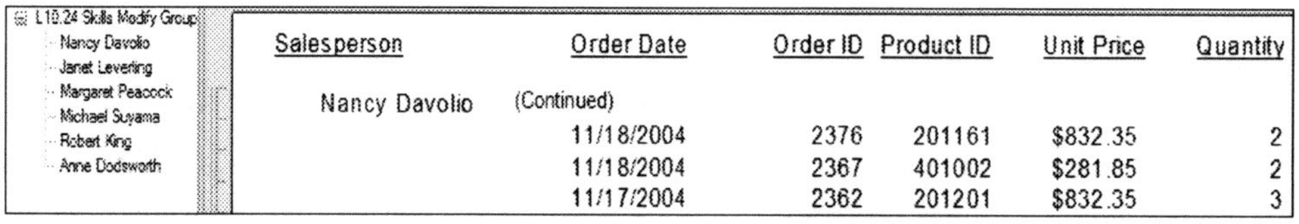

Salesperson	Order Date	Order ID	Product ID	Unit Price	Quantity
Nancy Davolio	(Continued)				
	11/18/2004	2376	201161	$832.35	2
	11/18/2004	2367	401002	$281.85	2
	11/17/2004	2362	201201	$832.35	3

Group tree:
- L10.24 Skills Modify Group
  - Nancy Davolio
  - Janet Levering
  - Margaret Peacock
  - Michael Suyama
  - Robert King
  - Anne Dodsworth

Figure 10-61 L10.25 Skills Modify group tree view report

9. Modify the L6.2 report to be used as a summary report. Save the report as `L10.26 Skills Summary report with conditional formatting.`

   - Suppress the field headings.
   - Remove the border from the Order Amount field in the group footer section.
   - Hide the details section.
   - Change the report title to `Summary of Customer Orders.`
   - Remove the bold from all of the objects in the group footer section.
   - Display the text `Level 1 Customer` if the Total Dollar Amount Of Orders field is > $75,000. (**Hint**: Use comparison conditional formatting.)
   - This type of report is often called a summary report because it does not print any detail records. Department managers and executives often request this type of report.

Your report should look like the one shown in Figure 10-62.

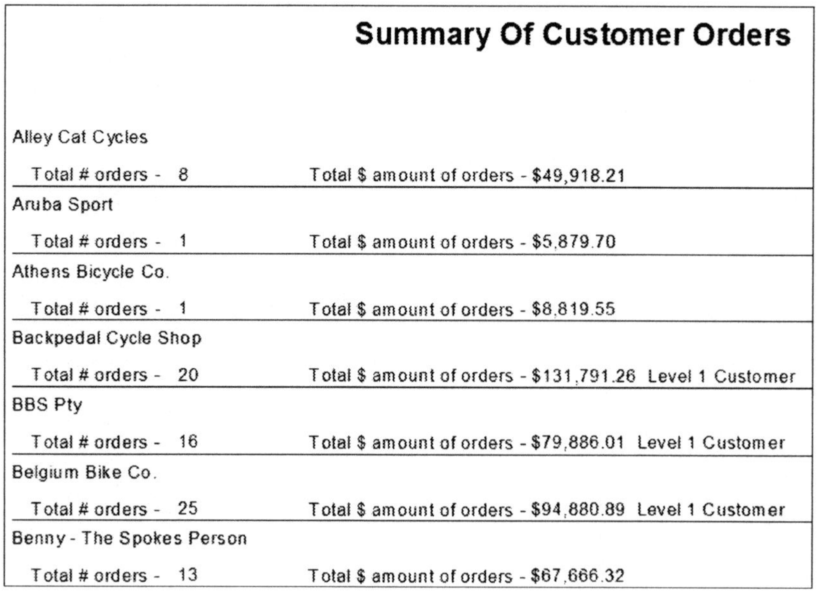

Summary Of Customer Orders

Alley Cat Cycles	
Total # orders - 8	Total $ amount of orders - $49,918.21
Aruba Sport	
Total # orders - 1	Total $ amount of orders - $5,879.70
Athens Bicycle Co.	
Total # orders - 1	Total $ amount of orders - $8,819.55
Backpedal Cycle Shop	
Total # orders - 20	Total $ amount of orders - $131,791.26 Level 1 Customer
BBS Pty	
Total # orders - 16	Total $ amount of orders - $79,886.01 Level 1 Customer
Belgium Bike Co.	
Total # orders - 25	Total $ amount of orders - $94,880.89 Level 1 Customer
Benny - The Spokes Person	
Total # orders - 13	Total $ amount of orders - $67,666.32

Figure 10-62 L10.26 Skills Summary report with conditional formatting

10. Add all of the reports that were created in this lesson to the Workbench.

CHARTS

Crystal Reports has an expert that you can use to create charts. There are 16 types of charts that you can create, including pie, bar and line. In this lesson you will learn the following:

☑ How to create all 16 chart types using the Chart Expert
☑ Basic chart formatting and editing techniques

To pass the RDCR201 exam, you need to be familiar with and be able to:

☑ Use the Chart Expert to create and modify charts
☑ Analyze trends in data

LESSON 11

Charts Overview

In addition to being able to format data in reports, charts allow you to present data in a graphical format which often makes the data easier to understand. Charts also allow data to be presented in formats that text-only reports cannot do as well. For example, charts can show trends over time, relationships or how one set of data compares to another set of data.

In previous lessons you created basic charts using a report wizard. As you saw, the chart options were very limited. When you need to create or modify charts that require more detail then the wizards provide, you should use the Chart Expert. It is very easy to get carried away when creating charts. Try to create charts that present the data in a meaningful way. Remember that sometimes, less is more.

There are four ways to open the Chart Expert as discussed below.

    ① Click the **INSERT CHART** button on the Insert Tools toolbar.
    ② Insert ⇒ Chart.
    ③ Right-click on an existing chart and select Chart Expert.
    ④ Click on an existing chart, then Format ⇒ Chart Expert.

Chart Considerations

There are two areas that need to be addressed before you start to create the chart. The two areas are the chart type and the source of the data for the chart. You will select the chart type on the Type tab on the Chart Expert, which is discussed below. Changing the chart type is easy. If you are not sure which chart type is the most appropriate, with a few mouse clicks, you can try out a few chart types and variations to see which is the best one for the data. The data source for the chart comes from one of the following: records in the details section of the report, a cross-tab, an OLAP grid or summary data.

The Chart Expert

This is the tool that allows you to create new charts and modify charts. It has wizard like characteristics because you click on the tabs to accomplish different tasks associated with creating and editing a chart. The biggest benefit of using the Chart Expert instead of the chart options on a wizard is that you have a lot of the chart options available from the beginning and the chart does not have to be based on data that will be printed on the report, like the wizards require. The options on each tab are covered in detail in this lesson because not understanding what all of the options are or knowing where they are, will take you longer to create a chart. As you read about the Chart Expert, you may gain a better understanding of the options if you have the Chart Expert open.

The six tabs on the Chart Expert (Type, Data, Axes, Options, Color Highlighting and Text) contain options for a variety of features that you can use to make the chart as effective as possible. Keep in mind that not all of these tabs are available for all chart types. The tabs and options are discussed below.

 You do not have to create a chart from an existing report. You can select the fields that you need on the Chart Expert.

Type Tab

The options on this tab let you select what the chart will look like. There are 16 chart types that you can select from, as shown in Figure 11-1. Many of these chart types have variations that you can select, which gives you more chart options. Each chart type is explained in Table 11-1. There are additional chart types, which Crystal Reports refers to as templates. You will learn about the other chart types later in this lesson.

In previous lessons you created a pie and bar chart using a wizard. If you have created charts in spreadsheet software, you are probably familiar with many of the chart types in Crystal Reports. When selecting the chart type, the most important consideration should be to select the chart type that will best display the data that will be presented in the chart. This is the first thing that you have to do. When you click on the chart type on the left, you will see variations of the chart on the right. Click on the chart style (variation) on the right that you want to use. Under the chart variations, you will see a description of the chart type.

Chart Type Options

At the bottom of the Type tab shown in Figure 11-1, you will see the first two options discussed below for the bar, line, area and histogram chart types. Most chart types also have the third option below.

① **Vertical** This is the default option. The elements will start at the bottom of the chart, as shown on the right side of Figure 11-1.
② **Horizontal** If selected, this option will change the direction of the elements on the chart. The bars will start on the left, instead of the bottom, as shown in Figure 11-2.
③ **Use Depth Effect** If checked, this option will display the chart in 3D format, as shown in Figure 11-3.

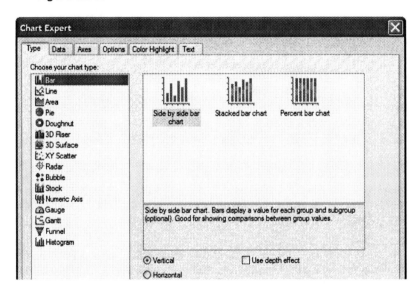

Figure 11-1 Chart Expert Type tab options

Figure 11-2 Horizontal chart options

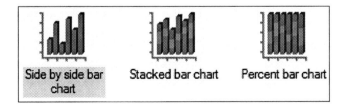

Figure 11-3 Use Depth Effect options

Chart Type	Description
Bar	Bar charts, as shown in Figure 11-4, compare data in intervals of time. This is probably the most used chart type. Stacked bar charts show each item as a percent of the total.
Line	Line charts show trends and changes over a period of time. The markers on the bottom three line chart types indicate the exact values. In Figure 11-5, the data is represented with lines. A good use of **3D LINE CHARTS** is when the data lines cross each other often. This makes a line chart easier to read.
Area	Area charts show how the data has changed over a period of time. Figure 11-6 shows how the four types of income (mail order, store, kiosk and Internet) make up the total income and how the income changes over the months. Area charts are almost identical to stacked line charts. The difference is that area charts are filled in below the trendline. Area charts are probably best suited for a few groups of data.
Pie	Pie charts only show information for one point in time. Figure 11-7 shows the various types of income for July. Each slice of the pie represents the percent for the item. The Multiple pie chart type will create a chart for each group.
Doughnut	This chart type is similar to pie charts. The difference is that there is a hole in the center, which contains the grand total of the data presented in the chart.
3D Riser	This is the 3D version of bar charts that shows data values side by side, separately or stacked. It can display several groups of data in shapes like a pyramid or octagon.
3D Surface	This is the 3D version of area charts. This chart type uses three sets of data. The surface of the chart has a curve.
XY Scatter	XY Scatter charts show how two values are related (like month of year and order amount) and how a change in one value affects the other value, as shown in Figure 11-8. This chart type lets you see the correlation between the items.
Radar	Radar charts compare sets of data relative to a center point and shows how far the data value is from the standard (the center point value). The values that are often used are group subtotals. The data from the X axis is usually plotted in a circle and the Y values are plotted from the center of the circle out.
Bubble	This chart type is similar to XY Scatter charts because it plots individual points. The difference is that bubble charts use different size plot points based on the data value. The larger the data value, the larger the size the plot point is.
Stock	This chart type is similar to bar charts. The difference is that the bars in stock charts do not have to touch the bottom of the chart. This type of chart is often used to display the minimum and maximum of stock prices, where each bar represents a different stock. Stock charts plot the high and low values for each element.
Numeric Axis	This chart type does not use a fixed X axis value or interval like many other chart types do. You can use a date/time field or numeric value for the X axis. This chart type is another way to create bar, line and area charts.
Gauge	This chart type looks like a fuel gauge in a car as shown in Figure 11-9. The needle in the chart points to the value that is being represented. If there is more than one value or group being represented, a gauge chart is created for each value or group. Multiple needles in one gauge means that there is more than one "On change of" value.
Gantt	This type chart is primarily used to display project management data like the start and end dates of tasks on a project plan. Gantt charts only work with date and date/time fields.

Table 11-1 Chart types explained

Chart Type	Description
Funnel	This chart type is similar to stacked bar charts because they show each item as a percent of the total. The difference is that the bars are in the shape of a funnel. The height of the bar represents the percent of the data. The width of the bar does not represent anything.
Histogram NEW	This chart type places the data (from the records) into buckets, based on the range that they fall into and displays a count of the records in each bucket, as shown in Figure 11-10. Usually, you will not see more than eight bars on a histogram chart, regardless of how many ranges (buckets) there really are.

Table 11-1 Chart types explained (Continued)

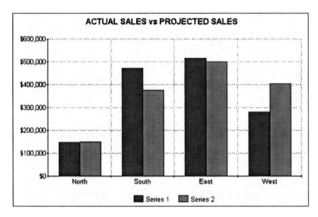

Figure 11-4 Bar chart

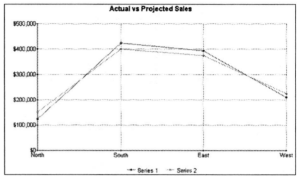

Figure 11-5 Line chart

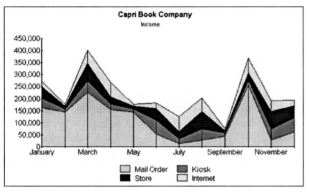

Figure 11-6 Area chart

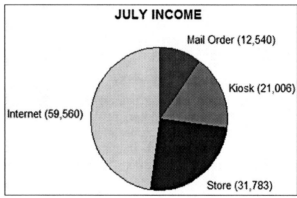

Figure 11-7 Pie chart

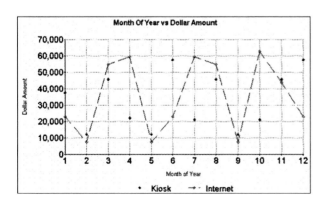

Figure 11-8 XY Scatter chart

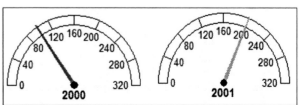

Figure 11-9 Gauge chart

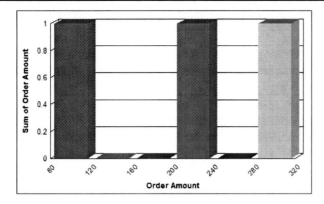

Figure 11-10 Histogram chart

It would be very helpful and a big time saver to me if at least one of the tabs on the Chart Expert would display the chart with the options that are selected, similar to what you see when you use the Chart Options dialog box to modify the chart. You will learn how to use the Chart Options dialog box later in this lesson.

Data Tab

The options on this tab let you select the source of the data for the chart. This is the second area that needs to be addressed before you create the chart. There are four ways (called layout options) to chart data, as discussed below. Depending on the chart type that was selected, not all of the data layout options will be available.

All four layout options have the **ON CHANGE OF** drop down list. The options in this list are how you decide when a new element (bar, slice of pie, point on a line, etc) will be added to the chart. This option lets Crystal Reports know that when the value in the field(s) listed below this option changes, you want a new element of the chart to be created.

Advanced Layout Options

This layout option is always available. Out of the four layout options, this is probably the most complex because it allows you to create a chart that is not based on data that will print on the report. If you created a report using the Blank Report option and have not added any fields to the report, the options on this tab will let you select the fields for the chart. This is how you would create a report that only has a chart. If you need to a create a chart based on records in the details section of the report, click on the Advanced layout option on the Data tab. You will see the options shown in Figure 11-11.

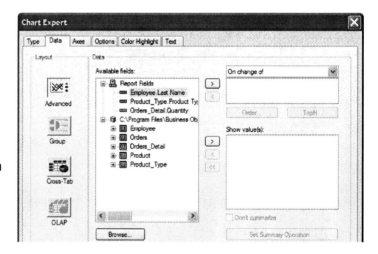

Figure 11-11 Chart Expert Data tab - Advanced options

 When you are working on exercises that use the options on the Advanced tab, you will see this instruction: **ADD THE FIELD TO THE FIRST LIST BOX**. This means to add the field to the list box that is under the On Change Of option shown above in Figure 11-11.

 If the report already has groups defined, you can still create an advanced chart because the options on this tab are not affected by the groups that are on the report.

The **AVAILABLE FIELDS** section of the Data tab contains the fields that are already on the report, including the summary, formula, running total fields, as well as, all of the fields in the tables associated with the report. This section is only available if the On Change of option is selected in the drop down list on the right.

 The summary and running total fields can only be added to the **SHOW VALUE(S)** list.

The **ON CHANGE OF** option allows you to select up to two fields to group the data in the chart on. This group is not a real group like the ones that you learned how to create earlier in this workbook. Each element on the chart represents one group. If you wanted to create a chart that displayed the orders by sales rep, you would add the sales rep (Employee Last Name) field to the box below this drop down list.

The On Change Of option works like the group option. If you select multiple fields to group on, the data from each group will be displayed (side by side or stacked, based on the chart type that is selected).

The **FOR EACH RECORD** option in the drop down list will cause a new element to be added to the chart for every record that would print on the report. If this option is selected, only one field can be added to the box below this drop down list. If there is not a lot of data in the table that the field that you select is in, it is okay to select this option because the chart will be legible. If there are a lot of records, more then likely it would be hard to read the chart if this option is selected. If this option is selected, fields that are added to the **SHOW VALUE(S)** list will not be summarized, the actual value in the field is what will appear in the chart.

You can reduce the records that are used to create the chart by using the Select Expert that you learned about in Lesson 5. If you realize that you need to do this, you can create the selection criteria after the chart has been created. You will learn how to do this later in this lesson.

 Gantt charts have to use the **FOR EACH RECORD** option. A start and end date must be added to the Show value(s) list.

The **FOR ALL RECORDS** option creates a chart with only one element, which is a grand total for all of the records that are on the report. You cannot add any fields to the box below the drop down list if this option is selected.

The **SHOW VALUE(S)** list contains the field(s) that the chart will create a summary for. The value from the summary calculation will be used as an element on the chart. If you add more than one field to this list, the chart will plot a separate line or bar for example, for each field in this list.

In the Orders by sales rep example, if you add the Order Amount field to the Show value(s) list, a total (summary) for each sales rep would be created.

Summary Calculations

Table 11-2 explains the default type of summary calculations that are applied to different field types.

Field Type	Default Calculation Type
Number	Summary
Currency	Summary
All others	Count

Table 11-2 Default summary calculations

You can change the summary calculation type by following the steps below.

① Click on the field that you want to change the calculation for in the Show value(s) list.
② Click the **SET SUMMARY OPERATION** button shown earlier in Figure 11-11. You will see the Edit Summary dialog box shown in Figure 11-12. You learned about this dialog box in Lesson 6.
③ The options in the **CALCULATE THIS SUMMARY** drop down list are the ones that are available for the data type of the field that you are changing. Select the type of calculation that you want.

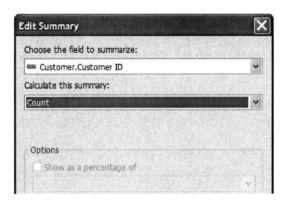

Figure 11-12 Edit Summary dialog box

The **ORDER** button on the Data tab will open the Chart Sort Order dialog box shown in Figure 11-13. The options on this dialog box work the same way that the options on the Insert Group dialog box that you learned about in Lesson 6. These options let you select the sort order for the element in the chart.

In the orders by sales rep example, if you selected on the Order Amount field and then clicked the Order button, you would be able to select how you wanted the total order amount for each rep to be displayed. If you were creating a bar chart and wanted to see the sales reps in order from high to low based on sales, you would select **DESCENDING**.

The **TOP N** button will open the Group Sort Expert, shown in Figure 11-14. The options on this dialog box are similar the ones on the **OTHERS** tab on the Change Group Options dialog box. [See Lesson 6, Figure 6-63] If you only wanted to include the top or bottom N records, groups or percents, you would select the options here. The options selected in Figure 11-14 would display the five sales reps that had the lowest number of sales.

If you want to include groups that are not part of the group sort, you can by checking the appropriate **INCLUDE** options on the right side of the dialog box. If checked, the **INCLUDE TIES** option will include groups that have the same summarized value if they meet the other selection criteria. Notice that you can also create formulas if the chart requires it.

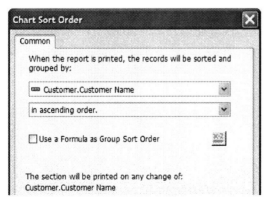

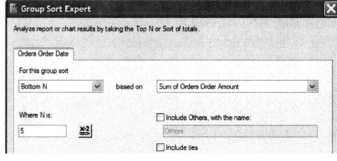

Figure 11-14 Group Sort Expert

Figure 11-13 Chart Sort Order dialog box

Group Layout Options

The group layout options create a chart that is based off of fields in a group header or footer section of the report. This chart layout type is only available if both of the conditions discussed below have been met.

① The chart must be placed in the report header or footer or in a group header or footer section that is on a higher level then the data in the group that the chart will be based on.
② The report has to have one group that has a summary or total field.

The options shown in Figure 11-15 let you select how the data in the group will be displayed in the chart. The options are explained below.

The options below the **ON CHANGE OF** drop down list are the fields (that have a summary or total field) that are in a lower level then the section of the report that the chart has been placed in. This option lets you select the group that the chart will be based on.

The 2004 Orders by shipping method report that you created in Exercise 6.4 has two groups: the Ship Via group and the Customer Name group. Both of these groups have summary fields.

If you put the chart in the report header or footer section, the On Change Of drop down list will have the options shown in Figure 11-15.

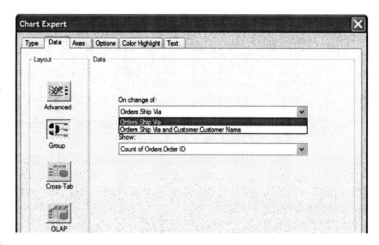

Figure 11-15 Chart Expert Data tab - Group options (On Change Of options for the two groups below the chart)

If the report has three groups with a summary or total field and you place the chart in the first group section, you would see the summary or total fields for the two groups below it. Just by looking at the options in Figure 11-16, you do not know if the chart is in a report section or a group section.

If you put the chart in the first group header or footer section or the report header or footer section and there is only one group below it that has a summary or total field, you would only see one option in the On Change Of drop down list as shown in Figure 11-16. These are the summary fields in the group header or footer section in the report.

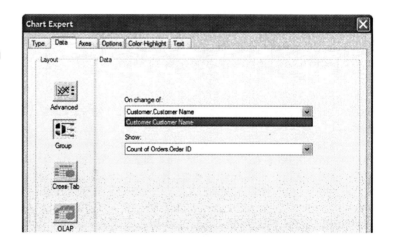

Figure 11-16 On Change Of options for one group below the chart

The fields in the **SHOW** drop down list are the summary and subtotal fields in the group selected in the On Change Of field. This is how you select the summary field in the group that will be used in the chart.

Cross-Tab Layout Options

This layout option is only available if the report has a cross-tab object in the same or corresponding section that the chart is placed in. By corresponding section, I mean if the cross-tab that the chart will be based off of is in the Group 2 footer section, the chart can be placed in the Group 2 header or footer section. The options shown in Figure 11-17 let you create a chart based on the data in the cross-tab.

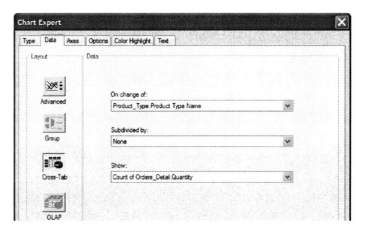

Figure 11-17 Chart Expert Data tab - Cross-Tab options

 If the report has more than one cross-tab object, you have to select the cross-tab object that you want to create the chart off of before you open the Chart Expert.

The options in the **ON CHANGE OF** drop down list are the first fields in the Rows and Columns sections of the Cross-Tab Expert or Wizard, regardless of how many fields each of these sections have. [See Exercise 7.9] The field selected in this drop down list is the first (or only) element that will be used as the primary X axis value.

Selecting a field in the **SUBDIVIDED BY** drop down list is optional, which is why the default option is **NONE**. The only field that is available in the Subdivided By drop down list is the one that was not selected in the On Change Of drop down list. Selecting a field will create a second X value, which will add a second series of data to the chart. This will let you create a chart that does a side by side comparison. Figure 11-18 shows a line chart with the first field in the Row section and the first field in the Column section from the cross-tab selected.

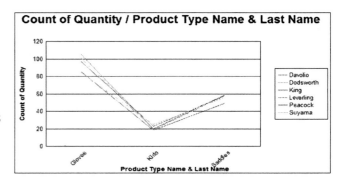

Figure 11-18 Line chart with the row and column fields selected

The options in the **SHOW** drop down list are the fields that are in the Summary Fields section of the Cross-Tab window. This field is used to determine the size of the elements in the chart, like the size of each slice in a pie chart or the height of each element on an area chart. The size refers to the height if the chart type is vertical or the width if the chart type is using the horizontal chart orientation.

OLAP Layout Options

Creating a chart that is based on OLAP grid data is very similar to creating a chart that is based on data in a cross-tab. The major difference is that charts that are based on OLAP grid data do not use summary fields. This layout option is only available if the report has data from an OLAP cube in the same or corresponding section that the chart is placed in, just like charts that are based on cross-tab data. The options shown in Figure 11-19 let you create a chart based on the data in the OLAP cube.

 If the report has more than one OLAP cube, you have to select the OLAP cube that you want to create the chart off of before you open the Chart Expert.

If checked, the **CHART OFF ENTIRE GRID** option will use all of the options that the OLAP grid used to create the report, to create the chart. Selecting this option causes the other data options on the window to be dimmed out. The only time that you would use the other options shown in Figure 11-19 is if you need to change the dimensions of the data that the chart will be created from.

The default **ON CHANGE OF** option is the first **DIMENSION** on the Rows/Columns tab on the OLAP Expert or Wizard. The drop down list contains the other dimension options that you can select from to use as the data for the X axis.

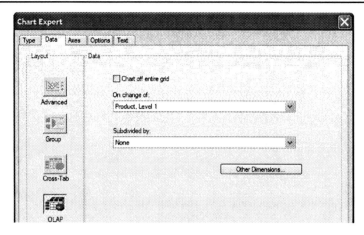

Figure 11-19 Chart Expert Data tab - OLAP options

 When creating a chart based on OLAP data, some chart types require multiple dimensions to be selected.

Selecting a field in the **SUBDIVIDED BY** drop down list is optional. The default for this field is None. Selecting a field will divide the data in the On Change Of option. The only field that is available in this drop down list is the one that was not selected in the On Change Of drop down list. Selecting a field from this list will cause a second series of data to be added to the chart. Figure 11-20 shows a bar chart with only one dimension selected (the field in the On Change Of drop down list). Figure 11-21 shows a 3D Riser chart with two dimensions selected.

 If you move the OLAP grid from a report section to a group section, the chart will move to the corresponding group section. Data in an OLAP grid will not change if it is moved from the report header or footer section to a group header or footer section, which means that the data in the chart will not change if it's moved.

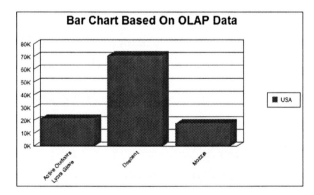
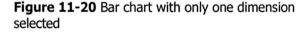

Figure 11-20 Bar chart with only one dimension selected

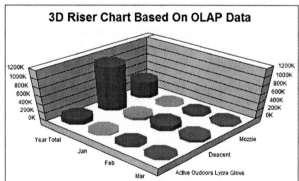

Figure 11-21 3D Riser chart with two dimensions selected

The **OTHER DIMENSIONS** button will open the Format Other Dimensions dialog box shown in Figure 11-22. You will use the options on this dialog box to limit the values in the dimensions that will be displayed on the chart. This is the equivalent of filtering the records that will be used to create the chart. For example, if you want to limit the products that appear in the chart to one product, click the **SELECT A MEMBER VALUE** button. You will see the Member Selector window. Select the option that you want, as shown in Figure 11-23 and click OK. The dimension that you select will be on the Format Other Dimensions dialog box. In this example, the only product that will appear on the report is Mozzie.

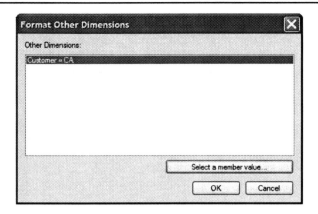

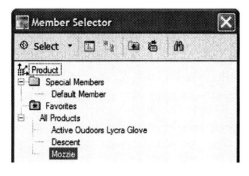

Figure 11-23 Member Selector window

Figure 11-22 Format Other Dimensions dialog box

Axes Tab

Depending on the chart type that is selected, you may not see the Axes tab shown in Figure 11-24. You will see this tab if the chart type selected uses the X and Y axis. For example, bar, line and area charts use the X and Y axis. Pie, doughnut and Gantt chart types do not.

The options on this tab let you select how the chart will display the data values that you see across the bottom of the chart (the X axis) and on the left side of the chart (the Y axis). If you are creating a 3D chart, you can also select the data values for the Z axis.

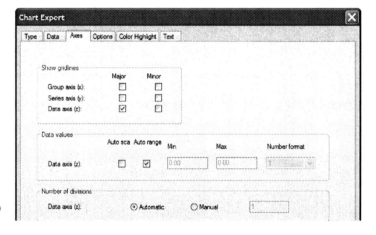

Figure 11-24 Chart Expert - Axes tab

If the chart that you are creating needed to display order totals by month, like the report that you created in Exercise 6.7, the months would be placed on the X axis because the report is grouped by month and the totals would be placed on the Y axis because they represent the quantity, as shown in Figure 11-25. If you were creating the same chart, but selected a 3D layout, the chart would look like the one shown in Figure 11-26, which also includes the data axis (the Z axis).

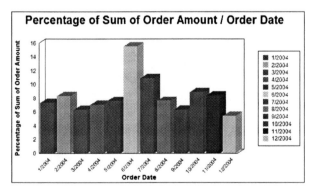

Figure 11-25 Bar chart with X and Y axis data

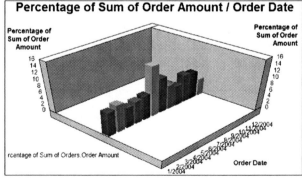

Figure 11-26 Bar chart with X, Y and Z axis data

Show Gridlines Options

You will see two or three axis options in this section depending on whether the chart is two or three dimensional.

The **Group Axis** option corresponds to the **ON CHANGE OF** field on the Data tab.
The **Series Axis** will only appear for three dimensional chart types.
The **Data Axis** option corresponds to the **SHOW** field on the Data tab.

If checked, the major and minor options will add gridlines to the chart. The **MAJOR** option will place the gridlines (with labels) on the axis, as shown in Figure 11-27. The **MINOR** option can only be used with numeric labels and will place the gridlines between the labels on the axis.

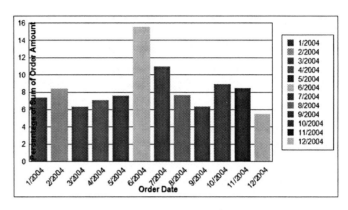

Figure 11-27 Bar chart with major gridlines added

 Some chart types will have a gridline on the Group axis whether you select the option or not.

Data Values Options

The options in this section of the Axes tab let you customize the **VALUES** on the Data axis.

The **AUTO RANGE** option is the default and lets Crystal Reports use the chart values to set the starting and ending values for the Data axis. If you want to customize the values, clear this option and enter the Min, Max and Number formats that you want.

MIN is the lowest value that you want to see on the axis. Usually this is zero, but you may have the need to use a different starting value.

MAX is the highest value that you want to see on the Axis. This value is usually larger than the largest value of the data on the axis.

 The danger in changing the max value in my opinion is that you would be basing the change on the current values being displayed on the chart. If the report is run later and for whatever reason has a larger value then the value that you entered in this field, the chart would not capture the largest value.

The **NUMBER FORMAT** option is only available if the Auto Range option is not checked. The options in the drop down list shown in Figure 11-28 let you select the format for the numbers that will be displayed on the chart.

 If you change the data value options and then recheck the **AUTO RANGE** option, the changes that you made will still be in effect, even though the options are not enabled.

If checked, the **AUTO SCALE** option lets you select the starting numeric value that the chart will use.

Number Of Division Options

The options in this section let you customize the number of gridlines (intervals) and labels that the data axis will have. Select the **MANUAL** option if you want to set the intervals.

Options Tab

Figures 11-29 to 11-31 show various versions of the Options tab. The options are different depending on the chart type that is selected.

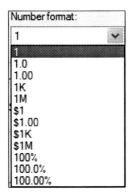

Figure 11-28 Number Format options

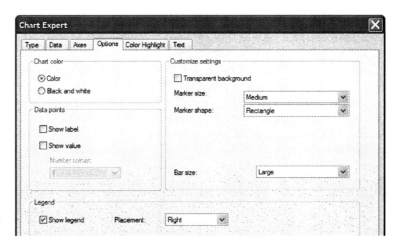

Figure 11-29 Options tab for a bar chart

The options in the **CUSTOMIZE SETTINGS** section let you select the size and shape for the legend in some chart types or the shape of the markers for bar and line charts. The **MARKERS** are the points on a chart that are connected by lines. This feature is often used in line charts, as you saw earlier in Figure 11-5. The last size option in this section lets you select the size of the element, for example, the size of a slice of the pie or the size of the bar as shown in Figures 11-30 and 11-31.

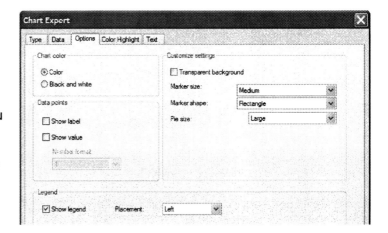

Figure 11-30 Options tab for a pie chart

The options in the **DATA POINTS** section let you select whether or not labels and values (the actual data) are displayed with the elements. Each element (slice) in the pie chart shown earlier in Figure 11-7 has a label and value. The value is in parenthesis for illustration purposes.

The options in the **LEGEND** section let you turn the legend on and off, as well as, select where you want the legend placed in reference to the chart. The legend is the color coded key that lets you know what the elements on the chart are referencing.

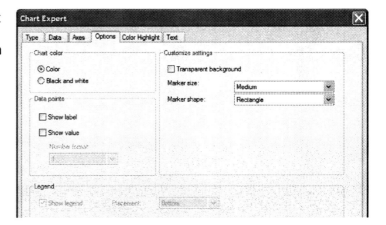

Figure 11-31 Options tab for a histogram chart

The area chart shown earlier in Figure 11-6 has the legend at the bottom of the chart. In Figure 11-30 above, the legend will be placed on the left side of the chart. Notice in Figure 11-31 above that the legend options are dimmed out. That means that the chart type cannot have a legend. There are also times when a chart looks better without a legend.

NEW Color Highlight Tab

The options on this tab allow you to conditionally format the colors for the elements on a chart. The options shown in Figure 11-32 should look familiar because they are similar to the options on the Highlighting Expert that you learned about in Lesson 10. The difference between them is that the Highlighting Expert works with objects on the report and the options on the Color Highlight tab on the Chart Expert work with elements on a chart. The options shown will change the color of the field to Teal if the percent of sales for the quarter is less than 20%.

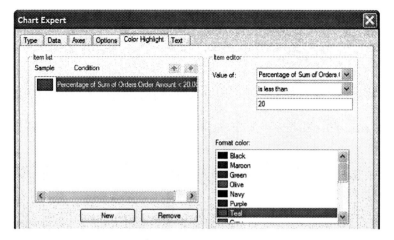

Figure 11-32 Color Highlight tab options

 The conditional formatting that you apply to an element does not change if the data for that element changes. For example, if you apply conditional formatting to the bottom section (for example, the mail order section) of the area chart shown earlier in Figure 11-6 and the data changes and the mail order element is no longer on the bottom, the formatting for the mail order element does not change. The new data that is in the bottom section of the area chart will change.

 Conditional formatting usually looks better on charts that are using data that is grouped.

Text Tab

The options on this tab will let you add text to a chart. As shown in Figure 11-33, the **AUTO TEXT** option is checked for all of the title fields and the text fields are dimmed out. This is because Crystal Reports automatically creates many of the titles based on the data that the chart is being created from. You saw this when you created charts with the wizards in Lesson 7. To change a title, clear the checkmark next to the title that you want to change and type in the title that you want.

You can change the font of a title by clicking on the title that you want to change in the **FORMAT** section and then click the Font button. Figure 11-34 shows the font options.

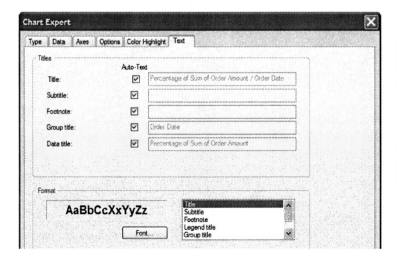

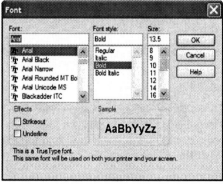

Figure 11-34 Font options

Figure 11-33 Text tab chart options

Parts Of A Chart

Charts can contain all or any of the options discussed below. It is important that you understand these options. These options can be added or deleted as needed. Figure 11-35 illustrates many of the parts of a chart that have already been discussed in this lesson. The parts of the chart illustrated in Figure 11-35 are explained below.

Title and **Subtitle** are a description of what type of data the chart is displaying.

X and Y Axis represent the vertical (Y) axis and horizontal (X) axis of the chart. The X axis often represents quantities or percents.

Gridlines make the chart easier to read if the values are close in range. You can have horizontal and vertical gridlines.

Scale shows the unit of measurement. The scale range is taken from the data that is displayed on the report. The scale is automatically created for you, but you can change it. Crystal Reports uses the Auto Scale and Auto Range options on the Chart Expert Axes tab to create the scale.

The **Legend** is used to help make the chart easier to read. Legends are color coded representations of different data elements on the chart.

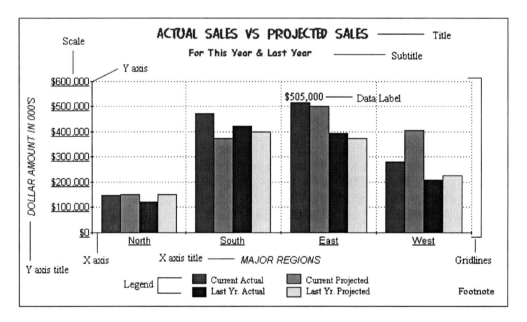

Figure 11-35 Parts of a chart illustrated

Adding A Chart To A Report

The way that charts are added to the report has changed from the previous version of Crystal Reports. This applies to the Insert ⇒ Chart option and Insert Chart button options. When either of these options are selected, you will see a shadow box like you see when you add an image to a report.
[See Exercise 4.3] Click in the section of the report that you want to place the chart in. If you select a section that the chart cannot be placed in, the cursor will change to a circle with a line through it. If this happens, you have to start the insert chart process over. Once you select a section of the report where the chart will be placed, one of two things will happen:

① The Chart Expert will automatically open.
② A bar chart will be added to the report with several options already selected. If this happens and the default options are not what you need, right-click on the chart and select Chart Expert on the shortcut menu.

The way that the above options are determined is not random. The scenarios below explain under what conditions the Chart Expert will or will not automatically open.

    ① If a chart is added to the report header or footer section of a report that has a group with a summary field, a bar chart based on the group will automatically be added to the report. The Chart Expert will not automatically open.

    ② If a chart is added to the report header or footer section of a report that does not have a group or a group that does not have a summary field, the Chart Expert will open automatically.

    ③ If a report has a cross-tab or OLAP object and it is not selected prior to inserting a chart, the Chart Expert will automatically open.

    ④ If a report has a cross-tab or OLAP object selected prior to inserting a chart, a bar chart based on the data in the cross-tab or OLAP object will be added to a new section of the report.

Like summary fields on the report, the section of the report that a chart is placed in determines the data that will be used to create the chart. If the chart is placed in the report header or footer section, the chart will contain data from the entire report. If the chart is placed in the group header or footer section, the chart will only contain data for the group.

Unless stated otherwise, if the exercise does not create a new report, place a chart object in the report header section of the report and open the Chart Expert after step 1 in each exercise.

When you view a chart on the design tab, you may see fields that you did not select. You will see real data on the preview tab. The chart in the design window does not represent data in the tables that the chart is using. I am telling you this because I do not want you to think that you are losing your mind when you see a chart in the design window, that doesn't display what you are expecting.

Exercise 11.1: Create A Bar Chart

1. Save the L7.7A report as `L11.1 Bar chart`.

2. Delete the existing chart. Select the Side by side bar chart type, then select the Group data layout option, if it is not already selected.

3. Select the Order Date field from the On Change Of drop down list if it is not already selected, then select the Order Amount field in the Show drop down list.

4. Add a major gridline to the Group axis option.

5. Select the Show value Data Points option, then change the Number format to $1. Place the Legend at the bottom of the chart. Your options should look like the ones shown in Figure 11-36.

6. Change the Title to `L11.1 Bar Chart`. Click OK and save the changes. The chart should look like the one shown in Figure 11-37. The chart looks good, but with a few changes, it would look better. Later in this lesson you will learn how to modify a chart.

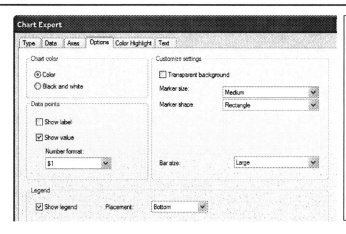

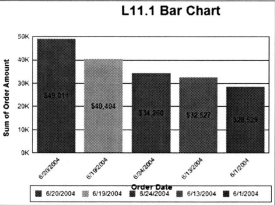

Figure 11-36 Options for the bar chart   **Figure 11-37** L11.1 Bar chart

Exercise 11.1A: Copy A Chart To A Group Section

Earlier you learned that if the same chart is placed in a group section of the report that it will only display data for the group. In this exercise, you will copy the chart that you created in Exercise 11.1 and place the copy in the group footer section of the report.

1. Save the L11.1 report as L11.1A Chart in group footer section.

2. Open the Section expert, click on the group footer section and click the **INSERT** button, then click OK. You should now see a group footer 1b section on the report.

3. Right-click on the chart and select Copy. Right-click and select Paste, then click in the group footer 1b section.

4. Open the Chart Expert for the chart in the group footer section and click on the Data tab. Add the Customer Name field to the first list box, then add the Order Amount field to the Show value(s) list.

5. Clear the Show value option on the Options tab.

6. Change the Title to L11.1A Chart in Group Footer Section.
Change the Subtitle to Customer Orders By Day.
Delete the text in the Group title field. Click OK and save the changes. The chart should look like the one shown in Figure 11-38. At the end of every group on the report, you will see a chart that only contains data for the records in that group. If you didn't want the chart in the report header section, you could delete it.

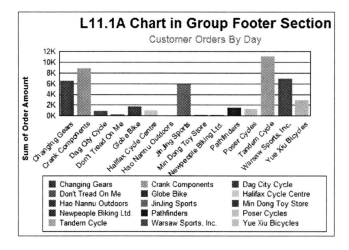

Figure 11-38 L11.1A Chart in group footer section

Exercise 11.2: Create A Line Chart

In this exercise you will create a chart that displays order totals by month.

1. Save the L10.10 report as `L11.2 Line chart.`

2. Select the Line chart type with markers at data points, then select the Group layout option.

3. Select the Sum Order Amount field in the Show drop down list.

4. Place the legend to the right of the chart. Select the large **MARKER SIZE** and the **DIAMOND** Marker shape.

5. Change the Subtitle to `L11.2 Line Chart.` Click OK and save the changes. The chart should look like the one shown in Figure 11-39.

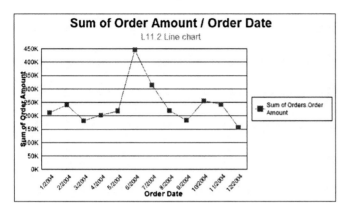

Figure 11-39 L11.2 Line chart

Exercise 11.3: Create An Area Chart

As mentioned earlier, you can add a chart to a report that does not have any data. You will learn how to do that in this exercise by creating a report that charts the sum of last years sales by region.

1. Create a new report and add the Customer table, then save the report as `L11.3 Area chart.`

2. Place a chart object in the report header section. The Chart Expert should open automatically. Select the Stacked Area chart type and check the Use depth effect option.

3. Add the Region and Customer Name fields to the first list box, then add the Last Year's Sales field to the Show value(s) list. The options on the Data tab should look like the one's shown in Figure 11-40.

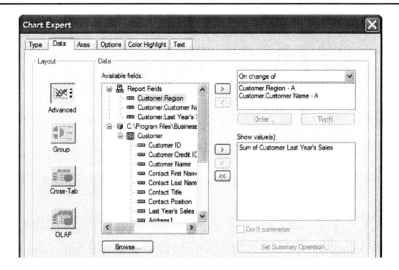

Figure 11-40 Area chart data tab options

4. Add a major gridline to the Group axis option, then change the option to show the legend at the bottom of the chart.

5. Change the Subtitle to `L11.3 Area Chart.` Delete the Group title and click OK.

Add The Selection Criteria

In addition to being able to create a report that does not have any other information besides a chart, you can also select the records that you want the chart to be based on.

1. Open the Select Expert, select the Region field and click OK.

2. Select the **IS ONE OF** value, then add the following regions: CA, NY, PA and BC. Click OK and save the changes. The chart should look like the one shown in Figure 11-41.

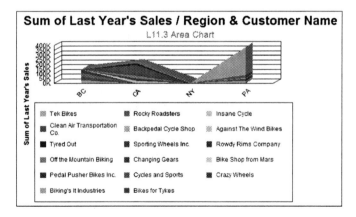

Figure 11-41 L11.3 Area chart

Exercise 11.4: Create A Pie Chart

In this exercise you will create a chart that displays the order totals for 2004, by quarter.

1. Save the L6.11 report as `L11.4 Pie chart.`

2. Select the Pie chart type and check the Use depth effect option.

3. Check the Show label and Show value options. Change the Number format to 1. Select **BOTH** for the Legend layout option.

4. Change the Title to `L11.4 Pie Chart,` then add the Footnote `2004 Orders By Quarter` and make the footnote italic. Click OK and save the changes. The chart should look like the one shown in Figure 11-42. The number under the date in the chart is the number of orders for that quarter.

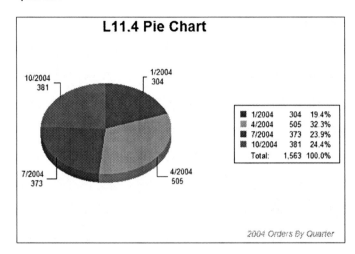

Figure 11-42 L11.4 Pie chart

Exercise 11.4A: Detach A Slice Of A Pie Chart

One way to emphasize a slice of a pie chart is to pull it away from the rest of the chart. This is sometimes referred to as "Exploding" a slice of a pie chart.

1. Save the L11.4 report as `L11.4A Explode a slice of the pie chart.`

2. Right-click on the chart and select Chart Expert.

3. Click on the Options tab and check the option **DETACH PIE SLICE,** then select the **LARGEST SLICE** option.

4. Change the Title to `L11.4A Explode a slice of a pie chart.` Click OK and save the changes. The chart should look like the one shown in Figure 11-43.

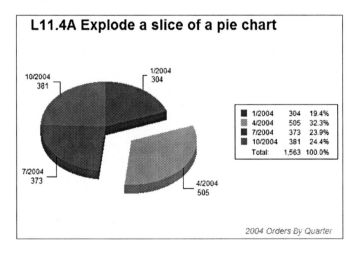

Figure 11-43 L11.4A Explode a slice of the pie chart

Exercise 11.5: Create A Doughnut Chart

In this exercise you will modify the pie chart that you created in Exercise 11.4 so that it will be a doughnut chart.

1. Save the L11.4 report as `L11.5 Doughnut chart`.

2. Select the Doughnut chart type.

3. Change the Title to `L11.5 Doughnut Chart`. Click OK and save the changes. The chart should look like the one shown in Figure 11-44.

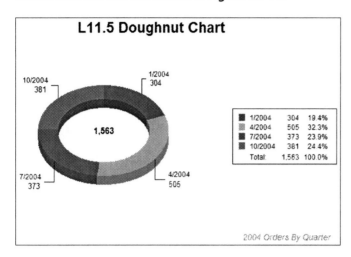

Figure 11-44 L11.5 Doughnut chart

 You can detach a slice of a doughnut chart, just like you can in a pie chart.

Exercise 11.6: Create A 3D Riser Chart

In this exercise you will create a chart that shows last years sales for three states (regions) that are over a certain dollar amount. In order to do that the report will need selection criteria.

1. Save the L11.3 report as `L11.6 3D Riser chart`.

2. Use the Select Expert to create the criteria shown in Figure 11-45, then refresh the data.

    {Customer.Region} in ["MA", "PA", "WI"] and
    {Customer.Last Year's Sales} >= $35000.00

Figure 11-45 Selection criteria

3. Select the 3D Riser bar chart type.

4. Display major gridlines for all axes. Show minor gridlines for the Data axis. Clear the Auto Scale option.

5. Change the Title to `L11.6 3D Riser Chart`.
Change the Subtitle to `Last Year's Sales >= 35,000`. Click OK and save the changes. The chart should look like the one shown in Figure 11-46.

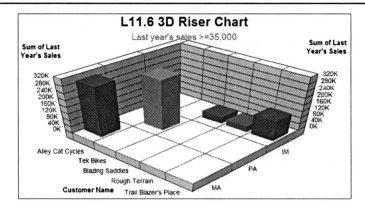

Figure 11-46 L11.6 3D Riser chart

Exercise 11.7: Create A 3D Surface Chart

In this exercise you will create a chart that shows a count of orders and order total amount by sales rep.

1. Save the L6.13 report as `L11.7 3D Surface chart.`

2. Select the 3D Surface honeycomb surface chart type, then select the Advanced layout option.

3. Add the Employee ID field to the first list box, then add the Order Amount and Group 1 Count Of Orders.Order ID fields to the Show value(s) list.

4. Add a major gridline to all axes.

5. Change the Viewing angle on the Options tab to **MAX VIEW**.

6. Add the Title `L11.7 3D Surface Chart.`
   Add the Subtitle `Sum of orders by Sales Rep.`
   Add the Footnote `For 2004.` Click OK and save the changes. The chart should look like the one shown in Figure 11-47.

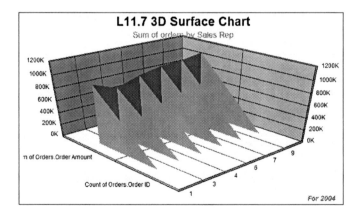

Figure 11-47 L11.7 3D Surface chart

Exercise 11.8: Create An XY Scatter Chart

In this exercise you will create a chart that plots the number of orders in 2004 by month and total dollar amount.

1. Save the L6.7 report as `L11.8 XY Scatter chart.`

2. Select the XY Scatter chart type, then select the Advanced layout option.

3. Add the Order Date field to the first list box, then add the Group 1 Distinct Count Of Orders.Order ID and Order Amount fields to the Show value(s) list.

4. Change the Marker shape to **DIAMOND**.

5. Change the Title to L11.8 XY Scatter Chart.
    Add the Subtitle 2004 Orders By Month. Click OK and save the changes. The chart should look like the one shown in Figure 11-48. As you can see, the markers are not diamond shape. This option does not seem to work on the Chart Expert. You will learn how to fix this in Exercise 11.23. If your report has diamond markers, there was a software update after this book was published.

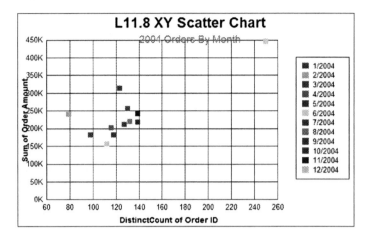

Figure 11-48 L11.8 XY Scatter chart

Exercise 11.8A: Show The Bottom 20% Of Orders

In the exercise that you just completed, the chart plotted the data for all 12 months. If the marketing department wanted to create a campaign to increase sales in the months that had the lowest number of sales, it could be difficult to tell which months fall into that category. If the chart was modified to only display the months that are in the bottom 20% of sales based on the total order amount by month, the chart would be easier for the marketing department to use.

You have already created a report that displayed the top five orders for a month. To create a report for the bottom 20% is very similar.

1. Save the L11.8 report as L11.8A Bottom 20 percent chart.

2. Open the Chart Expert and click on the Data tab.

3. Click on the Order Date field, then click the **TOP N** button.

4. Open the Group Sort drop down list and select **BOTTOM PERCENTAGE**. Change the Percentage field to 20 and check the **INCLUDE TIES** option. The options that are shown in Figure 11-49 will display the months that are in the bottom 20%, based on the number of orders placed that month. Click OK.

5. Change the Title to L11.8A Bottom 20% Of Orders.
    Delete the Subtitle.
    Change the Group title to Number of orders.
    Change the Data title to Total monthly order amount. Click OK and save the changes. The chart should look like the one shown in Figure 11-50.

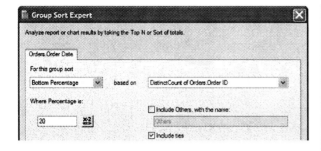

Figure 11-49 Group Sort Expert options

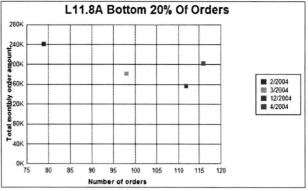

Figure 11-50 L11.8A Bottom 20 percent chart

 If you create a Top N report and do not add the records on the report that do not meet the Top N criteria to the "Others" group option, any grand total fields that are placed in the report footer will include totals for all records that meet the report criteria, whether or not they appear on the report. This means that if the records that do not meet the Top N criteria are not added to the "Others" option, the report grand totals will not be accurate. This may not be what you want. If you only want the grand totals to include records that print on the report, in this case the Top N records, you have to create running total fields and place them in the report footer instead of summary fields. [See Lesson 13, Running Totals]

Exercise 11.9: Create A Radar Chart

In this exercise you will create a chart that plots the order totals in 2004 by quarter.

1. Save the L6.11 report as `L11.9 Radar chart`.

2. Select the Radar chart type, then select the Group layout option, if it is not already selected.

3. Select the Sum of Orders.Order Amount field from the Show drop down list.

4. Check the Show value option, then select the circle Marker shape.

5. Change the Title to `L11.9 Radar Chart`.
    Add the Subtitle `Sum Of 2004 Orders By Quarter`. Click OK and save the changes.
    The chart should look like the one shown in Figure 11-51. This is a good example of not selecting the appropriate chart type for the data. This chart is somewhat hard to read.

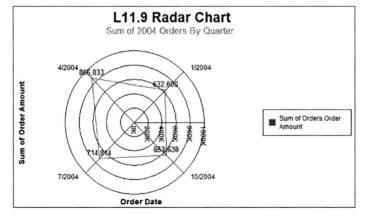

Figure 11-51 L11.9 Radar chart

Exercise 11.10: Create A Bubble Chart

In this exercise you will create a chart that plots the orders between 6/1/2004 and 6/15/2004. Even though the Bubble chart is similar to the XY Scatter chart, it requires three fields in the Show value(s) list.

1. Save the L7.2 report as `L11.10 Bubble chart`.

2. Change the Order Date selection criteria to between 6/1/2004 and 6/15/2004, then delete the Order Amount criteria and refresh the data.

3. Change the chart type to Bubble.

4. Add the Order Date to the first list box, then add the Order Amount field to the Show value(s) list.

5. Add the Order ID field to the Show value(s) list. Click on the field, then click the Set Summary Operation button. Change the summary type to Count and click OK.

6. Add the Order amount field to the Show value(s) list again. Click on the field, then click the Set Summary Operation button. Change the summary type to Average and click OK.

7. Add a major gridline to the Group axis option.

8. Change the Title to `L11.10 Bubble Chart`.
   Add the Subtitle `For Orders between 6/1/2004 and 6/15/2004`, then click OK.
   Save the changes and refresh the data. The chart should look like the one shown in Figure 11-52.

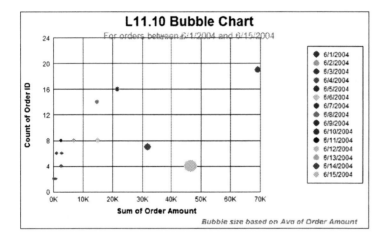

Figure 11-52 L11.10 Bubble chart

Exercise 11.11: Create A Stock Chart

The stock report that you will create will show the average order amount for five regions and the largest order in each region. Stock charts plot minimum and maximum values. The average value will be used as the minimum value and the largest order amount will be used as the maximum value.

The reason that I am using the average value for the minimum is because the lowest value would touch the bottom of the chart which defeats the purpose of the exercise of showing you how a stock chart really does look different then a bar chart.

Create The Selection Criteria

1. Create a new report and add the Customer and Orders tables to the report.

2. Click on the Links tab. The tables should be joined on the Customer ID field. If they aren't, create the link by clicking on the Customer ID field in the Orders table and dragging it to the Customer ID field in the Customer table. To make sure that link is correct, right-click on the link between the tables and select **LINK OPTIONS**. You will see the dialog box shown in Figure 11-53. Make sure that the link is exactly like the one illustrated.

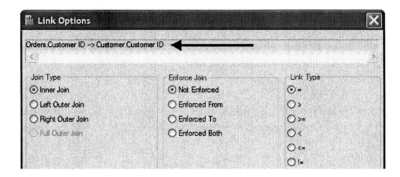

Figure 11-53 Link Options dialog box

3. Click OK twice to close both dialog boxes. If prompted to refresh the data, click OK.

4. Create selection criteria for the Region field to only include customers in the following regions: MA, PA, AL, ID, WI.

5. Save the report as L11.11 Stock chart.

Create The Chart

1. Add a chart object to the report header section and select the High-Low stock chart.

2. Add the Region field to the first list box.

3. Add the Order Amount field to the Show value(s) list. Click on the field, then click the Set Summary Operation button. Change the summary type to Maximum and click OK.

4. Add the Order Amount field to the Show value(s) list again. Click on the field, then click the Set Summary Operation button. Change the summary type to Average and click OK.

5. Check the Show value option. Do not display a legend.

6. Change the Title to L11.11 Stock Chart.
   Add the Subtitle Avg & Max order amounts for 5 states. Click OK and save the changes. The chart should look like the one shown in Figure 11-54.

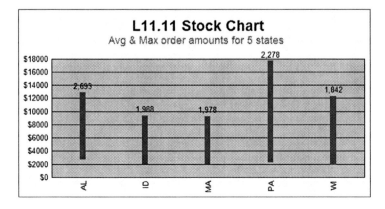

Figure 11-54 L11.11 Stock chart

Exercise 11.12: Create A Numeric Axis Chart

In this exercise you will create a chart that displays the sum of orders for one company during a specific date range. You will use the options on the Chart Sort Order dialog box to determine the frequency of the On Change Of option.

Create The Report

1. Create a new report and add the Customer and Orders tables to the report. Make sure the tables are linked liked they were in Exercise 11.11. Save the report as `L11.12 Numeric Axis chart`.

2. Create selection criteria for the Order Date field. The dates should be between 11/1/2004 and 11/30/2004, then create selection criteria that limits the report to only display information for the customer, To The Limit Biking Co.

3. Add the Order Date and Order Amount fields to the details section, then delete the date field from the page header section of the report if it's there.

4. Change the format of the Order Date field to XX/XX/XXXX, then sort the Order Date field in ascending order.

Create The Chart

1. Add a chart object to the report header.

2. Select the Numeric Axis - Date axis bar chart type, then select the Use depth effect option.

3. Add the Order Date field to the first list box. Click on the field, then click the **ORDER** button. Make sure the last option on the Chart Sort Order dialog box is set to **FOR EACH DAY** and click OK.

4. Add the Order Amount field to the Show value(s) list.

5. Add a minor gridline to the Data axis option.

6. Check the Show value option, then select the $1 Number format.

7. Change the Title to `L11.12 Numeric Axis Chart`. Add the subtitle `To The Limit Biking Co - Nov 2004`. Click OK and save the changes. The chart should look like the one shown in Figure 11-55.

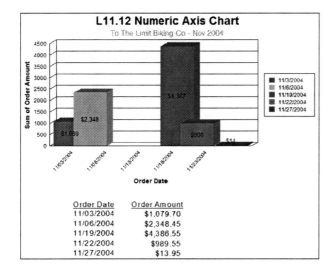

Figure 11-55 L11.12 Numeric Axis chart

Exercise 11.13: Create A Gauge Chart

In Lesson 10 you read how to create a report that displayed the words True or False in a Boolean field based on the employees salary. [See Lesson 10, Boolean Formulas] This was done to keep the employees actual salary private. In this exercise you will create a chart that will plot how many employees salaries are greater than 50K.

1. Save the L10.6 With a Boolean suppression formula report as `L11.13 Gauge chart`. (This L10.6 report is one that I created. If you haven't downloaded the files from the web site, see Lesson 1, Create A Folder For Your Reports)

2. Select the Gauge chart type.

3. Add the **BOOLEAN_STYLE** formula field to the first list box, then add the Employee ID field to the Show value(s) list.

4. Click on the Employee ID field and click the Set Summary Operation button. Change the summary type to Count and click OK.

5. Change the Title to `L11.13 Gauge Chart`.
   Add the Subtitle `Employee salary over 50K`. Click OK and save the changes. The chart should look like the one shown in Figure 11-56. The company has 15 employees. If you look at the needles on the chart, you will see that when added together, they equal 15.

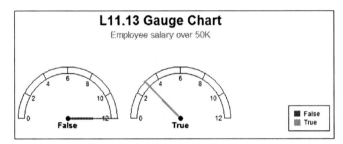

Figure 11-56 L11.13 Gauge chart

Exercise 11.14: Create A Gantt Chart

In Lesson 9 you created a report that calculated how many days it took to ship the customer orders. Gantt charts require a start and end date. In this exercise you will use the order date as the start date and the ship date as the end date.

The L9.9 Calculate order processing time report currently only has criteria that the order date is greater than or equal to a specific date. The Gantt chart would not be readable if all of the records that are currently on the report were displayed on the chart. To make the chart readable, you will select a few Order ID numbers to display on the chart.

1. Save the L9.9 report as `L11.14 Gantt chart`.

2. Create selection criteria that limits the report to the following Order ID numbers from the Orders Detail table: 1, 1015, 1020, 1069 and 1090.

3. Add a chart object to the report header and select the Gantt chart layout and the Use depth effect option.

4. Select the **FOR EACH RECORD** option from the drop down list on the Data tab, then add the Customer Name field to the first list box.

5. Add the Order Date and Ship Date fields to the Show value(s) list.

6. Add the Title `L11.14 Gantt Chart`. Add the Subtitle `Delay in shipping`.
   Click OK. Save the changes and refresh the data. The chart should look like the one shown in Figure 11-57.

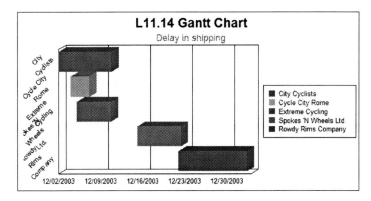

Figure 11-57 L11.14 Gantt chart

Exercise 11.15: Create A Funnel Chart
In this exercise you will create a chart that will display the daily order totals for the top five order days in June 2004.

1. Save the L7.7A report as `L11.15 Funnel chart`.

2. Delete the existing chart and add a chart object to the report header section.

3. Select the Funnel chart type, then select the Advanced layout option.

4. Add the Order Date field to the first list box, then add the Order Amount field to the Show value(s) list.

5. Change the Legend layout option to **BOTH**.

6. Change the Title to `L11.15 Funnel Chart`.
   Add the Subtitle `With total order amounts by day`.
   Add the Footnote `For the top 5 order days in June 2004`. Click OK and save the changes. The chart should look like the one shown in Figure 11-58. Leave the report open to complete the next exercise.

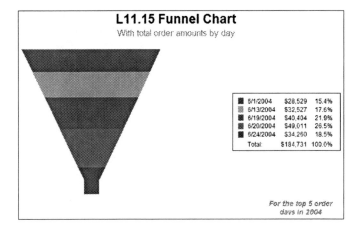

Figure 11-58 L11.15 Funnel chart

Exercise 11.15A: Modify The Funnel Chart

In the previous exercise, the legend displayed the daily order total and the percent. The chart may be easier to read if it also had information. In this exercise you will display the order date and the number of orders per day next to each bar on the chart.

1. Save the L11.15 report as `L11.15A Modified Funnel chart`.

2. Open the Chart Expert for the existing chart.

3. Delete the Order Amount field from the Show value(s) list and add the Order ID field to the Show value(s) list.

4. Click on the Sum Of Orders.Order ID field, then click the Set Summary Operation button. Change the summary type to Count and click OK.

5. Check the Show label and Show value options, then change the Legend layout option to Percentage.

6. Change the Title to `L11.15A Funnel Chart`.
   Change the Subtitle to `With # of orders per day`. Click OK and save the changes. The chart should look like the one shown in Figure 11-59.

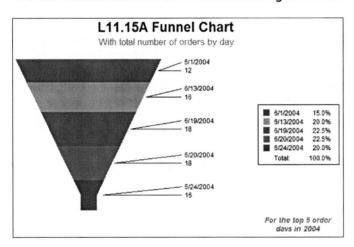

Figure 11-59 L11.15A Modified Funnel chart

Exercise 11.16: Create A Histogram Chart

In this exercise you will create a chart that shows how many orders per day were placed in 2004.

1. Save the L6.13 report as `L11.16 Histogram chart`.

2. Select the Histogram chart type, then select the Advanced layout option.

3. Add the Order Date to the first list box, then add the Order ID field to the Show value(s) list.

4. Click on the Sum of Orders.Order ID field, then click the Set Summary button and change the summary type to Distinct Count. Click OK.

5. Check the Show value option and change the Number format to 1.

6. Change the Title to `L11.16 Histogram Chart`.
   Change the Subtitle to `Count of orders per day`.
   Change the Data title to `Number of orders`. Click OK and save the changes. The chart should look like the one shown in Figure 11-60. As you learned earlier, a histogram chart does not display all of the data. A problem that I have noticed is that it is often difficult to know what data is actually being displayed.

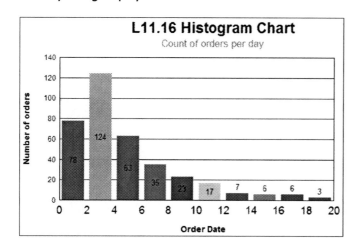

Figure 11-60 L11.16 Histogram chart

Exercise 11.17: Create Charts From Cross-Tab Data

Charts that are created from cross-tab data are often easier to create because the data has already been summarized. In this exercise you will create three charts and save them in the same report. Often, cross-tab data is stored in the report header. I find it easier to create additional report header sections and place each report in it's own section. That keeps the charts from overlapping when the report is viewed or printed.

Add More Report Header Sections

1. Save the L7.9 report as `L11.17 Cross-Tab data charts`.

2. Open the Section Expert and add three more report header sections.

Create The Quantity Sold By Product Type Chart

1. Add a chart object to the report header b section, then select the Side by side bar chart type, the Horizontal position and the Use depth effect option.

2. Make sure that the On Change Of option on the Cross-Tab layout window has the Product Type Name field selected. The Subdivided By field should be set to None and the Show drop down list should have the Quantity field selected.

3. Check the Show value option on the Options tab.

4. Change the Title to `Qty Sold By Product Type`.
   Add the Footnote `Report Header B`.
   Change the Group title to `Product Type`.
   Change the Date title to `Qty Sold`. Click OK and save the changes. The chart should look like the one shown in Figure 11-61.

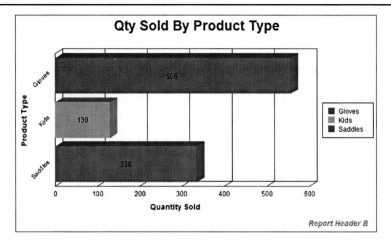

Figure 11-61 L11.17 Quantity sold by product type chart (Report Header B)

Create The Quantity Sold By Product Type By Sales Rep Chart

The chart that you just created provides a high level overview of how many of each product type was sold. The numbers shown, represent the totals across the bottom of the cross-tab. [See Lesson 7, Figure 7-34] The chart that you will create in this part of the exercise will display how many of each product type was sold by each sales rep.

1. Add a chart object to the report header c section, then select the Stacked bar chart type, the Horizontal position and the Use depth effect option.

2. Select the Employee Last Name field from the Subdivided By drop down list on the Cross-Tab data layout window.

3. Add a major gridline to the Group axis option.

4. Change the Title to `Product Type & Qty Sold By Sales Rep`.
   Add the Footnote `Report Header C`.
   Change the Group title to `Product Type`.
   Change the Date title to `Qty Sold`. Click OK and save the changes. The chart should look like the one shown in Figure 11-62. What you will notice is that each block on the chart is a running total, meaning that the sales rep Dodsworth did not have 186 glove sales. Instead, the sales rep sold the difference between 186 and 85 gloves.

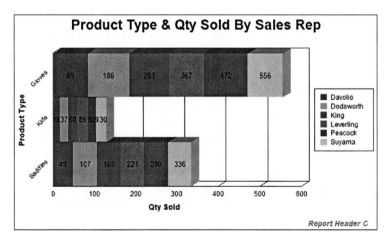

Figure 11-62 L11.17 Product type & Quantity Sold By Sales Rep chart (Report Header C)

Create The Percent Of Quantity Sold Chart

The chart that you will create in this part of the exercise will display the total quantity of products each sales rep sold and what percent of the total product quantity their sales represent.

1. Add a chart object to the report header d section, then select the Pie chart type and the Use depth effect option.

2. Add the Employee Last Name field to the first list box on the Advanced tab, then add the Quantity field to the Show value(s) list and change the summary type to Count.

3. Check the Show label and Show value options, then change the Legend layout option to Percentage. Explode the largest slice of the pie.

4. Change the Title to `Percent Of Qty Sold`.
   Add the Subtitle `The #'s on the chart represent the qty`.
   Add the Footnote `Report Header D`. Click OK and save the changes. The chart is on page 2 and should look like the one shown in Figure 11-63.

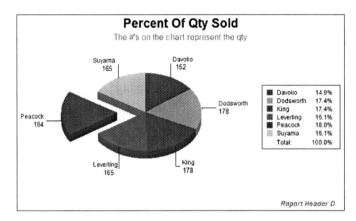

Figure 11-63 L11.17 Percent of Quantity Sold chart (Report Header D)

Exercise 11.18: Create Charts From OLAP Data

Creating charts based on data in OLAP cubes is similar to creating charts based on data in a cross-tab. In this exercise you will create three charts and save them in the same report, like you did in the cross-tab exercise.

Add More Report Header Sections

1. Save the L7.11 report as `L11.18 OLAP charts`.

2. Open the Section Expert and add three more report header sections.

Understanding OLAP Data Levels

When you create charts that use OLAP data, you will see the word "Level" a lot. I looked but didn't see anything in the Help file that explained what the levels are, so I figured that I would explain it here, so that when you are creating OLAP data charts on your own, you will be able to know which level to select to create the chart that you need. The information in parenthesis refers to the L7.11 OLAP report.

Level 0 contains the grand totals that are at the top of the OLAP report (the Year Total section).
Level 1 contains the totals (by month).
Level 2 contains the totals (by state).

The dimension that you select in the On Change Of drop down list is the data that is plotted on the X axis across the bottom of the chart. The dimension that you select in the Subdivided By drop down list is the dimension that has the totals that will appear on each element of the chart.

Create The Monthly Product Total Amount Chart

In this part of the exercise you will create a chart that shows the monthly sales amount for three products for all customers in the US.

1. Add a chart object to the report header b section, then select the Bar chart type and the Use depth effect option.

2. Open the On Change of drop down list and select Monthly, Level 1, then open the Subdivided By drop down list and select Product, Level 1.

3. Check the Show value option and select the $1 Number format.

4. Change the Title to `Monthly Product Totals`.
   Add the Subtitle `All customers in the US`. Click OK and save the changes. The chart is on the last page of the report and should look like the one shown in Figure 11-64.

The chart shows the product totals by month, which is Level 1. If you look at the grand total row for January in the report, [See Lesson 7, Figure 7-54] you will see the same totals that are displayed on the first three bars on the chart. If you scroll down the report to the February and March sections of the report, you will see the totals that are on the other bars are on the chart.

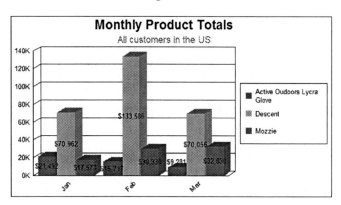

Figure 11-64 L11.18 OLAP Monthly Product Totals chart

Create The Monthly Product Total Amount For Customers In CA Chart

In this part of the exercise you will create the same chart that you just created. The difference is that you will limit the totals to sales in CA.

1. Complete steps 1 and 2 from the chart that you just created and place this chart in section c.

2. Click the **OTHER DIMENSION** button, then click on the Current Customer = USA dimension and click the **SELECT A MEMBER VALUE** button.

On the Member Selector window, you can see that currently all customers in the US will appear on the report.
If you selected a company name, the totals that appeared on the chart would be for that company only, as shown in Figure 11-65. This chart shows that the customer (Changing Gears) only purchased products in February.

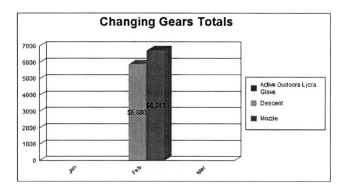

Figure 11-65 Monthly product totals for one customer

3. Click on the state, CA and click OK. The dimension on the Format Other Dimensions dialog box should be Customer = CA. Click OK to close the Dimensions dialog box.

4. Check the Show value option and select the $1 Number format.

5. Change the Title to `Monthly Product Totals`.
   Add the Subtitle `Customers in CA`. Click OK and save the changes. The chart should look like the one shown in Figure 11-66.

Figure 11-66 L11.18 OLAP Monthly product totals for customers in CA

Create The Monthly Product Total Amount Chart

In last part of this exercise you will create a pie chart that displays the total amount of sales in CA for the month of February.

1. Add a chart to the report header d section, then select the pie chart type and Use depth effect option.

2. Open the On Change Of drop down list and select Product, Level 1.

3. Open the Format Other Dimensions dialog box. Change the Customer dimension to CA, then change the Monthly dimension to Feb. You should have the options selected that are shown in Figure 11-67. Click OK.

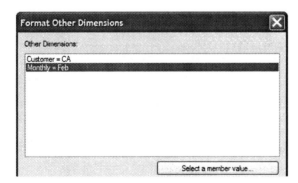

Figure 11-67 Format Other Dimensions dialog box options

4. Detach the largest slice of the pie, then check the Show value option and select the $1 Number format.

5. Change the Title to `CA Product Totals For Feb`. Click OK and save the changes. The chart should look like the one shown in Figure 11-68.

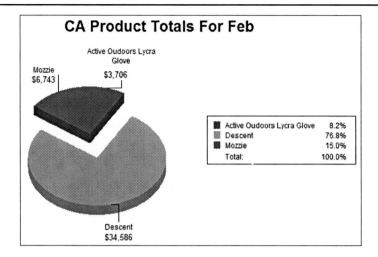

Figure 11-68 L11.18 CA product totals for Feb

 If the OLAP grid is in a report header or footer section, you cannot move the chart to a group header or footer section.

Exercise 11.19: Create A Color Highlighting Chart

In this exercise you will create a chart that will change the color of the bars on the chart to red, if the delay in ship time is greater than or equal to seven days or yellow if the delay in ship time is between four and six days. To reduce the number of order days to something that will make the chart readable, you will add selection criteria to the report.

1. Save the L9.9 report as L11.19 Highlighted chart.

2. Add selection criteria to the report so that only orders with an order date between 12/02/2003 and 12/05/2003 will appear on the report.

3. Add selection criteria to the report to only display orders that have a delay in days to ship greater than or equal to two, then refresh the data.

4. Select the Side by side bar chart type and the Use depth effect option.

5. Add the Order ID field to the first list box, then add the Sum of Delay in Days To Ship formula to the Show value(s) list.

6. Change the Title to L11.19 Color Highlighting Chart.
Add the Subtitle Yellow = 4-6 day delay, Red = 7+ day delay.
Add the Footnote Orders between 12/2/2003 & 12/5/2003.
Change the Group title to Order Number.
Change the Data title to Delay In Days To Ship.
Leave the Chart Expert open to complete the next part of the exercise.

Add The Color Highlighting To The Chart

In this part of the exercise you will create the criteria that will change the colors of the bars on the chart to red or yellow depending on the value in the Delay in Days To Ship field.

1. Click on the Color Highlight tab, then click the New button.

2. Open the first drop down list and select the Delay in Days To Ship field, then open the second drop down list and select Is greater than or equal to. Type a 7 in the last field.

3. Select Red as the Format color, then click the New button.

4. Open the first drop down list and select the Delay in Days To Ship field, then open the second drop down list and select Is between. Type a 4 in the first field and a 6 in the last field.

5. Select Yellow as the Format color. Click OK and save the changes. The chart should look like the one shown in Figure 11-69.

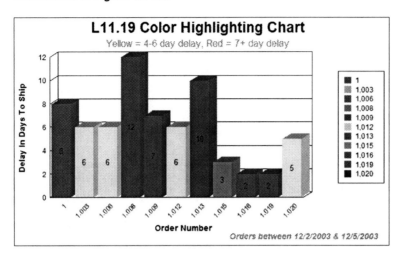

Figure 11-69 L11.19 Highlighted chart

Formatting And Editing Charts

There are a variety of techniques available to format and edit charts as a whole or individual parts of a chart, like the legend and axis titles. The majority of these options are in one of two places: the Chart Options dialog box or the Format Series dialog box. Other options are on the Chart menu.

Some of the formatting techniques that you will learn are resizing a chart or a specific element on the chart, changing the colors of elements on the chart, add color to the background of a chart and how to apply a template to a chart.

Zooming In And Out

Depending on the level of formatting intricacy, you may find it helpful to zoom in or out on the chart while you are modifying it. There are two ways to access the Zoom In option from the preview window as discussed below. Once you select the Zoom In option, the mouse pointer will change to a magnifying glass with a plus sign.

① Right-click on a blank space on the chart and select Zoom In.
② Click on a blank space on the chart, then Chart ⇒ Zoom In.

The Zoom options only work with bar and line charts.

The zoom feature in charts does not work the same way in Crystal Reports that it does in other software packages where you can click on the chart to zoom in or out. Instead, once you select the Zoom In option, you have to draw a box on the portion of the chart that you want to zoom in on. To zoom out, right-click on the chart, select Zoom Out, then click anyplace on the chart.

When you are finished zooming in or out, you have to select the option **SELECT MODE** from the shortcut menu or from the Chart menu. Doing this will change the mouse pointer back to the default, so that you can continue working.

After changing the mouse pointer back to the default, I was expecting the chart to go back to its original size. I didn't find that to be the case. To put the chart back to its original size, I click the Undo button once for each time that I zoomed in on the chart.

The **PAN** option is only available when a chart has been zoomed in on. This option allows you to scroll left or right on the chart.

Exercise 11.20: Resizing Charts

Charts and objects have the same sizing handles that images have. Like images, you can drag the chart to another section of the report or to a different location in the section that it is currently in. You can resize the chart manually or you can use the options on the Size and Position dialog box that you have learned about in Lesson 4. There are two ways to open the Size and Position dialog box as discussed below.

   ① Right-click on a blank space on the chart and select **SIZE AND POSITION**.
   ② Click on a blank space on the chart, then Format ⇒ Size and Position.

There are two options for resizing charts. You can resize the entire chart or you can resize individual elements on the chart. When you want to resize the entire chart, make sure that individual elements on the chart are not selected.

Resize The Entire Chart

If the default size of the chart is too small or too large, you can resize the chart by following the steps below.

1. Save the L11.15 report as `L11.20 Resized chart`.

2. Click on a blank space in the chart, then place the mouse pointer in the lower right corner of the chart and drag it to the 6 inch mark on the ruler.

 You can place the mouse pointer anyplace on the highlighted border of the chart to resize the chart in any direction that you need.

Resize One Object On The Chart

As you saw earlier in Figure 11-58, the text in the footnote was cut off. In this part of the exercise, you will resize the footnote.

1. Click on a blank space in the footnote object. (**Hint**: If the chart is not already selected, you have to click once to select the chart, then click again to select the footnote object.)

2. Place the mouse pointer on the top portion of the border and drag the frame up until you can see all of the text clearly in the frame. Save the changes. The chart should look like the one shown in Figure 11-70. You should now be able to see all of the content in the footnote.

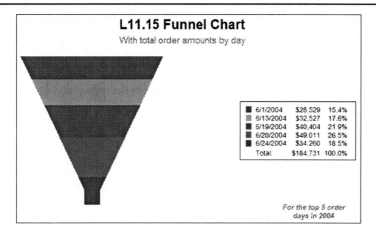

Figure 11-70 L11.20 Resized chart

Exercise 11.21: Use The Chart Expert Shortcut Menu Options

In Exercise 11.1A you placed a chart in the group footer section of the report. If you right-click on a chart in a group section on the preview window, when you select the Chart Expert option you will see the shortcut menu shown in Figure 11-71.

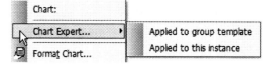

Figure 11-71 Chart Expert shortcut menu options

The **APPLIED TO GROUP TEMPLATE** option will allow you to apply the changes that you are about to make on the Chart Expert to all charts in all of the groups in the report.

The **APPLIED TO THIS INSTANCE** option allows you to only apply the changes that you are about to make to the group chart that you have selected. Remember that the preview window displays every occurrence of a chart that is in a group section.

Add Charts To The Report

The report that you will modify already has one group for the months. You need to create another group so that you can see how the options on the Chart Expert shortcut menu work. The group that you will create will be for the sales reps.

1. Save the L6.7 report as L11.21 Group chart changes.

2. Insert ⇒ Group. Open the first drop down list, select the Employee Last Name field and click OK.

3. Copy the three summary fields in the group footer order date section to the group footer last name section and save the changes.

Add Two Charts To The Report

1. Add a pie chart to the order date group header section.

2. Make the Group 1 Name field smaller, then make the chart smaller. Move the chart closer to the Group 1 Name field.

3. Change the Title to Monthly Order Amounts By Order Date. Delete the Subtitle. Click OK and save the changes. The chart should look like the one shown in Figure 11-72.

4. Add a bar chart to the last name group header section.

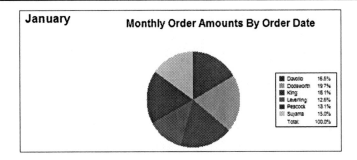

Figure 11-72 L11.21 Monthly orders by order date chart

5. Make the Group 2 Name field smaller, then make the chart smaller. Move the chart closer to the Group 2 Name field.

6. Add the Last Name field to the first list box on the Data tab. Add the Group 2 Distinct Count Order ID field and the Group 2 Percentage Order Amount field to Show value(s) list.

7. Add the Title `Sales Rep Totals By Order Date`. Click OK and save the changes. The chart should look like the one shown in Figure 11-73.

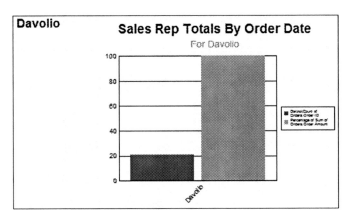

Figure 11-73 L11.21 Sales Rep totals by order date chart

Modify The Group Header 1 Charts

In this part of the exercise you will modify one of the group charts on the preview window and apply the change to all charts in the group.

1. Right-click on the chart for January in the order date group section (group header 1) and select Chart Expert ⇒ Applied to group template.

2. Change the location of the legend to the bottom of the chart. Click OK and save the changes. When you look at all of the charts in the group header 1 section (the charts for January, February, March etc.), you will see that the legend is now at the bottom of the chart as shown in Figure 11-74.

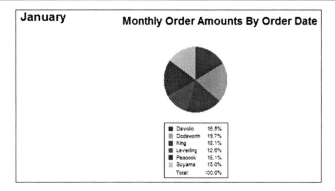

Figure 11-74 L11.21 chart with legend moved

Modify The Group Header 2 Charts

In this part of the exercise you will modify the chart for a particular sales rep.

1. Right-click on the chart for the sales rep whose last name is Dodsworth at the top of page 2. Select Chart Expert ⇒ Applied to this instance.

2. Check the Show Value option. Click OK and save the changes. The chart for Dodsworth should look like the one shown in Figure 11-75. Notice the values on the bars. The chart for Davolio should look like the one shown in Figure 11-76. This chart was not changed.

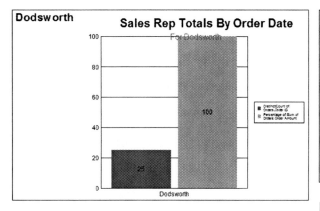

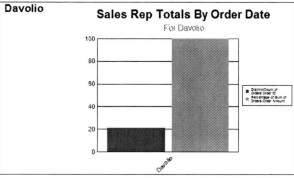

Figure 11-76 L11.21 Modified chart for Davolio

Figure 11-75 L11.21 Modified chart for Dodsworth

More Chart Types

As mentioned earlier in this lesson, there are more chart types then the ones on the Type tab on the Chart Expert. If you want to apply a different chart type, follow the steps below.

1. Right-click on the chart in a report that you want to change and select **LOAD TEMPLATE**. You should see the dialog box shown in Figure 11-77.

 You will not see the Load Template option if the **CUSTOM CHARTING** option was not installed when Crystal Reports was installed. If this is the case, you can run the setup again and install this option.

2. Click on a category on the left to view the chart types, then select the chart that you want on the right and click OK.

3. Customize the chart as needed.

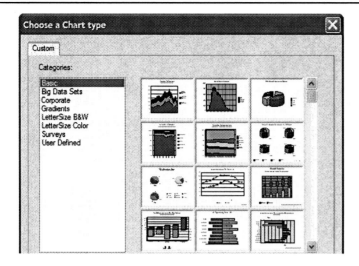

Figure 11-77 Choose a Chart type dialog box

Trendlines

Trendlines are added to a chart to better illustrate trends in data. They are often applied to bar charts. To add trendlines to a bar chart, select one of the options below. You will see the Trendlines dialog box shown in Figure 11-78. Select the type of trendline that you want from the **AVAILABLE TYPES** list and move it to the Show Trendlines list and click OK.

① Right-click on a bar in the chart and select Trendlines.
② Click on a bar in the chart, then Chart ⇒ Trendlines.

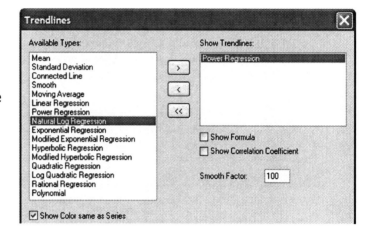

Figure 11-78 Trendlines dialog box

Exercise 11.22: Using The Underlay Following Sections Option

As you learned in Lesson 10, this option will let you place the content in one section of the report next to the content in the section below it. In this exercise you will apply this option so that the chart will print next to the data that it represents. This is often used with charts that are in the group header section of a report so that the records in the details section will print next to the chart.

The **UNDERLAY FOLLOWING SECTIONS** option on the Section Expert is better suited for reports that do not have a lot of fields in the details section. If you cannot get the chart and the fields in the details section to fit, you can select the landscape print option to have more space across the page.

In Exercise 11.1A you copied a chart to the group footer section. You will modify this report and apply the Underlay option to the group header section.

1. Save the L11.1A report as `L11.22 Chart with underlay option`.

2. Delete the group name field in the group header section.

3. Drag the chart in the group footer 1b section to the group header section and place it as far left as possible.

4. Resize the chart so that it ends at the 3.5 inch mark on the ruler.

5. Change the Title to L11.22 Chart With Underlay Option.

6. Move the fields in the details and group footer 1a sections over to the right so that they start to the right of the chart as shown in Figure 11-79.

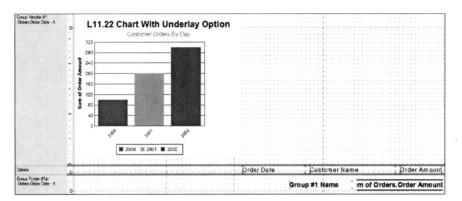

Figure 11-79 Details and group footer fields moved

7. Open the Section Expert and apply the **UNDERLAY FOLLOWING SECTIONS** option to the group header section. Delete the group footer 1b section. Click OK and save the changes. The chart should look like the one shown in Figure 11-80.

 If there is information in the group header section that you do not want to include in the underlay, create another group header section and place the chart in the new group header section as shown in Figure 11-81. You would still apply the underlay option to the group header section with the chart. The report would look like the one shown in Figure 11-82. Notice that the information in the first group header section did not move.

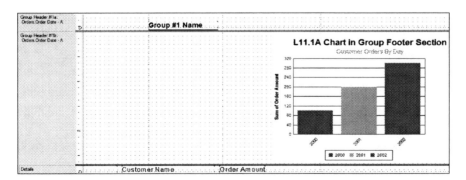

Figure 11-80 L11.22 Chart with the Underlay option applied

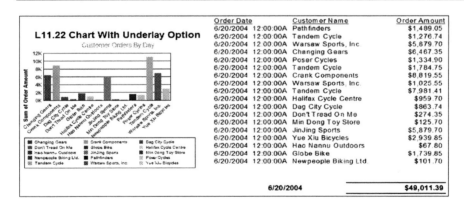

Figure 11-81 L11.22 Sample report layout for the chart in it's own group header section

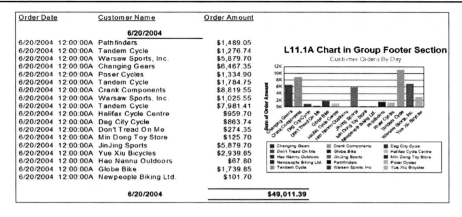

Figure 11-82 L11.22 Sample report in preview mode

Chart Options Dialog Box

The options on this dialog box pick up where the options on the Chart Expert leave off. I would like to see all of the following dialog boxes added to the Chart Expert: Chart Options, Choose A Chart and Chart Format. I think that would make creating and modifying charts easier.

Depending on the chart type, you will see slightly different options on the Chart Options dialog box. The options let you change the overall look of the chart. What I like most about the Chart Options dialog box is that you can see what your changes will look like without having to preview the report. This is very helpful when you need to experiment with several options. There are two ways to open the Chart Options dialog box as discussed below.

① Right-click on the chart and select Chart Options.
② Click on the chart, then Chart ⇒ Chart Options.

 If you click on the Help button on any tab on the Chart Options dialog box, you will see detailed information for all of the options on the tab.

Many of the settings on the Chart Options dialog box are the same as the ones on the Chart Expert. One difference that you will notice is that the settings have more options on the Chart Options dialog box then they do on the Chart Expert. The figures that follow show the tabs that you are most likely to use.

Appearance Tab

The options on this tab effect the general look of the chart.
Figures 11-83 to 11-85 show the appearance options for three types of charts.

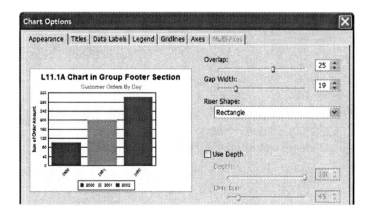

Figure 11-83 Bar chart appearance options

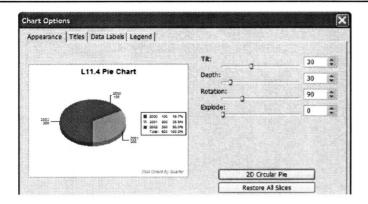

Figure 11-84 Pie chart appearance options

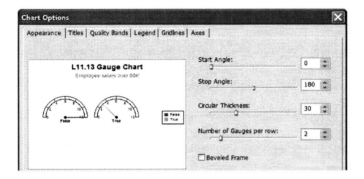

Figure 11-85 Gauge chart appearance options

Titles Tab

The options shown in Figure 11-86 let you add or modify the titles on the chart.

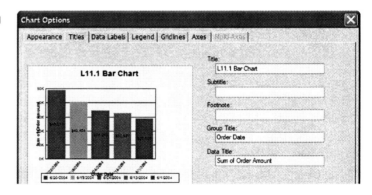

Figure 11-86 Titles tab options

Data Labels Tab

The options shown in Figure 11-87 let you add data labels to the chart, change the location of the labels and what the label will display.

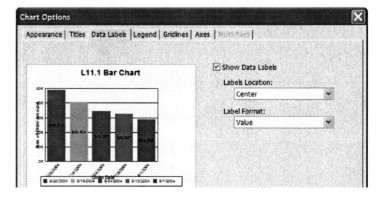

Figure 11-87 Data Labels tab options

Legend Tab

The options shown in Figure 11-88 let you modify the legend, add a frame around the legend, change the color of the items and swap the location of the series and groups.

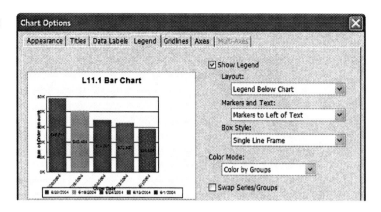

Figure 11-88 Legend tab options

Gridlines Tab

The options shown in Figure 11-89 let you add or remove major and minor gridlines for the group and data axes.

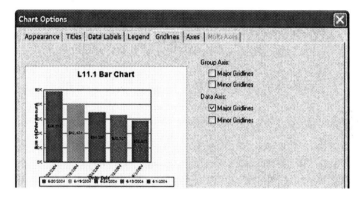

Figure 11-89 Gridlines tab options

Axes Tab

The options shown in Figure 11-90 let you select how the group axes line will be displayed on the chart. The axis line may not be visible after selecting the option if it is the same color as the frame of the chart.

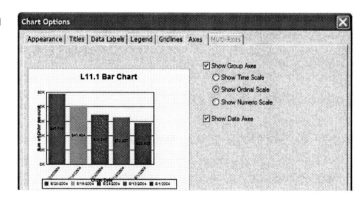

Figure 11-90 Axes tab options

Modifying Charts In The Preview Window

If you modify a chart in the preview window, in particular, a chart that is in the group header or footer section, by default the changes that you make will only be applied to that instance of the report. This does not happen when a chart is modified in the design window. Changes made to charts on the design window will be applied to all instances of the chart.

In Exercise 11.1A you added a chart to the group footer section that displays data for the top five order days in June. Because the chart is grouped by order date, the chart in the group footer section will appear five times on the report, once for each of the order date groups.

If you selected the chart for the second order date on the report and made changes to it from the preview window, the changes that you make would only be applied to that instance of the chart. The charts for the other four dates would not be changed. If you decide that you do want to apply the changes that you made to the one instance of the chart, to all of the charts in the same group, select one of the two options listed below. They work the same as the Applied to group template option that you learned about earlier in Exercise 11.21.

① Right-click on the chart that you made changes to on the preview window and select Apply Changes To All Charts.

② Click on the chart that you made changes to on the preview window, then Chart ⇒ Apply Changes To All Charts.

Edit X Axis Labels

If the labels across the X axis (at the bottom of the chart) are hard to read, right-click on the specific label on the preview window and select **EDIT AXIS LABEL** as shown in Figure 11-91. You will see the dialog box shown in Figure 11-92. Make the changes to the label and click OK.

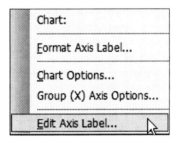

Figure 11-92 Label Aliasing dialog box

Figure 11-91 Axis label shortcut menu

Modify Parts Of The Chart Manually

So far, almost all of the chart modification techniques that you have learned have been selecting or changing options on a dialog box. You can also move or resize elements like the title or legend on the chart manually. Doing this allows you to have greater control over what the chart will look like.

If you make changes to the chart and then decide that you do not like them, you can use the **AUTO ARRANGE CHART** option. This option will reset the chart to it's default size, formatting and placement settings. You have to select the entire chart, not a specific element, for this option to appear on the chart shortcut menu.

Exercise 11.23: Move Labels On A Chart

In many of the charts that were created in this lesson, one or all of the axis labels are displayed on top of the values for the axis. Moving the axis labels would make the charts easier to read. In Exercise 11.8 you learned that the marker option on the Chart Expert does not work. You will learn another way to change the markers in this exercise.

1. Save the L11.8A report as `L11.23 Move labels on a chart`.

 Moving labels is easier to do in the preview window because you can see the live data in the chart.

2. Select the Total monthly order amount label and drag the label to the left until you can see all of the values on the axis.

3. Select the chart title, then make the frame of it smaller so that the frame is only over the chart, not over the legend.

4. Right-click on the chart title and select Chart Options, then click on the Titles tab. Change the Title to `L11.23 Move Labels On A Chart`. Click OK.

5. Right-click on the chart and select Chart Options. Change the **SIZE** to 50, then change the **SHAPE** to Diamond. Click OK and save the changes. The chart should look like the one shown in Figure 11-93. Compare this chart to the one shown in Exercise 11.8A. The markers should have a diamond shape and the labels should be easier to read.

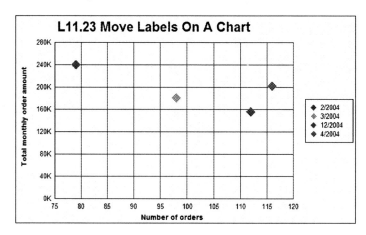

Figure 11-93 L11.23 Move labels on a chart

Customizing 3D Charts

As you saw earlier in Figure 11-84, the Appearance tab options let you tilt and rotate 3D charts. If you want or need more 3D chart formatting options, right-click on a chart like the 3D Surface or 3D Riser chart and select **3D VIEWING ANGLE**. You will see the dialog box shown in Figure 11-94.

You can scroll through the list of viewing angles to find one that you like. If clicked, the **ADVANCED OPTIONS** button displays additional options that let you customize the viewing angle even more, as shown in Figure 11-95. You can also view the Preset Viewing Angles on the left by clicking on the forward and backward (VCR style) buttons below the chart thumbnail, to the left of the Duplicate button. Another way to view them is by opening the drop down list under the chart thumbnail. The options on the **ROTATE**, **PAN**, **WALLS** and **MORE** tabs allow you to customize additional 3D options.

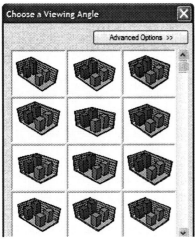

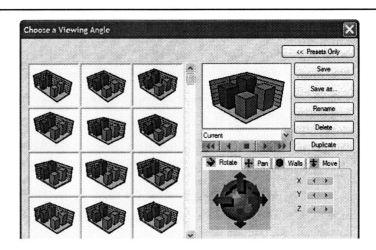

Figure 11-95 Advanced viewing angle customization options

Figure 11-94 Choose A Viewing Angle dialog box

 If you make any manual changes to a viewing angle, you will be prompted to save the changes with a new viewing angle preset name when you click OK. Entering a name on this dialog box will let you save a new viewing angle or replace an existing one. You do not have to do this to apply the changes that you have selected on the Choose a Viewing Angle dialog box. If you want to apply the changes to the chart without saving them as a viewing angle, click the Cancel button on the ENTER 3D VIEWING ANGLE PRESET NAME dialog box and the changes will still be applied to the chart.

Customizing Individual Elements On The Chart

Each element on a chart can be customized. For example, you can change the color of the report title or change the color of individual bars or slices of the chart. In Lesson 4 you learned about the Format Editor and how you can use it to customize fields on the report. Each of the elements on a chart also has a Format dialog box that has additional formatting options. Figures 11-97 to 11-101 show the Format dialog boxes for some of the more popular chart elements. You can open these dialog boxes by selecting either of the options discussed below.

① Right-click on the chart element that you want to modify and select the Format option on the shortcut menu shown in Figure 11-96.
② Click on the chart element that you want to modify, then Chart ⇒ Format.

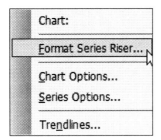

Figure 11-96 Bar element shortcut menu

 The name after the word Format on the shortcut menu will change depending on the type of element that is selected.

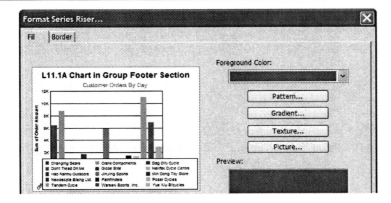

Figure 11-97 Bar format fill tab options

Selecting the options on the border tab shown in Figure 11-98 will place a dotted border around the chart. You have to select a color. I think the Color option should default to black instead of transparent, like it does on the Format Gridlines dialog box shown in Figure 11-101.

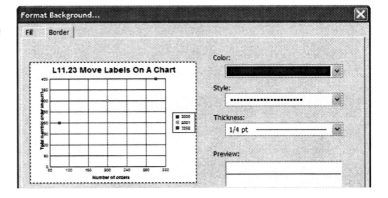

Figure 11-98 XY Scatter format border tab options

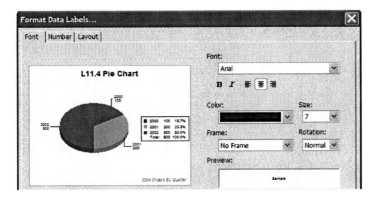

Figure 11-99 Format Data Label options

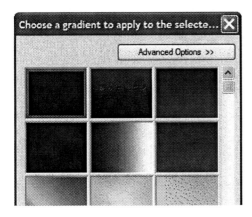

Figure 11-100 Bar gradient options

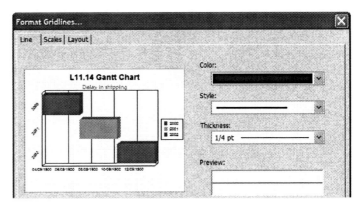

Figure 11-101 Format Gridlines options

Exercise 11.24: Apply Color To Chart Elements

This is probably one of the most used formatting options. In this exercise, you will apply color to parts of a chart.

1. Save the L11.21 report as `L11.24 Add color to charts`.

2. Click on the second bar (so that it is selected) on the chart in the group header 2 section, then right-click on it and select Format Series Riser. Change the **FOREGROUND** color to Yellow. (It's on the first row.)

3. Click the Pattern button and select the seventh option in the first row as illustrated in Figure 11-102. Click OK twice to close both dialog boxes and save the changes.

4. Open the Chart Options dialog box for the pie chart and make the following appearance changes: Tilt 45 and Explode 15, then click OK.

5. Right-click on the pie chart and select Format Background. Click the Gradient button and select the fourth option in the first column. Click OK twice to close both dialog boxes.

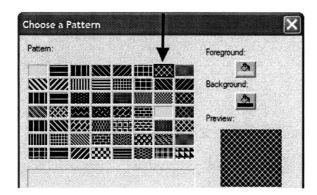

Figure 11-102 Pattern option illustrated

 If you click the **ADVANCED OPTIONS** button on the **CHOOSE A GRADIENT TO APPLY TO THE SELECTED AREAS** dialog box, you will see options that let you create your own gradients as shown in Figure 11-103. Compare this to the default options that were shown earlier in Figure 11-100.

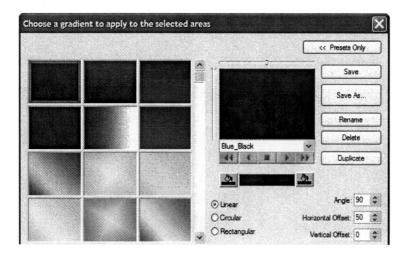

Figure 11-103 Gradient options

6. Save the changes. The pie chart should look like the one shown in Figure 11-104. The bar chart should look like the one shown in Figure 11-105.

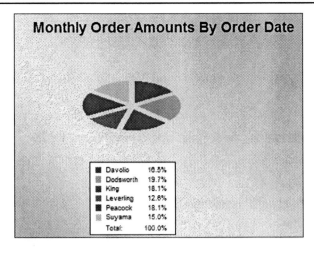

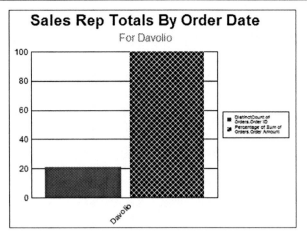

Figure 11-104 L11.24 Pie chart with the format options applied

Figure 11-105 L11.24 Bar chart with the format options applied

Chart Templates

If you have formatted a chart that has several options that you would like to use on other charts, you can save the options as a template, like the ones you saw earlier on the Choose A Chart Type dialog box. You can save a chart as a template by selecting one of the options below, then type in a name for the template.

① Right-click on the chart and select Save As Template.
② Click on the chart, then Chart ⇒ Save As Template.

To apply the template to another chart, click on the **USER DEFINED** category on the Choose A Chart Type dialog box shown earlier in Figure 11-77.

> By default, chart templates that you create are saved in the following location on your hard drive C:\Program Files\Common Files\Business Objects\3.0\ChartSupport\Templates\User Defined folder.
>
> If you want to change the location that the chart templates that you create are saved in, you can change the ChartSupportPath registry key, which is in this location.
> HKEY_LOCAL_MACHINE\Software\Business Objects\Suite11.0\Crystal Reports\

Test Your Skills

1. Create a new report that includes the following information for a chart, which should look like the one shown in Figure 11-106.

   - Add the Customer and Orders tables to the report.
   - Create a Side by side horizontal bar chart, with the Use depth effect.
   - Use the Region field as the On Change Of option.
   - Use the Last Year's Sales and Order Amount fields as the Show value(s) options.
   - Add the Title L11.25 Skills Bar Chart. Use the font size 14, no bold and the Comic Sans MS font. Add the Subtitle December 2003 Orders.
   - Add major gridlines to the Group and Data axis.
   - Use the Manual data axis option with an interval of 6.
   - Use the large Bar Size.
   - Only display orders in December 2003 that are in the CA, PA, NJ and WI regions.
   - Save the report as L11.25 Skills bar chart.

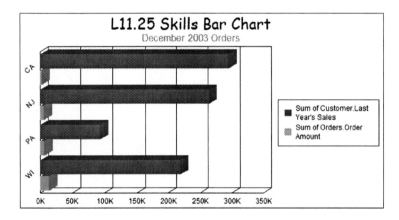

Figure 11-106 L11.25 Skills bar chart

2. Create a 3D Bar chart like the one shown in Figure 11-107.

   - The chart should show the total order amount for orders between December 1-10, 2003 for these three shipping methods: Loomis, Purolator and Parcel Post.
   - Change the Title to L11.26 Skills Orders For 3 Shipping Methods. Change the Subtitle to December 1-10, 2003.
   - Display major gridlines for all axes.
   - Save the report as L11.26 Skills Orders for three shipping methods chart.

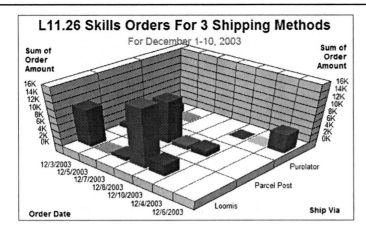

Figure 11-107 L11.26 Skills Orders for three shipping methods chart

3. Modify the L11.23 report. When finished, the report should look like the one shown in Figure 11-108.

    -   Insert a group header section under the existing one and create a pie chart that shows the top 10 orders for the month.
    -   Show the values for each slice of the pie. Detach the smallest slice of the pie.
    -   Include any top 10 ties.
    -   Place the legend at the bottom of the chart.
    -   Use the $1 Number format.
    -   Change the Title to L11.27 Top 10 Orders For the Month. Delete the Subtitle.
    -   Format the chart background with the gradient option of your choice.
    -   Sort the detail records in descending order on the Order Amount field.
    -   Save the report as L11.27 Skills Top 10 orders chart.

    The first 10 orders that are shown in Figure 11-108 are the same records that are on the chart.

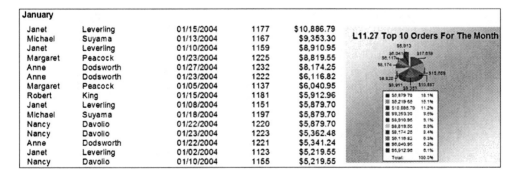

Figure 11-108 L11.27 Skills Top 10 orders chart

4. Add all of the reports that were created in this lesson to the Workbench.

PARAMETER FIELDS AND REPORT ALERTS

Parameter fields add interaction between the person running the report and the report. Parameter fields allow you to customize reports to better meet the users needs.

Report Alerts are a way to notify the person running the report that it contains information that they should be aware of.

In this lesson you will learn the following:

- ☑ How to use the Create New Parameter dialog box
- ☑ How to create three types of list of values
- ☑ How to use parameter fields with the Select and Section Experts
- ☑ How to create formulas for parameter fields
- ☑ How to create, edit and delete Report Alerts
- ☑ How to use Report Alerts in formulas
- ☑ How to view Report Alerts

To pass the RDCR201 exam, you need to be familiar with and be able to:

- ☑ Know the common string parameter field edit mask characters
- ☑ Know several ways to create list of values for parameter fields
- ☑ Know how to display (print) different types of parameter fields
- ☑ Create alerts

LESSON 12

Parameter Fields Overview

The reports that you have learned to create so far in this workbook did not require any input from the people that would run them. In Lesson 2 you learned that different users may need slightly different versions of the same report. Based on the report creation techniques that you have learned so far, especially the Select Expert, if one group of people needed to see a customer report for a specific date range and another group of people need to see the same report for specific customers, you would have to create two reports. This is the largest downside to only using the Select Expert to create selection criteria. Using parameter fields to get the criteria for the Select Expert, is a much better solution.

Think about this. If a user requested a report to only show data for one year, the date range would be entered as the criteria on the Select Expert. Now, the same user or a different user needs to see the same report, but for a different date range and specific customers. The easiest thing to do based on the report techniques that you have learned so far, is to open the existing report and save it with a new file name and change the selection criteria to the new date range and add customer criteria. As you can see, this could get out of hand rather quickly. If the original report used parameter fields to get the criteria from the person running the report, the report could be used for any date range and any customer. Another thing to think about is maintaining all of these reports. If a field needs to be added, you would have to add the field to more than one report.

If you created two parameter fields for the report, one for a date range and another one to select customers, both groups of people could use the same report. A popular type of parameter field is one that passes data to the Select Expert. In addition to being able to pass data to the Select Expert, a parameter field can also pass data to conditional and other types of formulas. This allows the person running the report to have control over the records that will appear on the report without having to know how to use the Select Expert or how to create formulas. All of the reports that you create that have criteria on the Select Expert can be enhanced by using parameter fields in place of specific (hard coded) values from a table or the value that you type in the second drop down list on the Select Expert. This would give the reports a lot more flexibility.

To help the person that will run a report that has parameter fields, you can include features like default values and drop down lists. For example, if you were creating a parameter field that needed to allow the user to select a country, you could set a default country if the report is often run using a specific country. You could also create a drop down list field that contains all of the countries and let the user select the country that they wanted to run the report for. Crystal Reports refers to this drop down list as a **PICK LIST** when referencing a parameter field. There are different types of pick lists and you will learn about them in this lesson.

An example of a pick list and how to combine existing reports (which means less reports for you to create or maintain) would be the reports that you created in Exercises 5.1 and 5.2. The report in Exercise 5.1 used the Select Expert to only display customers in one region. The report that you created in Exercise 5.2 displayed customers in two regions. These reports could easily be combined with the use of a parameter field. What would you do if the user needed to run the reports that you created in Exercise 5.1 or 5.2 for different regions next week? Someone, probably you, would have to save the current report with a new name and change the selection criteria for the new regions.

How Do Parameter Fields Work?

When a report is run that has a parameter field you will be prompted to select options, which creates all or part of the criteria that is needed to run the report. The information that is gathered from the parameter fields is passed on to various portions of the report like the Select Expert or a formula. The data in the parameter field is used to run the report.

Like the Select Expert, parameter fields ask questions that will determine what data will be displayed on the report. Using parameter fields, the following questions can be answered: Which three months do you want to see the sales reps totals for? Which country do you want to see sales for? Which customers ordered hats in December?

In addition to using parameter fields to gather the report selection criteria, parameter fields can be used to customize and format the report. For example, parameter fields can be used to select the sorting or grouping options, which you will learn how to do in this lesson or highlight records that meet a certain condition. If a report has confidential information, one of the parameter fields can require the person running the report to enter their User ID by using a special field as the basis for a parameter field. Based on the User ID, parts of the report would be hidden.

The Create New Parameter Dialog Box

Now that you know what parameter fields are, how useful they are and how they work, it is time to learn about the dialog box shown in Figure 12-1, which is used to create parameter fields. Table 12-1 explains the options on the Create New Parameter dialog box. Reports can and often do have more than one parameter field.

There are four ways to open the Create New Parameter dialog box as discussed below.

① Click on the Parameter Fields category in the Field Explorer, then click the **NEW** button on the Field Explorer toolbar.
② Right-click on the Parameter Fields category in the Field Explorer, then select **NEW**.
③ Click the Field Explorer button on the Standard toolbar to open the Field Explorer, then follow one of the options above.
④ View ⇒ Field Explorer, then follow option one or two above.

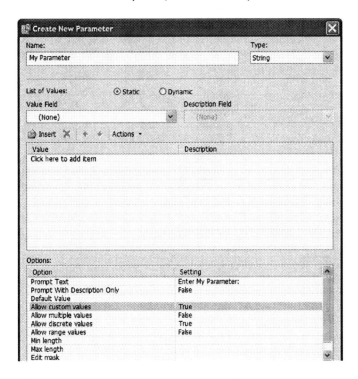

Figure 12-1 Create New Parameter dialog box

Option	Description
Name	This option lets you name the parameter field. The name is how you would reference the parameter field in a formula on the report. Try to use as descriptive a name as possible, while keeping the name as short as possible. You can use the name of the field in the table that the parameter field will query. You can also use the name of an existing formula. As you learned in Lesson 3, Crystal Reports adds a question mark to the beginning of parameter field names. [See Lesson 3, Field Type Symbols And Naming Conventions] (1)
Type	This option lets you select the data type for the parameter field. You should select the same data type as the field or data that the parameter field will be compared to. (1)
List of values	If you want to provide values for the parameter field, there are two types of values: Static values that do not change and dynamic values, which can change each time the report is run. (2)
Value Field	The options in this field are the fields from the tables that are connected to the report. This field has two purposes: To select the field for the comparison for the parameter field or select the field that will be used to import values for a static or dynamic list.
Description Field	This field allows you to specify text or another field that will be displayed next to the Value Field in the list. This is helpful when the value field option is an ID field. Often, the person running the report will not understand the values in an ID field. For example, you may need to use the Customer ID field, but display either the Customer ID field and the Customer Name field or display the Customer Name field by itself. The Customer Name field contains data that the person running the report understands.
Insert	Clicking this button will retrieve the data that is in the field selected in the Value Field, discussed above.
Actions	The options on this drop down list, as shown in Figure 12-2, are used to create a list of values or export values.
Value/Description	These two columns function like a table. These options let you select specific data from the field that is selected in the Value Field. Filling in the Description column is optional. If the field name that is in the Value column is not descriptive enough, you can enter text in the Description column to better explain the data in the Value column. You can also type values in this list.
Option/Setting	The options in this section let you customize the parameter field. The options will change depending on the data type that is selected. (2)

Table 12-1 Create New Parameter dialog box options explained

(1) This is a required option to create a parameter field.
(2) This option will be explained in detail later in this lesson.

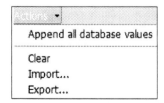

Figure 12-2 Actions drop down list options

Data Types

The data type that you select determines how the parameter field will be used in the report. For example, you cannot select a string data type to use for a parameter field that will be used in a comparison with a date/time field. Number, currency and string data types do not have the limitations that date, date/time and Boolean data types have.

Number and **Currency** data types can only use the numbers zero to nine and the minus sign. Any other values will generate an error message.

String data types can use all of the number data type options, plus letters and special characters.

Date And Time Data Types

Date fields may be the most used data type to limit the data that appears on a report. When you use the Select Expert to create criteria for a date field, you have several options including "Is greater than", "Is greater than or equal to" and "Is between". The Create New Parameter dialog box does not have the same exact options in terms of their names.

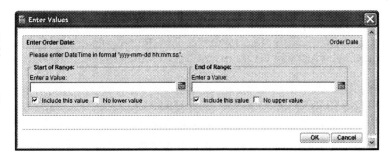

Figure 12-3 Date/Time parameter field options

The following three options will let you specify how to use dates on a parameter field. Figure 12-3 shows the options available for date/time parameter fields when the report is run.

① **INCLUDE THIS VALUE** If checked, this option will include the date that is entered in the parameter field as part of the selection process. Checking this option on the Start of Range field is the equivalent of the "Is greater than or equal to" Select Expert operator. Checking this option on the Start and End of Range fields is the equivalent of the "Is between" Select Expert operator.

② **NO LOWER VALUE** If checked, the value in the Start of Range field will not be used. (3)

③ **NO UPPER VALUE** If checked, the value in the End of Range field will not be used. (3)

(3) You cannot select both of these options at the same time. If you type 1/1/05 in the Start of Range field and 6/1/05 in the End of Range field and clear the No lower value option, all records that have a value that is less than the value in the End of Range field will be included on the report, even though a date was entered in the Start of range field. If the No upper value option is checked, all records that have a date greater than 1/1/05 will be included in the report.

If you need to create a date range, you have to set the **ALLOW RANGE VALUES** option to True on the Create New Parameter dialog box. By default, this option is set to False because the **ALLOW DISCRETE VALUES** option is set to True. These two options are mutually exclusive, meaning that only one of them can be set to True for the parameter field.

Boolean Parameter Fields

Boolean parameter fields are very similar to the Boolean formulas that you learned how to create in Lesson 10. Like Boolean formulas, Boolean parameter fields are used with a Boolean field in a table, which has one of two values: True or False.

Figure 12-4 shows the options that are available for Boolean parameter fields. In addition to being able to select a default value of true or false for the Boolean parameter field, you can enter a description for the true and false options. The description should help the person running the report decide which option is appropriate for the report that they are running.

Option	Setting
Prompt Text	Enter My Parameter:
Prompt With Description Only	False
Default Value	
Boolean group #	
Exclusive group	False

Figure 12-4 Boolean parameter field options

The **BOOLEAN GROUP #** option allows you to add the Boolean parameter field to a group of other Boolean parameter fields. Creating a Boolean group will remind you of a group of radio buttons that you have probably seen on dialog boxes in other applications, like the print range options on the dialog box shown in Figure 12-5.

The number that you enter in the field is the Boolean group that the parameter field that you are creating or editing should be associated with. If the report has five Boolean fields and two are needed to create one Boolean group, you would enter the same number in this field for these two parameter fields. You would enter a different number for the other three Boolean parameter fields so that they would be grouped together. The three options in Figure 12-5 would have the same Boolean group number.

This is similar to how summary fields appear on the Data tab of the Chart Expert, as shown in Figure 12-6. Notice how there are three fields that are in the Group 1 section and three fields in the Group 2 section. That would be the equivalent of two Boolean groups.

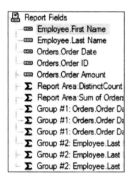

Figure 12-5 Radio button group example

Figure 12-6 Available group fields in a chart

The **EXCLUSIVE GROUP** option shown above in Figure 12-4 works with the Boolean groups on the report. This option lets you determine whether or not only one option in the Boolean group can be selected. Selecting **TRUE** for this option will only allow one option in the group to be selected. That option will be set to true and the other options will return a value of false. Figure 12-5 above is an example of this because you can only select one of the print range options. Selecting **FALSE** for the Exclusive Group option will allow more than one option in the group to be selected. Each option selected will be set to true and the others will be set to false.

Using Parameter Fields With The Select Expert

This combination may be the most used parameter field option. Many of the reports that you have created in this workbook used the Select Expert to specify which records appear on the report. In programming terminology, these reports are known as "hard coded" because all of the options needed to run the report are coded into the report. At one time this was the only programming option that was available. Today, there are other options and parameter fields is one of these options.

After you create the parameter fields, open the Select Expert and select the parameter field instead of the actual values in the table. For example, in Exercise 5.2 you created the criteria shown in Figure 12-7. Instead of selecting the specific states (regions) FL and OH, which is the hard coding that I was referring to earlier, you would select the parameter field from the drop down list. That is how the value in the parameter field is passed to the Select Expert.

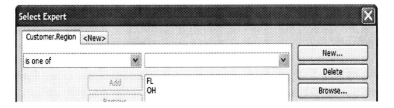

Figure 12-7 Select Expert criteria

 What you will find is that you cannot always use the same operator (Is greater than, Is between, etc) with parameter fields that you would when selecting actual values from a field. The majority of the time you will use the "Is equal to" operator with parameter fields on the Select Expert even when the parameter field will be used for a range of values like "Is between 1/1/04 and 1/31/04" or when the parameter field is used to select multiple values like "Is one of FL or OH".

When you open the drop down list on the Select Expert as shown in Figure 12-8, you will see all of the parameter fields that have the same data type as the field from the table. Parameter fields are always at the top of the list.

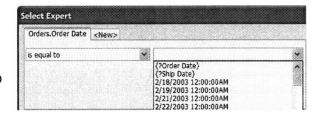

Figure 12-8 Select Expert with parameter field options

 If you do not see the parameter field that you are looking for when you open the drop down list on the right of the Select Expert, it usually means one of two things: 1) that you selected the wrong data type when you created the parameter field or 2) you associated the parameter field with the wrong field. Open the Edit Parameter dialog box, change the data type or field that the parameter field is associated to, then re-open the Select Expert.

 You will see the terms "pick list", "list of values" and "prompt". Depending on who wrote the article or documentation, these words when used in conjunction with parameter fields can be used interchangeably. To me, the first two mean the same thing, but prompt, refers to the questions asked on the Enter Values dialog box that you saw earlier in Figure 12-3.

When a report with parameter fields is refreshed, you will see the dialog box shown in Figure 12-9. These options let you decide if you want to use the parameter values that were selected the last time the report was run or if you want to select new values.

If the option **USE CURRENT PARAMETER VALUES** is selected, the report will run with the existing parameter values and you will not see the Enter Values dialog box.

If the option **PROMPT FOR NEW PARAMETER VALUES** is selected, the Enter Values dialog box that you saw earlier in Figure 12-3 will appear so that you can select new parameter values.

When the Enter Values dialog box appears, it will display the values that were selected the last time that the report was run. You only have to select values that you want to change. I tend to always select this option because it is a good way to double check to make sure that you have the options that you want to use when the report is run.

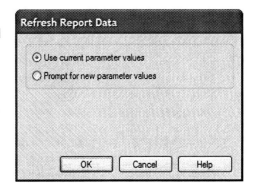

Figure 12-9 Refresh Report Data dialog box

Enter Values Dialog Box

This dialog box contains all of the parameter fields for the report as you saw earlier in Figure 12-3. If there is more than one parameter field on the dialog box, you will only be able to select options for the first prompt. Once you select an option for the first prompt, you will be able to select an option for the next prompt. The reason this happens is because sometimes the values in the next prompt are dependant on what was selected in the first prompt. This is known as CASCADING PROMPTS. For example, if the first prompt lets you select a country and the second prompt lets you select a state, the only values that will appear in the state drop down list are states that are in the country that is selected in the first prompt.

Parameter fields appear on the Enter Values dialog box in the order that they are created. You can change the order by right-clicking on a parameter field in the Field Explorer or on the Parameter Fields Category and selecting SET PARAMETER ORDER. The Enter Values dialog box can be customized. You can change the color, fonts and more, as you will learn later in this lesson.

> **Tips For Parameter Field Exercises**
> ① After saving the existing report with a new report name in step 1 of the parameter field exercises, open the Create New Parameter dialog box unless instructed otherwise.
>
> ② When you see the instruction "Press F5", after doing so, you should select the second option, PROMPT FOR NEW PARAMETER VALUES on the Refresh Report Data dialog box shown above in Figure 12-9 and click OK or press Enter.

Exercise 12.1: Create An "Is Equal To" Parameter Field

In this exercise you will enhance the L5.1 Region = CA report by creating a parameter field that will prompt for the state that will be used to run the report.

1. Save the L5.1 report as L12.1 Is Equal To parameter field.

2. Type Region in the Name field, then change the Type to String, if it is not already selected. Notice that the PROMPT TEXT option at the bottom of the dialog box has the name that you just entered.

3. Click OK and open the Select Expert, then open the second drop down list. At the top of the list you will see the parameter field that you just created, as illustrated in Figure 12-10. Select the Region parameter field and click OK.

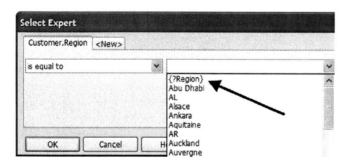

Figure 12-10 Parameter field illustrated on the Select Expert

4. Save the changes. Click Yes when prompted to generate the data, then preview the report. You will see the dialog box shown in Figure 12-11. This dialog box is created based on the parameter field(s) that the report has.

5. Type CA in the Region field and press Enter or click OK.

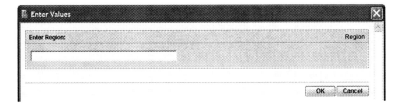

Figure 12-11 Enter Values dialog box

Unless the parameter field has an edit mask, string fields are not case sensitive, which means that you can type "CA" or "ca" and get the same results. When prompted to refresh the data, at this point it does not matter if you refresh the data because you refreshed it a minute or so ago. However, if you were running this report against live data, I would refresh the report every time it is run to make sure that I had the most current data. You will now see the six records in the CA region.

Run The Report Again

 Reports that have a parameter field will not automatically refresh when you switch from the design window to the preview window. You have two options: press the F5 key or click the **REFRESH** button on the Navigation Tools toolbar.

1. Click the **REFRESH** button on the toolbar above the report or press the F5 key. You will see the Refresh Report Data dialog box shown earlier in Figure 12-9. Select the second option and click OK. As you can see, the value that you entered last is still there.

2. Type your first name in the Region field and press Enter. Close the report and save the changes.

Unless your first name is a region in the table, you will not see any data on the report. This isn't what you want to happen. The majority of reports are created to retrieve data, not produce empty reports. If this report used a list of values for the region field, you would have been able to select a region from a list instead of typing it in. That is a better solution.

Exercise 12.2: Create An "Is Greater Than" Parameter Field

In this exercise you will enhance the L5.3 Order Date GTE 6-24-03 report by creating a parameter field that will prompt for the Order Date that will be used to run the report.

1. Save the L5.3 report as `L12.2 Is Greater Than parameter field`.

2. Type `Order Date` in the Name field, then change the Type to Date and click OK.

3. Open the Select Expert, then open the second drop down list.

As you will notice, you do not see the parameter field that you just created. That is because the Order Date field is a date/time field. I did this to demonstrate that Crystal Reports does try to help you as much as possible.

4. Close the Select Expert and reopen the parameter dialog box by right-clicking on the Order Date parameter field in the Field Explorer and selecting Edit. Change the Type to Date Time and click OK.

5. Open the Select Expert. Select the Order Date parameter field in the second drop down list and click OK. Press F5. You will see the Enter Values dialog box.

The display text is prompting you to enter the date and time in a specific format as illustrated in Figure 12-12. This format is the default for a date/time field. This isn't the easiest format to enter a date in. There are two options for entering a date. The date can be typed in or it can be selected from the calendar control.

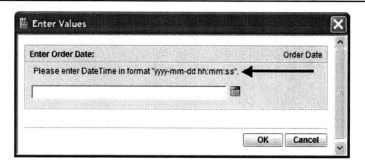

Figure 12-12 Date Time data entry format illustrated

If you entered data in a parameter field that isn't valid, the report would run, but not return any records, which would cause the report would be empty. This is why it is a good idea that parameter fields have a list of values as often as possible. All fields on the Enter Values dialog box are required. I have noticed that if you leave some types of fields empty and click OK, you will see an error message that says "The value is not valid".

 Notice the icon at the end of the Order Date field shown above in Figure 12-12. If you click on this icon you will see the calendar shown in Figure 12-13. Instead of typing in the date, you can use the calendar to select the date.

6. Select June 24, 2003 in the calendar. The next section explains the calendar control options. You should now see the date and time on the dialog box as shown in Figure 12-14.

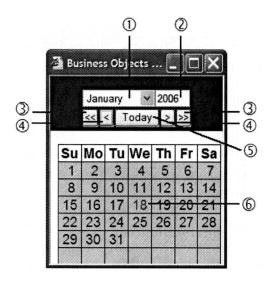

Figure 12-13 Calendar control

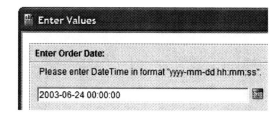

Figure 12-14 Order Date entered

7. Click OK. The report should have 3,602 records like the report shown in Exercise 5.3. Save the changes and leave the report open to complete the next exercise.

How To Use The Calendar Control

Navigating in this calendar is similar to other electronic calendars that you may have used. If you need a date in the month and year that is displayed on the calendar, click on the date in the calendar. The options are explained below.

① Open this drop down list to select a different month.
② If you need to change the year, you can type in the year that you need.
③ These buttons change the calendar to the previous or next year.

④ These buttons change the calendar to the previous or next month.
⑤ This button will take you to the current day. The current day is shown in red.
⑥ This is the current day.

Exercise 12.2A: Set A Default Date For A Parameter Field

If you know that the majority of times that a report is run that a certain value will be selected, you can set that value as the default. Setting a default value will still let another value be selected when the report is run. Default values are usually created to save time. In this exercise you will set a default date for the parameter field in the L12.2 report.

1. Save the L12.2 report as L12.2A Parameter field with a default value.

2. Open the parameter dialog box for the Order Date field. In the Options section of the Edit Parameter dialog box, click in the Setting column for the **DEFAULT VALUE** option and type 6/24/2003, as shown in Figure 12-15.

Option	Setting
Prompt Text	Enter Order Date:
Prompt With Description Only	False
Default Value	6/24/2003 12:00:00 AM ⬅
Allow custom values	True

Figure 12-15 Default Value option illustrated

3. Click OK. Save the changes and press F5. Select the second option on the Refresh Report Data dialog box and click OK. You will see the default date that you just added to the parameter field.

4. Select the date 7/15/2004 from the calendar and click OK. The report should have 1,977 records. Save the changes and close the report.

If you refresh the data, and select the **PROMPT FOR NEW PARAMETER VALUES** option, the default date that you will see on the Enter Values dialog box will be 6/24/2003.

 There isn't much use in saving the data with a report that has a parameter value, unless the report will be exported. Reports with parameter fields usually refresh the data.

 The remaining parameter field exercises in this lesson should not save the data with the report. After completing step 1 in the exercises, open the Report Options dialog box and clear the **SAVE DATA WITH REPORT** option.

𝐍𝐄𝐖 List Of Values

If you used a previous version of Crystal Reports, you will notice major changes in the list of values and the Create Parameter dialog box.

As you learned in Exercise 12.1, if a parameter field does not have a default value or a drop down list with values, it is possible that the person running the report will type in the values incorrectly. As much as possible, you should avoid creating parameter fields that allow this to happen. Instead, you should provide a list of values for the parameter field. There are three types of list of values that you can create for parameter field, as discussed below.

① **Static prompt** The values are stored in the report.
② **Dynamic prompt** The values are not stored in the report, they are stored in a database.
③ **Cascading prompt** The values are not stored in the report, they are stored in a database.

A list of values is the data that the person running the report will select from. You can use the same list of values for different prompts in the same report. For example, if the report prompted for a customer "Bill to" state and a "Ship to" state, you could use the same list of states for both parameter fields.

List Of Value Categories

There are two list of value categories as discussed below.

① **Unmanaged Lists** are stored in the report file. This type of list of values can use report fields or commands as the data source. If you are not going to publish the reports to the Business Objects Enterprise, you can use an unmanaged list of values.

② **Managed Lists** are stored in the Business Objects Enterprise. Managed list of values are based on a Business View, even if the report is not based on a Business View. [See Lesson 2, Business Views]

 The dynamic and cascading list of values exercises that you will complete in this lesson are not for reports that are published on the Crystal Reports Server or the Business Objects Enterprise.

Static And Dynamic List Of Values

As you learned in the exercises that you have completed earlier in this lesson, you can create parameter fields that require the person running the report to type in the data when prompted. You also saw that this type of parameter field can cause errors to be generated. This is not the best solution. You can create a static or dynamic list of values to use for the values for the prompt. Depending on the data, one type of list of values may be better suited then another. It is easy to get carried away and create all dynamic lists, but if a static list is better suited for the parameter field, you should use it. In addition to static and dynamic list of values, you can also create a cascading list of values, which is a type of dynamic list. You will learn how to create each type.

Static List Of Values

Out of the three types of list of values, static lists are the easiest to create. They are best suited for values that do not change or for data that is not stored in a field. An example of a static list of values would be a list of states. Keep in mind that static lists do not change unless you change them. This is the biggest drawback of a static list of values. I personally only use a static list of values if the list is small because the values are stored in the report which makes the report file size larger. The benefit of static lists is that they are retrieved faster.

In prior versions of Crystal Reports, a static list of values was the only type of list that was available. There are three ways to create a static list of values as discussed below. You can use any combination of these options to create the list that you need.

① Import the values from a field in a table.
② Type the list of values in manually.
③ Import the list of values from a text file.

Adding Values Manually

There are two ways to add values manually on the Create (or Edit) Parameter dialog box as discussed below.

① Click on the **CLICK HERE TO ADD ITEM** option in the Value column.
② Click the **INSERT** button.

Exercise 12.3: Create A Static List Of Values Manually

In this exercise you will create a static list of values manually. In Exercise 5.2, the report was limited to two regions; OH and FL. In this exercise you will limit the regions to five, but you will be able to select which of the five regions that you want to appear on the report from a drop down list.

1. Save the L5.2 report as `L12.3 Manual static list of values`.

2. Type `Region` in the Name field.

3. Select one of the ways discussed above to add a value and type `OH` in the first row in the Value/Description section of the dialog box, then type `Ohio` in the Description column.

If the data in the Value column contains an ID number, abbreviation or other data that the person running the report may not be familiar with, you should enter a brief explanation in the Description column. The information that you enter in the Description column will appear in the drop down list next to the content in the Value column. The description is only used for display purposes.

 You do not have to enter a value in the Description column for every option in the list, only those that you think the person running the report may not understand.

If you have entered a description for every value in the list, you can change the **PROMPT WITH DESCRIPTION ONLY** option at the bottom of the dialog box to True. If you do this, the only values that will appear in the list will be the values in the Description column.

If there is data in a report that you do not want everyone to see, you can create a list of values that will prevent everyone from seeing all of the data. For example, you may not want all sales reps to see sales outside of their region. In this example, you would create a parameter field that lists the regions that you want the sales reps to be able to view. You can create this type of list of values with static or dynamic lists.

4. Add the following regions to the Value column: CA, PA, WI and FL.

5. Change the **ALLOW CUSTOM VALUES** option at the bottom of the dialog box to False. In this report, you are only going to allow the report to be run for one of the regions that you added to the static list of values. You should have the options shown in Figure 12-16.

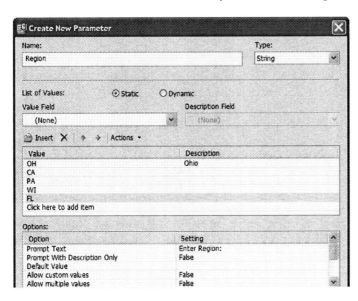

Figure 12-16 Parameter field options for a static list of values

6. Click OK. Open the Select Expert and select the Region parameter field, then remove the other values from the list and click OK.

You will see the Enter Values dialog box. If you open the drop down list, you will see the values that you added to the static list of values as shown in Figure 12-17. As you can see, the first option also displays the description that you entered. If you try to type in a value you will see that you can't. That is because the **ALLOW CUSTOM VALUES** option is set to False as shown above in Figure 12-16.

Also notice that the values are not in alphabetical order. They are in the order that they were added to the Value/Description table. In the next exercise you will learn how to change the order of values in a static list of values.

If the **ALLOW CUSTOM VALUES** option was set to True on the parameter dialog box shown earlier in Figure 12-16, you would see a field at the bottom of the Enter Values dialog box that would let you type in additional the values that you want, as shown in Figure 12-18. The person running the report could select an option from the drop down list and/or type in the value that they want. This would be useful for example, if the static list contained the 10 most used options, which would keep the list small, while providing additional flexibility.

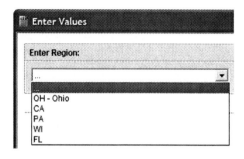

Figure 12-17 Static list of values

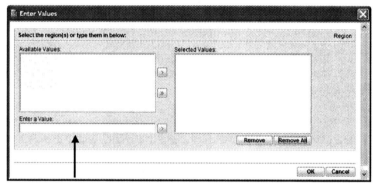

Figure 12-18 Result of the Allow custom values option set to true

7. Select PA from the list and run the report. You should have five records on the report. Save the changes and leave the report open to complete the next exercise.

Exercise 12.3A: Change The Sort Order Of The Static List Of Values

> There are two ways to change the sort order of a list of values. The instructions in this exercise are best suited for a list that does not need a lot of changes or for a list that you do not necessarily want in alphabetical order, but just in a different order then the list is currently in.
>
> An example of this would be if you wanted to put a specific value at the top of the list because it is the most used option and then put the rest of the list in alphabetical order. You may have seen this on a web-based form for a country field. You would see "USA" at the top of the drop down list because the company knows that most of their subscribers are in the USA. Below that option, the rest of the countries are in alphabetical order.

As you saw in the previous exercise, the states are not in alphabetical order. Most lists are in alphabetical order because it is easier to find the value that you need. In this exercise you will learn how to change the order of the items in the list.

1. Save the L12.3 report as L12.3A Reorder static list of values.

2. Open the Edit Parameter dialog box for the Region field.

3. Click on the CA value, then click the Up button as illustrated in Figure 12-19. Rearrange the other values in the column so that the entire list is in alphabetical order. Click OK, then press F5.

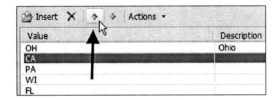

Figure 12-19 Reorder buttons illustrated

4. Select the second option and click OK. When you open the drop down list, the values will now be in alphabetical order. Save the changes and close the report.

How To Sort The Entire List At One Time

To sort the entire list at one time, click on the column heading (Value or Description) that you want to sort the list by. You will see an arrow as illustrated in Figure 12-20. If the arrow is pointing up, the values will be sorted in ascending order. If the arrow is pointing up and you click on the arrow, it will point down and the values will be sorted in descending order.

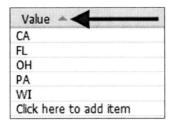

Figure 12-20 Column sorting options illustrated

Importing A Static List Of Values

The list of values that you created manually in Exercise 12.3 was small, so it did not take a lot of time to set up. Often, that is not the case and you could have 100 or more values for a static list. If the data for the static list exists in a table or text document, it is easier to import the list. If you know that you do not need all of the values in the list that you will import, you have the two options discussed below for removing the values that you do not need. You will have to evaluate which option is best, on a list by list basis.

① Import the list as is, then manually delete or change the options as needed on the parameter dialog box.
② Delete the values or make the changes to the list before importing it as a list of values. If the data that will be imported is in a table, it may not be possible or feasible to change the live data.

 If the list of values (static or dynamic) has a description, it will also be imported, if all of the values are imported. If the values are added individually from a database, the Description column will not be imported.

Exercise 12.4: Create An Imported Static List Of Values

In this exercise you will import values from a field in a table to create a static list of values.

1. Save the L5.2 report as `L12.4 Imported static list of values`.

2. Type `Region` in the Name field.

3. Open the Value Field drop down list and select the Region field.

4. Click on the Actions button and select the option, **APPEND ALL DATABASE VALUES**.

You will now see all of the values from the Region field from the Customer table. If there were values in the list that you did not want or need, you can delete them by clicking on the value that you do not want and then click the Delete button (which is the X after the Insert button).

5.   Change the Allow custom values option to False and click OK.

6.   Open the Select Expert and select the parameter field, then remove the other values from the list and click OK. Save the changes and close the report.

When you open this parameter drop down list you will see all of the values from the field in the table. If you changed any values, you will see the changes in the drop down list. The data in the table was not changed.

NEW Dynamic List Of Values

Dynamic and cascading prompts are probably one of the most talked about and most requested features in this version of Crystal Reports. These prompts allow for greater flexibility when creating reports. In Lesson 2, you learned some basic report design techniques. You also learned that different groups of people may need similar reports. One of the ways that you can create one report that works for slightly different needs is by incorporating dynamic and cascading prompts.

Unlike a static list of values that are not refreshed each time the report is run, dynamic and cascading list of values are refreshed each time the report is run. This means that if new values are added to the field in the table that the parameter field is getting the data from, the new values are also available in the parameter field. For example, if the dynamic parameter field is based on the product name field and 12 new products are added, those 12 products would also be available in the parameter field list. The opposite is also true. If values are deleted from the field in the underlying table, they would no longer be available in the parameter field list. Dynamic list of values are best suited for data that changes in a table, like new customers or a very large list of products.

 While you will not notice this completing the exercises in this workbook because the database is stored on your hard drive, dynamic and cascading lists take longer to be retrieved then static lists. Depending on the number of records in the table that the dynamic or cascading list is being retrieved from, you may notice a delay between the time that you open the drop down list and the time that you actually see the values appear in the list.

Exercise 12.5: Create A Dynamic Region List Of Values

In Exercise 12.4 you imported regions from a table associated with the report. When a customer is added that is in a region that does not currently exist in the values for the parameter field, the L12.4 report would not include the new region on the report, meaning that the report will not contain up to date information because static lists are not automatically updated. In this exercise you will create a dynamic list of values for the region field.

1.   Save the L5.2 report as L12.5 Dynamic region list of values.

2.   Type Region in the Name field, then select the **DYNAMIC** option.

3.   Click the Insert button. You will see a list of fields that are available for the dynamic list. Select the Region field.

The **EXISTING** option in the Data Source section is only available when the report already has an existing dynamic list.

The **DESCRIPTION** column works the same for dynamic lists as it does for static lists.

The **PARAMETERS** column is used when creating a dynamic cascading prompt. This is how you create the hierarchy between the fields that will be part of the cascading prompt. You will create this type of prompt later in this lesson.

4. Click OK. Open the Select Expert and select the parameter field, then remove the other values from the Region field.

5. Click OK and press F5. You will see that you can only select one value from the Region drop down list. Save the changes and close the report.

 If this report was going to be put into production, it would probably be a good idea to change the operator to "Is equal to" so that when you read the formula, it will match the objectives of the report. Otherwise, it may be confusing later if you have to edit the report. If you leave it as it is, when the report is run, only one region can be selected from the drop down list because the Allow multiple values option on the parameter dialog box is set to False.

NEW Cascading Prompts And List Of Values

Cascading prompts are created like dynamic prompts. Unlike the dynamic list of values, the cascading prompts contain related data and you must have at least two parameter fields to create cascading prompts. A cascading list of values will reduce the number of items to select from in the fields on the Enter Values dialog box.

The difference between dynamic and cascading prompts is that the option selected in the first prompt on the Enter Values dialog box is used to filter the values that will be displayed in the second prompt. An example of cascading prompts would be a list of suppliers and a list of products. The first prompt would be for the suppliers. Once a supplier is selected, the values in the second drop down list would only contain products for the supplier that was selected in the first prompt.

 When you create cascading prompts, Crystal Reports will automatically change the name of the parameter field. It will be renamed to a combination of the name that you gave the field and the name of the field that it is connected to in the prompt group. You can rename the parameter field in the Field Explorer back to what you had originally named it.

Exercise 12.6: Create Cascading Prompts For Countries And Regions

In this exercise you will create two prompts. The first one is for the country, the second one is for the region. The region drop down list will only show states (regions) that are in the country that is selected in the first prompt. The L6.6 report currently displays all countries and regions. The cascading prompts that you will create for this report will allow a specific country and specific region to be selected when the report is run.

1. Save the L6.6 report as L12.6 Cascading prompts for countries and regions.

2. Type Countries and Regions in the Name field, then select the Dynamic option.

3. Type Select a country, then select a region: in the **PROMPT GROUP TEXT** field.

4. Click the Insert button, then select the Country field. Click in the second row and select the Region field, then click OK.

5. Open the Select Expert, click on the Region field on the Choose Field dialog box and click OK. In this step, you have to select the last field that was added on the Create New Parameter dialog box.

6. Select the "Is equal to" operator, then select the Countries and Regions - Region parameter field and click OK. Press F5. Your dialog box should look like the one shown in Figure 12-21. Notice that the Region field is not available. When you select a country, the region field will be available.

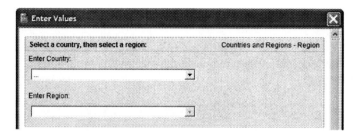

Figure 12-21 Dynamic cascading parameter options

7. Select USA, then select CA and click OK. There should be six records on the report. Save the changes and close the report.

Did you notice that the only states (regions) that you saw in the second drop down list are for the USA? If you select a different country, you will only see regions that are in that country. This is the dynamic cascading (filtering) effect.

Exercise 12.7: Create Cascading Prompts For Customers And Their Orders

Many people in a company may have the need to view a particular customers orders. This is the type of report that dynamic cascading prompts were designed to handle.

1. Save the L3.5 report as L12.7 Cascading prompts for customer orders.

2. Type Customer Orders in the Name field, then select the Dynamic option.

3. Type Select a customer, then select the Order # that you want to view in the Prompt Group Text field.

4. Select the Customer Name field in the Value column.

5. Change the **PROMPT TEXT** option to Select A Customer: as illustrated in Figure 12-22.

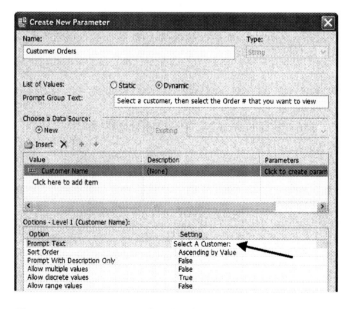

Figure 12-22 Options for the first parameter field

6. Click in the second Value row and select the Order ID field, then change the Prompt Text option to `Select the Order Number that you want to view:` and click OK.

7. Open the Select Expert, select the Order ID field and click OK.

8. Select the "Is equal to" operator, then select the Customer Orders - Order ID parameter field in the next drop down list and click OK.

9. Select the customer, Alley Cat Cycles, then select the order number 2300. The order numbers in the drop down list are for the customer that is selected in the first drop down list. Your dialog box should look like the one shown in Figure 12-23. Click OK and press F5. You should see the data for order number 2300. Save the changes and close the report.

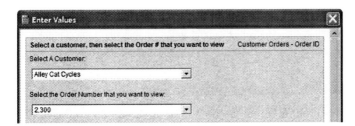

Figure 12-23 Cascading customer parameter options

 What may not be obvious is that once you click OK on the Create New Parameter dialog box, you can't go back and edit cascading parameter field options. For that reason, I create each of the fields for the group separately and then put them in a group parameter field, which you will learn how to do, later in this lesson. Doing this allows you to edit each of the fields in the parameter group if necessary.

Allow Range Values And Allow Multiple Values Options

The reports that you have created parameter fields for in this lesson have added a lot of interactivity between the user and the report. This allows the person running the report to have more control over the records that will appear on the report. What you have probably noticed is that each parameter field that you have created only allows one option to be selected. In some instances this can limit the data that displays on reports in a way that is not best suited for the user.

The Create New Parameter dialog box has two options that will allow more flexibility. The **ALLOW RANGE VALUES** option allows the parameter field to accept high and low values, like the "Is between" Select Expert operator. A good use of this option would be for a date range. The **ALLOW MULTIPLE VALUES** option allows more than one value to be selected from the parameter field. A good use of this option would be if you need to select more than one value from the same field. An example is if you needed to select several products to see which ones are not selling.

Allow Range Values Option

When you set this option to **TRUE**, you will be able to use one parameter field to accept two values, a start of range value and an end of range value. More than likely, you will use this to allow date ranges to be entered. When a parameter field has this option set to True, on the Select Expert you have to select the "Is equal to" operator, because the parameter field contains the start and end values in one field. A parameter field with the range value is the equivalent of the "Is between" operator.

By default, the start and end of range fields have the **INCLUDE THIS VALUE** option checked. This means that the values entered in both fields will be included in the record selection process. If you clear this option for either field, the value will not be included in the record selection process. This is the equivalent of the "Is greater than" and "Is less than" Select Expert operators.

Earlier in this lesson you learned about the **NO LOWER VALUE** and **NO UPPER VALUE** options. When the Allow range values option is set to True, these options are not checked. This means that only records that have a value between the start and end range values will be included in the record selection process.

These options were also discussed earlier in conjunction with date fields. These options also work with non date field ranges. If either of these options are checked, the input field is disabled and you can't enter anything in the field. These options can also be used like the "Is greater than" and "Is less than" Select Expert operators.

Only entering a value in the Start of range input field and checking the No lower value option will retrieve all records that have a value greater than (or equal to, if the Include this value option is also checked for the field) the value in the Start of range field.

Only entering a value in the End of range input field and checking the No lower value option will retrieve all records that have a value less than (or equal to, if the Include this value option is also checked for the field) the value in the End of range field.

Exercise 12.8: Use The Allow Range Values Option With Dates

In Exercise 12.2 you created a parameter field that only allowed one date to be entered. In this exercise you will modify that parameter field to allow a date range to be entered.

1. Save the L12.2 report as `L12.8 Date range parameter field`.

2. Open the Order Date parameter dialog box. At the bottom of the dialog box, change the Allow range values option to True and click OK. You should see the Edit Values dialog box. Close it and open the Select Expert.

3. Change the Order Date operator to "Is equal to", then select the parameter field and click OK.

4. Refresh the data and press F5. The reason that you have to refresh the report twice is because you are not saving the data with the report and reports with parameter fields will run with the last selected options by default. In order to change the options, the report must be refreshed.

5. Use the calendar control to select the start date 3/1/2004 and the end date 3/31/2004. You should have the options selected that are shown in Figure 12-24. Click OK. The report should have 159 records. Save the changes and close the report.

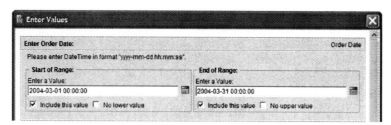

Figure 12-24 Date range parameter options

 You can also use the "Is not equal to" operator with range value parameter fields.

If you ran the report again and cleared the **INCLUDE THIS VALUE** option on the Start of Range field, there would be 139 records on the report. That means that 20 orders were placed on 3/1/2004. To verify that, check the Include this value option and change the End of Range value to 3/2/2004 and clear the Include this value option on the End of Range field. The reason that I entered 3/2/2004 is to be able to account for the time portion of the date/time field. In the real world, the time portion of a date/time field would probably have a value. I find this easier then typing in the equivalent of 11:59:59 PM as the end time.

If you wanted to run the report for one day, you would enter the same date in the start and end of range fields. You would have to include the equivalent of 11:59:59 PM on the End of Range field or you could enter the next day and use a time of 00:00:00.

 If you are running a monthly report and do not know if there are 30 or 31 days in the month, enter the first day of the month after the month you are running the report for in the End of range field and clear the Include this value option. Doing this will include all records for the prior month.

Using Range Values For Non Date Data

A lot of the time, the range value parameter field is used for dates. You can use range parameter fields for other types of data. Two other uses that come to mind are to only print records in a zip code range. Another use is if you wanted to print a list of customers whose last name started with a specific letter or was in a range of letters, like customers whose last name started with A through D.

Exercise 12.9: Use The Allow Range Value Option With Currency

In the previous exercise you used the Allow range values option with a date field. You can also use this option with numeric and currency fields. In this exercise, you will use the option to find all orders that are within a certain dollar amount range.

1. Save the L11.1 report as L12.9 Currency range parameter field.

2. Type Order Amount Range in the Name field, then change the Type to Currency.

3. Type Enter the order amount range for the report: in the Prompt Group Text field, then add the Order Amount field to the Value column.

4. Change the following options and click OK.
   Prompt Text - Select the order amount:
   Change the Allow range values option to True.

5. Open the Select Expert and click on the NEW tab. Select the Order Amount field and click OK. Select the "Is equal to" operator, then select the Order Amount Range parameter field and click OK.

6. Press F5. Select the first order amount over $1,000 for the Start of Range value. Select the first order amount over $2,000 for the End of Range value.

7. Clear the Include this value option for the End of Range field. Doing this will only display orders that have an order amount between $1,000 and $2,000. You should have the options shown in Figure 12-25. Click OK. There should be 36 records on the report. Save the changes and close the report.

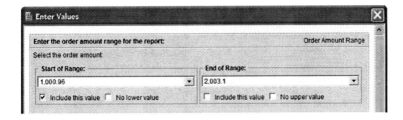

Figure 12-25 Currency range parameter options

Allow Multiple Values Option

When you set this option to TRUE, you will be able to select more than one value to the parameter field. This is the equivalent of the "Is one of" Select Expert operator. In Exercise 12.5 you created a dynamic list of values for the region field. When the report was run, only one region could be selected. You may often have a report request that requires that more than one value be included in the selection process. When the Allow multiple values option is set to True, you are creating what is called an ARRAY. This means that the field can contain more than one value.

If the ALLOW CUSTOM VALUES and ALLOW MULTIPLE VALUES options are set to True, values can be added from the AVAILABLE VALUES list box and typed in manually if the values in the Available Values list box is from a static list. This cannot be done with dynamic and cascading list of values.

Exercise 12.10: Use The Allow Multiple Values Option With A Static List Of Values

In Exercise 12.3 you created a static list of values by manually entering them. As you just learned, in addition to setting the Allow multiple values option to True, setting the Allow custom values option to True also, will allow the person running the report to select values from the static list and type in other values.

In this exercise, you will modify the parameter field to allow multiple values to be selected from the static list and allow other values to be entered.

1. Save the L12.3A report as `L12.10 Customer multi value parameter field`.

2. Open the Parameter dialog box for the Region field.

3. Change the following options and click OK.
   Prompt Text - `Select the region(s) or type them in below:`
   Change the Allow custom values and Allow multiple values options to True.

4. Open the Select Expert. Select the "Is equal to" operator on the Region parameter field and click OK. If you see a warning message that says the array must be subscripted, click OK and save the changes.

5. Press F5. Select the FL and PA regions from the Available Values list and add them to the Selected Values list.

If you hold down the CTRL key, you can click on multiple options in the Available Values list and then click the ADD button to add them to the Selected Values list box.

6. Manually add the TX and NY regions to the Selected Values list by typing one value in the Enter a Value field and then click the arrow button at the end of the field. Your dialog box should have the options shown in Figure 12-26. Click OK. There should be nine records on the report. Save the changes and close the report.

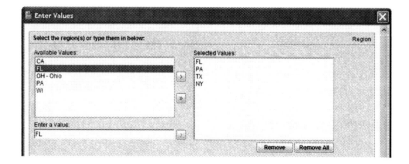

Figure 12-26 Multiple and custom value parameter options

Exercise 12.11: Use The Allow Multiple Values Option With A Dynamic List Of Values

In Exercise 5.9 you created a report that displayed all orders in 2004 that were shipped by two specific carriers. With a dynamic list, there is usually no need to allow custom values. In this exercise, you will modify this report to be able to select the carriers that will appear on the report.

1. Save the L5.9 report as `L12.11 Dynamic multi value list`.

2. Type `Ship Via` in the Name field, then select the Dynamic option.

3. Change the Prompt Group Text option to
    `Select the Ship Via option(s) for the report:`

4. Add the Ship Via field to the Value column, then change the Allow multiple values option to True and click OK.

5. Open the Select Expert and change the Ship Via operator to "Is equal to", then select the Ship via parameter field and click OK.

6. Add the last three shipping options to the Selected Values list as shown in Figure 12-27. Click OK and refresh the data. There should be 738 records on the report. The report may be easier to read if it was sorted on the Ship Via field.

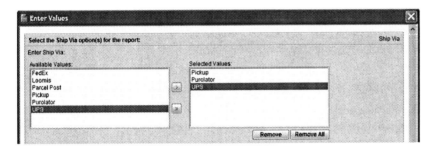

Figure 12-27 Shipping options selected

7. Sort the report on the Ship Via field in ascending order and rerun the report with the same options. The first shipping method on the report should be Pickup. Save the changes and close the report.

Combining Range And Multiple Values

What may not initially be apparent is that these two options can be combined on the same parameter field. Doing this allows for maximum flexibility and options when the report is run. On a report that uses a date parameter field, you can allow multiple date ranges to be entered. For example, if you wanted to be able to compare the orders for the first five days of three months, you could enter 1/1/04 to 1/5/04, 3/1/04 to 3/5/04 and 5/1/04 to 5/5/04 on the same parameter field. Another example would be if you wanted to see orders 1001 to 1050 and 1100 to 1124 on the same report. Setting the Allow range values and Allow multiple values options to true would allow you to create parameter fields for both of the examples just discussed.

Exercise 12.12: Combine Range And Multiple Values For A Date Field

In Exercise 12.8 the parameter field that you created only allowed one date range to be entered. In this exercise you will modify that parameter field to allow multiple date ranges to be entered.

1. Save the L12.8 report as `L12.12 Multiple date range parameter field`.

2. Open the Order Date parameter field dialog box.

3. Change the following options and click OK.
   Prompt Text - `Enter the Order Date range(s):`
   Change the Allow multiple values option to True.

4. Press F5. You should see the Enter Values dialog box. After you add the End of Range date, click the **ADD RANGE** button, then add the next date range. Add the following date ranges to the Selected Values list. 1/1/04 to 1/5/04, 3/1/04 to 3/5/04 and 5/1/04 to 5/5/04.

5. Your dialog box should have the options shown in Figure 12-28. Click OK. There should be 95 records on the report. Save the changes and close the report.

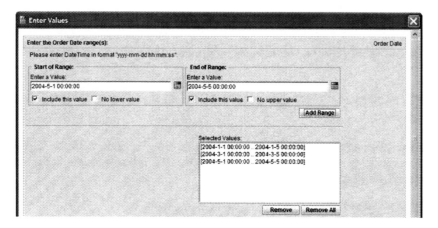

Figure 12-28 Range and multiple values parameter field options

Cascading Parameter Groups And Multi Value Parameter Options

Now that you have learned how to create cascading parameter groups and multi value parameter fields, the options that reports can have are almost endless. If you find that you cannot create the cascading parameter groups that you need, you can create individual parameter fields and add each one to the Select Expert and they will all appear on the Enter Values dialog box.

I prefer this method of one parameter field for each field that I need to query, because I do not have to rename the parameter fields after I create them. This is also very helpful if you need to rearrange the order that the fields appear in, on the Enter Values dialog box or if you need to add a new parameter field and place it between two existing parameter fields. This is what you will learn how to do in Exercise 12.13.

Exercise 12.13: Create Dynamic Cascading Prompts For Customers And Their Orders

In this exercise you will create cascading prompts for three fields: Customers, Order Date and Order Amount. The L6.2 report displays the orders by customer. Creating cascading prompts will let the person running the report select a customer and only display orders that meet the date range and order amount that they select. For example, the prompts that you will create in this exercise would let you see all orders placed on or after 1/1/04 for a specific customer that has orders greater than $1,000.

Create The Customer Name Parameter Field

1. Save the L6.2 report as `L12.13 Cascading prompts for customer orders.`

2. Type `Customer Name` in the Name field, then select the Dynamic option.

3. Type `Select the customer, date ranges(s) and minimum order amount` in the Prompt Group Text field.

4. Add the Customer Name field to the Value column, then click in the Parameters column. This is what tells Crystal Reports that you want to use this field on the Enter Values dialog box as a cascading prompt field. It should have the same name as the one you typed in the Name field.

5. Change the Prompt Text option to `Select A Customer:`. Click OK and save the changes.

Create The Order Amount Parameter Field

1. Type `Order Amount` in the Name field. Change the Type to Currency, then select the Dynamic option.

2. Add the Order Amount field to the Value column, then click in the Parameters column.

3. Change the Prompt Text option to `Select the smallest order amount that you want to see:`. Click OK and save the changes.

Create The Date Range Parameter Field

1. Type `Date Range` in the Name field. Change the Type to Date Time, then select the Dynamic option.

2. Type `You have to select at least one date range. Once selected, click the Add Range button:` in the Prompt Group Text field.

3. Add the Order Date field to the Value column, then click in the Parameters column.

4. Change the following options and click OK.
   Prompt Text `Select the beginning and ending order dates from the drop down lists:`
   Change the Allow multiple values and Allow range values options to True.

Modify The Select Expert Options

1. Open the Select Expert and change the Order Amount operator to "Is greater than or equal to", then select the Order Amount parameter field.

2. Change the Order Date operator to "Is equal to" and select the Date Range parameter field.

3. Click on the New tab and select the Customer Name field and click OK. Select the "Is equal to" operator, then select the Customer Name parameter field. The formula on the Select Expert should look like the one shown in Figure 12-29. Click OK. You should see the Enter Values dialog box.

```
{Orders.Order Amount} >= {?Order Amount} and
{Orders.Order Date} = {?Date Range} and
{Customer.Customer Name} = {?Customer Name}
```

Figure 12-29 Select Expert formula

Test The Parameter Fields

1. Select the Alley Cat Cycles company, then select the Order Amount 100.4.

2. Select the first and last dates in 2004. This will return all of this customers orders in 2004 that have an order total of $100.40 or more. You should have the options selected that are shown in Figure 12-30.

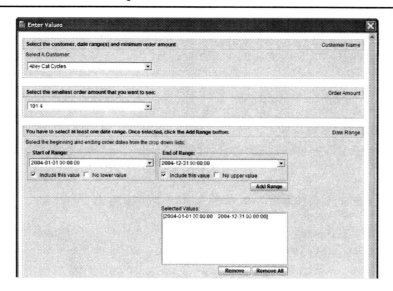

Figure 12-30 Report parameter options

3. Click OK. Press F5, then save the changes. There should be 29 records on the report.
    Leave the report open to complete the next part of the exercise.

Rearrange The Order Of The Parameter Fields

Earlier I mentioned that I think a benefit of creating individual parameter fields is that you can rearrange the order that they appear on the Enter Values dialog box. In this part of the exercise, you will change the order that the parameter fields appear on the Enter Values dialog box.

1. Right-click on the Parameter Fields option on the Field Explorer and select SET PARAMETER ORDER.

2. Click on the Order Amount parameter field and click the down arrow button. Your dialog box should look like the one shown in Figure 12-31.

3. Click OK, then press F5. The dialog box should look like the one shown in Figure 12-32.
    Compare this to the one shown earlier in Figure 12-30. Close the dialog box and save the changes.

Figure 12-31 Parameter order dialog box

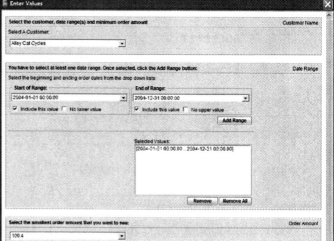

Figure 12-32 Modified parameter field order

 I don't know why, but you can only rename a parameter field from the Field Explorer. You cannot rename it from the Edit Parameter dialog box. The good thing is that if you rename a parameter field, it is renamed throughout the report.

Using Formula Fields In Parameter Fields

All of the formulas that you have created in this workbook have been static or hard coded, meaning that they do not change each time the report is run. There will be times when hard coded formulas will not produce the results that are needed. One way to tell if is you get requests for several reports that are very similar. This is often the case for reports that are used in what is known as "What-If" analysis.

For example, someone wants to see the potential revenue gain if they raise the price of the products by 5, 7 or 8%. Hard coded formulas could possibly require you to create three reports, one for each of the potential percent increases. Creating a parameter field that prompted for the percent of increase, allows the report to be flexible and not have to be changed.

A parameter field that is based off of a formula field will allow the user to be able to sort or group the report the way that best meets their needs. Instead of selecting a field name on the Record Sort Expert or Insert Group dialog box, you would select the formula field.

In addition to using formula fields for What-If analysis, you can also base parameter fields off of formula fields that are used to conditionally format data. An example of this is the suppression of data as shown in the L10.6 Suppress Salary GT 50000 report. Another example would be the conditional formatting that you created using the Highlighting Expert in Exercises 10.1 and 10.2.

NEW Top N Reports With Parameter Fields

In Exercise 7.7 and 11.8A, you created Top and Bottom N reports. Like other reports that have formulas, the options that you select on the dialog box to create a Top N report are hard coded. You can create a conditional formula and use it with the parameter field to be able to run the Top N report with different **N** values.

Exercise 12.14: Create A Parameter Field For A Top N Report

In this exercise you will create a formula that will be used as the basis for a parameter field that will let the person running the report select the **N** value. You will also remove the hard coded date range and add a parameter field to allow a date range to be selected each time the report is run.

Create The Parameter Field

1. Save the L7.7A report as L12.14 Top N parameter field.

2. Type Top N in the Name field, then change the Type to Number.

3. Change the following options:
   Prompt Text - Enter a number between 1 & 100 for the Top N value:
   Change the Default Value option to 5.
   Change the Min Value option to 1.
   Change the Max Value option to 100.
   You should have the options selected that are shown in Figure 12-33. Click OK and save the changes.

> When you have to create a Top, Bottom or Percent N parameter field you can select the Default, Min and Max Values that you want. If you know that the majority of times the users will run the report and select a specific N number, set that number as the default. It is not a requirement to have Min and Max Values.

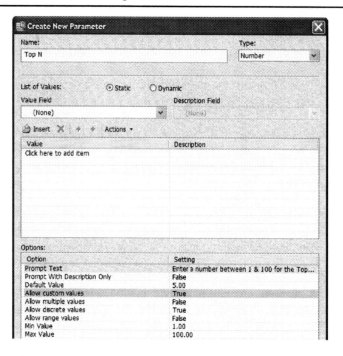

Figure 12-33 Top N parameter field options

Create The Top N Formula

1. Open the Group Sort Expert and click the Formula button.

2. Type `{?Top N}` as shown in the lower right hand corner of Figure 12-34. Click the Save and close button.

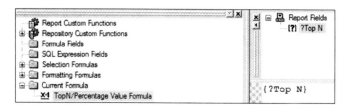

Figure 12-34 Top N Formula

3. Check the **INCLUDE TIES** option, then click OK to close the Group Sort Expert. Close the Enter Values dialog box.

> If the **INCLUDE TIES** option is not checked and there are ties, only one of the tied groups will be displayed on the report. I could not find a way to specify which of the tied groups will appear on the report or no way to indicate that there is another group with the same number. Therefore, I think the best solution is to always check this option.

The report needs more changes. The current report title will not be accurate because the person running the report has the option of selecting the Top N number and the order date range. Later in this lesson you will learn how to add a parameter field to the report, so that it can be printed.

Create The Order Date Range Parameter Field

In this part of the exercise you will remove the hard coded date range and replace it with a parameter field.

1. Open a new parameter field dialog box and type `Order Date` in the Name field, then change the Type to Date Time and select the Dynamic option.

2. Add the Order Date field to the Value column, then click in the Parameters column.

3. Change the following options and click OK.
Prompt Text - `Select the date range that you want to see orders for:`
Change the Allow range values option to True.

Modify The Select Expert Options And Parameter Field Order

1. Open the Select Expert. Select the "Is equal to" operator, then select the Order Date parameter field and click OK. Close the Enter Values dialog box.

2. Open the Parameter Order dialog box and put the parameter fields in the order shown in Figure 12-35, then click OK and save the changes.

Figure 12-35 Parameter Order dialog box options

Test The Parameter Fields

1. Press F5. Your dialog box should look similar to the one shown in Figure 12-36.

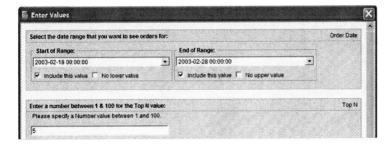

Figure 12-36 Top N parameter options

2. Run the report and make sure that it works. If you select a high N number, the chart will be difficult to read. More than likely, you would delete the chart.

Using Parameter Fields To Highlight Data

In Exercise 10.1 you used the Highlighting Expert to conditionally format data when a certain condition was met. The report created in that exercise may be more helpful if an option existed to select the value, in this case, the threshold to use for applying the conditional formatting. The report currently highlights records if the value in the Delay in Days To Ship field is greater than or equal to three.

Exercise 12.15: Create A Parameter Field To Highlight Rows Of Data

In this exercise you will modify the L9.9 report to prompt to select the delay in days to ship. You will also add a date range parameter. The background color of the row will change to yellow if the record meets the condition.

Create The Order Date Range Parameter Field

1. Save the L9.9 report as `L12.15 Highlight rows of data parameter field`.

2. Type `Date Range` in the Name field. Change the Type to Date Time and select the Dynamic option.

3. Add the Order Date field to the Value column, then click in the Parameters column.

4. Change the following options and click OK.
   Prompt Text - `Select the date range that you want to see orders for:`
   Change the Allow range values option to True.

Create The Highlight Rows Of Data Parameter Field

1. Open a new parameter field dialog box. Type `Delay in Days` in the Name field and change the Type to Number.

2. Change the following options:
   Prompt Text - `Enter the minimum number of Delay in Days To Ship that you want to see:`
   Change the Default Value option to 3.
   Change the Min Value option to 1.
   You should have the options shown in Figure 12-37. Click OK.

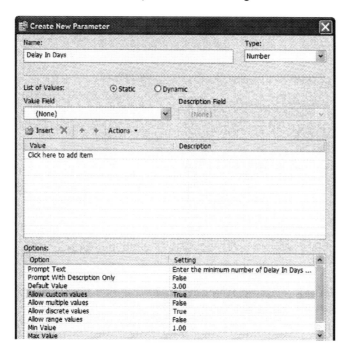

Figure 12-37 Delay in days parameter field options

Create The Row Color Formula

In this part of the exercise you will create the formula that will change the background to yellow for the rows that have a days to ship number greater than or equal to the number that is entered on the parameter field that you just created.

1. Open the Section Expert and click on the details section, then click on the Color tab.

2. Click on the Formula button and open the Report Fields tree in the Formula Workshop.

Notice on the left side of the Formula Workshop that the conditional formatting formula that you are creating is being applied to the background color option of the details section.

3. Type `If` in the Formula Text window and press the space bar, then double-click on the Delay in Dates To Ship formula field in the Report Fields section.

4. Press the space bar and type `>=`, then press the space bar.

5. Double-click on the Delay in Days parameter field in the Report Fields section, then press the space bar and type `Then crYellow Else crNoColor.` Your formula should look like the one shown in Figure 12-38. Click the Save and close button. Click OK to close the Section Expert, then save the changes.

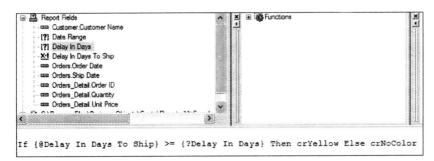

```
If {@Delay In Days To Ship} >= {?Delay In Days} Then crYellow Else crNoColor
```

Figure 12-38 Parameter field formula

 If you did not add the crNoColor option, rows that did not meet the criteria would have a black background and you would not be able to see the text.

Add The Date Range Parameter Field To The Select Expert

If you look at the Parameter Fields section of the Field Explorer you will see that the Date Range field does not have a green check mark next to it. That is because the field is currently not being used on the report.

1. Open the Select Expert and select the "Is equal to" operator.

2. Open the next drop down list and select the Date Range parameter field, then click OK.

Test The Parameter Fields

1. Save the changes and press F5.

2. Select the first date in 2004, for the Start of Range value, then select the last date in 2004 for the End of Range value. Notice that the default value that you set is in the Delay in Days To Ship field. You should have the options selected that are shown in Figure 12-39.

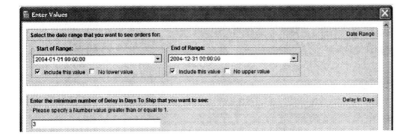

Figure 12-39 Delay in Days parameter field options

3. Click OK. The top of the first page of the report should look like the one shown in Figure 12-40. Every row that has a value of three or greater in the Delay in Days To Ship field has a yellow background.

Customer Name	Order Date	Ship Date	Order ID	Unit Price	Quantity	Delay In Days To Ship
Rough Terrain	01/01/2004	01/01/2004	1,121	$41.90	1	0
Rough Terrain	01/01/2004	01/01/2004	1,121	$809.87	1	0
Hooked on Helmets	01/01/2004	01/08/2004	1,122	$21.90	3	7
Hooked on Helmets	01/01/2004	01/08/2004	1,122	$479.85	2	7
Clean Air Transportation Co.	01/02/2004	01/02/2004	1,123	$1,739.85	3	0
Off the Mountain Biking	01/02/2004	01/09/2004	1,124	$19.90	3	7
Road Runners Paradise	01/02/2004	01/03/2004	1,125	$19.71	2	1
Road Runners Paradise	01/02/2004	01/03/2004	1,125	$36.00	1	1
Piatou Sport	01/02/2004	01/02/2004	1,126	$16.50	2	0
Piatou Sport	01/02/2004	01/02/2004	1,126	$1,739.85	2	0
Piatou Sport	01/02/2004	01/02/2004	1,126	$329.85	1	0
BBS Pty	01/02/2004	01/10/2004	1,127	$13.50	3	8
BBS Pty	01/02/2004	01/10/2004	1,127	$479.85	1	8

Figure 12-40 L12.15 Highlight rows of data parameter field report

Using Parameter Fields To Select The Sorting And Grouping Options

In Lesson 6 you learned how to sort and group data by selecting options on the Record Sort Expert and Insert Group dialog boxes. There will be times when a report needs to be sorted or grouped in several different ways. Rather then hard code this information and have to create several reports, one for each field the report needs to be sorted or grouped on, you can create a parameter field that will be used to find out what field the person wants the report to be sorted or grouped on. The value collected from the parameter field will be passed to the Record Sort Expert or Insert Group dialog box.

Parameter fields cannot retrieve a formula or table name. Therefore, you have to create a formula that uses the value in the parameter field as the field to sort or group on. The formula field is what you will select on the sorting or grouping dialog box.

Exercise 12.16: Create A Parameter Field To Sort The Records

In Exercise 3.1 you created a customer information report. As it is, the report is not sorted or grouped. In this exercise you will create a formula and parameter field that will allow the report to be sorted on one of the following three fields: Customer Name, Region or Country.

Create The Sort By Parameter Field

1. Save the L3.1 report as L12.16 Sort records parameter field.

2. Type Sort By Field in the Name field.

3. Type the values Customer Name, Region and Country in the Value column.
    Type State in the Description column of the Region value.

4. Change the following options and click OK.
    Prompt Text - Select the field that you want to sort by:
    Change the Allow custom values option to False.

Create The Sort Formula And Add It To The Parameter Field

1. Open the Formula Workshop and create a new formula. Type SortBy as the formula name.

2. Type the formula shown below, then click the Save and close button.

```
If (?Sort By Field) = "Customer Name" Then {Customer.Customer
Name}
Else
If (?Sort By Field) = "Region" Then {Customer.Region}
Else
{Customer.Country}
```

3. Open the Record Sort Expert, then add the SortBy formula field to the Sort Fields list box and click OK. The Enter Values dialog box shown in Figure 12-41 will open.

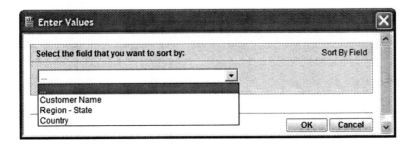

Figure 12-41 SortBy options

Test The Sort Parameter

1. Select the Customer Name option from the drop down list and click OK. The report should be sorted in Customer Name order.

2. Save the changes, then run the report again and sort the report by Region. Leave the report open to complete the next exercise.

Exercise 12.17: Create A Parameter Field To Group Data

In the previous exercise you learned how to sort the detail records using a parameter field. Selecting the field to group on via a parameter field basically works the same way. The difference is that you attach the formula field to the Insert Group dialog box instead of the Record Sort Expert.

In this exercise you will create a group for the customer information report from the previous exercise. One parameter field that you will create in this exercise will let you select which of the three fields; Customer Name, Region or Country to group on. You will create another parameter field that lets you select the group sort order, ascending or descending.

Create The Group Sort Parameter Field

1. Save the L12.16 report as L12.17 Group data parameter field.

2. Type Group By Field in the Name field.

3. Type the values Customer Name, Region and Country in the Value column.

4. Change the following options and click OK.
   Prompt Text - Select the field that you want to group by:
   Change the Default Value option to Region. You can select it from the drop down list.
   Change the Allow custom values option to False.

Create The Group Formula And Add It To The Parameter Field

1. Open the Formula Workshop and create a new formula. Type GroupBy as the formula name.

2. Click on the SortBy formula field under the Formula Fields node on the left of the Formula Workshop. Copy and paste the SortBy formula into the GroupBy formula.

3. Change the word "Sort" to Group in two places in the formula, then click the Save and close button.

Create The Group Sort Order Parameter Field

The parameter field that you will create in this part of the exercise will let the person running the report select the sort order of the group, either ascending or descending.

1. Open a new parameter dialog box and type `Group Sort Order` in the Name field.

2. Type the options `Ascending` and `Descending` in the Value column.

3. Change the following options and click OK.
   Prompt Text - `Select the order that you want to sort the groups in:`
   Change the Default Value option to Ascending.
   Change the Allow custom values option to False.

Change The Order Of The Parameter Fields

Parameter fields are displayed on the Enter Values dialog box in the order that they were created in. The more logical order in this exercise would be to have the Sort By Field last.

1. Change the order of the parameter fields so that the Sort By Field is last.

Create The Group And Add The Group Formula To The Insert Group Dialog Box

As you have noticed, the report that you are working on does not have any groups. In this part of the exercise you will create the group based on a formula field and sort the group based on a different formula field.

1. Click the Insert Group button on the Insert Tools toolbar.

2. Open the first drop down list and select the GroupBy formula.

3. Check the option, **USE A FORMULA AS GROUP SORT ORDER**, then click the Formula button and type the formula shown below.

```
If {?Group Sort Order} = "Ascending" Then crAscendingOrder
Else
crDescendingOrder
```

4. Click the Save and close button, then click OK to close the Insert Group dialog box.

Test The Parameter Fields

1. Click the Save button, then press F5. You should see the dialog box shown in Figure 12-42.

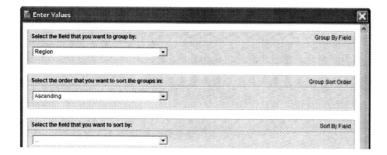

Figure 12-42 Group and field sort parameter options

2. Run the report a few times, selecting different options.

Boolean Parameter Fields

In Lesson 10 you learned how to create Boolean formulas. Boolean parameter fields, like Boolean formulas, can only have two values: True and False. Like the Boolean formulas, you do not have to display the options as true and false. If the Boolean parameter field is not a group, you can use the Description column to enter the text you want to display in the drop down list instead of the values, true and false.

Interestingly enough, you cannot use the Description column to change what is displayed in the drop down list on Boolean group parameter fields. Instead, the name of the Parameter field is used. Therefore, make good use of the name field.

Using A Parameter Field To Suppress Data

You have learned how to conditionally suppress data on a report. Suppression is often done with a Boolean field. Suppressing data is popular on reports that have a lot of detail records. Being able to select whether or not to suppress detail records allows one to run the report and only see the summary information. Doing this means that a report can be a detail report or a summary report. The Suppress (No Drill-Down) option on the Section Expert requires a Boolean formula when it will be used conditionally.

Exercise 12.18: Conditional Section Suppression Using A Parameter Field

In the last skills exercise in Lesson 10, the details section was manually suppressed to create a summary report. In this exercise, you will modify a report so that it can be run as a detailed report or a summary only report.

Create The Suppress Parameter Field

1. Save the L6.2 report as `L12.18 Suppress section parameter field`.

2. Type `Summary Report` in the Name field.

3. Type `Yes` in the first Value row, then type `No` in the second Value row.

4. Change the following options and click OK.
   Prompt Text - `Do you want to run a Summary Only report?`
   Change the Allow custom values option to False.

Modify The Section Expert Options

1. Open the Section Expert and add another page header section.

You need the additional page header section because the field headings will also have to be suppressed if the report will be run as a summary report.

2. Click on the Formula button for the Suppress (No Drill-Down) option for the page header b section, then type the formula shown below.

   `If {?Summary Report} = "Yes" Then True.`

This formula checks to see if the Summary Report parameter field has the value Yes. If it does, the page header b and details sections will be suppressed.

3. Highlight the formula and press CTRL + C, then click the Save and close button. This will let you copy the formula.

4. Click on the details section in the Section Expert, then click the Formula button across from the Suppress (No Drill-Down) option. Paste (Press CTRL + V) the formula into the Formula Text window, then click the Save and close button. Click OK to close the Section Expert.

Modify The Report

As mentioned earlier, when the report is run in the summary only mode, the field headings should not print. This is why you created the second page header section and added the suppression formula to the second page header section.

1. Move the field headings to the page header b section and save the changes. Press the F5 key. You should see the dialog box shown in Figure 12-43.

Figure 12-43 Summary only parameter dialog box

2. Select Yes to run a summary report. You should only see summary information on the report. Run the report again and select No.

Managing Data Entry In Parameter Fields

You have created several parameter fields in this lesson. While you took care and entered the data in the parameter fields correctly, it is unrealistic to think that people that run the reports will always enter the correct information in the parameter fields. If the reports are going to be part of an application, there are more options available for helping and guiding users to enter the data in parameter fields correctly then Crystal Reports provides. Crystal Reports does provide three types of options that you can use to help users enter data in the parameter fields correctly. These options are Min and Max field lengths, which use a range of values to limit the data. You have already used these options on date fields. The other options are Min/Max value and Edit Masks.

On string parameter fields the **MIN LENGTH** and **MAX LENGTH** options are used. The length refers to how many characters can be entered in the field. The number that you enter in the Max Length field should not be larger then the actual length of the corresponding field in the table. Any items in the Value column have to meet the min and max requirements.

The range limits **MIN VALUE** and **MAX VALUE** are primarily used for number and date fields. These options require that the data entered in the field be in a specific range. For example, if the min value is one and the max value is five, any number less than one or greater than five would not be accepted.

 If a number parameter field is populated with a static list of values and you do not want all of the values to be available, enter the min and max values for the range of data that you want to import before importing the values for the static list of values.

Edit Masks

In Lessons 9 and 10 you learned about masks. You learned that they are placeholders that determine how data will be displayed on a report. The Edit mask feature for parameter fields is similar. Edit masks are used to set the rules for how data has to be entered into a field. If an edit mask has 10 placeholders, that means that no more than 10 characters can be entered into the field. Each of the edit mask characters has its own rule. The characters can be combined in the same field as needed. For example, if you were going to use an edit mask for a country field, you may want to force the first character to be an upper case letter and the other characters could be a combination of upper and lower case letters.

Table 12-2 lists the mask characters that you can use. Edit masks provide a lot of flexibility for managing the data that is entered in parameter fields. An edit mask is a series of characters (placeholders) that control the type of data that can be entered in **STRING** parameter fields. The Edit Mask field was shown earlier at the bottom of Figure 12-1.

The edit mask **>AA** could be used for a state field. AA forces two alphanumeric characters to be entered in the field. **>** forces the characters to be uppercase.

If the values entered are not correct, you will see an error message. Often, the error messages are cryptic and can confuse the person that is trying to run the report. If I use an edit mask on a parameter field, I put as much information in the Prompt Text field as possible to help the person enter the correct data.

Character	Description
A	Requires that an alphanumeric character be entered.
a	Allows an alphanumeric character, but is not required.
0 (zero)	Requires a numeric character to be entered.
9	Allows a numeric character, but is not required.
#	Allows a digit, space, plus sign or minis sign, but is not required.
L	Requires a letter to be entered.
?	Allows a letter, but is not required.
&	Allows any character or space, but is required.
C	Allows any character or space, but is not required.
. , : ; - /	Allows separator characters, but is not required.
<	Converts the characters in the field to lower case.
>	Converts the characters in the field to upper case.
\	Causes the character that follows the \ to be taken as a literal.
Password	Does not display actual characters that are entered. Instead, circles appear when text is entered into this field.

Table 12-2 Edit mask characters

Adding Parameter Field Criteria To A Report

You have learned how to create parameter fields that add a lot of interaction. The one thing that is missing is adding the parameter field criteria to a report. With all of the parameter field selection combinations that a report can have, including the selection criteria on the report would be helpful. Single value parameter fields can be dragged from the Field Explorer on to the report like other fields.

Range value and multiple value parameter fields cannot be dragged onto the report and printed like single value parameter fields. If these fields are added to the report, only the first value in the field will print. Printing solutions for these types of parameter fields are discussed below.

Printing Parameter Range Fields

There are two functions, **MINIMUM()** and **MAXIMUM()** in Crystal Reports that let you print the range in a parameter field. These functions return the beginning and ending values. The formula below will print the date range on the report as long as the **NO LOWER VALUE** and **NO UPPER VALUE** options are not checked on the Enter Values dialog box. Replace the {?Date_Parameter} field with the name of the field that you need.

"Starting Date " & Minimum ({?Date_Parameter}) & " and Ending Date " & Maximum ({?Date_Parameter})

You can use the Minimum and Maximum functions for any type of range parameter field data. It is not just for date ranges.

Printing Multi Value Parameter Fields Using The Join Function

If you drag a multi value parameter field to a report, the only value that will print will be the first one. All of the values that are selected in a multi value parameter field are stored in one field and are separated by a comma in the array. The **JOIN** function will print all of the values in the array. The formula below will let you print all of the values in a multiple value parameter field. Replace the {?ShipVia} field with the name of the field that you need.

"Shipping Methods Selected: " + Join ({?ShipVia}, ", ")

Deleting Parameter Fields From A Report

You may need to delete a parameter field from a report. If you do, follow the steps below.

1. Right-click on the parameter field in the Field Explorer that you want to delete and select **DELETE**. You will see the message shown in Figure 12-44. This message is letting you know that once you delete the field it cannot be undone.

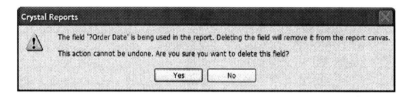

Figure 12-44 Delete parameter field message

2. Click Yes. You may see the message shown in Figure 12-45.

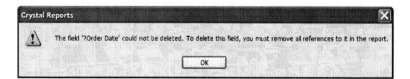

Figure 12-45 Unable to delete field message

This message is letting you know that the parameter field can't be deleted now because it is being used in the report. Before you can delete a parameter field, you have to delete it from the place(s) that it is being used in the report. In this example, it is being used on the Select Expert. If it was being used on the report to display the criteria that was used to run the report, you would have to delete it from there. It could also be used in a formula.

3. Click OK and delete the parameter field from all of the places that it is being used in the report. Once you do that, repeat step 1 above and the parameter field will be deleted, then save the changes.

Customizing The Enter Values Dialog Box

As mentioned earlier in this lesson, attributes of the Enter Values dialog box can be modified. You need to have some web design experience to modify the Enter Values dialog box, in particular, HTML (Hypertext Markup Language) and CSS (Cascading Style Sheets). This is beyond the scope of this workbook, but I wanted to let you know that the dialog box can be modified.

The file that you would modify is promptengine_default.css. This file is in the folder listed below if you selected the default installation path when you installed Crystal Reports.
C:\Program Files\Common Files\Business Objects\3.0\crystalreportviewers11\prompting\css\

If you plan to modify this dialog box, keep in mind that any changes that you make will be applied to all Enter Values dialog boxes that point to the CSS file that you modify, not just one report. You should make a copy of this file before making any changes to it. Some of the features that you can change are listed below in Table 12-3.

Enter Values Dialog Box Changes	
Font	Background color
Font size	Prompt text box
Font color	Prompt button
Border	Size of text in a drop down list

Table 12-3 Some of the Enter Values dialog box options that can be changed

Report Alerts

Report Alerts provide a way to notify the person running a report that the report contains data that meets a condition. These alerts can be informational, like 50 or more customers ordered a specific product in the date range that the report is using. Alerts can also be used as a reminder. For example, an inventory report could have an alert to let the person running the report know which products need to be reordered based on the quantity on hand.

Report Alerts are created with formulas that evaluate the conditions that you specify. A report can have more than one alert. Alerts are similar to using the Highlighting Expert and conditional formatting that you learned about in Lesson 10.

Report Alerts are only activated when the data is refreshed in the report. If the report is located on a Crystal Reports Server or in the Business Objects Enterprise and is scheduled, an email can be sent to a user when an alert is triggered.

 Unless instructed otherwise for the report alert exercises, after you save the report with a new name, open the **CREATE ALERT** dialog box, shown in Figure 12-46.
Report ⇒ Alerts ⇒ Create or Modify Alerts, then click the **NEW** button.

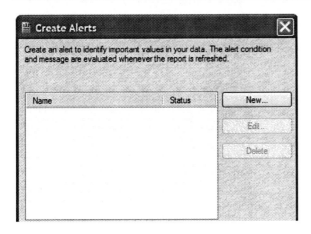

Figure 12-46 Create Alerts dialog box

Exercise 12.19: Create An Order Amount Less Than Alert

In this exercise you will create an alert that will let the person running the report know if there are orders on the report that are less than $250. This alert could be used by the sales department as a way to promote additional items.

Create The Alert

1. Save the L12.2 report as `L12.19 Order amount less than $250 alert`.

2. Type `Order Amount < 250` in the Name field.

3. Type `There are orders on this report that have an order total amount of less than $250` in the Message field.

 The Message field can have up to 254 characters.

4. Click the **CONDITION** button, then open the Orders table in the Reports Fields tree and double-click on the Order Amount field.

5. Press the space bar and type `< 250`. The formula should look like the one shown at the bottom of Figure 12-47.

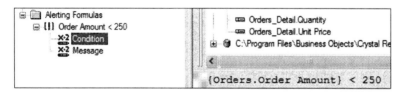

Figure 12-47 Order amount formula

Notice that alerts can have two types of formulas: one for the condition, like you just created and one for the message. The message formula allows you to include a field on the report as part of the message that is displayed. If you want to create a formula for the message, click on the Formula button on the Create Alert dialog box shown in Figure 12-48.

6. Click the Save and close button. Your dialog box should have the options shown in Figure 12-48. Click OK.

7. Click OK. You should see the alert that you just created in the dialog box shown in Figure 12-49. Click the Close button and save the changes.

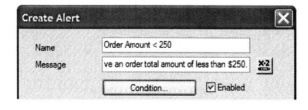

Figure 12-48 Create Alert dialog box options

Figure 12-49 Create Alerts dialog box

Test The Alert

1. Press F5 and select the first option and click OK. You should see the dialog box shown in Figure 12-50. This is the alert that you just created.

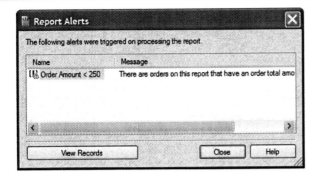

Figure 12-50 Report Alerts dialog box

 Report ⇒ Alerts ⇒ Triggered Alerts will also open the Report Alerts dialog box shown above in Figure 12-50.

2. Click the **VIEW RECORDS** button.

Notice that a new preview window opened. The name of the tab is the name of the alert. This is similar to drill down reports. The records on this tab are the ones that triggered the alert (met the condition) that you created. Close the report.

Exercise 12.20: Create A Delay In Shipping Greater Than Alert

In this exercise you will create two alerts: one that will notify the person running the report when the delay in shipping is greater than seven days. The second alert will notify the person if the delay in shipping is greater than four days and has and order amount of at least $500.

These alerts would be useful to sales people that need to let their customers know that their order has not shipped or to check on the order to find out why it has not shipped.

Create The Delay In Shipping > 4 Days Alert

1. Save the L12.15 report as `L12.20 Delay in shipping alert`.

2. Type `Delay is > 4 & Order amount >= 500` in the Name field.

3. Type `There are orders that took at least 5 days to ship and have an order amount of at least $500` in the Message field.

4. Click the Condition button, then double-click on the Delay in Days To Ship formula field.

5. Type the formula shown below.

   `{@Delay In Days To Ship} > 4 and {Orders.Order Amount} >= 500`

6. Click the Save and close button, then click OK.

Create The Delay In Shipping > 7 Days Alert

1. Click the New button on the Create Alerts dialog box.

2. Use the following information to create the alert.
   Name - `Delay is > 7.`
   Message - `There are orders that took at least 7 days to ship.`
   Formula - `{@Delay In Days To Ship} >= 7.`

3. Save the changes and press F5. Use the following parameters to run the report.
Start of Range Date - 1/1/2004
End of Range Date - 12/31/2004
Delay in days to ship - 4

When you run the report, you will see the Report Alerts dialog box. Depending on the date range that is selected, you may see one, both or no alerts. If you view the Delay is > 7 alert, all of the 358 records have a yellow background. That is because the parameter field for the delay in days to ship field has conditional formatting to change the background to yellow for rows that have a delay in days to ship, equal to or greater than the number that was entered on the Enter Values dialog box.

If you click on the preview tab, you will see the Report Alerts dialog box. If you click on the Delay is > 4 alert, another tab will open that displays the 465 records that meet the criteria for this alert.

 You can create conditional formatting that is based on whether or not the alert condition is met, just like you can create conditional formatting on parameter fields.

4. Leave the report open to complete the next exercise.

Editing And Deleting Report Alerts

Follow the steps below if you need to edit or delete a report alert.

1. Open the report that has the alert that you need to edit or delete.

2. Report ⇒ Alerts ⇒ Create or Modify Alerts.

3. In the Create Alerts dialog box, click on the alert that you want to edit or delete.

4. Click the **EDIT** button to modify the alert and make changes or click the **DELETE** button to delete the alert. Save the changes.

Alert Functions

In addition to creating the pop-up window notification alerts that you created in the previous exercises, Crystal Reports has three alert functions that you can use to create formulas to display the alert message on the report. These functions can also be used to apply conditional formatting, like changing the background color of records that trigger the alert.

① **IsAlertEnabled** This function will return a value of True if the **ENABLED** field on the Create Alert dialog box is checked. A value of False is returned if the Enabled field is not checked.
② **IsAlertTriggered** This function returns a value of True or False for each record. A value of True is returned if the record triggers the alert. A value of False is returned if the record does not trigger the alert.
③ **AlertMessage** This function contains the text that is in the Message field on the Create Alert dialog box, shown earlier in Figure 12-48 or the result of the formula that was created by the alert.

Exercise 12.21: Use The AlertMessage Function

In this exercise you will modify the L12.20 Delay in shipping alert report to print one of the alert messages on the report. You will use the AlertMessage function to print the message on the report. The alert message is not stored in a field that you can access. To print the alert message on the report, you have to create a formula that incorporates the AlertMessage function and then place the formula on the report to be printed.

1. Save the L12.20 report as L12.21 Print alert message on the report.

2. Open the Formula Workshop and create a new formula. Type `PrintAlertMessage` as the formula name.

3. Type this formula `AlertMessage ("Delay is > 7")`. The text in parenthesis is the name of the alert. Click the Save and close button.

4. Add a text box to the upper left hand corner of the page header section, then type `Alert Message:` and press the space bar.

5. Drag the PrintAlertMessage formula into the text box. This message is pretty long, so make the text field wider and save the changes. Preview the report. You should see the message shown in Figure 12-51.

Alert Message: There are orders that took at least 7 days to ship			
Customer Name	Order Date	Ship Date	Order ID
City Cyclists	12/02/2003	12/10/2003	1
Deals on Wheels	12/02/2003	12/02/2003	1,002
Deals on Wheels	12/02/2003	12/02/2003	1,002

Figure 12-51 L12.21 Print alert message on the report

Exercise 12.22: Use The IsAlertTriggered Function

In this exercise you will modify the 2004 Monthly orders by sales rep report to print the alert message in the group total section if the total number of orders for the month is greater than or equal to 425.

1. Save the L6.13 report as `L12.22 IsAlertTriggered function`.

2. Type `Above Order Total` as the alert name.

3. Create this condition `Count of Orders.Order ID >= 425`, then click the Save and close button.

4. Close both Create Alert dialog boxes, then open the Formula Workshop. Type `AlertTriggered` as the formula name.

5. Type the formula shown below, then click the Save and close button.

    ```
    If IsAlertTriggered ("Above Order Total") Then
    "* Great job! You exceeded the monthly number of orders *"
    ```

6. Drag the AlertTriggered formula field to the report and place it next to the Count field in the group footer section, then make the field wider. Save the changes and preview the report.

7. Click on the "3" in the group tree. You should now be on page 8 of the report. You should see the result of the formula, as shown in Figure 12-52. If you click on the "4" in the group tree, you will not see the message because the total number of orders is not greater than or equal to 425.

Totals for:	Nancy Davolio	
	Total # of orders - **433**	* Great job! You exceeded the monthly number of orders *
	Total # of pieces shipped - **883**	
	Total amount of orders - **$ 960,806.56**	

Figure 12-52 L12.22 IsAlertTriggered function report

 Report Alert formulas can be used for detail level or summary fields. They cannot be used with running total fields or shared variables.

Viewing Report Alerts

There are two ways to view alerts that have been triggered as discussed below.

    ① Refresh the data. You did this in the alert exercises above.

    ② Use the Report Alerts dialog box. This is covered below.

How To Manually Open The Report Alerts Dialog Box

1. Open and run the report that has the alert that you want to view, then close all open dialog boxes (You can open the L12.20 report.)

2. Report ⇒ Alerts ⇒ Triggered Alerts. You will see the Report Alerts dialog box shown earlier in Figure 12-50.

3. Select the alert for the records that you want to view. (You can select the first alert).

 You can select more than one alert at the same time. If more than one alert is selected at the same time, only records that meet the criteria for all of the alerts that are selected will be displayed on the new preview window.

4. Click the **VIEW RECORDS** button. You will see a new tab on the report that displays the records that triggered the alert(s).

Test Your Skills

1. Modify the L4.5 report to prompt to select a country.

   - The country prompt should allow multiple values.
   - Save the report as `L12.23 Skills select a country parameter field`.
   - The Enter Values dialog box should look like the one shown in Figure 12-53.

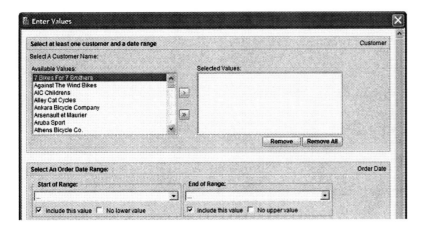

Figure 12-53 Enter Values dialog box options

2. Create a dynamic cascading parameter prompt for the L9.5 report.

   - Create parameter fields for the sales rep and order date fields.
   - The parameter fields should let you select a sales rep, then select an order date and only display orders for that sales rep with an order date greater than or equal to the date selected on the Enter Values dialog box. For example, run the report and select the sales rep Janet Leverling and the date, 1/2/2005. The first page of the report should look like the one shown in Figure 12-54. The report should have 127 records.
   - Save the report as `L12.24 Skills sales rep parameter field`.

	Employee	Order Date	Order ID	Customer #	Product #	Unit Price	Quantity	Line Item Total
3 1/2/2005 9	Janet Leverling							
		01/02/2005	2556	9	3304	$21.90	2	$43.80
	Total order amount for customer - **$ 43.80**							
40								
		01/04/2005	2561	40	4102	$13.50	3	$40.50
	Total order amount for customer - **$ 40.50**							
46								
		01/04/2005	2560	46	301221	$764.85	2	$1,529.70
		01/04/2005	2560	46	201161	$832.35	3	$2,497.05
		01/04/2005	2560	46	101202	$2,792.86	2	$5,585.72
	Total order amount for customer - **$ 28,837.41**							

Figure 12-54 L12.24 Skills sales rep parameter field report

3. Create a dynamic cascading parameter and multi value field prompt for the L5.9 report.

- Create a parameter field for the customer name. The parameter field should allow for more than one customer to be selected and have an order date range.
- Delete the Ship Via selection criteria.
- Save the report as L12.25 Skills customer parameter field.
- If you run the report for all customer names that start with the letter "A" in 2004, there should be 28 records on the report. The Enter Values dialog box should look like the one shown in Figure 12-55.

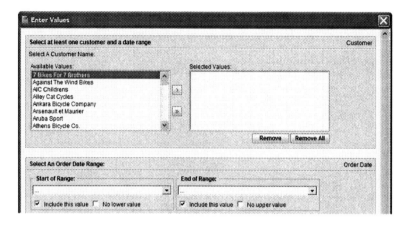

Figure 12-55 Customer and date range parameter field prompts

4. Modify the L5.3 report to allow a range of order numbers like 1002 to 1050 and 1100 to 1124 to be entered.

- Delete the Order Date selection criteria.
- If you run the report with the order number ranges listed above, there should be 115 records on the report. Figure 12-56 shows the Enter Values dialog box.
- Save the report as L12.26 Skills order number range.

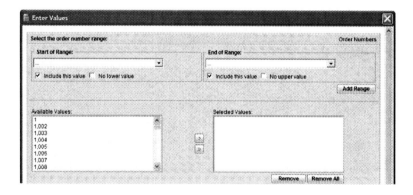

Figure 12-56 Order number range options

5. Create a new report to have an alert that notifies the user when the Units On Order is below 150.

- Add the tables and fields in Table 12-4 to the report.
- Use Reorder Alert as the name of the alert.
- The background color of the rows with a Units On Order amount below 150 should be silver.
- Save the report as L12.27 Skills reorder product level alert.
- Figure 12-57 shows the first page of the report.
- There should be 35 records on the Reorder Alert preview window.

Product	Purchases
Product ID	Units On Order
Product Name	Units In Stock

Table 12-4 Tables and fields for the L12.27 report

Product ID	Product Name	Units on Order	Units in Stock
1,101	Active Outdoors Crochet Glo	500	220
1,102	Active Outdoors Crochet Glo	0	450
1,103	Active Outdoors Crochet Glo	0	325
1,104	Active Outdoors Crochet Glo	0	265
1,105	Active Outdoors Crochet Glo	0	367
1,106	Active Outdoors Lycra Glove	0	440
1,107	Active Outdoors Lycra Glove	0	358
1,108	Active Outdoors Lycra Glove	500	266
1,109	Active Outdoors Lycra Glove	0	750
1,110	Active Outdoors Lycra Glove	500	112

Figure 12-57 L12.27 Skills reorder product level alert report

6. Modify the L12.6 report to allow multiple countries and regions.

    -   Save the report as L12.28 Skills multiple countries and regions parameters.
    -   If you run the report and select all countries that start with the letter "B" and then select all of the regions, the report should have 13 records.
    -   The Enter Values dialog box should look like the one shown in Figure 12-58.

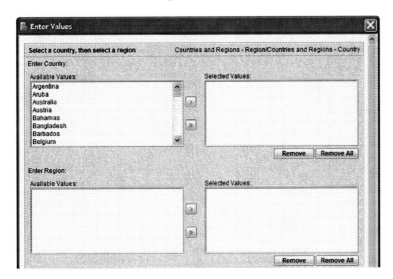

Figure 12-58 Enter Values dialog box options

7. Add all of the reports that were created in this lesson to the Workbench.

ADDITIONAL CRYSTAL REPORTS FUNCTIONALITY

Believe it or not, this workbook only covers a little more than half of the functionality that Crystal Reports has to offer report designers. You may be thinking that you have learned enough in the first 12 lessons to create all of the reports that you need. Some of the topics covered in this lesson, like the cross-tab and drill down reports build on what you have already learned in previous lessons. Other topics are being introduced for the first time. Many of the reports that you learn how to create in this lesson are known as or referred to as "Non standard report types".

In this lesson, you will learn how to:

☑ Use the Cross-Tab Expert
☑ Apply conditional formatting to a cross-tab object
☑ Create a template from scratch
☑ Add hyperlinks to a report
☑ Create Running Totals
☑ Create Hierarchical Groups
☑ Use the Group Sort Expert
☑ Create a form letter
☑ Use the Repository

To pass the RDCR201 exam, you need to be familiar with and be able to:

☑ Create and format a cross-tab
☑ Create a template without using a data source
☑ Add a hyperlink to a report
☑ Use the Running Total Fields dialog box
☑ Create a basic form letter
☑ Create a multi-column report
☑ Use the Repository to save reports on a Crystal Reports Server

Cross-Tab Expert Overview

In Lesson 7 you learned how to create a cross-tab report using a wizard. In this lesson you will learn more about cross-tab reports by learning how to use the Cross-Tab Expert. Cross-Tab reports let you summarize large amounts of data in columnar format, in a relatively small amount of space. Cross-Tab reports do not have to be the only object on the report. You can add a cross-tab object to a report that has standard data.

In addition to using the Cross-Tab wizard, there are three ways to add a Cross-Tab object to a report as discussed below.

    ① Right-click on a blank space on the report and select Insert Cross-Tab, then click in the report section where you want to place the cross-tab.
    ② Click the Insert Cross-Tab button on the Insert Tools toolbar.
    ③ Insert ⇒ Cross-Tab.

The Cross-Tab Expert has three tabs: Cross-Tab, Style and Customize Style. Many of the options on the first two tabs are on the Cross-Tab wizard.

Figure 13-1 shows the Cross-Tab tab.
Table 13-1 explains the options that are not on the Cross-Tab wizard.
Figure 13-4 shows the Style tab. The options on this tab are the same as the ones on the wizard.
Figure 13-5 shows the Customize Style tab. Tables 13-2 to 13-4 explain the options on this tab.

Cross-Tab Tab

The options shown in Figure 13-1 let you select the fields that will be used to create the cross-tab.

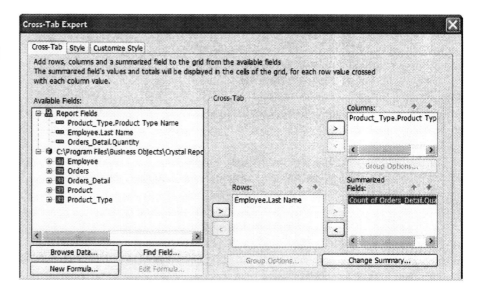

Figure 13-1 Cross-Tab options

Option	Description
New Formula	Opens the Formula Workshop so that you can create a formula that is needed for the cross-tab report.
Edit Formula	Opens the Formula Workshop, so that you can edit an existing formula. You can edit a formula that has been added to the cross-tab or a formula that is listed in the Available Fields list box.
Group Options	Opens the Cross-Tab Group Options dialog box shown in Figure 13-2. It is similar to the Insert Group dialog box that you have already learned about. After you click on a field in the Rows or Columns section, this button will be enabled and you can change the group options for the field.
Change Summary	Opens the Edit Summary dialog box shown in Figure 13-3. It works the same way that the Insert Summary dialog box works and will let you change the default summary type that was selected when the field was added to the Summarized Fields section.

Table 13-1 Options on the Cross-Tab tab explained

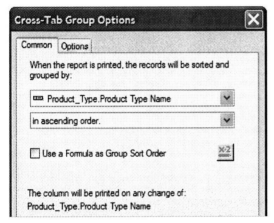

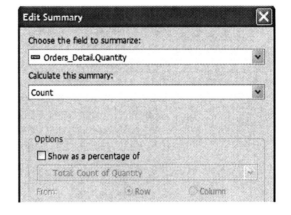

Figure 13-3 Edit Summary dialog box

Figure 13-2 Cross-Tab Group Options dialog box

Style Tab

The options shown in Figure 13-4 are the templates that you can use to format the entire cross-tab object at one time. These are the same templates that are on the Cross-Tab wizard.

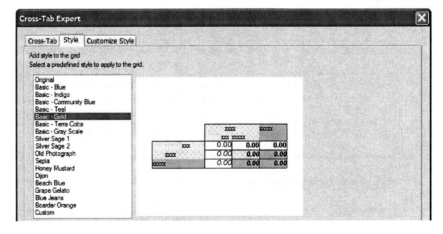

Figure 13-4 Style tab options

Customize Style Tab

The options shown in Figure 13-5 let you apply formatting to a specific section of the cross-tab like a row or to the entire cross-tab object. Each field in the Rows and Columns section is a group. The options in the Group Options section can be applied to each field.

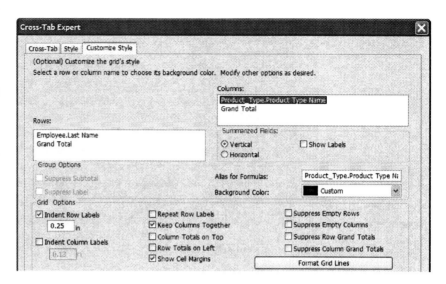

Figure 13-5 Customize Style tab options

Option	Description
Vertical/Horizontal	These options determine how the summarized fields will be displayed. There has to be at least two summarized fields to select one of these options. The **VERTICAL** option will stack the summarized fields in the same cell. You will see how this works when you complete the cross-tab exercise in this lesson. The **HORIZONTAL** option will place the summarized fields side by side.
Show Labels	If checked, this option will display the summarized field name in the row or column header.

Table 13-2 Summarized Field options explained

Option	Description
Suppress Subtotal	This option is only available if there are two or more fields in the Rows section or two or more fields in the Columns section. This option cannot be used on grand total fields. If checked, this option will suppress the subtotal for the row or column that is selected.
Suppress Label	This option is only available if the Suppress Subtotal option is checked. If checked, this option will suppress the group by fields label.
Alias for Formulas	This option lets you enter a different name for the field that is used on the cross-tab. The name entered in this field can be used in conditional formatting formulas instead of the name in the table.
Background Color	This drop down list box will let you select a background color for the row or column of data.

Table 13-3 Group Options explained

Option	Description
Indent Row Labels	Allows you to set how much space you want to indent the row labels.
Indent Column Labels	Allows you to set how much space you want to indent the column labels.
Repeat Row Labels	This option will force the row labels to be repeated on other pages when the width of the cross-tab requires more than one page.

Table 13-4 Grid Options explained

Option	Description
Keep Columns Together	This option will prevent a column from being split across two pages.
Column Totals on Top	This option will cause column totals to print at the top of the column.
Row Totals on Left	If checked, this option will cause the row totals to print on the left of the cross-tab object.
Show Cell Margins	This option will put white space on all four sides of the cell.
Suppress Empty Rows	If checked, rows that do not have data will not appear in the cross-tab.
Suppress Empty Columns	If checked, columns that do not have data will not appear in the cross-tab.
Suppress Row Grand Totals	If checked, the grand total row will not appear in the cross-tab.
Suppress Column Grand Totals	If checked, the grand total column will not appear in the cross-tab.
Format Grid Lines button	Clicking this button will open the Format Grid Lines dialog box shown in Figure 13-6. Table 13-5 explains the options on this dialog box.

Table 13-4 Grid Options explained (Continued)

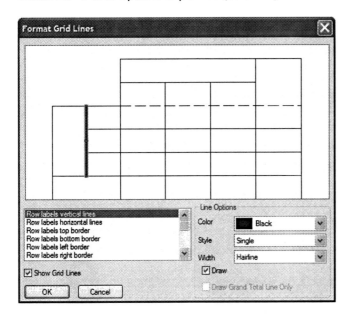

Figure 13-6 Format Grid Lines dialog box

Option	Description
Grid Line	Lets you select the grid line in the list box that you want to modify. The grid line(s) that you select will be highlighted in the grid at the top of the dialog box.
Show Grid Lines	Lets you turn the grid lines on or off.
Color	Lets you select a color for the grid lines.
Style	Lets you select a style for the grid lines.
Width	Lets you select a width for the grid lines.
Draw	Lets you select a specific grid line to hide.
Draw Grand Total Line Only	If checked, this option will only display grid lines on grand total rows or columns.

Table 13-5 Format Grid Lines dialog box options explained

Cross-Tab Shortcut Menu

Like many features in Crystal Reports, the cross-tab object has it's own shortcut menu. The **PIVOT CROSS-TAB** option lets you move the rows to where the columns are on the cross-tab and the columns to where the rows are on the cross-tab.

Formatting Formulas

You can create conditional formatting formulas in a cross-tab using the Format Editor, similar to how conditional formatting formulas are created for other fields on a report. In addition to being able to use the **CURRENTFIELDVALUE** and **DEFAULTATTRIBUTE** functions, cross-tabs can also use the **GRIDROWCOLUMNVALUE** function. This function lets you create a formula that depends on the value in a row that is related to the current cell. An advantage to using the GridRowColumnValue function is that you can use the Alias field name instead of the real field name. The examples below demonstrate how these functions can be used in a cross-tab or OLAP grid.

Example #1 The formula below will set the current field (cell) to yellow if it is greater than or equal to 25.

If CurrentFieldValue >= 25 Then crYellow Else DefaultAttribute

Example #2 The formula below will set the current field (cell) to yellow if it is greater than or equal to 100 and the Product Name is "Gloves".

If GridRowColumnValue {Product.Product Name} = "Gloves" and CurrentFieldValue >= 100 Then crYellow Else DefaultAttribute

 You can use the **HIGHLIGHTING EXPERT** to format data fields in a cross-tab.

Exercise 13.1: Use The Cross-Tab Expert

In this exercise you will recreate the cross-tab report that you created in Exercise 7.9. You will enhance the report by adding the following:

    ① Indenting the row labels.
    ② Modifying the grid lines.
    ③ Applying conditional formatting to change the background of cells that meet a specific condition.
    ④ Create a formula to calculate the total dollar amount of sales per product, per sales rep.

Create The Product Type Selection Criteria

The Cross-Tab wizard has a Record Selection screen that lets you create selection criteria. If you use the Cross-Tab Expert, you have different options. You can create a formula or create the selection criteria using the Select Expert.

1.   Open a new report, then add the following tables to the report: Employee, Orders, Orders Detail, Product and Product Type.

2.   Open the Select Expert. Select the Product Type Name field in the Product Type table and click OK. Select the "Is one of" operator, then add the gloves, kids and saddles options and click OK.

Create The Cross-Tab

1.   Add a cross-tab object to the report header, then right-click on the cross-tab object and select Cross-Tab Expert.

2.   Move the Last Name field in the Employee table to the **ROWS** section.

3. Move the Product Type Name field in the Product Type table to the **COLUMNS** section.

4. Move the Quantity field in the Orders Detail table to the **SUMMARY FIELDS** section.

5. Click the **CHANGE SUMMARY** button and change the summary type to Count and click OK.

Customize The Cross-Tab

The Customize Style tab has several options that you can use to change the appearance of the cross-tab.

1. Click on the Customize Style tab, then clear the **COLUMN TOTALS ON TOP** and **ROW TOTALS ON LEFT** options.

2. Check the Indent Row Labels option and type .25 in the box below it.

3. Click the Format Grid Lines button.

4. Select the Column label bottom border options, then select the Dashed style.

5. Click OK to close the Format Gridlines dialog box, then click OK to close the Cross-Tab Expert.

Test The Cross-Tab

1. Save the report as L13.1 Cross-Tab.

2. The report should look like the one shown in Figure 13-7. Leave the report open to complete the next part of the exercise.

	Gloves	Kids	Saddles	Total
Davolio	85	18	49	152
Dodsworth	101	19	58	178
King	97	23	58	178
Leverling	84	25	56	165
Peacock	105	20	59	184
Suyama	84	25	56	165
Total	556	130	336	1,022

Figure 13-7 L13.1 Cross-Tab report

Add Another Row Of Data To The Cross-Tab

In this part of the exercise you will create a formula that will calculate the total of each product, that each sales report sold.

1. Open the Cross-Tab Expert and click the New Formula button.

2. Type Item Total as the formula name, then type the formula shown below.

    {Orders_Detail.Unit Price} * {Orders_Detail.Quantity}

3. Save the formula, then click on it in the Available Fields list on the Cross-Tab Expert and add it to the Summarized Fields section. Click OK and save the changes. The cross-tab should look like the one shown in Figure 13-8.

If you are wondering why sales reps have the same quantity sold of a product but have different totals for the product, like the sales reps Leverling and Suyama do in the gloves column, it is because the products listed are categories of products, meaning that there are different types of gloves and each type of glove has a different price. I thought the same thing at first, that there was something wrong with the Item Total formula, so I created a detail report and looked at the raw data for the gloves and saw that there are different priced gloves.

	Gloves	Kids	Saddles	Total
Davolio	85 $2,735.59	18 $11,498.14	49 $1,929.29	152 $16,163.02
Dodsworth	101 $3,404.30	19 $11,625.66	58 $2,492.96	178 $17,522.92
King	97 $2,933.57	23 $15,069.70	58 $2,348.04	178 $20,351.31
Leverling	84 $2,668.06	25 $13,833.10	56 $2,235.63	165 $18,736.79
Peacock	105 $3,174.88	20 $10,830.79	59 $2,647.96	184 $16,653.63
Suyama	84 $2,486.31	25 $13,532.76	56 $2,026.98	165 $18,046.05
Total	556 $17,402.71	130 $76,390.15	336 $13,680.86	1,022 $107,473.72

Figure 13-8 Second row of data added to the cross-tab

When you see data that does not look right or somehow catches your attention, you should take the time to look at the raw data to see if you can find out why the data looks the way that it does. The L13.1 Cross-Tab test report (in the zip file) is the report that I created to figure out if there was really a problem with the formula.

Creating Conditional Formatting In Cross-Tabs

Creating conditional formatting in cross-tabs is not that much different then creating conditional formatting in other types of reports. In this part of the exercise, you will create conditional formatting on the quantity cells in the gloves column to change the background color to yellow if the quantity is greater than or equal to 100. This would be helpful to quickly be able to see which sales reps sold the most of this particular product.

1. In the first column of the cross-tab, right-click on the detail Quantity field and select Format Field.

2. Click on the Border tab, then click the Formula button across from the Background option.

3. Type the formula shown below, then click the Save and close button.

```
If GridRowColumnValue("Product_Type.Product Type Name") = "Gloves"
and CurrentFieldValue >= 100 Then crYellow Else DefaultAttribute
```

4. Click OK and save the changes. The gloves quantity for two sales reps should have a yellow background.

Printing Issues

Cross-Tab objects can have printing issues, in particular, cross-tab objects that require more than one page to print horizontally. The Cross-Tab Expert has the Repeat Row Labels and Keep Columns Together options that you learned about earlier in Table 13-4, that you can use to resolve some printing issues. If there are horizontal printing issues, there are three options that you can use to resolve them.

① **Horizontal Page Number** This special field counts the number of horizontal pages in a report. This field will not work if the cross-tab is in a section of the report that will not print page footers.

② **Repeat Horizontal Pages** This option is on the Common tab on the Format Editor dialog box. If checked, this option will force objects in the page header or page footer section to print on every horizontal page.

③ **Relative Positions** This option is on the Common tab on the Section Expert. Use it to control an object that is to the right of a cross-tab object. If checked, this option will cause the object next to the cross-tab to stay in the same relative position, regardless of how much the cross-tab grows.

Creating Templates From Scratch

As you learned in Lesson 7, templates are a way to change the overall appearance of a report. Templates can change the appearance of any or all of the following elements at one time: text objects, fields, lines, charts and more. If you create a report using a wizard you can apply a template to the report. The Template Expert also allows you to apply a template to a report. The templates that you have used so far in this workbook had a data source. In this lesson, you will learn how to create a template that does not have a data source.

Template Field Objects

Template Field Objects are used instead of fields from a table or other data source to create a template from scratch. Just like regular fields on a report can be modified using the Format Editor, so can Template Field Objects.

Template Field Objects are placeholders that contain the formatting for objects that will be used on the report. This formatting will be applied to the corresponding fields on the report when the template is applied to the report. By default, template fields do not display data. That is because they are not attached to a data source.

As you will see, when you add formatting to a template field, you can also create formulas. These formulas are stored in the Formula Fields section of the Field Explorer. When you create a template field and open the Format Editor, you will see tabs for all of the data types, as shown in Figure 13-9. The reason that you see tabs for all of the data types is because the template field has not been given a data type.

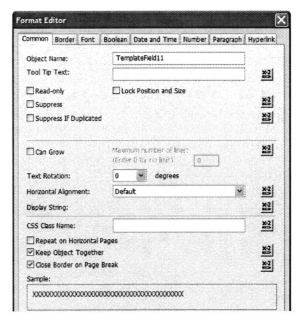

Figure 13-9 Format Editor dialog box for a template field

Exercise 13.2: Create A Template From Scratch

In this exercise you will create a template that has template fields for four data types: string, date/time, number and currency. You will create different formatting for each data type and then apply the template to an existing report.

1. Open a new report that does not have a database connection.

2. Add four template field objects to the details section of the report.

Rename The Template Fields, Add Summary Information And A Report Title

If you look in the Formula fields section of the Field Explorer, you will see the four template fields that you just created. If you leave them with these names, you will not know what type of field the formatting is for. It is a good idea to rename them to give them a more meaningful name.

1. Rename the fields as shown in Figure 13-10.

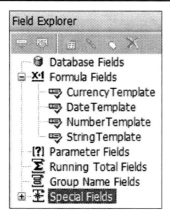

Figure 13-10 Renamed template fields

2. Add the Summary Information shown in Figure 13-11 to the report.

Figure 13-11 Template summary information

3. Add a text object above the field headings in the page header section and format it as shown in Figure 13-12. The font size is 18. Put a border around the title.

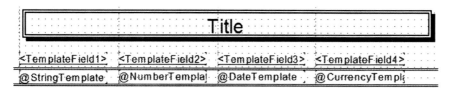

Figure 13-12 Template layout

Create Formatting For A String Field

1. Right-click on the StringTemplate field and select Format Template Field.

2. Change the font style to italic, then select the Can Grow option.

3. Change the Bottom border to Dotted and click OK.

Create Formatting For A Number Field

1. Right-click on the NumberTemplate field and select Format Template Field.

2. Change the Decimals option to 1, then clear the Thousands separator. This will cause the field to not display a comma. Click OK twice to close both dialog boxes.

Create Formatting For A Date/Time Field

1. Right-click on the DateTemplate field and select Format Template Field.

2. Change the Date formula to 03/01/1999 and click OK.

Create Formatting For A Currency Field

1. Right-click on the CurrencyTemplate field and select Format Template Field.

2. Change the Display Currency Symbol to fixed and click OK.

What I found interesting about templates when I first learned how to create one is that they are not as versatile as I thought they would be. I thought that if you create a template field for each field type that everything would be okay. For whatever reason, I also thought that if the template had a field for dates and if the report that the template was being applied to had two date fields that both date fields would automatically use the same date template field. That isn't how template fields work.

If you applied the template that you just created to the L3.3 report, shown in Figure 13-13 (which you will do later in this exercise), the report would look like the one shown in Figure 13-14.

Customer Name	Order Date	Ship Date	Order ID	Unit Price	Quantity
City Cyclists	12/2/2003 12:00:00A	12/10/2003 5:32:23F	1	$41.90	1
Deals on Wheels	12/2/2003 12:00:00A	12/2/2003 6:45:32AI	1,002	$33.90	3
Deals on Wheels	12/2/2003 12:00:00A	12/2/2003 6:45:32AI	1,002	$1,652.86	3
Warsaw Sports, Inc.	12/2/2003 12:00:00A	12/5/2003 12:10:12A	1,003	$48.51	3
Warsaw Sports, Inc.	12/2/2003 12:00:00A	12/5/2003 12:10:12A	1,003	$13.78	3

Figure 13-13 L3.3 report before the template is applied

Title			

Customer Name	Order Date	Ship Date	Order ID
City Cyclists	03-12-02 12:00:0(	12/10/2003	1
$41.90	1		
Deals on Wheels	03-12-02 12:00:0(	12/02/2003	1,002
$33.90	3		
Deals on Wheels	03-12-02 12:00:0(	12/02/2003	1,002
$1,652.86	3		

Figure 13-14 L3.3 report after the template is applied

As you can see, the Order Date and Order ID fields are not formatted as you would suspect, or at least not as I expected. I expected the Order Date field to have the same formatting that the Ship Date field has. I also expected the Order ID field, which is a number field, to not have commas.

The "trick" to creating a template is that you need one template field for each field on the report. Each template field must be in the same section and order in the template that the field is in the report that it will format. Exactly! That's what I said - "What is the point of creating a template? The only reason that I could think of is if you have the need to create a few reports that have the same fields in the same section and order and will sort one report by one field and the same report (with a different file name) sorted on a different field.

If the report that the template will be applied to has four fields in the details section, the template also has to have four fields in the details section with the same data types in the same order. Therefore, the template that you just created needs the following changes in order to be able to apply it to the L3.3 report.

Modify The Template

1. Move the NumberTemplate field after the CurrencyTemplate field.

2. Make the StringTemplate field wider.

3. Create another Date template field using the same formatting as the one you already created and place it after the string field.

4. Create another Number template field and place it before the CurrencyTemplate field. The template should look like the one shown in Figure 13-15.

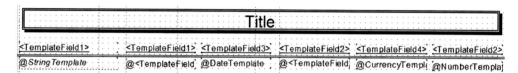

Figure 13-15 Modified template

Save The Template

As you learned in Lesson 7, if you want the template to appear in the Template Expert, you have to save it in the folder designated for report templates.

1. If the Save Data with Report option is checked, clear the option.

2. Save the template as `L13.2 Custom report template` in the Crystal Reports Workbook folder.

3. Save the template in the folder designated for report templates. [See Exercise 7.17]

4. Open the Template Expert. You should see the template as shown in Figure 13-16.

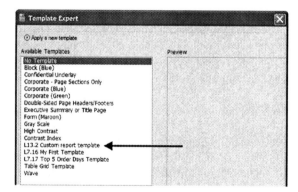

Figure 13-16 Custom template in the Template Expert

Apply The Template

1. Save the L3.3 report as `L13.2A Customer report with template`.

2. Apply the L13.2 Custom report template to the L13.2A report. As you can see, the Order ID, Unit Price and Quantity fields are not lined up correctly.

3. Line these three fields up correctly. Save the changes. The report should look like the one shown in Figure 13-17.

Title					
Customer Name	Order Date	Ship Date	Order ID	Unit Price	Quantity
City Cyclists	12/02/2003	12/10/2003	1	$ 41.90	1
Deals on Wheels	12/02/2003	12/02/2003	1002	$ 33.90	3
Deals on Wheels	12/02/2003	12/02/2003	1002	$ 1,652.86	3
Warsaw Sports, Inc.	12/02/2003	12/05/2003	1003	$ 48.51	3
Warsaw Sports, Inc.	12/02/2003	12/05/2003	1003	$ 13.78	3

Figure 13-17 L13.2A report with the template applied

Notice that even though the template has a placeholder for a report title, the report does not display a title. This is because the report did not have a report title before the template was applied. The same thing would happen if the report title object was placed in the report header section of the template and the title was in the page header section or if the report title was in the report header section and the template had the report object in a different section of the report. Template fields are only applied to fields in the section that they are in.

Add Values To Template Fields

Earlier I mentioned that you can add values to template fields. By default, template fields have a value of Space(10), which displays as blanks. I am not sure of the benefit one gets from adding a value to a template field, because you can apply the template to a report and see actual data. But just in case you want to add values to a template field to view the template, add the formula below to the template field. Open the Formula Workshop, then open the Formula Fields node and click on the template field that you want to add the formula to. The value that you add in quotes is what will appear when you preview the template. The first formula below is for a string field. The second formula is for a numeric field. When previewed, the template will look like the one shown in Figure 13-18.

```
WhileReadingRecords; "abcd";

WhileReadingRecords; "9,999.00";
```

<TemplateField1>	<TemplateField2>
abcd	9,999.00

Figure 13-18 L13.2 Template fields report with test data

Template Considerations

Templates apply formatting on an object by object basis. This is why you can get unexpected results when applying a template. For example, if the report that the template is being applied to does not have a chart, but the template does have a chart, a chart will be added to the report when the template is applied.

If the report has a field that does not have a corresponding template field, the field may not appear on the report once the template is applied. Fields in the details section that do not have a corresponding template field will be moved to a new details section. This is why you should always make a copy of any report that you want to apply a template to, even though you can undo one template change to reports. In addition to being able to compare the existing report to the one with the template applied, you will have a back up copy of the report should something go wrong.

If you search for `template considerations` in the help file, you will find more information on how different items are affected by templates.

In case you have extensive template needs, this link is for a document that has more information about templates. http://support.businessobjects.com/communityCS/TechnicalPapers/templates.pdf

Hyperlinks

If you have used the Internet, you have used hyperlinks, which are often called "Links". Crystal Reports has hyperlink functionality that you can add to reports. You may have already seen the Hyperlink tab shown in Figure 13-19, on the Format Editor.

In addition to being able to create a hyperlink to a website or email address, you can create a hyperlink to a file. You can also create hyperlinks to websites and email addresses that are stored in a table. Hyperlinks can be attached to objects like a chart or logo on the report.

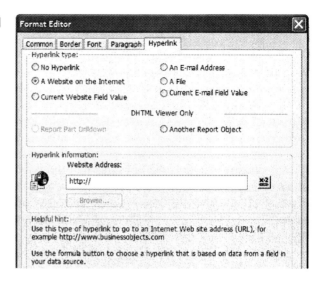

Figure 13-19 Hyperlink tab on the Format Editor

Hyperlink Options

 Before opening this tab, you have to select the object that you want to use for the hyperlink.

No Hyperlink   Select this option to remove the hyperlink.

A Web Site On The Internet   This option will allow you to create a hyperlink to a specific page on a web site.

Current Website Field Value   This option lets you create a hyperlink for website addresses that are stored in a field. Each record that appears on the report that has a web site will have a hyperlink to the web site.

An Email Address   This option will allow you to create a hyperlink to a specific email address.

A File   This option allows you to create a hyperlink to a file. This file can be another report or a document. The only stipulation is that the file has to reside in a location that the person running the report can access. Unless the person running the report has access to your hard drive, you should not create a hyperlink to a file on your hard drive.

Current E-mail Field Value   This option lets you create a hyperlink for email addresses that are stored in a field. Each record that appears on the report that has an email address will have a hyperlink to the email address.

Exercise 13.3: Create Hyperlinks

In this exercise you will create the following types of hyperlinks.

① A website on the Internet.
② An email address.
③ To a file.
④ To an email address stored in a field in a table.
⑤ To a website address stored in a field in a table.

1. Create a new report and add the Customer Name, Web Site and E-mail address fields from the Customer table to the report.

2. Add the Xtreme logo image to the report header section.

3. Save the report as `L13.3 Hyperlinks.`

Create A Hyperlink To A Website

1. Click on the logo, then Format ⇒ Hyperlink.

2. Select the option, A website on the Internet.

3. Click after the http:// in the Website address field and type `www.tolana.com.` You should have the options shown in Figure 13-20. Click OK and save the changes.

Figure 13-20 Website hyperlink options

Create A Tool Tip For A Hyperlink

1. Right-click on the logo and select Format Graphic.

2. Type `Go to www.tolana.com` in the **TOOL TIP TEXT** field on the Common tab and click OK.

Create A Hyperlink To An Email Address

1. Add a text object to the report header section and type
   `Click here to send an email to` and your first name.

2. Click on the text object, then Format ⇒ Hyperlink.

3. Select the An Email Address option, then type your email address in the E-mail Address field after the words mail to:. You should have the options shown in Figure 13-21. The only difference should be the email address. Click OK and save the changes.

Figure 13-21 E-mail Address hyperlink options

Create A Hyperlink To A File

In this part of the exercise you are going to pretend that your hard drive is a network server and create a hyperlink to a file on your hard drive. Yes, I know this contradicts what I said earlier about not creating links to a file on your hard drive, but everyone reading this workbook does not have access to the same server.

1. Add a text object to the report header section and type
   ```
   Click here to open the L8.17 Orders PDF file.
   ```

2. Click on the text object, then Format ⇒ Hyperlink.

3. Select the option, A File and click the **BROWSE** button.

4. Navigate to the Crystal Reports Workbook folder and double-click on the L8.17 Skills Top 5 orders PDF export file. You may have to change the Files of Type option to All files, to see the PDF file. You should have the options shown in Figure 13-22. Click OK and save the changes.

Figure 13-22 File hyperlink options

Create A Hyperlink To An Email Address In A Field

1. Right-click on the E-mail field and select Format Field, then click on the Hyperlink tab.

2. Select the Current E-Mail Field Value option. Notice that the section where you normally type in the information is dimmed out. That is because this type of hyperlink is tied to a field in the table. You should have the options shown in Figure 13-23. Click OK and save the changes.

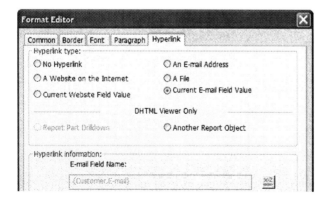

Figure 13-23 Email address field hyperlink options

Create A Hyperlink To A Website Address In A Field

1. Right-click on the Website address field and select Format Field, then click on the Hyperlink tab.

2. Select the Current Website Field Value option. You should have the options shown in Figure 13-24. Click OK and save the changes.

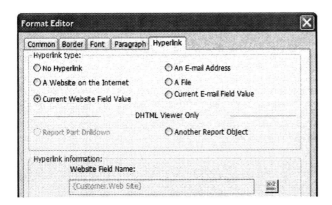

Figure 13-24 Website address field hyperlink options

Test The Hyperlinks

1. The report should look like the one shown in Figure 13-25. If you hold the mouse pointer over the logo, you should see the tool tip shown in Figure 13-26. If you are connected to the Internet, click on the logo. You should see the home page of Tolana Publishing.

Figure 13-26 Hyperlink tool tip illustrated

Figure 13-25 L13.3 Hyperlinks report

2. Click on the Email address text object in the report header. Your email software and a new email window should open. If it doesn't and you are sure that you created the hyperlink correctly, this could mean that your email software is not configured to open from a hyperlink.

3. Click on the hyperlink for the L8.17 file. Click Yes when prompted to proceed. The PDF file should open.

4. Click on the Email address for Pathfinders. If your email software did not open in step 2 above, it probably will not open when you click on this link.

5. Click on the Web Site address for City Cyclists. The Business Objects web site should open.

Running Total Fields

Running total fields are similar to the summary fields that you have already learned to create. While running total fields are similar to summary fields, they provide more options, which allows you more flexibility over the total fields that you create. There are four differences between running total and summary fields, as discussed below.

① Running total fields can be placed in the details section of the report, which would display a total up to the current record.
② Running total fields are only evaluated/calculated during the **WHILE PRINTING RECORDS** pass of the report is taking place. Crystal Reports uses a two pass system. This means that records in the "Others" group will not be counted in grand totals.
③ Running total fields are calculated at the detail level (record by record) and summary fields are calculated by group.
④ If a running total field is placed in the group header section, it will only include a total for the first record in the group because the other records in the group have not been processed at this point.

As you learned in Lesson 11, Top N reports do not have to include records that do not meet the Top N criteria. Records that do not meet the Top N criteria can be placed in the "Others" group. It is important to note that records in the "Others" group will be included in any grand totals on the report, whether or not the records in the "Others" group are printed on the report.

This is something that needs to be addressed during the report design phase. You have to find out if the people requesting the report want grand totals only for the records that meet the Top N requirements or all records including those in the "Others" category. Figure 13-27 shows the Create Running Total Field dialog box. If you only want report or grand totals for the records that meet the Top N condition, you have to use a running total field instead of a summary field.

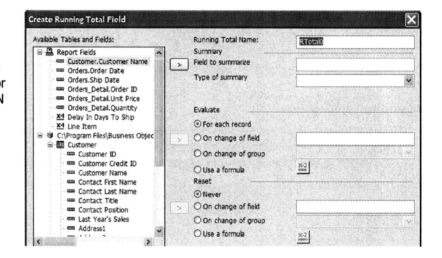

Figure 13-27 Create Running Total Field dialog box

You have probably figured out that there are a lot of good reasons to use running total fields instead of summary fields. You have also probably realized that selecting the appropriate type (summary or running total) of total field requires some thought. The other item that you have to consider is where the running total field will be placed on the report. Table 13-6 explains what the running total field will calculate depending on which section of the report it is placed in. The output will change depending on the Evaluate option that is selected.

Section	Which Records Will Be Calculated
Report Header	The first record on the report.
Page Header	All records up to the first record that will be printed on the current page.
Group Header	All records up to the first record of the current group.
Details	All records up to the current detail record.
Group Footer	All records up to the last record in the current group.
Page Footer	All records up to the first record on the next page.
Report Footer	All records on the report.

Table 13-6 Running total field output options explained

Like other dialog boxes that you have used, the Available Tables and Fields section contains the fields and formulas that you can use to create running total fields. The options in the summary section at the top let you enter a name for the running total field, select a field from the Available fields list and select the type of summary. The options in the Type of Summary field drop down list are the same as the ones for summary fields. The name of this field can be misleading because as you can see, a running total field does more than create totals. Like summary fields, it can provide counts, averages, percents and more.

The options in the **EVALUATE** section let you select when you want the running total field to be incremented. The **FOR EACH RECORD** option is most like a summary field calculation because the running total field is incremented after each detail record is processed.

The **ON CHANGE OF FIELD** option only increments the running total field when the value in the field is different than the value from the previous record. This is useful when the field that the running total is using can have several records that have the same value and you only want to count the value once. This is like the Distinct Count summary type that you have already used. If you are using a field like the Order ID field and the report uses the Orders and Orders Details tables, most of the time you should select the Order ID field from the parent table, which in this example is the Orders table.

When selecting this evaluation option, give some thought to the data that is in the field that you are using because records other then the first one that has the same data will not increment the running total field because this option excludes records. The key to using this option successfully, is to select a field that has a lot of unique values in it.

If you are going to use the **ON CHANGE OF FIELD** option, make sure that the records are sorted correctly, otherwise you will end up with unexpected results.

The **ON CHANGE OF GROUP** option can only be used on a report that has a group. This option will evaluate (increment) the running total field when the group changes.

If you need the field to be incremented based on a condition, select the **USE A FORMULA** option and click the Formula button next to the field. Then create a formula that the records must meet in order for the running total field to be incremented. An example of this would be if the report needed a total of orders that were not shipped in three days. The formula would check the Delay In Days To Ship formula field. If it was greater than three, add the order total to the running total field. If you needed a count of how many orders were not shipped that had an Delay In Days To Ship amount greater than three, you would create another running total field, use the count summary type and use the same formula for this running total field.

The options in the **RESET** section let you select when you want the running total field to be reset to zero. If you were using the running total field to get group totals, you would select the **ON CHANGE OF GROUP** option, then select the field and select the group from the drop down list. You could also create a formula that determined when to reset the running total field.

You should also use a running total field on reports that suppress records if there is a group selection formula. Report grand totals are calculated **BEFORE** the group selection formulas that have suppression are calculated.

The Create Running Total Field dialog box is also referred to as the Running Total Expert. It is also referred to as an "Expert" in the help file. Interestingly enough, neither the Reports menu or Expert Tools toolbar have an option for this dialog box.

There are three ways to open the Create Running Total Field dialog box as discussed below.

① Right-click on the field in the details section that you want to create a running total for and select Insert ⇒ Running Total.
② Right-click on the Running Total Fields category in the Field Explorer and select New.
③ Click on the Running Total Fields category in the Field Explorer and click the New button on the Field Explorer toolbar.

Exercise 13.4: Create Two Delay In Shipping Running Total Fields

In this exercise you will create two running total fields. You will create one to get an order total amount of orders that were not shipped in three days. The second running total field will count the number of orders that were not shipped in three days.

1. Save the L9.9 report as L13.4 Delay in shipping running totals.

2. Create the Line Item formula field that you created earlier in Exercise 13.1 and add it to the report after the Quantity field. Wrap the Delay In Days To Ship field heading to two lines.

Create The Order Total Amount Running Total Field

In this part of the exercise you will create a running total field that will only count the Unit of Price amount if the Delay in Shipping is greater than three days.

1. Right-click on the Line Item formula field and select Insert ⇒ Running Total.

2. Type Order Total Delay Amount in the Running Total Name field.

3. Select the Sum Type of Summary, if it is not already selected.

4. Select the Use a formula Evaluate option, then click the Formula button.

5. Double-click on the Delay In Days To Ship field, then type > 3 as the formula.

6. Highlight the formula and press the Ctrl and C keys. This will let you paste the code into the next formula that you will create.

7. Click the Save and close button, then click OK and save the changes.

Create The Order Count Running Total Field

In this part of the exercise you will create a running total field to get a count of the number of orders that were not shipped in three days.

If you preview the report you will see duplicate values in the Customer Name and Order ID fields. This means that some orders have more than one item. If this were live data, often the items that are available will ship immediately and the items that are not, will be delayed. Whatever the case is, you only want to count each order once. Therefore, using the Count summary option would not work. You would have to use the Distinct Count option on the Order ID field.

1. Open the Create Running Total Field dialog box and type Order Count in the Running Total name field.

2. Select the Order ID field as the Field to summarize.

3. Select the Distinct Count Type of Summary.

4. Select the Use a formula Evaluate option, then click the Formula button.

5. Paste the formula in by pressing the Ctrl and V keys.

6. Click the Save and close button, then click OK and save the changes.

 You could get the same results without a formula if the report was sorted on the Order ID field and you selected the **ON CHANGE OF FIELD** Evaluate option.

Add The Running Total Fields To The Report

1. Drag the Order Count and Order Total Delay Amount running total fields to the report footer section and create field headings for them.

2. Format the Order Total Delay Amount field to have a floating dollar sign. Save the changes. The last page of the report should look like the one shown in Figure 13-28.

Customer Name	Order Date	Ship Date	Order ID	Unit Price	Quantity	Line Item	Delay In Days To Ship
Souzel Bike Rentals	12/12/2003	12/16/2003	3,189	$15.50	2	$31.00	4
Tom's Place for Bikes	12/12/2003	12/12/2003	3,190	$53.90	1	$53.90	0
Coastal Line Bikes	12/12/2003	12/13/2003	3,191	$33.90	3	$101.70	1
Hikers and Bikers	12/12/2003	12/12/2003	3,192	$479.85	2	$959.70	0
Mountain View Sport	12/12/2003	12/12/2003	3,193	$11.90	2	$23.80	0
Total # of orders > 3 days shipping	709		Total order amount > 3 days shipping	$ 1,306,327.98			

Figure 13-28 L13.4 Delay in shipping running totals report

Exercise 13.5: Use Running Total Fields With Parameter Fields

As you learned in Lesson 12, parameter fields allow you to not hard code selection criteria, which makes the report much more flexible. The report that you created in Exercise 12.15 allows the user to select the date range and number of delay in days to ship. In this exercise you will modify that report to include the running total fields that you created in Exercise 13.4. You will also create summary fields that provide

totals for the entire report. These fields will demonstrate the difference between summary and running total fields.

1. Save the L12.15 report as `L13.5 Running total and parameter fields`.

2. Create the Line Item formula field, the Order Total Delay Amount and Order Count fields that you created in Exercise 13.4. Add the fields to the report footer section.

3. Create two summary fields, one for a count of orders and one for the total order amount of all records. Place these fields in the report footer section under the running total fields.

4. Run the report for all of 2004, with a delay in shipping days that is greater than or equal to four.

5. Save the changes. The last page of the report should look like the one shown in Figure 13-29. There should be 2,616 records on the report.

Customer Name	Order Date	Ship Date	Order ID	Unit Price	Quantity	Line Item	Delay In Days To Ship
Number of orders with a delay in shipping	529		Total order amount of delayed orders	$950,860.65			
Total number of orders	1,562		Total order amount of all orders	$2,861,205.48			

Figure 13-29 L13.5 Running total and parameter fields report

Running Total And Summary Field Limitation

The one limitation that both field types have is that they will not produce the correct result if the report suppresses data because both fields will include the suppressed records that will not be printed on the report. This happens because both fields perform calculations without taking into account conditional formatting formulas that the suppress option may have.

In Exercise 10.15 you modified a report and added a formula to the Suppress (No Drill-Down) option on three sections of the report. This was done because the report requirement was to only display groups that met a condition. You have to follow the same process for a running total field. The reason that you have to do this is because you only want running total fields to use records that will actually appear on the report.

If the report shown in Exercise 10.15 used a running total or summary field and did not have the suppression formula in the group header and footer sections, the report would look like the one shown in Figure 13-30.

Notice that the second company on this report is different then the one shown at the bottom of the L10.15 report. [See report, L13 Suppression (L10.15 report), in the zip file]

Backpedal Cycle Shop					
	02/08/2004	02/09/2004	$3,544.20	1279	$1,739.85
	02/08/2004	02/09/2004	$3,544.20	1279	$12.00
	02/08/2004	02/09/2004	$3,544.20	1279	$13.50
	02/19/2004	02/19/2004	$6,233.05	1311	$329.85
	02/19/2004	02/19/2004	$6,233.05	1311	$23.50
	02/19/2004	02/19/2004	$6,233.05	1311	$2,939.85
	07/02/2004	07/04/2004	$3,479.70	1802	$1,739.85
	08/15/2004	08/19/2004	$3,415.95	1972	$53.90
	08/15/2004	08/19/2004	$3,415.95	1972	$764.85
	08/15/2004	08/19/2004	$3,415.95	1972	$479.85
	11/16/2004	11/18/2004	$10,798.95	2358	$2,939.85
	11/16/2004	11/18/2004	$10,798.95	2358	$1,739.85
	11/16/2004	11/18/2004	$10,798.95	2358	$479.85
	12/18/2004	12/19/2004	$6,226.05	2507	$329.85
	12/18/2004	12/19/2004	$6,226.05	2507	$2,939.85
	12/18/2004	12/19/2004	$6,226.05	2507	$16.50
	01/04/2005	01/05/2005	$9,612.47	2560	$764.85
	01/04/2005	01/05/2005	$9,612.47	2560	$832.35
	01/04/2005	01/05/2005	$9,612.47	2560	$2,792.86
	02/02/2005	02/02/2005	$8,819.55	2685	$2,939.85
Total # orders -	20	Total $ amount of orders -	$131,791.26		
		Average order amount for customer -	$6,589.56		
BBS Pty					
Total # orders -	16	Total $ amount of orders -	$79,886.01		
		Average order amount for customer -	$4,992.88		

Figure 13-30 L10.15 report without suppression on the group header and footer sections

Hierarchical Group Reports

A hierarchical group is a special type of parent-child, one-to-many relationship. It shows the relationship between records that are in the same table. If it helps, think of the parent field as the field that is displayed in the group header section and the child fields will be displayed in the details section of the report. In Lesson 3 you learned about **RECURSIVE JOINS**. This type of join is required to create hierarchical report. [See Lesson 3, Recursive Joins]

Hierarchical groups are useful when you need to create a report where two fields in the same table relate to each other. This is what Crystal Reports refers to as a hierarchical group. This is how you can create organizational charts. An Employee table lists the employees that work for the company. It also contains who each employee reports to. Remember that the person that has someone reporting to them is also an employee.

In this example, the people that have someone reporting to them is the "parent" portion of the relationship. Employees that do not have anyone reporting to them are the "child" portion of the relationship. The Hierarchical Group Options dialog box shown in Figure 13-31 is used to create a hierarchical group report.

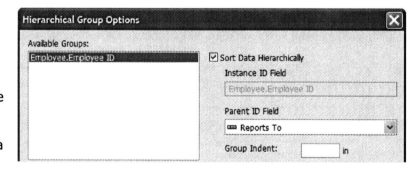

Figure 13-31 Hierarchical Group Options dialog box

The **AVAILABLE GROUPS** list contains all of the groups that the report has. The hierarchical report must be created using one of the groups that are listed in this section.

Once you select a group, check the **SORT DATA HIERARCHICALLY** option to indicate that you want to apply hierarchical sorting to the group that is selected.

The **INSTANCE ID FIELD** contains the field that will be used as the child field.

The **PARENT ID FIELD** contains the fields that can be used as the parent field. The parent record (in this example, the supervisor) will print first and then the employees that report to the supervisor will print below. All of the fields in this drop down list are the same data type as the group field.

The **GROUP INDENT** option lets you select how much the child records should be indented. Using this feature is optional. If the columns do not contain a lot of data and the Group Indent option is greater than zero, it is possible that some data will not line up properly with the field headings. One way to fix this is to make the Group Indent number smaller. Another option is to resize some of the fields on the report. Leaving this option set to zero means that the child records will not be indented, which will make it difficult to see who reports to who.

Hierarchical Report Requirements

In order to create a hierarchical report, the following three requirements must be met.

① The table must have two fields that represent the same data. This allows the data in one field to point to another record in the same table.
② The parent and child fields must have the same data type.
③ The report must be grouped on the child field.

Exercise 13.6: Create A Hierarchical Group Report

In this exercise you will create an organizational report that shows who each employee reports to.

1. Create a new report and add the Employee table, but do not add any fields to the report.

2. Create a group on the Employee ID field. Use the Options tab to create a group name formula that combines the Employee first and last name fields. [See Exercise 9.5]

3. Report ⇒ Hierarchical Grouping Options. You will see the Hierarchical Group Options dialog box.

4. Check the Sort Data Hierarchical option, then select the Supervisor ID field from the Parent ID Field drop down list.

5. Change the Group Indent option to .25. You should have the options shown in Figure 13-32. Click OK.

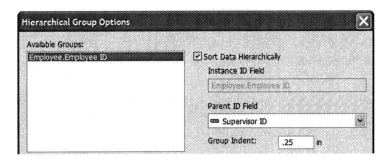

Figure 13-32 Hierarchical report options

6. Add the Position and Hire Date fields to the group header section, then format the Hire Date field so that the time does not show.

7. Save the report as L13.6 Hierarchical report. The report should look like the one shown in Figure 13-33.

Andrew Fuller	Vice President, Sales	07/12/1996
Steven Buchanan	Sales Manager	09/13/1997
Nancy Davolio	Sales Representative	03/29/1996
Janet Leverling	Sales Representative	02/27/1996
Margaret Peacock	Sales Representative	03/30/1997
Michael Suyama	Sales Representative	09/13/1997
Robert King	Sales Representative	11/29/1997
Laura Callahan	Inside Sales Coordinator	01/30/1998
Anne Dodsworth	Sales Representative	10/12/1998
Albert Hellstern	Business Manager	03/01/1998
Tim Smith	Mail Clerk	01/15/1998

Figure 13-33 L13.6 Hierarchical report

The Group Sort Expert

You have already used the Group Sort Expert to create and modify Top N reports. In addition to being able to create and modify Top N reports, the Group Sort Expert allows you to sort groups in ways other than ascending or descending order. You can sort groups based on values in a summary field in the group.

For example, in Exercise 6.2, you created a report that grouped the orders by customer. You also created two summary fields for the customer group; one for the customers total dollar amount of orders and one for the total number of orders. If someone needed to see the orders in high to low or low to high order based on the total dollar amount of the customer, you could sort the customer group on the Order Amount summary field. If you sorted the Order Amount summary field in ascending order, the customers with the lowest total dollar amount would appear at the beginning of the group.

In Exercise 6.7 you created a report that grouped the orders in 2004 by month. If you wanted to show the months with the highest monthly totals at the beginning of the report, you would sort the month group in descending order, on the Order Amount summary field. You will modify these two reports in this lesson.

Figure 13-34 shows the Group Sort Expert dialog box. When you open the dialog box you will see a tab for each group that the report has. You can sort on as many of the summary values in the groups as needed. Keep in mind that the sorting starts with the first tab and works it's way across the tabs.

In addition to the Top N, Bottom N, Top Percentage and Bottom Percentage options which you have already learned about, the **FOR THIS GROUP SORT** drop down list has the following options:

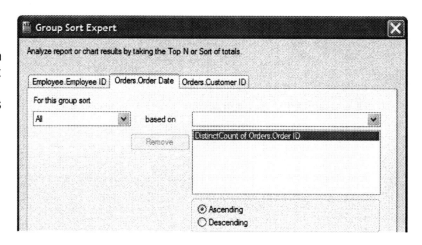

Figure 13-34 Group Sort Expert dialog box

NO SORT, which is the default and will use the sort options that were set up when the group was created.

The **ALL** option will include all of the groups and not suppress any groups like the Top N, Bottom N, Top Percentage and Bottom Percentage options will.

The options in the **BASED ON** drop down list are the summary fields that are in a group section of the report.

To create a Top or Bottom N report, the report must have the two items discussed below, before opening the Group Sort Expert.

    ① The report must have at least one group.
    ② The group that you want to use for the Top N report must have a summary field in it.

The way you know that the report has both of the options discussed above is that you can open the Group Sort Expert. Reports that do not meet the criteria will have the option to open the Group Sort Expert dimmed out.

There are two ways to open the Group Sort Expert as discussed below.

    ① Click the Group Sort Expert button on the Expert Tools toolbar.
    ② Report ⇒ Group Sort Expert.

Exercise 13.7: Sort The Report On The Customer Group By Order Amount Field

In this exercise you will change the sort order of the groups to show the groups that have customers with the lowest total order amounts at the top of this report. You will also sort the groups by the number of orders in descending order. This sort will happen within the order amount sort. This is helpful if two or more customers have the same order total amount.

1. Save the L6.2 report as `L13.7 Group sorted on two fields`.

2. Open the Group Sort Expert and select the All option.

3. Select the Order Amount summary field, then select the ascending option.

4. Select the Order ID count field, then select descending and click OK. Save the changes. The report should look like the one shown in Figure 13-35. As you look through the report, you should see all customers with the lowest order amount totals at the beginning of the report.

	Order Date	Ship Date	Order Amount	Order #	Unit Price
Jakarta Sunrise Sports					
	06/06/2004	06/07/2004	$2,699.55	3086	$899.85
Total # orders - **1**		Total $ amount of orders -	$2,699.55		
Super Bike					
	06/24/2004	06/26/2004	$2,699.55	3166	$899.85
Total # orders - **1**		Total $ amount of orders -	$2,699.55		
Tel Aviv Outdoors					
	06/08/2004	06/18/2004	$2,699.55	3098	$899.85
Total # orders - **1**		Total $ amount of orders -	$2,699.55		
Bordeaux Sports					
	05/14/2004	05/14/2004	$2,939.85	3021	$2,939.85
Total # orders - **1**		Total $ amount of orders -	$2,939.85		

Figure 13-35 L13.7 Group sorted on two fields report

As the report designer, it may be obvious to you how a report is sorted and grouped. Unlike the reports that you have created earlier in this workbook that have groups, reports that have groups that are sorted by a value in a summary field, may not be as easy for the reader to figure out how the report is grouped and sorted just by looking at it.

If you look at the report shown above in Figure 13-35, you will see the group name (the company name field) in the group header section. Many people will think that this is how the report is sorted even though the report is sorted by the values in the order amount summary field. You should do something to make sure that the person reading the report is aware of how the report is sorted or grouped. There are three options that I select from to help clarify how a report presents data. You can use any of the options below or come up with a different solution.

① Add how the report is grouped and sorted as a subtitle on the report. For example, Grouped by (field name) and sorted by summary (field name), where you fill in the (field name).
② Add how the report is grouped and sorted to the page or report footer section.
③ Add the summary value to the group header section.

Exercise 13.8: Sort The Month Groups In Descending Order

In this exercise you will sort the groups in descending order by the total monthly order amount.

1. Save the L6.7 report as L13.8 Sorted month groups.

2. Open the Group Sort Expert and select the All option.

3. Remove the Order Amount percentage criteria.

4. Select the Order Amount summary field, then select the descending option.

5. Save the changes. The report should look like the one shown in Figure 13-36. If you look in the group tree, you will be able to tell which month had the highest order amount, because it is at the top of the list.

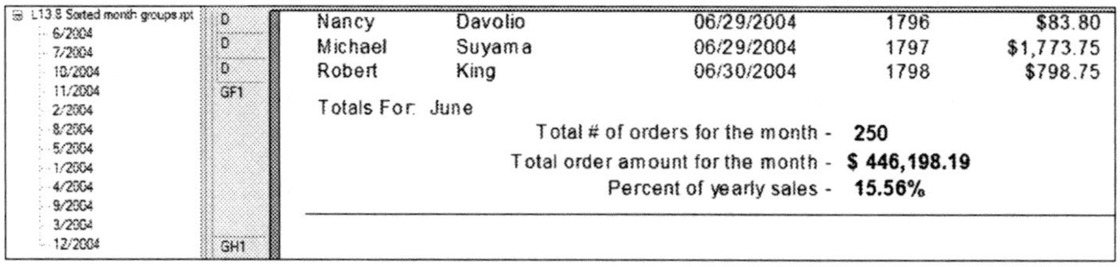

Figure 13-36 L13.8 Sorted month groups report

Creating Group Selection Formulas

Group selection formulas are used to filter groups that do not meet a condition. The formulas can be created by using the values in a group summary field or by using the values in the Group Name field. To use a Group Name field (which are stored in the Group Names Field folder in the Field Explorer), you have to use the Group Name function. The only time that you need to use this function is if the report has custom group names.

To create a group selection formula, select a summary field on the Select Expert instead of a detail field. In Exercise 13.7, you modified the report to sort the groups in ascending order. If you only wanted to see groups (in this example, customers) that have an order summary total amount less than $10,000 and are in the USA, you would create two selection criteria options: one on the Order summary total amount, which is a group summary field and one on the Region detail field.

Exercise 13.9: Create A Group Selection Formula

1. Save the L13.7 report as L13.9 Group selection formula.

2. Right-click on the Order Amount summary field in the group footer section and select the Select Expert option. Select the "Is less than" operator, then type `10000` in the next drop down list. This is the group selection formula.

3. Click on the New tab and select the Country field. Select the "Is equal to" operator, then select the USA region.

4. Delete the Order Amount greater than 2499.99 criteria.

5. The group selection formula should look like the one shown in Figure 13-37. Click OK and save the changes. The report should look like the one shown in Figure 13-38.

> Sum ({Orders.Order Amount}, {Customer.Customer Name}) < $10000.00

Figure 13-37 Group selection formula

	Order Date	Ship Date	Order Amount	Order #	Unit Price
Ride Down A Mountain					
	05/23/2004	05/23/2004	$12.00	3041	$12.00
Total # orders - 1		Total $ amount of orders -	$12.00		
Colin's Bikes					
	05/21/2004	05/22/2004	$13.50	3038	$4.50
Total # orders - 1		Total $ amount of orders -	$13.50		
Tony's Better Bikes					
	05/22/2004	05/22/2004	$17.50	3040	$17.50
Total # orders - 1		Total $ amount of orders -	$17.50		
Two Wheelin'					
	05/31/2004	06/02/2004	$23.50	3064	$23.50
Total # orders - 1		Total $ amount of orders -	$23.50		

Figure 13-38 L13.9 Group selection formula report

As you may expect, group selection formulas will suppress groups that do not meet the selection criteria. What I find interesting is that the summary field group totals are the same as if there were no suppressed groups. This is because there is a difference between suppressing groups and filtering records. Keep this in mind when creating group selection formulas.

Form Letters

Crystal Reports is being used more and more to create form letters instead of using word processing software. Form letters are usually customized for each person or company that they will be sent to. If a report already has the selection criteria that is needed for the form letters, make a copy of the report and delete the objects that are not needed.

Exercise 13.10: Create A Form Letter

In this exercise you will create a basic form letter similar to one that you have probably received in the mail. If you want, you can add other items like a company logo and date to a form letter.

1. Save the L12.15 report as `L13.10 Form letter`.

2. Delete all of the fields in the details section.

3. Open the Section Expert and click on the details section. Click on the Color tab, then click on the Formula button. Delete the formula at the bottom of the window, then click the Save and close button.

4. Check the **NEW PAGE AFTER** option in the details section. Click OK to close the Section Expert.

5. Add the fields from the Customer table to the top of the details section as shown in Figure 13-39. (**Hint**: The City, Region and Postal Code fields should be added to a text object).

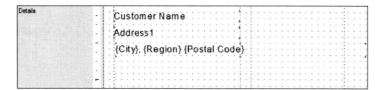

Figure 13-39 Return address fields for the form letter

6. Add the text and fields shown below to a text object below the return address fields. When you are finished, the details section should look like the one shown in Figure 13-40.

```
Dear {Customer Name},

We want to thank you for your order on {Order Date} in the amount
of {Order Amount}. We realize that this order took {?Delay In
Days} days to ship. The 15% off coupon at the bottom of this
letter is our way of saying thank you for not canceling the order.
We really appreciate your business.
```

Figure 13-40 Form letter layout

7. Format the Order Date in the body of the letter to xx/xx/xxxx. Format the Delay in Days to only print a whole number.

8. Save the changes and preview the report. Use the date range 1/1/2004 to 1/31/2004. Select 4 as the Delay In Days To Ship. The first form letter should look like the one shown in Figure 13-41. There should be 127 records (form letters).

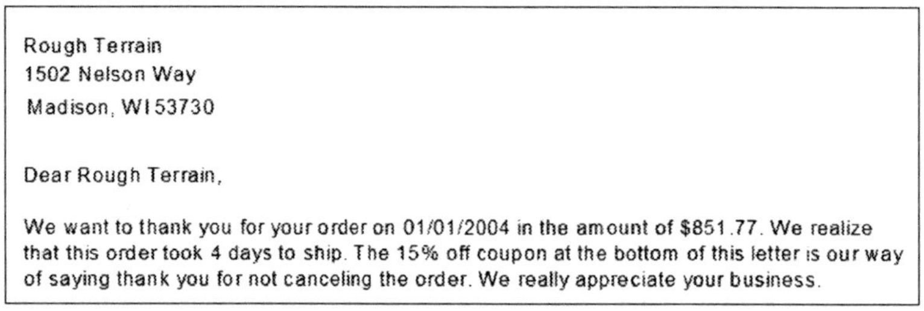

Rough Terrain
1502 Nelson Way
Madison, WI 53730

Dear Rough Terrain,

We want to thank you for your order on 01/01/2004 in the amount of $851.77. We realize
that this order took 4 days to ship. The 15% off coupon at the bottom of this letter is our way
of saying thank you for not canceling the order. We really appreciate your business.

Figure 13-41 L13.10 Form letter

Multi-Column Reports

In Lesson 7 you used the Mailing Label Report wizard, which let you create multi-column labels. You can use the options on the Layout tab shown in Figure 13-42, on the Section Expert to create multi-column reports.

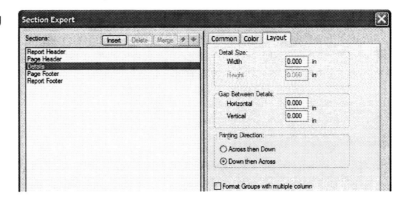

Figure 13-42 Layout tab options

The options on the Layout tab will let you create columns like the Mailing Label wizard does. Unlike word processing software that often has a "Number of columns" option, the Layout tab does not. You create the columns by using the **DETAIL SIZE** and **GAP BETWEEN DETAILS** options.

The **FORMAT GROUPS WITH MULTIPLE COLUMN** option if checked, will cause the group headers and footers to have the same width as the details section.

Summary Reports

The majority of reports that you have created in this workbook contained detail level records. This is the type of report that many people are use to seeing. Detail level reports provide a lot of information. There are times when this is too much information and someone will want to only see summary information. The L10.26 report that you created is a summary report. There are two main ways to create summary reports as discussed below.

① Use the Hide or Suppress report section options.
② Use a Parameter field.

Drill Down Reports

Drill down reports initially look like summary reports. The difference is that drill down reports do not use the Suppress (No Drill-Down) option. Keep in mind that the only data that will print or be exported when using the drill down feature is what is displayed on the selected preview tab.

Drill Down Report Problems

There are two problems that you may encounter when designing reports that will use the drill down feature as discussed below.

① Problems with the group headers.
② Problems with the column headings.

What I have noticed on reports that have at least three groups is that when you drill down, you will see more headers then you probably want or need. When you drill down on the top level group (group 1), you will see the headers for the second group. This may not be what you want when you drill down to the third level.

Using the Hide (Drill-Down OK) option on the Section Expert doesn't work well. The **DRILLDOWNGROUPLEVEL** function will allow you to control when group headers are suppressed. This function is used for printing. The original preview window will return a zero when this function is used. If you are drilling down on group 2, the function will return a 2.

When you drill down on the first group, you usually don't have a need to see the headers for the second group. To prevent this from happening, you would use the formula shown below to conditionally suppress the second level group headers. You would place this formula on the Suppress (No Drill-Down) option (in this example, you would place it on the group 2 header). When this formula is applied, the group 2 header will not appear when you drill down on the first level. The group 2 header will appear when you drill down on the third level, which is what you want to have happen.

```
DrillDownGroupLevel = 1
```

Column Heading Problems

On the first preview tab you will see column headings but no detail records if you use the Hide or Suppress option on the Section Expert. This happens when the column headings are in the page header section. When you drill down to the detail level, the data in the page header section does not appear. Yes, I was confused when I realized this also.

The number of groups on the report determines the solution. If the report only has one group, move the column headings to the group header section. Decide if they look better above or below the group name field if you plan to keep the group name field on the report.

If the report has more than one group, create a second details section and move the detail fields to the second section, then move the column headings to the first detail section and select the **SUPPRESS BLANK SECTION** option on the Section Expert.

The Repository

The repository is a database that report designers can use to store objects that will be used by more than one report or share with other people in the company. Actually, anyone that has a valid login account to the Crystal Reports Server or Business Objects Enterprise can connect to the repository. In some prior versions of Crystal Reports, there was a stand alone repository database. In Crystal Reports XI, the repository is part of Crystal Reports Server or Business Objects Enterprise, depending on what your organization has set up.

Interestingly enough, you can store images, parameter fields, SQL commands, lists of values, text objects, reports and even functions in the repository, but you cannot store formulas in the repository. Once connected to the repository you can create, change and delete folders using the Repository Explorer. A benefit of storing objects in the repository is that if the object is updated, all reports that use the object will be updated automatically.

Test Your Skills

1. Apply conditional formatting to the L7.10 Cross-Tab report.

   - Modify the report to include a group for Country = USA for each sales rep. Combine all other sales in a different group, called Other.
   - Remove the bold from the group names.
   - Save the report as `L13.11 Skills Cross-Tab`. It should look like the one shown in Figure 13-43.

		2003	2004	2005	Total
Davolio	USA	$39,485.69	$278,893.25	$109,053.25	$427,432.19
	Others	$32,377.01	$171,972.58	$28,975.17	$233,324.76
	Total	**$71,862.70**	**$450,865.83**	**$138,028.42**	**$660,756.95**
Dodsworth	USA	$23,107.06	$359,523.99	$119,880.97	$502,512.02
	Others	$5,942.88	$154,021.53	$20,372.78	$180,337.19
	Total	**$29,049.94**	**$513,545.52**	**$140,253.75**	**$682,849.21**
King	USA	$10,460.46	$335,306.18	$152,761.39	$498,528.03
	Others	$10,633.29	$177,100.42	$62,494.20	$250,227.91
	Total	**$21,093.75**	**$512,406.60**	**$215,255.59**	**$748,755.94**
Leverling	USA	$26,055.91	$324,864.09	$133,904.53	$484,824.53
	Others	$18,065.73	$116,491.40	$23,840.63	$158,397.76
	Total	**$44,121.64**	**$441,355.49**	**$157,745.16**	**$643,222.29**
Peacock	USA	$24,508.97	$295,308.43	$120,391.01	$440,208.41
	Others	$13,949.42	$150,842.13	$26,799.81	$191,591.36
	Total	**$38,458.39**	**$446,150.56**	**$147,190.82**	**$631,799.77**
Suyama	USA	$47,602.06	$347,551.55	$135,243.28	$530,396.89
	Others	$7,202.16	$149,329.93	$23,472.50	$180,004.59
	Total	**$54,804.22**	**$496,881.48**	**$158,715.78**	**$710,401.48**
Total		**$259,390.64**	**$2,861,205.48**	**$957,189.52**	**$4,077,785.64**

Figure 13-43 L13.11 Skills Cross-Tab report

2. Add running total fields to the L6.1 report.

   - Create two running total fields and place them in the report footer section. Create one for all USA orders and one for all Canadian orders.
   - Save the report as `L13.12 Skills Running totals`. That last page of the report should look like the one shown in Figure 13-44.

Customer Name	Address
Grand Total # of customers on this report -	269
Total # of orders in the USA -	90
Total # of orders in Canada -	10

Figure 13-44 L13.12 Skills Running totals report

3. Sort the L6.3 report by groups.

- Sort the groups by the Total amount of orders summary field in descending order.
- Filter the groups so that only customers with a total amount of orders over $50,000 appear on the report.
- Save the report as L13.13 Skills Group sort. The first customer on the report should be the one shown in Figure 13-45.

	Order Date	Ship Date	Order Amount	Order #	Unit Price
Backpedal Cycle Shop					
	02/08/2004	02/09/2004	$3,544.20	1279	$1,739.85
	02/08/2004	02/09/2004	$3,544.20	1279	$12.00
	02/08/2004	02/09/2004	$3,544.20	1279	$13.50
	02/19/2004	02/19/2004	$6,233.05	1311	$329.85
	02/19/2004	02/19/2004	$6,233.05	1311	$23.50
	02/19/2004	02/19/2004	$6,233.05	1311	$2,939.85
	07/02/2004	07/04/2004	$3,479.70	1802	$1,739.85
	08/15/2004	08/19/2004	$3,415.95	1972	$53.90
	08/15/2004	08/19/2004	$3,415.95	1972	$764.85
	08/15/2004	08/19/2004	$3,415.95	1972	$479.85
	11/16/2004	11/18/2004	$10,798.95	2358	$2,939.85
	11/16/2004	11/18/2004	$10,798.95	2358	$1,739.85
	11/16/2004	11/18/2004	$10,798.95	2358	$479.85
	12/18/2004	12/19/2004	$6,226.05	2507	$329.85
	12/18/2004	12/19/2004	$6,226.05	2507	$2,939.85
	12/18/2004	12/19/2004	$6,226.05	2507	$16.50
	01/04/2005	01/05/2005	$9,612.47	2560	$764.85
	01/04/2005	01/05/2005	$9,612.47	2560	$832.35
	01/04/2005	01/05/2005	$9,612.47	2560	$2,792.86
	02/02/2005	02/02/2005	$8,819.55	2685	$2,939.85
Total # orders - 20		Total $ amount of orders -	$131,791.26		
		Average order amount for customer -	$6,589.56		

Figure 13-45 L13.13 Skills Group sort report

4. Add hyperlinks to the L13.3 report.

- Create another report header section for the hyperlinks that you will create in this exercise.
- Use the Wingdings envelope and open folder images in the first row of the Character Map as the objects for the hyperlinks.
- Use the envelope image to create an email hyperlink that open an email window with your email address in the To field.
- Use the folder image to create a file hyperlink that opens the L13.1 report.
- Change the font size of both text objects to 28. The images should be larger.
- Add the appropriate text to the hyperlinks, so that the person running the report will know what the images link to.
- Save the report as L13.14 Skills hyperlink. The report header section should look like the one shown in Figure 13-46.

Figure 13-46 L13.14 Skills hyperlink report

5. Add all of the reports that were created in this lesson to the Workbench.

The End!

If you are reading this paragraph, I hope it means that you have completed all of the exercises in this workbook. If so, congratulations because you have covered a lot of material. If some topics seem a little fuzzy right now, that is to be expected. Hopefully you have gained some valuable Crystal Reports skills and techniques. As you have probably figured out, unless you are creating a basic list report, there are a lot of options and features are at your disposal to create reports that people will "like" to use.

INDEX

Other Titles In The Series

ISBN-10: 0977391248
ISBN-13: 978-0-9773912-4-0

ISBN-10: 0977391213
ISBN-13: 978-0-9773912-1-9
Covers versions 8 and 8.5. New cover coming soon.

ISBN-10: 0977391205
ISBN-13: 978-0-9773912-0-2

ISBN-10: 0977391256
ISBN-13: 978-0-9773912-5-7
Publication Date: July 2007

Coming In 2008

Certification manuals for Microsoft Word 2007, Excel 2007 and Access 2007

Crystal Reports for Visual Studio

Printed in the United States
84152LV00006B/97-98/A